Springer Texts in Education

Springer Texts in Education delivers high-quality instructional content for graduates and advanced graduates in all areas of Education and Educational Research. The textbook series is comprised of self-contained books with a broad and comprehensive coverage that are suitable for class as well as for individual self-study. All texts are authored by established experts in their fields and offer a solid methodological background, accompanied by pedagogical materials to serve students such as practical examples, exercises, case studies etc. Textbooks published in the Springer Texts in Education series are addressed to graduate and advanced graduate students, but also to researchers as important resources for their education, knowledge and teaching. Please contact Yoka Janssen at Yoka.Janssen@springer.com or your regular editorial contact person for queries or to submit your book proposal.

Devona M. Stalnaker-Shofner ·
Tanisha N. Sapp
Editors

A Comprehensive Guide for Counselor Education

Training Doctoral Learners and New Educators for Counselor Education and Supervision

Springer

Editors
Devona M. Stalnaker-Shofner
Antioch University
Yellow Springs, OH, USA

Tanisha N. Sapp
Liberty University
Lynchburg, VA, USA

ISSN 2366-7672 ISSN 2366-7680 (electronic)
Springer Texts in Education
ISBN 978-3-031-68357-2 ISBN 978-3-031-68358-9 (eBook)
https://doi.org/10.1007/978-3-031-68358-9

This Springer imprint is published by the registered company Springer Nature Switzerland AG
The registered company address is: Gewerbestrasse 11, 6330 Cham, Switzerland

—To Phyllis Wheatly and Black Herstory.

We are the legacy of our ancestors, and the contemporaneous creatives who paved a way forward for us.

We understood the assignment!

Foreword

As I sit down to pen this foreword, I am filled with a profound sense of responsibility and hope. My journey as a Black woman and first-generation college student in the field of counselor education has been one of struggle, resilience, and ultimately, triumph. Having navigated the often-turbulent waters of three research-intensive, predominantly White universities, I have witnessed firsthand the challenges the voices of persons with historically marginalized identities face in our profession. This path was made even more difficult by the lack of mentorship and support during my doctoral program–a common experience for many first-generation students and students of color. Yet, through perseverance and a commitment to creating the support systems I wished I had, I have seen the transformative power of mentorship, the strength found in community, and the potential for change when we dare to challenge the status quo.

This book, *A Comprehensive Guide for Counselor Education: Training Doctoral Learners and New Educators for Counselor Education and Supervision*, represents a crucial step forward in our field. It is a testament to the evolving nature of counselor education and a beacon for those who seek to create a more equitable, inclusive, and just profession. Moreover, it stands as a womanist homage to communities of color, recognizing and celebrating the wisdom, resilience, and collective care that have sustained us in the face of systemic oppression and white supremacy.

As the first African American woman to serve as president of the Association of Counselor Education and Supervision, I have strived to open doors and create pathways for others who have been historically underrepresented in our field. This text embodies that spirit of inclusion and progress, offering the guidance and support that I and so many others lacked in our early careers. It expands on how womanist collective care is not just beneficial, but necessary in confronting and dismantling the pervasive effects of white supremacy in academia and counselor education.

What sets this book apart is its unwavering commitment to social justice and equity. By framing the entire work through the lens of Diversity, Equity, Inclusion, Belonging, Accessibility, and Social Justice (DEIBASJ), the authors have created a resource that speaks to the heart of what our profession should aspire to be. This approach is not merely an add-on or an afterthought; it is the foundation upon which every chapter is built, reflecting the womanist principle of holistic care for the entire community.

As I read through the pages, I was struck by the intentionality with which the contributors were selected. The voices represented here are those that have often been silenced or marginalized in traditional academic spaces. By centering the experiences and wisdom of individuals from non-dominant groups, this book offers a perspective that is both refreshing and essential. The inclusion of statements of reflexivity (SOR) from each contributor adds a layer of transparency and vulnerability that is all too rare in academic texts, embodying the womanist ethos of authenticity and communal truth-telling.

Throughout my career, I have integrated womanist and critical race theories into my work, recognizing the gaps in traditional counselor education training. This book aligns beautifully with that approach, offering a nuanced and culturally informed perspective on every aspect of counselor education. From teaching and supervision to navigating the complexities of higher education, each chapter provides practical guidance while never losing sight of the larger goal of creating a more just and equitable profession.

As someone who lacked mentorship in my own doctoral journey, I have made it my mission to mentor countless Black women who have gone on to leadership roles and successful careers in counselor education. I am particularly heartened by the sections on personal and professional development. The chapters addressing wellness, imposter phenomenon, and leadership through a multicultural and social justice framework offer invaluable insights for those just starting their journey in the field. These are the conversations that are often missing from traditional training programs, yet they are crucial for the success and well-being of counselor educators, especially those from historically marginalized backgrounds and first-generation students.

The book's structure, divided into five comprehensive parts, provides a roadmap for success in counselor education. It covers everything from the fundamentals of teaching and supervision to the intricacies of developing CACREP-accredited programs. What impresses me most is how the authors have managed to infuse social justice principles and womanist collective care into every aspect of the counselor education process, from admissions policies to curriculum development.

I am particularly excited about the chapters that address working with counselors-in-training. The emphasis on creating access for persons with ascribed marginalized identities, mitigating attrition, and increasing student retention speaks directly to the challenges I have observed and worked to address throughout my career. By providing concrete strategies for inclusive advising and strengths-based remediation, this book offers a blueprint for creating counselor education programs that truly serve all students, including those who, like me, maybe the first in their families to pursue higher education.

As I reflect on my own journey and the state of our field, I am filled with cautious optimism. We have made significant strides, but there is still much work to be done in dismantling the structures of white supremacy that persist in our institutions. This book represents a significant step forward, offering a comprehensive guide that centers social justice, equity, and womanist principles in every aspect of counselor education.

To the students and new educators who will read this book: embrace the wisdom offered here. Allow it to challenge your assumptions, expand your perspectives, and inspire you to become agents of change in our field. Remember that your voices, experiences, and insights are valuable and necessary for the growth and evolution of counselor education. And to those who, like me, may feel alone or unsupported in their journey–know that this book is a testament to the fact that you belong in this field and that there are those of us fighting to create the supportive, collective environments you deserve.

To my colleagues in leadership positions: I urge you to engage deeply with the principles and practices outlined in this text. Let it serve as a catalyst for reflection on our current systems and a guide for creating more inclusive and equitable educational spaces. Consider how we can better support first-generation students and others who may lack traditional mentorship networks, and how we can implement womanist principles of collective care to combat the isolating effects of white supremacy in academia.

As we move forward, let us carry the spirit of this book with us–a spirit of inclusivity, critical reflection, and unwavering commitment to social justice and womanist collective care. Together, we can create a counselor education landscape that truly reflects and serves the diverse world in which we live and work, provides the support and mentorship that every student deserves, and stands as a powerful counterforce to the pervasive influence of white supremacy in our field and institutions.

Natoya Hill Haskins
William and Mary
Williamsburg, VA, USA

Preface–Building A New Table

Every great dream begins with a dreamer. Always remember, you have within you the strength, the patience, and the passion to reach for the stars to change the world.

—*Harriet Tubman*

Every idea, book, research project, or idea has a backstory, and this book is no different. It began with the creation of a manuscript that Dr. Stalnaker-Shofner submitted for publication, which was later *rejected*. Though the manuscript was not accepted, the feedback given was that the content would be "better suited as a book chapter." As I reflected on the feedback, I remembered the words of Pulitzer Prize-winning author Toni Morrison: "if there's a book that you want to read, but it hasn't been written yet, then you must write it." This was the impetus for the creation of this book you are reading now. It started as a random book proposal, and quickly gained momentum through word of mouth. It culminated in the contributions of more than 45 contributors with expertise and experience across multiple disciplines and the subject areas that are the content and foci for this book. Ultimately, and perhaps through providence, it led to my collaboration with my sister-colleague-friend, Dr. Tanisha N. Sapp, my esteemed co-editor and co-conspirator on this project and in so many other ventures.

As we began to conceptualize this book, we reflected on our experiences as doctoral learners and new counselor education and supervision (CES) professionals. One thing that stood out to both of us was that there was not a book that captured the total process of teaching in counselor education available. While we learned about best practices in teaching which were rooted in traditional pedagogy, there was neither a focus on addressing issues of equity or social justice, nor was there a holistic perspective exploring our lived experiences (and that of others) navigating academia, first as doctoral learners, then as new professionals and beyond. We also thought about what would have been helpful to know as we entered the profession as Assistant Professors in Counselor Education and Supervision and worked within the existing systems of higher education, especially as Black women. We also thought of the lack of representation within the subjective development of textbooks, research, and other literature in higher education and specifically, the CES profession. Thus, it was our purpose in this seminal work to be intentional in decentering whiteness and antiquated views of professional and academic writing. This book is a manifestation of not simply advocating for a seat at the existing table, rather it is *building a new table*, while burning down the table that is white supremacy, supported by the hegemony, oppression, and privilege pervasive in the systems of higher education.

A Comprehensive Guide for Counselor Education: Training Doctoral Learners and New Educators for Counselor Education and Supervision is a straight-forward book designed to chronicle the experiences you may have, while offering practical skills and guidance as you navigate the CES profession and higher education. We also want to emphasize the uniqueness of this book. First, this book is written entirely from a social justice perspective and is guided by the key tenets of Diversity, Equity, Inclusion, Belonging, Accessibility, and Social Justice (DEIBASJ). This book also is intentional in its utilization and incorporation of accessibility, as we strongly believe it to be an element (often overlooked) of social justice pathways toward inclusion. Secondly, this book is not only based on extant research regarding best practices for each subject area, but it is also written from the personal lived experiences of the contributors. Our hope is that this multi-faceted approach of incorporating research and contributor reflections through a social justice and equity lens will provide you with the most comprehensive framing of what it can be like to be a counselor educator.

Next, we want to take a moment to reflect on intent versus impact. We would also like to acknowledge that there are aspects of this book and its content that may elicit discomfort for you based on the identities you hold rooted in your lived experiences, and that's also a part of this book's social justice purpose. While this is not our intent, we recognize that even in our attempts to be inclusive, that there are parts that may still marginalize, disenfranchise, and negate some populations. We honor the impact and embrace the need for continued growth.

Another significant aspect of this book is the composition of the chapter contributors. As the book was being created, we were intentional in our selection process. Perhaps the most compelling feature is that all contributors are purposefully from non-dominant groups, with varying intersecting identities such as being female, queer, and/or a person of color. To maintain a social justice and inclusive practice, each contributor provides you with a statement of reflexivity (SOR) which reflects their positionality and intersectional identities including those of privilege and marginalization. The intention of the SOR is to ground the chapter in a culturally informed point of view and from a perspective of collaboration and dialogue. Thus, the central question we asked each contributor to consider as they authored their respective chapters was, "If you could send a letter to yourself at the beginning of your journey as a counselor educator, what would you say? How would you advise your former self about this profession and navigating higher education?"

As such, this book is divided into five parts: Teaching, Supervision, and Counseling Curriculum; Working with Students; Navigating Higher Education, Counseling Specializations; and Personal and Professional Development. Each chapter begins with an overview and the contributors SOR followed by a case scenario to help illustrate and demonstrate the salient points of the chapter. Within each chapter, you will find areas where you are tasked to stop and reflect on the content provided. It is meant to be a conversation and serve as an invitation for you to engage with the material. With this, we provide you with a general overview of the content within the book.

Part I: Teaching, Supervision, and Counseling Curriculum, begins in Chap. 1 where we establish and shape the social justice framework for the entire book. We further illuminate the principles specific to adult learning. We highlight the constructs of pedagogy, andragogy, and heutagogy, and the relationship of each to current best teaching and supervision practices (online and in-person). We introduce learner-centered praxis as an extension of social justice principles, in that learning is collaborative and inclusive of the learners' lived experiences, existing knowledge base, and their expressed learning goals and needs. Additionally, as we conceptualized this textbook, we as co-editors charged ourselves and the contributors to reflect on language and etymology of certain terms found in the counseling literature. For example, we examined the use of the terms *student* and *pedagogy*. While we recognize that the term *student* perpetuates the hierarchy distinct to pedagogy, we are cognizant of the necessity to shift language to promote inclusivity and equity in counselor education. Additionally, regarding the use of pedagogy, we recognized the inherent oppression linked to this term, and as such we have intentionally used the term *praxis* when appropriate to denote teaching models and approaches. Where possible, we integrate this language shift from *student* to *learner* or *counselors-in-training (CITs)*. Therefore, as you read this text, you will observe the terms learners and CITs are used interchangeably. *This is intentional.* It is our hope that this intentionality begins a conscious and collective shift in language, thus we create the change we want to see.

Next, is an exploration of the virtual learning experience of CITs in online programs, where we take adult learning concepts and apply them to best practices in online teaching and learning. One unique aspect that the co-editors would like to note is our intentional incorporation of the distinct nature and positionality of the counselor educator in Chap. 2, specifically how adult learning principles and practices are applicable to counselor education. Next, we shift the focus to providing you with an overview of clinical supervision within the degree program. Incorporating strategies and best practices for success. We conclude this section with Chap. 5, where we provide you with tools for effective anti-racist and socially just practices toward course development within your counselor education program. We offer practical guidance and replicable strategies for your consideration as you begin to conceptualize the requisite components of the course, as framed by the Council for Counselor Education and Related Programs (CACREP). Another important aspect of this book is its incorporation of the recently released 2024 CACREP standards.

Part II: Working with Counselors-in-Training, which explores all aspects of engagement with learners, from entry into the program and matriculation to degree completion. This part begins with Chap. 6, which outlines admissions and enrollment policies and practices. Further, we reflect upon the intentional development of an infrastructure emphasizing DEIBASJ principles and best practices. The overall goal is to create access to higher education for persons with historically marginalized identities, mitigate attrition as well as barriers to their education, and ultimately increase learner retention. Further, we explore engagement with learners through faculty advising. From a learner-centered perspective, we discuss how utilizing a relational approach can be facilitative of success and retention. We conclude this part with Chap. 8, where we delve into the counselor educator's role as a gatekeeper. We reflect on best practices in remediation and protocols that are learner-centered and strength-based. Such practices provide a framework that supports success and retention through collaboration, identifying CIT needs and resources, and clear communication of program academic and dispositional expectations.

Part III: Navigating Higher Education takes you through graduation and post-doctorate experiences. Through the sharing of personal anecdotes supported by research, the contributors highlight relevant professional experiences, with an understanding that each reader will have their own set of experiences. While our intention was to incorporate the lived experiences of underrepresented populations, we recognize that these experiences are not representative of all perspectives. This part begins with Chap. 9, where we explore some of the common pitfalls that you as a new CES may experience. We also want to offer you practical strategies to circumvent them if possible, or to facilitate their resolution. Next, we walk you through suggestions on how to best approach seeking employment and securing a faculty role. We highlight different teaching roles that are available to you as well as best suited to meet your career objectives. We also share possible encounters you may or may not experience in your first year as a new counselor educator. Within these chapters, we indicate our suggestions for tools and strategies that are designed to help prepare you for this journey. Additionally, we include the lived experiences of persons whose overlooked identities and voices are sorely under-represented in counselor education and typically silenced by oppressive dominant systems endemic to higher education. We specifically explore the unique perspectives of international learners and counselor educators, as well as the voices of learners and counselor educators with disabilities. Thus, to promote true accessibility, inclusion, and belonging, we elevate these voices within the context of this book. We conclude this section with Chap. 14, in which we notate the nuances of the promotion and tenure process, with the goal of better equipping and preparing you to navigate this process with the hope of a successful outcome.

Part IV: Counseling Specializations opens with Chap. 15 and concludes with Chap. 22. The opening chapter focuses on developing your understanding of the 2024 CACREP Standards. Additionally, we provide you with practical information and strategies to help you to develop a CACREP self-study for potential program accreditation. This chapter sets the foundation for the subsequent chapters in this section. The intention is to introduce you to each area and to provide you with guidance regarding best practices for creation of a specialization program or track. Further, another feature of the chapters in this section is our inclusion of helpful tools and strategies for curriculum development with an example program of study. We also provide you with some potential course suggestions that you may potentially incorporate as you create the structure of your program.

Part V: Personal and Professional Development where we begin with Chap. 23 and provide you with an overview of the leadership and administrative roles that CES's are likely to encounter. We offer examples of these roles and various leadership styles through a multicultural and social justice framework. From here, we transition to address the importance of maintaining your personal wellness as you impart knowledge and resources to CITs to facilitate their own wellness. We include this chapter because wellness, though promoted, is often an overlooked area of need. Lastly, we round out the book with Chap. 25 where we address the imposter phenomenon and offer tools for recognition, management, and prevention. As we close this textbook, we would be remiss if we did not return to the charge that we gave the contributors. As we have asked the contributors to write their chapters as though they were writing to their past selves, we conclude this book with our letter to you.

Within this book, there are various acronyms integral to your understanding of the structure within its context. We thought it prudent to introduce you to them here. While some of these acronyms may be new to you, others may be familiar. Therefore, when new terms and their acronyms are introduced, they will also be operationally defined within their respective chapters to ensure that we establish a common language that will be maintained throughout the book.

The common acronyms associated with counselor education are delineated below:

ACA	American Counseling Association
ACES	Association for Counselor Education and Supervision
BIPOC	Black and Indigenous People of Color
CACREP	Council for the Accreditation of Counselor Education and Related Programs
CE	Counselor Educator(s)
CES	Counselor Educator(s) and Supervisor(s)/ Counselor Education and Supervision
CIT	Counselor(s)-in-Training
CMHC	Clinical Mental Health Counseling
CRC/RC	Clinical Rehabilitation Counseling/Rehabilitation Counseling
DEIBASJ	Diversity, Equity, Inclusion, Belonging, Accessibility, and Social Justice
LGBTQQIP2SA	Lesbian, Gay, Bisexual, Transgender, Queer, Questioning, Intersex, Pansexual, Two-Spirited, Asexual
MCFC	Marriage, Couples, and Families Counseling
MSJCC	Multicultural and Social Justice Counseling Competencies

NBCC	National Board for Certified Counselors
SC	School Counseling

As a bonus feature of this book, each chapter references a link to the Springer page for this textbook. The link will connect you to supplemental material for each chapter. The intent is to give the reader access to a repository of references, resources, and supplemental items that will help you in your work as a counselor educator.

As you begin your journey to become a counselor educator, there is much to learn to help you through these experiences. This is the heart of this book, and it was written with you in mind. The book begins with you as a doctoral learner and guides you as you prepare to become a counselor educator. We hope this is everything you imagined it would be and that it serves you in the capacity as it was intended to serve.

Yellow Springs, USA Devona M. Stalnaker-Shofner
Lynchburg, USA Tanisha N. Sapp

Acknowledgements

First, we as co-editors of this textbook offer our respect in acknowledging the unceded and stolen land upon which each of us stands; we honor your loss and your legacy.

Next, we want to state our awareness that this work is not a singular effort. We are not self-made, we are *community-made*, and thus we acknowledge the love and support of our collective villages.

For Devona, my deep gratitude for the unceasing love and support of my husband, champion, and hunny bunny, Derrick. You have always encouraged me to pursue my dreams, and your love helps to make that possible.

For Tanisha, my deepest gratitude to my husband, Hip-Hop, and my children, for your sacrifice and unwavering support. When I want to quit or give up, you remind me of my why and tell me to keep going.

For our friends, colleagues, mentors, and the host of people in our communities who have impacted us with every step of this journey, we thank you. For the CES professionals who have paved the way for us and work alongside as co-conspirators in this fight, we have so much admiration for you and all you have done and continue to do. There are too many of you to name–and to do so would take up too many pages!. We especially want to honor our mentor, colleague, and friend, Dr. Mary Kate Reese, who shared her talent, wisdom, and purple pen to finish this project before leaving us too soon. We know she would be proud of this work and what we have become. There aren't enough words to share how invaluable each of you are and how much you have inspired us. We thank you!

Next, we want to acknowledge the counterintuitive narrative of *the illusion of inclusion*–the gracious and magnanimous gesture of the ascribed dominant group to *allow us* a seat at the table, and their admonishment for *us* to remember that it is *their table.* This book honors the strength in the legacy of our distant ancestors, as well as the recent work of our predecessors in this fight for inclusion, access, and social justice. Succinctly, if we are not invited to have a seat at *their table*, we will build our *own table!!*

Lastly, we want to acknowledge the cultural taxation specifically connected to the premise of this book and why it was created. As the co-editors of this textbook, this journey was not without its challenges. As Black women, there was a significant emotional cost to us as we labored to produce an unprecedented text, and we directly experienced marginalization and minimization leveled against us. More importantly, we were each reminded of our *why*, at times, in unexpected and always timely ways. We are grateful for these experiences and the persons who inspired us to persevere.

Contents

Editors and Contributors

About the Editors

Devona M. Stalnaker-Shofner, EdD, LPC, NCC, MHP, SAP (she/her/hers) is Associate Professor at Antioch University, School of Counseling, Psychology, and Therapy. She has been a counselor educator for more than 10 years and in professional practice as a licensed counselor for more than 20 years. Her clinical experience includes providing individual, group, and couples and family counseling to clients presenting with treatment concerns such as depression, anxiety, trauma, as well as substance use, addiction, and recovery. She also provides clinical supervision to counselors-in-training and new counseling professionals. Dr. Stalnaker-Shofner has served in various leadership roles within the counseling and counselor education professions. Her research and scholarship include numerous presentations at state, regional, national, and international conferences, as well as related publications. As a trainer, she has provided workshops on racial trauma and BIPOC mental health and wellness, and the decolonization of curriculum, teaching praxis, and educational policies to disrupt oppression and promote diversity, equity, inclusion, and access. Additionally, she serves as an educational and organizational consultant advising on implementing anti-racist and social justice practices for leaders and organizational policies and culture.

Tanisha N. Sapp, EdD, LPC, CST, NCC, ACS, CPCS (she/her/Dr.) is an Assistant Professor of Counseling at Liberty University in the Department of Counseling and Family Studies. Dr. Sapp is a counselor educator, professional counselor, trainer, and clinical supervisor focused on training the next generation of helping professionals. She is the owner of Tanisha Sapp, LLC where she provides professional development training, clinical supervision services, and individual and couples sex therapy. With over 20 years of experience in the helping profession, Dr. Sapp brings a wealth of experience, insight, and a unique perspective into counselor education.

Dr. Sapp is currently a member of the ACA ethics committee and serves on review panels for CACREP and NBCC where she offers her expertise to the profession in an effort to be the change she desires to see. Dr. Sapp has also served on a number of professional committees and provided leadership service to the profession and her community. Her areas of research, professional identity, and interests include: professional counselor identity, anti-racism in counseling and counselor education, DEIBASJ in counseling and counselor education, BIPOC sexual health and wellness, and professional advocacy in leadership.

Contributors

Samantha Airhart-Larraga Texas A&M University–Central Texas, Killeen, TX, USA

Bianca Augustine William & Mary, Williamsburg, VA, USA

Nicole Baker Morningside University, Sioux City, IA, USA

Rhea Bhatia Springfield College, Springfield, MA, USA

Katrina Y. Billingsley Albany State University, Albany, GA, USA

Lynn Bohecker Liberty University, Lynchburg, VA, USA

Deanna Burgess DePaul University, Chicago, IL, USA

Aja Burks Saybrook University, Pasadena, CA, USA

Janice Byrd The Pennsylvania State University, University Park, PA, USA

Erika Cameron Palo Alto University, Palo Alto, CA, USA

LaToya Chambers William & Mary, Williamsburg, VA, USA

Charmaine L. Conner Roosevelt University, Chicago, IL, USA

Ali K. Corey Antioch University, Yellow Springs, OH, USA

Dontè R. Corey True Living Counseling Services PLLC, Burlington, NC, USA

Syntia Santos Dietz Antioch University, Yellow Springs, OH, USA

Krista Dobson Yale University, New Haven, CT, USA

Natese Dockery The University of Kentucky, Lexington, KY, USA

Katherine Fort Antioch University, Yellow Springs, OH, USA

Mariaimeé Gonzalez Antioch University, Yellow Springs, OH, USA

Tiphanie Gonzalez State University of New York-Oswego, Oswego, NY, USA

Amoaba Gooden Kent State University, Kent, OH, USA

Stacy Henning Webster University, Webster Groves, MO, USA

Jehan Hill Stone Catchers Counseling, Downers Grove, IL, USA

Bridget Hollis Staten South Carolina State University, Orangeburg, SC, USA

Macie A. Hoover Buena Vista University, Storm Lake, IA, USA;
City University of Seattle, Seatle, WA, USA

Jung H. Hyun Agnes Scott College, Decatur, GA, USA

Letitia Johnson Antioch University, Yellow Springs, OH, USA

Krista Kirk Messiah University, Mechanicsburg, PA, USA

Cathy Lounsbury Antioch University, Yellow Springs, OH, USA

K. Lynn Pierce Mercer University, Atlanta, GA, USA

Latasha Matthews Illumination Counseling and Coaching, Lawrenceville, GA, USA

Joy Maweu Mwendwa Liberty University, Lynchburg, VA, USA

Amanda Minor Salve Regina University, Newport, RI, USA

Amy Morrison Antioch University, Yellow Springs, OH, USA

Katie Muirhead Salve Regina University, Newport, RI, USA

Amirah Nelson Jackson State University, Ridgeland, MS, USA

Jocelyn Novella Fairfield University, Fairfield, CT, USA

Christa J. Porter Kent State University, Kent, OH, USA

Taqueena S. Quintana Antioch University, Yellow Springs, OH, USA

Mary Kate Reese Walden University, Minneapolis, MN, USA

Brandy K. Richeson Liberty University, Lynchburg, VA, USA

Tracey E. Robert Fairfield University, Fairfield, CT, USA

Wendy Robinson Liberty University, Lynchburg, VA, USA

Kathleen M. Ruscitto Buena Vista University, Storm Lake, IA, USA

Keiko Sano Antioch University, Yellow Springs, OH, USA

Syntia Santos Dietz Antioch University, Yellow Springs, OH, USA

Tanisha N. Sapp Liberty University, Lynchburg, VA, USA

Brianne Scott Walden University, Minneapolis, MN, USA

Devona M. Stalnaker-Shofner Antioch University, Yellow Springs, OH, USA

Tyra Turner Whittaker Liberty University, Lynchburg, VA, USA

Jazmone Wilkerson Antioch University, Yellow Springs, OH, USA

Part I

Teaching, Supervision, and Counseling Curriculum

1 Diversity, Equity, Inclusion, Belonging, Accessibility, and Social Justice in Counselor Education

Katie Muirhead, Jehan Hill, Amanda Minor, Amirah Nelson, and Rhea Bhatia

> *We can disagree and still love each other unless your disagreement is rooted in my oppression and denial of my humanity and right to exist.*
>
> *James Baldwin*

Abstract

Diversity, equity, inclusion, belonging, and social justice are values at the center of effective and ethical counselor education. Best practices, ethical codes, textbooks, and research articles all discuss how important these topics are. However, there can be a gap between how DEIBASJ are discussed and how these dynamics are displayed in the profession. As a result, CES' can find themselves in complex situations while navigating these dynamics. This chapter discusses how doctoral learners, clinical supervisors, and counselor educators with historically marginalized identities can successfully navigate these political, social, and professional power structures and how counselor education professionals

K. Muirhead (✉) · A. Minor
Salve Regina University, Newport, RI, USA
e-mail: kathleen.muirhead@salve.edu

A. Minor
e-mail: amanda.minor@salve.edu

J. Hill
Stone Catchers Counseling, Downers Grove, IL, USA
e-mail: jhill2@niu.edu

A. Nelson
Jackson State University, Ridgeland, MS, USA
e-mail: amirahnelson@isu.edu

R. Bhatia
Springfield College, Springfield, MA, USA

D. M. Stalnaker-Shofner and T. N. Sapp (eds.), *A Comprehensive Guide for Counselor Education*, Springer Texts in Education, https://doi.org/10.1007/978-3-031-68358-9_1

can work to dismantle oppression across multiple roles. The authors include voices and contributions from people with intersecting cultural identities and experiences to help provide concrete guidance on maintaining wellness in the profession. Further, the authors of this chapter make every effort to abide by best practices as defined through the lenses of critical race theory, intersectionality, and social justice as defined in the introduction of this text.

Learning Objectives After reading this chapter, you will be able to:

1. Identify how people with historically marginalized identities can navigate challenges within oppressive systems and the protections they can put in place.
2. Integrate the importance of diversity, equity, inclusion, belonging, accessibility, and social justice within counselor education and supervision programs.
3. Implement concrete methods for consistently enacting effective and ethical practices that are cross-cultural and equitable.

1.1 Statement of Reflexivity

Five authors, each with differing and wide-ranging intersecting identities, constructed this chapter. As such, we recognize that within these intersections are areas of systemic marginalization and ascribed and inherent privilege. Each author brought their theoretical and applied expertise in the realms of social justice and multiculturalism, as well as their personal and professional lenses shaped by their unique identities. Dr. Muirhead identifies as a White, middle class, queer, fat, cisgender woman with a chronic illness. Dr. Hill is a multiethnic Arab American, naturalized citizen, cisgender woman with an invisible chronic illness. Dr. Minor identifies as a White, queer, cisgender, disabled, mental health counselor, academic, mentee, mentor, daughter, and partner. Her disabilities and queerness both often afford her to be stealth when wanted/needed, which comes with enormous advantages and, at times, isolation. Dr. Nelson is a Black, Muslim, American, cisgender woman with invisible disabilities. Ms. Bhatia is a third-year international doctoral learner, and she identifies as a heterosexual, cisgender, South Asian woman. Her experiences of growing up in one culture and living in a different one have informed her personal and professional work. While there is an authorship order listed, the authors approached the writing of this chapter from a collaborative and collectivist lens. Even considering this collaboration, the authors' worldviews, biases, and assumptions are situated in discreet contexts, and we encourage you to keep our positionality in mind throughout this chapter.

1.2 An Introduction and Developmental Framework for This Book

This chapter was not written in a vacuum. Authors, editors, and publishing structures all influenced the construction of the proceeding ideas, and each person contributed to the discourse with a diverse set of values, beliefs, biases, and worldviews. These dynamics will influence the material that is presented within these pages. As mentioned, we invite you to read this chapter and the entire textbook as a guide to help you navigate your unique situation and critically think about the material presented. As authors, we sought to address social justice and equity in a manner that: incorporates the values and best practices of the profession within the context of its noted downfalls; elevates the voices of people with historically marginalized and intersectional identities, particularly as they navigate academia; and provides concrete and actionable steps on how to identify and dismantle oppressive systems.

Constructs related to social justice, equity, and multiculturalism are discussed throughout. We incorporate terminology, ideas, and theories considered current best practice as of the chapter's submission to the best of our knowledge and expertise. Our awareness and knowledge, along with the collective understanding of socially-just ideas, will continue to develop long after these words make it to print. Considering this, we recognize that we may use ideas that will be identified later as harmful, regardless of our efforts and intentions. If you read this and find that a particular term or framework no longer represents best practice, we encourage you to do the work of seeking out the most relevant, equitable, extant socially-just ideology. As we commit to change, personal growth, and to do better, we are hopeful that the social structures will also continually move toward equitable, just, and compassionate treatment of all people and all identities. We also hope that this developmental stance will set the tone for how this chapter can be used. By the time you read this chapter, the authors and the power structures at large will have changed, and we are hopeful that you will join us in your own process of continual growth.

Stop and Reflect: *We encourage you to view this text with a critical eye as you read and engage with the presented material, even from sources with well-meaning intentions. Some questions you might ask when reading or viewing this material include: Who wrote the content I'm reading? What are their implicitly held or explicitly expressed interests, biases, and worldviews? What reactions might the writers have intended to elicit from me upon the reading of this material, and are these potentially biased or value-ladened? Does the writing and presented content represent me, my experiences, and my identities? With deeper engagement and further processing, you may be able to effectively discern the material that is useful to your growth, and that which is oppressive with the potential to create new or exacerbate existing barriers.*

Furthermore, as you reflect on the adoption of a developmental framework for yourself and others, you will want to consider the following: consistently engaging with cutting-edge ideas that are grounded in the voices, communities, and grassroots movements that are impacted predominant discourses; the courage required to remain curious about new ideas; and the humility needed to lean in when you realize you are wrong, misinformed, or operating near or at the edges of your competence. You may also want to keep in mind the utility of creating professional connections with those who are similarly committed to building community rooted in both compassion and accountability.

1.2.1 Establishing Working Terminology

An important starting point in establishing a common language is to address the discourse occurring (or not occurring) within our field. As we enter this dialogue, it is our ethical and professional responsibility to, at the very least, have a current understanding of the various elements and facets of social justice pedagogy and praxis (ACA, 2014; CACREP, 2024). However, for many within our profession, privilege can afford a willful blindness enabling our lack of active engagement with social justice discourse in favor of what is familiar and comfortable (Jun, 2018; Wilson et al., 2023). Therefore, we have included a discussion based on the terminology we feel represents a socially-just lens. We acknowledge that this is not comprehensive, and we may miss critical concepts. Also, your definition of social justice may differ from what is presented in this chapter and textbook. For our readers who identify with the phenomenology of being disenfranchised, we recognize this explanation of terminology can never do justice to your lived experiences.

For our readers with privileged identities, we strongly recommend that these terms be personally explored with cultural humility (see definition below). If you feel defensive as you are reading, view this unsettlement as an invitation to lean into the discomfort and to delve deeper. Seeing, questioning, investigating, and ultimately dismantling your privilege is a critical step, and it can be a jarring one. It is important to act with cognizance and deliverance. It is critical to recognize that people who experience perpetual disenfranchisement are constantly faced with performative allyship in the form of professed support and solidarity, without true active engagement and commitment (Kutlaca & Radke, 2023). This hollowness is greatly harmful. Bahrainwala (2020) shares several examples of performative allyship, such as when individuals in academia "opt out of setting meaningful thresholds for intervention and how these moments of inaction have consequences" (p. 135). Furthering this position, Hernández (2020) explores the "draining and violent experience of shepherding white colleagues through white allyship" (p. 150) and notes the following: "when performative white allyship is represented by centering oneself or expecting recognition, this can result in the perpetuation of white saviorism and white martyrdom that further re-centers whiteness" (p. 150). These authors point out the harm of inaction and underscore the importance of navigating discussions around allyship with competence. Helping profession researchers are calling for a movement from performative allyship toward critical allyship which includes concrete, decisive action and a dismantling of existing systemic oppression built into the structure of the profession (Gates et al., 2023; Hannon et al., 2023).

Below are several key terms that will be used throughout this textbook that we would like to operationally define for your consideration:

- **Accessibility** is unimpeded ingress to the functionality of a system, entity, or environment, and the ability to gain and utilize the related benefits such as products or services by all persons (Harvard University Diversity, Inclusion, and Belonging [DIB] Glossary of Terms, n.d.).
- **Allyship** involves using one's privilege(s) to work in solidarity and partnership with persons who are systematically marginalized to dismantle oppressive systems that create barriers to equity, basic human rights, access to resources and other necessities that give people the ability to thrive (Dickenson, 2021). Allyship is active, consistent, effective, genuine, and requires a strong relationship between the privileged person and those with whom they are in allyship.
- **Anti-racism** is the active process of identifying and eliminating racism by changing systems, organizational structures, policies and practices and attitudes, so that power is redistributed and shared equitably (ACES Human Rights & Social Justice Committee, 2023).
- **Belonging** is the intentional focus on the equitable treatment of all persons so as to promote a sense of one's full membership in the community, as well as fostering the ability to thrive (University of Hartford Diversity, Inclusion, and Belonging [DIB] Glossary of Terms, n.d.).
- **Cultural Humility** is viewed as a life-long process of self-reflection and self-examination (Tervalon & Murray-Garcia, 1998). Hook et al. (2013) later defines cultural humility as when "an individual has an interpersonal stance that is other-oriented rather than self-focused, characterized by respect and lack of superiority towards an individual's cultural background and experience" (p. 353).
- **Diversity** includes the complex identities that make us unique and include facets of self like race, ethnicity, culture, religion, spirituality, age, sex, gender, sexual orientation/affection, disability, social class, language, citizenship, size, and other areas that are integral to one's location of self.
- **Equity** occurs when people or groups are given open and unfettered access to requisite resources that facilitate one's ability to achieve equal outcomes. The important difference between *equity* and *equality* is their respective foci. While equity focuses on the fair end results, equality focuses on the unilateral distribution of resources, which can still have an inherent advantage for those with privilege.
- **Fundamental attribution error** refers to the often-unconscious bias to place more emphasis on perceived internal or innate characteristics to explain someone's behavior in each situation. It doesn't take into consideration the external factors that can, and often do, impact an individual or social group's behavior.

- **Implicit bias** categorizes social behavior as largely influenced by unconscious associations and judgments (Greenwald & Banaji, 1995), which results in "actions or judgments that are under the control of automatically activated evaluation, without the performer's awareness of that causation" (Greenwald et al., 1998, p. 1464).
- **Inclusion** means that everyone is included, visible, heard and their perspectives, experiences, and contributions are considered (Harvard University Diversity, Inclusion, and Belonging [DIB] Glossary of Terms, n.d.).
- **Intersectionality**, originally coined by Crenshaw (1989), references the multiple factors that impact discrimination, including the cross-section of various individual identities that inform how one views, discusses, and navigates through the world (Carbado et al., 2013).
- **Marginalization** is social exclusion, occurring when certain groups of people get denied access to varied areas of society. Types of marginalization include social, economic, political, educational and psychological means of exclusion or disregard (ACES Human Rights & Social Justice Committee, 2023).
- **Microaggressions** are the everyday verbal or nonverbal, slights, snubs, indignities or insults, whether intentional or unintentional, which communicate hostile, derogatory, or negative messages to target persons based solely upon their marginalized group membership" (Sue, 2010, p. 24). It is important to note here that research on microaggressions provides supporting evidence linking them to subsequent trauma reactions (Johnson et al., 2018; Kinavey & Cool, 2019; Sue, 2010).
- **Oppression** is the interconnectedness of prejudice with systemic/organizational power, which is the framework for the discrimination of groups of persons based on the marginalization and devaluation of various identity structures. Examples include sexism, classism, racism, ageism, ableism, heterosexism, and anti-fat bias (Vanderbilt University, 2021).
- **Patriarchy** is the prioritization of actions and beliefs that solely represent and endorse masculinity. It is systemic in the ways and methods through which power is distributed in society (jobs and positions of power given to men in government, policy, criminal justice, etc.) while also influencing how we interpersonally engage with people based on factors such as gender expectations, sexual dynamics, and space-taking (as adapted from the University of Hartford Diversity and Inclusion Glossary of Terms, n.d.).
- **Privilege** is the unearned benefits, resources, advantages, and favors that are given to people from certain social groups deemed dominant based on possession of perceived favorable identity. It operates on personal, relational, organizational, and society-wide levels, and is exerted at the expense of people who have been systematically disenfranchised. Privilege is often invisible to and unacknowledged by those who have it, and people with privileged identities often believe their privileges to have been earned. Additionally, it is the co-occurring belief that others could access the same privileges through merit and work ethic. Examples of privileged identities in Western cultures and countries are possessing white skin, heterosexuality, being cisgender,

male-identifying, Christian, those from a middle- or upper-class SES, persons who are middle-aged, and those whose first language is English (Vanderbilt University, 2021).

- **Social Justice** as defined by the ACA Code of Ethics (2014), is "the promotion of equity for all people and groups for the purpose of ending oppression and injustice affecting clients, students, counselors, families, communities, schools, workplaces, governments and other social and institutional systems" (p. 21).
- **White supremacy** is an historically-based and institutionally-perpetuated system of exploitation and oppression of persons of color by White-identifying and/or passing persons upholding a Eurocentric paradigm of ascribed entitlement for the purpose of maintaining and defending a system of wealth, power and privilege (as adapted from the ACES Human Rights & Social Justice Committee, 2023).

This list is meant to serve as a foundation for your reflections, which will ideally offer you a framework for the current understanding of social justice and equity that undergirds this chapter. In writing this chapter, the intent was to adapt and utilize these theoretical constructs in a way that is both realistic and accessible for the reader.

Stop and Reflect: *As you consider your existing intersectional identities, reflecting on areas of marginalization and privilege, you are invited to explore how your own experiences and meaning-making structures relate to the shared understandings and definitions below. Understand that your lived experience is nuanced and complex, and that blanket definitions may oversimplify the context of your experience. As such, you may want to identify in what ways CES' do better with a shared understanding as they consider the influence that language, feelings, or expressions best reflect different phenomenologies and worldviews? In what ways can those expressions be acknowledged and respected?*

Further, if you have areas of privilege, consider the following questions: In what ways have you engaged in performative allyship, or expressed commitment void of actionable effort, and in what ways could you have been more intentional in your ability to "show up?" In what areas do you need to increase your multicultural competence? As authors of this chapter, we want to invite you to consider in what ways you can consistently engage in advocacy and activism. Please note that your efforts ideally will be actionable, sustainable, collaborative, and equitable.

1.3 Social Justice and Equity in Counselor Education

Social justice, equity, and multiculturalism are all concepts that have played a role in CES, albeit to varying degrees. Societal and structural current events have influenced the counseling and counselor education profession's commitment to social justice and equity. We can see this influence in foundational ethics, the establishment of best practices, and the production of core research in counseling and counselor education. The 2014 ACA *Code of Ethics*, the 2024 CACREP

Standards, the ACA Advocacy Competencies (Toporek & Daniels, 2018), and the Multicultural and Social Justice Counseling Competencies (Ratts et al., 2016) form the foundation of ethical and culturally competent practice in counselor education and supervision. These documents address proper professional attitudes and guidelines around social justice, equity, advocacy, and multiculturalism. Several statements exist regarding the importance of social justice and advocacy to our professional identity, and several key suggestions have been offered relating to how we incorporate these values into practice have been offered. Despite these stated commitments, counselors and counselor educators continue to perceive gaps between the discourse and the day-to-day lived experiences in the profession (Chan et al., 2019; Gorritz, 2024; Nassar & Singh, 2020; Singh et al., 2020). It is not uncommon to encounter barriers and disconnects between basic and applied knowledge and the real-world implications that can contribute to counselor educators and supervisors contending with a pervading sense of false allyship and oversimplified "solutions" to offer CITs (Chan et al., 2019; Gorritz, 2024).

What is needed in the profession is clear: active, honest, consistent, and effective social justice and equity work in counselor education. Of particular emphasis is the importance of utilizing an intersectional and multidimensional approach to this work (Chan et al., 2019; Elliott & Downey, 2023). In the following sections of this chapter, we will address these issues from multiple vantage points to understand these complexities. First, we want to center our commitment to counselor educators and CES doctoral learners with systemically marginalized identities. In the recommendations that follow, we hope that you will find them useful in the context of your lived experience and the work you may have already been doing. We encourage you to approach these suggestions from a place where you can incorporate action where you have the emotional space, and that you set boundaries and find rest at times when your wellness and safety supersede the wider activism.

For those with privileged identities, we hope you read the following sections with just as much care and intention as any other chapter in this text to help inform your allyship. We want to provide concrete, feasible, and established methods for dismantling oppressive structures in the profession and establishing equity in relevant professional contexts. Our goal is to provide resources to facilitate the ability to navigate structures with existing barriers, and to identify ways to actively deconstruct inequitable systems where you have the access and ability to do so. We highly encourage you to adapt these practices to your purposes.

Stop and Reflect: *If you are someone who identifies with systemically marginalized identities, what parts of your unique situation could use a critical eye? Which systems you're a part of are not serving you? In your situation, is dismantling the identified system important and feasible or would seeking out ways to safely navigate the system be more helpful/feasible? Who could you seek out support and rest? Joy and community? If you are someone who identifies with systemically privileged identities, in what areas is there a gap between your knowledge and the action/activism that you incorporate? How is your inaction contributing to unjust systems?*

1.3.1 Advocacy and Change in Counselor Education

This section is dedicated to helping counselor educators, supervisors, and CITs who hold historically and systemically marginalized and/or privileged identities engage in effective social justice and advocacy work. We are called to serve clients and CITs with varying, intersecting identities, and our ability to render culturally competent mental health service, education, and clinical training starts with establishing professional structures founded in social justice and equity (Hannon et al., 2023). Elevating the voices and careers of those possessing systemically marginalized identities and ultimately dismantling oppressive systems can help us to overcome barriers to equity, thus leading to culturally competent practice, mentorship, praxis, and supervision. As you develop your professional identity while also navigating existing power structures, you will begin to encounter opportunities to engage in advocacy work in multiple areas. Counselor educators and supervisors inhabit leadership positions in CES organizations and associations on state, regional, and national stages as well as at varying levels within higher education; these positions afford us access and opportunity. It is incumbent upon us to use the inherent power of these positions to promote social justice and equity.

As we reflect on the journey of the counseling profession and its moral arc towards social justice, it is essential to trace the roots of this evolution. The history and origins of professional counseling can be traced back to Frank Parson's establishment of vocational guidance in 1908 (Jones, 1994). From there, the evolution of the Mental Health Counseling profession (Colangelo, 2009; Weikel, 1985) and Counselor Education (Savickas, 2011) are covered in multiple publications. As is common practice within colonized systems of power, the primary or exclusive credit was attributed to those with perceived and actual power, typically white men who presented or identified as cisgender, heterosexual, Christian, and not possessing any visible disability. This origin of exclusion is rooted in blind spots regarding our incorporation of the diversity of the human experience, in the systemic impacts of possessing various levels of privilege, and, at some points, in the conscious work of folks who wish to uphold their own power to the detriment of others. In one example of exclusion, we explore the development of the ACA *Code of Ethics* through time. The first version of the Ethical Standards distributed by the American Personnel and Guidance Association (APGA) in 1961 was six-pages long, and listed counseling as just one area of responsibility for a *professional helper* (APGA, 1961). It uses gendered language, excluding any reference other than *he*. Further, it does not include any language referencing social categories such as race, ethnicity, culture, gender, sexuality, disability, or other area. The inclusion of a more expansive view of culture within the counseling profession did not occur until much later (Hayes, 1996). By the 2004 iteration of the ACA Code of Ethics, the word *diversity* was incorporated 21 times (ACA, 2005). The word *advocate* and *dignity* were both mentioned once, and the term *advocacy* was included in the glossary. However, the phrase *social justice* was not included.

With the introduction of the 2014 ACA Code of Ethics, there was a shift in focus from the counselor's perspective to information pertaining more directly to the client's experience, as well as an emphasis on safety. The core professional values now list "enhancing human development throughout the lifespan," "honoring diversity," and "promoting social justice" (p 3). While there is a marked increase in the discussion and consideration for "diversity" and "multiculturalism" within the current iteration of the ACA *Code of Ethics*, the discussions pertaining to social justice concepts such as "power," "influence," "systemic barriers," and "authority" occur 10 times in total, and reference almost exclusively discussions related to the supervisee/supervisor, teacher/learner, and using client testimonials for personal counselor gain. Moreover, the words "privilege" and "oppression" are not mentioned. Thus, we have further work ahead related to an emphasis on core professional values based in social justice. This is just one example of many that can be extrapolated from the predominant counseling and counselor education literature. Below see some questions for further exploration to help structure your exploration of various discourses.

Stop and Reflect: *Consider the following questions when you are reading materials endorsed by the profession. Who is represented in this discourse and who is not? For those not represented, why are they not? Who was in leadership at the time this discourse was created and where is their worldview limited? What would have to happen for underrepresented voices to be better reflected in the discourse? What kinds of positions, roles, or work would I have to inhabit to be a part of the change needed?*

1.3.2 Social Justice Practice Within the Five Roles of Counselor Education

CACREP has delineated five key functions associated with being a counselor educator: teaching, supervision, counseling, research and scholarship, and leadership and advocacy (CACREP, 2024). One powerful way for us to provide concrete guidance on effective and consistent work towards social justice and equity in our counseling and educational praxis is to view the day-to-day responsibilities of counselor educators and supervisors through these CACREP-ascribed roles. The application of social justice and equity-based practices to each role enables you to effectively elevate accessibility and diversity in the collective move towards equity in education. For example, if your praxis is grounded in liberation, you can construct an action research study to collect data and publish scholarly work based on what you are already doing in the learning environment. In another example, you could apply Dollarhide's (2021) model for social justice supervision to your practices in other leadership roles. Each person's context is going to present unique dynamics and challenges, but as you read each section, we recommend the following:

- Find ways to be creative, thoughtful, and savvy with your time and resources.
- Establish accountability, consistency, and boundaries to ensure that you do not burn out. Advocacy that never materializes or quickly dissipates is often the most harmful.
- Surround yourself with a community of collaborators, co-authors, peer consultants, and others who you can share the load with. Some specific examples: rotate first author on projects, present together at conferences, co-instruct with colleagues you trust, etc. and become a part of a community of various expertise areas wherein you can lean on one another.
- Be thoughtful about when you can dismantle a system and when you may have to learn to navigate or survive within it. This can involve a certain amount of politicking, knowing when to pick your battles, and a sustained vision.
- Seek out funding and resources for your projects to:

  1. get compensated for your time and expertise, and
  2. ensure that financial resources are being directed to systemically marginalized CITs and clients.

Applying critical thinking and a "work-smarter" stance can help you to increase your effectiveness within and across domains. Lastly, your contemplation of the information presented in each section should be grounded in your own self-awareness. Identifying and actively dismantling your areas of prejudice and implicit biases is critical. For those with privileged identities, this awareness is essential as without specific attention to understanding of impact, we may not be cognizant of the potential harm we may cause. This harm can be perpetuated through ableist thinking, microaggressions, inaccurate assumptions, infantilization, euro- and ethnocentrism, nationalism, performative allyship, gaslighting, projection of our worldview and imposing our values on CITs, as well as being unaware of engaging in preferential treatment based on perceived privilege. If you are unclear on any of the terms in the above sentence, take the time to investigate their meanings and nuances.

Additionally, the self-awareness work needed around this type of growth should be done largely outside of professional interactions with willing peers, mentors, and teachers with experience and expertise. Asking colleagues or learners to help you with this growth, especially uncompensated, is likely harmful, crosses boundaries, and is an abuse of power. Consistent and earnest engagement in deliberative exploration to promote self-awareness can alleviate the potential for harm and prepare you to have difficult and necessary discussions in the learning environment, supervision, and other relevant arenas (Ivers et al., 2021). It can also be helpful to reflect on these interactions through the lens of who is expending emotional or intellectual labor during interactions.

1.3.2.1 Teaching

Within the ACA *Code of Ethics* (2014), the five professional values are framed by the concepts of human dignity and social justice, however, the ACA's commentary on the nature of social justice work is relegated to a brief mention of its importance and a common definition which states that social justice is "the promotion of equity for all people and groups for the purpose of ending oppression and injustice affecting clients, students, counselors, families, communities, schools, workplaces, governments, and other social and institutional systems" (p. 21). The deeper concepts behind social justice work—privilege, marginalization, oppression, etc.—are not detailed in the code and therefore cannot provide the needed nuance to effectively integrate these mandates. Counselor educators whose praxis is rooted in social justice, equity, and advocacy in education may find these voids within the professional values problematic; this may be especially so for educators possessing diverse and intersecting identities. The learning environment can be a primary tool utilized by counselor educators to highlight and explore the critical connection between counseling and social justice.

Accordingly, it becomes essential to have intentional and wide-ranging programmatic discussions about what and how social justice and equity are being incorporated into counseling curricula. While you will have to build some of that curriculum independently, there are also scholars and researchers who have provided frameworks for developing equitable and culturally competent materials (Baquet & Hill, 2021; Chapman-Hilliard & Parker, 2022; Medvide, 2022). This attention to detail may be of even greater importance for programs whose faculty have little visible diversity (i.e. sexuality, gender, race, disability), or are from similar geographic and demographic backgrounds, especially as structured support for learners with historically marginalized identities becomes a standard of the profession (Spellman et al., 2022). Some questions to ask as a faculty that may generate these intentional dialogues are:

- What meaningful training, engagements, or conversations have we had related to DEIBASJ, and what were our take-aways? Have these engagements been consistent or one-offs?
- What are the characteristics most or all of us have in common? What are our differences and how can these be utilized to enrich our CITs educational experiences and intentionally decolonize our educational practices?
- What perspective do we not have, or are we not considering as we make programmatic decisions? What are our collective and individual blind spots and what concrete actionable steps will we take to address these?
- Do our CITs see themselves in us, and why or why not?
- What concrete efforts are made to hire faculty and adjuncts who possess diverse identities, perspectives, and lived experiences/
- Is our conceptualization of faculty and our CIT body representative of diversity, or is it rooted in a colonized, antiquated, and narrow perspective that supports a hegemonic vision of who should have educational access?

- In what ways are our policies (including the language used to create them) and any related documentation facilitative of accessibility?
- Do our documents incorporate Universal Design (UD) and are there options for CITs with disabilities to access them without added effort, and if not, how do we implement such practices?
- What does our physical learning environment and university environment look like, and is it accessible and affirming for all CITs? How familiar are we with support services on campus?
- What is important to our faculty and CITs, and are we supporting those needs?
- In what ways do challenging conversations and discourse evoke discomfort, tension, sadness, loneliness, shame, or other feelings for faculty, and why?
- What are our sources in the class curricula? Are authors of our texts, articles, videos, etc. predominantly from one or a couple of worldviews/identities? If so, why do we pull inspiration from such a homogenous pool?

These represent some important considerations, and there are many more questions that you, your program faculty, and your department administration should ask when working towards a more socially-just curriculum based on your context.

From an individual perspective, many teaching approaches focus on social justice; some are explored in the later chapters of this text. We also want to note our belief that it is important to consider the critique of Malott and Porfilio (2011); it is key that we do not allow ourselves to stay stuck in pedagogical discourse and that we engage in action with a focus on social justice, hope, and radical love. That said, pedagogy Pedagogy is a foundational element to consider, and we must recognize that we may cause harm or leave CITs unprepared for the real world if our praxis is not refined for accessibility, equity, and rooted in diverse perspectives. Instead of delving into the teaching practices which are covered in other portions of this text, we will proffer concrete steps that you can use within your learning environment.

First, we must consider the feasibility of social justice action. This is especially poignant for counselor educators who have intersectional identities around which they experience systematic marginalization. It is important to recognize the mental, physical, emotional, and spiritual tolls as well as the professional risks they face as a person with underrepresented or historically marginalized identity in a non-affirming institutional system (O'Meara et al., 2020; Pérez & Carney, 2018; Pitcher, 2017; Podlucká, 2020; Simmons, 2017; Thacker et al., 2021). Research reflects that underrepresented faculty put in more work related to teaching, have less time for scholarship, and typically receive lower teaching reviews, which can all hinder tenure and promotion (Matthew, 2016; Pérez & Carney, 2018). These factors highlight the importance of self-care, especially nurturing social support and connections both within and outside of your colleagues (Pitcher, 2017; Podlucká, 2020; Simmons, 2017; Thacker et al., 2021). Wellness and self-care for CES doctoral learners and counselor educators are further explored in Chap. 24, however, we offer suggestions for educational tools that can be a helpful starting point when engaging cultural and justice issues in the learning environment:

- Setting up communication norms in the learning environment. This is best enacted when it is collaboratively constructed, and accountability is established around abiding by the norms.
- Recognizing your own work around cultural humility and growth and modeling your own willingness to engage with your growth edges.
- Saying CITs' names correctly and asking about pronouns.
- Making sure the components within the learning environment are accessible or utilizing Universal Design.
- Treating CITs as unique individuals and refraining from overgeneralizations or assumptions.
- Assessing learning using a variety of different modalities and refraining from work that is not professionally relevant and only serves as a hurdle.
- Making sure resources (books, handouts, media, etc.) cover a broad representation of voices and lived experiences.
- Incorporating discussions around social justice throughout your curriculum-not just the cultural focused class. Provide opportunities to dialogue about current events and nuanced systemic movements.
- Consistently using a variety of case studies that feature situations and clients from different backgrounds. Construct case studies with narratives from the community you're discussing and refrain from trying to speak to an experience that is not your own.
- Refraining from tokenism. In essence, not asking CITs with historically marginalized identities to speak for a larger group or culture that they are a part of, and providing space for CITs to share their perspective if they introduce it.
- Recognizing CITs' differing circumstances and modeling compassion.
- Giving space for CITs to share concerns with you without repercussions and model for CITs being called into conversations with curiosity and a willingness to shift your thinking when appropriate.

In addition to the aforementioned suggestions, Baquet and Hill (2021), Arthur and Achenbach (2002) and Jun (2018) suggest that incorporating a praxis that promotes both creative and experiential learning is helpful. Assignments and discussions that encourage CITs to collaboratively share their perspectives and provide space for making new, more complex meaning for CITs and faculty (Binkley & Minor, 2020) are vital outcomes to such learning praxis. Furthermore, the research of Jun (2018) focusing on educating counselors, notes the following: "It is no longer effective to teach multicultural competencies according to conventional teaching and learning models because they are not likely to provide a transformative learning experience, which has a higher probability of reducing prejudice, discrimination, and bias" (p. 346). Incorporating assignments that have real-world applications and implications is critical. One way to do this is through civic-engaged learning (Stoecker, 2018). This type of partnership can be a powerful tool in helping CITs recognize the importance of understanding the concept, connecting with the community, and making meaning. These partnerships are more than just sending CITs to a clinical placement. Community partners are working with a designated professor to accomplish a goal the community partner has identified. For example, CITs in a research class could be given an assignment such as working with a non-profit organization that has a need for program evaluation to determine the efficacy of a parenting program designed for immigrants. CITs could engage in data collection and analysis, which could subsequently facilitate their applying for federal funding for the program. Assignments that engage CITs in real-world learning provide a unique opportunity for the integration of social justice (Medvide, 2022). Additionally, utilizing tools such as multiple types of media, art, guest speakers, and panel discussions are helpful to provide CITs with worldviews, experiences, expertise, and perspectives that can augment assigned readings, and elevate the diverse and divergent voices. For a more robust exploration of teaching praxis, please refer to Chaps. 2 and 3, as well as the counseling specialization chapters in Part 4.

1.3.2.2 Supervision

There is a professional responsibility and ethical imperative to integrate social justice and multiculturalism into counseling supervision. However, guidance as to *how* to incorporate these constructs may vary based on the competency of the clinical supervisor (Fickling et al., 2019). CITs entering practicum and internship need supervisors and mentors whose approaches are rooted in social justice and intersectionality to facilitate the development of their self-efficacy (Mitchell & Butler, 2021). This can guide their efforts to navigate, challenge, and dismantle systemic barriers their clients or they, themselves, encounter. Though a best practice, there is currently no requirement for field experience sites to be centered in social justice or to engage in advocacy work (CACREP, 2024; Dollarhide et al., 2021). When reviewing the 2024 CACREP Standards that delineate supervisor qualifications, language focusing on multicultural competence or social justice is absent. Rather, qualifications focus broadly on years of experience and appropriate licensure/educational experiences. This lack of direction regarding supervision and social justice was the impetus for Dollarhide et al.'s (2021) development of a comprehensive supervision model framing decision-making and related interventions in a socially-just context.

We believe the Dollarhide et al. (2021) model for Social Justice Supervision (SJS) is transformative, as it weaves social justice as the foundation for all interactions in counseling, supervision, and education. When examining the supervision triad (i.e., supervisor, supervisee, and client), the model considers the interests and investment of each person and highlights the need for goals to be socially just. It also recognizes the requirement for oppressive structures to be examined, and that related interventions be selected and applied based on individual and systemic needs. It also notes an emphasis on critical reflection regarding intersecting identities and the creation of culturally affirming environments through the intentional exploration of positionality. The SJS Model is comprehensive and designed to be readily integrated into a wide variety of supervisory styles and theoretical approaches. Infusing the SJS Model into a supervisor's identity can lead to "culturally affirming social justice supervisors who model, teach, and hold themselves accountable for social justice can empower new ways of counseling practice, bringing more diverse counseling professionals into the field" (Dollarhide et al., 2021, p. 111). Supervision practices are discussed further in Chap. 4, as well as the counseling specialization chapters in Part 4.

1.3.2.3 Counseling

As counselor educators, our orientation and identity operate on two levels; our own counseling practices with our clients, and those that we teach to CITs. Our own counseling identities must align with the socially just frameworks that we use in educating CITs in their professional responsibilities (Field et al., 2019; Um & Wood, 2024; Westcott & Grimes, 2023). From a holistic viewpoint, many clients and CITs with historically marginalized identities may need the advocacy of counselors and counselor educators on multiple levels. The contemporary sociopolitical environment has unmasked the deep-rooted racism that BIPOC folks experience. This has resulted in current global social justice movements calling for a sustainable and multifaceted approach to addressing multiculturalism, social justice, and equity in the counseling profession. True integration of diversity in counseling and counselor education requires operationalizing the current policies and competency standards (Singh et al., 2020) so that counselors and counselor educators move beyond utilizing "social justice", "multiculturalism", "diversity" as buzzwords. When operationalizing and establishing concrete steps, intentionality, accountability, consistency, and feasibility are essential to our efforts to educate future counselors as they navigate their own cultural competence development. Additionally, we must apply these rigorous practices to our own clinical work and bridge any gaps between what is required by our ethical codes and standards and established best counseling practices. Below we offer guidance to effectively apply intentionality, accountability, consistency, and feasibility:

- **Intentionality**: Reflect on this question: In what ways have I deeply contemplated the ways that I can incorporate advocacy into my counseling practice on behalf of my clients? It is important to be thoughtful, to seek out discourses, voices, and consultation about your practices. Engaging in reactive clinical practices without applying intentionality can result in harm to clients.
- **Accountability**: Consider the ways in which you are holding yourself accountable for your actions and commitments. It is imperative that you can articulate your commitment to and demonstrate your engagement in social justice and equity work with clients, colleagues, and supervisors. This can be facilitated by surrounding yourself with trusted accountability partners.
- **Consistency**: How are you building enduring practices with lasting ability? Such efforts must be sustainable as well as consistently developed. Failing to do so could result in performative allyship which perpetuates harm.

- **Feasibility**: How will your social justice efforts be implemented? With a specific and clearly delineated plan of action that balances factors such as current roles, responsibilities, and time constraints, with your ability to incorporate interventions and paradigms that support social justice and equity.

To incorporate these elements effectively, adopting a lens of intersectionality has become an integral part of the necessary work (Chan et al., 2019; Interiano & Lim, 2018; Peters, 2017). Intersectionality expands the notion of social identity categories by exploring differences across dimensions of culture and social context such as race, ethnicity, gender identity, sexuality, ability status, spirituality, social class, affectional identity, and immigration status (Bowleg, 2012; Corlett & Mavin, 2014). It also emphasizes that intersectionality must fully operate with a clear attention toward power (Bowleg & Bauer, 2016). Counselors can and should use intersectionality to conceptualize and address multiple and overlapping levels of oppression (Carbado et al., 2013; Chan et al., 2019) and be highly cognizant of the power dynamics within and outside of the counseling room.

To fully understand power dynamics, it is key for our counseling practice to identify the dominant paradigms within the profession and ourselves (Hannon et al., 2023). Counseling practices rooted in Eurocentrism and perpetuating the expectations that our clients assimilate and acculturate to heteronormative and patriarchal ways rooted in white supremacist ideology inhibits quality of care for clients. It also fosters implicit bias, which impairs our ability to accurately diagnose and treat our clients. Addressing this gap through a multifaceted, non-hierarchical, non-patriarchal approach warrants several interventions that identify the institutional and cultural barriers that exist (Chan et al., 2019; Kuo et al., 2018). Below are suggestions for addressing these dynamics and integrating social justice, equity, and diversity into counseling for greater multicultural competency and effective practice:

- Remember to consider the impact of legal and political oppression/pressures facing clients and CITs (Shannonhouse & Myers, 2014).
- Consistently, respectfully, and humbly engage with persons from other cultures and reflect deeply about your experiences (Shannonhouse et al., 2018).
- Make sure that discussions with clients about culture and justice are natural parts of your counseling work. This permeates all aspects and stages of counseling from intake through termination.
- Operate with cultural humility. Understand that you are continually growing and learning, and temper expectations for perfection.
- Be willing to apologize earnestly and take concrete, ethical steps toward repairing when you're wrong.
- Seek and create a diverse network of people and nurture authentic, meaningful, and caring relationships that support each person's commitment to learning and growing. Consult with multiple trusted sources when you encounter a complex, difficult situation.

- Examine theoretical orientations and interventions through a socially-just, equity-based lens. Change or eliminate practices that are rooted in paradigms that don't serve your clients and constantly interrogate counseling protocol structures.
- Teach the above to your CITs and supervisees.

1.3.2.4 Scholarship

The production of scholarly works is an integral part of being a counselor educator and supervisor as noted by the 2024 CACREP standards. Publishing research involves engaging with oppressive systems and structures and people with privilege and power. As such, systemic barriers rooted in implicit bias can thwart the publication of research that is framed in social justice, equity, and multiculturalism. This weaponization of power and privilege in scholarship serves to control professional discourse and shared knowledge through constricting the research promoted, disseminated, and utilized. As such, it is important to understand how to successfully navigate through the bias and oppression within the publication process. Giordano et al. (2021) offer concrete guidance in this regard. Scholarly works receive favorable reviews if they:

1. have social validity, or are additive to the profession and/or society at large,
2. are doable in the publish-or-perish environment of many institutions, and
3. if researchers can successfully navigate the added barriers created by sexism, racism, and other isms within the profession (Arnold et al., 2016; Giordano et al., 2021; Lundine et al., 2018).

Additionally, the processes of creating and disseminating research are two different skill sets. Even if your research results are profound, they will not be read if you don't reach the proper audience. To publish research and share knowledge that others will appreciate, it is important to identify your intended audience, determine what venues will allow you to reach that audience, and promote yourself and your work in effective and efficient ways (Giordano et al., 2021).

While you navigate the power structures overseeing the publication of extant research, it is integral to remember that you also hold power as the researcher. The way you choose areas of study, select your participants and measures, and how the results are communicated each have the potential to promote social justice and equity or perpetuate oppression and create barriers. Researching with protocols steeped in rigor *and* social justice can result in disseminating research that is more representative of historically marginalized communities, thus increasing accessibility, inclusion, and diversity. There are existing paradigms that can help frame our work in this area. One widely recognized approach is action research, which is "any type of research that shifts the control for the study from the academic or professional researcher to the people who have traditionally been considered subjects of the inquiry" (Guiffrida et al., 2011). In action research, the research is framed by the practitioners, clients, and CITs themselves. Results are designed to challenge established oppressive paradigms, and data analysis and results directly enhance the lives of those it is studying (Guiffrida et al., 2011). Furthermore, the results of action research are shared in the community in a clear and easily applied way. When research incorporates philosophies like action research, critical race theory, liberation theory, and other socially just models, authors can effectively address prevailing oppressive systems and work toward dismantling racism, sexism, and other prevalent "isms" (Brown et al., 2019; Hylton, 2012). Navigating and developing research can be complex and, at times, daunting. We encourage you to hone your skills to produce meaningful research that is not only published, but that is grounded in social justice, advocacy, equity, and multiculturalism. A richer context of this topic can be found in Parts 3 and 5, specifically in Chaps. 11, 14, and 23 of this textbook.

1.3.2.5 Leadership and Advocacy

In 2018, the ACA adopted advocacy as one of the central pillars of a strategic initiative (Toporek & Daniels, 2018). The 2014 ACA *Code of Ethics* also clearly delineates the roles of counselors as advocates for the profession. And within the Advocacy Competencies (Toporek & Daniels, 2018), it states that counselor educators and doctoral learners should examine the relevance of multicultural considerations regarding clients, groups, issues, and approaches. This growth is promising. However, ACA has missed the mark on statements about topics such as undue police violence (Lee, 2020). While subsequent statements were released to clarify, it is hard to forget when statements are made that support an unclear agenda for justice related to historically disenfranchised groups.

For doctoral learners and counselor educators, mentorship is crucial and often linked with potential leadership opportunities. For those facing systemic and institutional oppression, it is understandable that advocacy and leadership may feel unattainable within counselor education. This shines additional light on the pressure of historically marginalized faculty and doctoral learners (Cartwright et al., 2021; Matthew, 2016). It also speaks to the research on women, specifically persons with underrepresented and historically marginalized identities, spending time on service that cuts into activities such as scholarship (O'Meara et al., 2020). Joining organizations like Chi Sigma Iota Counseling Academic and Professional Honor Society International and getting involved in counseling program leadership can be good ways to start your involvement in leadership (Osterlund & Mack, 2011). Studying the leadership efforts and narratives of experienced transformative and justice-minded leaders can provide a blueprint for your own efforts. One example is the Social Justice Action Project detailed by Makaiau et al. (2023). In addition, going to presentations that focus on mentorship, leadership, and advocacy are all potential ways to become involved.

Within national, regional, and state counselor education organizations, there may be opportunities to get involved in leadership that allows you to advocate for professional counseling or other areas of passion. At times, committees, subcommittees, or ad hoc committees are started based on issues brought to the executive boards. There are also typically volunteer opportunities at conferences which will allow you to meet others in our field and potentially get a reduced conference rate. In some cases, if money is an issue, there may be scholarship programs available. We recognize that these options may have been attempted, which can lead to disappointing dead ends or roadblocks for various reasons, such as accessibility, microaggressions, or simply a lack of response.

Joining mentorship programs within the field is another option to help network and move into leadership, and becoming an anti-racist, anti-oppressive mentor to new professionals can facilitate the continuation of justice-centered mentorship (Cisneros et al., 2023). Often, the mentors have actively said they are willing to mentor CITs or new faculty in these situations. Typically, the organization tries to pair up mentor/mentees based on stated interests. These can be enriching opportunities. Mentorship with respect to retention of learners, particularly BIPOC learners and learners with diverse and intersecting identities is explored more in Chap. 8. Additionally, the importance of establishing mentorship early in the learner's journey is explored further in Chap. 6. Other opportunities to support BIPOC faculty have recently garnered attention. For example, the North Atlantic Region for Counselor Education and Supervision (NARACES), has offered Affinity Groups for individuals who identify as BIPOC at both its regional and national conferences. Seeking out opportunities like the BIPOC affinity space (which offers the chance to avoid the White gaze) or various interest networks allow specific groups an escape to perhaps process, celebrate with peers, or plan, depending on the group. Chapter 23 provides a deeper dive into leadership and advocacy.

Stop and Reflect: *Consider some of the following questions to help inform your work and show up in culturally competent ways. Am I asking emotional or intellectual labor from someone (especially someone who identifies with a systemically marginalized identity) when I could take that labor upon myself? If someone is expending emotional or intellectual labor on my learning and awareness, did they consent to that labor? What specific resources (books, podcasts, articles, narratives, etc.) would I seek out to do my own work in this area? What from my own life or experience has led to this gap in my knowledge?*

1.4 Navigating Counselor Education with Systemically Marginalized Identities

Higher education has perpetuated a system of disenfranchisement and oppression for CITs with historically marginalized identities (Sherman & Slate, 2020; Weddle-West & Bingham, 2010). This is further exacerbated by limited access to representation when examining diverse faculty members and course material which is often situated within the dominant culture (Delgado et al., 2012). Marginalization extends across many intersecting identities, including social class (O'Hara & Cook, 2018), disability (Rivas, 2020), and among the LGBTQQIP2SA+ population (Bryan, 2018). Counselor educator programs must do more than acknowledge these barriers and the adversity present within the system by proactively addressing systemic barriers. Barriers can be context bound and complex to analyze, however, meaningful progress should bridge the gap between theoretical discourse and concrete action. Further, recommendations for navigating or mitigating institutional barriers should be specific and informed by the experiences of folks who have managed these dynamics. To assist folks who may be subject to inequitable institutional dynamics, the chart below indicates real barriers that professionals in counselor education have faced, as well as guidance for how to address the identified barrier based on their experiences. The experiences of the folks in these excerpts do not represent a one-size-fits-all answer to every situation but may provide a foundation for helping you navigate the spaces you inhabit (Table 1.1).

Stop and Reflect: *Consider the following questions as you navigate your roles and responsibilities. In what realms do you feel you have strengths when it comes to a socially just, equitable, and culturally competent practice? In what realms do you feel you have gaps in your knowledge or the action you take? What prevents you from addressing these gaps in the present? How can you allocate your time and energy to address them? If the barriers to more competent practice stem from a system, what parts of the system are preventing you? What power, role, or actions could you take to influence these steps?*

Table 1.1 Identified barriers in counselor education and practices for addressing barriers

Identified barrier	Lived experience of identified barrier	Best practices for addressing barriers
Performative allyship	"I wanted… institutions to follow up on their words through their actions and bridge that gap. I wanted them to hold themselves accountable for the choices they made to not care and be performative"	• Actively commit to allyship and advocacy • Exercise and increase personal awareness of biases • Inquire about specific examples of social justice equity work to ascertain genuine commitment to DEIJABSJ (Kutlaca & Radke, 2023) • Incorporate terminology that goes beyond the broadest, most well-known terms in social justice equity work, so that you create a culture facilitative of dialogue and aid with personal awareness (Kutlaca & Radke, 2023)
Lack of community	"I found people communally and mentors who weren't even teaching but were somewhere in the department. It was about navigating spaces where I didn't feel seen or valued. I found what I needed in the community and through other people who took me under their wing"	• Actively seek community and sources of social support upon which you can rely. You may need to be creative. (Erby & Jones, 2024) • Find equitable social connections and community. Consider finding supports that are not attached to your position at an institution (Erby & Jones, 2024)

(continued)

Table 1.1 (continued)

Identified barrier	Lived experience of identified barrier	Best practices for addressing barriers
Fatigue and burnout	"[Social justice, equity, and cultural work is] a never-ending battle. I say this because when issues are brought up in class and across the learning materials discussed in the courses, I always say 'we as a profession have long way to go, though we have made strides. Finding the *strides* made in counselor ed is a struggle because I don't have dates and events on a timeline to present as if to say, 'this is what we've done'"	• Consider the impact of emotional labor on persons with historically marginalized identities, and as a countermeasure identify potential protective factors (Jeung et al., 2018) • Create a personal and institutional work balance for advocacy that is adaptable and sustainable (Çarkit, 2024) • Prioritize rest! *Rest, joy, and wellness can be radical acts of resistance.* Attend to any barriers and develop a realistic plan for coping with stress (Hersey, 2022) to help reduce the potential for fatigue and burnout
Lack of representation and accessibility	"I realized how little anti-fat bias is actually addressed or ever talked about when diversity is addressed. I feel like I'm not even sure what I need because I've never stopped to think that I could even ask for things to be different [...] I've lived with all of these uncomfortable and sometimes heart-breaking experiences caused by other people/my surroundings but always got the message that I didn't have a right to be upset"	• Critically examine whose voices are represented at the institutional level and whose are not, in all aspects of learning. This includes the leaders, community members, texts, videos, and other representations of lived experience (Woodbridge, 2023) • If your identities and lived experiences are not represented, be thoughtful and strategic about in what ways you engage in advocacy and identify community partners (from within or outside of the institution) who will support you

1.5 Conclusion

Counselor education and supervision is a complex field with many opportunities as well as challenges. We hope that this has provided you with a starting framework for a comprehensive view of social justice, equity, and diversity dynamics in the field, along with practical, usable guidance. After reading this chapter, we highly recommend that you ask yourself the questions posed throughout, and bring to your programs, CITs, supervisees, and colleagues any insights you gained along the way. Creating an edifying community of professionals dedicated to social justice, equity, diversity, and multiculturalism is imperative to our work. We invite you to create those communities in the places you work. Further detail regarding the ways that systemic barriers manifest in admissions processes, curriculum development, faculty hiring practices, and dynamics within the learning environment, as well as other imperative counselor education processes, will be reviewed in future chapters. We hope that your introduction to these concepts will help you to navigate later chapters in greater depth and assist in your reflections on these topics as they relate to your specific context.

References

ACES Human Rights and Social Justice Committee. (2023). *Association for counselor education and supervision diversity, inclusion, equity, human rights and social justice statement*. Association for Counselor Education and Supervision. https://acesonline.net/diversity-equity-inclusion-and-justice/

American Counseling Association. (2005). *ACA code of ethics*. https://www.counseling.org/knowledge-center/aca-archives/code-of-ethics-archives

American Counseling Association. (2014). *2014 ACA code of ethics*. https://www.counseling.org/docs/default-source/default-document-library/ethics/2014-aca-code-of-ethics.pdf?sfvrsn=55ab73d0_1

American Personnel and Guidance Association. (1961). *Ethical standards*. https://www.counseling.org/knowledge-center/aca-archives/code-of-ethics-archives

Arnold, N. W., Crawford, E. R., & Khalifa, M. (2016). Psychological heuristics and faculty of color: Racial battle fatigue and tenure/promotion. *The Journal of Higher Education, 87*(6), 890–919. https://doi.org/10.1080/00221546.2016.11780891

Arthur, N., & Achenbach, K. (2002). Developing multicultural counseling competencies through experiential learning. *Counselor Education & Supervision, 42*(1), 2–14. https://doi.org/10.1002/j.1556-6978.2002.tb01299.x

Bahrainwala, L. (2020). The web of White disengagement. *Women & Language, 43*(1), 135–140. https://doi.org/10.34036/WL.2020.013

Baquet, S. N., & Hill, J. (2021). Cross-cultural distance dialogues in counselor education: Collaborative pedagogy. *Teaching and Supervision in Counseling, 4*(2), Article 4. https://doi.org/10.7290/tsc04xwpi

Binkley, E. E., & Minor, A. J. (2020). Constructivist pedagogy to promote cultural learning in counselor education. *Journal of Creativity in Mental Health, 16*(3), 348–359. https://doi.org/10.1080/15401383.2020.1763222

Bowleg, L. (2012). The problem with phrase women and minorities: Intersectionality—An important theoretical framework for public health. *American Journal of Public Health, 102*, 1267–1273. https://doi.org/10.2105/AJPH.2012.300750

Bowleg, L., & Bauer, G. (2016). Invited reflection: Quantifying intersectionality. *Psychology of Women Quarterly, 40*(3), 337–341. https://doi.org/10.1177/0361684316654282

Brown, K. S., Kijakazi, K., Runes, C., & Turner, M. A. (2019, February). Confronting structural racism in research and policy analysis: Charting a course for policy research institutions. *The Urban Institute*. https://www.urban.org/sites/default/files/publication/99852/confronting_structural_racism_in_research_and_policy_analysis_0.pdf

Bryan, S. E. (2018). Types of LGBT microaggressions in counselor education programs. *Journal of LGBT Issues in Counseling, 12*(2), 119–135. https://doi.org/10.1080/15538605.2018.1455556

Carbado, D. W., Crenshaw, K. W., Mays, V. M., & Tomlinson, B. (2013). Intersectionality. *Du Bois Review, 10*(2), 303–312. https://doi.org/10.1017/S1742058X13000349

Çarkıt, E. (2024). Counselor burnout, person–environment fit, and job crafting among school counselors: A person-centered approach. *Journal of Counseling & Development, 102*, 302–317. https://doi.org/10.1002/jcad.12513

Cartwright, A. D., Stark, M. D., Boswell, J. N., & Oller, M. L. (2021). Black female doctoral students' mentorship experiences in counselor education. *Journal of Counseling and Leadership, 8*(2), 87–99. https://doi.org/10.1002/ceas.12262

Chan, C. D., Cor, D. N., & Band, M. P. (2019). Privilege and oppression in counselor education: An intersectionality framework. *Journal of Multicultural Counseling and Development, 46*(1), 58–73. https://doi.org/10.1002/jmcd.12092

Chapman-Hilliard, C., & Parker, B. (2022). Embodied social justice learning: Considerations for curriculum development and training in counseling programs. *Journal for Social Action in Counseling & Psychology, 14*(1), 77–93. https://doi.org/10.33043/JSACP.14.1.77-93

Cisneros, D., Anandavalli, S., Brown, E. M., Whitman, J. S., & Chaney, M. P. (2023). Antiracist mentorship: A multicultural and social justice approach to mentoring students identifying as Black, Indigenous, and Persons of Color in counselor education. *Journal of Counselor Leadership & Advocacy, 10*(1), 63–75. https://doi.org/10.1080/2326716X.2022.2162462

Colangelo, J. J. (2009). The American mental health counselors association: Reflection on 30 historic years. *Journal of Counseling & Development, 87*(2), 234–240. https://doi.org/10.1002/j.1556-6678.2009.tb00572.x

Corlett, S., & Mavin, S. (2014). Intersectionality, identity and identity work. *Gender in Management, 29*(5), 258–276. https://doi.org/10.1108/GM-12-2013-0138

Council for Accreditation of Counseling and Related Educational Programs. (2024). *2024 CACREP standards*. https://www.cacrep.org/wp-content/uploads/2024/04/2024-Standards-Combined-Version-4.11.2024.pdf

Crenshaw, K. (1989). Demarginalizing the intersection of race and sex: A Black feminist critique of antidiscrimination doctrine, feminist theory and antiracist politics. *University of Chicago Legal Forum, 1989*(1), 139–167.

Delgado, R., Stefancic, J., & Harris, A. (2012). *Critical race theory: An introduction* (2nd ed). NYU Press. http://www.jstor.org/stable/j.ctt9qg9h2

Dickenson, S. R. (2021, January 28). *What is allyship?* National Institute of Health Office of Equity, Diversity, and Inclusion. https://www.edi.nih.gov/blog/communities/what-allyship

Dollarhide, C. T., Hale, S. C., & Stone-Sabali, S. (2021). A new model for social justice supervision. *Journal of Counseling & Development, 99*(1), 104–113. https://doi.org/10.1002/jcad.12358

Elliott, J. A., & Downey, L. E. (2023). Broaching intersectionality and social justice: Incorporating Fruitvale Station into multicultural counselor education. *Journal of Creativity in Mental Health, 18*(4), 604–615. https://doi.org/10.1080/15401383.2022.2035294

Erby, A. N., & Jones, C. T. (2024). A mixed methods study of Black/African American counselor wellness. *Journal of Counseling & Development, 102*, 96–106. https://doi.org/10.1002/jcad.12498

Fickling, M. J., Tangen, J. L., Graden, M. W., & Grays, D. (2019). Multicultural and social justice competencies in clinical supervision. *Counselor Education and Supervision, 58*, 309–316. https://doi.org/10.1002/ceas.12159

Field, T. A., Ghoston, M. R., Grimes, T. O., Sturm, D. C., Kaur, M., Aninditya, A., & Toomey, M. (2019). Trainee counselor development of social justice counseling competencies. *Journal for Social Action in Counseling & Psychology, 11*(1), 33–50. https://doi.org/10.33043/JSACP.11.1.33-50

Gates, T. G., Bennett, B., & Baines, D. (2023). Strengthening critical allyship in social work education: Opportunities in the context of #BlackLivesMatter and COVID-19. *Social Work Education, 42*(3), 371–387. https://doi.org/10.1080/02615479.2021.1972961

Giordano, A. L., Schmit, M. K., & Schmit, E. L. (2021). Best practice guidelines for publishing rigorous research in counseling. *Journal of Counseling & Development, 99*(2), 123–133. https://doi.org/10.1002/jcad.12360

Gorritz, F. (2024). Addressing elements of White supremacy in counselor education: The path forward for racial justice in the counseling field. *Counselor Education & Supervision, 63*(2), 131–144. https://doi.org/10.1002/ceas.12297

Greenwald, A. G., & Banaji, M. R. (1995). Implicit social cognition: Attitudes, self-esteem, and stereotypes. *Psychological Review, 102*(1), 4–27. https://doi.org/10.1037/0033-295X.102.1.4

Greenwald, A. G., McGhee, D. E., & Schwartz, J. L. K. (1998). Measuring individual differences in implicit cognition: The implicit association test. *Journal of Personality and Social Psychology, 74*(6), 1464–1480. https://doi.org/10.1037/0022-3514.74.6.1464

Guiffrida, D. A., Douthit, K. Z., Lynch, M. F., & Mackie, K. L. (2011). Publishing action research in counseling journals. *Journal of Counseling & Development, 89*(3), 282–287. https://doi.org/10.1002/j.1556-6678.2011.tb00090.x

Hannon, M. D., White, E. E., & Fleming, H. (2023). Ambivalence to action: Addressing systemic racism in counselor education. *Counselor Education & Supervision, 62*(2), 108–117. https://doi.org/10.1002/ceas.12264

Harvard University. (n.d.). *Glossary of diversity, inclusion, and belonging terms.* https://edib.harvard.edu/files/dib/files/dib_glossary.pdf

Hayes, P. (1996). Addressing the complexities of culture and gender in counseling. *Journal of Counseling & Development, 74*(4), 332–338. https://doi.org/10.1002/j.1556-6676.1996.tb01876.x

Hernández, L. H. (2020). Silence, (in)action, and the downfalls of White allyship. *Women & Language, 43*(1), 147–152. https://doi.org/10.34036/WL.2020.015

Hersey, T. (2022). *Rest is resistance: A manifesto.* Little, Brown Spark.

Hook, J. N., Davis, D. E., Owen, J., Worthington, E. L., & Usey, S. O. (2013). Cultural humility: Measuring openness to culturally diverse clients. *Journal of Counseling Psychology, 60*(3), 353–366. https://doi.org/10.1037/a0032595

Hylton, K. (2012). Talk the talk, walk the walk: Defining critical race theory in research. *Race Ethnicity and Education, 15*(1), 23–41. https://doi.org/10.1080/13613324.2012.638862

Interiano, C. G., & Lim, J. H. (2018). A "chameleonic" identity: Foreign-born doctoral students in U.S. counselor education. *International Journal for the Advancement of Counselling, 40*(3), 310–325. https://doi.org/10.1007/s10447-018-9328-0

Ivers, N., Johnson, D., & Rogers, J. (2021). The association between implicit racial bias and mindfulness in mental health practitioners. *Journal of Counseling and Development, 99*(1), 11–23. https://doi.org/10.1002/jcad.12350

Jeung, D. Y., Kim, C., & Chang, S. J. (2018). Emotional labor and burnout: A review of the literature. *Yonsei Medical Journal, 59*(2), 187–193. https://doi.org/10.3349/ymj.2018.59.2.187

Johnson, R., Leighton, L., & Caldwell, C. (2018). The embodied experience of microaggressions: Implications for clinical practice. *Journal of Multicultural Counseling and Development, 46*(3), 157–171. https://doi.org/10.1002/jmcd.12099

Jones, L. K. (1994). Frank Parsons' contribution to career counseling. *Journal of Career Development, 20*(4), 287–294. https://doi.org/10.1007/BF02106301

Jun, H. (2018). *Social justice, multicultural counseling, and practice: Beyond a conventional approach* (2nd ed.). Springer. https://doi.org/10.1007/978-3-319-72514-7

Kinavey, H., & Cool, C. (2019). The broken lens: How anti-fat bias in psychotherapy is harming our clients and what to do about it. *Women & Therapy, 42*(1–2), 116–130. https://doi.org/10.1080/02703149.2018.1524070

Kuo, P., Woo, H., & Washington, A. (2018). Professional identity development of international counselor education doctoral students. *Journal of Counselor Leadership and Advocacy, 5*(2), 153–169. https://doi.org/10.1080/2326716x.2018.1452079

Kutlaca, M., & Radke, H. R. M. (2023). Towards an understanding of performative allyship: Definition, antecedents and consequences. *Social & Personality Psychology Compass, 17*(2), 1–12. https://doi.org/10.1111/spc3.12724

Lee, K. (2020, May 18). *ACA statement on undue police violence.* American Counseling Association. https://www.counseling.org/news/updates/2020/05/18/aca-statement-on-undue-police-violence

Lundine, J., Bourgeault, I., Clark, J., Heidari, S., & Balabanova, D. (2018). The gendered system of academic publishing. *The Lancet, 391*(10132), 1754–1756. https://doi.org/10.1016/S0140-6736(18)30950-4

Makaiau, A. S., Halagao, P. E., & Thao, G. (2023). Creating transformative leaders of social justice in education. *Multicultural Perspectives, 25*(1), 52–59. https://doi.org/10.1080/15210960.2022.2136181

Malott, C. S., & Porfilio, B. (Eds.). (2011). *Critical pedagogy in the twenty-first century: A new generation of scholars.* Information Age Publishing.

Matthew, P. A. (2016, November 23). What is faculty diversity worth to a university? *The Atlantic.* https://www.theatlantic.com/education/archive/2016/11/what-is-faculty-diversity-worth-to-a-university/508334/

Medvide, M. B. (2022). Teaching cultural competence and social justice in a mental health counseling graduate course: Reflection and review of the literature. *Journal for Social Action in Counseling & Psychology, 14*(1), 94–105. https://doi.org/10.33043/JSACP.14.1.94-105

Mitchell, M. D., & Butler, S. K. (2021). Acknowledging intersectional identity in supervision: The multicultural integrated supervision model. *Journal of Multicultural Counseling & Development, 49*(2), 101–115. https://doi.org/10.1002/jmcd.12209

Nassar, S. C., & Singh, A. A. (2020). Embodying the multicultural and social justice counseling competency movement: Voices from the field. *Journal of Multicultural Counseling and Development, 98*(3), 253–260. https://doi.org/10.1002/jcad.12320

O'Hara, C., & Cook, J. M. (2018). Doctoral-level counseling students' experiences of social class microaggressions. *Counselor Education and Supervision 57*(4), 255–270. https://epublications.marquette.edu/edu_fac/523

O'Meara, K., Sayer, L., Nyunt, G., & Lennartz, C. (2020). Stressed, interrupted, and underestimated: Experiences of women and URM faculty during one workday. *Journal of the Professoriate, 11*(1), 105–137. https://caarpweb.org/wp-content/uploads/2020/07/stressed-interrupted-and-underestimated.pdf

Osterlund, L. C., & Mack, M. (2011). Promoting advocacy and leadership in counselor education through an innovative student and alumni association. *Vistas, 29*, 1–15. https://www.counseling.org/docs/default-source/vistas/vistas_2011_article_29.pdf?sfvrsn=ba1724f5_11

Pérez, J. F., & Carney, J. V. (2018). Telling of institutional oppression: Voices of minoritized counselor educators. *Counselor Education & Supervision, 57*(3), 162–177. https://doi.org/10.1002/ceas.12108

Peters, H. C. (2017). Multicultural complexity: An intersectional lens for clinical supervision. *International Journal for the Advancement of Counselling, 39*(2), 176–187. https://doi.org/10.1007/s10447-017-9290-2

Pitcher, E. N. (2017). 'There's stuff that comes with being an unexpected guest': Experiences of transacademics with microaggressions. *International Journal of Qualitative Studies in Education, 30*(7), 688–703. https://doi.org/10.1080/09518398.2017.1309588

Podlucká, D. (2020). Transformative anti-ableist pedagogy for social justice: Charting a critical agenda for inclusive education. *Outlines-Critical Practice Studies, 21*(1), 69–97. https://doi.org/10.7146/ocps.v21i1.118234

Ratts, M. J., Singh, A. A., Nassar-McMillan, S., Butler, S. K., & Rafferty McCullough, J. (2016). Multicultural and social justice counseling competencies: Guidelines for the counseling profession. *Journal of Multicultural Counseling and Development, 44*(1), 28–48. https://doi.org/10.1002/jmcd.12035

Rivas, M. (2020). Disability in counselor education: Perspectives from the United States. *International Journal for the Advancement of Counselling, 42*(4), 366–381. https://doi.org/10.1007/s10447-020-09404-y

Savickas, M. L. (2011). *Career counseling*. American Psychological Association.

Shannonhouse, L. R., & Myers, J. E. (2014). Global links and gaps in counselor education programs: Establishing a baseline. *The Professional Counselor, 4*(4), 353–362. https://doi.org/10.15241/lss.4.4.353

Shannonhouse, L. R., Myers, J. E., & Barrio Minton, C. A. (2018). Cultural immersion in counselor education: Trends, prevalence, and common components. *Journal of Multicultural Counseling & Development, 46*(4), 283–296. https://doi.org/10.1002/jmcd.12115

Sherman, J., & Slate, J. R. (2020). Differences in graduation and persistence rates over time for African-American students at Texas 4-year universities. *Athens Journal of Education, 7*(4), 353–364. https://doi.org/10.30958/aje.7-4-2

Simmons, S. L. (2017). A thousand words are worth a picture: A snapshot of trans postsecondary educators in higher education. *International Journal of Qualitative Studies in Education, 30*(3), 266–284. https://doi.org/10.1080/09518398.2016.1254303

Singh, A. A., Appling, B., & Trepal, H. (2020). Using the multicultural and social justice counseling competencies to decolonize counseling practice: The important roles of theory, power, and action. *Journal of Counseling and Development, 89*(3), 261–271. https://doi.org/10.1002/jcad.12321

Spellman, K., Dillenbeck, J., Edwards, N. N., & Bohecker, L. (2022). Supporting marginalized students in counselor education and supervision programs. *Journal of Counselor Leadership & Advocacy, 9*(1), 32–44. https://doi.org/10.1080/2326716X.2021.2007429

Stoecker, R. (2018). *Liberating service learning and the rest of higher education civic engagement*. Temple University Press.

Sue, D. W. (Ed.). (2010). *Microaggressions and marginality: Manifestation, dynamics, and impact*. Wiley.

Tervalon, M., & Murray-García, J. (1998). Cultural humility versus cultural competence: A critical distinction in defining physician training outcomes in multicultural education. *Journal of Health Care for the Poor and Underserved, 9*(2), 117–125. https://doi.org/10.1353/hpu.2010.0233

Thacker, N. E., Barrio Minton, C. A., & Riley, K. B. (2021). Marginalized counselor educators' experiences negotiating identity: A narrative inquiry. *Counselor Education and Supervision, 60*(2), 94–111. https://doi.org/10.1002/ceas.12198

Toporek, R. L., & Daniels, J. (2018). *American counseling association advocacy competencies: Endorsed by ACA 2003 (Lewis, Arnold, House & Toporek) and updated in 2018*. American Counseling Association. https://www.counseling.org/docs/default-source/competencies/aca-advocacy-competencies-updated-may-2020.pdf?sfvrsn=f410212c_6

Um, B., & Wood, S. M. (2024). The influence of professional identity and social justice training on counseling trainees' social justice advocacy. *Journal of Counselor Leadership & Advocacy, 11*(1), 46–59. https://doi.org/10.1080/2326716X.2023.2292229

University of Hartford. (n.d). *Diversity and inclusion glossary of terms*. https://www.hartford.edu/about/diversity-inclusion/deij-learning-resources/deij-glossary.aspx

Vanderbilt University. (2021). *Understanding privilege and oppression*. https://www.vanderbilt.edu/oacs/wp-content/uploads/sites/140/Understanding-Privilege-and-Oppression-Handout.doc

Weddle-West, K., & Bingham, R. P. (2010). Enhancing recruitment, persistence and graduation rates of students of color from P-22: The roles of senior administrators in higher education. *National Forum of Applied Educational Research Journal, 24*(1), 7–20.

Weikel, W. J. (1985). The American mental health counselors association. *Journal of Counseling and Development, 63*(7), 457–460. https://doi.org/10.1002/j.1556-6676.1985.tb02833.x

Westcott, J. B., & Grimes, T. O. (2023). Applications of relational-cultural theory for social justice in mental health counseling. *Journal of Mental Health Counseling, 45*(1), 1–19. https://doi.org/10.17744/mehc.45.1.01

Wilson, J. Z., Chihota, C., & Marks, G. (2023). Teaching White privilege: An auto-ethnographic approach. *International Journal of Inclusive Education, 27*(14), 1642–1658. https://doi.org/10.1080/13603116.2021.1909154

Woodbridge, L. M. (2023). The power of language: A call to critically analyze the discourse of the human service professions. *Journal for Social Action in Counseling & Psychology, 15*(2), 36–49. https://doi.org/10.33043/JSACP.15.2.36-49

Kathleen N. Muirhead Ph.D., LMHC, (she/her/hers) is an Assistant Professor at Salve Regina University in the Clinical Counseling Program. Her scholarly work and research interests center around equitable, socially just, and rigorous practices for counselor educators and counselor education programs. As a clinician she works to address systemic barriers for people who have co-occurring substance use and mental health diagnoses, as well as folks with eating disorders. Her passion is in the integration of social justice advocacy across the counseling curriculum and in mentoring first generation students and folks who experience marginalization in navigating higher education and the helping professions.

Jehan A. Hill Ph.D., LPC, (she/her/hers) is counselor at Stone Catchers Counseling. Her scholarly work highlights methods of advocacy, activism, and culturally responsive counseling practices to better support historically marginalized and oppressed communities in the educational system. As a counselor, she seeks to understand the client's worldview holistically to foster resilience and personal growth. Her counseling approach is grounded in trauma-informed and culturally responsive practices.

Amanda J. Minor Ph.D., (she/her/hers) is currently an Associate Professor and Department Chair in the Counseling, and Expressive Arts Graduate Department at Salve Regina University in Newport, RI. She is also a domestic violence counselor. Amanda teaches and works from a socially just, trauma-informed, humanistic perspective. She serves within various service roles in the counselor education profession, her university, and her community with a focus on justice, equity, accessibility, and sustainably changing the system.

Amirah R. Nelson Ph.D., LPC (she/they) is a LPC with over 10 years of experience. Her research focuses on social justice, diversity, equity, and inclusion practices, Black women, and race-based trauma, and has presented on the state, regional, national, and international levels in these areas. Dr. Nelson currently teaches at Jackson State University as an Assistant Professor where she consistently utilizes her social identities to educate learners about advocacy and systemic issues. As a counselor educator, she is committed to teaching learners about fostering enduring relationships in the counseling professional and ways to promote healing.

Rhea Bhatia (she/her/hers) is a doctoral candidate, South Asian international student, cisgender woman. Her experiences of growing up in one culture and living in a different one inform her personal and professional world.

2 Successful Teaching Strategies

Nicole Baker

Education must begin with the solution of the teacher-student contradiction, by reconciling the poles of the contradiction so that both are simultaneously teachers and students.

Paulo Freire

Abstract

New counselor education and supervision faculty are hired with the expectation that they have been trained on how to plan, prepare, and deliver course instruction. Conversely, new CEs may believe that there will be extensive training and support provided by the university related to course design. However, counselor educators often find that this is not the case, as many are left with a copy of an old syllabus and well wishes before being thrown into the learning environment. This chapter will provide new counselor educators with practical strategies for how to plan, prepare, and deliver engaging and quality instruction in the learning environment.

Learning Objectives After reading this chapter, you will be able to:

1. Identify the specific needs unique to adult learners.
2. Integrate actionable teaching interventions and strategies to create an engaging, learner-centered, and supportive learning environment.
3. Solve common challenges counselor educators may face in the learning environment.

N. Baker (✉)
Morningside University, Sioux City, IA, USA
e-mail: bakernicole630@gmail.com

D. M. Stalnaker-Shofner and T. N. Sapp (eds.), *A Comprehensive Guide for Counselor Education*, Springer Texts in Education, https://doi.org/10.1007/978-3-031-68358-9_2

2.1 Statement of Reflexivity

My career as an educator has spanned teaching in primary, elementary, and middle school educational settings, to my current work as a professor teaching in undergraduate and graduate teacher preparation programs. My background, experience, research, and training has been in how to teach others using engaging teaching strategies and how to meet the needs of adult learners. The lens through which I view successful teaching strategies for CITs is shaped by my education and experience as an elementary and middle school teacher, turned professor; this is at the heart of my positionality and ultimately informed my approach to writing this chapter. As I penned this chapter, I sought to highlight the teaching methodologies I learned through my undergraduate education, and then to subsequently examine how those methodologies apply to adult learners through my graduate work and research. Though my background is not in counseling, my contribution to this text is based on my research and expertise in education methodologies geared towards adult learners. As such, it is important for me to acknowledge my contribution to this project from the position and perspective of an educator without the lived experience of a *counselor* educator. Thus, the content of this chapter was developed in collaboration with the co-editors of this book to ensure a cohesive counselor educator voice.

2.2 Case Scenario

Dr. Brown is a counselor with 10 years of experience working in a community mental health center. They recently earned their Doctorate in Counselor Education and Supervision and were offered an adjunct faculty position at their alma mater teaching the course they took as a CIT in their master's program. Dr. Brown is excited for this new opportunity and is looking forward to the upcoming new faculty orientation meeting to be held a few weeks before the semester begins. Upon attending the orientation, Dr. Brown was disappointed to learn that the orientation only consisted of taking their new faculty photograph, touring the campus, and meeting the university and department administration. While those things were all important, there was no mention of how to manage the learning environment, nor was there guidance as to where to go for help. Additionally, there was no information provided about the services available for support in their course design and instruction. When Dr. Brown asked the department leadership as to how to prepare for the class, they were given a copy of the most recent course syllabus. Dr. Brown noticed that the syllabus looked familiar and realized that it had not been updated to reflect the current key performance indicators (KPIs) as outlined in the 2024 CACREP Standards. "This cannot be it," Dr. Brown thought, "Surely there are more materials and teaching support items for me to use." Seeing none, Dr. Brown spent the final week before the semester began throwing together whatever materials they could find to begin the semester.

2.3 Introduction

As a new counselor educator, you are both excited and nervous. Perhaps you are thinking that someone will help you navigate higher education and what it means to be a faculty member; however, most faculty members' experiences are contrary to that belief. Historically, there may be a lack of sufficient training to prepare faculty members to teach during the onboarding process at higher education institutions, as well as a subsequent lack of faculty development once hired (Irby & O'Sullivan, 2017). Typically, new faculty members are provided with an old, and sometimes outdated copy of the syllabus, and left to navigate how to teach the course. You likely are a content area expert in your field of study, however, your knowledge and expertise must be supplemented with knowing how to deliver that content effectively to others. To this end, Lowenthal et al. (2012) surmises that "faculty are prepared as scholars, not teachers (p. 150)." While you may be able to recite relevant statistics, and speak confidently about your content in your field, knowing how to *teach others* about your field is a different skill set. This chapter will introduce you to concepts and skills to prepare you to teach at the graduate level.

2.3.1 Terminology

The field of education has a plethora of terminology and acronyms that can sometimes be confusing. In this chapter, we will focus on the diverse terrain of educational methodologies, unpacking the fundamental teaching approaches prevalent in higher education: andragogy, pedagogy, and heutagogy. These approaches encapsulate the intricate art and science of teaching. As you navigate each approach, the counselor educator should look at the level of instructor involvement needed in each class, the level of CIT involvement needed in each class, and the maturity and autonomy of your CITs. Each approach will be described in further detail below. As we consider each approach, it is important to note that they are not linear and operate on a continuum (see Fig. 2.1).

At one end is pedagogy, a teacher-centered learning approach. As the educator in this approach, you are the *sole subject-matter expert*. You design the learning process and provide the materials needed to achieve predefined learning outcomes. Using a pedagogical approach often involves one-way communication via lectures, where students predominantly absorb information without active engagement unless prompted (Alabisi & Vucetic-Trifiro, 2023). Therefore, you are doing most of the work while your students listen and may take notes. In this approach, students usually do not engage unless invited by the educator. This approach may be better suited for teaching new or difficult material and concepts.

In the middle of the continuum is andragogy, or self-directed learning. In the andragogical approach, you are the *facilitator of learning*. As with the pedagogical approach, in this approach you also design how the course content will be taught, however, you also foster an environment where learners navigate diverse learning

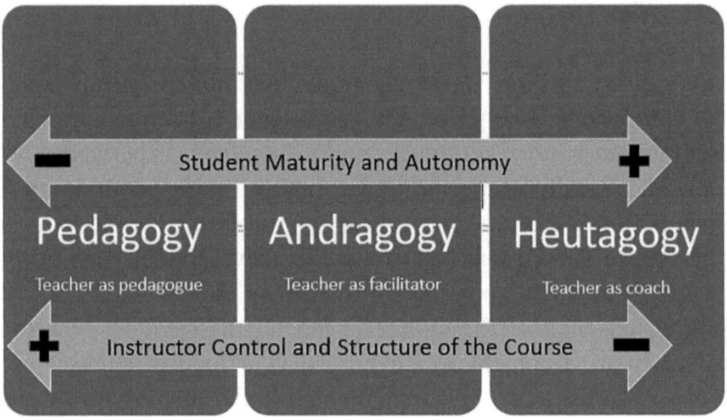

Fig. 2.1 Learning environment delivery approaches

paths. While this method may involve brief lectures, emphasis lies in learners actively interacting with the content and the educator. Essentially, learners will engage in a dialogue with you and their peers, and complete activities that reinforce the material covered during the class lectures and reading material (Alabisi & Vucetic-Trifiro, 2023). Andragogy may be better suited for more important topics that specifically address learner and program outcomes, as well as for concepts that require critical thinking and problem solving (Glassner & Back, 2020).

Finally, on the opposite end of the continuum is heutagogy, or self-determined learning. With heutagogy, the educator is viewed as the *learning coach.* You empower learners to utilize information they have learned while cultivating an environment where curiosity and collaborative exploration thrive (Alabisi & Vucetic-Trifiro, 2023). With a heutagogical approach, learners take substantial ownership of their educational journey. This approach is best suited for advanced learners with life experience or experience in the field of study (e.g. adult learners and doctoral learners) (Glassner & Back, 2020).

When considering which approach will work best for your CITs, you need to evaluate CITs' level of maturity and autonomy. If your CITs exhibit lower levels of maturity and autonomy, a pedagogical approach may be warranted. Thus, your course may be very structured and planned from beginning to end. Conversely, if your CITs are autonomous, mature, and take ownership of their learning experience, learners may benefit more from an andragogical, heutagogical, or mixed approach (Patel, 2019). Here, your class period may have less structure and include more discussions and experiential activities. Depending on the content and CIT's previous exposure to the content, it is not uncommon for you to flow between the three approaches within a given class session. While one approach may be more prudent within a specific topic, it is important that you remain flexible and tailor your approach to suit the needs of your CITs.

In reflecting on these models and considering social justice practices in counselor education, it is important to note that pedagogy is fraught with oppression

(Freire et al., 2018). Goodman et al. (2015) explore pedagogy and power, specifically noting that in the banking approach to education, students are not expected, nor are they given permission, to question, critique, analyze, discuss, assess, or evaluate information, thereby perpetuating the status quo in terms of both knowledge and power. Thus, to dismantle oppressive practices in teaching and education, Freire et al. (2018) proponed the concept of *critical pedagogy*. This term upends traditional pedagogy, in that the educator approaches instruction not from a position of power as the sole expert, rather engages in frequent dialogue with the learners. This promotes a collaborative learning environment where learning becomes a reciprocal process. Through a social justice lens, traditional pedagogy is seen as an extension of the hierarchy and imperialism that is inherent within teaching practices in which censorship and control are used to cultivate and ensure student obedience, deference, reverence, submission, and compliance (Freire et al., 2018). This top-down approach ultimately restricts the learning and growth potential in learners.

Therefore, through a social justice conceptualization of teaching and learning, the hope is to move the needle from pedagogy to the more aspirational praxis of heutagogy, or learners' self-direction. This paradigm seeks to minimize power differentials, promotes the inclusion of multiple phenomenologies, and encourages mutuality, respect, belonging, equity, and relational principles to learning and educator-student dynamics to foster connection and facilitate learning that is experiential and bi-directional. It may even be better to describe this learning as multidirectional, in that all persons engaged in learning can offer relevant and important personal experiences and can contribute to the educational discourse occurring in the learning environment. Through an exploration of teaching models that are more consistent with a social justice approach to learning infused throughout this textbook, the hope is that you ultimately feel prepared to begin to dismantle systemic oppression on a micro, meso, or macro level in both counselor education and higher education in your own way.

2.4 Adult Learners

As a new counselor educator, you will be working with adult learners. Therefore, it is important to know your audience when teaching. To effectively teach, understanding your audience is pivotal.

- Who are your CITs?
- What diverse cultural backgrounds and experiences are represented in your class?
- What beliefs are held by you and your CITs that may impact CIT engagement and learning?
- How will you adapt your instruction to meet the diverse needs of your CITs?
- What do your CITs already know about your content?

Recognizing and valuing these differences is integral to cultivating an inclusive learning environment. Each CIT's distinct experiences and perspectives contribute inherent value to the class and its content.

While it is crucial that you avoid generalizations, research offers insights into the diverse needs of adult learners. Malcolm Knowles is widely noted as one of the first theorists to study adult learners and developed the Adult Learning Theory (Knowles, 1984). Knowles believed that adults need reasoning and explanations for the material they learn, and that instruction should be task-oriented or problem-oriented, rather than learning through rote memorization or isolated learning (Knowles, 1984).

Even in your daily life, no one likes wasted time. Everything we do, we do with a purpose. Our assignments in class should be no different. Assignments should serve a purpose and be relevant and useful. Aligning assignments with purpose and relevance mirrors how we function in everyday life. Accordingly, Knowles (1984) delineated Four Principles of Teaching Adult Learners:

1. Involvement: Adults need to be a part of the planning and evaluation of their own instruction.
2. Experience: Learners' individual backgrounds and experiences provide the basis for learning activities.
3. Problem-centered: Learning should not be content-oriented, but rather problem-centered.
4. Relevance: Topics should include content that has immediate relevance and/or impact to their job or personal lives.

Additionally, Knowles (1984) outlined Five Assumptions of Adult Learners, emphasizing:

1. A motivation to learn,
2. Student orientation to learning,
3. Student readiness to learn,
4. Adult learning experiences, and
5. Student self-concept.

Stop and Reflect: *Let's take a moment to digest this information. Think about your own experiences as an adult learner. Have you always understood the purpose behind your course assignments? Can you think of ways to improve those assignments based on the information you have learned so far?*

Since most CES will primarily teach graduate level learners at the master's level, you may find it easier to connect the content to real-world applicable experiences to enhance CIT learning. Additionally, while lectures may be an easier and more comfortable approach, remember, you must consider the needs of the adult learner. The adult learner must take new information and *use it* in some way for the information to be stored in the brain (Caine & Caine, 1991). The adult brain organizes facts and skills in isolation, like those in a lecture, differently from information that was used and experientially applied. Both are needed for the adult learner to commit information to memory, and to apply the knowledge to the content area. While the core content of what you cover should be the same to meet your course objectives, the *way in which you deliver that content* should be catered to meet the needs of the CITs in your class this semester.

Stop and Reflect: *Dr. Brown facilitated their class using a lecture-based format, in a manner congruent with the way they were taught when they were in their doctoral program. Dr. Brown spent countless hours writing lectures to cover the course content in its entirety. Using this approach seemed ineffective, as Dr. Brown would often observe CITs glancing at their phones, typing on their laptops, or even fighting off sleep. The CITs were not engaged in the lectures. This disheartened Dr. Brown. As you reflect on the case, which of Knowles's Principles of Teaching Adult Learners or Knowles's Assumptions of Adult Learners were present in class lessons? Where were there opportunities to insert some adult learning principles?*

2.4.1 Engaging Teaching Practices for Adult Learners

When deciding how you will deliver your content, there are a few things to consider. The first is the length of the course and how often the course meets. You also need to consider the length of each class session. Does your school operate in a traditional 17-week long semester? Do you meet once a week or every other week? Do classes meet for one hour per session, or four hours per session? Designing your course structure largely depends on how the course is offered. One suggestion is to conceptualize your class as "chunks." As you plan your "chunk," consider the main focus and identify related subtopics. From here, you want to thoughtfully select the most pertinent material to share, as well as how to share it. For example, begin the class with heavier content, and content that may require focus and attention, as learners will be most alert and receptive at the beginning of the class. You may also want to consider the time of day that you are meeting, and the impact this has on CIT engagement. Regardless of if the class is first thing in the morning or after your CITs already had a full day of work, the key to having an attentive class is to keep your lessons active and engaging. A guideline to creating an engaged learning environment is to plan for at least one experiential activity for every hour of class you meet.

If your content works best in a lecture format, think of ways to keep CITs active and engaged *during* the lecture. Some ways to do this can be through guided notetaking, graphic organizers, or skeleton notes. Skeleton notes are notes that follow along with your lecture, but you intentionally delete key words and ideas that CITs can fill in the blanks as you are lecturing. Interactive polls are another great way to keep CITs engaged and to increase engagement during a lecture.

Slido, Poll Everywhere, and Mentimeter are examples of polling platforms you may use. The polls can be embedded within your PowerPoint or other medium and can significantly increase engagement with the material.

Aside from lecturing, there are many other ways for you to present content in your class. Many educators choose mini-lectures, followed by interactive and engaged activities to get CITs involved. Some common activities to use would be class discussions, debates, and collaborative group work. Some common activities that work in almost every class are outlined below.

- ***Gaming***: Especially on days where you cannot help but lecture a good portion of the content, a good way to break up the lecture and to re-engage the CITs into being active in your learning environment is through a gaming format. Rather than just reading back key points and ideas from the lecture, engage CITs by having them interact in a game-like format. There are templates online to create simple games like Jeopardy, Who Wants to Be a Millionaire, Family Feud, or Are You Smarter Than a 5th Grader. For online options, interactive gaming sites like Kahoot and Quizizz allow CITs to answer questions in real time using their laptops, tablets, or phones and you can track individual CIT progress. There are premade games to choose from or you can design your own game. Plickers is a website that allows you to enter quiz questions. For CITs to answer the questions, they hold up printed QR Codes and the counseling educator scans the codes using the app. The app will display answers in real time on your projector in the learning environment. Online gaming is a great way for you to assess your CITs, as many of them give you feedback right away to let you know if CITs are understanding the content, or if reteaching may be needed.
- ***Pause and Interact***: Just taking a minute away from your lecture or stopping to ask CITs to engage in some way, is a great way to break up the class. There are many simple ways to get CITs to engage.
- ***Turn and Talk***: During a lecture or when you feel yourself talking too much, ask CITs to turn to the person next to them to reflect on what you just covered.
- ***Think-Pair-Share***: Pose a question to your class. Ask your class to *think* individually of the answer or response to your question in their head. After a minute or two, ask CITs to *pair* with a person next to them to discuss the same question. After two to five minutes, then ask the class to come together to *share* as a whole group. You will be likely to get more dynamic discussions since CITs have already discussed it with their partner. It also takes the pressure off the CITs who may be too shy to speak in front of the whole class and in doing this requires all CITs to participate, engaging all CITs at once.
- ***Other online tools***: Answer Garden is another tool to increase CIT engagement. You can pose a question to your CITs and have CITs answer from their laptops or phones. You can ask content-related questions or even just temperature-check type of questions to see how CITs are doing. CIT responses are displayed in real time.

- ***Think Maps***: This can be done as a whole class on your whiteboard, as groups, or as individuals by writing with dry erase markers on the desk (test your desk material first to make sure it erases!) or by using an online tool like Google Slides. You give CITs the prompt and CITs write words or phrases in response to your prompt.
- ***Movement***: Especially if your class meets for several hours at a time, movement is a great way to engage the class. One way to do this is to use *parking lots* in your class. Parking lots are a space in the learning environment, usually a bulletin board or anchor chart of some kind, where CITs can "park" their ideas by adding questions as learning is happening. It is a living document that educators and CITs can reference throughout the duration of the class. Another simple way to add movement to your class is to write questions on pieces of paper and hang those around the room. CITs can travel from paper to paper, posing answers to your questions.

Stop and Reflect: *After a few weeks of looking out at sleepy eyes and distracted CITs, Dr. Brown decided to try a few new teaching strategies. They started small by giving CITs a handout to complete the skeleton notes while following along with the lecture. Then they moved to more interactive skeleton notes, where CITs were filling in missing pieces during the lecture, which seemed to increase engagement. Dr. Brown also had CITs participate more in small group discussions as well as role-playing. This led to CITs connecting with the material in a more meaningful way. For further consideration: How might you think creatively to gain and maintain CITs' attention for the duration of your class?*

2.4.2 Meeting the Needs of Adult Learners

As with engaging teaching practices, you want to make sure you can meet the needs of your CITs. Two ways to do this is through motivation and attention to learning differences. Learner motivation is important for success, retention, and attrition. As you begin the course and learn more about each of your CITs, you want to find out what motivates them. Some CITs may be motivated just by gaining new knowledge. For others, it may be that they are the first in their family to go to college, they are fulfilling a dream or goal, or they may be entering their second career, reenergized. Regardless of the CIT's motivation, you must look for ways to increase their intrinsic motivation and show CITs that your class is relevant, meaningful, and important. The power of relationships is critical to increasing CIT motivation and as a CES, you must work to build relationships with your CITs. Consider the following questions: *What do I have in common with the CITs? What are the things that they typically enjoy? How can I work their experiences and interests into the learning environment?*

You want to be authentic in your approach. Show the CITs that you care about their learning and their outcomes. While you are holding CITs accountable, you are also a counselor, and you are human. Therefore, it is important to show compassion as well. Take notes and remember things that were said during your class introductions so that you can incorporate this information within future discussions. CITs will recognize that you remembered something about them and see that you care. This will increase their motivation.

One final component to increasing student motivation is understanding their backgrounds and experiences. Know that their experiences are likely different from your own. There is a difference between the CIT who chooses not to do the work and the CIT that is engaged and trying but is unable to grasp the concepts. The motivation for these two CITs is different. While you want all your CITs to be successful in your class, your definition of success may be different than your CITs' definition of success. You will have to be able to accept this difference and meet the CITs where they are at.

2.4.3 Understanding Differences with Adult Learners

Sometimes you will have CITs in your class who learn differently. It is important to reflect on your method of teaching to see if it meets the needs of each CIT. Factors that may influence CIT learning and engagement are a lack of prior knowledge or exposure to a topic, lack of motivation, or possibly *how* the material was presented. When individual CITs perform poorly on assessments, the use of reflection can help CITs find the missing pieces and barriers to their learning. When an entire class performs poorly on assessments, more in-depth reflection may be necessary. Analyze the data you have available to you. One way to analyze your data is to perform an item analysis of the assessment. Which question or questions did most CITs answer correctly? Which question or questions did most CITs struggle? Then, reflect on your teaching. Did you thoroughly cover the content? Could you have taught the content in a different way? Is reteaching necessary?

As you reflect on how you teach the material to your CITs, you also want to consider the format of how you delivered the content to CITs. It may be beneficial to explore the different ways in which people learn. Using a single method of instruction, may simultaneously reward some CITs, and penalize others. If your teaching method caters to primarily one type of learning style, it will not serve all students (Blouin et al., 2008). Gardner (1983) described nine main learning styles: bodily-kinesthetic, verbal-linguistic, naturalistic, visual-spatial, interpersonal, intrapersonal, existential, musical, and logical-mathematical.

There are online inventories that can help your CITs identify the learning style that best suits them. As the counselor educator, it is best if you can vary your teaching style and delivery format often so that you are meeting the needs of more CITs. You may also decide to administer a learning inventory at the beginning of the course, to help you understand the best teaching approaches that correspond to the CIT's learning styles. Another alternative is to query the class to self-identify their ideal or preferred learning modality. You can also learn this information just by having a conversation with any CITs who have been having challenges in the class. Having conversations with CITs demonstrates your commitment to the CIT's learning and success. Keep in mind that learning styles can grow and change over time, even from concept to concept (Gorski & Pothini, 2018).

2.4.4 Challenges to Learning

Over time, how we conceptualize what defines a student has evolved. We have come to understand that the narrow definition of student no longer applies, as learners can include new college graduates, change-of-career learners, or retirees. Learners are managing multiple roles and responsibilities, and at times, these factors and the complexities of their intersectionality can pose a barrier to learning. In addition to being a learner, they may also be an employer or employee, a parent or caretaker, a life partner, a coach, or any combination of a myriad of roles. At any time, any one of these roles may take priority over education. Juggling the different identities can adversely impact the learner's ability to focus on their learning. The multiplicity of these roles can result in time being a barrier to their success.

As counselor educators, we have a unique opportunity to offer support and resources that may facilitate CIT success. One such opportunity is to redirect CITs who need additional support to their faculty advisor. Another resource that can be offered to CITs is to refer them to the Office of Disability Support for guidance, and if warranted, intervention. While information specific to learners with disabilities, their unique needs, and adjunctive support is detailed in Chap. 13, a potential intervention is offered here for your consideration. For example, an intervention that is within your control as a counselor educator is to provide CITs with a detailed syllabus outlining policies and procedures, as well as delineating course assignments and due dates. Doing so can help CITs to organize their time and plan accordingly. It is also critical to provide the syllabus in a timely manner so that CITs can begin to plan ahead. Given the multiple roles our CITs play, it is important to remember adult learning principles when designing your assignments and consider: *Are your assignments relevant? Can CITs use and apply the assignment once working in the field? Is the assignment important? Is there a purpose to the assignment?* CITs will be more willing to prioritize their schoolwork when you can help them see the value in completing it.

2.4.5 Assessment and Feedback

Ongoing assessment of your CITs and your own personal analysis of assessment data is important. There are several ways to assess CITs. First, the assignments you choose to use in your class are one form of assessment. It is important to ensure that each assignment is consistent with the specified learning objectives aligned with the CACREP Key Performance Indicators (KPIs) for your course. These assignments are a way for CITs to apply what they have learned through reading material, course lectures, supplemental materials, as well as their own resources.

Additionally, our feedback to CITs can be one of the most important and integral parts of a CIT's learning. Feedback must extend beyond a mere, "Good job" with an ascribed letter grade. Just assigning a grade without any qualitative feedback is not helpful to CIT learning and growth. In your role as faculty and content expert, your feedback can offer your knowledge and practical experiences to the CITs. Effective counselor educators will extend the learning beyond the learning environment by providing valuable and meaningful feedback to CITs. This can be done with thorough comments, questioning, and practical guidance on CIT assignments by offering feedback on both what they did well as well as growth areas. Additionally, you may extend the learning by asking open-ended questions to facilitate CITs' ability to reflect and to think more critically about the topic. Both assessment and feedback are further addressed in Chap. 5.

2.4.6 Rubrics

Rubrics can be a vital tool to provide structured feedback. Rubrics outline exactly what is expected of the CITs on each assignment, as well as serve as a tool for the counselor educator to grade CITs consistently, and not subjectively. Rubrics are a good reference point, offering CITs a clearer picture as to where they lost points and why, as well as how to improve their future efforts. The incorporation of a rubric with your feedback and comments on the CIT's assignment can add greater depth and value.

In general, as you design your rubric, you will want to consider the following: *What is the essence of the assignment related to CIT learning?* In other words, what is the "meat" of your assignment and what are the important takeaways? As you begin to construct the rubric, you want to assign the most points to these key learning areas, followed by designating fewer points for things like format, presentation, style, and grammar.

2.4.7 Formative and Summative Approaches to Feedback

In the learning environment, there are many ways to assess CITs as you teach so as the educator, you know how CITs are doing. These formative assessments allow you to evaluate how CITs are doing after specified intervals in the learning process.

In the class there are many ways to assess CITs as you go. These are formative assessments, or assessments that let you know how CITs are doing after you covered one topic, as opposed to a summative assessment that would be in summary of the entire semester. There are many simple formative assessments that you can use in your college learning environment that pull double-duty of both assessing your CITs, as well as serving to engage your CITs in an activity in the class. Administering assessments are only helpful if you analyze the results and use those results to determine the next steps. If all CITs are successful on the formative assessment, that tells you that the class is ready to move on. If CITs are still struggling with the concepts, it may be time to slow down and reteach. You will reach more learners and move CITs towards mastery when you are continually assessing. Some ideas for assessment in the learning environment are outlined below.

2.4.7.1 Exit Tickets

Exit tickets are a task you give your CITs before they are allowed to exit the class. They are typically given at the end of class, or before taking a break in a longer class session. Exit tickets can be administered in a variety of ways. You could pose a question to ask CITs. CITs answer the question on a piece of paper and submit the answer before they leave. You may also have CITs complete an exit ticket using a pre-formed template, or even just on a sticky note. CITs can stick their answer to the door as they exit. Using a sticky note has the benefit of allowing you to quickly assess the entire class at once, as they are all on display together. You may also begin to group CITs based on their level of understanding by putting the sticky notes into piles. Further, in a later class, you can assign a group activity to CITs who are ready to progress to the next topic, while you focus on re-teaching the CITs who have struggled with the material. Another format for an exit ticket is the 3-2-1 prompt, which encourages CITs to write three things they have learned, two major take-aways, and one question they would like to submit to be answered. The CIT questions can be used to open the next class session. One final suggestion is to frequently change the format of your exit ticket, which will keep the activity from becoming stale and will aid in increasing CIT engagement.

2.4.7.2 Temperature Checks

A "temperature check" is a check in with CITs to see how they are feeling about the course content. It is a beneficial practice to regularly conduct temperature checks. Some CITs will not share their struggles with their professor, unless invited to do so. Counselor educators can get a sense of CIT understanding through methods like a thumbs up for, "I'm all good," or thumbs down for, "I need help." It is also good to offer a sideways thumb for, "I think I'm good, but I am not ready to move on." You can also have CITs rate their level of understanding using a scaling question like, "Using a scale of 1–5 to rate your current understanding, where 5 represents the most complete understanding and 1 the least, how would you rate yourself with today's content?" You can also ask the following temperature check question: "Before I move on, what question(s) do you have, or what question(s) do you think someone else may have?" It is also good to ask CITs what is working well for them and what they wish could be different. You might even ask CITs what remains unclear, or how you could teach this differently next time. You can also invite CITs to share their feedback anonymously in your class using polls or another evaluative method. Often these CIT requests can be easily integrated, which can also have the added benefit of validating their concerns, as well as increasing their motivation and engagement.

Stop and Reflect: *Dr. Brown incorporated a midterm exam and a final exam as the only assessments within the course. However, after the midterm exam, Dr. Brown was shocked due to the CITs' low scores. As Dr. Brown reflected on their teaching throughout the first half of the semester, they recognized that CITs were participating and seemed to grasp an understanding of the concepts, but this was not reflected on the midterm exam. After the midterm, Dr. Brown implemented daily exit tickets to review the main topic covered in each class lecture and used the results to plan the content for the following class lecture. With this strategy, Dr. Brown was able to identify the gaps in CITs' knowledge as they were teaching and when CITs were reassessed during the final exam, Dr. Brown saw a significant increase in CIT scores. How will you assess your CITs and use the data to drive your instruction?*

2.5 Conclusion

Teaching at the master's and doctoral level is no easy task. Often counselor educators rely on trial and error to see what works and what does not work. However, being an effective CES requires planning and organization. While you may not be able to predict everything that would happen within your class, if the tools provided in this chapter are utilized, you should be able to meet your CITs where they are to successfully teach your course. For additional information on navigating the common pitfalls you may experience as a new CES, see Chap. 9.

References

Alabisi, A., & Vucetic-Trifiro, C. E. (2023). Pedagogy, andragogy and heutagogy: How are they related? *E-Journal of Business Education & Scholarship of Teaching, 17*(2), 1–7. https://www.proquest.com/scholarly-journals/pedagogy-andragogy-heutagogy-how-are-they-related/docview/2878448011/se-2?accountid=12085

Blouin, R. A., Joyner, P. U., & Pollack, G. M. (2008). Preparing for a renaissance in pharmacy education: The need, opportunity, and capacity for change. *American Journal of Pharmaceutical Education, 72*(2), 42. https://doi.org/10.5688/aj720242

Caine, R. N., & Caine, G. (1991). *Making connections: Teaching and the human brain.* Association for Supervision and Curriculum Development.

Freire, P., Ramos, M. B., Macedo, D. P., & Shor, I. (2018). *Pedagogy of the oppressed* (50th anniversary ed.). Bloomsbury Academic.

Gardner, H. (1983). *Frames of mind: The theory of multiple intelligences.* Basic Books.

Glassner, A., & Back, S. (2020). Exploring heutagogy in higher education. *Springer.* https://doi.org/10.1007/978-981-15-4144-5_5

Goodman, A., Joshi, H., Nasim, B., & Tyler, C. (2015). *Social and emotional skills in childhood and their long-term effects on adult life.* http://www.eif.org.uk/wp-content/uploads/2015/03/EIF-Strand-1-Report-FINAL1.pdf

Gorski, P. C., & Pothini, S. G. (2018). *Case studies on diversity and social justice education* (3rd ed.). Routledge.

Irby, D. M., & O'Sullivan, P. S. (2017). Developing and rewarding teachers as educators and scholars: Remarkable progress and daunting challenges. *Medical Education, 52*(1), 58–67. https://doi.org/10.1111/medu.13379

Knowles, M. (1984). *The adult learner: A neglected species* (3rd ed). Elsevier.

Lowenthal, P. R., Wray, M. L., Bates, B., Switzer, T., & Stevens, E. (2012). Examining faculty motivation to participate in faculty development. *International Journal of University Teaching and Faculty Development, 3*(3), 149–164. https://www.proquest.com/scholarly-journals/examining-faculty-motivation-participate/docview/1727484723/se-2?accountid=12085

Patel, J. V. (2019). Paradigm shift-pedagogy to andragogy to heutagogy in higher education. *Weekly Journal of Higher Education by Association of Indian Universities, New Delhi, 56*(30), 23–29.

Nicole Baker Ph.D. Ed.D. (she/her/hers) is a life-long educator with teaching experience from the smallest preschoolers up to graduate and doctoral level college students. Her education includes a Baccalaureate Degree in Elementary Education, Master's Degree in Educational Leadership, and Doctorate Degree in Education and Ethical Leadership. She spent 14 years teaching in the elementary grades and has spent the last 18 years teaching at the college level. Nicole has held positions such as Department Chair for the College of Education, Curriculum Developer, and Faculty Development coordinator.

Best Practices for Online Education

3

Ali K. Corey and Amy Morrison

> *Education is the most powerful weapon which you can use to change the world.*
>
> *Nelson Mandela*

Abstract

This chapter will provide an overview of best practices in utilizing a learner-centered approach for course design, instructional time, community building and learner evaluation that are unique to the online teaching environment. A case study will highlight examples of how to integrate specific approaches. Recommendations are given to support instructors in the implementation of best practices for online counselor education.

Learning Objectives After reading this chapter, you will be able to:

1. Compare and contrast current best practices for online teaching in counselor education.
2. Evaluate the appropriate application of pedagogical, andragogical, and heutagogical approaches to online learning through a social justice lens.
3. Construct core elements of a graduate course such as syllabus development, assignment creation, and learner evaluation and feedback for online teaching utilizing a learner-centered approach.

A. K. Corey (✉) · A. Morrison
Antioch University, Yellow Springs, OH, USA
e-mail: acorey@antioch.edu

A. Morrison
e-mail: amorrison4@antioch.edu

D. M. Stalnaker-Shofner and T. N. Sapp (eds.), *A Comprehensive Guide for Counselor Education*, Springer Texts in Education, https://doi.org/10.1007/978-3-031-68358-9_3

3.1 Statement of Reflexivity

We approach this chapter as authors both having taught in higher education at predominately White institutions (PWIs) for over 10 years, and we currently teach almost exclusively online. We are both White-identified, cisgender women, active parents, and engaged life-long learners. In recognizing our positionality, we are compelled to contextualize our background as having been educated primarily within traditional systems that emphasize a Eurocentric, hierarchical, and patriarchal approach to educating and training CESs who are then expected to replicate these same philosophies and approaches to learning in their teaching praxis. Our identities also include being of Eastern European descent and from low-middle socioeconomic backgrounds. We acknowledge that these identities intersect and inform our lens as educators, and as such, we can recognize our ascribed privilege of race, and acquired privilege with respect to digital access, and education. The realities of being women, parents, counselors, as well as continuous adult learners drives our passion and support for online education, with particular emphasis on the access it can provide for persons who experience systemic oppression because of the intentional marginalization of their intersecting identities. In our writing of this chapter, it is our intent to present to you current and established best online teaching practices that can foster pathways for learner and faculty intersectional identities to be visible, acknowledged, respected, and included as a requisite part of educational discourse. As educators and learners, we are aware of the complexity of online education and in response, make explicit our bias toward relational educational approaches and learner-centered teaching practices.

3.2 Case Scenario

Jamie is a full-time CIT in the second semester of their online counselor training program. During their first semester in the program, their grades were exceptional. In the current semester, Jamie struggled to submit assignments on time in your Counseling Theories course. The work was submitted one to two days late, and often the work did not meet the requirements delineated in the assignment rubric. After reaching out to Jamie multiple times without a response, you have connected with their other professors for the semester and discovered the same problem existed in those classes. Finally, after a few weeks Jamie responded, and you were able to set up a meeting.

During that meeting, Jamie becomes emotional once they begin to talk about the struggles that have been making things difficult this semester. At first, Jamie focuses on feelings of disconnect and loneliness. They report struggling to get to know any of the other CITs in the program and feeling as though there is little to no community connection. Jamie states that it is difficult to "teach myself the material" and that it has just gotten harder this semester with three classes. Jamie also states that they identify as non-binary and that this has continuously been a struggle with their classmates and feeling as though no one can remember to utilize their correct pronouns and that there is no one else "that is anything like me" in the program. Jamie also reports experiencing some challenges at home, finally admitting that their partner has recently moved out, leaving Jamie lonely at home as well. Near the end of the meeting, Jamie shares that they are very passionate about becoming a counselor but afraid that online learning is not going to work and that scheduling conflicts make it impossible to do a face-to-face program.

3.3 Introduction

Online counselor education has seemingly exploded over the last decade, especially in response to the COVID19 pandemic. However, many educators have not been trained in best practices for online approaches to this work. While there is a dearth of current research addressing this need, it is the hope of these authors that we will be able to share our professional experiences and integrate current best practices on how to teach online courses in counselor education from a learner-centered approach.

Learner-centered higher education can be defined as those institutions and programs "which prioritize the needs and interests of graduate learners, rather than focusing first and foremost on the interests of higher education institutions and the demands of the research enterprise" (aau.com). Many counselor education programs do, in general, attempt to take a learner-centered approach to curriculum and course development. However, one might argue that being intentional about this is even more important in online learning. To be learner-centered, a program and course would focus on individual learner needs, strengths and learning goals to co-create the learning experience. As an online professor, you would need to be intentional about connecting with each learner individually to understand their specific needs. Additionally, as an online CES, you might allow for flexibility in assignments, methods of meeting standards, and resources provided in order to take a learner-centered approach to assessment of learning. Finally, you would take a learner-centered approach to course development by inviting and integrating learner feedback on assignments with a willingness to make changes as necessary.

With this in mind, much of what is shared in the following chapter can be seen as a guide and/or options from which to develop your courses rather than a strict design which you might be expected to follow as best practice. Online education becomes a dance in which we move fluidly back and forth between meeting the course requirements and individual learner needs. We begin the first step in our dance by reviewing educational theoretical frameworks and online implications for each approach, specific to counselor education, with an emphasis on being learner-centered.

3.4 Models of Praxis in Counselor Education

As mentioned in Chap. 2, CES' may take different approaches based on the identities and needs of CITs. Utilizing a pedagogical, andragogical or heutagogical approach will depend on multiple variables that impact the learning experience. In determining their approach, CES' should consider the factors of dependence, learning resources, focus of the learning, motivation of the learner, the role of the instructor overall and what impacts the online learning environment may have on the educational process (Halupa, 2015). In the next section, we will provide you with an overview of the major teaching models used in higher education as a whole, with specific information to their use in counselor education. Further, we offer the applicability of each model with adult learners. Lastly, we offer you a teaching model that is based on the principles of social justice, educational equity, inclusion, and accessibility. It is our hope that the information to follow provides you with the foundational knowledge you will need as a future CES as you begin to conceptualize and craft your teaching philosophy.

3.4.1 Pedagogy

Online implications for a pedagogical educational model include a clear and directed course schedule that is set by the instructor. As the instructor, you choose all course material including course readings and media, as well as the pacing and organization of the materials (Holmes & Abington-Cooper, 2000). Within this structure, an online CES will want to make sure materials are available online through university libraries and internet links. A pedagogical approach ensures that specific materials are covered and therefore a knowledge base is expanded. In the role of expert, you as CES may choose to record video lectures or meet with the class synchronously to review course content and share examples of their theoretical approach and counseling skills. The pedagogical model is objective-based and aligns with an external source of motivation, thus employing motivational and behavioral reinforcement (Skinner, 1968). This includes learner evaluation, grades, testing and assessment, all of which can be incorporated into the online learning environment through varied online tools (Halupa, 2015). CITs have clear expectations for course completion, and for learner and instructor interactions. Overall, the online pedagogical educational approach emphasizes a clearly organized learning process that clarifies a path for obtaining knowledge and being successful in the course.

3.4.2 Andragogy

Andragogy, or learning that is self-directed, has specific implications for online education. The term was first proffered by Knowles (1984) to describe adult learning based on his observations. Blondy (2007) asserts that the unique needs of adult learners must be incorporated into online learning environments. This may require you as the instructor to facilitate a reflective process at the beginning of the course and request that learners identify what their unique needs and situations are, and how these may apply to the course material and overall learning process. The andragogical approach views adult learners as independent, autonomous, and self-directed. Learners draw upon their own lived experiences and interactions with their peers and within their communities. These experiences are used as resources for learning, Additionally, learners may seek out resources and materials that directly apply to their learning process. As an online instructor, you have the opportunity to incorporate forms of peer interactions such as peer check-ins, small group conversations, and 'walk and talk'. These serve to increase learner engagement. Further online andragogical considerations include experiential learning activities applied to novel material that allows for opportunities to connect with and build upon individual and collective learner experiences. Andragogy is competency-based, as learners focus on strengthening skills and abilities. Adult learners are intrinsically motivated and value internal resources such as self-esteem, confidence, being recognized and feeling successful (Holmes & Abington-Cooper, 2000). Being an online instructor can provide a unique opportunity to develop creative ways to acknowledge learner contributions and engagement in the course. This can include noting learner contributions in a summary recording of a text-based online discussion or using a learner quote in a course announcement. The role of the instructor is that of facilitator, one who provides learner-centered materials, creates an online climate for collaboration and learner voice, and displays qualities of openness and respect (Brookfield, 2013). The learning relationship is reciprocal, and the instructor learns just as much from the learners as the learners are learning from the instructor.

3.4.3 Heutagogy

Heutagogy is described as learning that is self-directed, self-determined, and transformative. Learners are independent and interdependent, learning on their own as well as in an interconnected manner with others, including peers, instructors, and the community. Heutagogical practices encourage learners to identify the potential to learn from novel experiences and manage and determine their own learning (Halupa, 2015). With heutagogy, learning is neither planned out nor sequential; it is process-oriented as opposed to problem-based. Furthermore, learning is capacity-based, which builds upon established competencies and expands them beyond a specific discipline. The instructor may present the course materials, however, resources for learning are viewed as unlimited, varied, and multidimensional. Online heutagogical implications include collaborative reviewing and revising course objectives by both the instructor and the learner. This also creates space for the use of flexible learning contracts, and these may incorporate adaptable learning materials, learner-directed questions, and assignments. Other options for learning strategies based on learner input and choice, include the development of individualized learning goals, as well as negotiated learner assessment (Blaschke, 2012). Learning goals may include self-reflection, developing habits of mind, and expanding a point of view. Learners value experience and interaction with others, and this can be supported by a 'double loop' learning strategy. This strategy works by encouraging the learner to question their personal values and assumptions while acquiring new ways of learning. Thus, preparing learners to better negotiate complex issues and engage in life-long learning (Blaschke, 2012). With heutagogy, online materials and engagement are co-created with learners, and the content that is generated can be shared online and with other communities of learning. As the instructor, you can serve as a mentor supporting the learner's ability to actively engage with the material and take risks experimenting with their acquired knowledge. Through incorporating diverse instructional approaches, the instructor creates a supportive environment, thereby offering opportunities for the learner to use various methods for finding applicable resources and information to facilitate their overall learning. For the adult learner, motivation is rooted in a sense of self-efficacy, as well as understanding how to learn, be creative, and the ability to use these qualities in situations both known and unfamiliar. Heutagogy is often understood as a progressive next step in learning after andragogy. CITs who are learning online will need an introduction to the primary principles and role expectations of the heutagogical learning framework. Continuous check-ins with the instructor as well as supported peer interaction should be established. Although some learners may embrace the liberation of this educational approach, being empowered in the learning process and determining your own direction may be a new idea for many learners. As such, offering an empathic response is recommended to hearing expressed discomfort and questions of uncertainty from learners.

As we develop curriculum and establish course sequence, including both clinical and non-clinical instruction, it can become clear that there is benefit in utilizing all three educational approaches, and at specific junctures in the learner's education. As you develop your courses, considering learner development from their first semester to last will aid you in stratifying the approaches both within each course and over the curriculum as a whole. This incorporation of the three learning approaches can also be done within the course itself. For example, first semester learners may need more pedagogical approaches where instruction is clearly defined, course materials are established, and assignments articulately delineated. First semester learners may also need an andragogical approach where they can begin to collaborate with others and take steps toward self-directed learning. Learners in their last semester may benefit from all three educational approaches with an emphasis on andragogy and heutagogy and less emphasis on pedagogy (Fig. 3.1).

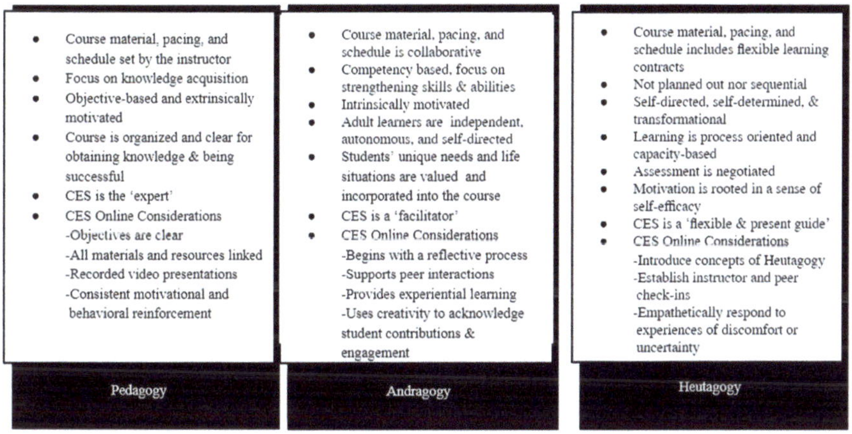

Fig. 3.1 A comparison of the major teaching models

Stop and Reflect: *Jamie states that it is difficult to "teach myself the material" and that it has just gotten harder this semester with three classes. It would appear that using a more pedagogical approach with Jamie would be needed. In using this approach, it is important to include opportunities for self-reflection, connection with one's peers, as well as interaction with the professor. Clear objectives and assignment descriptions along with lecture/discussion-based videos and/or opportunities for synchronous meeting times to review the course material will also likely increase Jamie's experience of connection to the course material, professor and peers.*

3.5 Community of Inquiry–Teaching from a Social Justice Framework

Anderson et al. (2019) developed the concept of Community of Inquiry, which is a communication and interaction framework designed to facilitate critical reflection for the learner and critical discourse between learner and instructor. There are key elements to this framework as depicted in the below graphic. The first is social presence, which explores the extent to which the instructor or learner are able to project authenticity. The next is cognitive presence which is defined by the extent to which the instructor or learner is able to construct meaning from the learning. Lastly, there is instructor presence, which focuses on the instructor's teaching and pedagogical approach. Instructor presence is directly related to social and cognitive presence through course design, facilitation, and direction. Through these three categories, learners can reach meaningful and educational outcomes (Anderson et al., 2019). As this textbook is focused on the development of CES faculty, in the following section we offer a deeper exploration of instructor presence.

3.5.1 Instructor Presence in the Online Learning Environment

An instructor's presence is an essential component to the learner's learning experience. As described above, instructor presence is the combination of social, cognitive and instructor presence. This can include perceived competence with the material and learning system, physical and emotional presence in the learning environment, and the ability to create community and connection utilizing self as a tool. According to Hinkley et al. (2021), the following were essential components of instructor presence in the online counseling learning environment that effectively leads to learner success.

- Creating connection with and between learners
- Having an intentional and consistent approach to grading
- Utilizing a "care-first" approach that invites learners to share personal experiences
- Ensuring that you are approachable for additional support and communication
- A focus on compassion and grace in approach in order to provide learners the benefit of the doubt while upholding course and learning standards.

Additionally, instructor presence may be experienced differently in the synchronous versus asynchronous learning environments. We will explore these nuances in the next section.

3.5.2 Synchronous Sessions and Instructor Presence

While there is little empirical evidence describing the best practices in online synchronous instruction, it is likely that more data will be available over time as a result of recent shifts in higher education. Conklin and Garrett Dikkers (2021) report that learners prefer and value opportunities to connect synchronously with their instructors. Therefore, it is important to consider how to make the best use of these interactions to ensure a positive learner experience. While many of the same recommendations made for face-to-face instruction can clearly apply to the synchronous online learning environment, there are additional aspects to consider. To ensure effective synchronous learning experiences, learner engagement, instructor presence, learner peer interactions, and course content are important focuses. Accordingly, Sharp et al. (2022), recommended the following practices to promote instructor efficacy:

- Arrange your physical space and optimal lighting to enhance the audiovisual experience for the learners.
- Familiarize yourself with the online platform and its tools and consider how to best integrate innovative and interactive tools into class sessions.

- Conceptualize yourself as a learning tool. This means that you should present your most authentic, best self in class sessions. Consider your physical presence, a workspace that projects a professional image, and your engagement with the learners and the course material. Set ground rules as a group and foster a sense of accountability within the online class community.

3.5.3 Asynchronous Courses and Instructor Presence

One of the major challenges associated with asynchronous instruction is creating a sense of community and instructor presence. Research suggests that both course design and instructor engagement are essential elements of creating instructor *presence* in online synchronous courses (Conklin & Garrett Dikkers, 2021; Ekmekci, 2013; Kupczynski et al., 2010). Kupczynski et al. (2010) noted that while facilitation of discourse and direct instruction were ranked as most important for learner success, course instructional design and organization were the most identified reasons for learner struggles and course failure. Additionally, you should consider developing structure through meaningful assignments, as well as creating engaging activities. Lastly, using thoughtful discussion prompts can create a sense of instructor guidance and support for the learner. Instructor presence may then be created through being visible to, engaged with, and caring for the learners every step of the way throughout the learning experience (Ekmekci, 2013). This can be done through creating strong connections to the learners through constant and timely communication as well as encouraging peer interaction. Recommendations for creating instructor presence in the asynchronous environment include but are not limited to (Conklin & Garrett Dikkers, 2021; Ekmekci, 2013).

- Use multiple methods to connect with learners such as email, announcements, and instructional video lectures, which can promote a sense of connection for the learner.
- Send a weekly text or video message as a way to debrief previous course activities, transition to upcoming activities, and provide overall context for what learners are currently doing in the class.
- Give the perception that you care about the learners through empathic messaging via email, announcements, and videos which are conversational in tone and can convey "I am here for you through the learning process."
- Timely feedback is imperative, and ideally should be rendered within a 12–24-h window. Provide substantive feedback on learner assignments; this can be facilitated by preparing rubrics. You can also develop common feedback remarks, which can streamline this process.
- Lastly, actively monitor and facilitate asynchronous discussions.

3.5.4 Aesthetic Considerations for Teaching Online

Continuing with a learner-centered approach in combination with the community of inquiry model (COI) we see where aesthetic considerations find their place in almost every aspect of the online learning experience. The overlapping components in the COI model (instructor presence, cognitive presence, and social presence) include setting the climate, supporting discourse, and selecting content. Aesthetic considerations support concepts of universal design which attends to different learning needs and inherently increases inclusion.

Moreover, aesthetics has been included in education as an important element for creating a welcoming environment, uplifting historically marginalized identities, engaging learners, fostering learning relationships and addressing power dynamics (Brookfield, 2013). Furthermore, aesthetics in education are steeped in social justice principles articulated by Dewey (1934/2005) who suggested that learning is an active process based in experience, Freire (1973), who saw enactment and visioning as a counter to passive acceptance, hooks (1994) who supported arts-based experiences, especially writing and storytelling, as an import part of interpersonal freedom in education, and Lorde (1984) who viewed poetry as liberation and a path for learning and unlearning, especially for historically marginalized communities.

The learning management system (LMS) becomes a platform and creative space for you as the CES. Although it may be overwhelming when thinking about the myriad of tools and programs to implement, when we return to the learner-centered perspective incorporating an aesthetic lens becomes clearer. Here are some questions for consideration:

- What does a learner see when they first click on my class?
- What images, colors, or quotes have I included to welcome learners?
- How is my online class platform inviting and open to creating community?
- How is my online class platform encouraging creativity and expression?
- Do learners look forward to opening and reviewing the course site? Why or why not?
- Do learners feel engaged by the set-up and organization of the course?
- Do learners feel a sense of belonging when they view my class?
- How do I support non-verbal communication online through imagery, sound or video?

Lastly, CES' may consider including aesthetics in their communications with CITs. This may occur through including images, sound recordings, or videos in emails, announcements, as well as videos introducing or summarizing the week. Including aesthetics can be a bridge to connecting with CITs and increase a sense of humanity, trust, and engagement in the online course.

Stop and Reflect: *Reflecting back to Jamie, let's consider the learning management system (LMS) being used. Jamie continues to struggle with feelings of disconnection in the course, with course instruction content, and colleagues. Additionally, Jamie has experienced being misgendered by colleagues and frustration around incorrect pronouns use. In general, the LMS provides a typical landing page or overview page for the course. This can be your first opportunity as a CES to welcome your CITs and begin creating community and connection. Including a variety of photos that represent diversity as well as color choices for text and sections of the page offers a visual welcome. Highlighting quotes that represent diverse voices can also exhibit appreciation and acceptance. These components will help to increase comfort levels for CITs when they see themselves represented in the course material, and they see you as the CES taking steps to intentionally be welcoming.*

3.6 Considerations for Course Development in Online Teaching

Along with considering a model for your praxis as a CES, and the development of a teaching philosophy that aligns with how you see yourself as an educator, we offer you practical steps and best practices with respect to course development, and the unique nuances of online education and the virtual learning environment. We discuss the integral components of course development, such as syllabus development, learner engagement, assignment construction, and the essentials of timely feedback, all through the lens of social justice, accessibility, and equity.

3.6.1 Syllabus Development

Syllabi have historically been utilized as a contract, a statement of expectations, and a way to document what will be covered in a course and how learner work will be evaluated. In an online course, the syllabus is the first form of communication between the learner and instructor. We must consider who the syllabus is meant to serve and design it as such, focusing on integrating university expectations with learner-centered information. It is an opportunity for the faculty member to demonstrate not only what they are expecting from the learners but also to share their values, their ideas around how learning will happen in the course, and to establish the learning community norms from the beginning.

Most often the university/college and department/program will have required parts of the syllabus that are expected to be integrated into the syllabi of all university courses. This might include information related to learner services, such as the library, writing center, or disability services. Integral university policies may also be included, such as those regarding plagiarism and attendance. Lastly, there may be department or program requirements related to participation and late work. CACREP requires that all syllabi include a course description with the standard learning outcomes (SLOs) based on the current iteration of CACREP standards clearly stated. Additionally, the assignments that meet these standards must be clearly documented. It is essential that you are well-versed in the requisite aspects of the syllabus prior to putting your own expectations and personality into the document. From this point, it is important that you include the following information: course readings, media required for the course, assignment descriptions, evaluation procedures and timelines for assignments and their submission. Many professors include a course schedule to ensure that learners have a place to refer to for pertinent information such as the aforementioned. According to Snow et al. (2018), "Distance counselor education faculty will find their syllabi growing longer with more detail as they work to integrate traditional assignments with the e-learning and videoconferencing tools in order to create engaging, predictable, and enjoyable interactive learning experiences" (p. 140). Most importantly, *how* you communicate this information and what is included in these descriptions should indicate your intention to create an equitable learning environment for all learners.

3.6.1.1 Decolonization

Another important consideration in syllabus development is decolonization as an extension of a social justice foundation in education. Goodman and Gorski (2014) conceptualize decolonization as:

> Decolonizing multicultural counseling and psychology recognizes that this focus on culture directs our attention down the power hierarchy to focus almost entirely on the experiences and identities of disenfranchised people. This phenomenon is, in many ways, a distraction rooted in Western epistemologies. A decolonizing view, instead, pushes us to gaze up the power hierarchy, where inequalities are embedded in systems and structures that privilege the few at the expense of the many. (p. 2)

Decolonization touches every aspect of higher education. If we are to approach decolonization from a bottom-up perspective as noted above in Goodman and Gorski (2014), then beginning with syllabus development is a logical place to begin to elevate equity in education. Accordingly, creating an equity-based syllabus to begin to decolonize our courses, thus communicating a commitment to social justice practices in our classrooms. According to Wasik et al. (2019) "Culturally responsive online instructors use cultural knowledge and responsive teaching to validate learner experiences" and this should first occur in the syllabus (p. 49). It is important that we focus on language that demystifies programmatic and university policies, sets the tone for a welcoming environment for learners that communicates care, validates the commitment to learner success, and creates a partnership between instructors and learners. Examples of ways to facilitate collaboration include respectful communication, demonstrating your willingness to work with and support learners throughout their learning process, and ensuring that there is a clear anti-discrimination policy and supporting practices within the course. While instructors who teach in face-to-face learning environments may do these types of things in the first class, online professors must recognize that the syllabus is the first (and maybe one of the few) opportunities they will have to set norms of inclusion and equity-based practice.

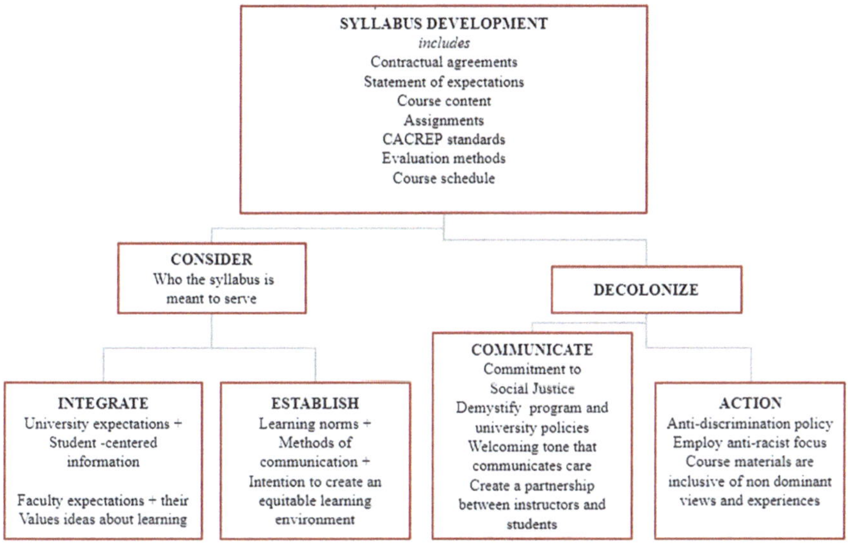

Fig. 3.2 Best practices for course syllabus construction through a decolonized lens

Additionally, it is recommended that it is best practice to focus on decolonizing your syllabus to ensure a focus on anti-racist classroom communities. In choosing readings and resources, it is important to recognize who has written the books and articles to ensure that the dominant narrative is not the only one heard. Videos, podcasts, blogs and online articles may serve to integrate additional ways of imparting information beyond peer-reviewed resources (Wasik et al., 2019). Additionally, it is recommended that the instructor assess each syllabus utilizing an antiracist checklist or rubric. A myriad of examples are readily available in seminal research, as well as resources available online (Fig. 3.2).

Stop and Reflect: *In considering Jamie's case, perhaps if the syllabus had been created through an equity-based lens, which may have encouraged a sense of trust that may have allowed them to approach you with concerns sooner. Early and supportive intervention provided by the instructor may have mitigated Jamie's noted challenges, particularly with respect to the importance of adhering to the usage of correct pronouns. Additionally, a clearly delineated statement of anti-racism and anti-discrimination in the syllabus provides a point of reference for the faculty to initiate classroom discussions about co-creating a learning environment that is supportive and inclusive of all CITs.*

3.6.2 Course Participation and Assignments

One of the challenges in creating an effective learning environment online is creating assignments that reflect the readings and integrate course content while demonstrating learner understanding, critical thinking and engagement with the material presented. Additionally, in the online classroom it is important to consider how one might utilize assignments to create the learning community and therefore whether the assignments will be done independently or if they will require interaction with other learners or communities.

One method for creating course assignments is to start with the end in mind. Ask yourself, "what do I want learners to know and to be able to do with what they have learned when they complete this course?" Creating these goals and objectives will provide the destination, and from there you must create the path that the learners will take. When considering which types of assignments will help learners achieve specific objectives, it is also important to consider ways to ensure that the assignments are varied and that we integrate reflection, experiential learning activities, quizzes and/or tests, along with papers, presentations and discussion. Additionally, varying the format of the assignments to include videos, audio and written responses will increase learner engagement with the material and assignments.

Online classes can be taught in different formats, utilizing a mix of asynchronous and synchronous modalities. As we have already discussed, asynchronous work involves learners independently engaging with the material in order to meet expectations. Synchronous work might include instructor led lectures and discussions as well as group/paired projects or clinical sessions. It is important that the expectation of synchronous and asynchronous participation in the class is clearly communicated in the course description, in the syllabus and in the first communications from the instructor. Regardless of teaching modality, the faculty should consider cognitive presence, social presence and instructor presence as previously discussed in this chapter above to create a community of learners who are committed to participating in collaborative, higher-level thinking thereby facilitating deep and meaningful learning (Garrison et al., 2000). It is important to provide a clear indication of participation expectations, whether through synchronous chats and meetings and or discussion forums, as well as communication on how you will engage in those experiences with the learners.

3.6.2.1 Assignments

Assignments in online counseling classes can be clearly grouped into two categories, clinical vs. non-clinical. Non-clinical assignments may include discussion forums, tests, papers, reflection journals, case studies, presentations, and other integrations on learning technology or tools. Clinical assignments might include peer practice sessions or role plays and recorded clinical sessions for supervision. It is important that learners are familiar with the tools that they will be using for assignments in your classes. It may be helpful to provide a brief overview of the types of assignments and how they will be submitted at the beginning of the semester. This can be augmented with subsequent updates as well as reviewing this information just prior to their due date. Clarity provides learners with the ability to focus on content and quality without being inundated with technological challenges.

Class content and desired learning outcomes should drive the types of assignments integrated into counseling classes. For online learning, it is important to consider variety in the assignments, as well as how the assignments will be completed. Assessment and testing may be completed through online testing centers, using proctors or allowing learners to utilize materials when completing a timed or untimed assessment (Smith et al., 2018). One method to ensure learner competency may be to require learners to retake the quiz or test until they are able to get a passing percentage, thereby facilitating the development of a foundation of learning requisite material. Larger assignments may include multiple ways of demonstrating learning, such as integrating reflection, research, and experiential activities into papers and presentations. For these types of assignments, it may be helpful to utilize scaffolding by breaking the larger assignment into manageable parts and possibly providing specific due dates for each part (Smith et al., 2018). Andragogical approaches to online teaching and learning encourage allowing adult learners a choice in the ways in which they can demonstrate competency. This may mean providing alternatives for an assignment such as reflections, recordings, or presentations. Additionally, it is important to clearly outline how each of the options meets course objectives and will be evaluated. Finally, providing templates and examples will help learners to develop a clearer picture of what is expected of them.

To create community and connection, instructors may choose to assign asynchronous discussions, synchronous group meetings, paired assignments or group presentations and papers. How one decides to assign partners or groups may depend on the knowledge that the instructor has of the learners as well as the learning objectives of the assignment. There may be times when the instructor allows learners to choose their own groups and others when the faculty may assign groups based on experience, identity, and/or interests (Smith et al., 2018). Whether to utilize homogeneous vs. heterogeneous groups, and even the consideration of allowing learners to self-identify into affinity groups, should be a choice that is clearly and intentionally communicated to learners. Assigning groups and partners early allows learners to prepare and plan effectively in order to best avoid scheduling conflicts resulting from negotiating different time zones, as well as managing family and work obligations. Again, it is important to clearly identify the expectations of co-creating assignments as well as the method of evaluation. Smith et al. (2018) report that to give group assignments the best chance at success, it is important that the instructor provide resources that will help the group members to connect effectively and efficiently. Therefore, providing access to online tools is an essential component of preparing learners for the group experience.

Another consideration is clinically-based assignments, such as practice sessions and/or counseling sessions from clinical placements. These can allow faculty to evaluate the CITs' clinical skills and their ability to integrate theory based on best practices. Often clinical practice sessions are recorded, and faculty are able to evaluate sessions through the use of rubric-based feedback. Currently the Counselor Competency Scale-Revised (CCS-R) provides a standard way of evaluating these clinical practice sessions through asynchronous feedback (Flynn & Hays, 2015). According to Snow et al. (2018), asynchronous methods are not well suited for modeling, teaching, and assessing interpersonal skills. However, synchronous videoconferencing technologies provide the same opportunity as residential settings to conduct fishbowl class exercises, break CITs into groups to practice clinical skills, conduct role plays, apply procedural learning, and give CITs immediate, meaningful feedback about their skills development.

While they strongly encourage utilizing synchronous methods of teaching and evaluating clinical skills, faculty can utilize videos, audio-recordings and time-stamped comments on videos to provide meaningful feedback to CITs when real-time supervision is not possible.

Stop and Reflect: *For Jamie, the assignment of peers for group discussions may be an important opportunity to create a less threatening learning environment for this CIT. Two options for this could be to either utilize affinity groups or to elicit requests from CITs for group composition. This might look like a simple email asking CITs to identify other CITs in the course that they believe would most support their learning experience based on the course material and assignment. These requests would be kept confidential and would be utilized by the instructor to create the discussion groups.*

3.6.3 Evaluation and Feedback

Hinkley et al. (2021) advises that faculty with high success rates provide prompt “positive, constructive, and corrective feedback to learners’ (p. 130). Successful faculty were also intentional in looking for ways to help learners succeed, including supplemental materials or tips (Hinkley et al., 2021). Prompt instructor feedback has been identified as the single most important indicator of learner success in online classes and is critical for the quality of an online course. Prompt feedback, both formal and informal, allows learners to either request additional support if needed or be assured that they understand the material and are moving in the right direction to assure competency (Northrup, 2009; Wasik et al., 2019). Prior to providing feedback, it is important that the learner is clear about what they will be evaluated on and how the evaluation will be provided (Wasik et al., 2019). As we discussed previously, the assignment description is an essential piece of the evaluation process as it clarifies exactly what is expected of the learner. Additionally, the rubric provides clear and concise guidelines for how the learner can reach a required standard. Finally, the learner must be clear on how they will be receiving their feedback in order to ensure access and understanding.

The way in which feedback can be provided to the learner can vary; however, it is especially important in an online classroom that the feedback is clear and understandable. As you consider your feedback to the learner, the first step to ensuring clarity is the creation of an assignment rubric that articulates the course expectations and delineates the criteria that learners' need to address to be successful. A clear rubric also describes the learner's performance based on varying levels of competency. It is recommended that there are multiple levels of competency and that the performance ratings are both quantitative (numerical) and qualitative (narrative). Criteria might include aspects of an assignment such as integration of the literature, use of basic counseling skills, APA formatting and grammar as a few examples. It is important that you predetermine the levels of competency and ensure that while there is the possibility for varied levels of success you are not going down a rabbit hole by listing too many criteria levels.

While points earned provide a quantitative understanding of "success" on an assignment, it is the qualitative feedback that is essential to learner learning. Through qualitative feedback, the learner can more fully understand what errors they made, and how to incorporate in future work the noted growth areas. Furthermore, although qualitative feedback may be incorporated in the rubric criteria, it is strongly recommended to provide a narrative summary of your feedback on the assignment. One suggestion that will enhance learner receptivity to the feedback offered is to utilize a voice recording or a video.

In counseling classes, CITs are often evaluated on their counseling skills through role plays or clinical videos. Feedback for these assignments should contain rubrics as well; however, it is most helpful if you are able to provide time-stamped feedback within the CIT's recording that allows them to go back to their videos and clearly identify their successes as well as areas for improvement. Additionally, you might view the CIT's video jointly and provide live feedback; this can contribute to a growth-fostering relationship with the CIT. Finally, it is important to ensure that the feedback is provided in such a way that helps the CIT improve the next time. Many of us have heard of the "sandwich" method for providing feedback, where constructive feedback is provided between two pieces of positive feedback. This can also promote CIT receptivity to, and integration of feedback by making the constructive feedback more palatable.

Another way to provide feedback is through cooperative learning, which involves the inclusion of peer feedback. Via this method, learners are able to support each other, create connections, and learn how to effectively provide critical feedback to each other. This skill is incredibly important for their professional development and growth (Smith et al., 2018). While ideally this can be an opportunity for learners to learn through the process of providing feedback, it also has some innate risks. To ensure that the feedback provided is aligned with the assignment expectations, it may be necessary for you as the instructor to facilitate these sessions between learners or request that feedback is sent to you as well. Engaging in discussions about how to best provide feedback (i.e. the sandwich method) is essential to creating a learning environment for the learners that is collaborative and supportive, with the goal of improving learner performance.

Stop and Reflect: *In the case of Jamie, personal and timely feedback could have been incredibly helpful for Jamie to provide the experience of being visible and validated as a part of their experience in this course. It may also be important to invite Jamie to have individual conversations related to their assignments, both before and after they are due to ensure that they feel supported in the learning process. Lastly, it is recommended to be intentional in the creation of a peer-pairing* **with** *Jamie as a part of the cooperative learning experience for feedback. This can facilitate the opportunity to create connection, engagement within the course, and enhance Jamie's overall academic performance.*

3.7 Conclusion

We conclude this chapter with a few key takeaways that we hope will provide you with a framework as you begin to teach online as well as a refresher for those who have already been working in this environment. It is our hope that the learner-centered focus remains a key aspect of the work, regardless of the format in which one is teaching, and that information shared here will help support learner and faculty success in the virtual classroom.

We began with the importance of integrating theoretical perspectives from pedagogical, andragogical and heutagogical approaches throughout the course design as this will provide opportunities for varied learner experience and interaction with course material, peers and the instructor. Highlighting how course design and aesthetics play an important role in ensuring learner understanding and engagement with the material, we encourage you to include elements that will include and invite all learners. Additionally, this is the first place that an instructor is able to communicate a community of acceptance and support which is essential to learner success. We clarify how the syllabus guides the course, this is especially true in the online learning environment. Intentional creation of varied learner experiences through assignment design will support learner engagement, reflection and critical thinking around course material. We promote experiential learning assignments and processing space as they are a critical component of integrating clinical experiences into online training. Instructor presence is described and can be created in both the asynchronous and synchronous learning environments through intentional course design, consistent and supportive communication, timely assignment feedback and the use of peer dialogue or feedback groups. Lastly, you as CES have an opportunity from the creation of the syllabus and the online learning platform to ensure that CITs like Jamie are met with a sense of inclusion and acceptance. Intentionality around peer groups, timely and personal feedback, as well demonstrating faculty availability for discussion and support will likely create opportunities for this CIT, and others like them, to engage with the course material and ultimately be successful in the course.

References

Anderson, T., Rourke, L., Garrison, D. R., & Archer, W. (2019). Assessing teaching presence in a computer conferencing environment. *Journal of Asynchronous Learning Networks, 5*(2), 1–17. https://doi.org/10.24059/olj.v5i2.1875

Blaschke, L. M. (2012). Heutagogy and lifelong learning: A review of heutagogical practice and self-determined learning. *The International Review of Research in Open and Distance Learning, 13*(1), 56–71. https://doi.org/10.19173/irrodl.v13i1.1076

Blondy, L. C. (2007). Evaluation and application of andragogical assumptions to the adult online learning environment. *Journal of Interactive Online Learning, 6*(2), 116–130. https://www.ncolr.org/jiol/issues/pdf/6.2.3.pdf

Brookfield, S. (2013). *Powerful techniques for teaching adults*. Jossey-Bass.

Conklin, S., & Garrett Dikkers, A. (2021). Instructor social presence and connectedness in a quick shift from face-to-face to online instruction. *Online Learning, 25*(1), 135–150. https://doi.org/10.24059/olj.v25i1.2482

Goodman, R. D., & Gorski, P. C. (Eds.). (2014). *Decolonizing "multicultural" counseling through social justice*. Springer.

Dewey, J. (2005). *Art as experience*. Berkley Publishing Group (Original work published 1934).

Ekmekci, O. (2013). Being there: Establishing instructor presence in an online learning environment. *Higher Education Studies, 3*(1), 29–38. https://doi.org/10.5539/hes.v3n1p29

Flynn, S. V., & Hays, D. G. (2015). The development and validation of the comprehensive counseling skills rubric. *Counseling Outcome Research and Evaluation, 6*(2), 87–99. https://doi.org/10.1177/2150137815592216

Freire, P. (1973). *Education for critical consciousness*. Seabury Press.

Garrison, D. R., Anderson, T., & Archer, W. (2000). Critical inquiry in a text-based environment: Computer conferencing in higher education. *The Internet and Higher Education, 2*, 87–105.

Halupa, C. (2015). Pedagogy, andragogy, and heutagogy. In C. Halupa (Ed.), *Transformative curriculum design in health sciences education* (pp. 143–159). Medical Information Science Reference. https://doi.org/10.4018/978-1-4666-8571-0

Hinkley, P., Shaler, L., Chamberlin, B., Peters, C., Davis, J., & Kuhnley, A. (2021). Effective strategies for promoting faculty and student success in online counselor education programs. *International Journal of Online Graduate Education, 4*(1).

Holmes, G., & Abington-Cooper, M. (2000). Pedagogy vs. andragogy: A false dichotomy? *The Journal of Technology Studies, 26*(2), 50–55. http://www.jstor.org/stable/43603946

Hooks, B. (1994). *Teaching to transgress: Education as the practice of freedom*. Routledge.

Knowles, M. S. (1984). *Andragogy in action: Applying modern principles of adult learning*. Jossey-Bass.

Kupczynski, L., Ice, P., Wiesenmayer, R., & McCluskey, F. (2010). Student perceptions of the relationship between indicators of teaching presence and success in online courses. *Journal of Interactive Online Learning, 9*(1), 23–43.

Lorde, A. (1984). *The master's tools will never dismantle the master's house*. Penguin Books.

Northrup, P. T. (2009). Online learners' preferences for interaction. In *The perfect online course: Best practices for designing and teaching* (pp. 463–473).

Sharp, S. R., Rutherford, G. L. II, & Echols, K. I. (2022). Creative science through inquiry: Improving teacher self-efficacy and outcome expectancy through adaptable, mystery-based professional development. *International Journal of Innovation in Science and Mathematics Education, 30*(1).

Skinner, B. F. (1968). *The technology of teaching*. Appleton-Century-Crofts.

Smith, A. C., Warren, J. M., Ting, S. M. R., & Taliaferro, J. D. (2018). *Developing online learning in the helping professions: Online, blended, and hybrid models*. Springer Publishing Company.

Snow, W. H., Lamar, M. R., Hinkle, J. S., & Speciale, M. (2018). Current practices in online counselor education. *Professional Counselor, 8*(2), 131–145.

Wasik, S., Barrow, J., Royal, C., Brooks, R., Dames, L., Corry, L., & Bird, C. (2019). Online counselor education: Creative approaches and best practices in online learning environments. *Research on Education and Psychology, 3*(1), 43–52. https://dergipark.org.tr/en/pub/rep/issue/43787/524049

Ali K. Corey Ph.D., LMHC (she/her/hers) is an Associate Professor at Antioch University, School of Counseling, Psychology, and Therapy. She has been a counselor educator for more than 10 years, and in professional practice as a licensed counselor for almost 20 years. Her clinical experience has been primarily with children and adolescents, her leadership work has included program development and expansion, and her scholarship has focused on leadership development for counselors and counselor educators.

Amy Morrison Ph.D., LMHC, ATR-BC (she/her/hers) is Associate Professor at Antioch University, School of Counseling, Psychology, and Therapy. She is the Co-Founder and Program Director of the Art Therapy Concentration in the Clinical Mental Health Counseling Program. She has taught in higher education and has been a practicing mental health counselor and art therapist for 20 years. Her clinical focus includes contemplative and attachment psychology, intersubjectivity, parenting, and life transitions during adulthood. She is an advocate for experiential, transformative learning, and social justice education and has presented nationally and internationally on these topics.

Clinical Supervision Within the Degree Program

4

Tanisha N. Sapp, Wendy Robinson, and Latasha Matthews

Each one, teach one.

W. E. B. DuBois

Abstract

This chapter will address best practices in clinical supervision for CITs enrolled in practicum and internship. It will focus on monitoring efforts, supervision planning, engagement with CITs, and setting up the CIT to have a successful and meaningful clinical experience that best prepares them for clinical practice or teaching. It will also address the use of technology in teaching and supervision, the use of software such as TEVERA and Supervision Assist designed to assist the counselor educator and supervisor during the supervision process.

Learning Objectives After reading this chapter, you will be able:

1. Implement best practices that are used to provide clinical supervision for CITs enrolled in practicum and internship.
2. Evaluate the development of requisite CIT counseling knowledge, awareness, and skills, and the appropriate application of such, to facilitate preparedness to enter the counseling profession.
3. Identify the ways one can utilize technology as an adjunctive tool for clinical supervision.

T. N. Sapp (✉) · W. Robinson
Liberty University, Lynchburg, VA, USA
e-mail: tsapp6@liberty.edu; cestextbookemail@gmail.com

W. Robinson
e-mail: wrobinson54@liberty.edu

L. Matthews
Illumination Counseling and Coaching, Lawrenceville, GA, USA
e-mail: info@illuminationcc.com

D. M. Stalnaker-Shofner and T. N. Sapp (eds.), *A Comprehensive Guide for Counselor Education*, Springer Texts in Education, https://doi.org/10.1007/978-3-031-68358-9_4

4.1 Statement of Reflexivity

We approached this chapter with an understanding that we do not know everything about the subject matter. While we have varying roles ranging from core faculty to adjunct faculty, we recognize the varying degrees of experience we each bring to the chapter while embracing our unique positionality. For example, each of us are counselor educators, supervisors, and private practitioners. Collectively we have a wealth of experience and expertise in our respective niche, yet we also recognize clinical skills are not inherently transferrable into supervision skills.

We also recognize the cultural implications of practice and the blind spots we each carry. We felt this was important to address, given that this book was written during a double pandemic. Additionally, we recognize this chapter is written through the eyes of inherent privilege and based on a foundation of systemic oppression. We recognize our privilege as counselor educators and scholar practitioners among the different intersections that encompass our counselor identities. Dr. Tanisha N. Sapp and Ms. Latasha Matthews are Black cisgender female counselor educators and supervisors. Dr. Wendy Robinson is a White, cisgender female counselor educator and supervisor. Drs. Sapp and Robinson both currently serve as core faculty members at a faith-based Predominantly White Institution (PWI). Additionally, Ms. Matthews is currently an adjunct professor at a faith based PWI. Each author has their own unique experiences as the student, educator, and site supervisor, which allows us to address these roles and identified perspectives. Additionally, both Dr. Sapp and Ms. Matthews graduated from online programs. While Dr. Robinson graduated from a campus-based program, each author has extensive training and experience with teaching in online programs and utilizing technology in counseling, education, and supervision. Thus, careful attention was paid to reduce author bias, while still acknowledging the lived experiences to maintain the integrity of the chapter.

This chapter's intention was to focus on the educator while differentiating the supervisor's role and respecting the differences among counselor preparation and education programs. Additionally, we aimed to be honest in providing a truthful experience. This was done in careful consideration to preserve the integrity of the educator, program, and institution. It was our intent to maintain the profession's standards while reaffirming the importance of gatekeeping through a multicultural lens.

4.2 Case Scenario

You are a new CES faculty member teaching your first practicum course at your university. There are 12 CIT's in your class and your university requires that you provide weekly individual supervision to CITs during their practicum experience. Additionally, you are teaching four other content courses at your university to fulfill your contractual obligation. During the first group supervision session, you find out that three CITs are working at their site without a supervisor present. Another CIT informs you that they have been seeing clients prior to the start of the semester and they are currently seeing 10 clients a week alone. You asked your faculty mentor for support, but they were unable to help. You continue to provide support for the CITs in the course.

A few weeks later, a different CIT reports that they have not received individual supervision at their site by the site supervisor. You attempted to reach the site supervisor, but they will not return your calls or emails. However, you noticed that the CIT has submitted timesheets and skills evaluations signed by the site supervisor. The CIT insists that the documents were completed by the site supervisor. Something doesn't feel right about this to you, so you consult your faculty mentor. However, your mentor refers you to your department chair who states that the university has never had these experiences before, so they are unsure what to do. You begin to feel overwhelmed by the complexity of these issues and the need for additional support. You begin to wonder if you can handle this job.

During one of the final group supervision classes, one of the CITs shared a videotaped session where they dominated the session and overshared the intimate details of their life experiences with clients to build rapport. During feedback, this CIT was defensive and began to cry. They stated that they cry at their site and when going home from their site every day. The site supervisor has not expressed any concerns about the CIT's emotional regulation. However, when you reached out to the site supervisor, they stated that the CIT has been unable to retain clients and shows poor boundaries. Although this was verbally reported to you, the site supervisor was hesitant to put this in writing stating that they "did not want to affect the CIT's placement in the program." As you address your concerns with the CIT, the CIT is not receptive to feedback and accuses you of "sabotaging my education." Given these concerns, you do not believe the CIT should pass the course, but your Department Chair and Field Placement Office state that there is "insufficient evidence" to support not passing the CIT. You find yourself stuck.

4.3 Introduction

As a counselor educator you will find yourself playing various roles from that of the educator, supervisor, and perhaps even the therapist. While each of these roles are important, they come together as one during the supervision experience. However, it is also important that you are aware of the differences between these roles specific to counselor education (Luke, 2019). This chapter explores each of these roles and the best practices for success. The authors discuss these roles while considering the cultural implications and use of technology in counselor supervision. As you explore each position, consider them within the context of the scenario presented above.

4.4 Welcome to the Academy

As a new counselor educator, you will be faced with a multitude of challenges differentiating your roles between educator and supervisor (we will talk more about this in the applicable sections below). This may be further exacerbated by the limited information provided within the 2014 ACA *Code of Ethics* outlining the role of the counselor educator as the supervisor. While there is a wealth of information pertaining to the ethical practices of the supervisor, there is sparse information connected to the role of the counselor educator as the supervisor during field placement. While Section F of the ACA *Code of Ethics* focuses on supervision, training, and teaching, it does not adequately address the role of the counselor educator as a supervisor (McKibben et al., 2022). Furthermore, Section F.7.i. of the 2014 ACA *Code of Ethics* is the only subsection that specifically addresses field placement. It states:

> Counselor educators develop clear policies and provide direct assistance within their training programs regarding appropriate field placement and other clinical experiences. Counselor educators provide clearly stated roles and responsibilities for the student or supervisee, the site supervisor, and the program supervisor. They confirm that site supervisors are qualified to provide supervision in the formats in which services are provided and inform site supervisors of their professional and ethical responsibilities in this role. (p. 14)

As written, the ACA notes the responsibility of supervision lies with the site supervisor. However, Section 4 of the 2024 CACREP standards mandates that the counselor educator serve in the role of clinical supervisor for counselors in training. While CACREP's standards in this regard are also limited in scope, the ACES *Ethical Guidelines for Counselor Supervision* (Hart et al., 1993) provide the most detailed guidance regarding the role of supervisor for the counselor educator as they define the supervisor as

> Counselors who have been designated within their university or agency to directly oversee the professional clinical work of counselors. Supervisors also may be persons who offer supervision to counselors seeking state licensure and so provide supervision outside of the administrative aegis of an applied counseling setting. (p. 2)

4.4.1 Differences Between the Counselor Educator and Site Clinical Supervisor

While there are many similarities and roles that overlap between the CES and site clinical supervisor, there are also distinct differences between the two roles. However, it is ultimately up to the counseling program to define these differences. As such, we have attempted to mention the key differences between these roles. We do not intend this list to be considered exhaustive, but rather as a point of reference for a new CES.

There are many similarities along with some distinct differences between the roles and responsibilities of the CES and Site Clinical Supervisor. These roles and responsibilities are ultimately defined by the counseling program as noted in section F of the CACREP 2024 Standards (CACREP, 2024). Therefore, we have attempted to mention some key differences between these roles, though we do not intend this list to be considered exhaustive, but rather as a point of reference for a new CES.

First, both CES and site clinical supervisor have responsibilities to train and develop the CIT's counseling skills and professionalism while gatekeeping in the profession (Borders & Brown, 2022; Luke, 2019). Typically, both will evaluate the CIT through a formal assessment to ensure that the CIT is meeting professional counseling standards through program requirements to progress to the next level or initiate remediation to support the CIT's development. Even though both are evaluating the same requirements, there can sometimes be tension as one may identify issues that the other does not see or disagrees with.

Second, the CES typically only observes the CIT during the scheduled class time with only required case presentations, which is limited, whereas the site clinical supervisor has more access to the CIT for more frequent observations. Further, the site clinical supervisor has access to feedback from clients along with other staff members. However, the access of the CIT's work and professionalism does not negate issues identified by the CES. This can just be challenging in getting everyone on the same page to best support the development of the CIT. Third, the CES and site supervisor will engage in multiple tasks/roles to foster the growth and academic professional development of the CIT through observation, coaching, mentoring, and evaluation while creating an environment that is safe to make mistakes and learn. However, how they perform these roles may look different.

Lastly, the site clinical supervisor is ethically responsible for the care of each client that the CIT is providing services to during the field placement course. Therefore, the CES may provide feedback and suggestions on client care, however, ultimately the CES should refer to the site clinical supervisor for final guidance. The exception to this best practice would occur if CES identified a potential ethical concern at which the CES would need to engage the site clinical supervisor in further discussion to protect and advocate for the CIT. An example of this may be if the CIT is being asked to engage in a clinical practice that is well beyond the training and competency of the CIT and may potentially cause harm to the client. For the purposes of this textbook and chapter, we will focus on your role as the CES providing supervision of CITs within the context of counselor education.

4.5 Evaluation

One of your most important roles as a CES will be to evaluate the CITs in your course. In accordance with the 2024 CACREP standards, standard 4.F states that "formative and summative evaluations of the learner's counseling performance and ability to integrate and apply knowledge are conducted as part of the learner's practicum and internship" (CACREP, 2024, p. 17). The task of evaluation is often complex involving multiple layers and considerations and completed during multiple points of the field placement process. While informal evaluations of core knowledge, awareness, and skills are completed throughout the practicum and internship courses, more formal summative assessments are completed either quarterly or during midpoint and at the end of the academic semester. Some programs choose to utilize an end of field placement assessment capturing the material learned throughout the entire program. No matter the type of assessment, both the CES and site clinical supervisor are responsible for assessing the CIT's competency and preparedness to enter the counseling profession.

It is often challenging to find balance of encouragement and working through the learning curve of CITs' abilities in field placement, as counseling does not have a step-by-step approach creating subjectiveness in the evaluation process. Counseling is an art that can be conducted in a multitude of approaches and styles that promote CITs' authenticity while meeting client needs. And then there is a reality that CITs are often struggling with adequately demonstrating counseling skills and knowledge at varying stages of field placement. Therefore, it is important to assess through a developmental lens, however, maintaining high standards and accountability for making improvements is vital to effectively gatekeeping the profession and adequately preparing the CIT.

Stop and Reflect: *Most people become counselors to support others not necessarily to challenge and confront, and this is no different for you, the CES. Yet, it could be argued that support is best demonstrated when stretching your CITs through the evaluative process with sometimes hard truths in a caring and respectful manner. This in fact could be the definition of support. Therefore, reframing how you approach and think about evaluation can create an opportunity to maximize the growth and development of CITs during their time with you. In addition, assessing your own belief about the benefits of evaluation can make this complex task a little easier or if you do not then gate slipping could occur along with being a barrier to what the CIT needs from you. Further exploration of evaluation will be explored in more detail as we examine your role as an educator and supervisor.*

4.5.1 Your Role as the Educator

One of the things you will find as you step into your new role as a counselor educator is that, well, the lines between your various intersecting professional identities become obscure. It is the hope of these authors that we may be able to shed light and help provide clarification as to what this may look like in the context of clinical supervision. As you navigate the content of this chapter, it is important to note that while many examples may be addressed, this is not an exhaustive list of experiences. Let's walk through some of the activities you can expect to experience when operating in your role as the educator in the field placement course from start to finish.

First, let's dive into *course prep.* This is not to be confused with the course prep that you learned about in Chap. 2. Once you are assigned your course, you want to review your roster to verify the CIT and site placement information. Whether you are teaching the course online or on campus, you will want to create a way to maintain information on the CIT and site information from the field placement office. This could be achieved with a notebook or file folder for each CIT or use technology with a spreadsheet with specific information on the CIT's placement site. This system can be utilized to document data on the CIT throughout the course such as observations in interactions with peers, receptiveness to feedback, scheduled presentations, etc. Documentation is important and necessary in field placement to support your evaluations, so it is vital to create an organization system that works best for you, and you may have to experiment to find it. Once you organize the site placement information, you will need to communicate with the Clinical Site Supervisor to introduce yourself and begin establishing a collaborative partnership along with reminders of the course to ensure you are all on the same page regarding expectations.

Next, we will discuss facilitating the field placement course. This will vary by program and institution, though there are best practices to consider in organizing and conducting the course. However, the 2024 CACREP standards, standard 4.T requires a field placement program to conduct regular contact with CITs through group supervision that averages 1 1/2 h per week (CACREP, 2024). This requirement may be facilitated by either the CES or a CES doctoral learner providing clinical supervision under core faculty supervision or that of affiliate faculty.

Typically, the first couple of weeks of the course whether it is practicum or internship, will focus on logistics such as setting expectations and reviewing requirements to create a foundation for success. Further, the first couple of weeks will parallel group dynamics with a focus on formation of the group so spend time with activities to create connection within the group and you. Similar to the formation of a working group, a working field placement course will promote an environment that is safe to be authentic and engage in risk taking that is necessary for developmentally growing and promoting the CIT. Therefore, spend time reviewing requirements and teaching is needed, do not forget to carve out time for building safety and security within the group as it is not uncommon for CITs in field placement courses to have high levels of anxiety and angst in performing at this stage in their development. (Borders & Brown, 2022). Finding your teaching and facilitation style may also take risks so expecting some failures along with success is normal for new CES and seasoned ones, too. We like to set up experiments at the beginning of the course to try new approaches based on feedback and learning from each time we teach or new information from research and fellow colleagues. This can be exciting while possibly falling flat, but you will not know without trying. Convey this message to CITs as this is a parallel process of what they will experience within the site placement while working with clients. What a great opportunity to demonstrate vulnerability and putting to practice what you are teaching.

Facilitating course content may be challenging due to the multifaceted requirements to expose and develop a well-rounded counselor-in-training. Again, this is not an exhaustive examination though some content areas to consider in creating your integrative approach in guiding exploration of CIT's presentation of work with a client. There are different approaches to how you can choose to structure the feedback segment when reviewing a CIT's client video. Regardless of your specific style or approach, it is vital to cover areas including cultural awareness, theory, ethics, diagnosis, treatment planning along with the CITs' ability to demonstrate foundational and advanced counseling skills.

In addition to counseling skills and knowledge, you will also be responsible for teaching about professional dispositions. Professional dispositions depict the CIT's ability to conduct oneself in a manner that represents the ethical and professional standards of the counseling profession. We recommend going over the dispositions in detail during the first two weeks of the course along with explaining the importance, and then providing reminders when you begin reviewing CITs' client work. Often dispositional issues will arise during feedback as it is anxiety provoking to be vulnerable to show one's work and then receive live feedback from both you and peers, though this is necessary for growth of the CIT. Therefore, educating prior to showing work may mitigate some of the CIT's response, though if the CIT cannot self-manage then this is a red flag that needs attention. You will find more information on how to manage common issues with CITs later in this chapter.

Developmental scaffolding should be utilized in your approach to each of the different clinical courses. Practicum is the CITs first encounter with real clients. There tends to be a lot more support and encouragement required by you. You will find that focusing more on foundational and advanced counseling skills is necessary while providing exposure and beginning to integrate content from all the courses within the program such as conceptualizing clients, applying ethical and multicultural considerations, diagnosing along with effective treatment planning through biopsychosocial spiritual lens. Then as the CIT is promoted to the next clinical course the expectations and requirements will increase such as demonstrating more consistency with effective counseling skills while understanding the why behind the skill while simultaneously improving integration and conceptualization skills. By the second semester of internship the CIT should be demonstrating more consistency in all content areas as determined by the 2024 CACREP standards, standard 3.E (CACREP, 2024).

Lastly, as you prepare to close your course, here are a few things to consider. Make sure to close the group. This can be done with an activity of sharing takeaways from the course and time with peers along with growth areas for the next phase of one's clinical training. The choice is yours though it is recommended to do a closure activity. Further, most CES programs will require an end of the semester formal evaluation that would be beneficial to submit to the CIT prior to the end of the course. Provide some time for individual meetings if CITs have questions or would like further discussion of your feedback. Next, you will have logistics to complete such as reviewing hour reports and site placement supervisor evaluation. Errors may occur that may require you to follow up. Finally, if you identified concerns about a CIT's development and/or disposition, it is best to document your observations along with any actions taken then supply them to your field placement office.

4.5.2 Your Role as the Supervisor

As a new counselor educator, understanding and attending to multiple roles as clinical supervision and teacher in practicum and internship can be overwhelming and requires a change in your thinking, skills, and professional identity (Borders, 1992, as cited in Steiny, 2017; Luke, 2019). Learning the administrative aspects of graduate level course work is consuming, though this is compounded in clinical courses due to the many hats one must wear, often simultaneously. Therefore, identifying roles with clear expectations is necessary. Defining counselor educator supervision and understanding the developmental stages of CITs is imperative to one's ability to effectively facilitate clinical courses. Essentially you would ask yourself the following questions: Who am I as clinical supervisor? What is my understanding of the developmental stages of CITs during the different phases of their clinical field placement experience? These are important questions to answer to create your framework as a clinical supervisor and educator.

Clinical supervision has been defined as, "Supervision is a disciplined, tutorial process wherein principles are transformed into practical skills, with four overlapping foci: administrative, evaluative, clinical, and supportive" (Powell & Brodsky, 2004, p. 11). Bernard and Goodyear (1992; as cited in Bernard & Goodyear, 2024) expanded the definition noting,

> Supervision is an intervention provided by a senior member of a profession to a more junior member or members.... This relationship is evaluative, extends over time, and has the simultaneous purposes of enhancing the professional functioning of the more junior person(s); monitoring the quality of professional services offered to the clients that she, he, or they see; and serving as a gatekeeper of those who are to enter the particular profession. (p. 9)

Understanding how to guide, mentor, coach, and evaluate CITs while inspiring self-motivation, recognizing and owning growth areas and developing professionally is imperative to the role of CES facilitating clinical courses. As with any new role, a new CES, you will make mistakes as you learn the expectations along with navigating course content and providing supervision. Kindness to self is important so you have the space to grow and learn from your own mistakes, as it is given you will make them. So, think about how you will balance your expectations within this reality?

Clinical courses require the CES to create and facilitate an environment of safety to promote CITs to step outside of one's comfort zone to grow and fail with guidance and understanding. This is often a vulnerable situation for CITs to navigate the transition from knowledge to application of learning and practicing how to become a counselor. Subsequently, new CES experience discomfort and anxiety (Grant et al., 2012) in their new role just like CITs in applying your learning to overseeing the development of the CIT. Consideration of the learning curve is necessary for you and your CITs as you will both engage in trial and error to solidify your style and approach to this new role.

The key to effective supervision is the same as effective counseling—relationship-building. Borders and Brown (2022) noted the quality of the supervisor-supervisee relationship is "heart and soul of the supervision experience" (p. 66). Therefore, the supervisory relationship is essential to promote self-efficacy and competency among CITs. This may seem simple, yet many CES will lean heavily into the educator role as it can be easier to focus on didactic teaching where the CES is the expert compared to creating a collaborative relationship that focuses on processing and challenging the CIT and their work (Corey et al., 2021; Steiny, 2017). Thus, building effective relationships and an environment that is conducive to risk taking at the onset of your clinical course will be most beneficial. Therefore, we recommend that you begin the course with a strong focus on engagement while clearly reviewing the requirements and expectations of the course. Balance will be the key to managing your two different roles: the educator and supervisor.

Take some time to explore ways to build effective clinical supervision relationships and avoid simple introductions as time is limited. Instead, you may want to start your class with an ice breaker then an experiential learning opportunity to introduce and begin connecting CITs/supervisees. This allows the CIT/supervisee the opportunity to learn more about you as well as you an opportunity to learn about them and offers a culturally humble approach to building an effective supervisory relationship (Bernard & Goodyear, 2024; Corey et al., 2021; Hardy & Bobes, 2016). Creating a space to share about self is good though adding additional information such as goals for the course along with needs and gaps in their counseling abilities can be beneficial twofold. First, in that CITs connect when sharing struggles or concerns along with learning they are not alone as most will have similar beliefs. Second, you will gain data about each CIT to create a baseline along with identification of how to best support CIT needs. This information is beneficial in evaluation as you can recall what the CIT shared then build on it as a soft entry for feedback. In addition, focusing on themes such as: CIT needs, creating safety, encouraging bravery and risk taking may alleviate angst and fear while fostering vulnerability and safety through normalizing the CITs' feelings and thoughts. Do not be afraid to be bold and take risks on Day One! You are modeling these skills to CITs, and they will gain more from your vulnerability and risk-taking action than merely your words.

Lastly, another factor to consider is that learners at the graduate-level are often perfectionists, high achievers, and strong academic performers, which again you may relate to as a recent graduate. This topic will be explored in more detail in Chap. 10 focused on common pitfalls. Consequently, CITs may struggle receiving constructive feedback that may be perceived as critical to building counseling skills and conceptualization of clients along with applying theory within treatment planning can be overwhelming. Therefore, challenging high performing CITs' ability to accept that they are not good at counseling yet is critical to their growth. Explaining this new reality during the first class is often beneficial along with reminders throughout the course. Specifically, explaining developmentally that the CIT must learn to walk before running can be helpful. Though often CITs have unrealistic expectations of self, revealing and exploring the dissonance may increase the CIT's openness and ability to gain the most from your feedback. This feedback is what is desired most by CITs (Fickling et al., 2017).

4.5.3 The Importance of Timely and Qualitative Feedback

CES must be able to provide constructive feedback to CITs while also challenging the other CITs in the course to provide the same. This may sound like an easy task, however, many CES struggle for a variety of personal and professional reasons including: Fear of being judged and not being liked, fear of complaints by CITs to the administration, fear of confrontation in front of a group of CITs, fear of hurting a CIT's feelings. Thus, your anxieties and fears may drive your decision-making surrounding the delivery of your feedback to the CIT. Therefore, your feedback should be accurate, direct, and honest. Feedback that downplays a CITs genuine performance is not beneficial to the CIT or the counseling profession, and ultimately does not serve the best interest of the client. Additionally, allowing the other CITs in the course to provide surface-level feedback that feels good to the CIT and does not challenge the growth of the CIT in question is not conducive to either CITs learning. Therefore, it is imperative for counselor educators to conduct a self-examination to identify and combat barriers to growing and developing CITs. The truth is that the counselor educator may provide honest feedback that is not received well by a CIT and the CIT may file a complaint against you. In turn, your administration may question your tactics causing you to feel the need to defend your position. While this does not feel good for the counselor educator, it is important to remember that you cannot ethically protect the counseling field and grow the CITs without providing effective supervision which includes providing honest feedback. Therefore, you are encouraged to manage your fears while attempting to do the right thing to avoid this pitfall. The CES is not their CIT's therapist. However, the CES would benefit from open dialogue with CITs regarding the frustrations experienced in the counseling session and consider that parallel process that could exist. As a point of reflection, the CES might consider the parallel process that exists and address this with the CIT. A parallel process occurs when the dynamics present in the supervisory relationship mirror those in the client-counselor relationship. Here is an example:

Hello CIT,

I want to discuss something that has come up in our recent supervision and provide feedback. I've noticed that there might be a parallel process occurring that mirrors what you are experiencing with your client. During our discussions about your client, I have picked a sense of frustration and impatience that mirrors what you've stated that you experience with your client. It is important that we explore this parallel process because it might impact the effectiveness of your work counseling work.

It is essential in your CES role to explore and mention the similarities mentioned that might resonate in the CIT own personal experience. As CES it would be beneficial to spend time providing encouragement to the CIT regarding the frustrations that arise in the counseling session. As stated in previous sections, these dialogues and conversations are not easy, in fact they can cause stress and anxiety for both the CES and the CIT. Therefore, it is important for both the CES and CIT to maintain wellness practices and self-care.

4.6 Establishing Your Self-care and Wellness

As previously discussed, it is important that the CES maintains self-care and wellness practices The 2014 ACA *Code of Ethics* mandates in the introduction to Section C that "counselors engage in self-care activities to maintain and promote their own emotional, physical, mental, and spiritual well-being to best meet their professional responsibilities" (ACA, 2014, p. 8). In keeping with this, here are a few practical steps to get you started.

First, let's define wellness. According to Myers et al. (2000), wellness is "a way of life oriented toward optimal health and well-being, in which body, mind, and spirit are integrated by the individual to live life more fully within the human and natural community" (p. 251). It is important to note that this definition is fluid, therefore you must determine what wellness looks like for you. Most importantly, give yourself permission to change your wellness plan as you evolve and mature during your tenure as a CES.

Once you have defined what wellness looks like to you, you must identify the barriers you faced during the supervision process. Some examples specific to the scenario above are: CIT pushback, systemic processes, poor boundaries, lack of administrative support, and perhaps your unwillingness to ask for help or have an ability to recognize that help is needed. It is also important that you are able recognize the multicultural implications that surround those with the innate responsibility to wear the superhero cape, whether they want to or not. This most often includes historically marginalized populations including BIPOC.

For many, asking for help requires a level of vulnerability that may not have been accessed yet. Therefore, to implement this first step, having the ability to take a deeper look inside yourself is important. Keep it real, be honest, and speak your truth. Shake off any fear or meaning attached to seeking help and go for it. Taking care of you does not equate to being incompetent, it simply requires having clear boundaries. Consequently, the second step is about boundaries. Having clear boundaries is essential to developing a healthy wellness and self-care routine. Boundaries for CES can look like taking time off (WOAH! That's a big one), taking a vacation without access to phones, emails, or any communicative devices, time management strategies to reduce distractions, and not allowing your inner critic to take up real estate in your head to trick you into believing you are incompetent. This also includes setting boundaries with your CITs, peers, and your university administration. You matter.

Monitoring your own self efficacy is vital for new CES'. Therefore, utilizing program directors, faculty mentors (or your university equivalent), or the institution's field placement office is key to success in this area. You may even look to seek additional support from colleagues outside of your university and within professional organizations, specifically organizations geared towards clinical supervision. For example, ACES conducts a monthly CES roundtable to support faculty providing supervision of CITs. Your state may also have similar resources available to you.

Above all else, the CES is the intervention. Therefore, if you are not well, you cannot bring out the best in the CITs you serve. Therefore, your total wellness supersedes any of the tips we have provided above. How do you achieve total wellness? We are so glad you asked. The answer is simple, get you a therapist! Seriously, go get a therapist and do your own work. Having someone you can talk to allows you to release what you hear and experience in the learning environment so that you can fill your cup and return to the learning environment. This is also a space to navigate the parallel processes between supervisor and CIT, CIT stories, secondary trauma, and other various experiences.

4.7 Use of Technology in Supervision

Your university utilizes an online platform to host faculty group supervision for both practicum and internship courses. CITs, faculty, and site supervisors are required to know how these programs work along with submitting appropriate documentation into the system. CITs complete the field application in this system and send it to the site supervisor to sign, which triggers the field placement office to review the final submission once everything is complete. This academic year, you find that you are assigned to teach the 1st semester of internship. As you go through your roster, you notice one CIT has not submitted any hours during the entire practicum semester. You reached out to the CIT who is adamant that they have submitted their hours, and their site supervisor has approved all of the necessary paperwork. They insist that there must be "something wrong with your system."

4.7.1 Introduction

Technology is ever-changing and evolving over time. This is no different for the use of technology within CES programs. There are various platforms that exist to serve the needs of our programs. While each institution will ultimately determine the platform(s) that best align with their curricular needs, we thought it ideal to shed light on three popular programs and how they are used in Faculty/Site Supervision within field placement courses outlined in Fig. 4.1. We recognize that there are multiple platforms and programs available and by mentioning these programs, we do not profess to be experts in the use of such programs or endorse any one program over another.

1. Tevera(™) is a web-based software platform designed to streamline and manage various aspects of academic and clinical education programs (Tevera, 2023). It's commonly used in fields such as social work, counseling and healthcare education. The platform provides tools for tracking a learner's progress, managing field placements, and facilitating communication between learners, educators, and field supervisors.
2. Supervision Assist is a software solution focused on simplifying and improving the supervision process in various professional settings, particularly in healthcare, counseling and education (Supervision Assist, 2024). The system is designed to help supervisors monitor and assess the performance of supervisees, track supervision hours, and facilitate communication between supervisors and those under supervision.
3. Motivo is a telehealth platform specifically designed for clinical supervision in the mental health field (Motivo, 2024). It offers a HIPAA complaint environment for remote supervision sessions. Motivo's goal is to increase accessibility to quality supervision by overcoming geographical barriers, enabling supervisors and supervisees to connect virtually.

Stop and Reflect: *The aforementioned platforms raise several considerations. First the integration of technology into academic and professional supervision settings highlights the ongoing need and desire for digitalization but also speaks to the need for balance and efficiency. It is important to continue to find ways to foster the human touch in these critical interactions while considering the accessibility benefits that come from utilizing various platforms. Additionally, the adoption of such platforms underscores the importance of secure and compliant platforms in the field that deal with sensitive information. As we embrace these digital platforms it is crucial to assess their implications for counselor educators, supervision and the overall implications on human interactions.*

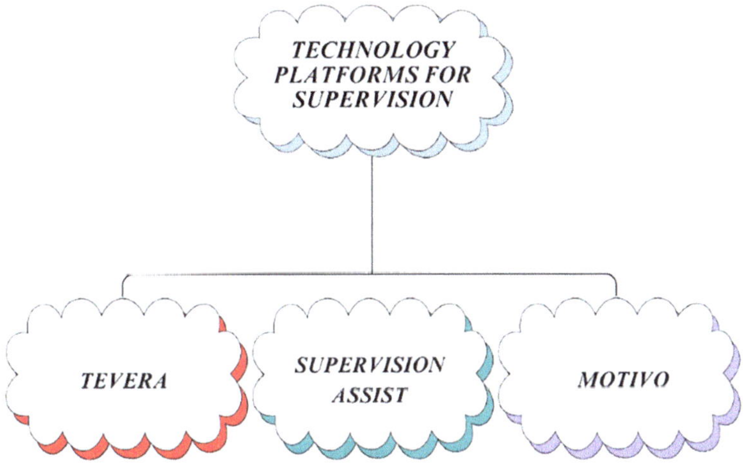

Fig. 4.1 Technology platforms used for supervision in CES

4.8 Best Practice Guidelines for Supervision

In the scenarios for this chapter, the CES has a responsibility to advocate for the profession in addition to supporting the CIT and managing their own wellness. There were several attempts made by the CES to give the CIT feedback and share the outcome with the department. The role of ethical gatekeeping mandates that the CES is to protect the public from harm while also providing CITs with transparent feedback regarding how their personal struggles (i.e. unresolved mental health challenges) could impact their ability to provide adequate care for clients. Effective feedback and remediation support from the CES could positively impact the CIT personally and professionally. It is important for the CES to continue to advocate for the CIT by talking to a peer mentor regarding best practices using remediation to protect the profession, the CIT, and the public. The ACA *Code of Ethics* (ACA, 2014) and 2024 CACREP standards (CACREP, 2024) charge counselor educators and counselor education programs with monitoring the development of CITs to include gatekeeping providing feedback and remediation as needed. The new CES would benefit from peer support and mentorship, as well as referring to the program and/or faculty handbook and/or University policy on how to approach issues of impairment and competency. In addition to faculty support, the CES would benefit from seeking personal therapy as well as professional academic mentorship for accountability and support. The new CES should examine their schedule and conduct a self-assessment to ensure they are able to care for themselves as they honor their contractual obligations.

The CES must explore their own self-care strategies to determine if their self-care plan is sufficient for their new role. The new CES must be honest and vulnerable while asking for support. Thus, the following self-care tips are recommended: understand your current risk factors for burnout, create a wellness plan, create a daily routine, engage your interest and seek consultation. Furthermore, exploring the domains of wellness (as identified by Myers et al., 2000) to ensure that you are giving the necessary attention to the areas that support and cultivate your academic development and success is also beneficial.

The new counselor educator would benefit from professional counseling to assess and address secondary traumatic stress, feelings of inadequacy, and the emotional toll that supporting CITs can have on your emotional well-being. Additionally, the new CES could benefit from journaling, practicing mindfulness and expressions of gratitude which can highlight the impact they have made in the profession as well as with the CITs they are serving and will serve in the future.

4.8.1 Managing the Site and Clinical Site Supervisors

Next, it is important to consider your approach to working with the CIT's site supervisor(s) based on the above scenarios. Unfortunately, many CES have not been trained in how to effectively manage, lead, and develop relationships with site supervisors. A different skill set is required to manage these external relationships along with the course, university, accreditation, license requirements. Depending on the university that you work with, there may be different requirements of the CES related to the management of clinical sites and site supervisor relationships. Therefore, your first step is to obtain a clear understanding of these requirements from your department leadership. This may take more than one conversation to get your needs met, so you are encouraged to inquire until you have a good handle on it. Once the expectations have been defined, then you should create a plan of execution. We encourage you to seek mentoring from a seasoned faculty to get ideas on what they do. There is no reason to create from scratch when others already have a plan and have been doing it for a while. Try some things and determine what is best for your style.

This expectation of managing relationships with clinical site supervisors and sites can be time consuming so we are providing some practices that work for us. First, establishing an effective partnership with the clinical site supervisor is highly beneficial. In most cases the clinical site has received information and even agreed to it with your clinical field placement office, though that does not mean they are tracking all the information when the practicum or internship starts. Therefore, it is good to reinforce in your first communication. Your communication may be an email, phone call or even physical visit depending again on your department's requirement. Regardless of the method, it is helpful to include field placement requirements of them and their CITs along with role definitions for both you, the faculty supervisor and the site supervisor. Clear roles and responsibilities identified may mitigate confusion and possible conflict if an issue arises. The communication is best to send in the first week of the course with your introduction and thank you for the site and clinical site supervisor's willingness to guide and direct CITs.

In addition, remind the clinical site supervisor that this is a team approach to ensure that the CIT is meeting appropriate developmental milestones consistent with their current level of clinical training. Request the clinical site supervisor to contact you immediately with any observable and/or evaluative clinical and/or dispositional concerns. You both have an obligation to maintain high standards of the counseling profession within this learning phase of field placement. As basic as this first step may seem, it is one that is often overlooked and not prioritized. This can lead to challenges that may have been avoided with clear communication from day one of the new term.

Second, you want to create a working relationship with the clinical site supervisor, and this again is done through communication, communication, and more communication. The importance of communication cannot be overstated. Communication may occur in a variety of ways from written, verbal, or face-to-face visits. Regardless of how it occurs, it needs to happen. Consistent communication throughout the clinical course is necessary to ensure the CIT is developing at a level to allow their continuation within clinical courses. Keeping an open dialogue with the clinical site supervisor may identify and address early on any deficiencies in developmentally appropriate counseling skills demonstration and professional disposition. The clinical site is significant in providing a foundation for the CIT to gain the necessary experience and skills to provide effective counseling to clients. Therefore, the CES must be diligent to not only ensure the clinical site supervisor has a good understanding of the course requirements but that there is an open line of communication and desire to work in the best interest of the CIT's development.

Third, address CIT or site concerns sooner than later. Trust your intuition and inquire with the site supervisor if you have any notation that there is a problem. Many issues can be remedied at this junction since most of them will fall under simple miscommunication. So, attending to any issues immediately may alleviate long term challenges and undue stress for you, the CIT, and the clinical site supervisor. Though, you will need to determine if the issues should be addressed by you directly with the site supervisor or if the issue warrants soliciting support from the clinical practicum/internship office or your program director may be warranted. Therefore, it is always good practice to consult if you are ever in doubt or just need some reassurance of your plan of action.

Once the best course of action has been identified to address concern, prepare for the meeting. Create your talking points to guide the conversation and this will start your documentation. Just like you would guide CITs working with clients, always document even if it is a minor miscommunication. If there is a future issue, then documentation will be necessary to provide evidence of a pattern and support next steps. Focus on facts of the concern(s) to minimize defensive responses and quickly get to core issue(s). For example, a CES suspects the CIT is conducting unethical behaviors and the CES has concerns the site supervisor is not addressing the CIT. The CES begins the conversation with a statement about concerns and makes an inquiry if the site supervisor has observed similar issues. It is not uncommon for a clinical site supervisor to lack some awareness so always approach as a collaborative partner. Once the issue(s) has been discussed then identify the next steps with the CIT that were agreed upon by both you and the clinical site supervisor. Document the CIT's receipt of feedback and any comments along with the action plan. Do not forget to document the follow-up and outcomes along with any additional interventions. If this is a pattern with the clinical site supervisor, then escalate the issue with documentation to the clinical office to address and decide if site/site supervisor is appropriate for the department's counseling program.

Attending the differences of opinions of a CIT may be highly uncomfortable for a CES, though the concerns should not be avoided for one's comfort. An avoidant approach is detrimental to the CIT and the counseling professional. Both the CES and site supervisor have responsibilities to move through the discomfort and attempt to work together to address the concerns. Often, though, the CES will be positioned to lead the discussion. The CES may be at a disadvantage in this scenario, since the CES only saw a video of the CIT conducting a session while the site supervisor may be engaged in the CIT's daily practice. In a situation like this the CES should convey one's concerns and request the site supervisor to be aware. Remembering this is a partnership so it is possible the site supervisor has not paid attention to the CES' concerns, though now with an awareness the site supervisor can focus more to see if there is any validity to the CES concerns.

As noted in the scenario, a clinical site supervisor may take offense to the CES acknowledging a deficiency that they did not identify. Consider the defensiveness of the clinical site supervisor as their issue, and your role is to facilitate a productive discussion focused on the CIT's needs. It is important to do your best and not personalize the situation, though let's be real, this is easier said than done. Try to take a deep breath and remind yourself that this is not about you, and there may be external issues facing the site supervisor or not. The reason behind the defensiveness is not necessary to know however, like managing a challenging client, your counseling skills will be beneficial to de-escalate the situation to regulation to reset the focus back to the best interest and needs of the CIT. Further, you will have feelings and thoughts from this uncomfortable encounter, please honor it and then attend to them at a different time with a supervisor, counselor, or colleague. Lack of attention to the experience(s) can build up over time leading to fatigue and burnout, so creating your own wellness plan will benefit you.

4.8.2 Managing the CIT

Gatekeeping is a key role for both the CES and clinical supervisors. However, the role of the gatekeeper could vary based on the setting. The ACA *Code of Ethics* states that it is important for the supervisor to ensure supervisees meet required professional standards prior to entering the counseling profession. The CES is responsible for ensuring and safeguarding adequate admission standards, ongoing academic assessment, remediation, and if deemed necessary, termination from the program. The standards for gatekeeping for site supervisors include skill assessment, professional practice, counselor wellness, client care, remediation, and termination. Although the functions overlap it is important for site supervisors and CES to have a cohesive and collaborative relationship to set the CIT/supervisee up for success in their academic and professional career.

Another challenging area for the CES may fall in the evaluation of the CIT's competency in clinical skills as this is a shared responsibility with the practicum/internship site supervisor. The CES is responsible to evaluate a CIT's ability to demonstrate clinical skills; however, the CES only has access to what the CIT presents in class as opposed to the site supervisor who has ongoing access to observe the CIT's actual clinical work and performance. Therefore, if the CES identifies potential issues with CIT's clinical skill competencies then the CES would need to coordinate with the site supervisor to verify concerns then decide next steps within the university's program policies.

Counselors must display qualities and characteristics that align with professional standards outlined in the ACA *Code of Ethics*. Therefore, in addition to evaluating the competency of the CIT's ability to demonstrate clinical skills, a CES is also required to assess the personal qualities and characteristics of CITs to ensure one is capable to engage in effective therapeutic relationships with clients and do no harm (Haddock & Whitman, 2019; Luke, 2019). The CES may need to engage with the site supervisor to investigate the validity of the impairment concerns. Subsequently, the CES should follow procedure to report concerns with the university.

4.9 Conclusion

In this chapter, we explored the importance of providing adequate and effective supervision to CITs within your counseling program. We addressed the necessity of providing timely, qualitative feedback to CIT's and some of the barriers you may face when providing feedback. While we have touched on the use of technology, we are aware that it is not all inclusive. Therefore, we suggest doing your own research in this area to further your learning as technology is ever changing. We also recognize that while we mention programs within this chapter, those programs may be obsolete at the time of the printing of this book. Lastly, we provide you with best practices for working with sites, site supervisors, and CITs. It is our hope that this information provides you with some direction as you begin your journey as a new CES.

References

American Counseling Association. (2014). *2014 ACA code of ethics*. https://www.counseling.org/docs/default-source/default-document-library/ethics/2014-aca-code-of-ethics.pdf?sfvrsn=55ab73d0_1

Bernard, J. M., & Goodyear, B. K. (2024). *Fundamentals of clinical supervision* (7th ed.). Pearson.

Borders, L. D., & Brown, L. L. (2022). *The new handbook of counseling supervision*. Routledge.

Corey, G., Haynes, R., Moulton, P., & Muratori, M. (2021). *Clinical supervision in the helping professions: A practical guide* (3rd ed.). American Counseling Association.

Council for Accreditation of Counseling and Related Educational Programs. (2024). *2024 CACREP standards*. https://www.cacrep.org/wp-content/uploads/2024/04/2024-Standards-Combined-Version-4.11.2024.pdf

Fickling, M. J., Borders, L. D., Mobley, K. A., & Wester, K. L. (2017). Most and least helpful events in three supervision modalities. *Counselor Education and Supervision, 56*(4), 289–304. https://doi.org/10.1002/ceas.12086
Grant, J., Schofield, M. J., & Crawford, S. (2012). Managing difficulties in supervision: Supervisors' perspectives. *Journal of Counseling Psychology, 59*(4), 528–541. https://doi.org/10.1037/a0030000
Haddock, L. R., & Whitman, J. S. (2019). *Preparing the educator in counselor education: A comprehensive guide to building knowledge and developing skills.* Routledge.
Hardy, K. V., & Bobes, T. (2016). *Culturally sensitive supervision and training: Diverse perspectives and practical applications.* Routledge.
Hart, G., Borders. L. D., Nance, D., & Paradise, L. (1993). Ethical guidelines for counselor supervisors. *ACES Spectrum, 53*(4).
Luke, M. (2019). Supervision in the counselor education context. In J. E. A. Okech & D. J. Rubel (Eds.), *Counselor education in the 21st century: Issues and experiences.* American Counseling Association.
McKibben, W., George, A., Gonzalez, O., & Powell, P. W. (2022). Exploring how counselor education programs support site supervisors. *Journal of Counselor Preparation and Supervision, 15*(2), 1–26. https://digitalcommons.sacredheart.edu/jcps/vol15/iss2/1
Motivo. (2024). https://motivohealth.com/
Myers, J. E., Sweeney, T. J., & Witmer, J. M. (2000). The wheel of wellness counseling for wellness: A holistic model for treatment planning. *Journal of Counseling and Development, 78*(3), 251–266.
Powell, D. J., & Brodsky, A. (2004). *Clinical supervision in alcohol and drug abuse counseling: Principles, models, methods* (rev. ed.). Jossey-Bass.
Steiny, N. (2017). Collaborative training tools for supervisors and supervisees. In K. V. Hardy & T. Bobes (Eds.), *Promoting cultural sensitivity in supervision: A manual for practitioners.* Routledge.
Supervision Assist. (2024). https://supervisionassist.com/
Tevera. (2023). https://tevera.com/

Tanisha N. Sapp Ed.D., LPC, CST, NCC, ACS, CPCS (she/her/Dr.) is an Assistant Professor of Counseling at Liberty University in the Department of Counseling and Family Studies. Dr. Sapp is a counselor educator, professional counselor, trainer, and clinical supervisor focused on training the next generation of helping professionals. She is the owner of Tanisha Sapp, LLC where she provides professional development training, clinical supervision services, and individual and couples sex therapy. With over 20 years of experience in the helping profession, Dr. Sapp brings a wealth of experience, insight, and a unique perspective into counselor education.

Dr. Sapp is currently a member of the ACA ethics committee and serves on review panels for CACREP and NBCC where she offers her expertise to the profession in an effort to be the change she desires to see. Dr. Sapp has also served on a number of professional committees and provided leadership service to the profession and her community. Her areas of research, professional identity, and interests include: professional counselor identity, Anti-Racism in counseling and counselor education, DEIBASJ in counseling and counselor education, BIPOC sexual health and wellness, and professional advocacy in leadership.

Wendy Robinson Ph.D., LPC, CCTP (she/her/hers) is an Associate Professor of Counseling at Liberty University. Dr. Robinson has 20 years in the management and training of counselors and counseling programs. Dr. Robinson is also a certified clinical trauma professional with extensive experience working with individuals and couples. Her areas of research and interest include professional counselor identity, professional ethics, and trauma work.

Latasha Matthews M.A., LPC, CPCS, (she/her/hers) is known as America's Emotional Wellness Expert; she is the CEO and Clinical Director of Illumination Counseling and Coaching and Why 2 Live Well. Latasha has over 15 years' experience as a speaker, therapist, Coach, and author and she also provides continuing education training for clinicians and corporate training on wellness, DEI, EQ, and trauma informed resilience in the workplace. She has trained 1000's of individuals globally on the importance of setting healthy boundaries to live well.

Course Development

5

Jung H. Hyun and Tiphanie Gonzalez

> *The power of [non-standard English] speech is not simply that it enables a resistance to white supremacy, but that it also forges a space for alternative cultural production and alternative epistemologies–different ways of thinking and knowing that were crucial to creating a counter-hegemonic worldview.*
>
> *bell hooks*

Abstract

This chapter will focus on preparing CES doctoral learners and new counselor educators for the process of developing a course within a counselor education program. It will cover various components of the syllabus, including an introduction to learning assessments. As a newly hired counselor educator, you may find teaching graduate-level courses challenging. Teaching CITs involves not only preparing class materials and activities to facilitate their learning but also ensuring that: (1) the course objectives align with the mission of the university, the department, and the program; (2) the course elements guide CIT's learning meaningfully and congruent with their learning style; and (3) CIT's performance meet the national and state standards of counselor preparation programs. In this chapter, we will share best practices for course development and provide suggestions for creating an optimal learning roadmap.

J. H. Hyun (✉)
Agnes Scott College, Decatur, GA, USA
e-mail: jhyun@agnesscott.edu

T. Gonzalez
State University of New York-Oswego, Oswego, NY, USA

D. M. Stalnaker-Shofner and T. N. Sapp (eds.), *A Comprehensive Guide for Counselor Education*, Springer Texts in Education, https://doi.org/10.1007/978-3-031-68358-9_5

Learning Objectives After reading this chapter, you will be able to:

1. Develop graduate courses that are grounded in a decolonized and socially just framework while ensuring alignment with requisite CACREP standards.
2. Identify the necessary components for incorporation in course syllabus design.
3. Construct appropriate evaluative measures to formatively and summatively assess CIT learning and performance.

5.1 Statement of Reflexivity

In writing this chapter, there were many factors influencing our approach to writing and the final product we present here. We started with identifying our positionality and delineating its influence in our respective perceptions, perspectives, and our overall understanding and application of our acquired knowledge and expertise. Dr. Jung (June) H. Hyun, and Dr. Tiphanie Gonzalez both identify as cisgender women of color and counselor educators. Culturally our rich and diverse upbringings and our varying employment experiences have influenced our individual and collective perspectives and respective approaches to course development in counselor education programs. Dr. Hyun was born and raised in South Korea, and after completing her undergraduate studies worked as an English teacher in secondary schools for two years. She immigrated to the U.S. as an international student. She obtained her master's degree in School Counseling and her doctorate in Counselor Education and Supervision. Dr. Hyun's diverse employment experiences have directly influenced how she approaches curriculum development. Her roles as program chair and CACREP liaison both have contributed to her knowledge and expertise in curriculum development, as well as program assessment and evaluation.

Dr. Gonzalez identifies as an Afro-Latina of Puerto Rican descent, and US-born American raised in The Bronx, New York. Her work experience includes working with urban youth from the inner-city within primary and secondary school settings. She obtained her master's degree in counseling services, with a specialization in School Counseling and her doctoral degree in Counselor Education. As an educator, she has experience with curriculum development and classroom management, which she brings to this chapter. Both Drs. Hyun and Gonzalez have adapted their knowledge and professional and cultural experiences to curriculum development. As such, they have a keen awareness of the importance of inclusivity in education and are fully committed to developing anti-racist curriculum. Both hope that this chapter's writing can provide you with a roadmap as you develop counselor education curriculum.

5.2 Case Scenario

You are starting your first year as an Assistant Professor of Clinical Mental Health Counseling. One of your assigned courses is Multicultural Counseling. In the early stages of preparation, you created a lesson plan for what material you feel it is essential to include based on the 2024 CACREP standards. First, you spoke to other faculty in the department who have taught the course in the past and asked to see their syllabi. You were able to see which textbooks, assignments, and other activities have been used prior. Also, you were able to see the style and format that was the foundation for the development of their syllabi which is different from the syllabi design with which you are familiar from both your master's and doctoral programs. You met with your mentor and expressed feeling a bit overwhelmed with the course prep and design. You share, "My doctoral program really taught me how to teach…strategies, classroom management, ways to engage learners, but not necessarily the nuts-and-bolts of how to prep a class." With some exasperation, she sighed and said, "I'm not sure where to begin."

5.3 Introduction

Embarking on the journey of course development can be a daunting task, especially for those without prior teaching experience. Sexton (1998) recognized that "history and tradition have been the primary pedagogical guidance for counselor educators" (p. 69). Over the years, scholars in the field of counselor education and supervision have tirelessly endeavored to establish robust theoretical foundations for teaching. Starting with Nelson and Neufeldt (1998) suggesting a constructive approach to promote a learner active engagement in their learning, numerous other dedicated researchers such as Dollarhide et al. (2007), Granello (2000), Grant (2006), and Moate and Cox (2015) have delved into developing effective praxes to train future counselors.

In the ever-evolving landscape of counselor education, the 2024 CACREP Standards delineate the essential components of counseling-related preparation programs. Whether operating at the macro level, involving the development of counseling programs aligned with the CACREP standards and state licensure regulations or at the microlevel, where the task may entail creating new courses, revising existing ones, or updating the course as needed, this chapter aims to serve as your guiding compass. In this chapter, we will provide a comprehensive framework for course development, one that places a strong emphasis on the lenses of social justice, advocacy, and antiracism.

5.4 Considerations Prior to Course Development

As you embark on your journey as a new CES, there are several critical considerations that should shape your course development process. Using the ecological systems theory (Bronfenbrenner, 1979), you can conceptualize your classroom as a dynamic system that brings together your world and the learner's world. Here are the key aspects to contemplate. First, you should reflect on the CIT's identities, worldviews, and purpose in the program while asking yourself: Do they have prior experience in the helping professions (i.e., counseling, psychology, social work)? Are they traditional or non-traditional learners? What are their cultural identities and backgrounds? What about their visible and invisible identities? How do their identities shape their worldview? Lastly, what is their motivation for becoming a counselor? Answers to these questions will assist you in creating a safe learning environment for CITs to engage in the learning process and developing optional learning opportunities.

Next, based on your program's course delivery method, you want to think about the classroom setting. Consider the following questions: How long is the semester/ quarter? Are you teaching online? If so, is the course asynchronous, synchronous, or hybrid? Are you teaching in person? How long is each class? What day and time is each class held? Answers to these questions will help you design course components and provide information to accommodate CITs' needs.

Finally, consider yourself the instructor and reflect on how your identity and worldview intersect with those of your CITs at the institution. Recognize both the commonalities and differences. Awareness of your own perspective is essential in fostering an inclusive and respectful classroom environment. Acknowledge the presence of implicit bias and work towards minimizing its impact on your teaching. Embrace antiracist practices to create an equitable learning environment. Further, you want to be aware of the historical colonization of higher education and consider how you can actively dismantle antiracist practices in your teaching. Recognize the power dynamics present in the classroom.

With a clear understanding of these interconnected factors, you can approach course development with purpose and sensitivity. It's akin to planning a road trip to great destinations; you need to know your destination, the company you are traveling with (your CITs), what to pack (course content), things to do (teaching methods), and potential stopovers (learning opportunities). All these considerations come together in the syllabus, which serves as your roadmap for this educational journey.

5.5 Developing the Course Map

The course syllabus serves as a comprehensive roadmap for both instructors and CITs, guiding them through the educational journey ahead. It functions as a detailed itinerary, outlining the ultimate destination of the course, describing the significant events and milestones that will be encountered along the way, and specifying the competencies that CITs are expected to achieve by the end of this journey. An effective syllabus provides a clear structure while maintaining instructor flexibility to adapt to CITs' learning needs and any changes in the learning environment. It also reflects the professor's belief in learner success (Slattery & Carlson, 2005).

Within the context of individual classes, the course syllabus takes on a distinct role as a binding agreement between you and the CIT (Gannon, 2018; Slattery & Carlson, 2005). This mutual commitment underscores the importance of involving CITs in its development, as their input can lead to valuable adjustments and accommodations. Examples of such adjustments include flexible assignment deadlines, recognition of CIT's pre-existing knowledge, and exploration of topics of particular interest to the CIT.

When crafting an effective syllabus, it is essential to consider nine key components identified by Slattery and Carlson (2005): (1) identifying information, (2) course description, (3) course goals (and objectives), (4) ways to meet course goals, (5) grades, (6) schedule, (7) rationale, (8) motivational messages, and (9) university support services. In addition to these nine components, it is advisable to incorporate your university, department, and/or program's vision and mission as the tenth component. These components need not be developed in a strict chronological order and can be organized according to the guidelines presented in the Road Trip Metaphor (see Table 5.1). By meticulously crafting your course syllabus with these components in mind, you create a document that not only serves as a roadmap for learning but also fosters a collaborative and empowering learning environment.

Table 5.1 Road trip metaphor

Road trip	Course development	Syllabus components
Who plans the trip?	You (and the program)	Identifying information
Name of the road trip	Title of the course	Course description
Where are we going?	Competencies/standards	Course goals, objectives, and rationale
What are we going to do during the road trip? Stops and activities	Objectives learning activities	Course schedule ways to meet course goals
Things to pack	Course materials	Textbooks, readings, and/or bibliography
Check in (road trip diaries): how do you know you are on the right track to or arrive at the final destination?	Assignments evaluation	Grades and motivational messages
Resources		University support services

5.5.1 Who Plans the Trip?

As described in the case scenario, this is You! The important part is you are not alone. You can reach out to your mentor, program chair (or director), and colleagues who taught the course before. Depending on the styles of the instructor, they may share all materials that they use for the course or just the syllabus. In both cases, you are the captain of the trip, but you want to make sure that you have support. In the syllabus, the identifying information is the section about the instructor. This includes your contact information such as name, title, email, telephone number, office location, and office hours. Providing your contact information allows for CITs to know when and how you will be available for individual conversation to answer any questions, concerns, or provide clarity to CITs regarding the course (Gannon, 2018). This information can be helpful as a way for you to receive feedback from CITs and adjust your teaching to meet the CITs' needs with provided feedback (Gannon, 2018). If you don't have to have office hours, provide a tool for the CITs to schedule an appointment. Applications such as Microsoft Outlook or Calendly can allow CITs to schedule an appointment linked directly to your calendar.

5.5.2 Name of the Road Trip

As a counselor who loves facilitating group counseling, one of the most enjoyable moments is when group members collaboratively come up with a creative, engaging name for their counseling group. In the context of decolonization and promoting learner engagement, it would be ideal if our CITs could contribute to shaping the course title based on their expectations and goals. However, it is important to recognize that in most cases, the course title is predetermined by the program and the university.

The course description in the syllabus encompasses crucial details such as the course title and course number. Ensuring alignment with the university's official course catalog is essential, as this information serves as a foundational reference point. Additionally, this section may also include important course dates. While specific requirements related to this information can vary depending on your university and program, it is vital to incorporate the course format (e.g., in-person, online, hybrid, etc.) within the section to provide CITs with a clear understanding of how the course will be delivered.

5.5.3 Where Are We Going?

The final destination of a road trip often aligns with its title, serving as a clear endpoint. In the context of course development, this destination is analogous to what we envision our CITs achieving by the end of the semester or quarter, represented by competencies, or in simpler terms, our goals. It's imperative that every aspect of your course, both what you and your CITs engage in, is intricately linked to these overarching goals. Moreover, these goals should harmonize seamlessly with the broader vision and mission of both the institution and the program. The university's mission and vision act as guiding beacons, shaping the mission of your program and affirming the significance of your course. By incorporating the university's mission and vision within the syllabus, you not only emphasize the systemic context of the course but also raise CITs' awareness of its broader institutional impact. As a new instructor of the course, it is important to note that in most cases, these goals are pre-established by the program. So, what comes next in the course development journey?

5.5.4 What Are We Going to Do During the Trip?

This section marks the crux of the course development process, and it corresponds to what Slattery and Carlson (2005) referred to as "Ways to Meet Course Goals" (p. 161). Within this section, you will craft specific objectives, articulate your expectations, compile the essential readings, and outline assignments. In the context of our road trip metaphor, think of it as determining the various routes you might take from point A to B. Are you going to drive all the way to B from A? Will you opt for detours to fully immerse yourself in the journey? While the answers to such questions during a road trip may depend on factors like time and budget, the focus is on creating objectives that serve as guiding markers for CITs to reach their goals in course development. This involves selecting appropriate learning materials, designing engaging activities to enrich their learning experience, and formulating assignments that allow CITs to demonstrate their competencies in the course development.

If the goals of the course indicate the final destination, the objectives of the course specify the measurable actions CITs must take to meet the goal of the course. Objectives are statements that include a subject and action verb, describing what you want to see in your CITs at the end of the course. They are learner-oriented and begin with the subject stem "Students will…" followed by the action verbs. For the verbs, you want to consider, *The Taxonomy of Educational Objectives, Handbook I: Cognitive Domain* (Bloom et al., 1956), commonly known as, Bloom's Taxonomy. Bloom's Taxonomy provides a hierarchy of cognitive learning consisting of six major classes: Knowledge, Comprehension, Application, Analysis, Synthesis, and Evaluation.

One of the major critiques of Bloom's Taxonomy is that it is a learning process that is not as clear cut as it seems (Anderson & Krathwohl, 2001). For example, there seems to be an assumption that *Evaluation* is the highest cognitive learning level and other cognitive learnings such as *Knowledge, Comprehension, Application, Analysis, and Synthesis* need to happen before *Evaluation.* In addition, even Bloom accepts the functions of the categories with the hierarchy overlap in some areas (Krathwohl, 2002). Further, Anderson and Krathwohl (2001) stated while Bloom's Taxonomy describes cognitive systems of learning, the metacognitive system is not considered in his original model. Other scholars have provided variations to Bloom's Taxonomy. Anderson and Krathwohl's (2001) revision included the metacognitive system and presented a three-dimensional model, clarifying the learning objectives. Marzano and Kendall (2007) presented a two-dimensional model which also includes metacognition in the learning process, assessing the Domains of Knowledge (Information, Mental Procedures, and Psychomotor Procedures) and Levels of Processing (Retrieval, Comprehension, Analysis, Knowledge of Utilization, Metacognitive System, and Self-System). While there are critics that oppose using the hierarchical aspects of the taxonomy, Bloom's revised taxonomy (Anderson & Krathwohl, 2001) seems one of the most widely used tools to help scaffold learners' learning objectives related to gaining knowledge (Bonner, 2016). Please visit the following resources to review action verbs that can be used for crafting objectives in your course: Iowa State University (n.d.) and Krathwohl (2002).

As previously mentioned, the 2024 CACREP standards serve as a comprehensive framework, defining the essential components of counseling-related courses. In particular, Section 3 of the 2024 CACREP standards encompasses the following eight core domains that should be addressed in your course development: Professional counseling orientation and ethical practice, social and cultural identities and experiences, lifespan development, career development, counseling practice and relationships, group counseling and group work, assessment and diagnostic process, and research and program evaluation (CACREP, 2024). Additionally, in section 5, you will find curriculum standards tailored to your program's area of specialized practice, whether it is school counseling, rehabilitation counseling, clinical mental health counseling, or another area of specialized practice (CACREP, 2024). These specialized practice-specific standards must also be considered as you embark on course development. For programs that are not accredited by CACREP, it is essential to research the licensure/certification requirements of your state. This ensures that your program aligns with these requirements, ultimately aiding your CITs in becoming eligible for licensure/certification.

While many course objectives may have already-established, the key lies in demonstrating how these objectives align with the most recent standards. As stipulated by the 2024 CACREP Standards, counselor education programs must document how each of the numbered standards is covered in the curriculum. Therefore, your focus should be on ensuring that the readings, learning objectives, and assignments you incorporate into your course effectively meet these standards. In the forthcoming chapters, we will delve deeper into the CACREP Standards and specialty programs. However, let us now shift our attention to the section where you will spend the majority of your time during the course development process.

Stop and Reflect: *As you construct your syllabus and design your course, you develop the learning objectives. Here is an example of potential learning objectives for a Multicultural Counseling course in the School Counseling program:*

- *CITs will identify factors that influence the social, familial, emotional, and behaviors problems and the connection between these issues and academic achievement.*
- *CITs will demonstrate theory specific techniques of personal/social counseling in schools.*
- *CITs will design an intervention plan to promote academic development and increase graduation rates and evaluate it.*

Do you use action verbs within the objectives? Are they measurable? Discuss if the objectives are crafted appropriately. If not, how would you want to change and why?

5.5.5 Stops and Activities

While not every learning activity may need to be explicitly detailed in the syllabus, it can be highly beneficial to provide an overview of the topics you intend to address, both for your own planning and for the CITs' understanding. Typically, this information is organized in a table format labeled as the "Course Schedule.“ Within this table, you should include key elements such as class dates, the specific subjects to be covered, assigned readings, due dates for assignments, and their alignment with established standards.

When crafting these learning activities, it is essential to consider the diverse backgrounds, prior experiences, and existing knowledge of your CITs. These activities should serve as valuable tools to enhance learner learning and promote the practical application of the knowledge they acquire throughout the course. Chapters 2 and 3 of this textbook provide valuable insight and guidance on this aspect of course development.

While it may not be a direct component of your course development process, an essential element that must find a place within the syllabus is information about university support services. As CITs engage in learning activities and work towards meeting standards through assessments, there may be occasions when they require additional support. To draw an analogy to our road trip, just as we make stops for necessities like bathroom breaks, refueling, groceries, and rest during a journey, our CITs, each with their unique backgrounds and life experiences, may also require specific resources.

Understanding the diverse needs of your CITs, it becomes imperative to identify and provide access to vital university support services. These services may encompass the library, writing center, counseling services, and other forms of support, such as those offered by the veterans' office or disability services. While not all CITs may require these resources, it is crucial to clearly indicate their availability and how to access them for those who do. This proactive approach ensures that every learner has access to the necessary support systems to thrive in their educational journey.

Stop and Reflect: *In the case scenario, reaching out to other faculty in the program and asking for a prior version of the syllabus allows you to get a clearer idea of how to organize your updated iteration. You will also want to research which textbook would be the best fit for the course. A good tip is to start with the textbook's table of contents to use as a guide in building the course schedule. You also want to include additional readings that complement the textbook content which can reinforce what is being discussed or introduce a supplemental element to facilitate CIT learning. We invite you to consider further the following question: What other things would you want to consider in preparing the course?*

5.5.6 Things to Pack

Selecting learning materials for your course is a critical step in the course development process. Your syllabus should provide comprehensive information about textbooks and additional learning resources. Some programs may offer a list of approved textbooks that align with CACREP standards, but you also have the flexibility to choose textbooks from other programs that meet your specific content goals. When selecting a textbook, it is essential to ensure that it covers the required content thoroughly. Beyond textbooks, consider incorporating supplemental readings, videos, webinars, and other materials to enrich the learning experience.

Equity should be the next consideration in the selection of learning materials. Research has shown that textbook costs can be a significant barrier for learners, particularly historically underserved learners (Jenkins et al., 2020). As a result, some instructors opt not to use a traditional textbook and explore Open Education Resources (OER) as an alternative to reduce financial burdens on learners.

Incorporating a social justice framework is imperative in counselor education. Counselors are expected to be culturally competent and practice cultural humility. As a counselor educator, your role extends to modeling and promoting multicultural competencies among CITs. This aligns with the 2014 ACA *Code of Ethics*, which emphasizes infusing multiculturalism and diversity into all courses and workshops for the development of professional counselors (ACA, 2014). To achieve this, it is vital to select textbooks authored by culturally diverse writers and diversify course materials to expose CITs to a range of perspectives across various modalities. This inclusive approach should extend to decolonizing the course syllabus and curriculum.

Historically, pedagogy in counselor education has often perpetuated a Eurocentric, predominantly White framework, as exemplified by the limited diversity in the scholars and theories presented (Cheaito, 2022; Singh et al., 2020; Tuck & Yang, 2012). To address this, it is crucial to critically examine and contextualize the scholars and theories featured in your curriculum. Consider integrating multicultural and social justice theories, such as Relational Cultural Theory, Critical Race Theory, intersectionality theory, and Liberation Psychology (Singh et al., 2020). These theories provide a foundation for applying a Multicultural and Social Justice Counseling Competency framework and dismantling Western and Eurocentric conceptions of counseling.

Recognizing how colonization has shaped counseling theories and practices, the next step is to actively decolonize them. This involves continuously evaluating your curriculum and course syllabi to identify areas that perpetuate harm or reinforce racist ideas in BIPOC communities. Selection of learning materials, case scenarios, and assignments should prioritize accurate and adequate representation of diverse populations.

For instance, with Relational Cultural Theory (RCT; Miller, 1976), you can address power imbalances in the counseling relationship. When teaching intersectionality (Crenshaw, 1989), you deepen CITs' understanding of privilege and oppression systems. Critical Race Theory (CRT; Bell, 1995) and Liberation Psychology (Martín-Baró, 1994) can inform assignments that empower CITs to develop interventions or community projects for BIPOC clients to identify their healing paths. Feedback from both BIPOC CITs and colleagues should be actively sought to inform ongoing improvements. This should be done thoughtfully without leaning into BIPOC emotional labor to help inform your learning and awareness. As counselor educators, the journey involves unlearning colonized views and relearning ways to incorporate the voices and experiences of BIPOC communities, ensuring that your work contributes to accurate and inclusive representation in the counseling profession.

Stop and Reflect: *As you reflect on the need to thoughtfully and intentionally decenter whiteness in your course, consider reviewing the "Decolonize My Counseling Psychology Syllabus Checklist" (Academics for Black Survival and Wellness, n.d.) and actively seek ways to incorporate diverse voices from historically marginalized and disenfranchised populations, populations within your course. While these populations are typically the target of counseling theories, they are largely absent in the existing literature. Additionally, find ways to intentionally use theories such as CRT and RCT as frameworks to conceptualize your andragogical approach to learning, and to conceptualize the experiences of diverse persons and populations within your course.*

5.5.7 How Do You Know You Are on the Right Track?

Drawing from a straight-forward analogy, just as you recognize your arrival at a destination during a road trip when you see the corresponding address on a building or place, in your course, you will determine whether your CIT have successfully acquired the targeted knowledge areas or course objectives through their performance in assessments. Your course syllabi meticulously outline the specific knowledge and skills you intend to observe in CIT' performance throughout the course.

In the syllabus, the grading section plays a pivotal role in the assessment framework. This section encompasses various aspects, such as the chosen grading system (e.g., points system, weighted grades), attendance policy, weekly topics (commonly for graduate classes meeting once a week in person), and strategies to achieve course goals. Moreover, as suggested by Slattery and Carlson (2005), it is advisable to include motivating messages in the syllabus to convey your enthusiasm for the course and inspire CITs to engage actively in the subject matter while envisioning their successful completion. While these messages may not be mandatory components, well-defined expectations can contribute to reducing undesirable learner behaviors, such as tardiness, as discussed by Appleby (2003).

Assignments serve as a dual-purpose tool, benefiting both you and your CITs by enabling the assessment of their progress in terms of competencies. Assessments primarily focus on evaluating individual learner development within the classroom context, providing insights into their growth and learning. Conversely, program assessments serve a broader purpose, evaluating the overall effectiveness of the program itself, including its curriculum and teaching methodologies. In the sections that follow, we will delve into each of these aspects in greater detail, shedding light on their significance and practical implementation.

According to the 2024 CACREP Standards, faculty in counselor education programs maintain a consistent evaluation of each CIT's progress throughout the program, assessing their acquisition of both knowledge and skills (CACREP, 2024, p. 9). Furthermore, the standards laid out by CACREP emphasize the need for multiple evaluations at different points in time (CACREP, 2024, p. 9). These standards also specify the use of Key Performance Indicators (KPIs), which are described as "student learning outcomes chosen by program faculty to represent student knowledge and skills related to program objectives" (CACREP, 2024, p. 34). KPIs play a crucial role in assessing the CIT's learning within the eight core areas and their chosen program of specialized practice. While CACREP mandates a minimum of nine KPIs for CITs in entry-level program specialized practice areas (eight foundational curricular areas and one for each specialized practice area) (CACREP, 2024, p. 9), it is possible that your course may require additional assessments to ensure that CITs effectively demonstrate their competencies in alignment with the course objectives.

Typical course-level assessments include papers, presentations, and tests (Minton & Gibson, 2012). When considering assessments, you should ensure that the assessments used in the course do not discern or distinguish CITs' strengths. For example, if the sole assessment in a course is the final paper, the knowledge of CITs with deficiencies in writing may not be fairly evaluated. Although writing is considered as a primary method to analyze CITs' knowledge in counselor education, it should not be used as the only measurement tool when assessing CITs' progress in their knowledge, skills, and dispositions. Most course-level assessments are accompanied by a rubric. Rubrics are defined as a tool used to "articulate the expectations for assignments by listing the criteria and describing levels of quality from excellent to poor" (Reddy & Andrade, 2010, p. 435). Rubrics consist of three parts: (1) criteria to be evaluated: (2) definition of quality; and (3) a scoring strategy (Reddy & Andrade, 2010). The rubric can also allow CIT to map out what to accomplish in a specific assignment aligned with the course objectives (Minton & Gibson, 2012).

Finally, it is essential to strike a balance that provides a meaningful learning experience without overpacking the curriculum when determining the appropriate workload and assignments for your course. The Carnegie Unit suggests that one credit hour of coursework typically represents 2–3 h of learner work per week, both in and out of the classroom (Shedd, 2003). Therefore, when designing your course, it is crucial to consider this workload estimation to ensure that CITs can feasibly manage their coursework while also engaging in meaningful learning experiences. To effectively design your course workload, you can utilize resources like the credit hours calculator (American International College, 2024) and the course workload estimator (Center for Teaching Excellence, n.d.). These tools can help you estimate the amount of time CITs will need to dedicate to your course.

Stop and Reflect: *As you review the course, you also want to make sure not to overwhelm your CITs by adding too many readings and assignments, while still maintaining the rigor of the course. Once you have decided on the reading and course schedule, you will begin to develop the content. Assessment of the CIT's knowledge of content must be clearly explained in the assignment instructions and rubric.*

5.6 Conclusion

Developing a course is a fundamental pillar of counselor education, holding direct implications for the training of future counselors and the broader counseling profession. The impact of your course design extends not only to your CITs but also to their future clients, shaping the quality of mental health care provided. As a counselor educator, it is essential to grasp the intricacies of course development and equip yourself with assessment and evaluation skills to ensure effective instruction.

Importantly, the journey of course development does not conclude once the initial course is created. Instead, it unfolds as an ongoing and dynamic process, continuously refined with each teaching iteration. Embrace the invaluable input from your CITs and colleagues, incorporating their feedback into course revisions to enhance the learning experience. In doing so, you are actively shaping yourself into an effective counselor educator, dedicated to fostering the growth and competence of future counselors. Your commitment to this endeavor will have a lasting impact on the field of mental health counseling.

References

Academics for Black Survival and Wellness. (n.d.). *Decolonize my counseling psychology syllabus checklist.* https://img1.wsimg.com/blobby/go/933462b1-6242-4899-aa4d-d3e2d945c1b4/downloads/DecolonizingSyllabus.pdf?ver=1661359508478

American Counseling Association. (2014). *2014 ACA code of ethics.* https://www.counseling.org/docs/default-source/default-document-library/ethics/2014-aca-code-of-ethics.pdf?sfvrsn=55ab73d0_1

American International College. (2024). *Credit hours calculator.* https://www.aic.edu/academics/credit-hours-calculator

Anderson, L. W., & Krathwohl, D. R. (Eds.). (2001). *A taxonomy for learning, teaching, and assessing: A revision of Bloom's taxonomy of educational objectives* (2nd ed.). Pearson.

Appleby, D. (2003). Purposes and components of course syllabi. In *The evolving syllabus: Motivating students and maximizing success.* Symposium conducted at the annual meeting of the American Psychological Association, Toronto, Canada.

Bell, D. (1995). Who's afraid of critical race theory? *University of Illinois Law Review, 4*, 893–910.

Bloom, B. S., Engelhart, M. D., Furst, E. J., Hill, W. H., & Krathwohl, D. R. (1956). *Taxonomy of educational objectives: The classification of educational goals.* Allyn & Bacon.

Bonner, M. W. (2016). Grading rigor in counselor education: A specifications grading framework. *Educational Research Quarterly, 39*(4), 21–42.

Bronfenbrenner, U. (1979). *The ecology of human development: Experiments by nature and design.* Harvard University Press.

Center for Teaching Excellence. (n.d.). *Course workload estimator.* Rice University. https://cte.rice.edu/resources/workload-estimator

Cheaito, A. (2022, June 23). Decolonizing the field and history of psychology: A global reckoning. *Psychology Today.* https://www.psychologytoday.com/us/blog/global-reckoning/202206/decolonizing-the-field-and-history-psychology

Council for Accreditation of Counseling and Related Educational Programs. (2024). *2024 CACREP standards.* https://www.cacrep.org/wp-content/uploads/2024/04/2024-Standards-Combined-Version-4.11.2024.pdf

Crenshaw, K. (1989). Demarginalizing the intersection of race and sex: A Black feminist critique of antidiscrimination doctrine, feminist theory and antiracist politics. *University of Chicago Legal Forum, 1989*, 138–167.

Dollarhide, C. T., Smith, A. T., & Lemberger, M. E. (2007). Counseling made transparent: Pedagogy for a counseling theories course. *Counselor Education and Supervision, 46*(4), 242–253. https://doi.org/10.1002/j.1556-6978.2007.tb00029.x

Gannon, K. (2018, September). How to create a syllabus. *The Chronicle.* https://www.chronicle.com/article/how-to-create-a-syllabus/

Granello, D. H. (2000). Contextual teaching and learning in counselor education. *Counselor Education and Supervision, 39*(4), 270–283. https://doi.org/10.1002/j.1556-6978.2000.tb01237.x

Grant, J. (2006). Training counselors to work with complex clients: Enhancing emotional responsiveness through experiential methods. *Counselor Education and Supervision, 45*(3), 218–230. https://doi.org/10.1002/j.1556-6978.2006.tb00144.x

Iowa State University. (n.d.). *A model of learning objectives.* https://www.celt.iastate.edu/wp-content/uploads/2015/09/RevisedBloomsHandout-1.pdf

Jenkins, J. J., Sanchez, L. A., Schraedley, M. A. K., Hannans, J., Navick, N., & Young, J. (2020). Textbook broke: Textbook affordability as a social justice issue. *Journal of Interactive Media in Education, 1.* Article 3, 1–13. https://doi.org/10.5334/jime.549

Krathwohl, D. R. (2002). A revision of Bloom's taxonomy: An overview. *Theory into Practice, 41*(4), 212–218. https://doi.org/10.1207/s15430421tip4104_2

Martín-Baró, I. (1994). In A. Aron & S. Corne (Eds.), *Writing for a liberation psychology.* Harvard University Press.

Marzano, R. J., & Kendall, J. S. (2007). *The new taxonomy of educational objectives.* Corwin Press.

Miller, J. N. (1976). *Toward a new psychology of women.* Beacon Press.
Minton, C. A. B., & Gibson, D. M. (2012). Evaluating student learning outcomes in counselor education: Recommendations and process considerations. *Counseling Outcome Research and Evaluation, 3*(2), 73–91. https://doi.org/10.1177/2150137812452561
Moate, R. M., & Cox, J. A. (2015). Learner-centered pedagogy: Considerations for application in a didactic course. *The Professional Counselor, 5*(3), 379–389. https://doi.org/10.15241/rmm.5.3.379
Nelson, M. L., & Neufeldt, S. A. (1998). The pedagogy of counseling: A critical examination. *Counselor Education and Supervision, 38*(2), 70–88. https://doi.org/10.1002/j.1556-6978.1998.tb00560.x
Reddy, Y. M., & Andrade, H. (2010). A review of rubric use in higher education. *Assessment & Evaluation in Higher Education, 35*(4), 435–448. https://doi.org/10.1080/02602930902862859
Sexton, T. L. (1998). Reconstructing counselor education: Supervision, teaching, and clinical training revisited. *Counselor Education and Supervision, 38*(1), 2–5. https://doi.org/10.1002/j.1556-6978.1998.tb00552.x
Shedd, J. M. (2003). The history of the student credit hour. *New Directions for Higher Education, 2003*(122), 5–12. https://doi.org/10.1002/he.106
Singh, A. A., Appling, B., & Trepal, H. (2020). Using the multicultural and social justice counseling competencies to decolonize counseling practice: The important roles of theory, power, and action. *Journal of Counseling & Development, 98*(3), 261–271. https://doi.org/10.1002/jcad.12321
Slattery, J. M., & Carlson, J. F. (2005). Preparing an effective syllabus. *College Teaching, 53*(4), 159–164. https://doi.org/10.3200/CTCH.53.4.159-164
Tuck, E., & Yang, K. W. (2012). Decolonization is not a metaphor. *Decolonization: Indigeneity, Education, & Society, 1,* 1–40. https://journals.scholarsportal.info/pdf/19298692/v01i0001/nfp_dinam.xml_en

Jung (June) H. Hyun Ph.D., LMHC, NCC (she/her/hers) is an Associate Professor in the CMHC program at Agnes Scott College. Her scholarly pursuits center around presenting and publishing in the areas of multicultural counseling as well as social justice issues and fostering the resiliency of Asian American Native Hawaiian and Pacific Islanders. She is actively engaged in leadership roles in the counseling profession on a national level. She is a licensed mental health counselor in the State of Washington providing play therapy for children and adolescents and parenting workshops for Asian American populations.

Tiphanie Gonzalez Ph.D. (she/her/hers) is an Associate Professor of Mental Health Counseling in the Counseling and Psychological Services department at the State University of New York (SUNY) Oswego. As both a counselor and counselor educator, she has held various positions in the profession. Having the opportunity to train as a School Counselor, Mental Health Counselor, and College Counselor has provided her with the experience of seeing the similarities and differences of the counseling role in these settings. This includes the similarities and differences in how we discuss, work with, and advocate for people of different intersectional identities.

Part II

Working with Counselors-in-Training

6 Strategies for Recruitment, Admission, and Retention

Bianca Augustine, Natese Dockery, and Devona M. Stalnaker-Shofner

Invest in the human soul. Who knows, it might be a diamond in the rough.

Mary McLeod Bethune

Abstract

Admissions and enrollment are vital aspects of counselor education. Counselors-in-training/Learners) are the foundation of graduate programs. As counselor educators, it behooves us to understand best practices for the attraction, recruitment, enrollment, and retention of graduate Learners to counselor education programs. This chapter will discuss the overall admissions process, with specific focus on best practices for learner success grounded in the 2024 CACREP standards. We connect these practices to recommendations that serve to improve learner retention and their academic success. Lastly, this chapter will provide guidance for working with the Admissions Office, Student Affairs Office, and other supporting personnel in the university regarding how to develop at minimum socially just policies rooted in the offered recommendations, and ideally how to create a culture that supports diversity, inclusion, and accessibility.

B. Augustine (✉)
William & Mary, Williamsburg, VA, USA
e-mail: braugustine@wm.edu

N. Dockery
The University of Kentucky, Lexington, KY, USA

D. M. Stalnaker-Shofner
Antioch University, Yellow Springs, OH, USA
e-mail: dstalnakershofner@antioch.edu

D. M. Stalnaker-Shofner and T. N. Sapp (eds.), *A Comprehensive Guide for Counselor Education*, Springer Texts in Education, https://doi.org/10.1007/978-3-031-68358-9_6

Learning Objectives After reading this chapter, you will be able to:

1 Utilize current best practices for developing an admissions process for counselor education programs based on the 2024 CACREP standards.
2 Integrate best practices in collaboration with learner-related entities with a focus on recruiting more diverse applicants, and subsequently admitting, supporting, and retaining these learners.
3 Evaluate the current university, department, and program processes regarding the evaluation, assessment, and implementation of policies that promote learner retention and academic success.

6.1 Statement of Reflexivity

For Dr. Augustine, as graduate of a CACREP-accredited counselor education and supervision Ph.D. program, who is now employed as an Assistant Professor, the lens through which she views CIT recruitment, retention, admissions, and enrollment are two-fold. Her experiences informed the lens through which she viewed the extant research and recommendations for best practices. She reflected on her experience as a prospective learner reviewing the websites of available CACREP-accredited programs. As a part of this search, she was intentional in examining the diversity and research interests of university faculty, as well as the availability and accessibility of supplementary financial resources that could support her doctoral studies.

For Dr. Dockery, who recently successfully defended her dissertation and is a new entrant into the academy, the admissions and enrollment processes she experienced are still fresh. As she finishes her doctoral studies and begins her faculty journey, she actively reflected on the ways in which the admissions process could have been better for her, and ways that counselor education programs can improve their admissions and retention processes for future learners, particularly those with diverse lived experiences and historically marginalized identities.

For Dr. Stalnaker-Shofner, as a counselor educator, admissions and enrollment are an important part of her work, although as a doctoral learner, she could not have imagined how much of a part of her work it would be. Through this work, she has come to believe that learner success is inextricably linked to the enrollment practices and admissions criteria. Further, she believes that the professional obligation of gatekeeping begins with admissions, and that learner retention requires supportive programs and initiatives that will allow learners to develop and flourish.

These perspectives have culminated in the writing of this chapter and the lens through which its content is presented—as an assistant professor, a recent CES doctoral graduate on the cusp of her faculty career, and as an experienced counselor educator.

6.2 Case Scenario

As a counselor educator charged with supporting admissions, you encountered the application of Jorge, a 40-year-old, Honduran, male-identifying individual seeking admission into the CMHC program. Jorge is a first-generation college learner, divorced, and has primary custody of his two elementary school-aged children. He completed 20 years of military service and plans to use his GI Bill to fund his graduate education. His undergraduate GPA was 3.00, and his GRE score on the combined Verbal and Quantitative sections was 270. Jorge obtained his bachelor's degree while serving full-time in the military and is employed full-time as a transition counselor with the Army. In his current employment, he helps veterans secure employment and address mental health concerns that may inhibit their ability to secure civilian employment opportunities. Jorge has strong letters of recommendation and a well-written resume and admissions essay/personal statement, highlighting his experiences with counseling veterans from diverse backgrounds.

6.3 Introduction

One of the roles of CES that is often overlooked in doctoral programs is that you are also expected to engage in the recruitment, admission, and enrollment process as a part of your academic unit's admissions committee. This is outlined by the 2024 CACREP Standards as "Entry-level admission decision recommendations are made by the counselor education program" (CACREP, 2024, p. 4, Standard 1.J). In this chapter, we will begin with an exploration of best practices for the development of admissions policies, and the connection they have to learner recruitment and retention. We explore the admissions process and discuss factors for consideration as you develop your academic unit's admission criteria in alignment with both your university's admission policies and the 2024 CACREP standards. Additionally, we examine best practices for the intentional recruitment and retention of learners who are representative of the diverse populations which are served in the counseling profession, with particular care to include underrepresented and historically marginalized populations. Further, we explore the importance of learner support services such as mentorship and faculty advisement, and how these services contribute to overall academic success. The chapter concludes with helpful resources as you consider your work in this area. Although this chapter primarily focuses on admissions and enrollment, it will also address aspects of gatekeeping, as well as learner retention and success, and serves as a segue to the deeper exploration of both in Chaps. 7 and 8, respectively.

6.4 Best Practices for Developing Admissions Policies

First, let's explore the development of program admissions policies. One important factor to consider is that most programs incorporate CACREP standards in different ways. Remember that best practices are like good research—generalizable, replicable, and a foundation for critical evaluation, with the goal of enhancing policies and aligning them with best practices. With this in mind, we explored the extant literature related to the admissions process. According to McCaughan and Hill (2015), the admissions review process represents the first opportunity for counselor educators to formally evaluate the suitability of applicants for the profession. CACREP provides general guidelines for admissions to counselor education programs (both master's and doctoral programs), specifically that admissions decisions "include consideration of each applicant's (1) career goals, (2) aptitude for graduate-level study consistent with program delivery type, and (3) potential success in forming effective counseling relationships with diverse populations" (CACREP, 2024, p. 4, Standard 1.J). How universities approach this is often specific to their existing admissions policies with a primary focus on the needs and goals of their respective counselor education programs. Thus, in this chapter we will provide a general overview of best practices regarding admissions and enrollment that sets the foundation for learner retention and program success.

While there is research on the importance of having admission criteria, there appears to be a paucity of research as to how best to incorporate criteria for admissions, particularly for the field of counselor education (Ju et al., 2020). One specific aspect noted in the literature as a best practice is having an admissions rubric to standardize the admissions process. Rubrics can mitigate subjectivity through establishing standardized criteria to provide both a qualitative and quantifiable manner for assessing applicants.

Additional best practices for admissions include:

- Advocating for the emphasis of non-academic sources for learners such as letters of recommendation, goal statements, individual interviews, and work experiences that are a part of the learner's application. This allows for the ability to move away from the prioritizing of GPA and/or GRE scores, which upholds a reductionist approach to admissions rooted in academic oppression. As test scores are not predictive of aptitude, performance, or success (Dorans & Cook, 2016), this de-emphasizing practice exemplifies a more socially just approach and promotes educational accessibility.
- Additionally, McCaughan and Hill (2015) propone the assessment of professional and personal readiness as an admissions criterion. This practice coupled with the applicant's academic preparedness is a multidimensional approach to effectively screen potential learners. This is offered as a best practice by McCaughan and Hill (2015) as it places greater emphasis on the personal characteristics of applicants, in greater congruence and alignment with the requisite characteristics necessary to be an effective and competent counselor (i.e. empathy, acceptance, warmth, genuineness, and sensitivity).

- Another best practice is the incorporation of a baseline assessment of applicant of counseling skills (i.e. role plays, submitted recordings) and interpersonal skills. Including these performance barometers allows programs to identify professional dispositions issues prior to admission. Further, adding this practice to both the application review process *and* more importantly, during the applicant interview.
- Eakins and Eakins (2017) enjoin broadening the admissions process to address equity and accessibility challenges inherent in current admissions practices. This is explored further in a later section of this chapter.
- Lastly, Hipolito-Delgado et al., 2021 suggest transparency in the admissions process for prospective entrants, as to do so advances check-and-balance measures, thus holding the program and university accountable in their work implementing socially just best practices.

Lastly, one final component that must be considered during admissions is the importance of gatekeeping as a professional and ethical mandate. Gatekeeping begins with the recruitment of learners and the program's admissions policies and processes. Ziomek-Daigle and Christensen (2010) notes that specifically within the academic environment, counselor educators serve as gatekeepers in selecting, retaining, and remediating learners who have the potential to become effective, ethical counselors. This is why admissions and enrollment are such vital aspects of being a counselor educator. While gatekeeping may be one of the least enjoyable aspects of being a counselor educator for some, it is arguably the most important.

Stop and Reflect: *As you revisit the case scenario, you may want to reflect on Jorge's application materials such as his stated goals, work history, and expressed commitment to education in addition to the delineated admissions criteria. Consideration of these factors as contributors to aptitude, and potentially more predictive, is an example of balancing the importance of rigor thoughtfully applied to an applicant's academic potential. Through a more constricted view of his potential for academic success, one would only consider his GPA and GRE scores, while admirable, they alone may exclude Jorge from admissions based on the established (and antiquated) criteria for many graduate programs. Based on the prior recommendations, best practice would be to not only evaluate his past academic performance, but also his potential for success. This could include considering his successful military career and current work with career counseling (which could be indicative of professional dispositional characteristics). Additionally, it may be helpful to have a demonstration of how he might apply counseling skills, which could be assessed during the admissions interview and integrated role-play activity.*

6.5 Best Practices for Learner Recruitment

For persons applying to any graduate program, the admissions process can be very stressful. Thus, demystifying the admissions process with transparency for learners is vital. In examining admissions policies and practices used by counselor education programs, one way to be transparent is to provide applicants with specific prompts to address as they write their admissions essays. An additional consideration addresses the program's front-facing information, such as their website and printed program material. As applicants typically review and apply to multiple counselor education programs, they will likely visit the program's website to review program-specific information (i.e. vital statistics) as well as the program's faculty biographies. It is important for counselor education programs to have consistently updated information so that prospective learners can accurately review and assess program faculty information (i.e. current faculty, curriculum vitae, research interests and agenda, course specializations).

When thinking of factors that can influence an applicant's decision to apply to your counselor education program, consider opportunities to showcase the benefits of your program such as the potential for them to build relationships with faculty. This could be fostered through activities such as hosting a *meet and greet* with faculty and/or current learners in the program. The meet and greet can be a space for prospective entrants to ask questions and receive insight into the program's culture. Hipolito-Delgado et al. (2021) found that learners appreciated the authentic relationships they were able to gain through conversations with current faculty members, which applicants found to be both empowering and encouraging.

6.6 Best Practices for the Recruitment and Enrollment of Diverse Learners

Many counselor educators have expressed skepticism about the use of traditional academic criteria (e.g. GPA, GRE scores) in selecting applicants for admission to counseling programs (Leverett-Main, 2004; McCaughan & Hill, 2015). In surveying counselor educators, Leverett-Main (2004) found that GRE scores were ranked as the least useful predictor of learner success, even lower than letters of recommendation. In addition to questions about predictive validity, there is also the concern that a heavy emphasis on GRE scores may create a disparate impact for historically marginalized and non-traditional graduate learners.

When recruiting diverse learners, it is important to keep in mind that factors such as early exposure to counselor education programs, responsiveness to learner needs, finances, program and university commitment to diversity, community relationships as well as program location may influence the recruitment process (Ju et al., 2020). Additionally, terminal degree programs may not be on many learners' radars due to a lack of awareness of this as an available and accessible opportunity. This may especially be true for potential learners from historically marginalized populations and underrepresented groups. These learners may be unaware that counselor education may be a viable option. Therefore, accessing these communities is imperative to ensure the recruitment and retention of diverse learners. One recommendation is to proactively engage identify diverse learners in their living and learning communities, invite them to consider applying to a counselor education program, and provide them with useful resources (i.e. funding opportunities, evidence supporting the need for diversity in mental health and counselor education). This may stoke interest and a sense of being able to actively and meaningfully contribute to their communities. These diversification efforts will support the broadening of counselor education and the counseling profession.

Additionally, Hipolito-Delgado et al. (2021) found that the motivation for learners from varying backgrounds to apply to counselor education programs stems from a desire to diversify the field. Hipolito-Delgado et al., (2021) also noted the limited publication of research that discusses the motivation of diverse learners applying to counselor education programs. This may be important for programs to consider when thinking about recruiting such learners. Therefore, counselor education programs should be intentional when recruiting learners by demonstrating a commitment to diversity (Hipolito-Delgado et al., 2021). Furthermore, programs can demonstrate their commitment to diversity by integrating multicultural perspectives and intersectionality into their curriculum as well as promoting open dialogue that highlights the importance of diversity and inclusion within the faculty and learner body. Moreover, Hipolito-Delgado et al. (2021) found that learners appreciated programs that demonstrated an authentic commitment to multicultural issues, social justice, and intersectionality, and steered away from programs that lacked these considerations as an integral element of their mission.

As counselor educators, we are charged by CACREP to be inclusive in our admissions and enrollment processes to create a diverse student body (CACREP, 2024, Standard 1.H), with the aspiration that such a practice will subsequently provide a more representative body of counseling practitioners. Therefore, it is imperative for counselor education programs to focus their efforts on the identification, recruitment, enrollment, and retention of such learners. However, one of the challenges in meeting this mandate are the policies and practices that systemically marginalize and disenfranchise learners based on cultural, educational, economic, social, geographical, linguistic, gender, ability or other identities. Such practices impede these learners' ability to access and admission to institutions of higher education, leaving individuals with diverse and intersectional identities to be underrepresented in the counseling profession. Thus, the issues of attraction and recruitment, and ultimately enrollment and retention center around learner *accessibility* rather than *aptitude.*

As a countermeasure, we propose that counselor education programs consider broadening the admissions policies and practices to facilitate the process of diversification. Accordingly, these programs would cast a wider net resulting in greater inclusivity and greater access to more educational opportunities. For example, a cohort model approach to recruitment and retention has been previously suggested (Eakins & Eakins, 2017). This approach can serve to address the mandate of having representation of diverse learners (Eakins & Eakins, 2017). Also worth noting is this model's endorsement of mentorship and other requisite support services for BIPOC learners. Additionally, the cohort model should integrate a multiculturally-aware developmental approach with specific measures and markers of learner success. Thus, the success of this model will greatly depend on the support that is offered to the learners, particularly in relation to the issues of adjustment, incongruency, and isolation that they may experience, as well as any other academic or social difficulty that may hinder their experience and progress (Tinto, 1993, as cited in Eakins & Eakins, 2017). Though the afore-referenced research highlights the need for racial diversification, we assert that a cohort model can also be employed to increase representation and access for *all* persons with varying intersectional identities. Below, we provide recommendations for the recruitment of diverse learners with various historically marginalized identities rooted in the unique lived experiences that may impact their overall educational experience. As such, we urge programs to examine the layered forms of diversity within each identity group to ensure that their unique life experiences are considered and supported. Specific consideration and application of our recommendations are explored further in Chaps. 8 and 12. In Fig. 6.1, we offer an illustrative summary of the recommended best practices discussed in this section based on the research of Goldberg et al. (2022), Hsueh et al. (2021), and McCallen and Johnson, (2020).

Stop and Reflect: *Referring back to the case scenario, Jorge's story offers a valuable opportunity for a university with the goal to recruit and retain diverse learners, in alignment with their commitment to educational equity, accessibility, and inclusion. Jorge is a nontraditional learner, and his significant life experiences may make him an excellent candidate for admission despite his lower GPA and GRE scores. It is also important to note that he worked full-time and attended school full-time, which is an indicator of his aptitude for success.*

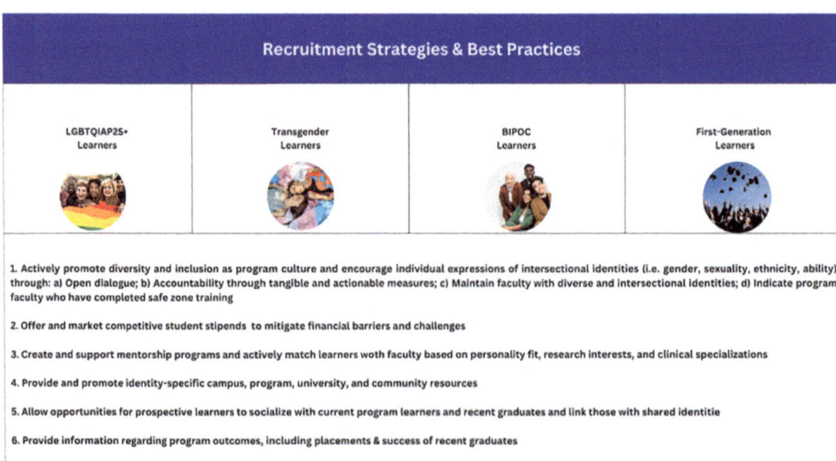

Fig. 6.1 Best practices for recruitment of diverse learners

6.7 Best Practices for Learner Retention

Though it is typically associated with diversification strategies, revising policies to intentionally promote learner retention can offer the program, the university, and its body of learners benefits on multiple levels beyond diversity, inclusion, and accessibility. First, proactively mitigating attrition serves the circular benefit of increased completion rates, which can also be used as a marketing tool to attract new learners as well as to retain current learners (Hsueh et al., 2021). Ultimately, there is a financial incentive for universities to mitigate learner attrition, as retention of current learners is fiscally prudent. As you seek to enhance your program's retention efforts, specifically those that also support diversification, this afore-referenced rationale may be an ideal way to frame your suggested policies. In short, the development and implementation of supplemental resources and programs that enhance learner retention by addressing their academic success can also create pathways that facilitate the pipeline of funneling quality professionals to the counseling field. Some suggestions we offer and explore here involve counselor education programs providing their learners with additional support through the following programs and initiatives: (1) intentional assistantship assignments and pairings, (2) established mentorship programs, (3) social support networks, and (4) faculty advisement. Each of these can be uniquely engaging opportunities to form relationships and connections with learners that can ultimately improve overall program retention.

6.7.1 Assistantship Programs

Many counseling graduate programs offer learners the opportunity to enhance their counseling identity while further developing their curriculum vitae through graduate assistantships (GAs). These opportunities often entail teaching assistantships or research assistantships. In addition to providing experience to foster development of CIT professional identity, GAs are also a source of financial relief for many learners. As graduate programs are inherently cost-prohibitive, thus supporting elitism, the provision of GAs makes a graduate-level education attainable for a wider range of individuals across varying socioeconomic backgrounds. This also is aligned with best practices that are socially just. Additionally, GAs can provide learners with a valuable opportunity to gain practical experience (Preston et al., 2020). To foster learner retention, we advise counselor education programs to consider the value inherent in intentionally assigning graduate assistantships. For example, many counselor education programs require a personal statement, in which the applicant discusses their career goals; this may also provide an opportunity for applicants to identify faculty members with whom they wish to work. By assigning program entrants to assistantships consistent with their career and research goals, their professional identity development is better fostered (Preston et al., 2020). Similarly, assigning learners to work with faculty with whom they share research interests may allow for the natural development of a mentorship relationship as the learner is able to contribute to research consistent with their interests. The practice is an extension of mentorship, which is discussed further in the following section.

6.7.2 Mentoring Programs

When researching information related to mentorship, it became evident that far more literature currently exists related to mentorship than for other programs described in this section. As with graduate assistantships, established mentorship programs may benefit graduate learners in a myriad of ways (Hutson et al., 2022; McCallen & Johnson, 2020). For example, through mentoring CES-in-training, the skills associated with conducting and publishing research can be fostered and better prepare these learners for work in academia. However, this option for support is often overlooked (Anekstein & Vereen, 2018; Hutson et al., 2022). In their recognition of the importance of mentorship, ACES developed guidelines to promote research mentorship in counselor education programs (Wester et al., 2009). According to the ACES guidelines, mentorship programs may be formal or informal, and should be structured in a way that provides mentees with both relational and instructional support. This mentorship model can also be applied to mentorship relationships focused on teaching or clinical counseling. Through research-focused mentorship programs, learners' knowledge of the research process is enhanced through collaboration with program CES faculty. We want to note here that learner mentorship through faculty advisement is further explored in Chap. 7.

Similarly, mentorship of counseling and teaching skills in CES-in-training can further the development of their professional identity. Teaching-focused mentorship programs foster the development of a teaching philosophy, while allowing CES-in-training to explore various teaching modalities and resources. Additionally, clinically-focused mentorship programs provide CES mentees with an opportunity to further develop their counseling skills with respect to a given theoretical counseling approach.

Furthering their support of mentorship programs, ACES highlights the importance of their relational aspect to learner academic, and ultimately, their professional success (Wester et al., 2009). Counseling competence, as well as the development of a professional counselor identity, can be fostered with faculty mentors' thoughtful provision of individualized support to their mentees. As learners have differing aspirations, skill levels, and clinical experience, faculty mentors should be intentional in collaboratively developing an individualized mentorship plan with their mentees. For instance, consider the following questions:

- *Does the mentee wish to learn more about developing their research agenda?*
- *Does the mentee hope to collaborate on a conference presentation with their faculty mentor?*
- *Is the mentee's goal to learn new clinical interventions, or become more active in professional organizations?*

To ensure the best possible outcomes and to foster a beneficial mentorship relationship, goals and expectations should be developed *collaboratively* and *early* within the mentoring relationship, thus aligning faculty mentor and mentee in a common and shared purpose. Agreement upon explicit expectations for the mentorship relationship is also shown to promote an environment of openness and successful mentor–mentee matching (Huskins et al., 2011). This transparency is integral to equity and inclusion.

Furthermore, mentorship can provide a reciprocal relationship that is equally beneficial to the mentor. As they establish the mentorship relationship, it is important that both faculty mentors and their mentees are self-aware regarding their limitations (Anekstein & Vereen, 2018). To model self-awareness for their mentees, faculty mentors may consider disclosing their limitations with new mentees. Additionally, mentors should work collaboratively and openly with mentees to identify ways in which the mentee can continue to enhance their development in areas that may not be a specialization for that mentor.

Moreover, there is research to indicate that effective mentors possess certain attributes (Huskins et al., 2011). One such attribute is utilizing direct and open communication, which promotes congruence and alignment in the mentorship relationship between mentor and mentee. Additionally, effective mentors provide active support to their mentees (Hutson et al., 2022; Meagher et al., 2011). Developing specific programming can facilitate creating a supportive environment. For instance, Anekstein and Vereen (2018) suggests hosting annual or semi-annual writing and research weekends. Having this specific time dedicated to research mentorship would allow the mentor and mentee to work collaboratively and intentionally towards the mentee's research goals.

6.7.3 Social Support Programs

Through the development of social support networks, learners' mental health and sense of community are fostered (Hutson et al., 2022; Wang et al., 2018). Though there is limited research in this area, published studies delineates the benefits of implementing social programming into counselor education programs to foster a sense of community and belongingness (Jensen et al., 2018; Trent et al., 2021). Through the intentional integration of programming aimed at connecting first-year learners with current faculty and established peers within the program, positive learner-faculty relationships, peer support, and cohesion are fostered (Jensen et al., 2018). Regularly scheduled social events that create opportunities for learners, faculty, and program administrators to connect facilitates the development of supportive relationships. Findings of extant research also recommend the collaborative engagement of learners and faculty in a community service project to develop a sense of community (Jensen et al., 2018). Welcome events, picnics, ice cream socials, or game-nights may also provide an opportunity for learners, specifically those in their first year, to cultivate relationships and a sense of community early on in their academic journey. Research has demonstrated that such social supports are identified by diverse learners, specifically those with historically marginalized racial identities, as playing a critical role in their program retention and attrition (Trent et al., 2021). As the first year of graduate education is the most impactful in facilitating retention, we suggest that social programming for *all* learners be used to aid in the development of relationships; this recommendation is supported by the research of Jensen et al. (2018). This may be especially useful as learners may have relocated to a new geographical region for their studies, and therefore may lack a social support system in close geographic proximity. Furthermore, as graduate education tends to be costly, special consideration should be made in ensuring that social programs are free or low-cost for all learners.

6.7.4 Faculty Advisement

Through the advising process, learners gain increased opportunities for support and both academic and professional success (Dipre & Luke, 2020; Hutson et al., 2022). Therefore, intentionality in the advisement of any learner in a counselor education program is a vital component of retention efforts. Unfortunately, this important aspect of the learner experience is not always prioritized within counselor education programs (Furr, 2018). The American Counseling Association's *Code of Ethics* (2014) explicitly states that it is the responsibility of counselor educators to provide career advice to learners, in addition to exposing CITs to opportunities that may enhance their knowledge and development as professional counselors. As all learners are unique, it is the responsibility of the faculty advisor to adjust their approach to best suit the needs of individual learners (Dipre & Luke, 2020).

While the literature suggests numerous ways of incorporating advising into the counselor education learners, Relational Cultural Theory (RCT) is listed as a beneficial and effective framework (Dipre & Luke, 2020). Moreover, RCT provides a socially just framework with an inherent emphasis on relationship-building, which is key in learner retention. As RCT prioritizes social connections, it facilitates the building of meaningful relationships between faculty advisors and their advisees. Furthermore, RCT posits that growth-fostering relationships are dependent on the individuals' development and maintenance of mutual empathy and empowerment (Dipre & Luke, 2020). Therefore, advisement through an RCT lens lessens the power differential between the faculty advisor and the learner, while encouraging a lifelong engagement in learning. This practice is also a key characteristic of effective and multiculturally-informed counselors and counselor educators. Chapter 7 will delve further into best practices regarding the provision of faculty advisement (Fig. 6.2).

As we bring this section to a close, you may note that these practices may scaffold and/or overlap. The development of academic programming using any combination of the afore-referenced best practices creates an intentional wraparound approach to learner support, and when effectively implemented bolsters learner success.

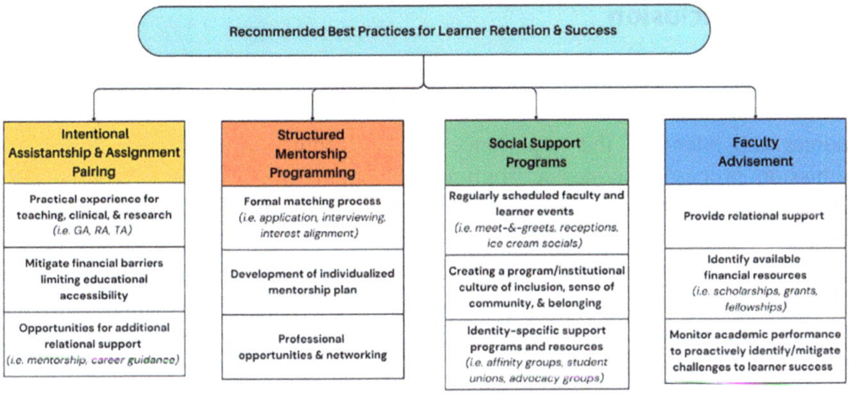

Fig. 6.2 Learner retention and academic success best practices

In summary, best practices related to learner retention may include:

- Intentionally assigning learners to graduate assistantships that align with their stated interests and goals.
- Implementation of mentorship programs.
- Integration of social programming to foster a sense of belonging and community.
- The provision of advising through an RCT lens.

Stop and Reflect: *As a result of the aforementioned admissions and retention strategies, Jorge was able to begin his graduate journey in the counseling program at your university. However, his success in the program will be greatly fostered by the development of a social support system. As previously mentioned, Jorge is a nontraditional learner, who is also a divorced, single parent. Best practices to foster his success may include assigning him to a research assistantship that allows him to work with a current faculty member whose research focus is veteran mental health, which is aligned with Jorge's prior work experience and preferred client population. This will provide him with a mentor that has a similar research interest and aligns with his aspirational goals. Additionally, enrolling Jorge into your department's mentorship program will provide him with additional resources as he develops his professional identity as a counselor. Furthermore, given his overlaying diverse and intersectional identities, utilizing RCT as a foundation of his student advisement in the program may serve to enhance his academic experience, thereby increasing the likelihood of his retention and ultimately success in the program.*

6.8 Conclusion

In this chapter, we provide you with recommendations for best practices for inclusive admissions and retention processes. Additionally, we provide strategies to address and attend to the importance of gatekeeping in admissions. Since the admission process provides a frontline opportunity for counselor educators to gauge the readiness of individuals for the counseling profession, it is important to ensure this process is equitable to provide access to all learners. Therefore, we believe that with these processes in place, counseling education programs may be one step closer to providing the community with adequate representation of the diverse populations we serve as counselors and counselor educators.

References

American Counseling Association. (2014). *2014 ACA code of ethics*. https://www.counseling.org/docs/default-source/default-document-library/ethics/2014-aca-code-of-ethics.pdf?sfvrsn=55ab73d0_1

Anekstein, A. M., & Vereen, L. G. (2018). Research mentorship: Implications for the preparation of doctoral students. *The Journal of Counselor Preparation and Supervision, 11*(2), Article 6.

Council for Accreditation of Counseling and Related Educational Programs. (2024). *2024 CACREP standards*. https://www.cacrep.org/wp-content/uploads/2024/04/2024-Standards-Combined-Version-4.11.2024.pdf

Dipre, K. A., & Luke, M. (2020). Relational cultural theory–Informed advising in counselor education. *Professional Counselor, 10*(4), 517–531.

Dorans, N. J., & Cook, L. L. (Eds.). (2016). *Fairness in educational assessment and measurement.* Routledge.

Eakins, A., & Eakins, S. L. (2017). African American students at predominantly White institutions: A collaborative style cohort recruitment & retention model. *Journal of Learning in Higher Education, 13*(2), 51–57.

Furr, S. (2018). Faculty review, promotion, and tenure process. In J. E. A. Okech & D. J. Rubel (Eds.), *Counselor education in the 21st century: Issues and experiences* (pp. 105–128). American Counseling Association.

Goldberg, A. E., McCormick, N., Matsuno, E., Virginia, H., & Beemyn, G. (2022). Transgender graduate students: Considerations, tensions, and decisions in choosing a graduate program. *Journal of Homosexuality, 69*(9), 1549–1575.

Hipolito-Delgado, C. P., Estrada, D., & Garcia, M. (2021). Disrupting the narrative on recruiting graduate students of color in counselor education. *Teaching and Supervision in Counseling, 3*(1), Article 4.

Hsueh, L., Werntz, A., Hobaica, S., Owens, S. A., Lumley, M. A., & Washburn, J. J. (2021). Clinical psychology Ph.D. students' admission experiences: Implications for recruiting racial/ethnic minority and LGBTQ students. *Journal of Clinical Psychology, 77*(1), 105–120. https://doi.org/10.1002/jclp.23074

Huskins, W. C., Silet, K., Weber-Main, A., Begg, M. D., Fowler, V. G., Hamilton, J., & Fleming, M. (2011). Identifying and aligning expectations in a mentoring relationship. *Clinical and Translational Science, 4*(6), 439–447. https://doi.org/10.1002/j.1556-6978.2013.00034.x

Hutson, J., Nasser, R., Edele, S., Parrish, G., Rodgers, C., Richmond, S., Marano, M., & Curtis, R. (2022). Predictors of persistence, retention & completion for first-generation graduate students. *Journal of Organizational Psychology, 22*(1), 99–114. https://doi.org/10.33423/jop.v22i1.5022

Jensen, J., Midgett, A., & Doumas, D. (2018). Evaluation of a program designed to increase retention in counselor education: Reaching year two. *Journal of Counselor Preparation & Supervision, 11*(2), Article 5.

Ju, J., Merrell-James, R., Coker, J. K., Ghoston, M., Casado Pérez, J. F., & Field, T. A. (2020). Recruiting, retaining, and supporting students from underrepresented racial minority backgrounds in doctoral counselor education. *The Professional Counselor, 10*(4), 581–602. https://doi.org/10.15241/jj.10.4.581

Leverett-Main, S. (2004). Program directors' perceptions of admission screening measures and indicators of student success. *Counselor Education and Supervision, 43*(3), 207–219. https://doi.org/10.1002/j.1556-6978.2004.tb01843.x

McCallen, L. S., & Johnson, H. L. (2020). The role of institutional agents in promoting higher education success among first-generation college students at a public urban university. *Journal of Diversity in Higher Education, 13*(4), 320–332. https://doi.org/10.1037/dhe0000143

McCaughan, A. M., & Hill, N. R. (2015). The gatekeeping imperative in counselor education admission protocols: The criticality of personal qualities. *International Journal for the Advancement of Counselling, 37*, 28–40. https://doi.org/10.1007/s10447-014-9223-2

Meagher, S., Taylor, L., Probsfield, J., & Fleming, M. (2011). Evaluating research mentors working in the area of clinical translational science: A review of the literature. *Clinical and Translational Science, 4*(5), 353–358. https://doi.org/10.1111/j.1752-8062.2011.00317.x

Preston, J., Trepal, H., Morgan, A., Jacques, J., Smith, J. D., & Field, T. A. (2020). Components of a high-quality doctoral program in counselor education and supervision. *Professional Counselor, 10*(4), 453–471.

Trent, F., Dwiwardani, C., & Page, C. (2021). Factors impacting the retention of students of color in graduate programs: A qualitative study. *Training and Education in Professional Psychology, 15*(3), 219–229. https://doi.org/10.1037/tep0000319

Wang, J., Mann, F., Lloyd-Evans, B., Ma, R., & Johnson, S. (2018). Associations between loneliness and perceived social support and outcomes of mental health problems: A systematic review. *BMC Psychiatry, 18*(1), 1–16. https://doi.org/10.1186/s12888-018-1736-5

Wester, K. L., Border, L. D., Briggs, C., Chang, C., Haag-Granello, D., Hays, D., Pepperell, J. & Spurgeon, S. (2009, June). *ACES research mentorship guidelines*. http://www.acesonline.net/aces-research-mentorship-guidelines

Ziomek-Daigle, J., & Christensen, T. M. (2010). An emergent theory of gatekeeping practices in counselor education. *Journal of Counseling & Development, 88*(4), 407–415. https://doi.org/10.1002/j.1556-6678.2010.tb00040.x

Bianca Augustine, Ph.D., LPC, CCTP, is a Clinical Assistant Professor at William and Mary in Williamsburg, Virginia. Her expertise lies in mental health counseling, particularly with individuals from oppressed identity groups, with an emphasis on those across the Black diaspora and those with sexual/affectional and gender-expansive identities. Dr. Augustine has a private counseling practice, in which she focuses on wellness through liberatory practices, sexuality, relationships, identity development/affirmation, trauma, and grief. Her research interests include Acceptance and Commitment Therapy for racialized trauma, intergenerational trauma, resilience/resistance, and the experiences of marginalized groups in CES and counseling.

Natese Dockery, Ph.D., LPC, NCC is an Assistant Professor of Mental Health and Well-being and Extension Specialist at The University of Kentucky, School of Human Envi-ronmental Sciences. She is a licensed professional counselor who has extensive experience working with clients struggling with anxiety, depression, trauma, and other mental health concerns. Her research interests are in social determinants of health, health equity, and all aspects of providing clients with culturally appropri-ate and aware care.

Devona M. Stalnaker-Shofner, EdD, LPC, NCC, MHP, SAP (she/her/hers) is an Associate Professor at Antioch University, School of Counseling, Psychology, and Therapy. She has been a counselor educator for more than 10 years, and in pro-fessional practice as a licensed counselor for more than 20 years. Her clinical ex-perience includes providing individual, group, and couples and family counseling to clients presenting with treatment concerns such as depression, anxiety, trauma, as well as substance use, addiction, and recovery. She also provides clinical su-pervision to counselors-in-training and new counseling professionals. Dr. Stal-naker-Shofner has served in various leadership roles within the counseling and counselor education professions. Her research and scholarship includes numerous presentations at state, regional, national, and international conferences, as well as related publications. As a trainer, she has provided workshops on racial trauma and BIPOC mental health and wellness, and the decolonization of curriculum, teaching praxis, and educational policies to disrupt oppression and promote diver-sity, equity, inclusion, and access. Additionally, she serves as an educational and organizational consultant advising on implementing antiracist and social justice practices for leaders and organizational policies and culture.

Faculty Advisement

7

LaToya Chambers

Invest in the human soul. Who knows, it might be a diamond in the rough.

Mary McLeod Bethune

Abstract

Faculty advisement is important in promoting learner development and successful outcomes in their program of study. Perhaps more importantly, good advising has the potential to reduce attrition rates. This chapter focuses on understanding what advising is, the components of advising, the role of advising in retention efforts, culturally inclusive advising related to supporting underrepresented and non-traditional learners, and the intersection of advising and mentorship.

Learning Objectives After reading this chapter, you will be able to:

1. Understand the definition, purpose, importance, and components of advising, especially as it relates to retention efforts.
2. Integrate culturally inclusive advising to support underrepresented and non-traditional learners as well as the nuances of a supportive advising relationship with such learners.
3. Expand one's understanding of learner advisement to include mentorship as an element of the advising relationship.

L. Chambers (✉)
William & Mary, Williamsburg, VA, USA
e-mail: lchambers@wm.edu

D. M. Stalnaker-Shofner and T. N. Sapp (eds.), *A Comprehensive Guide for Counselor Education*, Springer Texts in Education, https://doi.org/10.1007/978-3-031-68358-9_7

7.1 Statement of Reflexivity

As a Black, cisgender woman in higher education, I feel personally connected to experiences of marginalization, isolation, racism, oppression, and trauma as part of an underrepresented population and person of color. As an individual with two graduate degrees, I am also aware of education as a privilege and how it can impact the dynamics of relationships with learners and people in general. As a Licensed Professional Counselor with a doctorate, I have experienced relationships with faculty advisors within two different graduate counseling programs who were, often, representative of the dominant culture. I approach this chapter as an author and individual tasked with providing advising services to graduate counselors-in-training (CITs) in a master's level counseling program. As both a counselor educator and faculty advisor, I am responsible for providing support to CITs throughout the duration of their program of study which includes degree mapping/planning, providing support and linking to resources, monitoring progress, and providing feedback to promote professional development.

7.2 Case Scenario

You are a counselor educator in a graduate Clinical Mental Health Counseling Program that is delivered online with required residencies twice per year. At the start of the semester, you are assigned an advisee who registered for three classes in their first term. You were provided little information regarding the advisee; however, you had access to their educational records, which contained their course schedule, application materials to the program, the results of their admission interview and acceptance details, and some basic demographic information. You were also aware that your advisee did not declare any specializations or emphases for their degree and that they would just be pursuing the general Clinical Mental Health track. Based on the available information, you knew the following: your advisee is a 32-year-old, cisgender African American woman named Kara and uses the pronouns "she/her." Your advisee received an undergraduate degree in psychology and completed her degree with a 3.5 GPA. Her admission essay reflected graduate level writing ability, and her resume indicated at least five years of work experience in the behavioral health field as a mental health technician.

After reviewing the documents, you reached out to Kara to schedule the initial advising session. During that session, you provided her with information about the purpose and importance of advising, what advising entails, your role and responsibilities to Kara as your advisee, and where to find important resources online for the graduate program and college. You also exchanged contact information, addressed questions and concerns from Kara, and asked her what her expectations and needs were from you as her advisor. You collaborated with Kara to discuss the frequency and format of future meeting sessions along with the purpose of the meetings. You also obtained additional information from Kara, which revealed that she is currently working full-time which is why she chose an online program. She is also a married mother of two children, ages 5 and 9. Kara's partner also works full-time at a night-shift job. Kara is currently receiving financial aid and one scholarship. She was diagnosed with a learning disability in elementary school but has had no significant issues with academic coursework.

7.3 Introduction

Counselor Education and Supervision (CES) doctoral programs bear the responsibility of preparing future professionals to teach, supervise, conduct research, and engage in advocacy and leadership activities in the field (CACREP, 2024). Counselor educators are also tasked with conducting faculty advising; however, this role has not always been well understood or prioritized as a function of counselor education. Universities and counselor educators often have agendas and responsibilities that take precedence over advising, and there is not much incentive supporting faculty members in carrying out advising activities (i.e. additional remuneration, course release). CES faculty are often preoccupied with teaching, research, and other responsibilities directly linked to faculty evaluation and the need to sustain employment (He & Hutson, 2017; Zhang et al., 2019). Additionally, stereotypes persist regarding the level of interest and concern faculty have in advising learners, as well as questions related to advisor competence. The latter may be somewhat substantiated as research shows many counselor educators do not receive any specific training or instruction on how to advise learners (Dillon & Fisher, 2000). Further complicating matters surrounding advising also include conflicts in scheduling opportunities and a lack of learner understanding about the need and purpose of advising services (Volino et al., 2015). Despite its challenges, faculty advising can be a crucial component for successful learner outcomes.

7.4 What Is Faculty Advising?

There is no single, agreed-upon definition of faculty advising; however, existing literature does highlight the similarities across definitions. Older definitions of faculty advising often focused on activities related to guiding learners in choosing the correct courses to complete their academic programs (Zhang et al., 2019). Over time, definitions have increasingly evolved to reflect a more purposeful intent behind advising learners to reflect more specific and holistic perspectives. For example, Volino et al. (2015) point to literature asserting that faculty advising involves actions that support and promote professional identity and service, learning beyond the program of study, and learner confidence. Bloom et al. (2018) describe advising as a collaborative process in which learners are supported in gaining the most benefit from their education to reach their personal and professional goals. In Harborth's (2015) interview with Charlie Nutt, the executive director of the National Academic Advising Association, he was quoted as saying "Advisors are now providing direction focused on moral, social, economic, and

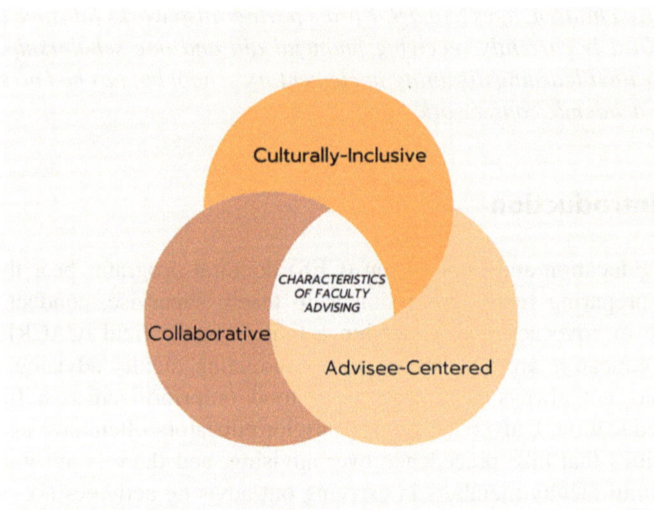

Fig. 7.1 Characteristics of faculty advising

educational development of learners" (p. 18). When discussing the progression to a more holistic model of advising, Nutt goes on to assert that this approach, "supports learner development and learning, and it far exceeds just sharing registration details" (Harborth, 2015, p. 18).

For our purposes, faculty advising for counselor educators will be defined as a collaborative, culturally inclusive, learner-centered process that entails 1) relationship- building, 2) mentorship, 3) degree planning assistance, 4) career information and guidance, 5) support and resource referral to promote program completion, 6)professional identity development, and 7) successful engagement in professional activities (see Fig. 7.1). Additionally, one cannot disregard the importance of faculty advising in CIT retention, as discussed in Chaps. 7 and 8. According to Zhang et al. (2019), programs and colleges often rely heavily on learner enrollment and retention for economic sustainability. Therefore, effective faculty advising is crucial in the support of program completion, especially for non-traditional CITs and those from underrepresented groups.

7.5 The Role of Faculty Advising in Learner Retention

According to Litalien and Guay (2015), up to one-fourth of masters-level learners and up to one-half of doctoral learners do not complete their academic programs. This may be especially true when there is the absence of a supportive faculty relationship, which has been shown to reinforce retention (Gilmore et al., 2016; Joy et al., 2015). Blanchard and Haccoun (2020) also assert the type of support plays a factor in reducing attrition. Positive support was more beneficial than counterproductive support such as micromanaging. This substantiates other studies which suggest advising should contribute to the professional development of learners beyond the program of study in which they can independently function in their professional duties after graduation. As we consider this research and reflect on the significance of an advising relationship with CITs that is strong and supportive, it is also important to consider the impact of cultural factors which may necessitate the use of culturally inclusive practices.

7.6 The Role of Culture in Advising

Although graduate faculty members' perceptions of attrition often point to individual learner characteristics or motivation, Gilmore et al. (2016) and Felder et al. (2014) identify several factors that indicate the issue of attrition is much more complex. These include variables such as socioeconomic status, race, gender, and ethnicity. Additionally, Gardner's (2010) findings note that non-traditional learners may be enrolled part-time, maintaining some form of employment, and have additional roles and responsibilities that may impact their ability to complete their degree program.

Felder et al. (2014) indicates that learners from underrepresented groups can often feel further marginalized and disconnected. These experiences may contribute to attrition despite their personal motivation, ability, and skills. Though there is increasing awareness of the need to recruit and retain a diverse learner body including underrepresented groups such as women, learners of color, and LGBTQQIP2SA populations, *how to* address the needs of those learners and support them once they are enrolled requires further attention (Purgason et al., 2016). This requires us to consider the unique needs of learners from underrepresented groups. Schlosser et al. (2011) attest to the multicultural nature of advising. Faculty cannot assume advising these learners can be conducted in the exact same manner as advising learners from the dominant culture (Butler et al., 2013), especially since learners from underrepresented groups have to navigate the nuances of diversity-related issues (Haizlip, 2012). As previously stated, attrition rates are significant for graduate learners in general, but non-traditional and underrepresented groups of learners are at an even higher risk of dropping out of their programs of study.

In support of the need for a culturally inclusive approach to advising is the research of Miller and Stone (2011), which noted that doctoral learners of color made decisions about pursuing careers in counselor education or remaining in a program of study based on faculty relationships. Therefore, a supportive relationship with a faculty member is important for graduate learner success and is even more critical for underrepresented groups of graduate learners (Haizlip, 2012). More often than not, this supportive relationship is developed through working with the faculty advisor (Schlosser et al., 2011).

Underrepresented groups of graduate learners also must contend with the realization that they are more likely not to see themselves reflected in the individuals that hold positions of power at their universities, including the faculty with whom developing supportive relationships is so crucial to their success. Additionally, advisors may be unsure and uncomfortable about initiating and holding conversations about culture with advisees from underrepresented groups (Locke & Bailey, 2014) since the faculty advisors for these learners are more likely to be representative of the dominant culture (Miller & Stone, 2011). Fortunately, being from the same or a similar background is not a prerequisite for effective, culturally appropriate advising (Haizlip, 2012; Miller & Stone, 2011). Additionally, the benefits of underrepresented graduate learners finishing their program of study far outweigh the challenges. Diversity needs to be reflected throughout the counseling field, both in counselor education programs and amongst those providing clinical services to diverse clientele (Purgason et al., 2016). Although diversity encompasses numerous characteristics, research has been conducted on particular groups with regards to retention and advising issues.

7.6.1 Lower-Income Background and Status

College has become increasingly unaffordable for many learners, and this is especially so for those pursuing advanced degrees. Coupled with the stigma of poverty and uncertainty about taking on considerable debt to complete such degrees, a lack of financial resources can prevent degree program enrollment altogether. Nguyen and Herron (2021) point out that lack of financial resources can impact mental wellness and the ability to fully engage in academic pursuits or access resources needed for school such as textbooks. The lack of financial resources also contributes to higher attrition rates than those with adequate or abundant resources and can negatively impact the ability to build relationships with other learners and faculty which foster the sense that one belongs (Goldrick-Rab, 2016). Feelings of isolation and disconnectedness negatively impact retention, especially for those from underrepresented groups. Therefore, understanding the constraints of limited financial resources is critical for faculty advisors to build relationships with these CITs. Additionally, faculty advisors need to maintain awareness of these issues in case linkage to appropriate college resources for additional support is warranted since the lack of finances can contribute to leaving the program of study.

7.6.2 Learners with Disabilities

Though we have a chapter that addresses learners and faculty with disabilities (Chap. 13), it seems prudent to note the unique advising concerns associated with this group. There have been significant increases in enrollment for learners with disabilities (National Center for Education Statistics, 2019), yet this population remains underrepresented in higher education settings. However, enrolling in a program of study and completing a program of study are two different matters. Learners with disabilities are more likely to fail to complete their degree programs (Lee et al., 2015). This has far-reaching implications for the future of these learners. Higher education attainment is usually positively correlated to employment and earning potential (Bureau of Labor Statistics, 2014). Research indicates the need for support and access to resources as a main contributing factor in decreasing attrition for learners with disabilities regardless of whether or not the learner reports having a disability. It is crucial that colleges, faculty, and staff have an understanding of the importance of supporting these learners with programs and services (Newman et al., 2021); this is further explored in Chap. 13. Additionally, the stigma of having a disability imposed on many learners needs to be understood as a potential barrier for access to resources and support. The faculty advisor plays a key role in providing support to learners with disabilities, especially regarding retention issues. According to Thompson-Ebanks (2014), learners reported support services including faculty advising positively impacted their educational experiences. Therefore, faculty advisors play a key role in ensuring that CITs can access and utilize the services and support that will help them complete their degree programs.

7.6.3 First-Generation College Learners

The definition of a first-generation college learner varies across the literature. For example, some sources identify a first-generation college learner as the first family member to attend college (Peralta & Klonowski, 2017). Other definitions specifically limit the family member element to the learner's parents (Longwell-Grice et al., 2016). First-generation college learners face obstacles that their peers who have had some exposure and preparation related to secondary education do not. This can include difficulty completing degree programs and limited financial resources (Martin, 2017). They tend to struggle earlier on in graduate studies (Roksa et al., 2018) and face significant threats to overall wellness (Covarrubias & Fryberg, 2015). Additionally, first-generation college learners may struggle with accepting their opportunities to obtain higher education while witnessing other family members that were not afforded the same (Jenkins et al., 2013).

7.6.4 Learners with Racially and/or Ethnically Historically Marginalized Identities

Ongoing initiatives to increase diversity in higher education are often aimed at the recruitment and retention of racial minorities including Black, Latine/x, and Native American/Indigenous/First People learners. Racial minorities are highly underrepresented in graduate education (Gonzales et al., 2013). Despite increases in enrollment, this does not always translate to retention and program completion as with other underrepresented groups. Several unique challenges impact learners of color including how they navigate issues surrounding racial identity, try to overcome alienation to achieve a sense of belonging, build supportive relationships with faculty and peers (especially in the absence of role models that look like them), and increase personal resiliency to cope with their environments (Trent et al., 2021). As discussed in Chap. 6, the climate of the educational institutions and the availability of adequate support such as faculty advising and/or mentorship directly influences retention for BIPOC learners. Noy and Ray (2012) found that women of color report gaining the least advantages from primary advisors and often seek out support and guidance from others who end up acting as secondary advisors. Also, having access to inclusive, safe spaces that promote a culture of acceptance and diversity are important. BIPOC learners often contend with racism and discrimination. When coupled with a perception that the collegiate environment is also unsupportive, not inclusive, and lacking care and concern, the chances that these learners will complete their studies decrease (Trent et al., 2021). Although the terms "students of color" or "racial minorities" are used as catch-all phrases, they in no way are intended to insinuate that learners with historically marginalized identities have the exact same issues or experiences, despite any similarities. The information presented below highlights these nuances.

7.6.4.1 Black/African American Learners

Black CITs enrolled in counseling and related programs only comprise about 13% of the learner enrollment (Okahana & Zhou, 2019). In addition to the barriers shared by other groups of underrepresented learners, Black CITs also must contend with the results of complex, historical, and ongoing traumas imposed by living in the United States. Racism, oppression, microaggressions, isolation, and stereotypes are often the challenges Black learners must overcome in addition to negative self-talk, imposter syndrome, and low self-esteem facilitated through anti-Blackness (Ragland Woods et al., 2021). This is especially true for Black learners enrolled at predominantly White institutions (PWIs). Beyond the potential impact on completing graduate studies, the effects of racism can negatively impact overall wellness and quality of life by inducing physical, psychological, and emotional problems (Evans et al., 2020).

7.6.4.2 Latiné/x Learners

Faced with similar challenges like other racial minorities such as racism, oppression, and stereotypes, Latiné/x learners are also underrepresented in graduate school programs (Kamimura-Jimenez & Gonzalez, 2018) despite belonging to the fastest-growing ethnic population in the United States (Espino, 2014). Unfortunately, the rates of attrition and failure to complete programs of study are significant. Additionally, many Latiné/x learners are also first-generation college learners (Santa-Ramirez, 2021) which brings another set of unique challenges.

7.6.4.3 Native American/Indigenous/First People Learners

Before we begin, it is important to note that there was intentionality in the use of the terms *Native American/Indigenous/First People.* However, for the purposes of this section and in alignment with the terminology used by the literature and that which is consistent with APA 7th ed formatting, I will use the term Native American. Native American graduate learners are significantly underrepresented in institutions of higher education as well, and the low numbers of professionals in counseling and related programs are significant. This is concerning considering the importance of having Native American clinicians available to treat Native American populations in need of behavioral health services. There are several contributing factors correlated with this underrepresentation (Goforth et al., 2016) such as significant historical and intergenerational trauma in this country, both having a profoundly negative impact. The history of war, genocide, colonization, racism, oppression, and loss of language (Campbell & Evans-Campbell, 2011) have all been detrimental to Native American populations. Furthermore, barriers to recruiting and retaining Native American learners begin well before entrance into higher education and include problems in primary school, with social support, and with financial resources. Ways to increase retention include creating culturally inclusive environments, having diverse faculty and learners, and creating supportive resources for Native American learners (Goforth et al., 2016).

7.6.4.4 Asian American and Pacific Islander (AAPI) Learners

Asian American and Pacific Islander (AAPI) learners experience unique challenges in higher education. Often, they are mischaracterized as high achievers in academia, and this stereotype reinforces the fallacy of AAPI persons as monolithic. Unfortunately, the *model minority* stereotype coupled with pressure to do well and live up to high expectations can negatively impact mental wellness (Panelo, 2010). AAPI learners also face experiences in higher education similar to other ethnic groups including racism, stereotypes, and microaggressions (Bauman, 2018). Additionally, there have been increases in anti-Asian sentiments and racism since the COVID-19 pandemic (Jiang, 2020) along with pandemic related academic challenges for AAPI learners (Key, 2020).

7.6.4.5 Learners with Sexually and/or Affectionally Historically Marginalized Identities

LGBTQQIP2SA learners continue to encounter underrepresentation along with numerous other issues including discrimination and marginalization (Moran et al., 2018). Negative effects on mental wellness and academic performance are often triggered by microaggressions directed at LGBTQQIP2SA learners (Kulick et al., 2017) coupled with higher education environments which are less inclusive than they should be by centering dominant-culture identities (Duran, 2019). Additionally, homophobia and transphobia are not adequately addressed; this is further supported by the research of Chen et al. (2021). In their research, Chen et al. (2021) reported that sexual minorities reported feeling that their institutions provided less support to them due to their identity and gender. Lesbian and gay CITs reported feeling a lack of safety due to microaggressive behaviors and discrimination directed toward them (Pollock & Meek, 2016). This is particularly problematic considering the importance of supportive environments and a sense of belonging in learner retention efforts. Stout and Wright (2016) also point to the need for inclusion by finding that a decrease in sense of belonging for LGBTQQIP2SA learners is associated with wanting to terminate enrollment.

7.6.4.6 International Learners

Though Chap. 12 of this textbook explores the experiences of international learners and faculty, it also seems important to note here the uniqueness of the needs of these learners. International learners also face significant challenges that may impact retention in higher education. Leaving one's home to study in the United States often results in the loss of one's primary support system. Additionally, these learners are also faced with experiences of racism, microaggressions, and discrimination (Yang et al., 2021). International learners are often subjected to the stress of fitting into a new culture. Reid and Dixon (2012) point to cultural differences as a factor in the isolation from peers and faculty members that international learners also face.

Despite ongoing initiatives in higher education surrounding diversity, inclusion, equity, and awareness, underrepresented learner populations continue to struggle with cultural barriers which significantly impact academic experiences and the ability to complete programs of study. Colleges and universities with goals of recruiting and retaining diverse learners must provide resources to promote those endeavors. Supportive relationships with faculty and culturally inclusive faculty advising practices for all CITs and all learners are crucial in battling attrition rates. However, as previously stated, many faculty members acting as faculty advisors are not specifically trained on how to deliver advising services. Therefore, the rest of this chapter is devoted to providing some suggestions on facilitating that process in the absence of official guidance at the institutional level as well as in counselor education and supervision programs. In response to this lack of guidance, it is proposed that counselor educators work with their institutions and departments to develop or obtain guidance related to advising protocol for CITs in their program.

7.7 The Academic Advising Process in Counselor Education

7.7.1 Rapport/Relationship Building and Orientation

The aforementioned discussion has already highlighted the importance and role of supportive relationships for learner success. Regardless of how institutions assign CITs to counselor educators, the very first step in the faculty advising process should be to establish a connection and rapport with the CIT to begin building a positive, supportive relationship, and Ford et al. (2021) recommend that faculty advisors are intentional with this process. Bloom et al. (2007) found there were certain characteristics of the advising relationship that learners appreciated. Advisees reported satisfaction when advisors showed genuine care and concern, demonstrated a vested interest in learner success, and were approachable and accessible. Bloom et al. (2007) further note that advisors should provide some orientation to their advisees during initial contacts, including informing them of their role as the advisor, preferred methods of contact, what academic advising entails, and initiate a discussion pertaining to expectations for both the advisor and advisee. It is also during this phase that advisors need to reinforce the importance of faculty advising, especially within the context of successful program completion. CITs should be encouraged to familiarize themselves with program requirements and engage in activities to reinforce this such as reading the institution and program policies, procedures, and requirements along with identifying institutional resources that may be beneficial to the learner.

7.7.2 Information-Gathering and Needs Assessment

It is proffered here that faculty advising should be an advisee-driven and holistic process. To be effective in your role as a faculty advisor, you must be able to adequately assess your advisees and gather data to determine how to best implement this practice. Appropriate assessments entail obtaining demographic and background information, data related to resources and supports, strengths, and any deficits or unmet needs advisees may have. Additionally, advisors need to also inquire about advisees' interests and goals. Bloom et al., (2018, para. 2) referred to this process as Appreciative Advising which entails "the intentional collaborative practice of asking generative, open-ended questions that help learners optimize their educational experiences and achieve their dreams, goals, and potentials". The purpose of information-gathering is to assist the faculty advisor in determining how to best support the advisee and what other resources or collaborative relationships will be needed. While there are various theories, styles, and models for faculty advising (Zhang et al., 2019), they will not be addressed within the scope of this chapter. However, you are strongly encouraged to explore these models on your own to find one that works for you. Additionally, it may be beneficial for your role as a faculty advisor to develop a level of self-awareness regarding your personal advising style and what may work best for your advisees by engaging in some self-reflection regarding your own traits, characteristics, strengths and deficits. Just as you should conduct needs assessments for advisees, one should be conducted for yourself to determine what support is needed from the program or institution to ensure your success in your role as a faculty advisor.

Stop and Reflect: *In the case scenario for this chapter, you can begin the advising process by accessing the available documentation about your advisee. You can then move on to the rapport/relationship building and orientation phase, by scheduling the initial session, providing pertinent information, and orientating your advisee to the advising process. You will want to begin to create a supportive relationship by collaborating with your advisee, asking questions, and obtaining her input about expectations. During the same session, you can also engage in the information gathering/needs assessment phase by obtaining additional information about your advisee that was not initially known prior to their first meeting. You want to note that your advisee is a part of an underrepresented and non-traditional learner group in higher education. You also want to learn more about your advisee in terms of potential work/life balance and resiliency. Finally, you will need to obtain information about disability and financial aid status. All of these facts can be utilized to guide how you will approach advising with your advisee and which resources may be important for them to access while enrolled in their program of study.*

7.7.3 Degree Planning

Perhaps one of the most important aspects of the academic advising relationship is providing information and guidance related to course scheduling. Walker et al. (2017) found that learners desired clear communication and guidance from their advisors about course and program requirements. Therefore, it is imperative that faculty advisors understand graduation requirements in order to provide adequate support and assistance. Learners also appreciated advisors that focused on long-term goals and "the big picture" instead of term-by-term advising. Faculty advisors should work with CITs as early as their first term entering the program to complete a degree plan which details the sequence of courses CITs will take throughout the program of study and any other requirements needed for graduation. This provides the CIT with the ability to identify and keep track of the completion of core courses, electives, practicum, internships, and any other graduation requirements such as exit exams. Degree planning also provides a way for CITs and faculty to monitor academic progress and address any issues as they arise. Faculty advisors should involve CITs in the degree planning process and allow them to take as much autonomy as possible in planning their courses. Per Walker et al. (2017), learners desire collaborative relationships with advisors. Furthermore, one of the main differences between undergraduate and graduate advisees is that graduate advisees desire more input and control over picking courses instead of having faculty advisors control that process (Christian & Sprinkle, 2013). Plans should be specific and identify the year and term coursework is expected to be completed. Additional pertinent information such as transfer courses, etc. should be included. Plans should also be updated as needed to reflect changes. Due to the significance of ensuring CITs are enrolling and completing the correct courses, it may be beneficial for advisors to establish a standard for how they will maintain contact with

CITs and how often. When faculty advisors are unsure regarding course information, sequencing, etc., it is imperative they reach out for support and assistance. Some institutions provide degree planning tools and software (Samaranayake et al., 2023) which may take this work off of the advisor. However, due to financial constraints, this may not be an option for smaller institutions or those with limited budgets. Therefore, faculty advisors need to be able to provide course planning assistance to CITs in the absence of technology resources that could perform this task.

Stop and Reflect: *You can engage your advisee in the degree planning process by providing clear communication about required coursework and resources to reinforce those communications. Additionally, you can encourage your advisee to participate in their plan by identifying courses that interest them. You can engage your advisee in looking at the "big picture" regarding long-term goals. Finally, you can establish a method of monitoring your advisee's progress toward their goals by setting minimum expectations about how often they would check in.*

7.7.4 Ongoing Support

Providing support to CITs can take on many forms from resource referral to career guidance. As previously discussed, there are numerous benefits of supportive relationships for graduate learners. Blanchard and Haccoun (2020) and other researchers identify some of these benefits including increasing retention and ease of adjustment to graduate school along with contributing to the learner's overall well-being and success. They also identify more concrete support efforts such as linking to networking opportunities and providing resources as a form of support. Faculty advisors can also display affective/emotional support for graduate learners who experience uncertainty or lack of confidence (Blanchard & Haccoun, 2020). Graduate school can be extremely stressful as learners often struggle with extracurricular stressors including problems with finances and conflicts with others (Charles et al., 2022). Therefore, emotional support may take place in numerous ways including affirmations, reassurance, encouraging words and behaviors, compassion, flexibility, and listening. However, it is important that advisors maintain a healthy balance regarding support and be careful not to become too controlling as micromanagement was found to be counterproductive (Blanchard & Haccoun, 2020). It is also important that faculty advisors recognize the importance of a comprehensive support system and take measures to ensure that learners are linked with other supports such as peers (Janta et al., 2014) along with institutional and professional supports as needed. By conducting the previously mentioned needs assessment, advisors can gain insight regarding which supports may be beneficial for CITs. Per Walker et al. (2017), advisors should maintain awareness of learner needs and identify how to help meet those needs. Faculty advisors should also communicate and collaborate with course instructors as needed to provide support to graduate learners, especially for those from underrepresented groups. Figure 7.2 offers a graphic representation of the best practices explored in this section.

Stop and Reflect: *You can engage in the ongoing support of your advisee by making time to meet with them on a consistent basis for follow up and to monitor progress. You can provide positive reinforcement, listen to their concerns, provide them with concrete plans of action, and link them to resources to support their continued enrollment in the program. You can also engage your advisee in discussion geared towards personal and professional development related to self-care; by doing so, you are promoting the building and use of skills that will benefit your advisee not only as a CIT, but as a professional counselor. Self-care is further explored in Chap.* 24.

7.7.5 Faculty Advisor's Supportive Role in Remediation When Needed

CES faculty act as gatekeepers for the counseling profession and have a duty to uphold standards. Therefore, when problematic CIT behaviors arise, educators and supervisors are compelled to intervene by implementing appropriate remediation strategies (CACREP, 2024) which are thoroughly addressed in Chap. 8. Although there are no concrete, specific instructions on how to remediate learners, Henderson and Dufrene (2017) identified several common methods of remediation including completing assignments, taking additional classes, participating in individual therapy, and meeting regularly with program faculty to monitor progress. In fact, they noted that remediation plans often required learners to meet with their advisors in addition to other faculty members. Therefore, the faculty advisor plays a crucial role in supporting CITs through remediation processes, especially regarding feedback and emotional support. Because of the role advising plays in retention efforts, remediation marks a critical point for the CIT in their academic journey as unsuccessful remediation attempts lead to dismissal.

Although many faculty members with advising responsibilities may not receive specific training on how to carry out those responsibilities, it is clear the process is necessary, especially for graduate level in CITs. Faculty advising is critical in retention efforts. The support provided is also instrumental in growth and development which is a necessary component in the transition from CIT to professional counselor. With the increase in hybrid and fully online educational programs, the need for faculty advising does not decrease. Instead, CITs enrolled in distance education may require even more supportive resources. Additionally, faculty members concerned about time constraints may also be able to utilize group advising along with individual sessions. More suggestions about advising as a part of the retention and remediation process are offered in Chap. 8.

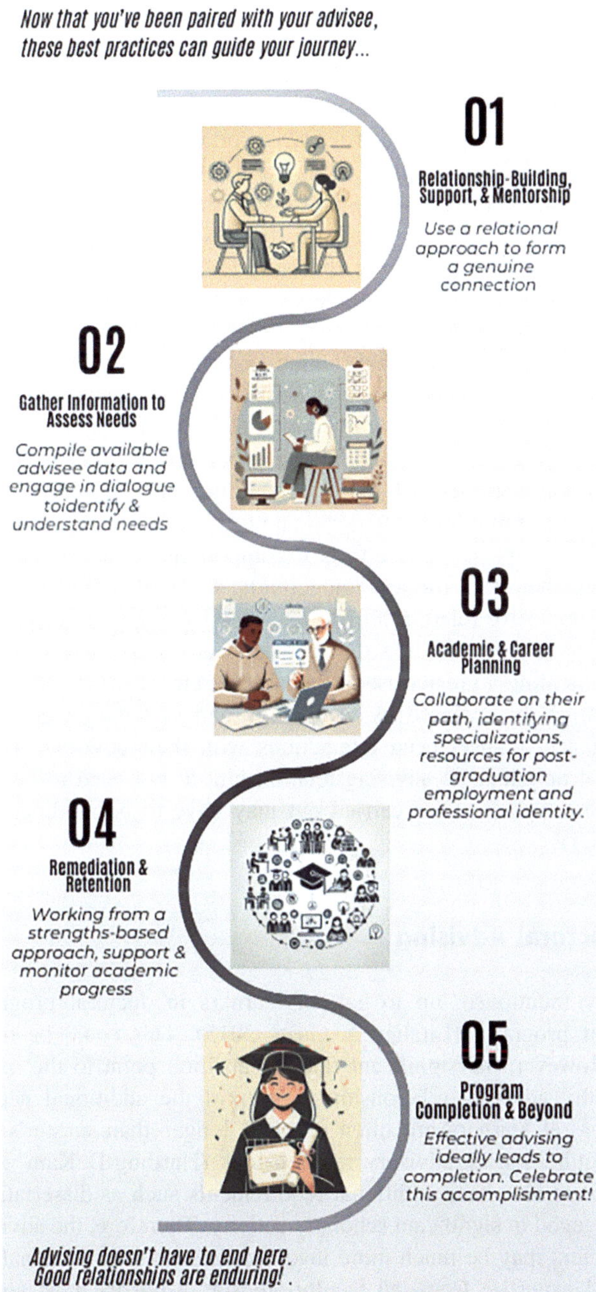

Fig. 7.2 Best practices for faculty advisement

7.7.6 E-Advising

Distance learning is an attractive option for many non-traditional learners who would otherwise be limited in opportunities to obtain their degree when face-to-face attendance is required. Examples include those with full-time jobs, limited means to travel, and other time-consuming responsibilities that do not align with rigid schedule requirements (Burns et al., 2019). Although navigating technology as a distance learner may be challenging for some, surprisingly, it is usually not the most stressful aspect of distance education for most. Instead, online learners report more challenges related to feeling disconnected, managing school along with other responsibilities outside of the classroom, and coping with overall feelings of uncertainty pertaining to academic potential and abilities (Kara et al., 2019). Additionally, having to engage with online systems more frequently than people can increase frustration. Therefore, connecting distance learners with appropriate support becomes an important way to combat attrition (Johnson et al., 2018). Distance learners need access to faculty advising perhaps even more than traditional learners due to the increased risk of not completing their program of study (Burns et al., 2019) and needing longer to acclimate to the online environment.

Faculty advisors must make efforts to support distance learners as much, if not more, than their face-to-face counterparts. CITs attending online programs need strong, supportive relationships to decrease isolation and enhance retention. Advisors may need to modify how they engage in advising activities for these CITs such as implementing a greater use of technology, etc. However, the actual human connection cannot be replaced by technology and systems (Aversa & MacCall, 2013) as distance learners need interactions with their advisors. Therefore, the components of an adequate advising relationship do not need to be reduced, but the method in which they are carried out may have to be modified to meet the needs of the CIT.

7.7.7 Doctoral Advising

As previously mentioned, up to half of learners in doctoral programs do not complete their programs (Litalien & Guay, 2015). This could be for a number of reasons. However, the significant rates of attrition point to the importance of a strong faculty advising relationship to support the additional needs of these learners. Doctoral learners are often enrolled longer than master's level learners which require longer advisory relationships (Harding-DeKam et al., 2012). Doctoral learners also have additional requirements such as dissertation and may already be engaged in significant scholarly activity. Therefore, the advising process for these learners may be much more involved and require additional knowledge, guidance, and expertise from the faculty advisor. Advisors must also recognize the unique dynamics of the power differential in advising relationships and how the use of power and authority could help or hinder learners, especially doctoral learners (Harding-DeKam et al., 2012).

7.7.8 Intersection of Advising and Mentorship

Although close bonds can be formed within the supportive nature of the faculty advising relationship, and many advisors do end up being mentors to their CITs, not all advisors automatically take on this role. Torrens et al. (2017) defines mentorship as "dyadic relationship where a senior member (mentor) guides a junior member (mentee/protégé) through formal and informal professional development experiences to help expand professional, psychosocial, political, academic, and resource-gathering skills" (p. 1). According to Lunsford (2012), mentorship involves multiple types of support including career guidance and psychosocial support. However, learners value mentoring relationships, and they have a positive impact on learner success and productivity. Conversely, poor mentorship can be detrimental. According to Santa-Ramirez (2021), "Mentors should be more personable with their advisees, provide genuine care, and build trust, rapport, and meaningful friendships while simultaneously assisting in their development as scholars and academics" (p. 8).

7.8 Conclusion

Despite ambiguity and little uniform guidance on how to provide faculty advising services, the research clearly indicates the importance of advising relationships for graduate learners. Strong faculty advising relationships have several benefits including boosting retention and fostering personal and professional development for CITs. Underrepresented and non-traditional groups particularly benefit from supportive relationships and faculty advising due to the additional unique challenges of navigating graduate school for these populations. At the heart of sufficient advising, outside of providing expertise and guidance, is a compassionate and caring disposition on the part of the advisor to foster a sense of belonging and increase confidence which is crucial to graduate school success. Thus, building relationships, gathering information about strengths, needs, and deficits, degree planning, and ongoing support are key actions in providing adequate advising services. Finally, advisors that eventually become effective mentors to their CITs positively impact success outcomes, development, and productivity.

The aim of this chapter was to define faculty advising, describe its importance in CIT retention efforts, and describe cultural factors associated with providing advising services to diverse populations. Readers should now be able to identify ways to engage in culturally competent faculty advising which includes establishing adequate rapport with CITs including understanding the unique needs and concerns of underrepresented populations, properly assessing needs and assisting with degree planning, and adequately understanding how positive mentorship adds to successful faculty advising relationships.

References

Aversa, E., & MacCall, S. (2013). Profiles in retention part 1: Design characteristics of a graduate synchronous online program. *Journal of Education for Library & Information Science Education, 54*(2), 147–161.

Bauman, D. (2018, November 14). *Hate crimes on campuses are rising new FBI data show*. Chronicle of Higher Education. https://www.chronicle.com/article/hate-crimes-on-campuses-are-rising-new-fbi-data-show/

Blanchard, C., & Haccoun, R. R. (2020). Investigating the impact of advisor support on the perceptions of graduate students. *Teaching in Higher Education, 25*(8), 1010–1027. https://doi.org/10.1080/13562517.2019.1632825

Bloom, J. L., Cuevas, A. E. P., Hall, J. W., & Evans, C. V. (2007). Graduate students' perceptions of outstanding graduate advisor characteristics. *NACADA Journal, 27*(2), 28–35. https://doi.org/10.12930/0271-9517-27.2.28

Bloom, J. L., Hutson, B. L., & He, D. Y. (2018, October 26). *What is appreciative advising? Appreciative advising*. https://www.appreciativeadvising.net

Bureau of Labor Statistics. (2014). *Persons with a disability: Labor force characteristics—2013* (Department of Labor Publication No. 14–1076).

Burns, E., Kimmel, S., & Discala, J. (2019). E-advising: Expanding advising for distance LIS students. *Journal of Library & Information Services in Distance Learning, 13*(4), 369–385. https://doi.org/10.1080/1533290X.2019.1705454

Butler, S. K., Evans, M. P., Brooks, M., Williams, C. R., & Bailey, D. F. (2013). Mentoring African American men during their postsecondary and graduate school experiences: Implications for the counseling profession. *Journal of Counseling & Development, 91*(4), 419–427. https://doi.org/10.1002/j.1556-6676.2013.00113.x

Campbell, C. D., & Evans-Campbell, T. (2011). Historical trauma and Native American child development and mental health: An overview. In M. C. Sarche, P. Spicer, P. Farrell, & H. E. Fitzgerald (Eds.), *American Indian and Alaska Native children and mental health: Development, context, prevention, and treatment* (pp. 1–25). ABC-CLIO.

Charles, S. T., Karnaze, M. M., & Leslie, F. M. (2022). Positive factors related to graduate student mental health. *Journal of American College Health, 70*(6), 1858–1866. https://doi.org/10.1080/07448481.2020.1841207

Chen, C. Y. C., Panebianco, A., & Verkuilen, J. (2021). Exploration of the experiences of sexual and gender minority students in school psychology programs. *Psychology of Sexual Orientation and Gender Diversity. Advance Online Publication, 10*(1), 44–55. https://doi.org/10.1037/sgd0000485

Christian, T. Y., & Sprinkle, J. E. (2013). College student perceptions and ideals of advising: An exploratory analysis. *College Student Journal, 47*(2), 271–291.

Council for Accreditation of Counseling and Related Educational Programs. (2024). *2024 CACREP Standards*. https://www.cacrep.org/wp-content/uploads/2024/04/2024-Standards-Combined-Version-4.11.2024.pdf

Covarrubias, R., & Fryberg, S. A. (2015). Movin' on up (to college): First-generation college students' experiences with family achievement guilt. *Cultural Diversity and Ethnic Minority Psychology, 21*(3), 420–429. https://doi.org/10.1037/a0037844

Dillon, R. K., & Fisher, B. J. (2000). Faculty as part of the advising equation: An inquiry into faculty viewpoints on advising. *NACADA Journal, 20*(1), 16–23.

Duran, A. (2019). Queer and of color: A systematic literature review on queer students of color in higher education scholarship. *Journal of Diversity in Higher Education, 12*(4), 390–400. https://doi.org/10.1037/dhe0000084

Espino, M. M. (2014). Exploring the role of community cultural wealth in graduate school access and persistence for Mexican American PhDs. *American Journal of Education, 120*(4), 545–574. https://doi.org/10.1086/676911

Evans, A. C., Levin, S., & McClain, A. (2020, August 18). *Mental-health leaders: We must end pandemic of racism*. American Psychological Association. https://www.apa.org/news/press/op-eds/end-pandemic-racism

Felder, P. P., Stevenson, H. C., & Gasman, M. (2014). Understanding race in doctoral student socialization. *International Journal of Doctoral Studies, 9*, 21–42.

Ford, J. R., Kelly, A. C., & Bloom, J. L. (2021). Challenges and opportunities: Reinventing faculty advising in the era of COVID-19. *Journal of Appreciative Education, 26*(8), 32–42.

Gardner, S. K. (2010). Contrasting the socialization experiences of doctoral students in high-and low completing departments: A qualitative analysis of disciplinary contexts at one institution. *The Journal of Higher Education, 81*(1), 61–81.

Gilmore, J., Wofford, A. M., & Maher, M. A. (2016). The flip side of the attrition coin: Faculty perceptions of factors supporting graduate student success. *International Journal of Doctoral Studies, 11*, 419–439.

Goforth, A. N., Brown, J., Machek, G., & Swaney, G. (2016). Recruitment and retention of Native American graduate students. *School Psychology Quarterly, 31*. https://doi.org/10.1037/spq0000160

Goldrick-Rab, S. (2016). *Paying the price: College costs, financial aid, and the betrayal of the American dream*. University of Chicago Press.

Gonzales, L. M., Allum, J. R., & Sowell, R. S. (2013). *Graduate enrollment and degrees: 2002 to 2012*. Council of Graduate Schools.

Haizlip, B. N. (2012). Addressing the underrepresentation of African Americans in counseling and psychology programs. *College Student Journal, 46*, 214–222.

Harborth, A. (2015). The developing role of student advising: An interview with Charlie Nutt. *Journal of Developmental Education, 39*(1), 18–20.

Harding-DeKam, J. L., Hamilton, B., & Loyd, S. (2012). The hidden curriculum of doctoral advising. *NACADA Journal, 32*(2), 5–16. https://doi.org/10.12930/0271-9517-32.2.5

He, Y., & Hutson, B. (2017). Assessment for faculty advising: Beyond the service component. *NACADA Journal, 37*(2), 66–75. https://doi.org/10.12930/NACADA-16-028

Henderson, K. L., & Dufrene, R. L. (2017). Remedial interventions used with students enrolled in counseling graduate programs. *Journal of Counselor Preparation & Supervision, 10*(1), 1–22.

Janta, H., Lugosi, P., & Brown, L. (2014). Coping with loneliness: A netnographic study of doctoral students. *Journal of Further and Higher Education, 38*(4), 553–571.

Jenkins, S. R., Belanger, A., Connally, M. L., Boals, A., & Durón, K. M. (2013). First-generation undergraduate students' social support, depression, and life satisfaction. *Journal of College Counseling, 16*(2), 129–142. https://doi.org/10.1002/j.2161-1882.2013.00032.x

Jiang, S. (2020, November). *Asian and Asian American college students' educational and career dilemmas during COVID-19: CCWT student intern report #1*. Center for Research on College-Workforce Transitions. https://ccwt.wisc.edu/wp-content/uploads/2022/04/ccwt_report_Asian-and-Asian-American-College-Students-Educational-and-Career-Dilemmas-during-COVID-19.pdf

Johnson, E., Morwane, R., Dada, S., Pretorius, G., & Lotriet, M. (2018). Adult learners' perspectives on their engagement in a hybrid learning postgraduate programme. *The Journal of Continuing Higher Education, 66*(2), 88–105.

Joy, S., Liang, X., Bilimoria, D., & Perry, S. (2015). Doctoral advisor-advisee pairing in STEM fields: Selection criteria and impact of faculty, student, and department factors. *International Journal of Doctoral Studies, 10*, 343–363.

Kamimura-Jimenez, M., & Gonzalez, J. (2018). Understanding PhD Latinx career outcomes: A case study. *Journal of Hispanic Education, 17*(2), 148–168. https://doi.org/10.1177/1538192717753037

Kara, M., Erdogdu, F., Kokoc,, M., & Cagiltay, K. (2019). Challenges faced by adult learners in online distance education: A literature review. *Open Praxis, 11*(1), 5–22. https://openpraxis.org/articles/10.5944/openpraxis.11.1.929

Key, J. (2020, August 4). *Pandemic may delay college graduation for students of color.* USCDornsife. https://dornsife.usc.edu/news/stories/3279/coronavirus-covid-19-may-delay-graduation-students-of-color/

Kulick, A., Wernick, L. J., Woodford, M. R., & Renn, K. (2017). Heterosexism, depression, and campus engagement among LGBTQ college students: Intersectional differences and opportunities for healing. *Journal of Homosexuality, 64*(8), 1125–1141.

Lee, I. H., Rojewski, J. W., Gregg, N., & Jeong, S. O. (2015). Postsecondary education persistence of adolescents with specific learning disabilities or emotional/behavioral disorders. *The Journal of Special Education, 49*, 77–88. https://doi.org/10.1177/0022466914524826

Litalien, D., & Guay, F. (2015). Dropout intentions in PhD studies: A comprehensive model based on interpersonal relationships and motivational resources. *Contemporary Educational Psychology, 41*, 218–231.

Locke, D. C., & Bailey, D. F. (2014). *Increasing multicultural understanding* (3rd ed.). Sage.

Longwell-Grice, R., Adsitt, N. Z., Mullins, K., & Serrata, W. (2016). The first ones: Three studies on first-generation college students. *NACADA Journal, 36*(2), 34–46. https://doi.org/10.12930/NACADA-13-028

Lunsford, L. (2012). Doctoral advising or mentoring? Effects on student outcomes, mentoring & tutoring. *Partnership in Learning, 20*(2), 251–270. https://doi.org/10.1080/13611267.2012.678974

Martin, J. M. (2017). It just didn't work out: Examining nonreturning students' stories about their freshman experience. *Journal of College Student Retention: Research, Theory & Practice, 19*(2), 176–198. https://doi.org/10.1177/1521025115611670

Miller, J. K., & Stone, D. J. (2011). Voices of family therapy doctoral students of color: Aspirations and factors influencing careers in academia. *Journal of Multicultural Counseling and Development, 39*, 101–113. https://doi.org/10.1002/j.2161-1912.2011.tb00144.x

Moran, T. E., Chen, C. Y. C., & Tryon, G. S. (2018). Bullying victimization, depression, and the role of protective factors among college LGBTQ students. *Journal of Community Psychology, 46*(7), 871–884. https://doi.org/10.1002/jcop.21978

National Center for Education Statistics. (2019). *Digest of Education Statistics, 2017* (NCES 2018-070). https://nces.ed.gov/fastfacts/display.asp?id60

Newman, L. A., Madaus, J. W., Lalor, A. R., & Javitz, H. S. (2021). Effect of accessing supports on higher education persistence of students with disabilities. *Journal of Diversity in Higher Education, 14*(3), 353–363. https://doi.org/10.1037/dhe0000170

Nguyen, D. J., & Herron, A. (2021). Keeping up with the Joneses or feeling priced out?: Exploring how low-income students' financial position shapes sense of belonging. *Journal of Diversity in Higher Education, 14*(3), 429–440. https://doi.org/10.1037/dhe0000191

Noy, S., & Ray, R. (2012). Graduate students' perceptions of their advisors: Is there systematic disadvantage in mentorship? *The Journal of Higher Education, 83*(6), 876–914.

Okahana, H., & Zhou, E. (2019). *Graduate enrollment and degrees: 2008–2018.* Council of Graduate Schools.

Panelo, N. (2010). The model minority: Asian American students and the relationships between acculturation to western values, family pressures and mental health concerns. *The Vermont Connection, 31*(16). https://scholarworks.uvm.edu/tvc/vol31/iss1/16

Peralta, K. J., & Klonowski, M. (2017). Examining conceptual and operational definitions of "first-generation college student" in research on retention. *Journal of College Student Development, 58*(4), 630–636.

Pollock, S. L., & Meek, G. S. (2016). What about our lesbian/gay students? Results of a survey exploring the experiences of counseling students who are lesbian and gay. *Journal of LGBT Issues in Counseling, 10*(4), 227–241. https://doi.org/10.1080/15538605.2016.1233841

Purgason, L. L., Avent, J. R., Cashwell, C. S., Jordan, M. E., & Reese, R. F. (2016). Culturally relevant advising: Applying relational-cultural theory in counselor education. *Journal of Counseling & Development, 94*(4), 429–436. https://doi.org/10.1002/jcad.12101

Ragland Woods, C. C., Chronister, K. M., Perez Grabow, A., Woods, W. E., & Woodlee, K. (2021). Racial battle fatigue: The experiences of Black/African American, Biracial Black, and Multiracial Black identified graduate students. *Journal of Black Psychology, 47*(4–5), 219–243. https://doi.org/10.1177/00957984211002615

Reid, L. M., & Dixon, A. L. (2012). The counseling supervision needs of international students in U.S. institutions of higher education: A culturally-sensitive supervision model for counselor educators. *Journal for International Counselor Education, 4*, 29–41.

Roksa, J., Feldon, D. F., & Maher, M. (2018). First-generation students in pursuit of the PhD: Comparing socialization experiences and outcomes to continuing-generation peers. *The Journal of Higher Education, 89*(5), 728–752.

Samaranayake, S., Gunawardena, A., & Meyer, R. (2023). An interactive decision support system for college degree planning. *Athens Journal of Education, 10*(1), 101–115.

Santa-Ramirez, S. (2021). Sink or swim: The mentoring experiences of Latinx PhD students with faculty of color. *Journal of Diversity in Higher Education*. https://doi.org/10.1037/dhe0000335

Schlosser, L. Z., Lyons, H. Z., Talleyrand, R. M., Kim, B. S. K., & Johnson, W. B. (2011). A multiculturally infused model of graduate advising relationships. *Journal of Career Development, 38*, 44–61.

Stout, J. G., & Wright, H. M. (2016). Lesbian, gay, bisexual, transgender, and queer students' sense of belonging in computing: An Intersectional approach. *Computing in Science & Engineering, 18*, 24–30.

Thompson-Ebanks, V. (2014). Personal factors that influence the voluntary withdrawal of undergraduates with disabilities. *Journal of Postsecondary Education and Disability, 27*(2), 195–207.

Torrens, O. D., Salinas, C., & Floyd, D. L. (2017). Examining the value of mentorship and men of color staff members of a community college. *Mentoring & Tutoring: Partnership in Learning, 25*(5), 509–527.

Trent, F., Dwiwardani, C., & Page, C. (2021). Factors impacting the retention of students of color in graduate programs: A qualitative study. *Training and Education in Professional Psychology, 15*(3), 219–229. https://doi.org/10.1037/tep0000319

Vollmo, L. R., Candelario, D. M., & Bridgeman, M. B. (2015). Development and implementation of an advising program's meet-and-greet session. *American Journal of Pharmaceutical Education, 79*(10), 150. https://doi.org/10.5688/ajpe7910150

Walker, R. V., Zelin, A. I., Behrman, C., & Strnad, R. (2017). Qualitative analysis of student perceptions: "Some advisors care. Some don't." *NACADA Journal, 37*(2), 44–54. https://doi.org/10.12930/NACADA-15-027

Yang, C., Chen, C., Chan, M., Wang, C., Luo, H., & Lin, X. (2021). Training experience in the US school psychology program: Understanding Asian international students' assets, challenges, and coping. *Contemporary School Psychology, 25*, 299–310. https://doi.org/10.1007/s40688-020-00320-x

Zhang, X., Gossett, C., Simpson, J., & Davis, R. (2019). Advising students for success in higher education: An all-out effort. *Journal of College Student Retention: Research, Theory & Practice, 21*(1), 53–77. https://doi.org/10.1177/1521025116689097

LaToya Chambers Ed.D., LPC, CAADC, CPCS (she/her/hers) is a Licensed Professional Counselor, Certified Advanced Alcohol and Drug Counselor, and Certified Professional Counselor Supervisor. She is currently a Clinical Assistant Professor in the Online Counseling Program at William & Mary. Dr. Chambers has over 15 years of experience in the fields of mental health and substance use disorders with diverse populations including active-duty service members and veterans. She has worked in a variety of settings including outpatient community clinics and the Department of the Army.

Remediation and *Gatekeeping* 8

Ali K. Corey and Devona M. Stalnaker-Shofner

Only when we're drowning do we understand how fierce our feet can kick.

Amanda Gorman

Abstract

Remediation is one of the most challenging aspects of education and training, and it is one of the most important roles of a counselor educator and supervisor. This chapter focuses on understanding remediation as a gatekeeping responsibility for counselor educators and supervisors, identifying challenges to academic success for learners, and identifying effective remediation strategies to support learner growth and professional development.

Learning Objectives After reading this chapter, you will be able to:

1. Explain the ethical aspects of learner remediation, particularly from a gatekeeping perspective, through case scenarios, discussion, and identification of relevant ethical standards and concepts.
2. Develop methods using available resources that will address common challenges to learner academic success thereby improving retention.
3. Explore strategies related to the implementation of a learner professional development plan to support their academic performance enhancement and also to mitigate factors that may pose a barrier to their academic success and program retention.

A. K. Corey (✉) · D. M. Stalnaker-Shofner
Antioch University, Yellow Springs, OH, USA
e-mail: acorey@antioch.edu

D. M. Stalnaker-Shofner
e-mail: dstalnakershofner@antioch.edu

D. M. Stalnaker-Shofner and T. N. Sapp (eds.), *A Comprehensive Guide for Counselor Education*, Springer Texts in Education, https://doi.org/10.1007/978-3-031-68358-9_8

8.1 Statement of Reflexivity

As authors who both have had experience serving in a learner support administrative role, we approach the crafting of this chapter with this experience providing a frame of reference for our shared perspective on academic support services focused on remediation and retention. It was in this capacity that we developed and refined the policies we discuss in this chapter with respect to working with learners to address gatekeeping challenges, and then pivoting away from remediation as the principal focus to a more learner-centered approach to improve program retention and academic success. Though we shared this common experience serving in this role, it is important to articulate the impact of our intersectional identities and our positionality.

Dr. Stalnaker-Shofner's principal identity is as an unapologetically Black woman. This one dominant facet of self directly impacts her other areas of intersectionality and positionality, as previously delineated in the opening of this textbook. Though there are acknowledged areas of privilege, it is her primary identity as a Black woman that has most impacted her professional experiences and the writing of this chapter.

Dr. Corey approached this chapter based on her experiences in higher education, which includes holding both faculty and administrative roles. She identifies as a White, cisgender woman, and in recognizing her positionality, she offers her background and prior experiences primarily within traditional higher educational systems that are rooted in a Eurocentric, hierarchical, and patriarchal epistemology as context for her framing of the chapter context and her approach to writing. Also integral to her intersectionality is possessing an identity that also includes being of Eastern European descent and from a low-middle socioeconomic background. In offering her acknowledgment that these identities have informed her lens as a counselor educator, and as a chapter contributor, she recognizes her ascribed privilege of race, and acquired privilege with respect to education.

8.2 Case Scenario

Beginning in the Fall semester of Beverly's second year in the program, they demonstrated professional disposition concerns related to the impact of self on others, interpersonal relationships with peers and faculty, and a lack of multicultural sensitivity. Over the course of Beverly's matriculation in your program, similar concerns were documented by program faculty. Additionally in your course, you noticed Beverly displayed academic concerns which ultimately could result in their inability to successfully complete the course. In response to the documented concerns, a meeting with Beverly, their faculty advisor, and your Program Director was held, and an initial professional development plan was developed for the following academic year. The following Fall semester, Beverly was reassessed, and it was determined that they had successfully completed all elements of the plan. By the following Spring, Beverly entered field placement. After six weeks, Beverly began missing faculty group supervision and stopped showing up at their site as scheduled, thus abandoning clients. Beverly met with their faculty advisor and the Program Director, and it was determined that additional remediation was needed. The remediation plan specified that Beverly attend all remaining group supervision meetings and maintain a consistent schedule at their site. Within one month, Beverly had missed an additional faculty group supervision meeting, and they continued to not show up at their site resulting in missed client sessions. The site was at the point where they were ready to terminate Beverly, which subsequently would impact their ability to be able to complete the program.

8.3 Introduction

Remediation is one of the least enjoyable aspects of education and training, and it is one of the most important roles of a CES. Gatekeeping in counselor education is an ethical obligation to the profession, the client, and the community. Additionally, it is a designated responsibility per the 2024 CACREP Standards that counselor education programs "have and follow a written policy for student retention, remediation, and dismissal from the program consistent with institutional policies and procedures, the counseling profession's ethical codes, and standards of practice" (CACREP, 2024, Standard 1.O). As well, the 2014 ACA *Code of Ethics* defines gatekeeping as "the initial and ongoing academic, skill, and dispositional assessment of student competency for professional practice, including remediation and termination as appropriate" (ACA, 2014, p.20). Henderson and Dufrene (2013) further specify that gatekeeping is noted twice in the ACA 2014 *Code of Ethics*, first as a directive for supervisors (F.6.b) and second as a directive for counselor educators (F.9.b); however, this still seems to not be as strident of an endorsement of its importance as discussed in Chap. 4.

For many CES', gatekeeping can be a source of significant anxiety and stress, perhaps because some institutions, agencies, and organizations do not always have clear policies regarding gatekeeping. Many programs rely on the judgment of individual educators and supervisors to enforce the ethical codes and CACREP standards when CITs present with *problems of professional competence* (Rust et al., 2013), *problematic behavior* (Kress & Protivnak, 2009), or evidence of *impairment* or *incompetence* (Gizara & Forrest, 2004). Additionally, in our professional experience, we have found that what is seen as problematic can be subjective at times, making the process murkier. Generally, members of the counseling profession focus on support and strengths rather than evaluation and consequences (Bhat, 2005; Lumadue & Duffey, 1999); thus, fulfilling the duties of a gatekeeper can be a reluctant and difficult role to navigate (Schuermann et al., 2018). In this chapter, we will share our experiences with gatekeeping punctuated by the current body of literature regarding understanding remediation as a gatekeeping responsibility for educators and supervisors. We also identify challenges to learner success and offer tips for successful remediation that not only supports learner growth and learning, but also can enhance program retention rates.

8.4 Remediation

Remediation as defined in Henderson (2010) is "a documented, procedural process that addresses observed inabilities in student performance with the intent to provide [learners] with specific means to remedy their inabilities" (p. 176). As previously noted, remediation as a form of gatekeeping is an accreditation and ethical mandate (Henderson & Dufrene, 2013). Additionally, the 2024 CACREP Standards require that programs utilize "procedures for student remediation" as a part of retention policies. Therefore, within counselor education programs, professional performance evaluation processes should be comprehensive, ongoing, and based on behaviorally specific student assessment categories (Lumadue & Duffey, 1999).

8.4.1 Behaviors Requiring Remediation

Professional disposition issues can be a significant factor for remediation. Redekop and Wlazelek (2012) define professional dispositions as "those characteristics or variables that define an effective counselor." As a new CES, addressing professional disposition issues at the course level is a necessary first step of the remediation process. Henderson (2010) offers the following suggestions for addressing professional disposition concerns: respect, multicultural acceptance, use of sound judgment, self-reflection, boundaries with others, flexibility, advocacy for self and profession, personal responsibility, and lifelong learning. Additionally, Henderson and Dufrene (2012, 2013) note the most common professional disposition issues requiring remediation are: (1) receptivity to feedback; (2) counseling skills (basic and/or advanced); (3) ethical behaviors such as boundary issues with clients, supervisors, and/or colleagues, integrity/academic honesty, and multicultural competency; (4) openness to self-examination, such as awareness of impact on self/others, self-reflective abilities, and personal responsibility; and (5) personal difficulties such as physical or mental health impairment (depression, anxiety, substance use), intrinsic characteristics (interpersonal skills, maturity, conflict management, flexibility, cooperativeness, stress management, expression and management of emotion), and financial concerns. Wolf et al. (2014) further expound on this list to define impairment in CITs as an inability or unwillingness to integrate professional standards, remove personal bias, control emotional and psychological dysfunction, and withhold personal agendas or issues while engaging in the counselor relationship with clients so as not to cause harm. They argue that as CES', we cannot separate academic from nonacademic inter- and intrapersonal issues, and we must be able to integrate these effectively within our remediation policies.

8.4.2 Common Interventions Used in Remediation

There are three primary ways that CES have historically engaged in remediation efforts to manage professional disposition concerns demonstrated by CITs, which are delineated below. The principal interventions of personal counseling, sanctioned clinical supervision, and program dismissal, are each explored in order to examine their efficacy with respect to learners' retention in the program and their academic success.

8.4.2.1 Personal Counseling

In a historical review of the literature, there is seminal research with respect to the need for and the requirement of learners to seek personal counseling within the degree program. For instance, Pope and Tabachnick (1994) identified support for the use of personal therapy by psychology graduate students as a requirement for licensure and/or as a mandate for resuming practice after violations of professional standards. Though their research primarily focused on psychologists, it is referenced in this chapter for its general applicability to all helping professions who engage in psychotherapy, including mental health counseling. In their study, about psychologists' opinions regarding mandating personal therapy, the results indicated that 70% of the participants believed that graduate and professional schools should "probably" or "absolutely" require therapy for therapists-in-training (Pope & Tabachnick, 1994). Additionally, 54% of participants believed that state licensing boards "probably" should make personal therapy a requirement for licensure, indicating the belief that personal counseling in graduate school might reduce future violations of professional standards. Moreover, 87% of participant favored enabling licensing boards to require therapists who violate professional standards to obtain therapy as a condition of continuing or resuming clinical practice (Pope & Tabachnick, 1994). The research offered by Pope and Tabachnick seems to warrant a rethinking of remediation policy and practice. Thus, the issue of mandating personal counseling as a tool for remediation to address ethical violations can serve as a foundation for the models of intervention used today.

8.4.2.2 Sanctioned Clinical Supervision

Another remediation effort used in counseling degree programs is sanctioned clinical supervision. This is a risk-management strategy to resolve professional impairment, address current ethical violations and offenses, and prevent future violations. Sanctioned supervision is defined as teaching and training that occurs through a series of meetings and over a period of time and involves counselors' disclosure of their work with clients" (Kress & Protivnak, 2009, p. 40). It is also a "systematic review of the licensee's clinical work [which] should occur with an eye toward recidivistic tendencies" (Walzer & Miltimore, 1993, p. 571).

Rapisarda and Britton (2007) proposed a model of sanctioned supervision that required the development of a process for selecting and training potential supervisors with specific guidelines for evaluation and planning, monitoring of progress, assessing the final disposition, and any further recommendations for the sanctioned professional. The strength of this model is that it critically reviews deficits in the current structure and the organization of existing sanctioning processes and provides a comprehensive and carefully reviewed corrective action plan to address ethical violations.

8.4.2.3 Dismissal

The final remedial effort used in counseling degree programs is dismissal. The decision to dismiss any learner from a counseling program is not only difficult to make but also challenging due to the possibility of the learner pursuing litigation in response to their dismissal. While it is an essential piece of gatekeeping and the final step in any unsuccessful remediation efforts, counselor educators often struggle in this area (Bradley & Post, 1991; McAdams et al., 2007; Wolf et al., 2014). While the fear of litigation is based on historical occurrence, cases such as Harris versus Blake (1986) and Keeton versus Anderson-Wiley (2011) both demonstrate that as long as due process is followed, the universities will be supported in their decision. The due process must be both substantive, not based on prejudice or performed arbitrarily, and procedural, performed with adequate notice (Wolf et al., 2014). Therefore, the implementation of effective remediation plans is essential not only to provide restorative pathways for learner academic improvement, but also to protect the program when or if dismissal is necessary.

As you reflect on the primary remediation options presented, you may find yourself questioning the multicultural appropriateness of these interventions, specifically, are they socially just? The black-and-white nature and general blanket applicability to their implementation seems to suggest that such approaches support a more colonized way of addressing remediation. As we progress through the chapter, this is an important consideration to keep under advisement, particularly as we move into exploring the structure and utility of models of remediation.

Stop and Reflect: *In the opening case scenario for this chapter, we highlighted the issues related to Beverly's need for a remediation plan. A potential remediation plan for Beverly could include interventions such as additional supervision in the form of monthly meetings with their advisor, additional multicultural training, six sessions of personal counseling, and a requirement to earn a B + or higher in all remaining courses in the degree program.*

8.5 Models for Remediation

As we begin to consider approaches to remediation that coalesce aspects of the aforementioned interventions into cohesive models, one critical framing question is: "What is the intended goal or outcomes of the utilization of this method of remediation?" Essentially, is it deficit- or strengths-based, and is the final outcome one that is not only appropriate but socially just? We propose that a strengths-based remediation model should be steeped in multicultural awareness, promote equity, and have an intended goal of supporting the learner's success through improved academic performance and/or a solid grounding in the professional dispositions of counseling practice. Below, we explore three proposed remediation models and invite you to reflect on their foundational principles and whether they integrate a DEIBASJ framework for learner support.

8.5.1 Monitoring and Dismissal Model

Frame and Stevens-Smith (1995) propose one of the first remediation processes established as a best practice for gatekeeping in counselor education. In their examination of enhanced monitoring and dismissal processes in counselor education programs, the researchers consider the concept proponed by Witmer and Young (1996) that well counselors produce well clients. The researchers reviewed the effectiveness of a monitoring and dismissal model developed by the University of Colorado at Denver's Counseling Psychology and Counselor Education Division. The essential feature of the model is the Personal Characteristics Evaluation Form, which is a 5-point Likert scale designed to assess " nine personal characteristics of ethical and competent counselors, to include: ability to be open, flexible, positive, cooperative, willing to use and accept feedback, awareness of impact on others, ability to deal with conflict, ability to accept personal responsibility, and the ability to express feelings effectively and appropriately (Frame & Stevens-Smith, 1995). In this model, learners would be assessed midterm and at the conclusion of each semester of enrollment and must obtain a rating of "3" or above in each category. If a learner receives at least one rating of *below-standard (2 or below)*, recommendations for remediation should be discussed with the assessing professor. If a learner receives more than one evaluation with a *below-standard* rating during any one semester or a *below-standard* rating from more than one professor over any two-semester time frame, then remediation or program dismissal should be discussed. Lastly, if a learner receives three or more *below-standard* ratings in one semester, the learner should meet with an advisory panel to review dismissal from the graduate program. Learner personal or professional behavior deemed grossly inappropriate or detrimental based upon your program's definition could result in dismissal from the program. In the evaluation of the effectiveness of the model, Frame and Stevens-Smith (1995) noted that 93% of learners and faculty surveyed agreed that learners monitoring was important, 81% of learners and faculty indicated their belief that faculty have an ethical responsibility to monitor learners, and 86% of the faculty reported that they had become more deliberate and intentional in their evaluation of learners' personal and professional dispositions as a result of the monitoring-dismissal process.

8.5.2 Decision-Making Model

Another remediation model is Letourneau's (2015) decision-making model which is described as "a collaborative and multi-perspectival decision-making model for addressing problematic behaviors in counseling learners" (p. 211). This seven-step model draws upon Frame and Stevens-Smith (1995) feminist model and infuses Goodrich and Shin's (2013) culturally responsive intervention, along with principles from Cottone's (2001) social constructivist ethical decision-making model. First, Step 1 is recognizing the problem. This involves identifying and gathering information from the reporting individual, faculty, supervisors, and other pertinent persons, using a multi-perspective approach. Step 2 is defining the problem. In this step, decision-makers reference ethical codes, accreditation standards, and established competencies and determine whether the learner's behaviors are aligned within these professional norms (Letourneau, 2015).

Next, Step 3 of Letourneau's (2015) model is determining potential courses of action, whereby decision-makers reference the existing body of literature for guidance in generating possible action steps. Then, in Step 4, the decision-makers choose a course of action that considers the interests of all stakeholders and gives precedence to client and learner welfare, respectively. Step 5 is the review process. This step requires the decision-makers to examine their agreed-upon course of action for "emotional, rational, cultural, and social influences" (Letourneau, 2015, p. 214). Step 6 is the implementation and evaluation process. This step involves the decision-makers acting upon the decision and observing related consequences through continual examination. Lastly, in Step 7, the decision-makers continue reflecting. They "reflect on their choices, the consequences and outcomes of those choices, and the influences of which they are aware and unaware" (Letourneau, 2015, p. 214), which may bring to light other issues or newly-arising concerns.

8.5.3 Emergent Theory of Gatekeeping

Ziomek-Daigle and Christensen (2010) constructed the afore-named approach as a multi-phasic gatekeeping process. Phase 1 is the pre-admission screening. During this phase, applicants' academic aptitude is assessed by a records review, and their interpersonal skills are evaluated through individual and/or group interviews. Phase 2, or post-admission screening, involves continual evaluation of learners' academic aptitude and interpersonal skills. This evaluation is based on learners' academic performance within the program-culminating exams like the Counselor Preparation Comprehensive Examination (CPCE), and professional dispositions. During Phase 3, the remediation plan is developed when learners present with academic struggles requiring additional support and assistance to facilitate success. This may involve intensified supervision (e.g., additional monitoring, repeating coursework), and personal development (e.g., personal counseling, leave of absence). Lastly, Phase 4, or remediation outcome, looks at three categories of possible outcomes and related measures for each: *successful, unsuccessful,* and *indifferent/*

neutral. A successful outcome utilizes the foundational strengths-based philosophy of counseling, and the resolution to the remediation involves facilitating the learner's academic and professional growth such that they are ultimately able to complete their studies and transition to professional practice as a counselor. An unsuccessful outcome would again be grounded in a strengths-based approach; however, efforts to intervene and return the learner to solid academic standing have not yielded that intended outcome. This could ultimately mean dismissal from the degree program. Lastly, an indifferent/neutral outcome involves indication that the remediation plan yielded marginal results. This may be due to a number of factors; however, the research supports the impact of barriers that may have impeded progress. Examples include managing multiple roles and responsibilities that may at times result in constraints on time, ability to engage, and overall wellness. It is at this point that one as the CES may want to consider incorporating revisions to the plan that address potential barriers to success.

8.6 A Model for Professional Gatekeeping and Learner Remediation

Considering the case scenario presented at the beginning of the chapter, there is a need for a comprehensive approach to identifying and remediating problematic behavior in learners. In accordance with current CACREP standards and ACA ethical guidelines, a review process should be developed and implemented within the program. To address these issues, we recommend the following model:

1. Faculty or program administration will identify learners exhibiting academic and professional disposition concerns and record these concerns. This could be done using a specifically developed form or by similar means to capture that data.
2. Designate committee (e.g. academic success committee) and a person who will serve as chair. They will as a team review the documented concerns and facilitate a faculty panel discussion of the identified concern(s).
3. If warranted, a formal Academic Review Meeting will be held, and the Program Director notified. During this meeting, the concerns are noted with the learner and advisor, and a Professional Development Plan (PDP) is created.
4. The committee chair and the learner's faculty advisor will monitor the learner's progress and follow-up accordingly, ideally to achieve a satisfactory resolution (i.e., plan completed, revisions needed, an escalation to meet with the Program Director, or dismissal if warranted).

8.6.1 Suggestions for Model Implementation

Next, we offer a few guidelines for implementing this model. While these guidelines are provided as a process, you may use these within your program as you see fit. We propose that there be a designated member of the committee who will provide guidance and continued monitoring and tracking of learner referrals and implemented plans. Additionally, they will serve as the point of contact between the program administration and committee. This is aligned with the requirements captured in the 2024 CACREP Standards, specifically that throughout a student's program, faculty and program administration are required to document student who present with academic, clinical, or disposition concerns (CACREP, 2024, Standard 2.C.1.e, 2.C.2.c.).

To address the mandate for documentation, the noted learner concerns could be formally recorded in a form specifically designed to capture and track such reports. The completed form then becomes a part of the learner's academic file. The committee will review the form, and if after identifying the presenting issue(s) it is determined that a more formal meeting is required, the committee will subsequently notify the learner to request a formal meeting. The Program Director will also be apprised of the committee's decision.

In the Academic Review Meeting, all documented academic, clinical, and/or dispositional concerns will be of focus. The participants in this formal meeting include the learner, the committee chair, and the learner's faculty advisor (who can also serve as the learner's advocate). Additionally, any other relevant supporting personnel such as representatives from the Office of Disability Services or other academic support professionals, can be invited to the meeting. The purpose of the meeting is to review the documented concerns as well as any related issues, and to subsequently establish criteria for remediation. The potential outcomes could include placement on academic review status with a clear PDP, up to a recommendation for program dismissal. Additionally, the committee will work with the learner to identify barriers to success. As a result of this meeting and in collaboration with the learner, a developmental plan will be created which delineates the requisite steps that the learner must take to return to a satisfactory standing in the program and/or with the university. The plan should be placed in the learner's record, and the committee chair and/or the faculty advisor will monitor learner adherence to the plan. If any part of the agreed-upon plan is not fulfilled, the committee chair has the option to recommend interventions that could include a revised PDP that involves more progressive remediation up to potential dismissal from the program.

While most learner concerns may be addressed in this process, there are more egregious offenses or ethical violations that will require immediate intervention. In these cases, the learner may bypass the faculty panel and meet with the Program Director. Examples of such offenses include blatant academic dishonesty, a breach of confidentiality, and boundary violations that result in harm to the client. Figure 8.1 provides an illustrative graphic summarizing the major points of this section.

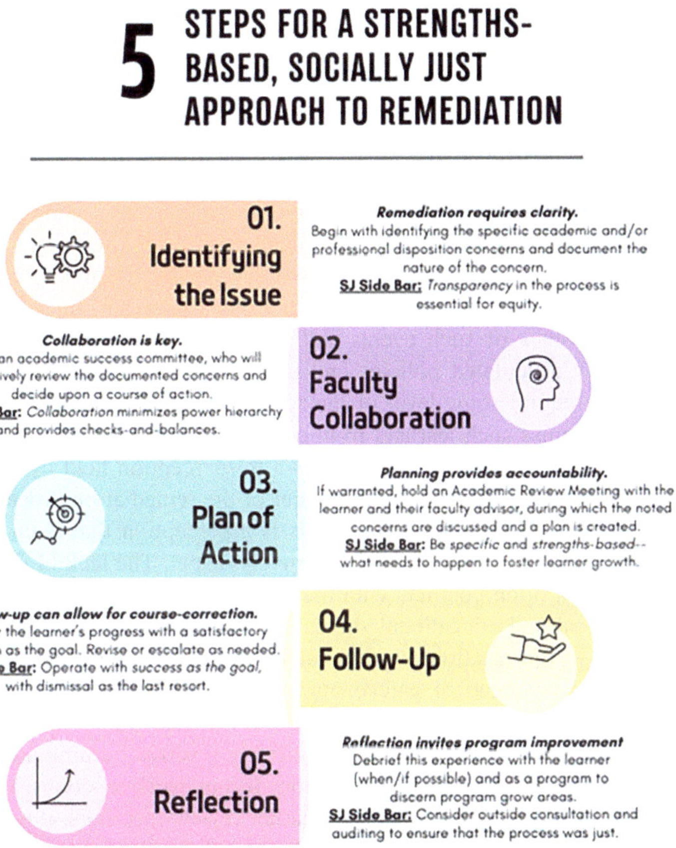

Fig. 8.1 Strengths-Based, Socially-Just Approach to Remediation

Stop and Reflect: *In the opening case scenario, Beverly met with the committee chair and PD to discuss a remediation plan. Beverly's progress on the plan will be monitored by the committee chair, in conjunction with their faculty academic advisor. If there is an additional concern identified while Beverly is in remediation, or if they are not meeting the plan's delineated and mutually agreed upon interventions, then the committee chair could make a follow-up recommendation in consultation with the advisor and other committee members. This could include Beverly's dismissal from the program. As you consider the role of gatekeeping through remediation, what other factors might you want to consider as you craft the plan?*

8.7 Conclusion

According to McAdams et al. (2007), counselor educators must actively engage in gatekeeping as a function of their role. Consistent with the extant literature (Brear & Dorrian, 2010; Dugger & Francis, 2014; Foster & McAdams, 2009), gatekeeping is emphasized as "a chief ethical responsibility of the profession, intended to prevent client harm, ensure counselor competence, and uphold accreditation and licensure standards" (Schuermann et al., 2018, p. 62). Furthermore, Ziomek-Daigle and Christensen (2010) note that despite the unknowns related to learner remediation and potential dismissal from a program, there is no way to predict the outcomes of such events and processes. Thus, there is a significant need for clearly articulated policies and procedures to address learners of concern who may require some level of intervention to either promote success or to appropriately dismiss such learners from counseling programs.

It is also important to note that there is a misperception held by learners (and even some faculty) of the purpose and intent of the remediation process, which is viewed as punitive and demoralizing. This is a perception that counselor educators and program administration need to actively dispel. The lack of understanding about remediation often conflicts with the actual gatekeeping responsibilities proscribed by ethical and educational standards. Schuermann et al. (2018) note that learners who see remediation as punishment; however, when learners were educated about and informed of gatekeeping procedures, they were more likely to view remediation in a more positive light and as a critical part of their professional and educational growth. We concur that utilizing positive framing and supportive efforts may help to mitigate this perception. In our work as counselor educators with the administrative role of chairing learner review meetings, it was our experience that learners once educated about the remediation process and its intended purpose, were able to actively engage in the remediation process from a more proactive stance. Further, in collaboration with faculty, learners were able to be their own best advocates by identifying supports they may need as well as potential obstacles and barriers impeding their learning and professional development. It seems important to end this chapter with a note that counselor educators are *counselors* at heart and that denotes deep caring, compassion, and a belief in the capacity of people to change and grow. It is this same caring spirit that needs to be projected to learners who are most vulnerable and in need.

References

American Counseling Association. (2014). 2014 ACA Code of Ethics. https://www.counseling.org/docs/default-source/default-document-library/ethics/2014-aca-code-of-ethics.pdf?sfvrsn=55ab73d0_1

Bhat, C. S. (2005). Enhancing counseling gatekeeping with performance appraisal protocols. *International Journal for the Advancement of Counselling, 27*, 399–411.

Bradley, J., & Post, P. (1991). Impaired learners: Do we eliminate them from counselor education programs? *Counselor Education and Supervision, 31*(2), 100–108. https://doi.org/10.1002/j.1556-6978.1991.tb00148

Brear, P., & Dorrian, J. (2010). Gatekeeping or gate slippage? A national survey of counseling educators in Australian undergraduate and postgraduate academic training programs. *Training and Education in Professional Psychology, 4*, 264–273. https://doi.org/10.1037/a0020714

Cottone, R. R. (2001). A social constructivism model of ethical decision making in counseling. *Journal of Counseling & Development, 79*(1), 39–45.

Council for Accreditation of Counseling and Related Educational Programs. (2024). *2024 CACREP Standards*. https://www.cacrep.org/wp-content/uploads/2024/04/2024-Standards-Combined-Version-4.11.2024.pdf

Dugger, S. M., & Francis, P. C. (2014). Surviving a lawsuit against a counseling program: Lessons learned from Ward v. Wilbanks. *Journal of Counseling & Development, 92*, 135–141. https://doi.org/10.1002/j.1556-6676.2014.00139.x

Foster, V. A., & McAdams, C. R., III. (2009). A framework for creating a climate of transparency for professional performance assessment: Fostering learner investment in gatekeeping. *Counselor Education and Supervision, 48*, 271–284. https://doi.org/10.1002/j.1556-6978.2009.tb00080.x

Frame, M. W., & Stevens-Smith, P. (1995). Out of harm's way: Enhancing monitoring and dismissal processes in counselor education programs. *Counselor Education and Supervision, 35*, 118–129. https://doi.org/10.1002/j.1556-6978.1995.tb00216.x

Gizara, S. S., & Forrest, L. (2004). Supervisors' experiences of trainee impairment and incompetence at APA-accredited internship sites. *Professional Psychology: Research and Practice, 35*, 131–140.

Goodrich, K. M., & Shin, R. Q. (2013). A culturally responsive intervention for addressing problematic behaviors in counseling students. *Counselor Education and Supervision, 52*, 43–55. https://doi.org/10.1002/j.1556-6978.2013.00027.x

Henderson, K. L. (2010). The remediation of learners in counseling graduate programs: Behavioral indicators, terminology, and interventions (Doctoral dissertation). Retrieved from https://scholarworks.uno.edu/td.

Henderson, K. L., & Dufrene, R. L. (2012). Learner behaviors associated with remediation: A content analysis. *Counseling Outcome Research and Evaluation, 3(1)*, 48–60. https://doi.org/10.1177/2150137812437364

Henderson, K. L., & Dufrene, R. L. (2013). Learner behaviors and remediation: An empirical study. *Journal of Professional Counseling: Practice, Theory, and Research, 40*(2), 2–14.

Kress, V. E., & Protivnak, J. J. (2009). Professional development plans to remedy problematic counseling student behaviors. *Counselor Education and Supervision, 48*, 154–166. https://doi.org/10.1002/j.1556-6978.2009.tb00071.x

Letourneau, J. L. H. (2015). A decision-making model for addressing problematic behaviors in counseling learners. *Counseling and Values, 61*, 206–222. https://doi.org/10.1002/cvj.12038

Lumadue, C. A., & Duffey, T. H. (1999). The role of graduate programs as gatekeepers: A model for evaluating student counselor competence. *Counselor Education and Supervision, 39*(2), 101–109.

McAdams, C. R., III., Foster, V. A., & Ward, T. J. (2007). Remediation and dismissal policies in counselor education: Lessons learned from a challenge in federal court. *Counselor Education and Supervision, 46*, 212–229. https://doi.org/10.1002/j.1556-6978.2007.tb00034.x

Pope, K. S., & Tabachnick, B. G. (1994). Therapists as patients: A national survey of psychologists' experiences, problems, and beliefs. *Professional Psychology: Research and Practice, 25*(3), 247–258.

Rapisarda, C. A., & Britton, P. J. (2007). Sanctioned supervision: Voices from the experts. *Journal of Mental Health Counseling, 29*(1), 81–92.

Redekop, F., & Wlazelek, B. (2012). Counselor dispositions: An added dimension for admission decisions. *Ideas and research you can use: VISTAS 2012.*

Rust, J. P., Raskin, J. D., & Hill, M. S. (2013). Problems of professional competence among counselor trainees: Programmatic issues and guidelines. *Counselor Education and Supervision, 52*, 30–42. https://doi.org/10.1002/j.1556-6978.2013.00026.x
Schuermann, H., Avent Harris, J. R., & Lloyd-Hazlett, J. (2018). Academic role and perceptions of gatekeeping in counselor education. *Counselor Education and Supervision, 57*, 51–65. https://doi.org/10.1002/ceas.12093
Walzer, R. S., & Miltimore, S. (1993). Mandated supervision: Monitoring and therapy of disciplined health care professionals. *Journal of Legal Medicine, 14*, 565–596. https://doi.org/10.1080/01947649309510930
Witmer, J. M., & Young, M. E. (1996). Preventing counselor impairment: A wellness approach. *Journal of Humanistic Education and Development, 34*(3), 141–155.
Wolf, M. R., Green, S. A., Nochajski, T. H., & Kost, K. A. (2014). Graduate learner impairment: The impact on counselor training programs. *Journal for International Counselor Education, 6*, 61–74.
Ziomek-Daigle, J., & Christensen, T. M. (2010). An emergent theory of gatekeeping practices in counselor education. *Journal of Counseling and Development, 88*, 407–415.

Ali K. Corey, Ph.D., LMHC is an Associate Professor at Antioch University, School of Counseling, Psychology, and Therapy. She has been a counselor educator for more than 10 years, and in professional practice as a licensed counselor for almost 20 years. Her clinical experience has been primarily with children and adolescents, her leadership work has included program development and expansion, and her scholarship has focused on leadership development for counselors and counselor educators.

Devona M. Stalnaker-Shofner, EdD, LPC, NCC, MHP, SAP is an Associate Professor at Antioch University, School of Counseling, Psychology, and Therapy. She has been a counselor educator for more than 10 years, and in professional practice as a licensed counselor for more than 20 years. Her clinical experience includes providing individual, group, and couples and family counseling to clients presenting with treatment concerns such as depression, anxiety, trauma, as well as substance use, addiction, and recovery. She also provides clinical supervision to counselors-in-training and new counseling professionals. Dr. Stalnaker-Shofner has served in various leadership roles within the counseling and counselor education professions. Her research and scholarship includes numerous presentations at state, regional, national, and international conferences, as well as related publications. As a trainer, she has provided workshops on racial trauma and BIPOC mental health and wellness, and the decolonization of curriculum, teaching praxis, and educational policies to disrupt oppression and promote diversity, equity, inclusion, and access. Additionally, she serves as an educational and organizational consultant advising on implementing antiracist and social justice practices for leaders and organizational policies and culture.

Part III

Navigating Higher Education

Common Pitfalls for New Counselor Educators and How to Prevent Them

9

Tanisha N. Sapp, Wendy Robinson, and Latasha Matthews

You should never view your challenges as a disadvantage. Instead, it's important for you to understand that your experience facing and overcoming adversity is actually one of your biggest advantages.

Michelle Obama

Abstract

This chapter provides practical guidance for six common pitfalls experienced by new counselor educators and supervisors. Examples include burnout, boundary setting, self-care, gatekeeping, and navigating complaints made by CITs.

Learning Objectives After reading this chapter, you will be able to:

1 Identify the common pitfalls experienced by CES faculty in higher education.
2 Appraise how burnout is experienced by counselor educators, factors contributing to its development, as well as how to mitigate the related symptoms when they arise.
3 Outline the areas of vulnerability and susceptibility for counselor educators to experience the challenges of common pitfalls.

T. N. Sapp (✉) · W. Robinson
Liberty University, Lynchburg, VA, USA
e-mail: tsapp6@liberty.edu; cestextbookemail@gmail.com

W. Robinson
e-mail: wrobinson54@liberty.edu

L. Matthews
Illumination Counseling and Coaching, Lawrenceville, GA, USA
e-mail: info@illuminationcc.com

D. M. Stalnaker-Shofner and T. N. Sapp (eds.), *A Comprehensive Guide for Counselor Education*, Springer Texts in Education, https://doi.org/10.1007/978-3-031-68358-9_9

9.1 Statement of Reflexivity

We approach this chapter with a degree of humility and vulnerability. While we recognize we do not know everything about the subject matter, we also recognize our collective experiences, including the pitfalls associated with them. We also recognize the cultural implications of practice and the blind spots we each carry. Careful attention was given to reduce author bias while still acknowledging the lived experiences to maintain the integrity of the chapter.

We also recognize the cultural implications of practice and the blind spots we each carry. We felt this was important to address, given that this book was written in a double pandemic. Additionally, we recognize that this chapter is written through the eyes of inherent privilege and based on a foundation of systemic oppression. We recognize our privilege as counselor educators and scholar practitioners among the different intersections that encompass our counselor identities. Dr. Tanisha N. Sapp and Ms. Latasha Matthews are African American cis-gender female counselor educators and supervisors. Dr. Wendy Robinson is a White, cis-gender female counselor educator and supervisor. Drs. Sapp and Robinson both currently serve as core faculty members at a faith based Predominantly White Institution (PWI). Additionally, Ms. Matthews is currently an adjunct professor at a faith based PWI. Each author has their own unique experiences as being the student, educator, and site supervisor, which allows us the opportunity to address these roles and identified perspectives. Additionally, both Dr. Sapp and Ms. Matthews graduated from online programs. While Dr. Robinson graduated from an on-campus program, each author has extensive training and experience with teaching in online programs and utilizing technology in counseling, education, and supervision. Thus, careful attention was given to reduce author bias while still acknowledging the lived experiences to maintain the integrity of the chapter.

This chapter's intention was to focus on the educator while differentiating the supervisor's role and respecting the differences among counselor preparation and education programs. Additionally, we aimed to be honest in providing a truthful experience. This was done with careful consideration to preserve the integrity of the educator, program, and institution. It was our intent to maintain the profession's standards while reaffirming the importance of gatekeeping through a multicultural lens.

9.2 Introduction

As CES, it is a matter of when pitfalls will happen, not a matter of if they will happen. This chapter explores various pitfalls that future counselor educators may experience through the lens of current CES and each scenario should be explored with humility. It is important to note that this chapter is rooted in the empathy that is inherent in being a counselor and CES. Within each scenario, CES are provided with three possible solutions to approach the situation with the requisite humility and vulnerability. These potential solutions are depicted as *Pocket Solutions* and illustrated throughout the chapter. While the pitfalls are numbered, they are not ranked or presented in any particular order of importance.

9.2.1 Pitfall #1

CES' have the honor and pleasure of impacting lives in our clinical practices and with CITs by teaching, supervising, and providing critical feedback that will help shape them as future counselors. Oftentimes while wearing multiple hats, CES' tend to forget the importance of setting boundaries and limits that align with the 2014 ACA *code of ethics* and known best practices for supervisors, mentorship, and overall wellness. Consider the following scenario:

You are excited about the contributions you have been making as an adjunct professor teaching field placement courses over the last 5 years. You are proud that you have recently secured a contract with your third university. After signing your contract with your newest university, you thought "how will I balance teaching at three universities while running a group practice?" Because you are an adjunct, you assumed that you would have more flexibility. You enjoy your roles as a practice owner, counselor, and counselor educator; however, you are finding it very difficult to stay on top of the grading and support for CITs and your practice. Lately you find yourself always tired, cranky, and anxious. You also notice that you are feeling more stressed than usual. When asked to teach an additional course at one of your other universities, you gladly accept it and rationalize your choice by saying "it won't always be stressful and busy. Once I pay off my debt and secure a full-time position, I won't have to take on so many classes". You recognize that you have always had a difficult time saying no to others, and you don't want people to think you can't handle your responsibilities. You are embarrassed and fearful about sharing your concerns with others in the counseling departments because you do not believe they will understand.

9.2.1.1 Discussion

In the above scenario, the CES demonstrates poor boundaries and self-care. As the counselor educator added more universities to their workload, they became increasingly overwhelmed and questioned how they would balance their practice and teaching. It is important for CES' to be aware of the balance needed to manage teaching and provide support for clients. The Code of Ethics does not explicitly reference limits around this topic; however, failure to maintain balance can result in the counselor educator experiencing problems with professional competency. The 2014 ACA *Code of Ethics* states in standard C.2.g:

> Counselors monitor themselves for signs of impairment from their own physical, mental, or emotional problems and refrain from offering or providing professional services when impaired. They seek assistance for problems that reach the level of professional impairment, and, if necessary, they limit, suspend, or terminate their professional responsibilities until it is determined that they may safely resume their work. Counselors assist colleagues or supervisors in recognizing their own professional impairment and provide consultation and assistance when warranted with colleagues or supervisors showing signs of impairment and intervene as appropriate to prevent imminent harm to clients (p.9).

In the scenario, the CES displays signs of problems with professional competency due to a lack of managing their own wellness demonstrated by being tired, stressed and anxious. The CES inability to establish professional work boundaries may negatively impact one's ability to build and maintain relationships with the CITs they serve. To address this concern, the CES first must have awareness of professional competency problem(s). This can be challenging so it is beneficial to establish early before challenges in the CES career to identify colleagues that are honest to assist you when something seems to be off. Then you must be open and willing to receive consultation to examine boundary setting, which may include specific guidance on how to balance both roles effectively.

Additionally, the CES in the scenario above has difficulties saying no due to fear of appearing incompetent. This fear impedes the CES' willingness to say no and seek support from peers or supervisors, which may increase incompetency in the CES that they are attempting to avoid. If you are unable to set boundaries, you will have a difficult time setting realistic expectations for yourself which can be a detriment to your ability to meet professional expectations. This will not change with a full-time position.

Before we can adequately take care of ourselves, we must first know ourselves to identify and understand our individual needs. The dimension of wellness highlights the importance of examining physical, social, intellectual, vocational, spiritual, and emotional wellness (Myers & Sweeney, 2005). It is important for CES to identify growth areas that could positively impact their efficacy in this role. Thus, the importance of developing strategies to help you set limits and establish boundaries by creating a schedule that highlights dedicated time to grade, meet with CITs, and participate and engage in wellness.

The CES could benefit from tools that help with organization and productivity. Project management tools such as Asana, Trello and Zoho Projects could be useful resources to help CES manage tasks, time and projects. In addition, using bullet journals, business planners, and the university calendar could help the CES track when assignments are due at each university. Lastly, working with a mentor, coach, or gaining department support can provide accountability and help you prioritize tasks while also reducing the stress of your workload.

Finally, seeking counseling to help you explore the factors that contribute to your difficulties with setting boundaries. Personal counseling would be beneficial to help CES have greater self-acceptance and the ability to change and uncover self-defeating thoughts, habits, and behaviors. In the above scenario, the CES stated that they were embarrassed and fearful about sharing their concerns with others in the counseling departments because they did not believe they would understand. Personal counseling would allow CES the safety to express and manage emotions. Counseling would also uncover any unresolved issues with depression and anxiety with which the CES is experiencing.

9.2.1.2 Pocket Solutions

Here are three possible solutions to address common pitfalls related to boundaries, help-seeking behaviors, and potential problems with professional competency (see Fig. 9.1).

9.2.2 Pitfall #2

Fear is a major pitfall for the new CES. Counselor educators set high expectations for themselves in an effort to manage all aspects of their new role. Often, fear manifests from one's core beliefs surrounding perfectionism and how we *should* be as a new CES. For example, a CES *should* be able to effectively manage all elements of their role. In general, counselors believe they must be strong and *should* be able to put their experiences to the side to help others. There may

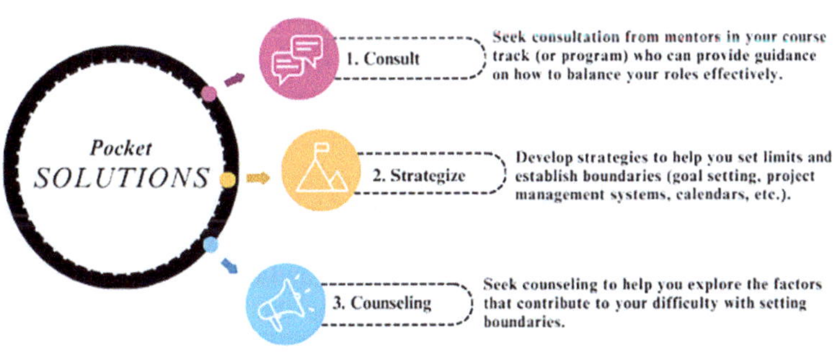

Fig. 9.1 Possible solutions for Pitfall #1

be fears of perceived judgment from administration and colleagues. Consider the following scenario:

You were recently hired as CES in your first full-time CORE faculty position. You are in your first semester of the academic year and learning the expectations of your new role along with the culture of the university and department. You are expected to teach a full course load while maintaining an active research agenda. Additionally, it is conference season, and you are presenting at three conferences. Also, you learned that there are additional departmental responsibilities that you are required to support, such as academic advising and admissions. In the middle of the semester, you experienced a family emergency that required your immediate attention. You struggled with balancing your family's emergent needs and your own anxiety related to it. As a new faculty member wanting to prove yourself and feeling uncertain about the department culture, you decide to brute force your way through the semester and refuse to solicit support out of fear of being perceived as weak and incompetent. As a result, your personal mental health and professional work begin to decline and as your self-doubt increases, you begin to lose passion for the profession.

9.2.2.1 Discussion

BIPOC faculty members in the field of counselor education navigate a unique set of experiences that encompass cultural, social-political, and vulnerabilities. As a new counselor educator, they often bring a wealth of diverse perspectives and backgrounds, enriching the learning environment for both CITs and colleagues. The educators may face challenges related to cultural representation and inclusion with academic settings, striving to bridge gaps and create an inclusive space for all. Socio-political factors can also play a significant role, as BIPOC faculty encounter systemic barriers or biases that impact their professional journey. Vulnerabilities, including the potential for microaggressions or stereotypes, may add an extra layer of complexity to their roles. However, their experiences contribute invaluable insights to the counseling landscape, fostering a more comprehensive understanding of diverse cultural nuances and the impact of social-political dynamics on mental health practices.

Reality check! Everyone has different seasons of challenges in life that require an evaluation of their work responsibilities (i.e., significant loss, too much on their plate, positive changes such as starting a new CES role, etc.). The CES in the above scenario is no different. Both positive and negative events may create stress that requires a new CES to seek consultation from a colleague or supervisor. While negative events such as family loss are often easier to navigate, positive events such as a new addition to the family or a leadership role in a professional organization may be harder to approach. However, stress triggered by positive and negative changes present challenges to balancing self-care and one's responsibilities.

Another compounding aspect to this pitfall is the belief that a CES should not be vulnerable in a professional environment. Subsequently, this belief may be reinforced by the department's culture, which requires navigating a balance of departmental expectations and your personal needs and beliefs.

Reality check! First, there may be a need to determine if this is a perceived belief or a reality of your university or program culture. If your university culture does not permit or encourage vulnerability, you would need to evaluate the next steps. One way to approach the issue is to engage in consultation. Solicit support from a seasoned faculty member that you deem objective to explore the differences between perceived versus rational beliefs on this message. Second, you are strongly encouraged to have difficult conversations with your department leadership to advocate for yourself. Taking risks is difficult for everyone, although learning to advocate for yourself is necessary to maintain job satisfaction, job efficacy and decrease the potential for burnout and fatigue. Third, your presentation of the concerns may impact your administration's reception to the identified issues. Therefore, you are encouraged to be prepared with facts and know what you want to gain from the conversation. While collaboration is good, your administration will need you to have reasonable solutions for their consideration. Questions or solutions to consider may include: Is there an ability to teach one less course for your teaching load and add an additional course next term? Did "I" take on too much, or do I need to release a responsibility (e.g. an upcoming presentation or committee commitment)? Do you have what you need currently, and can you ask for it specifically? The answer may be no, although you may never know if you do not ask. There may be a solution of which you are unaware, and by not taking the risk of having the conversation you could have missed the opportunity to receive support.

The next area to consider is not saying "no" when necessary and warranted. Learning how to set boundaries and the value of saying "no" is vital to longevity in effectiveness in your new role. One way you can set healthy boundaries in your new CES position is to determine if the expectations on your list are required by your administration or self-imposed. Self-imposed expectations can be fueled by your own desire to be viewed as competent without giving yourself permission to learn and grow in your new role. These may be irrational beliefs that need to be identified and explored in supervision and/or your own personal counseling.

On the other hand, there may be an underlying cultural norm in your counseling department that you may need to consider while learning to set healthy boundaries. One example is the belief that if you say "no" to a request, then you may not receive additional opportunities such as being able to teach your desired courses or having access to additional financial incentives. Therefore, as a new CES, you will need to be able to weigh the risks and benefits associated with setting healthy boundaries.

The final area to address is the lack of a wellness plan prior to starting the new role as a CES. There is a lot of talk about self-care and wellness, in fact, we address this in greater detail in Chap. 24. While counselors know the importance of self-care and wellness theoretically, the reality is that many counselors often do not take their own advice and forego wellness as a requisite. We believe that a wellness plan needs to be created within the doctoral program and reviewed and updated as necessary throughout your career. It is not a matter *of if,* but *when* a counselor educator becomes overwhelmed, stressed, burned out, fatigued, etc.

Therefore, having a wellness plan along with self-care strategies in place may mitigate the impact of these stressors. While it is important to cover foundational needs such as exercise, sleep, eating, etc., maybe more vital is identifying and engaging a support system. In fact, Myers and Sweeney (2005) indicate that having social support is the strongest predictor of wellness. A support system may be friends or professional colleagues. Additionally, it is strongly recommended that you have a personal counselor who is objective and will call you out on your *stuff*. Yes, we all have our *stuff*, and this does not go away. However, it may change as you grow in your professional identity. Lastly, find someone who will encourage and support you, and more importantly someone who will help you identify and challenge your blind spots. We all have them, and they are often what gets in our own way.

9.2.2.2 Pocket Solutions

Here are three possible solutions to address common pitfalls related to balancing expectations, fear and vulnerability (see Fig. 9.2).

9.2.3 Pitfall #3

CES are responsible to ensure that CITs are professionally competent to meet and maintain professional ethical standards. This is achieved through assurance that the CIT is equipped, prepared along with effectively assessing and evaluating CITs counseling skills and disposition toward the counseling professional Gatekeeping is a vital part of the CES role (ACA, 2014) that was explored in more detail in Chap. 8.

You have been teaching for many years and have a good reputation with CITs and staff. Currently, you have a CIT in your internship class that is preparing to graduate at the end of the semester. The CIT is struggling with their ability to set boundaries with their clients on a consistent basis. Throughout the semester, you have spoken with the CITs about the importance of boundary-setting and you believe that they

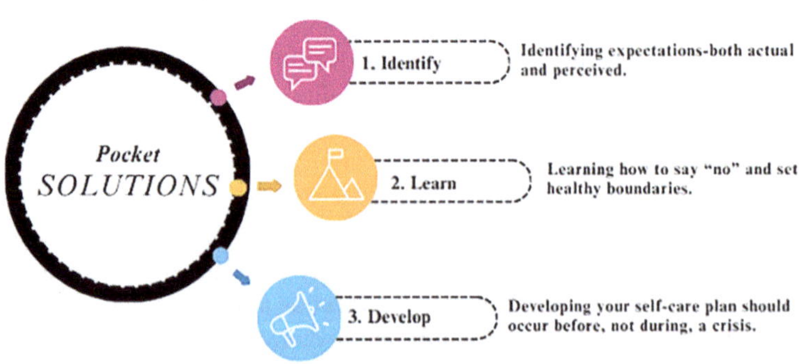

Fig. 9.2 Possible solutions for Pitfall #2

will eventually learn this skill. Therefore, you decide not to take any formal action or develop a remediation plan. Although the CIT's behaviors do not change, you remain quiet and convince yourself that speaking up now would ruin your great reputation at your institution.

9.2.3.1 Discussion

In the scenario above, the CES is engaging in gateslipping. Gateslipping occurs when the CES is aware that the CIT is not meeting professional standards though the CES is choosing not to take steps to remediate the deficiencies. Further, the CES in this scenario is "hopeful" the CIT issue will eventually work itself out, yet there is no plan to create change. In addition, the CIT has not demonstrated any progress in mitigating the issue from previous discussions. Lastly, and the most important issue in this scenario is the CES choosing to avoid addressing the issue to protect their own reputation.

You may examine this situation and quickly conclude that you would never do this, and maybe you would not. Though there could be many barriers for the CES that result in gate slipping such as personal factors, department culture, etc. Regardless of the reasons, avoidance of addressing the CIT and creating a plan to modify the ineffectiveness of the CIT counseling skills and disposition is unethical.

As a result of the CES unwillingness to take formal action, the CIT will enter the profession unequipped and ethically challenged. This is unfair and a disservice to CIT and their future clients. Therefore, direct and constructive feedback is necessary for the CES to promote competency along with documentation. When the CIT is not demonstrating an ability to receive feedback and apply adequately, then the CES needs to take the next steps identified within the department's academic policies for evaluation of formal intervention such as remediation.

Assumptions are often made of CES that they know how to effectively communicate difficult content. However, this may not be true, so it is reasonable and encouraged to solicit support through a mentor, colleague or department administrator to process and create a plan on how to best address the concerns. Asking for help does not equate to incompetence. Actually, the opposite is true that knowing growth areas and seeking help is indicative of a competent professional so ask.

Lastly, personal factors may contribute to the CES lack of willingness to challenge and require the CIT to demonstrate the necessary changes. Imposter syndrome is a legitimate issue for a lot of professionals, and it does not discriminate against novice or seasoned CES. People pleasing is another barrier to effectively guide and direct CITs, and therefore needs to be addressed as a growth area for the CES. These personal factors may need more support than work colleagues can provide, so seeking one's own counseling is beneficial.

9.2.3.2 Pocket Solutions

Here are three possible solutions to address common pitfalls related to gatekeeping and gateslipping (see Fig. 9.3).

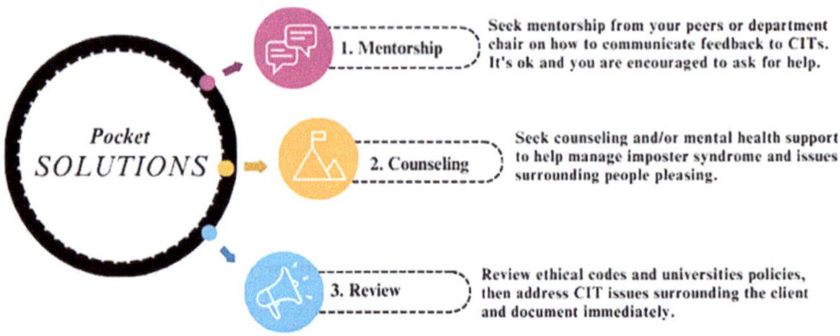

Fig. 9.3 Possible solutions for Pitfall #3

9.2.4 Pitfall #4

A challenging aspect of the CES role is addressing CIT when counseling skills deficiencies and professional counselor dispositions are identified especially when the CIT is emotionally dysregulated. Often a CES will avoid addressing concerns with the CIT and engaging in gate slipping, which is a detriment to the CIT and the counseling profession. Here we will examine a scenario of the CES avoiding addressing deficiencies within CITs resulting in poor gatekeeping.

You are teaching a first-semester internship course, and you identify a CIT who is unable to adequately demonstrate and apply the basic counseling skills consistent with CITs at this stage of development. During the most recent case presentation, you observed the CIT talking over the client, giving advice, and missing a lot of what the client was saying in session. Additionally, when reviewing the tape in class, the CIT was unable to identify the appropriate skills they could have used instead. You and the other CITs in the course provided feedback to this CIT during class, and the CIT's response was defensive and argumentative demonstrating an inability to receive feedback. The CIT became increasingly upset with you and their peers and began to yell and scream demonstrating an inability to regulate their emotions and behaviors inconsistent with professional counselor dispositions. Despite having other case presentations scheduled, you decided to end class early. Later that week, you spoke with the CIT's site supervisor and received feedback about their deficits in counseling skills that are consistent with your observations.

9.2.4.1 Discussion

A common pitfall is that the counselor educator does not immediately identify and attend to the CIT's deficiency in counseling skills and professional dispositions by documenting the concerns before the situation escalates. This also presents an ethical dilemma regarding gatekeeping and remediation (ACA, 2014, Standard F.6.b) and (CACREP, 2024, Standard 2.C). Since this is an internship, it would be beneficial for the CES to make an inquiry to the practicum professor (if different) to determine if any deficiencies were previously identified and documented. If there were deficiencies identified, and not addressed in the practicum course, then this becomes a significant detriment to the CIT, current CES, and most importantly, their client. This also presents an ethical dilemma regarding the imperative of nonmaleficence, to do no harm (ACA, 2014, Standard A.4.a). As CES, you have an obligation to inform the CIT of any observed deficiencies and provide them with feedback and an opportunity to make improvements. Without notification and documentation, the situation presented in the case scenario above would be considered the CIT's first instance thus making it difficult to apply any remedial efforts.

In the above scenario, proactively and preemptively attending to the CIT's issue with an individual meeting delineating clear and specific expectations can support the CIT's development while upholding ethical and professional standards as a gatekeeper. Even if you believe the concerns are minor, it is always best to document if support for the CIT is needed when there is potential for a pattern to be established. Additionally, as a CES, you would educate and demonstrate how to respectfully address the CIT's the lack of receptivity to feedback within the group setting just like a counselor would challenge a client who is resistant to feedback within a group setting.

Another pitfall in this scenario is that the CES failed to consult with the CIT's site supervisor to monitor the CIT's performance during field placement which is an integral component and core responsibility within the 2024 CACREP standards (CACREP, 2024, Standard 4.J). The site supervisor can be a partner in holding the CIT accountable to the action plan developed with the CIT in collaboration with the CES. In addition, the site supervisor can provide additional documentation of persistent issues or subsequent improvements that may strengthen your documentation. Since the site supervisor has more opportunities to observe the CIT in clinical sessions and obtain feedback from clients, you may want to utilize this option.

One final pitfall is for the CES to pass the CIT along to avoid conflict. In the scenario above, the CES did not address the observed deficiencies or dispositional concerns with the CIT, site supervisor, or their program administration. This approach is unfair to the CIT who relies on you to teach, mentor, and provide accountability. As a result, the CIT may be ill-equipped for the next internship course. Moreover, passing the CIT with significant deficiencies has the potential to be deleterious to future clients and the counseling profession. In this scenario, by allowing the CIT to continue without providing interventions to remediate the observed deficiencies, the CES is engaging in gateslipping (Homrich & Henderson, 2018).

9.2.4.2 Pocket Solutions

Here are three possible solutions to address common pitfalls related to the inability to address CIT deficiencies, a lack of intervention, and gateslipping (see Fig. 9.4).

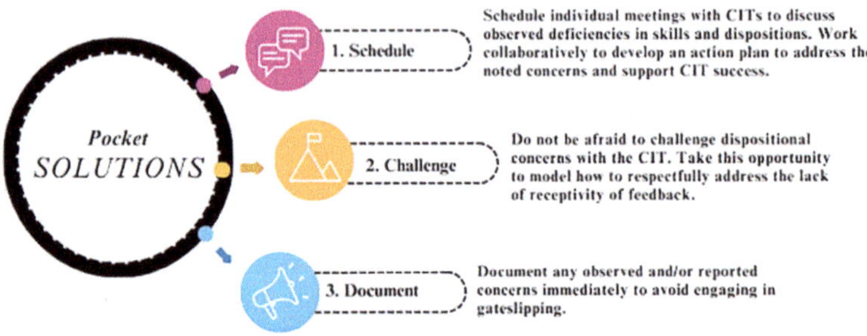

Fig. 9.4 Possible solutions for Pitfall #4

9.2.5 Pitfall #5

The next pitfall we will address is related to compounding and complex CIT concerns. As a CES, you may encounter complex issues with CITs which require evidence to support your findings. Thus, it is important that you maintain complete and accurate records of your interactions with CITs as you never know when they may be requested. While some circumstances may be clear cut, others may require you to example multiple possibilities. Therefore, taking care to consider all of the facts involved while looking at the whole learner is imperative. Consider the following scenario where we examine a complex issue related to documentation, remediation, and explicit cultural bias.

A Black male CIT reported that he was experiencing anxiety as he neared the end of his final internship course. He stated that he was reprimanded at his site because he was unable to work with a White male client who was self-referred due to depression. After probing further, the CIT shared that during the intake interview he observed that the client had a Swastika tattoo on the back of his neck. The CIT reviewed the client's history, which included being raised by a father who was a member of an Aryan Nations white supremacist group. The CIT stated that he was triggered and feared working with the client. He stated that his site supervisor was unwilling to listen to his concerns. He stated "she doesn't understand what it's like being a Black man working with a client that is racist. She won't listen to me." The site supervisor contacted you stating that she reprimanded the CIT for refusing to work with the client. She stated that this was not the first time that the CIT refused to work with a client, and he had an ethical obligation as a CIT to not discriminate against his clients and to honor his commitments. You learned that the previous occurrence was a similar situation. The site supervisor informed you that she completed the CIT's final evaluation and that she did not believe that the CIT was ready to enter the field.

9.2.5.1 Discussion

In addressing the scenario above the CES must consider multiple dimensions of the situation. Firstly, it is crucial to acknowledge the CIT's experience of anxiety and the challenges he faced when confronted with the client expressing racist ideologies and the impact of the CIT's personal identity, being a Black male in relation to working with a client harboring racist beliefs. Sensitivity to cultural competence and the psychological toll of such encounters on the CIT is paramount. The CES should also evaluate the effectiveness of the site supervisor's response, considering if the site supervisor adequately addressed the CITs' concerns and provided a supportive environment. Ethical considerations, including the obligation to avoid discrimination and honor commitments, must be weighed against the potential harm to the CIT's well-being. Moreover, the CES should investigate the supervisors' claim about the CIT's refusal to work with clients, evaluating if this is a recurring pattern or if this is a unique situation. The CES should integrate the ethical decision-making model and encourage the CIT to articulate the specific ethical dilemma faced, emphasizing the clash between his duty to serve clients without discrimination and his need to protect his own well-being. Furthermore, the CES should address the site supervisors' concerns about the CIT's readiness to enter the field by examining the CIT's overall performance, ethical reasoning, and the ability to navigate challenging situations. Ultimately the counselor educator should collaboratively work toward resolution where both ethical standards and the CIT's well-being are addressed, possibly involving additional training on navigating sensitive clients' issues with diverse clients. The goal is to foster a nuanced understanding of the ethical complexities involved, empowering the CIT to make informed decisions aligned with ethical standards while also acknowledging the importance of self-care and cultural competence in the counseling profession. This reflective process can contribute to the CIT's professional growth and ethical competence.

9.2.5.2 Pocket Solutions

Here are four possible solutions to address common pitfalls related to compounding and complex CIT concerns (see Fig. 9.5).

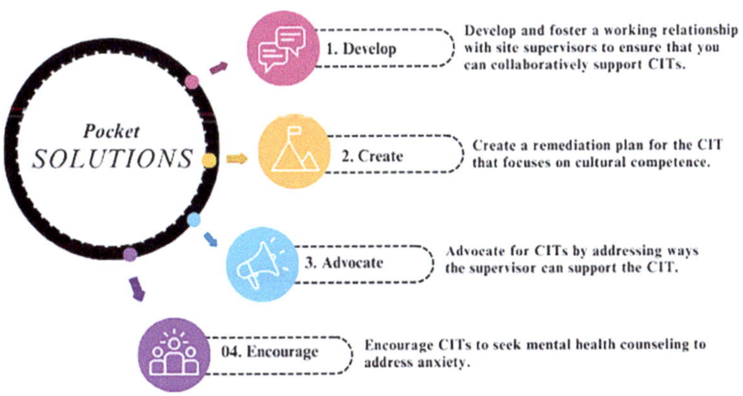

Fig. 9.5 Possible solutions for Pitfall #5

9.2.6 Pitfall #6

Taking responsibility for an incident and being defensive to the feedback is a pitfall many CES will experience at some point during their career. It is important to examine one's role in the situation. We all make mistakes, so it is imperative to identify and own them. There may have been extraneous circumstances, or you just did not measure up in your responsibilities. Whatever the reason, seek truth in the evidence and make changes accordingly. Being open to growth and development is vital to being an effective counselor educator, and this presents an opportunity to model growth and development to CITs. Remember as a new and/or seasoned counselor educator, we are all a work in progress. Consider the following scenario:

You have been notified that several CITs in your course have filed a complaint against you stating that you have not provided clarification for the grade posted on a presentation assignment. They stated that the grade was posted with minimal feedback, and they requested more information, but you did not respond. After a second email request to you did not result in a sufficient answer, the CITs filed their complaint. The complaint was reviewed by your department leadership and your grading was overturned. Additionally, department leadership agreed with the CITs' complaints, and they provided feedback for you to increase the justification of point deductions and content in the CIT's feedback.

9.2.6.1 Discussion

In this scenario, the CES would need to take responsibility for their actions or inaction. Acknowledging your error to the CITs without an excuse if there is merit to their complaint is important. This not only makes you human, but it also models an acceptance of personal responsibility and appropriate professional dispositions. Unlike other professions, the individual is critical to the counseling process, and there are times when a CIT will be in the role of the counselor and make an error in session. Teaching a CIT how to make mistakes without making excuses will be beneficial to their development as a future counselor. Another pitfall may be getting stuck in resentment of the CIT and faculty leadership. The negative response may lead to increased defensiveness, expending unnecessary energy and experiencing angst about your standing in the department. Your regret may diminish work satisfaction and effectiveness, leading to more errors. Having a support group and/or personal counselor is suggested to process your emotions and thoughts while identifying if you need to take any additional steps.

9.2.6.2 Pocket Solutions

Here are three possible solutions to address common pitfalls related to CIT complaints (see Fig. 9.6).

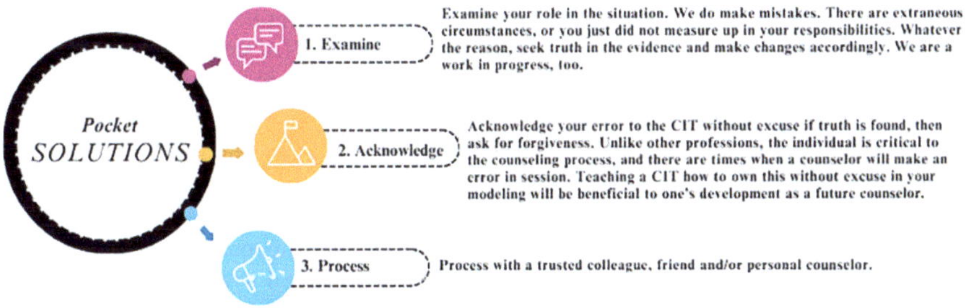

Fig. 9.6 Possible solutions for Pitfall #6

9.3 Conclusion

In closing this chapter offers valuable insights into challenges faced by new counselor educators and supervisors by addressing seven common pitfalls. The Chapter raises awareness by highlighting burnout, gatekeeping, boundary issues, self-care and the challenges navigating complaints made by CITs. The Chapter also gives practical guidance on how to navigate these challenges ethically. By incorporating the strategies provided and maintaining self-care and healthy boundaries, new counselor educators can maintain wellness, enhance their resilience and contribute positively to the education and supervision of future counselors.

References

American Counseling Association. (2014). *2014 ACA Code of Ethics*. https://www.counseling.org/docs/default-source/default-document-library/ethics/2014-aca-code-of-ethics.pdf?sfvrsn=55ab73d0_1

Council for Accreditation of Counseling and Related Educational Programs. (2024). *2024 CACREP Standards*. https://www.cacrep.org/wp-content/uploads/2024/04/2024-Standards-Combined-Version-4.11.2024.pdf

Homrich, A. M., & Henderson, K. L. (Eds.). (2018). *Gatekeeping in the mental health professions*. American Counseling Association.

Myers, J. E., & Sweeney, T. J. (2005). The indivisible self: An evidence-based model of wellness. *The Journal of Individual Psychology, 61*(3), 269–279.

Tanisha N. Sapp, EdD, LPC, CST, NCC, ACS, CPCS is an Assistant Professor of Counseling at Liberty University in the Department of Counseling and Family Studies. Dr. Sapp is a counselor educator, professional counselor, trainer, and clinical supervisor focused on training the next generation of helping professionals. She is the owner of Tanisha Sapp, LLC where she provides professional development training, clinical supervision services, and individual and couples sex therapy. With over 20 years of experience in the helping profession, Dr. Sapp brings a wealth of experience, insight, and a unique perspective into counselor education.

Dr. Sapp is currently a member of the ACA ethics committee and serves on review panels for CACREP and NBCC where she offers her expertise to the profession in an effort to be the change she desires to see. Dr. Sapp has also served on a number of professional committees and provided leadership service to the profession and her community. Her areas of research, professional identity, and interests include: professional counselor identity, Anti-Racism in counseling and counselor education, DEIBASJ in counseling and counselor education, BIPOC sexual health and wellness, and professional advocacy in leadership.

Wendy Robinson, Ph.D., LPC, CCTP is an Associate Professor of Counseling at Liberty University. Dr. Robinson has 20 years in the management and training of counselors and counseling programs. Dr. Robinson is also a certified clinical trauma professional with extensive experience working with individuals and couples. Her areas of research and interest include professional counselor identity, professional ethics, and trauma work.

Latasha Matthews, MA, LPC, CPCS is known as America's Emotional Wellness Expert; she is the CEO and Clinical Director of Illumination Counseling and Coaching and Why 2 Live Well. Latasha has over 15 years' experience as a speaker, therapist, Coach, and author and she also provides continuing education training for clinicians and corporate training on wellness, DEI, EQ, and trauma informed resilience in the workplace. She has trained 1000s of individuals globally on the importance of setting healthy boundaries to live well.

Finding and Landing the Job

10

Aja Burks and Charmaine L. Conner

Teaching is the profession that teaches all the other professions.

—Unknown

Abstract

This chapter addresses successful job-seeking and interviewing strategies for new graduates seeking their first position as a professor in higher education. The typical job process in higher education begins a year before graduation. In doctoral programs, you are trained to become a scholar in the field, and minimal attention is given to the job search process. In this chapter, we focus on three core areas to land the job you want: Mindset, Finding (the job), and Landing (the job). We hope to prepare you as doctoral learners to understand the importance of your mindset with regard to securing employment. Furthermore, we share helpful guidelines to utilize before submitting your application. Lastly, we conclude with a detailed explanation of the interview, negotiation, and onboarding processes.

Learning Objectives After reading this chapter, you will be able to:

1 Identify the requisite application materials commonly used in the counselor education field to include in your employment portfolio.
2 Build professional relationships rooted in authenticity through effective networking.

A. Burks (✉)
Saybrook University, Pasadena, CA, USA
e-mail: ajaburks@transformativemindcounseling.com

C. L. Conner
Roosevelt University, Chicago, IL, USA
e-mail: cconner@roosevelt.edu

D. M. Stalnaker-Shofner and T. N. Sapp (eds.), *A Comprehensive Guide for Counselor Education*, Springer Texts in Education, https://doi.org/10.1007/978-3-031-68358-9_10

3 Implement the tools offered in this chapter to facilitate your engagement with the employment search process, from initial searches through your salary and employment negotiation process.

10.1 Statement of Reflexivity

As the authors of this chapter and counselor educators, we have learned through experience and guidance ways to effectively engage in the employment search process and have used these experiences to inform its writing. We further used our experiences and successes to highlight the tools and strategies that we have found to be helpful, as well as those supported by research and rooted in best practices. It is also important to note that our respective employment searches were also framed by our shared identities as Black women. While we share some commonalities with respect to our identities and experiences, there are also some significant differences that have also framed our writing. Through candid dialogue and discourse, we openly reflected on our experiences as we deliberated on how to create a chapter that was thorough and authentic. As a part of our discussions, we reflected on our individual positionalities and experiences and their impact on us and crafted the chapter content with intentionality and honored our identities and experiences. As we wrote, we took time to reflect on how we were experiencing the presented material, which led to further dialogue as we processed this impact. We acknowledge that due to our unique experiences, we also have our own biases and assumptions, and as we navigated the writing process, we also engaged in journaling which allowed us to reflect more deeply on how our biases impacted the chapter content.

10.2 Case Scenario

You are in the last year of your doctoral program. You have decided to enter the job market and search for a position in counselor education. You have shared with your chair that you have multiple interests in the field of CES and are certain that academia is the right direction for you. Your research is focused on urban counseling agencies, and you have a strong curriculum vita (CV) that consists of presentations, publications, and clinical experience. You are ready to start preparing your various statements and to request letters of recommendation. You are also open to relocation. You are aware that the job market is very competitive this year and you just want to secure a position in the field that you love.

10.3 Introduction

Congratulations! You have advanced to the end of your doctoral journey, and now you are embarking on the journey to secure employment as a CES faculty, moving from doctoral learner to colleague. There are many important aspects to this process for you to consider, and this chapter will run through each to help you succeed in finding and landing the job. In this section, we will focus on setting yourself up to begin searching for the job that you would like to have.

For the past three to four years, you have established yourself as a doctoral learners. You were trained under the best and brightest in your program, and now it is your time to take your talents and knowledge to another place that will value your training and work in the field. While this is a natural process in the doctoral journey, now is when you must prepare yourself for your new title as "Dr." and your new role as a CES faculty (Kelsky, 2015). You may experience feelings of uncertainty about your new identity, and this is quite common. Questioning who you are, who you are becoming, and your ability to meet your professional obligations is a natural part of the process of developing your professional identity; we explore this more in Chap. 25.

As you dive into this journey, staying true to who you are as a person will guide you to the place of employment you desire. Many doctoral learners navigating the job market find themselves wanting to fit into the box of what the university wants in a faculty member thus sacrificing their own professional priorities. An additional consideration for some individuals who hold a historically marginalized identity is the challenge of navigating additional barriers related to their identities and how these can impact their role as new faculty. Understanding who you are as a person, your personality, your strengths, your growth areas and also the specific challenges you may encounter will ultimately determine how you navigate your employment search in higher education.

10.4 Being Intentional: Knowing What You Want

Before you navigate the job market, it is imperative to understand what you want in a position, what type of position you are seeking, and what type of support you believe you will need as new faculty to facilitate your success. Being intentional in your job search means targeting positions that match your skills and career goals, allowing you to highlight your unique qualifications effectively (Johnson & Rehg, 2021). This strategic approach not only enhances your chances of securing a suitable position but also ensures long-term job satisfaction and professional growth. It is important to know what your "hard no's" are, as well as to what experiences you are open to. Would you consider relocating to a more rural area? Are you open to online programs? Do you want to work in a teaching-centered or research-focused program? Below are some points for you to consider as you begin your job search.

10.4.1 Location

Essential to an effective job search is to start with knowing not only whether or not you are willing to relocate, but also knowing where you are willing and able to move for a position. What specific geographical areas will you consider? What contributes to making this decision (i.e. quality of life, cost of living, availability of leisure activities)? Having an idea of where you want to be can streamline your search.

10.4.2 Access to Culture/Identity

One area that may be very important to you is to be able to access things you identify with culturally. Having a historically marginalized identity may mean that where you choose one chooses to look for positions is directly related to access to self-preservation. Living in a world that you are repeatedly told is not made for you can have a mental and emotional toll for many. There is also the possibility that you will be the only faculty member in your program with more visible marginalized identities such as race and gender. Creating and nurturing a social support system can be helpful to your success. Knowing where you can access activities and persons with similar cultural identities can mitigate feelings of isolation which are often experienced as "the only one" in a department and/or program. If cultural identity support is important to you, we encourage you to investigate this as a part of your job search.

10.4.3 Institutional Culture

In addition to geographical access to culture and identity supports, the culture of the institution is important to understand. Institutional culture will look different everywhere. In what type of environment do you want to work? Are you looking for a supportive environment that fosters the development of its new faculty utilizing resources and programs such as faculty mentorship? What resources are available to you to support your professional growth? What are the faculty dynamics? One tip for this is to ask open-ended questions to individuals about their experience on campus. For example, you can ask: "Can you tell me a time where you had to navigate a tough situation at work? How did that go? What did you learn from it?".

Stop and Reflect: *As you stand on the precipice of transitioning from doctoral learner to CES faculty and colleague, the journey ahead is not only one of professional advancement but a profound transformation of identity. The realization that you are not merely seeking employment but positioning yourself to become an active contributor to the academic community adds a nuanced layer to this transition. The clarity in your career path, rooted in a love for CES, serves as a guiding beacon, shaping not only your aspirations but also influencing the institutions and roles you seek. Considering this, we invite you to reflect on the following questions: What are your long-term career goals in counseling education? How do your values and aspirations align with the types of positions discussed in this chapter?*

10.5 Classifications of Institutions of Higher Education

There are different types of institutions that may be of consideration to you as you begin your search, and it will be important to understand what type of university and program best aligns with your expressed goals.

The Carnegie Classification of Institutions of Higher Education® is the framework for recognizing and describing institutional diversity in higher education (Indiana University Center for Postsecondary Research, n.d.). It also denotes colleges and universities' level of research activity by offering a hierarchical taxonomy of research universities categorized by type of programming. The classifications are broken down into seven categories, but for the purpose of this chapter, we will focus on four: Doctoral Universities, Master's Colleges and Universities, Baccalaureate Colleges, Specialized Institutions. You can access the Carnegie Classification® system online (https://carnegieclassifications.acenet.edu).

Another type of institution of higher education is the teaching institution. These institutions primarily emphasize teaching, and they may be classified as Master's College & Universities or Doctoral/Professional Universities within the Carnegie Classification®. Teaching institutions are focused on student development, while research institutions are focused on the dissemination of research (Brown et al., 2022).

Understanding the nuances of the different types of institutions will be essential in your job search and in your prioritization of your career needs and professional goals. As you search, you will want to get a full understanding of both the institutions and program faculty expectations. For instance, most universities require that core faculty engage in four domains of activities: scholarship, teaching, contributions to the profession, and institutional citizenship. However, what makes this more nuanced is the emphasis that is placed on any one of these domains. Additionally, you need to have a clear understanding of what the expectations are related to faculty workload. If you are curious about the type of institution you are applying to, you can go to the university and program website to get more information on their focus. When you are researching the school, look at the profiles of the faculty members and read their CV if available.

10.6 Types of Positions

In the vast landscape of academia, aspiring educators can navigate a diverse array of university teaching positions, each offering unique opportunities. One prominent category is the Tenure-Track Professor position, an esteemed role that entails conducting research, publishing scholarly works, and delivering high-quality instruction. These positions are longer contracts (i.e. six to seven years) with annual reviews periods that lead to tenure (Whitaker, 2019). In addition to tenure track positions, there are non-tenure track positions you will see available. Similar to tenure track positions, nontenure-track can have longer contracts; however, they are not connected to receiving tenure. Non-tenure track positions typically involve a heavier emphasis on teaching and the specific demands of academic programs. Within the context of counseling programs, which often have a significant clinical teaching component, there is a potential for the establishment of non-tenured clinical positions. These positions are designed to support the intensive practical training that CITs require, aligning faculty responsibilities more closely with the hands-on, experiential learning that is integral to these programs (Finklestein, 2016). The term rank is used to describe different positions a program could have available. The positions are:

- **Adjunct**: A part-time teaching role that provides flexibility for professionals to share expertise without a long-term commitment. Adjunct professors typically bring practical experience to the classroom. As a new graduate, this is a position you may have interest in.
- **Assistant Professor**: An early career faculty position with a balance of teaching and research responsibilities. Assistant professors work towards establishing a strong research portfolio and demonstrating excellence in teaching. As a new graduate, this is a position you may have interest in.
- **Associate Professor**: A mid-career faculty position with a balance of teaching and research responsibilities. Assistant professors work towards establishing a strong research portfolio and demonstrating excellence in teaching.
- **Clinical Professor**: A faculty member with expertise in counseling, contributing to both teaching and practice. Clinical professors often bring practical insights and clinical experience to the classroom.
- **Full Professor**: A senior faculty member representing the pinnacle of academic achievement. Full professors have demonstrated sustained excellence in teaching, research, and service over an extended period.
- **Instructor**: Typically, an entry-level position, instructors focus on teaching responsibilities and may have limited involvement in research. This role often serves as a foundation for those starting their academic careers.
- **Lecturer**: Focused primarily on teaching responsibilities, lecturers contribute to the educational experience without the extensive research obligations associated with tenure-track positions.

- **Visiting Professor**: A temporary faculty position filled by a scholar from another institution. Visiting professors bring expertise to the host institution for a specific duration (most likely a semester or a school year), often contributing to teaching and research during their stay.

Job postings may include the term "open rank." An open rank position indicates that the university is willing to hire at any faculty level, including assistant, associate, or full professor (Kelsky, 2015). The decision regarding the specific rank is typically determined by evaluating the candidate's qualifications and experience.

Stop and Reflect: *Understanding the classifications of institutions of higher education becomes pivotal as you navigate the job market. Whether it be a research-intensive university, a liberal arts college, or a community college, each offers unique opportunities and expectations. Deliberating on the type of position you desire, whether a tenure-track role, a lecturer position, or a clinical faculty appointment, involves a thoughtful consideration of your skills, preferences, and long-term goals within the diverse landscape of higher education. Considering this, we invite you to reflect on the following questions: What factors are most important to you when considering different counseling education positions? How do teaching, research, and service expectations align with your professional strengths and preferences?*

10.7 Where to Look

One of the best places to look for job opportunities in counseling education is through professional organization websites. The ACES is the professional organization for our field. On the professional organization website, you can locate the jobs that are available under the job listing section. You can also look at other professional organizations, such as the ACA and American Mental Health Counseling Association (AMHCA). In addition to professional organizations, jobs are also listed on websites and their related printed media for publications like *The Chronicle of Higher Education* and *Diverse: Issues in Higher Education.* Other websites for your consideration include academicjobsonline.com, insidehighered.com, and linkedin.com.

10.7.1 Finding the Job

Earlier in the chapter, we focused our time on our mindset, knowing who we are and what we want in a position. In this section, we will focus on a successful search for available positions that meet your needs and goals. When you start your employment search process, it is important to consider broadening your options by applying to multiple positions at various universities. As you navigate through multiple job descriptions, organization will be important.

One of the most efficient ways to stay organized is to create a spreadsheet with the following: identifying information about the university, and your employment search criteria. Having this information in one central document will allow you to keep track of the openings you are considering and to see the positions side-by-side. Within your spreadsheet, the main labels you may want to consider using include the name of the university, the location of the university, job title, salary, tenured or non-tenured track, application deadline, contact information of search chair, application review start date, website, application requirements, application status, type of interview, and offer. Next, you want to have a section on the spreadsheet that is dedicated to your career needs and your own ratings of each university and its opening. A suggestion is to have a pre- and post-interview rating for your interest in the position. An example of factors that may be important to you can include the university's mission to DEIBASJ.

10.7.2 Cover Letter

As the job market for available faculty positions is quite competitive, it will be essential to separate and distinguish yourself as the best fit for the university, department, and program and their expressed criteria. This is where a good cover letter can help. The cover letter introduces yourself to the search committee, enumerate exactly how you meet their listed position requirements, and shows why you are the best fit for the position. The cover letter is the search committee's first impression of you. Think of the cover letter as a 1.5-page abstract of who you are as a professional, as well as the most important aspects about your fit for the position and what you can offer to the program. In the cover letter, you want to explicitly state how you fit the details in the job description. Programs that explicitly state in their job description what they are looking for in a candidate are looking for an individual to fill a hole missing on their faculty team. You want to put in the cover letter how you fill this missing link.

As you think about how to construct your cover letter, you will want to ensure that your letter is tailored to the university you are applying to. Lastly, you want to highlight your accomplishments that can benefit the program and ultimately the CIT. The cover letter affords you the opportunity to gracefully and pointedly highlight your accomplishments, and how these set you apart from other applicants. One tip for your cover letter is to start with a strong, memorable sentence.

10.7.3 Curriculum Vita

A curriculum vita (CV) is a document that delineates the history of your professional academic and clinical accomplishments and experiences that span your career. thus far. Additionally, your CV ideally should provide pertinent information such as education history and related degrees conferred, teaching experience, summary of research projects and publications, honors and awards received, and professional service. Similar to the cover letter, you will want to tailor your CV to the specifics of the position to which you are applying. For example, if the position requirements emphasize a strong research focus, then you will want to position your research history earlier in your CV. If the position is heavily focused on teaching, then you would want to strategically emphasize your teaching experience with higher positioning on your CV. One tip is to make sure your CV is easy to read and has a clear and concise format.

10.7.4 Statements

In academia, job postings typically ask for different types of statements that will inform search committee of your guiding principles and philosophies, approaches and practices, as well as your core beliefs regarding your professional experiences These statements are an opportunity to expound on the line items in your CV in a clear concise explanation of who you are professionally. There are different types of statements you can provide in your job materials. Below we outline the most common.

10.7.4.1 Teaching Philosophy/Statement

A teaching philosophy focuses on who you are as an instructor, the philosophy that undergirds your praxis, and noteworthy examples of each in your experience. You want to offer a succinct but compelling portrait of your talents, dedication to CIT learning, and commitment to your professional growth in this area. Your statement needs to be clear and concise, highlighting to the reader key aspects of your teaching identity that would be beneficial to their department and program.

Furthermore, you want to showcase your experience and how you incorporate your philosophy into your teaching. You can list the courses you have taught and how those experiences have been informed by your philosophy of teaching. If you have specific skills, training, and related qualifications to teach a specific course, you will want to integrate this into your philosophy, particularly if this is of value to the search committee. If you have developed any courses, you can share what went into the overall development and how it aligns to your philosophy of teaching. If the job description shares the courses you would teach, you write your approach to teaching those courses.

10.7.4.2 Research Statement/Agenda

It is not uncommon for search committees to request the inclusion of a research statement or agenda. A research statement is a document delineating your scholarly accomplishments and your proposed plan for your future research efforts. In your research statement, you want to provide a road map of your past work, present research work and future agenda. In addition to your road map, you want to explain why your research agenda is important to the field in a concise summary.

Make sure that your research agenda follows your research timeline. This is easy for the search committee to read and follow your CV. In addition to your order, be sure to cite your work in your research statement. If you know the goals of the department, be sure to speak to how your research agenda aligns with the program's needs.

10.7.4.3 Diversity Statement

A recent development congruent with the current trends and societal shifts, more search committees are requesting the inclusion of a diversity statement as a part of the application portfolio. The purpose of a diversity statement is to offer demonstrable and concrete examples of your efforts to facilitate multicultural approaches to learning, advance advocacy and social justice initiatives, as well as your efforts to advance the basic principles of DEIBASJ. In your diversity statement, you can offer your perspectives based on your diversity work, commitment, and experience, and how it shapes and informs your professional development, or share your personal experiences as a person from a historically marginalized group.

In your diversity statement, it is important to provide specific and concrete examples of your commitment to DEIBASJ. You want to discuss your experiences with working with diverse populations and your engagement in service, advocacy, and activism. If you have helped CIT from historically marginalized groups, you want to highlight these experiences and discuss how they shape your teaching and research. Lastly, you want to write about your commitment to achieving equity and diversity in your work.

For each statement you write, you want to write about your experience clearly and concisely. This is where you are firm in what you bring to the academic space. Be honest and factual in your statements. One essential tip is to tailor your statements to each university or institution and for the specific position to which you are applying. This will allow you to stand out from other applicants vying for the same position.

10.7.4.4 Writing Sample

In addition to the statements, you must include in your packet, you may be asked to provide a writing sample. This request usually is indicative of a program's desire for a candidate with strong writing skills. Factors that search committees may consider include writing style, tone, content, and grammar. When you are choosing a writing sample, please consider the following in your selection: the recency of the work, the nature of the work (i.e. published research paper, a paper submitted for an assignment), its ability to highlight your writing talents, or a sample that articulates your lived experiences related to one of you submitted statements (Fig. 10.1).

Stop and Reflect: *Determining where to look for a job is a strategic decision. While academic job boards, university websites, and professional associations are traditional avenues, the importance of networking cannot be overstated. Engaging with conferences, workshops, and online communities establishes connections that may prove invaluable in the job search process. Considering this, we invite you to reflect on the following questions: How can you tailor your application materials,*

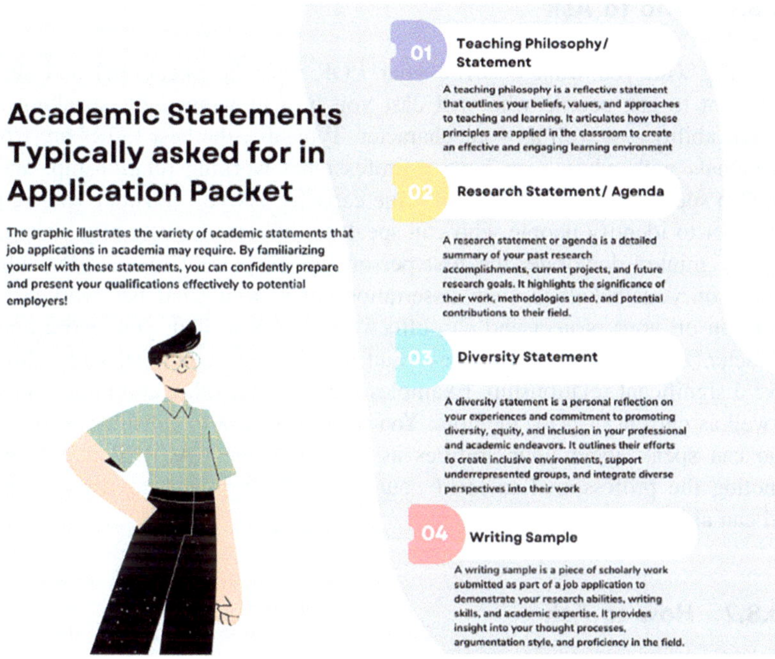

Fig. 10.1 Summary of teaching portfolio contents

including cover letters and statements, to effectively communicate your passion for counseling in higher education? What unique contributions do you bring to a counseling position within an academic setting?

10.8 Letters of Recommendation and References

Letters of recommendation (LOR) and references (i.e. professional, personal, academic) are a standard requisite for many faculty positions. The LOR should highlight the best parts of you. It will speak to your academic and professional achievements and character from the perspective of someone who has such knowledge. LORs, though a weighted component of the application, usually are reviewed as the last element of the application packet; however, there are programs that will read your LORs to begin to formulate their initial impressions of you and your candidacy. As you contemplate this element of your application, please consider the following factors.

10.8.1 Who to Ask

Choosing who you want to write your LOR must be intentional and strategic. You want to ask people who will cast you in a glowing light, speaking highly of your abilities as well as your character. Typically, the best LORs are from the individuals with whom you have a professional working relationship, and who can also speak to your character in some capacity. As you consider your requests, you want to identify people who can speak to different aspects of your work. As a newly minted doctorate, the first person you may want to consider authoring a letter on your behalf is your dissertation chair. Your chair has worked closely with you on your project and can effectively speak to both your work and your character. Another person you may want to ask is an individual with whom you have a significant relationship. Examples include your other committee members, as well as current or prior mentors. You may also want to consider asking people who can speak about your abilities as related to the CACREP five core areas denoting the professional roles of counselor educators and counselor education and can also speak to your skills.

10.8.2 How to Ask

Even though you have a relationship with your recommenders, it can still be hard to ask for their assistance with writing the letter. The best approach is to initiate a conversation with the potential recommenders to ask directly for their written support. This can be in the form of verbal communication (preferred), or via email. As you consider who and how to ask, consider the recommenders' availability. Further, you want to be explicit in your request. One way to do this is to collate documentation such as your CV, performance reviews, and writing samples. Doing so will assist your recommenders in writing the strongest and most illustrative letter on your behalf. One tip we suggest is to ask your recommenders early in your process. Avoid waiting until the last minute! Remember, your recommenders will need time to formulate their thoughts and write their letters, and this is a factor you must consider.

10.8.3 Website/Portfolio

As the world continues to advance with technology, counselor educators are choosing to create websites that can highlight their professional identity and accomplishments. If you are considering developing a website as part of your portfolio as a counselor educator, you want to address the 5 pillars of counselor education (counseling, supervision, teaching, research, and leadership and advocacy.) You also want to have a place explaining the purpose of the site as well.

10.9 Self-care

Self-care is a concept that has become re-popularized in the counseling profession over the last several years (ACA, 2014). Self-care can be defined in many ways. We have chosen to define self-care as simply being intentional about one's choices made throughout the day that contribute to your overall mental/emotional/physical health. We encourage you to create your own definition of self-care. Additionally, you will want to identify different ways you can engage in these practices. This is explored more in Chap. 24. You may be wondering why this is important in the job search process…keep reading!

The job search process is very *stressful!* As you begin this process, you are likely a doctoral candidate or have recently completed your degree, and you are balancing multiple roles and responsibilities such as clinical practice, supervision, research, and/or service. As an applicant, you will be constructing cover letters, personal statements, diversity statements, research statements, teaching philosophies, securing letters of recommendation, and editing your CV (Cartwright et al., 2018; Rutter & Jones, 2007). These tasks are time-consuming, and the pressure placed on you as a job seeker may have an impact on your self-care. We would like to offer some suggestions for self-care and coping strategies:

- Setting aside job application prep time
- Ensuring that you have at least one hour to yourself each week
- Planning your meals
- Talking with friends about topics unrelated to counselor education
- Identifying and engaging in a hobby.

These strategies should be aligned with your needs. This may require you to be creative and think of your own methods for self-care. We invite you to participate in the following exercise. Reflect on how you might maintain your mental and emotional health throughout the job search. Consider the following questions:

- What does self-care mean to me?
- How do I know when I am well?
- How do I know when I am unwell?
- What are three things I can do in the immediate future to take care of myself?

These prompts will help you to begin to conceptualize your own self-care plan. Now that you have a self-care plan, please remember this: you are the only person who is responsible for taking care of yourself! This may require developing firm boundaries. There are times when people will attempt to encroach on your established boundaries, and it will be incumbent upon you to manage this.

Another issue that may arise is related to how you see yourself, and of equal importance, how you perceive that others view you. This self-doubt, known as imposter syndrome. You want to avoid as much as possible allowing imposter syndrome to take a foothold in your mind, as this phenomenon may sneak up on you. Remember this: you are good enough! Imposter Syndrome is further explored in Chap. 25.

Stop and Reflect: *Finding a job in a competitive market necessitates meticulous preparation of statements and letters of recommendation. Crafting a compelling narrative in cover letters and statements of teaching philosophy becomes crucial in conveying not just your qualifications but also your passion for CES. Seeking letters of recommendation involves tapping into the network of mentors and colleagues who can authentically vouch for your capabilities. Considering this, we invite you to reflect on the following questions: How do you plan to prioritize self-care throughout the job process? What strategies can help you manage stress and maintain a healthy work-life balance during the application and interview stages?*

10.10 Networking–Fostering a Genuine Connection

Again, the job search is a stressful time period. The job search requires significant focus on being marketable, researching the institution/department/program, and networking. Networking can be a key factor in the job search process. Yet this can sometimes be a hollow endeavor. Many jobseekers and even employers have reported desiring more genuine connections (Cartwright et al., 2018). Fostering a genuine connection is one of the most difficult processes to navigate during the job search. In this section, we will offer tips for building authentic connections in the job search, as well as how to navigate conversing with peers who are also in the job market.

We invite you to reflect on a time when you had a real connection with someone, thus allowing you to be authentically you. What factors or conditions contributed to that experience? How was emotional safety cultivated, thus fostering a level of comfort that lends itself to being more genuine? As you continue to read, keep the answers to these questions at the forefront of your mind.

Here is a scenario for you to consider: it is the annual ACES Conference, regional ACES conferences, or the annual ACA conference, and you have signed up to participate in the Career Link and University Job talks. The career link process is an opportunity for job seekers and employers to meet and have informal or formal initial interviews during a conference. University job talks are an opportunity for job seekers to hear from a representative of a counselor education program seeking to fill an open position. Both of these events are important for you as a job seeker; it will be important to develop a process for how you want to authentically discuss who you are and why you are a good fit for the job.

Below are some strategies that may support you in making a genuine connection with prospective employers at conferences. Our first suggestion is to do your research on the prospective employer *before* initiating any contact. Specific tasks include examining the job description, conducting a preliminary investigation into the institution that is hiring, reviewing faculty profiles and becoming familiar with their work (Rutter & Jones, 2007). After completing this research, you will want to identify similarities between their work and your career goals. You might even consider attending a presentation that faculty from prospective employers will be leading to gain a deeper understanding of how they conceptualize their work. Another way to foster genuine connection is utilizing your current professional network—remember, people know people and these connections matter! By communicating your interests with mentors, professors, and colleagues at other universities, this may create additional opportunities to connect with faculty who may be able to assist you as you navigate the job market.

Another opportunity for networking and connection is to consider fellowships such as the NBCC Minority Fellowship Program, and Emerging Leaders Program such as the ones offered by the ACES division as well as by its regions. There are a number of potential fellowships that may be available to you—do your research and find the right fit for you and your professional goals.

10.11 Landing the Job

In the previous section, we discussed how to find a job. We also reviewed the importance of self-care and establishing a genuine connection through networking. This section will integrate what we previously shared, and help you gain a deeper understanding of the important elements of landing the job, specifically the interview process, choosing the best fit, and negotiating offers.

10.11.1 Job Interviews

As a candidate for a faculty opening in counselor education, you may likely have multiple interviews. There are a few steps to consider regarding the interview process. First, it is not uncommon for CMHC programs to register and attend a related conference with the expressed purpose of finding candidates for their open faculty positions. During these conferences, they may also post the open position on the conference job board to generate interest. If potential candidates are identified, then the program representative may schedule an informal interview with candidates during the conference. The next step after this is usually to schedule a phone interview or virtual interview; this is usually the formal first step in the interview process. During this phone or virtual interview, you will want to focus on the following:

- Providing thoughtful and clear, yet concise answers to the questions that are posed. Intentionally highlighting key points outlined in your cover letter that speaks to how you meet the criteria for the opening. You want to keep your answers succinct lasting at the longest 2 min per question. (Bolles, 2020).

- Asking follow-up questions when additional clarity is needed
- Being prepared to "counter-interview" and as a candidate have your own questions prepared for the interviewers
- Ensuring that you are in a space conducive to the interview and the privacy needed (i.e. quiet, well-lit, professional).

Another suggestion we offer is for you to consider practicing your interviewing skills with a trusted professor, mentor, or friend—someone who will give you honest feedback for you to consider integrating. Certain professional counseling organizations may offer you the opportunity to participate in mock interviews to prepare you for the interview process. Take advantage of every opportunity to hone your interview skills to help improve your odds of moving to the next phase.

After the initial interview, there is typically a waiting period; during this time, the search committee is narrowing down the candidate pool and determining whom they would like to interview further and extend an invitation for an on-campus interview, the next phase of the interview process. In the wake of the 2019 Coronavirus pandemic, on-campus interviews for counselor education programs have had to evolve and utilize alternatives to accomplish the task of on-campus interviewing. Currently, the campus interview may occur either in-person or virtually, and there are specific nuances to both that you must consider. This will impact your overall approach to and strategy for interviewing. Some of these include the time of day, the length and pacing of the scheduled day, if there is a planned lunch or dinner (make sure not to imbibe), and most importantly, your teaching demonstration, the next integral step in the interview process.

During the scheduled virtual or in-person interview, you will be required to complete a teaching demonstration. This is probably one of the most critical aspects of this process—and the one most fraught with nervousness. For your teaching presentation, you may be given a specific prompt around which you will build your lecture, or you may be given the opportunity to choose the topic for yourself. The lecture is usually one hour in length, and can be a part of an actual class, or presented to the search committee and invited attendees.

Teaching presentations typically involve candidates showcasing their teaching skills, methodologies, and approaches to a specific audience, often composed of faculty members, administrators, and CIT(s). The goal is to demonstrate the candidate's effectiveness as an educator, their ability to engage CIT(s), and their commitment to fostering a positive learning environment. Here's some aspects of what the teaching presentations might involve.

1. **Teaching Philosophy**
   Candidates may start by presenting their teaching philosophy, outlining their beliefs about education, CIT learning, and the role of the professor.

2. **Sample Lecture of Class Activity**
   Candidates might be asked to deliver a sample lecture or engage in a class activity relevant to their field. This provides an opportunity to showcase their teaching style, communications skills, and ability to convey complex concepts.
3. **Use of Technology**
   Candidates may demonstrate their proficiency in using educational technology. This could include multimedia presentations, online resources, or interactive tools that enhance the learning experience.
4. **Assessment Strategies**
   Candidates might discuss their methods for assessing CIT learning, including the types of assignments, exams, and projects they use to evaluate comprehension and critical thinking skills.
5. **CIT Engagement and Interaction**
   Emphasis may be placed on how candidates foster CIT engagement and interaction in the classroom. This could involve discussing approaches to discussions, group activities, or CIT participation.
6. **Inclusive Teaching Practices**
   Candidates may address how they promote inclusivity and diversity in their teaching, ensuring a welcoming and supportive environment for CIT(s) from various backgrounds.
7. **Handling Challenges**
   Candidates might be asked how they handle challenges in the classroom, including addressing diverse learning needs, handling conflicts, or adapting to unexpected situations.
8. **Feedback Improvement**
   Candidates may discuss how they collect feedback from CIT(s) and colleagues and how they use this feedback to improve their teaching methods.
9. **Integration with Research**
   Depending on the institution, candidates may be encouraged to discuss how their teaching aligns with their research activities and contributes to the overall academic mission of the department and university.

It is crucial for candidates to be well-prepared, engaging, and responsive to questions and feedback during the teaching presentation as it is a key component in evaluating their sustainability for a position. Below we offer practical suggestions for both virtual and in-person interviews.

- Be yourself! Being authentic will likely enhance your confidence and also allow for the institution to better determine if you are a good fit.
- Try to channel your nervousness into a heightened focus that will help you attend to the details of the interview.
- Dress comfortably, but professionally. It will be a long day and there will be many people to meet and tasks to complete. Another tip is to have with you cleaning wipes (in case of spills) and other essentials (i.e. breath mints,

sewing kit, deodorant). Show your range during your teaching presentation. Consider incorporating multiple teaching methods that align with your teaching philosophy and approach.

- Utilize your research presentation as an opportunity to talk about what you have done and where your research is going. You will especially want to communicate a strong research agenda.
- Be prepared to answer confrontational questions. The current socio-political climate has led to some institutional changes, and counseling programs may desire to understand your position on hot button issues.
- Ask questions! Intentionality is key here, and any unanswered questions during the initial call can be asked during this interview (Vick & Furlong, 2015).
- Each of the afore-mentioned suggestions can be helpful as you navigate both in-person and virtual interviews. However, there are some specific recommendations for virtual on-campus interviews that we offer below: Check the stability and quality of your internet connection. Interviewers will likely be turned off by grainy and choppy video quality.
- If you are not in a professional setting, consider creating a virtual background or sprucing up your actual setting with fresh or faux flowers or an assortment of books strategically placed in your setting.
- Look directly into the camera; this is equivalent to making eye contact during an in-person interview.
- Ensure, as best as possible, that you are in a quiet space. You might have to get creative and secure a room in the library or a hotel room. Smile! Unlike in-person interviews, the search committee members will not be able to observe your body language so easily. Be intentional about smiling and presenting a range in your affect.

Whew! Now that the interview day is over you might feel relief or you might feel nervous about next steps. Either way, there is a waiting period before the decisions have been made. We hope that you showed up authentically and that you will be receiving a phone call about an offer.

Stop and Reflect: *Navigating the job search is not merely a professional endeavor but a holistic journey that demands self-care. Balancing the demands of the applications, interviews, and self-reflection requires moments of introspection and rejuvenation. Networking becomes a two-fold process- not only connecting with potential employers but also fostering a supportive community that understands the challenges inherent in the pursuit. Landing the job is a culmination of these efforts, a testament to the alignment of your skills and aspirations with the institution's needs. Negotiating the offer is a delicate dance, requiring a clear understanding of your worth, the institution's expectations, and a collaborative spirit to ensure a mutually beneficial arrangement. Considering this, we invite you to reflect on the following questions: How can you align your skills, values, and goals with the ideal counseling position in higher education? In what ways can you showcase your unique contributions during the application and interview process?*

10.12 Negotiating the Offer

After successfully completing the phone and campus interview phases, the search committee has decided to extend you employment! This is an exciting moment, and there is still work to be done. It is a common occurrence for job candidates to either fail to negotiate their salary all together or they are not strategic and committed to their target salary in the negotiating efforts, and many simply accept the first salary offer along with terms of employment (i.e. teaching load, benefits packages, research support). The art of negotiating involves asking for what you want. You must be assertive, firm, and very clear about your needs. Understanding the current market for your desired position and the typical offerings outlined in a contract letter is essential. Having this information at your disposal can significantly boost your confidence when discussing and negotiating the terms of your offer. Being well-prepared allows you to advocate effectively for a package that aligns with industry standards and meets your professional needs (Formo & Reed, 2011). Remember, you are your best advocate, and it is important to work through your fears and anxiety about asking for too much. Asking for more does not always involve a higher salary. You can make a variety of requests. Common requests during the negotiation process include, but are not limited to:

- Course releases
- Securing technology (i.e. computers, software, remote support)
- Travel reimbursement
- Professional membership fees
- Relocation costs
- Benefits for family
- Parking fees
- Office location.

Another important factor of the negotiation process is doing your research. Research the cost of living and salary range for similar faculty positions in counselor education, the general salary ranges within the profession, salary ranges at the institution. Regarding this, it may be difficult to access this information if the institution is not publicly-funded. In these cases, you may benefit from consulting with a mentor (Vick & Furlong, 2015). Your mentor (e.g., dissertation chair, mentor, other counselor educator) has been through this process and has likely served on search committees. They will be able to give you sound advice in regard to negotiating a competitive offer. In addition to conducting research and consulting with a mentor, you want to be time-bound in how you navigate the negotiation process. Essentially, do not rush the process and you also want to avoid taking too much time to decide. The person facilitating the offer will want to know that you put effort into your requests. Maintaining professionalism is important throughout this process. Approach the negotiation with a collaborative yet professional tone. Be firm but respectful. Remember that negotiations are a normal part of the hiring

Fig. 10.2 The interview process

process. Be willing to compromise on some aspects. Understand that the institution may have constraints, finding a middle ground can be essential for a successful negotiation. Remember that negotiation is a collaborative process, and a successful negotiation results in a mutually beneficial arrangement. Approach the process with professionalism, clarity, and a willingness to find common ground (Fig. 10.2).

Stop and Reflect: *As you embark on this transformative journey, you are not just seeking a job, you are forging a path towards becoming a colleague and contributing member of the academic community. Each step in this process, from self-reflection to networking, is a deliberate stride towards a future where your passion for CES is not just a personal pursuit but a shared endeavor within the vibrant tapestry of higher education. Considering this, we invite you to reflect on the following questions: What aspects of a job offer are non-negotiable for you, and where might you be open to negotiation? How can you effectively communicate your needs and expectations during the negotiation process?*

10.13 Conclusion

The journey from preparing for the job market to successfully finding and landing a position in academia is a multifaceted process that demands strategic planning, resilience, and a commitment to professional growth. As we have explored various aspects of the job search in higher education, from self-reflection and networking to crafting compelling application materials and negotiating offers, it is evident that the pursuit of a career in academia involves not only technical expertise but a nuanced understanding of the academic landscape. Embracing the transition from CIT(s) to colleague requires a holistic approach, recognizing that the path to securing a position is dynamic and influenced by a myriad of factors.

Reflecting on one's strengths, values, and career aspirations sets the foundation for a targeted job search, while effective networking establishes connections that can prove instrumental in navigating the competitive landscape. Crafting impactful application materials, including well- crafted statements and letters of recommendation, becomes a pivotal step in presenting oneself as a qualified and passionate candidate. The process of finding a job extends beyond the traditional realms of job boards and applications; it involves actively engaging with academic communities, attending conferences, and leveraging online platforms to build a professional presence.

Landing the job is a culmination of these efforts, a testament to the alignment of skills, values, and goals with the institution's mission. The negotiation phase is an opportunity for candidates to advocate for their worthwhile fostering a collaborative spirit for a mutually beneficial arrangement. In the ever-evolving landscape of higher education, adaptability and a commitment to continuous learning are key. By embracing the challenges and opportunities presented throughout the job search process, individuals not only secure a position but contribute meaningfully to the vibrant tapestry of academia. May this chapter serve as a guiding beacon for those navigating the exciting and transformative path toward finding and landing a fulfilling position in higher education. We encourage you to re-engage the reflection questions throughout the chapter. We also hope that this information has been useful for you and that you will integrate the content into your upcoming search.

References

American Counseling Association. (2014). *2014 ACA code of ethics*. https://www.counseling.org/docs/default-source/default-document-library/ethics/2014-aca-code-of-ethics.pdf?sfvrsn=55ab73d0_1

Bolles, R. N. (2020). *What color is your parachute?* Ten Speed Press.

Brown, N., Clark, T., Aubrey, H., Anderson, K., Jordan, T., Hill-Eley, D., Swanson, H., & Cameron, E. (2022). The Carnegie classification system and American higher education funding policies: An analysis of information resource collections at selected research institutions. *Edulearn22 Proceedings*, 1170–1173. https://doi.org/10.21125/edulearn.2022.0315

Cartwright, A. D., Avent, H. J. R., Munsey, R. B., & Lloyd, H. J. (2018). Interview experiences and diversity concerns of counselor education faculty from underrepresented groups. *Counselor Education & Supervision, 57*(2), 132–146. https://doi.org/10.1002/ceas.12098

Finklestein, M. J. (2016). *The academic job search handbook*. University of Pennslyvania Press.

Formo, D. M., & Reed, C. (2011). *Job search in academe: How to get the position you deserve*. Taylor & Francis Group.

Indiana University Center for Postsecondary Research (n.d.). *The Carnegie classification of institutions of higher education,* (2021 Ed).

Johnson, R. L., & Rehg, J. A. (2021). *The hiring process in higher education: An insider's guide for success*. Routledge.

Kelsky, K. (2015). *The professor is in: The essential guide to turning your Ph.D. into a job*. Three Rivers Press.

Rutter, M. E., & Jones, J. V. (2007). The job club redux: A step forward in addressing the career development needs of counselor education students. *Career Development Quarterly, 55*(3), 280–288.

Vick, J. M., & Furlong, J. S. (2015, January 20). *A guide to campus interviews: What you need to practice (repeatedly) to make a good impression.* The Chronicle of Higher Education. http://www.chronicle.com/article/A-Guide-to-Campus-Interviews/151279

Whitaker, M. (2019). *How to read a faculty job ad.* The Chronicle of Higher Education. https://www.jentheiss.com/resources

Aja Burks, Ph.D., LMSW is core faculty at Saybrook University, owner of Transformative Mind Counseling LLC, and founder of the Michigan Black Therapy Fund, which provides free services to Michigan's Black community. She holds a Ph.D. in Counselor Education and Supervision from Wayne State University and a master's in clinical social work from Michigan State University. Dr. Burks focuses on treating anxiety, depression, and trauma, and is an active speaker on mental health, implicit bias, and anti-racism. She serves on multiple committees addressing multicultural counseling and anti-racism.

Charmaine L. Conner, Ph.D., LPC, NCC, CCPT-S, CPRT-S is the Department Chair and Assistant Professor at Roosevelt University in the Counseling and Human Services Program. She has been a counselor educator for 5 years, and in professional practice as a licensed counselor for more than 10 years. Her clinical experience includes providing individual and group counseling to children and adolescents who have presented with treatment concerns such as depression, anxiety, trauma, and academic issues.

11 The First Year

Brandy K. Richeson

Nothing can dim a light that shines from within.

Maya Angelou

Abstract

Over the last decade, there has been an influx of CEs joining the ranks of higher education. Becoming a new faculty member can be both rewarding and stressful, as it offers the opportunity of maturing from a doctoral learner, to learning the roles and responsibilities that come with being a counselor educator. This chapter discusses the critical first year of employment as a new CES faculty member, navigating the expectations around service commitments, teaching and research, challenges that may arise, and the importance of boundaries and self-care.

Learning Objectives After reading this chapter, you will be able to:

1. Outline the expectations and responsibilities associated with being a counselor educator.
2. Identify possible personal and professional challenges that can occur while navigating the first year.
3. Explore the importance of implementing self-care strategies and setting boundaries to help to remain physically and mentally healthy while maintaining the workload.

B. K. Richeson (✉)
Liberty University, Lynchburg, VA, USA
e-mail: bricheson@liberty.edu

D. M. Stalnaker-Shofner and T. N. Sapp (eds.), *A Comprehensive Guide for Counselor Education*, Springer Texts in Education, https://doi.org/10.1007/978-3-031-68358-9_11

11.1 Statement of Reflexivity

As an African American, cisgender woman in higher education, I am called to reflect on the fear and pain around my experiences with unfair and discriminatory practices, misogynistic behaviors, and systemic racism in the workplace. I find myself heavy at times with the burden of the many responsibilities that are placed on Black, educated women like the implicit expectation and explicit requirement to be a fortress of strength in adversity, as well as an unapologetic role model for those who come behind. My intersectionalities, while beautiful, tempt others to place me in their box of stereotypes, that are often hurtful reminders of how I am viewed. As a counselor educator and clinician, I use that hurt as motivation to give back, to pay it forward, and to provide opportunities for those in need. My experiences speak to my process of being mentored at an Historically Black College/University (HBCU), where excellence was the standard. My mentorship was under a seasoned professor and mentor, who prepared me well for academia by providing me with ample opportunities for growth and improvement during my first year as a counselor educator. My time with him taught me how to successfully work with my own mentees in a way that sets them up for success. I approached this chapter guided by my experiences as a counselor educator, former mentee, and current mentor, tasked with providing an outline of the expectations for novice faculty. This discussion of the critical first year of employment includes my interpretation of the requisite CE roles including service, teaching, and research commitments, while also highlighting challenges that make creating boundaries and practicing self-care all the more important.

11.2 Case Scenario

You are a new *counselor educator in a graduate counseling program that offers a doctoral track that is delivered in an on-campus format. The first class that you are assigned to teach is a multicultural class. You are provided with the course syllabus, textbook and additional supplemental readings to begin your preparation for the course. After reading through the syllabus and reviewing the course assignments and textbook, you realize that the text is extremely outdated, including derogatory terms like "Indian", "Mulatto", "Gypsy" and "Transvestite". You immediately request a meeting to speak to your department chair about the textbook because your class is starting in two weeks. In the meeting with your chair, you find out that the book is the designated text and it must be used for your course. Upon asking about the procedure to have the book replaced, you find out that all newly proposed texts must go through a book audit which takes a full semester to process. Being that you recently graduated from a program with CACREP accreditation, you are aware that teaching the course with the designated textbook is a social justice issue. You are new to the university and don't want to cause any problems, but you now also feel anxious about teaching your first course as a CES.*

11.3 Introduction

Congratulations on obtaining employment as a CES faculty member! The first year in a professorship can be a rite of passage that involves an almost immediate shift in maturity and responsibility from your days of being a doctoral learner. You may even begin to question your ability to do the job well, as you wrestle with feelings of inadequacy. This concept can impact learners and new educators and is referred to as imposter syndrome. This will be discussed further in Chap. 25. Employment as a counselor educator can be both satisfying and rewarding, as you see gains in your growth, while also being challenging, due to limited opportunities for self-care and work-life balance (Magnuson, 2002). Doctoral training, and understanding of your professional identity, as well as the demands and responsibilities of the position during the first year, are integral to your success (See Chap. 10 where this is further discussed). According to the 2024 CACREP Standards, your doctoral program has set you in motion to be in a position of leadership in the profession (CACREP, 2024), thus preparing you for this critical first year. As a novice CES faculty member, it is imperative that you understand the expectations and requirements of the position, anticipate and prepare for first year challenges, and identify boundaries and self-care strategies to be successful in your position. When unsure, ask questions!

11.4 Expectations

As you begin your new career as CES faculty member, it is essential that you have a clear understanding of the expectations and responsibilities for the first year. Having this knowledge also puts you in a position to have a better understanding of how tenure works at your institution (See Chap. 14). The level of research your university subscribes to will often define what aspects of the position are most important, but ultimately whether you are employed in a brick and mortar, or online institution (See Chap. 3), the three overarching responsibilities of full-time counselor educators are teaching, research and scholarship, and service. While these are standard university requirements, they may vary based on the institution and program type (Table 11.1).

11.5 CACREP Requirements

11.5.1 Professional Identity

Your identity as a faculty member will be a huge part of your matriculation during your first year. Your professional identity is dynamic, it is affected by many factors, including your intersectionalities, and is continually changing, and developing over time (Gholampour & Ayati, 2020). Institutional support and understanding of professional standards around identity formation is necessary for your success. The

Table 11.1 Year one expectations

Requirements	Professional identity development
Teaching	Learner-based teaching Learner-centered engagement Social justice teaching practices
Research	Establish research agenda Learner collaborations Presentations Networking
Scholarship and service	Institutional commitments Sponsor learner organizations Membership in professional organizations mentoring Mentoring

CACREP (2024) supports the growth of faculty identity by ensuring in standards 1.H. and 1.S. that institutions make "continuous and systematic efforts to recruit" and "retain" diverse students and faculty "that enhance and support the diversity of the program" (pp. 4–5). Similarly, they promote a unified counseling identity by requiring that core faculty identify with the counseling profession. Each core faculty member must:

1. have sustained memberships in professional counseling organizations;
2. relevant professional counseling credentials; and
3. show evidence of sustained professional engagement through at least two of the following: (a) professional development and renewal activities related to counseling, (b) professional service and advocacy in counseling, (c) ongoing counseling practice, or (d) research and scholarly activity in counseling commensurate with their faculty role (CACREP, 2024, p. 6; Standard 1.Z).

There are numerous benefits to having CACREP's blueprint for professional identity. For you, it helps to highlight what your expectations will be, and it can also be used as a template that allows you and your learners to learn the importance of professional identity. It further ensures that you understand the connection between the above standards and your success during your first year.

11.5.2 Leadership and Advocacy

The CACREP has identified expectations for leadership and advocacy that can support you during your first year. As a newly graduated individual, you want to familiarize yourself with standards in the Doctoral Section dedicated to leadership and advocacy (CACREP, 2024, Standard 6.B.5). A part of your professional identity should be based on your roles as a leader and advocate. Some of the highlighted areas speak to being a leader in your CES program, when consulting and working in the profession, as well as in your knowledge of accreditation standards and processes. As it relates to advocacy, you are expected to advocate for the profession in your role as a clinician and CES, when working with clients, and as it relates to social justice issues and practices (CACREP, 2024). Being a leader and an advocate in the profession is another part of your growing professional identity. This means including diverse materials in your classroom, speaking up to, and for, your learners, and addressing those microaggressions when they come your way (Yes, even when it makes you uncomfortable!). In the words of Kirk Franklin, "It don't feel good, but growing never does", so keep your head up, stick your chest out and go and be the advocate and leader that you have been called to be!

11.5.3 Teaching

With teaching often being the most highly weighted role in academia, a good development of teaching skills is critical in your role as a new counselor educator (Pietrzak et al., 2008). Waalkes et al. (2021), states that teaching requires time and practice to develop and must be done in conjunction with balancing the role of faculty and maintaining boundaries with learners (See Chap. 2). According to Swank and Houseknecht (2019), "teaching requires time and practice to develop the knowledge, skills, professional behaviors, and dispositions of a competent, learner-centered counselor educator" (p. 86). Just remember, with time and practice, comes growth.

In your initial role as teacher, it is typical to rely on content and teacher-focused ways of teaching that tend to offer you comfort, while relieving anxiety. As you develop your style, it's important to move towards learner-based teaching, developing more interaction and processes, which ultimately allows for greater self-efficacy in your capacity to teach. In relation to classroom techniques, you will likely begin with more didactic teaching skills, using more content related information that allows teaching larger amounts of information. With growth, you will become more learner-centered, offering engagement that speaks to multiple learning styles and development (Hoidn, 2017). Ultimately, the goal is for you to grow as a new faculty member, while also setting learners up for success.

From a social justice approach to teaching, it's important that you integrate texts and materials that include diverse voices and perspectives in your teaching. Utilizing diverse curriculum, praxis, and classroom management styles can be paramount in providing a more individualized approach to education for learners. Decolonizing, or undoing traditional, colonial practices include confronting and challenging past practices that still influence the educational system. This may include communicating and theorizing with scholars across the globe (Morreira et al., 2020). Indigenizing your classroom can help with reflection on the structure of educational institutions, and the roles they play within the larger society. It can also assist with empowerment, and connections to place and community. I want to encourage you to develop your classroom into a brave space that fosters learner strength and validates their lived experiences. This is beneficial to creating scholars who form their identities built on diverse contributions, histories, and worldviews (Pete, 2016).

Stop and Reflect: *In the case scenario for this chapter, you can use the outdated text as "a teachable moment". The scenario addresses several important factors for you as the professor. It incorporates aspects of teaching, research and scholarship, service and social justice. Because you are working with CES doctoral learners who are learning how to operate within systems, in the role of counselor educator, this is a great opportunity to pull them into the dialogue about the text. As a part of the class, you present the textbook and you divvy up portions of it to your learners for review. In class, you hold discussions around the derogatory names in the text, and then honor them with the appropriate wording. In your quest for a more individualized approach to education, you have learners to share their observations and opinions of their assigned portions of the text, creating an environment that is ripe for decolonizing Western, colonial systems and language, while also allowing your CES doctoral learners to challenge influences from the past, that are still showing up today. Your final assignment for the text includes learners researching an updated text that respects diversity and differences. The class will vote on the text that most meets the needs of teaching learners about social justice practices and then propose it to the university as a replacement for the multicultural course. You introduced the learners to a better understanding of leadership and advocacy, while creating an atmosphere of learning with a purpose!*

11.5.4 Research and Scholarship

Research is a substantial expectation in the academy. Your university's classification is typically what determines the weight and depth that research holds at your institution, as well as designating what will be required of you. Establishing a research agenda will be instrumental to your success in research and scholarship. Your research agenda helps to lay the foundation for your current and future research.

As a new professor, your dissertation will likely be the most recent research that you have completed, and it should certainly be the research that you are the most well- versed in. You worked hard on your dissertation, so explore different avenues to get as many publications as you can from it. Not only can you benefit from your dissertation, but you can also provide scholarship opportunities for learners who may also be interested in your topic. As you grow your work, invite them to present and to write with you, as a way to introduce them to research and writing. Look at you contributing to the future generation of counselor educators!

Another great way to collaborate on research topics is networking. During your first year be sure to form connections with your colleagues, especially others who are also new. Not only is the support system beneficial, but it also provides an opportunity for additional research options for both you and your colleagues. It's important for you to attend as many conferences as you can and network with faculty in other programs and other universities, whose interests align with your own.

Networking is also a great way to expand your professional endeavors and it can introduce you to diverse topics that you didn't know that you were interested in. Because of the benefits of today's technology, opportunities to collaborate on scholarship and research across geographic, disciplinary, and stakeholder contexts, (Morreira et al., 2020) can be helpful in unraveling colonized research and practices. Gerlach (2018) shares that additional ways to aid in decolonizing research and scholarship include affirming and implementing Indigenous epistemologies and working with scholars that combine Indigenous and Western methodologies. Both are great ways to implement social justice strategies, while modeling diverse practices in scholarship and research with learners. Remember, research is something that will be on-going, so as you grow and mature in your position, your areas of interest and collaboration can expand, providing additional research opportunities.

11.5.5 Service

As a new Counselor Educator, you will be expected to make service contributions. Providing service allows you to give beyond your scholarship and teaching requirements. Service options can consist of donating your time and/or resources to the institution, the community, or providing a professional service.

One way to provide academic service is to work on committees within your institution. While you will likely be appointed to the new faculty committee, you will also have an opportunity to participate on at least one other committee that is of interest to you. Committee service can include working on assessments, curriculum development, or sponsoring a student organization. It is important that you research which committees are available for you to join as many universities will typically limit committee work for novice faculty.

Another way to provide a service is to work with a local community organization. As a faculty member, you can work with learners to provide seminars and presentations based on data that benefit your community. You can also incorporate community service aspects into your lessons, giving your learners the opportunity to meet a need in the community. These are my personal favorites, as they teach learners the importance of advocacy.

The final form of service that will be addressed is professional. Professional service can be provided in many ways to include working to organize conferences, sitting on professional committees, or editorial boards, or serving on accreditation committees to help establish standards for the profession. As you embark on finding a service that speaks to you, be sure to inquire about the workload, time commitment and requirements, before making a final decision. Remember, this is your first year and you have a lot to learn, so take it easy. Teaching, research and scholarship, and service are expectations for those fulfilling the role of counselor educator and are used as a part of the requirements for tenure in the academy. As you fulfill your conditions of employment, do yourself a favor and be sure to

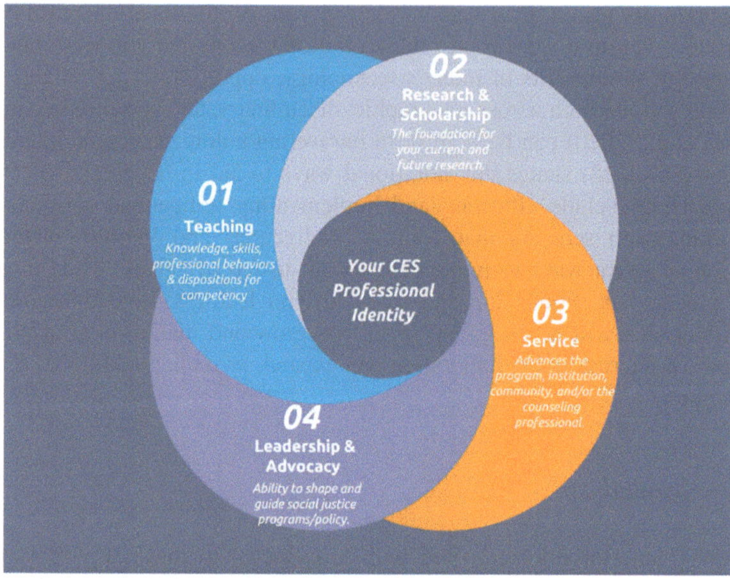

Fig. 11.1 CACREP requirements for counselor educators

track the work that you are doing by updating your curriculum vita (CV) as these opportunities occur (Fig. 11.1).

Stop and Reflect: *Faculty roles are often defined by institutional cultures. The expectations of teaching, research and scholarship, and service, requires achieving the right balance for you to be successful in your first year. It's important to make connections between what is acceptable within your discipline, versus what is encouraged by your institution. As you walk into your first year managing your expectations, it's important to note that teaching, research and scholarship, and service do not have to be in conflict with one another. You can work smarter to create teaching opportunities where they can co-exist. This may happen with the creation of a class service project, where your learners are expected to include some parts teaching, and some parts research and scholarship in an experiential learning community. Because navigating the first year is challenging, in and of itself, it's important to have meaningful experiences with your learners that can help to make the work more fun for them, and for you.*

11.6 Meeting Expectations

It can be difficult to meet all the demands of the first year, no matter how hard you try. Successful mentorship can improve your odds if you have the right mentor. A good mentor can provide guidance, advice and socialization for you during your first year, increasing your chances for success.

11.6.1 Mentoring

The mentoring relationship is a formal relationship that typically lasts for your first two years of professorship. Essentially, you would be partnered with a more senior faculty member, whose job is to show you the ropes. Activities that you can expect to participate in include shadowing your mentor, attending committee meetings, working on projects together and regular meetings to discuss various topics. You can use your meeting time to ask questions, gather information and discuss the expectations of your institution. Ideally, your mentor will teach you strategies for success during your first year. A good mentor provides opportunities for you to network, collaborate and to begin recognizing your areas of strength and potential, while helping to prepare you for promotion and tenure (Borders et al., 2011).

11.6.2 Self-care and Boundaries

Transitioning from being a doctoral student into a new CES position can be challenging. The demands of the teaching loads, research and scholarship, and service can be overwhelming to meet, causing stress, and possible burn-out, as you adjust to your new work-life balance. As a new professional in the field, you may experience feeling inadequate, or like an imposter. Don't worry, you're in good company, as most first year faculty experience these same feelings.

Burnout can occur causing exhaustion, depersonalization and/or cynicism, as well as reduced personal and/or professional efficacy in the workplace (American Psychological Association, 2018; Maslach & Leiter, 2016). This can occur when your ideas of your work life do not match what you actually experience in your work setting. These situations can cause a decrease in satisfaction and trust, causing cynicism to occur. According to a 2023 Healthy Minds Network Study, 64% of participating faculty reported being burned out due to work (Vyletel et al., 2023). The bad news is that burnout can occur. The good news is that I am going to share with you some ways that you can combat burnout or mitigate the effects.

The first is the importance of creating boundaries in helping you traverse your new responsibilities, and to do it well. As a novice faculty member, it is important that you set boundaries. I imagine you're thinking, "How do I set boundaries as a new employee who is excited to be employed in my field of study?" It is because you are new that you need to maintain boundaries for yourself to avoid taking on more than you can handle in your first year. Remember how I previously addressed the importance of asking questions for better understanding of what your university will require of you? Once you have that information, focus on those aspects of the job, and those aspects only, so that you can have a successful first year, meeting (exceeding, if you are feeling fancy) the tasks that you were assigned. Do not volunteer, or accept additional roles, or allow yourself to be pressured into taking on additional responsibilities (you can thank me later). Your employer has laid out the requirements for your first year of employment and I can assure you

Table 11.2 Meeting expectations

Methods	Outcomes
Formal mentoring	Guidance Collaboration Networking Support system Areas of strength Areas for improvement
Self-care	Track stressors Set boundaries Create a plan for success Utilize healthy coping responses

that meeting their expectations will require time, patience and energy. Creating boundaries that allow you to focus on your assigned tasks will be detrimental to your success.

Work stress can be harmful to your mental and physical health, so it is important to create a plan to minimize work related stress. One way to do that is to be mindful of tracking your stressors. This can be done by journaling and recognizing patterns, and your responses to situations. You can also work to develop healthy responses to stressors. This can include making healthier choices when stressed. Instead of eating unhealthy foods, choose healthier options. You can also exercise, make time for what's important to you and build healthy sleeping habits. Discussing situations with your support system (supervisor, friends, mentor) to create a plan to combat stress can also be helpful. Lastly, take time to recharge and focus on activities that bring you peace of mind. Activities such as walking, meditation, mindfulness, and deep breathing can all be beneficial in managing work-related stress (Table 11.2).

Stop and Reflect: *As you consider the case scenario and information provided above, remember that there is always more to do, and some of those things you may not know how to do. To tackle the inner imposter, take a moment to reflect on what has you feeling uneasy and how you can get the job done. Stop to acknowledge your strengths and celebrate your accomplishments (you did get the job, after all). Another strategy is to reframe those negative thoughts. If necessary, jot down the negatives and turn them into positives. Use your superpowers for good! If you get too overwhelmed, remember to set those boundaries we discussed. Use the plan that you created to remind you of your priorities! Lastly, reach out to your support system (including your mentor), to discuss how you're feeling and what you're going through. Dealing with the stress of a new position can be overwhelming, but you have the tools to be successful. Figure out what works for you and stick to it. You got this!*

11.7 Conclusion

Navigating the critical first year can be challenging and can push you out of your comfort zone. Meeting the expectations of a new CES program can be daunting without proper mentorship. Having a mentor to guide you through your first year can be instrumental in your success. A good mentor will provide you with opportunities to collaborate on service projects, teaching and research and provide helpful feedback that will teach you strategies for success during your first year. In reflection, it is my hope that this chapter, and its suggestions, will offer you guidance as you navigate your role as a new faculty member. Hopefully, you found aspects of the chapter that resonated with you. A tacit role that is a part of being a faculty member, with intersecting and historically marginalized identities, will be to share what you have learned as you mentor the next generation of counselors and counselor educators and supervisors, as they enter the academy. As you continue, it is my hope that you will refer back to this chapter as often as necessary to guide you in your professional growth. "Let me be the first to congratulate you again. Once you have completed your first year, do a little jig, pat yourself on the back, and treat yourself to something that makes you happy. You did it!"

References

American Psychological Association. (2018, October 14). *Coping with stress at work.* https://www.apa.org/topics/healthy-workplaces/work-stress

Borders, L. D., Young, J. S., Wester, K. L., Murray, C. E., Villalba, J. A., Lewis, T. F., & Mobley, A. K. (2011). Mentoring promotion/tenure-seeking faculty: Principles of good practice within a counselor education program. *Counselor Education and Supervision, 50*, 171–188. https://doi.org/10.1002/j.1556-6978.2011.tb00118.x

Council for Accreditation of Counseling and Related Educational Programs. (2024). *2024 CACREP standards.* https://www.cacrep.org/wp-content/uploads/2024/04/2024-Standards-Combined-Version-4.11.2024.pdf

Gholampour, M., & Ayati, M. (2020). Factors affecting the development of a teacher's professional identity: A narrative-research of a teacher's life events. *Journal of Educational Sciences, 27*(2), 1–22. https://doi.org/10.22055/EDUS.2020.34294.3078

Gerlach, A. (2018). Thinking and researching relationally: Enacting decolonizing methodologies with an Indigenous early childhood program in Canada. *International Journal of Qualitative Methods, 17*, 1–8. https://doi.org/10.1177/1609406918776075

Hoidn, S. (2017). *Student-centered learning environments in higher education classrooms.* Palgrave Macmillan.

Magnuson, S. (2002). New assistant professors of counselor education: Their 1st year. *Counselor Education & Supervision, 41*(4), 306–320. https://doi.org/10.1002/j.1556-6978.2002.tb01293.x

Maslach, C., & Leiter, M. (2016). Understanding the burnout experience: Recent research and its implications for psychiatry. *World Psychiatry, 15*(2), 103–111. https://doi.org/10.1002/wps.20311

Morreira, S., Luckett, K., Kumalo, S., & Ramgotra, M. (2020). Confronting the complexities of decolonising curricula and pedagogy in higher education. *Third World Thematics: A TWQ Journal, 5*(1/2), 1–18. https://doi.org/10.1080/23802014.2020.1798278

Pete, S. (2016). 100 ways: Indigenizing & decolonizing academic programs. *Aboriginal Policy Studies/Commentary, 6*(1), 81–89. https://doi.org/10.5663/aps.v6i1.27455

Pietrzak, D., Duncan, K., & Korcuska, J. S. (2008). Counseling students' decision making regarding teaching effectiveness: A conjoint analysis. *Counselor Education and Supervision, 48*(2), 114–132. https://doi.org/10.1002/j.1556-6978.2008.tb00067.x

Swank, J., & Houseknecht, A. (2019). Teaching competencies in counselor education: A delphi study. *Counselor Education and Supervision, 58*(3), 162–176. https://doi.org/10.1002/ceas.12148

Vyletel, B., Voichoski, E., Lipson, S., & Heinze, J. (2023, August 23). *Exploring faculty burnout through the 2022–23 HMS faculty/staff survey.* American Psychological Association. https://www.apa.org/ed/precollege/psychology-teacher-network/introductory-psychology/faculty-burnout-survey#:~:text=Burnout%20was%20higher%20among%20women,were%20satisfied%20with%20their%20job

Waalkes, P. L., Hall, D. P., Swindle, P. J., & Stickl Haugen, J. (2021). Beginning counselor educators' experiences of teaching mentorship. *Teaching & Supervision in Counseling, 3*, 78–88. https://doi.org/10.7290/tsc030108

Brandy K. Richeson, Ph.D., LPC, LSC, NCC, ACS (she/her/hers) is an Assistant Professor and the Co-Chair of the Faculty of Color Connections Committee in the Counselor Education and Family Studies Department at Liberty University. She has held leadership roles with the Virginia Association for Counselor Education and Supervision, as well as the Standards Revision Committee for CACREP. Her scholarly work includes presenting at local, state, national and international conferences in the areas of school counseling, social/emotional health in children, anti-racist practices, epigenetics, continuous traumatic stress in marginalized populations, depression, anxiety, sexuality, and substance abuse.

The International Learner and Counselor Educator

12

Keiko Sano, Syntia Santos Dietz, Krista Kirk, and Joy Maweu Mwendwa

Better than a thousand days of diligent study is one day with a great teacher.

Japanese Proverb

Abstract

This chapter introduces some of the fundamental challenges and obstacles international counseling learners and CES face as they navigate the field of counselor education and academia in the United States. The authors share their personal experiences, lessons learned, and recommendations for other learners, faculty, and administrators, supported by current literature in this area. The authors suggest the use of two diversity models to increase self-awareness of multicultural sensitivities in working with international individuals by understanding their unique needs and barriers and by acknowledging their own and systemic stereotypes, assumptions, and biases.

K. Sano (✉) · S. Santos Dietz
Antioch University, Yellow Springs, OH, USA
e-mail: ksano@antioch.edu

S. Santos Dietz
e-mail: sdietz@antioch.edu

K. Kirk
Messiah University, Mechanicsburg, PA, USA
e-mail: keadour@liberty.edu

J. Maweu Mwendwa
Liberty University, Lynchburg, VA, USA
e-mail: jmmaweu@liberty.edu

D. M. Stalnaker-Shofner and T. N. Sapp (eds.), *A Comprehensive Guide for Counselor Education*, Springer Texts in Education, https://doi.org/10.1007/978-3-031-68358-9_12

Learning Objectives After reading this chapter, you will be able to:

1. Outline the unique experiences that international CES faculty and CITs face within counselor education programs.
2. Support the development of counselor education curricula that is inclusive of the unique lived experiences of international CES faculty and CITs with the goal of enhancing the cultural sensitivity of counseling programs.
3. Identify strategies to advocate for the incorporation of educational and professional support for international CES faculty and CITs to enhance retention outcomes.

12.1 Statement of Reflexivity

As we reflect on our experiences and how those come to bear on the writing of this chapter, we note that two of the authors of this chapter are immigrants, and two were born to their immigrant parents. The first author was born and raised in Japan, the second author was born and raised in Honduras, the third author was raised by an immigrant parent from India and a first-generation immigrant from Lebanon, and the fourth author was born to Kenyan parents and raised both in Kenya and in the United States. We wrote this chapter together as female counselor educators with international backgrounds and experience in teaching, supervising, and counseling in multiple countries outside the United States. We share experiences of working closely with international students and faculty in higher education institutions and in clinical settings, where we are often asked to be their advisor and/or mentor, while institutions, admissions, or other faculty members may not have enough resources, knowledge, or strategies to support them. international students and faculty have unique needs that require counselors, faculty, and administrators; a broad set of skills to not only help them survive in a foreign environment but also to thrive utilizing their talents in service to the profession both locally and globally. Through writing this chapter, we have increased our understanding of ourselves, acknowledged the work we have done in support of our international students and faculty, and valued our passion for the profession from a global perspective by learning from each other and sharing our experiences, as well as supporting and processing them together. In this chapter, we share our personal and collective learning journey, aiming to inform other internationals on their own journeys and those in positions to support them.

12.2 Case Scenario 1

Chen is a Chinese male doctoral candidate in your CACREP accredited Ph.D. in CES program and one of your advisees. He is currently finalizing his dissertation and applying for a CES faculty position while also attending to his graduate assistantship responsibilities. Chen's two younger siblings have recently moved in with Chen to attend an undergraduate program nearby. As the first-born son pursuing a terminal degree, Chen is depended upon to bring esteem to the family name and to be a father figure and role model to his younger siblings. Additionally, Chen's pursuit of a Ph.D. in Counselor Education was not readily accepted by his family based on their belief system which is also reinforced by the stigma surrounding counseling. Since Chen chose to deviate from his parent's desire for him to major in computer science or medicine, this has added pressure to perform academically. Chen also reports that he feels misunderstood by his U.S. friends when they question his strong familial ties that, from the mainstream perspectives, only add to the dysfunction and enmeshment. On top of this, during the pandemic, Chen reported that he and his siblings experienced physical and verbal attacks by people in their local community because they were Asian. Chen explained that the anti-Asian violence that he and his siblings endured was frightening for them because they have never experienced physical violence that was overtly and openly directed toward them. Chen stated that he felt hopeless and feared for his and his siblings' lives. Since the attacks, Chen reported feeling anxious and having some difficulty leaving his home for basic life needs such as going to purchase groceries or get a haircut.

Chen informed you that he was offered a faculty position at an institution across the state; however, he has been informed that hiring has been frozen for all positions. Other scheduled interviews have also been halted, and many inquiries have not responded to him. Chen just received notice from the International Student Office in his school that he may need to return to his home country since his optional practical training (OPT) is delayed. Chen explained to different stakeholders that since he is graduating this semester, he is not eligible to register for the additional semester needed to maintain his status as a full-time graduate learner and remain on a valid Student Visa in the U.S. Chen asked if you could advocate for him, and you informed him that you were unaware of the expectations surrounding his international learner status and you were unsure who to connect him to for additional support. He stated that he felt alone and unprepared on this journey as an international learner and future CES.

12.3 Case Scenario 2

Dr. Madalitso, originally from Malawi, was recently hired as a counselor educator at a teaching university. They had completed a master's in Guidance and Counseling at a top university in South Africa that had offered her a scholarship. Additionally, they completed their Doctorate in Counselor Educator and Supervision at a southeastern US university with a CACREP accredited program. Subsequent to their degree completion, Dr. Madalitso, they were hired as an Assistant Professor at an U.S. university, which is a significant accomplishment and a source of pride within their family and community.

They are in their fourth week of classes in the current academic term. Dr. Madalitso is quickly realizing that their new faculty role at a northern Midwest university is a completely different environment than that of the institution where they earned their CES doctorate. Relocation was required for this position, and they rented a small apartment close to the university which allowed for connection to the campus as well as an easier commute. This was important as they did not have any established community or personal relationships outside of that with their colleagues. Dr. Madalitso lives in a rural area, and it takes two hours to drive to a larger city. There, they can get a few commodities such as ethnic food and requisite hair products that are specific to African hair. Dr. Madalitso is the only person of color in the department. The department chair recently approached them and requested that they facilitate a presentation focusing on racial justice concerns. This request has created anxiety for them and is especially distressing since they have already experienced overt discrimination at the university and in their community. They have heard racial slurs directed at them, and learned that this experience was not an anomaly, based on news reports from other BIPOC individuals. They have not received adequate support as a new faculty member or found someone else like her in her school whom she can freely process her cultural adjustment with.

Her graduate CITs mostly liked her engaging and storytelling lecture style. Many of them have made an effort to pronounce their names correctly, while others have avoided saying their names altogether. When she asked a colleague how she should handle this situation, she was advised to consider selecting an English name to use instead. She loves her name since it represents part of her indigenous identity. Moreover, after a slight consideration of this name change, she quickly remembered that she must maintain her legal name since she desires to apply for a green card once she is eligible.

12.4 Introduction to the CES International Learner

The international learner population in the United States has dramatically increased over the last 20 years. According to the Institute of International Education (2023), the United States hosts over 15% of the world's international learner population: the current 6.4 million learners in 2023 boasts a significant increase as compared to 1.6 million learners in 2000. This rise has forced institutions to become more aware of the unique needs and specific experiences of international learners, and how these needs often have gone unmet (Barton & Ryan, 2020; Coates & Dickinson, 2012; Franken, 2012). International learners, specifically those from non-European countries, appear to face more acculturative stress (Houshmand et al., 2014), social isolation and discrimination (Freeman & Li, 2019; Leon & Chmiel, 2013), homesickness (Poyrazli & Grahame, 2007), and language-related issues (Arthur, 2013) in comparison to their European counterparts. Subsequently, the challenges experienced by these learners can affect academic performance and competency in their occupational fields (Sherry et al., 2010). Specifically, in CES, international doctoral learners feel pressure to assimilate into US culture, and are forced to "reject" (Li & Liu, 2020, p. 207) their histories, backgrounds, and values which are—essential experiences to their learning. Additionally, international CES doctoral learners experience a level of tension that domestic learners do not face; this can be seen in the unique power dynamics of clinical supervision, which seems to involve higher professional requirements for these learners (Ng & Smith, 2009). This is also evident in the restrictions and expectations inherent in the university systems through which these learners navigate. With the added challenge of having limited exposure to U.S. culture, including learning communication styles and interpersonal dynamics, international CES doctoral learners subsequently feel less confident in their supervision practices than domestic CES doctoral learners; Woo et al. (2015) argue that this lack of confidence is a result of CES programs ignoring the unique needs of international learners.

Despite the obvious challenges that international learners may face, previous literature clearly identifies that their presence in the U.S. stimulates cultural, financial, and academic growth. Urban and Palmer (2014) argue that international learners in CES doctoral programs are an unequivocal resource for integrating intercultural purpose and delivery in higher education curricula. International CES doctoral learners offer the experience of reciprocal cultural learning, which helps to develop domestic learners' multicultural competence (Jones, 2017; Yan et al., 2014). Unfortunately, many of these learners will work with non-immigrant counselor educators, which heightens the sense that international CES doctoral learners feel to assimilate in order to integrate into these often unfamiliar academic environments (Li & Liu, 2020). This results in the rich experiences of international learners being minimized or undervalued. In spite of this, the number of international learners traveling to the US has continued to increase over the years (Cantwell et al., 2009), with many programs beginning to increase their efforts to integrate intercultural elements. When international, intercultural, and global dimensions are included in the philosophy of postsecondary education, this process has been referred to as internationalization (Knight, 2004, 2018).

Stop and Reflect: *In the first case scenario, Chen attempts to address the emotional pressures they are experiencing as an international learner by acknowledging expectations from his family as well as the difference in the cultural norms of Hong Kong and those of the U.S. Understanding the conflicting cultural values, and the systemic barriers posed, offers context to understand Chen's unique challenges and other critical experiences related to their identity as an international CES doctoral learner. As you consider this case, we invite you to note the following: (1) the internalized values and beliefs reinforced by Chen's culture of origin, and how they may conflict with the cultural norms and expectations inherent in U.S. culture; (2) identify possible systemic barriers to Chen's success; and (3) consider how your feelings, initial assumptions, and potential biases influence your reflections of the case scenario.*

12.5 Introduction to the International Counselor Educator

International learners may choose to pursue degrees in the U.S. for a number of reasons: a desire for academic and professional growth, or a need for intellectual stimulation, economic improvement, and greater freedom or stability (Interiano & Lim, 2018; Kim et al., 2011). Their decision to leave or stay in the U.S. post-graduation is just as difficult as their initial decision to enroll in a U.S.-based graduate program (Kim et al., 2011). The completion of a doctorate presents a significant transition for these learners as they become new CES professionals and begin to explore employment opportunities. International learners face added challenges in their decision-making process, not just limited to choosing a job, rather also the consideration of the significance of deciding to stay in a foreign country with a culture different, and at times divergent from their own. Deciding to separate from loved ones, their community of support, spiritual leaders, and their known culture can result in higher levels of stress. Research from Khanal and Gaulee (2019) noted that international CES faculty experience potential impediments in the form of language barriers, culture shock, reverse culture shock, and overt and covert racism, and that these challenges can have implications throughout their professional journey.

The number of international doctorate recipients in the U.S. continues to increase; this includes those completing doctoral programs in counseling-related disciplines (Interiano & Lim, 2018). The Institute of International Education (2023) identified the U.S. as the leading destination for international learners, even as these learners are faced with a broad number of academic and nonacademic challenges (Khanal & Gaulee, 2019). These include reports of dissatisfaction, and feeling unwelcome (Horne et al., 2018), experiencing alienation or separation (Burdett & Crossman, 2012; Gardner, 2013), and encountering racial discrimination (Lee, 2015). Regarding doctoral learners, Ugwu and Adamuti-Trache (2017) state that the challenges they experience include having to adapt to a new culture, learning a new language, and the related language barriers, as well as other cultural, social, and academic barriers. The experience of being an international learner or faculty is influenced not only by factors such as country of origin and language, but also by one's cultural history and background and the current events occurring in the host country (Khanal & Gaulee, 2019). In other words, the experience of a European, White, French-speaking international is not the same as that of a Black, Spanish-speaking, Latinx/e international.

Other important considerations impacting the life and well-being of international CES doctoral learners and faculty are those related to immigration and institutional policies, practices, and regulations, which can be systemic obstacles that may hinder the success of CES doctoral learners and new CES faculty (Andrade, 2017). The process, time, cost, and restrictions of obtaining the appropriate paperwork and respective visas are extensive (Andrade, 2017). This is especially true for the transition between being a learner and becoming an employee and barriers manifest in things such as financial costs associated with education, lack of access to or the decentralization of information, oppressive practices, misinformation, and lack of support. Those things combined with the implications of where the international CES doctoral learner or counselor educator is from and how they are viewed within the context of current events within their host country (e.g., travel bans, global pandemic restrictions, etc.) have a great influence on international doctoral learners' decision to stay or leave upon conferral of their degree (Todoran & Peterson, 2019). This can potentially impact the living conditions, mental health, and overall well-being of international CES and faculty.

Stop and Reflect: *In considering the case scenario of Dr. Madalitso, it is noted that they have been asked to carry additional workload duties and responsibilities, specifically for assisting international counseling graduate and CES doctoral learners because of a lack of available support for these learners in their programs, as well as within the institution, and their community. They understand international learners' challenges because of what has been stated by the administration as their "shared experiences" (even international learners are not a monolith). The emotional capital expended in supporting other learners while also holding at times similar experiences as an international faculty can exact its own personal cost. As you consider this case, we invite you to ponder the following: (1) what explicit or implicit messages may be contributing to Dr. Madalitso's increased workload? And (2) what challenges may manifest and potentially impact Dr. Madalitso's decision to stay or to change their current employment?*

12.6 Internationalization of Counselor Education

It is evident that a different set of skills and knowledge are needed to respond efficiently to the characteristics of our current, dynamic, fast-paced, globalized, diverse world. This is especially true for the counseling field, which aims to provide the most accurate and effective support to the new generation of global citizens. Counselors and counselor educators are challenged to learn to work effectively with culturally diverse clients (Arthur & Achenbach, 2002), and in this regard, Pedersen and Leong (1997) originally highlighted the realities of cultural context, personal and professional ethnocentrism, and culturally encapsulated assumptions that may have diminished decision making and effectiveness in counseling. Over three decades later, the process of internationalization has become a key element for success in all fields, including counseling.

Internationalization in counseling and counselor education encompasses the fundamental elements of respect and cultural sensitivity, instead of assuming the Western perspectives are universal thereby spreading the Western ideology to the world. It can be argued that these elements may only be accomplished through collaboration, equal partnerships (Leung et al., 2009), and growth-fostering relationships (Avent Harris et al., 2019; Dietz & Baker, 2019) through international collaboration, the theoretical foundation of practice, training and development, professional advocacy, and social advocacy (Ng & Noonan, 2012). International education and international counseling involve the consideration of a global multidimensional perspective, the importance of indigenization and respect for one another, the urgent need for mutual collaboration through equal partnerships and growth-fostering relationships, and the common goal of improving knowledge and practice (Avent Harris et al., 2019; Dietz & Baker, 2019; Ng & Noonan, 2012).

For example, inviting counselor educators outside of the country as a keynote, guest speaker, or workshop facilitator can offer both faculty and learners an opportunity to learn diverse aspects of counseling and its training from global perspectives. Another idea is to invite counselors-in-training outside of the country to the classroom remotely to have live class discussions. Having direct interactions with CITs from outside the country can assist in the formulation of relationships; however, simply inviting them does not mean a collaborative relationship has been yet built. Counselor educators need to create shared objectives clearly and intentionally as to promote cultural exchange rather than create a cultural hierarchy. To learn about various cultural aspects in counseling and counselor education, one must not simply obtain new knowledge or understanding from different cultural backgrounds, but one must also increase self-awareness in their stereotypes, biases, and assumptions. Thus, developing skills to increase self-awareness in diverse contexts is a critical key to developing multicultural competence.

Another example of mutual collaboration can be utilizing international faculty members to lead study-abroad opportunities in their home countries. When the international faculty is present on such trips, potential stronger connections and understanding of the international service opportunities can occur for both learners and faculty. The international faculty's skill sets, cultural responsiveness, and unique insights are displayed as real-world examples for other faculty and learners who are present. Learning abroad programs with the support of the program and the institution will build trust and respect between the faculty and learners. Furthermore, the prolonged engagement of program faculty with the prospective learners in their home country could promote interest in and access for masters and doctoral learners to consider an U.S. counseling program because they know someone from "home" is there for additional support.

Counselor educators play an important role in creating opportunities and guiding the learning process to promote cultural competence development among future generations of counseling professionals and future counselor educators (Avent Harris et al., 2019; Dietz & Baker, 2019; Jurgens & McAuliffe, 2004). The cultivation of supervision and teaching readiness in CES doctoral learners is of utmost importance for future employment as a counselor educator. The 2024 CACREP standards identifies five core areas that represent foundation knowledge for CES graduates, two of which outline supervision competencies and teaching competencies (CACREP, 2024). Even so, international CES doctoral learners report feeling underprepared for teaching despite its key role in assessment as future counselor educators (Li & Liu, 2020). Rather than normalizing issues associated with cross-cultural experiences, programs tend to focus narrowly on the issues in supervision without attempting to meet the learners' needs long before they are responsible for supervising and teaching CITs.

Stop and Reflect: *Both Chen and Dr. Madalitso's challenges can be caused by cultural gaps and a lack of multicultural relevancy in counselor education. The success of international CES doctoral learners and counselor educators influences and is influenced by their families as well. In reviewing the above two case scenarios: (1) Identify possible biases in internationalizing counseling and counselor education; (2) Based on your own cultural identities, what might being an ally with Chen or Dr. Madalitso look like for you?*

12.7 Diversity Models for Inclusion

Multiculturalism influences the philosophy of counseling education depending on the level of faculty commitment to being culturally sensitive and competent (Hoshmand, 2004). Although a study found that international counseling faculty often identify themselves as "foreigner" or "immigrant" rather than their racial or ethnic identities (Sano, 2019), the societal system often categorizes individuals into racial/ethnic groups in the United States without considering their unique international identities. For example, Japanese-born international counselor educators associate with the challenging experiences of other international counselor educators more than U.S.-born Japanese counselor educators.

International CES doctoral learners and counselor educators often study and work with professionals who were born and raised in the U. S., and their pedagogy (Li & Liu, 2020), supervision (Sano, 2019), and ethical practice (Li & Ai, 2020) are influenced by those U.S. born counselor educators and supervisors. In pursuing academic and career success in a foreign land, they are forced to be assimilated into the cultural norms to fit in with the unfamiliar academia and the field of professional counseling and counselor education. Even though international counselor educators may have rich multicultural experiences, their cultural norms can be questioned or ignored rather than being encouraged to present their uniqueness in an environment where cultural sensitivity is lacking. As a result, they are less likely to be accessible or expressive of their unique culture. As a result, international faculty often have limited opportunities to explore their identities in the U.S.

For international CES doctoral learners and novice international CES faculty, learning to apply Eurocentric pedagogy and theories of counseling and supervision in unfamiliar classroom environments can increase their sense of self-doubt. When they are not confident or develop their sense of belonging, their own sense of safety in the learning environment can be difficult to develop, which can influence their assertiveness and transformation of their knowledge to practice. Counselor educators' relationships with their counselors-in-training and quality of teaching are related to their own sense of safety (Hernández et al., 2009); however, international CES doctoral learners and counseling faculty do not always feel safe due to their nonnegotiable identity as foreign individuals (Sano, 2019) in unfamiliar cultural contexts in the counseling profession and in counselor education.

International CES doctoral learners and educators find gaps in counseling approaches between the U.S. and their culture (Azuma, 1984; Mocan-Aydin, 2000) and challenges in integrating their Western approaches (Raguram et al., 2002) into their culture of origin. Because immigrants tend to partake in the visiting culture to fit in the new culture and survive in the new environment (Navas et al., 2007), international counseling faculty may focus more on fitting with the given cultural norms rather than developing or constructing their teaching praxess or clinical supervision styles. As their assimilation and acculturation progress and become familiar with the new culture in the U.S., they face consequences in re-entering their home countries due to their difficulty adapting (Li & Gale, 2018) and re-adjusting (Brabant et al., 1990) to their culture of origin as a result of their cultural exposure in the U.S. Therefore, international learners and counselor educators often do not decide to return to their home countries if they have the option and continue to work in the U.S., where they continue to experience marginalization and isolation (Ju et al., 2020).

CACREP emphasizes diversity both nationally and internationally (CACREP, 2024), and counseling programs and institutions emphasize recruiting and admitting diverse populations, including international learners and faculty. However, they may mistakenly focus on "having" international individuals rather than assisting them in retaining and thriving personally and professionally. The challenges of globalization in the field of counseling can be because of multiculturalism or internalization based on Western perspectives instead of inclusion or collaboration with international learners and faculty.

Furthermore, international Counselor Educators and Counselors-in-Training often face other challenges such as the following.

- Face racism, discrimination, and microaggression.
- Language proficiency and communication difficulties. Preparation for classes takes longer and hesitation in pursuing publication opportunities.
- Lack of support:
  - Institutional support including Admission Office (knowledge, resources, and support for the Student/Employment VISA, OPT, and those for their family members).
  - Department support is needed to advocate and be an ally.
  - Support and understanding of the tenure process due to the lack of long-term networks.
  - Funding opportunities (Grant and scholarship).
  - Support system outside of the institution.
- Misunderstanding key life requests because of cultural differences (deaths, marriage, births, religious or ritual events). For example—policy handbooks might indicate that time off for bereavement is given only for immediate family members; however, an International Faculty Member from a collectivistic society might have strong and deep ties to a grandparent or aunt who played a crucial role in their life. This loss might be as close to a parental loss. At times,

the international faculty might hold a leadership role that necessitates them to attend a family function to lead a ritual or say a blessing.

- The barrier to understanding the USA financial system and post-graduate systems that lend to the overall success of international faculty. For example, not knowing much about financing, credit, investments in the USA, etc. means that the international faculty is learning as they go and starting at times from scratch to build credit which is linked to housing needs. Struggling with these personal areas impacts the overall well-being of the international faculty.
- Intersectionality confusion – misunderstanding or expectations on international faculty to better understand USA/Western nuanced social issues like microaggressions. For example, a black international faculty who was born and raised in a dominant cultural context in their national home country might miss certain nuances about the racism landscape and related cultural implications on either side.
- Cultural gaps in ethical practices and classroom management, as well as helping, teaching, and supervisory relationships.
- Lack of recognition of "Counseling" professionals in their home country, including licensing requirements and portability difficulties.
- Tokenism—representing their country/continent.
- Feel responsible for advocating for ALL international learners in the program, especially if they have struggled to connect with other faculty. For example, international learners in a doctoral program who desire to research an international topic for their dissertation might not have many options for their dissertation committee selection except for this international faculty.

Due to the limited role models who share similar international identities and cultural backgrounds within the program, cultural mismatch with theories of counseling and supervision, and mistrust from their peers and learners in the classrooms (Sano, 2019), international CES doctoral learners and counselor educators experience further isolation from their institution and program. While they experience a lack of understanding or available support for their successful career development or positive classroom experiences, they are often assigned international learners in their programs to offer support for their development. Because of limited empirical evidence in applying specific models for counselor educators and administrators, we suggest integrating the RESPECTFUL Model (D'Andrea & Daniels, 2001) and the ADDRESSING model (Hays, 2016) to facilitate the inclusion of international counselor educators and doctoral learners in counseling programs utilizing a multicultural competence framework.

12.7.1 RESPECTFUL Model

The RESPECTFUL model (D'Andrea & Daniels, 2001) was developed for counselors to comprehensively and integratively recognize clients' multidimensional factors. This framework aims to consider individuals' development and diversity factors of counselors and clients present in the counseling process. This model identifies 10 domains that recognize the uniqueness and complexity of individuals and their development from multiple perspectives. Each RESPECTFUL factor contributes to the development of the individual as a whole and impacts their wellbeing: (R) religious-spiritual identity; (E) ethnic-cultural-racial background; (S) sexual identity; (P) psychological maturity; (E) economic class background; (C) chronological-developmental challenges; (T) threats to one's personal well-being; (F) family history and dynamics; (U) unique physical characteristics; and (L) location of residence. This model considers that these factors influence individuals' developmental challenges and concerns in addition to affecting their self-perspectives. This model can be the fundamental guide for administrators, faculty, program chairs, and hiring committees to assess cultural identities, personally and interpersonally, to check their biases and increase their culturally responsive approach without unconsciously imposing their own values, beliefs, stereotypes, or assumptions.

12.7.2 ADDRESSING Model

The ADDRESSING model (Hays, 2016) reflects socio-cultural diversity, which also helps counselors recognize and understand individuals' multicultural influences in combination with the following nine factors: (A) age; (DD) developmental and acquired disabilities; (R) religion; (E) ethnicity; (S) socioeconomic status; (S) sexual orientation; (I) indigenous heritage; (N) national origin; and (G) gender. Furthermore, Hays (2016) emphasizes the following six essential pieces of knowledge:

> (1) We all have biases; (2) We're all biased, but we do not all belong to dominant cultural groups; (3) When bias is reinforced by powerful groups and social structures, the results are systems of privilege and oppression; (4) Nonprivileged (minority) members are socialized to be aware of the lines separating those who have privilege from those who do not; (5) Privileged members of these systems are socialized to ignore the lines and differences; (6) Privilege creates access to important information for people with ascribed privileged and withholds this access from those who have been marginalized. (pp. 24–33)

Comparing these multidimensional factors in the interpersonal contexts helps us begin recognizing our own privilege (Agent identity) and considering the experience of others who do not have such privileges (Target identity). These agent and target identities are identified in the social context, institutional policies, systemic aspects, and cultural norms. For example, U.S.-born administrative staff may not be aware of the experience of an international faculty, yet they may unconsciously interact with them based on their assumptions and stereotypes. This tendency may mistakenly reinforce systemic oppression by imposing their own values and worldviews onto international learners and faculty.

12.8 Integration and Adaptation of the RESPECTFUL and ADDRESSING Models

Counselor's awareness of their own cultural values and beliefs and their clients' worldview, as well as their use of culturally appropriate intervention strategies, are critical competencies in multicultural and social justice counseling (Arrendondo et al., 1996). These competencies are paramount to counseling practice but are also essential to counselor education and the development of future generations of counseling professionals locally and globally. Thus, we suggest that institutional administrators and faculty consider their own multicultural and social justice competencies, particularly their awareness, as they choose to work with international CES doctoral learners and faculty and commit to their growth, advancement, success and overall well-being. The following two case studies aim to increase the understanding of international CES doctoral learners and faculty needs and challenges by applying the RESPECTFUL and ADDRESSING models (Fig. 12.1).

Stop and Reflect: *Instead of perceiving Chen's and Dr. Madalitso's identities from a monocultural worldview, consider each of them from multicultural lenses. For example, consider the following: (1) How might her race/ethnicity manifest differently in the U.S. as opposed to their countries of origin? (2) How likely would they face racial discrimination and microaggressions in the U.S.? (3) Are there any considerations of gender dynamics in their country of origin that can be different from the U.S. culture? (4) How may Chen and Dr. Madalitso hold both perspectives and gaps together?*

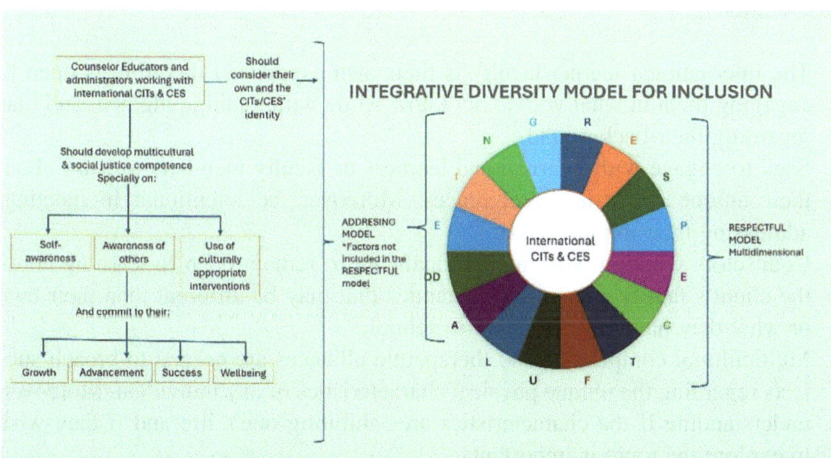

Fig. 12.1 Integrative diversity model for inclusion. *Note* This model captures the different factors to consider when working with international CITs and CES based on the RESPECTFUL and ADDREESING models

As you consider the *implications* of exploring your privilege, oppression, culturally-influenced beliefs, values, stereotypes, assumptions, blind spots, biases, and countertransference reactions in interacting with Chen and Dr. Madalitso as individuals and as professionals, key considerations to note are: expectations from their family of origin and community in their country of origin; current support system that can be similar to and different from their culture of origin; and ways to be an ally by being aware of your privileges and oppression, as well as your positionalities in the society and organization.

12.9 Toward Nurturing and Flourishing of International Learners and Faculty

International learners and faculty have unique challenges that can vary based on different factors. While international identities can share common experiences (e.g., leaving home, having to navigate a new culture/language, immigration), they are very culturally, linguistically, and individually different. Some of these differences are connected to one's background in terms of travel history, ties to one's own country, and time in the U.S. (e.g., acculturation). We suggest considering both the RESPECTFUL (D'Andrea & Daniels, 2001) model and the ADDRESSING model (Hays, 2016) to emphasize the importance of expanded cultural identities without limiting to what one model suggested. Table 12.1 offers a sample activity to facilitate the utilization of both models, respectively. Accordingly, when working with international learners and faculty, review the following considerations:

1. The international learner/faculty is their own expert and therefore is open to engaging them in what you do not know while withholding judgment and bias regarding their background.
2. Seek to engage with international learners or faculty members to learn about their unique needs and preferences. Moreover, be intentional in meeting/addressing their unique needs.
3. Counselors working with internationals are to remain open to learning about the client's family history and dynamics that may be different than their own or what they have learned about in school.
4. Multicultural competence and therapeutic alliances are needed to broach subjects regarding the unique physical characteristics of any individual. Moreover, understanding if the characteristics are inhibiting one's life and if they wish to explore the topic is important.
5. Celebrate the international faculty/learners who can speak more than one language and welcome the diversity that comes with different expressions of teaching and supervision (narrative style, proverbs, and song). Beyond CACREP's call and support for such diversity, all students—international and U.S. learners—need international faculty perspectives to help them prepare for the global world.

Table 12.1 Reflection exercise toward inclusion and support

Integrative diversity model for inclusion	Your identity Who you are	International learner/ faculty Identity What do you know about them?	Implications for your work (e.g. How does your privilege/ oppression may manifest?) What do you need to consider?	Cultural responsive strategies for inclusion and support How can you help?
RESPECTFUL model				
R: Religious-spiritual identity				
E: Ethnic-cultural-racial background				
S: Sexual identity				
P: psychological maturity				
E: Economic class background				
C: Chronological-developmental challenges				
T: threats to one's personal well-being				
F: family history and dynamics;				
U: unique physical characteristics				
L: location of residence				
ADDRESSING model (Only factors that not covered by RESPECTFUL model)				
A: Age and generational influences				
DD: Developmental disabilities and other disabilities				
E: Ethnic and racial identity				
I: Indigenous heritage				
N: National origin				
G: Gender				

Note Use this table to reflect on your process when working with CITs or CES with the ultimate goal of implementing culturally responsive strategies for inclusion and support towards their wellbeing and advancement (D'Andrea & Daniels, 2001; Hays, 2016)

6. Regarding language and accents, negatively highlighting, or gossiping about an international faculty/learner, one's accent is unacceptable. Everyone has an accent. Instead, be aware of your own biases, acknowledge the work it takes to learn a different language in order to teach and supervise in that language then, invite the international faculty to discuss how best they can be supported in teaching and supervising learners from another background.
7. Encourage and support international faculty/learners to publish. Their expertise and voice are needed both locally and internationally in the counseling profession. Furthermore, understand that publications will help your international faculty to succeed in academia. In essence, their success occurs if the departments/institutions succeed. Support publication efforts by:
   (a) Funding international faculty to publish on international topics.
   (b) Invite collaboration of international topics and international faculty research interests with other international faculty outside your institution.
   (c) Provide mentoring sessions on publishing to your international faculty, facilitate publisher workshops, and offer editing services
8. Increase your knowledge and be willing to learn about different counseling topics about marriage and family structures. Invite the international learner/faculty, if they are open to this, to teach a class section on the marriage process from their cultural background (Ex. Lifespan class lecture).
9. Note that international learners have limited access to scholarships and loans since they do not hold U.S. citizenship, so they have to pay out-of-pocket and out-of-state tuition. In addition to tuition fees, counseling learners who are international learners pay money for textbooks, attend conferences, counseling professional association memberships, and pay for counseling supervision costs that are not normally addressed in handbooks or prior to admissions but are necessary parts of the overall development of an international learner's identity as a counselor educator. Faculty can be a part of supporting international learners in obtaining funding by personally recommending international learners via reference letters and networking privilege.
10. Note that legal information for internationals is usually very decentralized and at times even disconnected. Therefore, looking for ways to have the most accurate up-to-date information, resources, and contacts is important (e.g., department/program rules or opportunities may not be the same, applicable, or available for internationals according to the international learner office and immigration laws).
    (a) It is not always easy to obtain a U.S. VISA for international learners/faculty. VISA approvals are not automatically awarded to everyone who applies. Once in the U.S., one has to navigate through the different VISA statuses if they switch from being a learner to another VISA (green card, H1B).
    (b) A program can facilitate an immigration workshop with a seasoned immigration lawyer for the international faculty and learners.

11. It is very important to ask and get to know your faculty members and understand their preferences and needs. If they would like to be addressed by a non-English name, ask them to teach you how to pronounce it and put effort into practicing their name.
12. Offer resources and safe spaces for international faculty members to learn what it means to be them in the U.S. (e.g., being Black, Latinx/e, Muslim, LGBTQQIP2SA).
13. Provide opportunities for the international faculty/learner to build a support system. Examples of these can include:
    (a) Connect international faculty with a faculty mentor in the department to help them understand the culture of the department.
    (b) Provide a safe place to share—another connection outside the department or institution that will relate to the international faculty.
    (c) Fund to attend major counseling conferences that have an International Faculty Network to provide connection.
    (d) Particularly important for counselors, engage the international learner/faculty about social support. Ask them what would be helpful for them (e.g., is the person interested in finding more internationals, more like-minded people, spiritual/religious sites, more people with similar cultural backgrounds?).

12.10 Conclusion

International learners enrolled in counseling programs are increasing, yet there is limited research surrounding their academic and professional experiences, their career choices, the factors contributing to their success, and their cultural representation in academia. Because various factors can influence the unique experiences of international CES doctoral learners and faculty we believe that the first step to inclusion is for counselor education program faculty to increase their own self-awareness, develop program curricula that can be embraced and utilized in multicultural contexts, and become knowledgeable about international counselor education and practice beyond the borders of the U.S. Utilizing the aforementioned models within this chapter as a foundational framework is critical to foster a deeper exploration of the cultural identities that extant Eurocentric models may not embrace. Counselor education as a field is called to be aware, reflective, and prepare to take action towards the advancement and well-being of international counselors in training and faculty.

References

Andrade, M. S. (2017). Institutional policies and practices for admitting, assessing, and tracking international students. *Journal of international students 7*(1), I–VI. https://doi.org/10.32674/jis.v7i1.241

Arrendondo, P., Toporek, R., Brown, S. P., Jones, J., Locke, D., Sanchez, J., & Stadler, H. (1996). Operationalization of the multicultural counseling competencies. *Journal of Multicultural Counseling and Development, 24*(1), 42–78. https://doi.org/10.1002/j.2161-1912.1996.tb00288.x

Arthur, N. (2013). *Counseling international students: Clients from around the world.* Springer.

Arthur, N., & Achenbach, K. (2002). Counselor preparation: Developing multicultural counseling competencies through experiential learning. *Counselor Education & Supervision, 42*, 2–14. https://doi.org/10.1002/j.1556-6978.2002.tb01299.x

Avent Harris, J. R., Dietz, S. S., & Crumb, L. (2019). Relational cultural theory: A guiding framework for study abroad experiences. *Teaching and Supervision in Counseling, 1*(2), 113–126. https://doi.org/10.7290/tsc010208

Azuma, H. (1984). Psychology in a non-western country. *International Journal of Psychology, 19*, 45–55. https://doi.org/10.1080/00207598408247514

Barton, G., & Ryan, M. (2020). What does reflection look and feel like for international students? An exploration of reflective thinking, reflexivity and employability. *Journal of International Students, 10*(S2), 1–16. https://doi.org/10.32674/jis.v10iS2.2848

Brabant, S. C., Palmer, E., & Gramling, R. (1990). Returning home: An empirical investigation of crosscultural re-entry. *International Journal of Intercultural Relations, 14*(4), 387–404. https://doi.org/10.1016/0147-1767(90)90027-T

Burdett, J., & Crossman, J. (2012). Engaging international students. *Quality Assurance in Education, 20*(3), 207–222. https://doi.org/10.1108/09684881211240286

Council for Accreditation of Counseling and Related Educational Programs. (2024). *2024 CACREP standards.* https://www.cacrep.org/wp-content/uploads/2024/04/2024-Standards-Combined-Version-4.11.2024.pdf

Cantwell, B., Luca, S. G., & Lee, J. J. (2009). Exploring the orientations of international students in Mexico: Differences by region of origin. *Higher Education, 57*, 335–354. https://doi.org/10.1007/s10734-008-9149-x

Coates, N., & Dickinson, J. (2012). Meeting international postgraduate student needs: A programme-based model for learning and teaching support. *Innovations in Education and Teaching International, 49*(3), 295–308. https://doi.org/10.1080/14703297.2012.703018

D'Andrea, M., & Daniels, J. (2001). RESPECTFUL counseling: An integrative model for counselors. In D. Pope-Davis & H. Coleman (Eds.), *The interface of class, culture and gender in counseling* (pp. 417–466). Sage.

Dietz, S. S., & Baker, S. B. (2019). Study abroad as a cultural competence development tool: Case study Honduras. *International Journal for the Advancement of Counselling, 41*(1), 104–124. https://doi.org/10.1007/s10447-018-9348-9

Franken, M. (2012). Re-situation challenges for international students 'becoming' researchers. *Higher Education, 64*, 845–859. https://doi.org/10.1007/s10734-012-9532-5

Freeman, K., & Li, M. (2019). "We are a ghost in the class": First year international students' experiences in the global contact zone. *Journal of international students, 9*(1), 19–38. https://doi.org/10.32674/jis.v9i1.270

Gardner, S. K. (2013). The challenges of first-generation doctoral students. *New Directions for Higher Education, 163*, 43–54. https://doi.org/10.1002/he.20064

Hays, P. A. (2016). *Addressing cultural complexities in practice: Assessment, diagnosis, and therapy* (3rd ed.). American Psychological Association.

Hernández, P., Taylor, B., & McDowell, T. (2009). Listening to ethnic minority AAMFT approved supervisors: Reflections on their experiences as supervisees. *Journal of Systemic Therapies, 28*(1), 88–100. https://doi.org/10.1521/jsyt.2009.28.1.88

Hoshmand, T. L. (2004). The transformative potential of counseling education. *Journal of Humanistic Counseling, Education & Development, 43*, 82–90. https://doi.org/10.1002/j.2164-490X.2004.tb00045.x

Houshmand, S., Spanierman, L. B., & Tafarodi, R. W. (2014). Excluded and avoided: Racial microaggressions targeting Asian international students in Canada. *Cultural Diversity & Ethnic Minority Psychology, 20*(3), 377–388. https://doi.org/10.1037/a0035404

Horne, S. V., Lin, S., Anson, M., & Jacobson, W. (2018). Engagement, satisfaction, and belonging of international undergraduates at U.S. research universities. *Journal of International Students, 8*(1), 351–374. https://doi.org/10.5281/zenodo.1134313

Institute of International Education (2023). Global mobility trends. *Project Atlas*. Retrieved from https://www.iie.org/research-initiatives/project-atlas/explore-global-data/

Interiano, C. G., & Lim, J. H. (2018). A "Chameleonic" identity: Foreign-born doctoral students in U. S. counselor education. *International Journal of Advance Counseling, 40*(3), 310–325. https://doi.org/10.1007/s10447 018-9328-0

Jones, E. (2017). Problematising and reimagining the notion of 'international student experience.' *Studies in Higher Education, 42*(5), 933–943. https://doi.org/10.1016/j.ijintrel.2021.04.007

Ju, J., Merrell-James, R., Coker, J. K., Ghoston, M., Pérez, J. F. C., & Field, T. A. (2020). Recruiting, retaining, and supporting students from underrepresented racial minority backgrounds in doctoral counselor education. *The Professional Counselor, 10*, 581–602. https://doi.org/10.15241/jj.10.4.581

Jurgens, J. C., & McAuliffe, G. (2004). Short-term study-abroad experience in Ireland: An exercise in cross-cultural counseling. *International Journal for the Advancement of Counselling, 26*, 147–161. https://doi.org/10.1023/B:ADCO.0000027427.76422.1f

Knight, J. (2018). The changing landscape of higher education internationalization—For better or worse? *Perspectives: Policy and Practice in Higher Education, 17*(3), 84–90. https://doi.org/10.1080/13603108.2012.753957

Knight, J. (2004). Internationalization remodeled: Definition, approaches, and rationales. *Journal of Studies in International Education, 8*(1), 5–31. https://doi.org/10.1177/1028315303260832

Khanal, J., & Gaulee, U. (2019). Challenges of international students from pre-departure to post-study: A literature review. *Journal of International Students, 9*(2), 560–581. https://doi.org/10.32674/jis.v9i2.673

Kim, D., Bankart, C. A. S., & Isdell, L. (2011). International doctorates: Trends analysis on their decision to stay in US. *Higher Education, 62*(2), 141–161. https://doi.org/10.1007/s10734-010-9371-1

Lee, J. J. (2015). International student experiences of neo-racism and discrimination. *International Higher Education, 44*, 3–5. https://doi.org/10.6017/ihe.2006.44.7916

Leon, R. A., & Chmiel, J. (2013). Counseling international students: Clients from around the world. *Journal of International Students, 3*(2), 190–192. https://doi.org/10.32674/jis.v3i2.511

Leung, S. A., Clawson, A., Norsworthy, K. L., Tena, A., Szilagyi, A., & Rogers, J. (2009). Internationalization of the counseling profession: An indigenous perspective. In L. H. Gerstein, P. P. Heppner, S. Ægisdóttir, S.-M.A. Leung, & K. L. Norsworthy (Eds.), *International handbook of cross-cultural counseling: Cultural assumptions and practices worldwide* (pp. 111–123). Sage.

Li, D., & Ai, Y. (2020). Ethics acculturation of international counseling students. *Journal of International Students, 10*(4), 1103–1109. https://doi.org/10.32674/jis.v10i4.1442

Li, D., & Liu, Y. (2020). International counseling doctoral student teaching preparation: A phenomenological study. *Counselor Education and Supervision, 59*(3), 200–215. https://doi.org/10.1002/ceas.12184

Li, P. F., & Gale, J. (2018). Reentry experiences and professional developments of international marriage and family therapy graduates in Taiwan. *Contemporary Family Therapy, 40*(4), 380–393. https://doi.org/10.1007/s10591-018-9464-z

Mocan-Aydin, G. (2000). Western models of counseling and psychotherapy within Turkey: Crossing cultural boundaries. *The Counseling Psychologist, 28*, 281–298. https://doi.org/10.1177/0011000000282007

Navas, M., Rojas, A. J., García, M., & Pumares, P. (2007). Acculturation strategies and attitudes according to the Relative Acculturation Extended Model: The perspectives of natives versus immigrants. *International Journal of Intercultural Relations, 31*(1), 67–86. https://doi.org/10.1016/j.ijintrel.2006.08.002
Ng, K. M., & Noonan, B. M. (2012). Internationalization of the counseling profession: Meaning, scope and concerns. *International Journal for the Advancement of Counselling, 34*, 5–18. https://doi.org/10.1007/s10447-011-9144-2
Ng, K. M., & Smith, S. D. (2009). Perceptions and experiences of international trainees in counseling and related programs. *International Journal for the Advancement of Counselling, 31*(1), 57–70. https://doi.org/10.1007/s10447-008-9068-7
Pedersen, P. B., & Leong, F. T. L. (1997). Counseling in an international context. *The Counseling Psychologist, 25*(1), 117–122. https://doi.org/10.1177/0011000097251012
Poyrazli, S., & Grahame, K. M. (2007). Barriers to adjustment: Needs of international students within a semi-urban campus community. *Journal of Instructional Psychology, 34*(1), 28–45. https://www.redorbit.com/news/education/907480/barriers_to_adjustment_needs_of_international_students_within_a_semiurban/index.html/
Raguram, R., Venkateswaran, J. R., Ramakrishna, J., & Weiss, M. G. (2002). Traditional community resources for mental health: A report of temple healing from India. *British Medical Journal, 325*, 38–40. https://doi.org/10.1136/bmj.325.7354.38
Sano, K. (2019). *Foreign-born doctoral-level counselor supervisor's use and experience of supervision theories/models* (Doctoral dissertation). Retrieved from ProQuest. (27805292).
Sherry, M., Thomas, P., & Chui, W. (2010). International students: A vulnerable student population. *Higher Education, 60*, 33–46. https://doi.org/10.1007/s10734-009-9284-z
Todoran, C., & Peterson, C. (2019). Should they stay or should they go? How the 2017 U.S. travel ban affects international doctoral students. *Journal of Studies in International Education, 24*(4), 440–455. https://doi.org/10.1177/1028315319861344
Ugwu, D. N., & Adamuti-Trache, M. (2017). Post-graduation plans of international science and engineering doctoral students attending U.S. universities. *Journal of international students, 7*(1), 1–21. https://doi.org/10.32674/jis.v7i1.242
Urban, E., & Palmer, L. B. (2014). International students as a resource for internationalization of higher education. *Journal of Studies in International Education, 18*(4), 305–324. https://doi.org/10.1177/1028315313511642
Woo, H., Jang, Y. J., & Henfield, M. S. (2015). International doctoral students in counselor education: Coping strategies in supervision training. *Journal of Multicultural Counseling and Development, 43*(4), 288–304. https://doi.org/10.1002/jmcd.12022
Yan, Z., Finn, K., Cardinal, B. J., & Bent, L. (2014). Evaluation of a 6-week peer education program to promote healthy living among international students. *Medicine and Science in Sports and Exercise, 46*(5), 493–494. https://doi.org/10.1249/01.mss.0000494945.02671.00

Keiko Sano, Ph.D., LMHC, NCC (she/her/hers) is a Core Faculty member of the Counselor Education and Supervi-sion program at Antioch University. She was born and raised in Japan and has worked with individuals and families with international backgrounds for over 25 years in Japan, Australia, Hong Kong, and the United States. Her passion for counseling and counselor education in global contexts leads to her strong research interest in culturally sensitive approaches by focusing on the diversity of counse-lors, counselors-in-training, supervisors, and counselor educators, in addition to deconstructions of traditional theories of counseling, supervision, and counselor education.

Syntia Santos Dietz, Ph.D., NCC (she/her/ella) is a Licensed School Counselor and is an Associate Professor at An-tioch University. She has held varying leadership roles such as program coordinator in the school counseling program at the Universidad Pedagógica Nacional Francisco Morazán (UPNFM) in her native country of Honduras, creating a School Counseling Program at her institution, as well as co-founder/director of the Latinx Mental Health and Social Justice Institute. Her research includes cultural competence, school counseling, and international counseling and counselor edu-cation addressing mental health counseling for historically marginalized popula-tions and how future counselors can support them.

Krista Kirk, Ph.D., LMHC, NCC, ACS, BC-TMH is an Associate Professor of Counseling at Messiah University. She has been a counselor educator for almost 10 years, and she has worked clinically for over 15 years. In addition to being a professor, she runs a private practice in the New York City metropolitan area where she seeks to meet the needs of under-served populations.

Joy Maweu Mwendwa, Ph.D. (she/her/her) is an Associate Professor in the Department of Counselor Education and Family Studies at Liberty University. With over two decades in the counseling profession, she has worked in varied settings including a college counseling center, community mental health, churches, and internationally in Kenya, Tanzania, and Malawi. As an LPC (VA), she mostly works with women of color, immigrants, in-ternational students, and international professionals. Her research interests are qualitative and indigenous research methodologies, the development of the pro-fession of counseling internationally, and multicultural competence.

Counselors-in-Training and Counselor Educators with Disabilities

13

Tyra Turner Whittaker, Bridget Hollis Staten, and K. Lynn Pierce

> *A good teacher is like a candle—it consumes itself to light the way for others.*
>
> *Mustafa Kemal Atatürk*

Abstract

This chapter seeks to illuminate the experiences of CITs and counselor educators with disabilities, both having very specific nuances from admission to the educative process, interviewing and hiring practices, and the impact of world views on teaching philosophy.

Learning Objectives After reading this chapter you will be able to:

1. Identify representative disabilities that are common in academic settings.
2. Describe best practices for working with counselors-in-training and counselor educators with disabilities.
3. Apply critical thinking and concepts learned to "real life" scenarios in counseling programs and in working with counselor education.
4. Integrate disability-affirming approaches rooted in multicultural considerations and awareness.

T. T. Whittaker (✉)
Liberty University, Lynchburg, VA, USA
e-mail: tnwhittaker@liberty.edu

B. Hollis Staten
South Carolina State University, Orangeburg, SC, USA
e-mail: bhollis@scsu.edu

K. Lynn Pierce
Mercer University, Atlanta, GA, USA
e-mail: pierce_k03@mercer.edu

D. M. Stalnaker-Shofner and T. N. Sapp (eds.), *A Comprehensive Guide for Counselor Education*, Springer Texts in Education, https://doi.org/10.1007/978-3-031-68358-9_13

13.1 Statement of Reflexivity

Acknowledging our positionality in crafting this chapter is critical. The first two authors, Tyra Turner Whittaker and Bridget Hollis Staten are middle-class African American, cisgender females without a disability. We are keenly aware that in many regards, we come from a privileged status. Our 26 years of academic training and professional experience in rehabilitation counseling, especially with individuals from the BIPOC community sharpen the lens through which we view working with counselors-in-training (CITs) and faculty with disabilities. Our positionality as members of the BIPOC community shapes our sensitivity and collective conscience toward working with persons with disabilities. We also acknowledge the potential presence of implicit bias as authors without a disability, which may influence how we view this chapter's content. The overarching goal of this chapter is to adopt an anti-ableist stance by centering and honoring the diverse voices of CITs and faculty with disabilities which is aligned with the focus of this text.

The third author, K. Lynn Pierce, is White, queer, and identifies as a disabled academic. She has physical disabilities, chronic illness considerations, and assistive technology needs and aligns with crip culture, Say the Word, and disability identity and pride movements. She is a CRC and has experience working with disability community (particularly chronic illness, late diagnosis, and rare condition populations), mentoring CITs and counselor education students with disabilities, and work experience in disability services in higher education. She approaches work with disabled individuals from a place of empowering self-determination and a disability justice lens.

13.2 Language Statement

While person-first language has been typical within academic environments, it is not representative of the language choice of many within the disability community. Both person-first language and identity-first language are intentionally used throughout this chapter, with the identity-first language used more heavily in sections addressing disability culture to reflect the expressed preferences of some members of the disability community as well as align with the social justice and anti-ableist framework of this book. Readers will notice a "shift" in the language used in the following sections: (a) Ableism and Disability-Related Bias in Counselor Education, (b) Disability Culture, (c) Language, (d) Affirming Models of Disability and Disability Justice, (e) Disability Identity Development Model, and (f) Disability Justice.

13.3 Case Scenario #1

Jennifer, a first-year CIT who is deaf, comes to your class and asks to meet with you concerning her disability and the need for accommodations. You schedule a meeting with her and her signer. During the meeting, you realize that Jennifer has not provided you with any written documentation. However, you continue the meeting because her disability is obvious and there may not be a need for documentation. As Jennifer describes her disability and need for accommodations, she expresses that her signer will be with her at all times even in class.

You begin to review the syllabus and realize that some of your coursework and assignments are not set up in a way to adjust for her accommodations. For example, one of your assignments includes a final paper summary from an immersion experience at an equestrian farm where CITs will experience horseback riding and therapy. This is just one assignment that may be challenging for Jennifer. As you sit and listen to her additional needs for accommodations, she needs extended time on tests and a space for her signer to be included.

13.4 Case Scenario #2

You have just signed your new contract as an assistant professor in the Department of Counseling at the university. You also have a new diagnosis of Attention-Deficit/Hyperactivity Disorder (ADHD). Although you have dealt with the symptoms of ADHD for a long time, this is the first time that you have been officially diagnosed. You are not worried about this new diagnosis as you have used many strategies to counteract the perceived negative symptoms of the disability. Your Department Chair has assigned you to a committee and made you the committee chair. This committee requires you to work with other faculty on CITs needs in the department. It requires you to meet with faculty, create an agenda for each meeting, and report on committee outcomes. You have always preferred to work alone on tasks as it allows you to move at your own pace. It also allows you not to depend on others and helps you to control your interactions. You have always had challenges with turning in work on time during your doctoral program and you have not managed to learn time management the way you need to. This committee assignment pulls you out of your comfort zone and challenges your disability.

13.5 Introduction

Diversity, equity, inclusion, justice, and belonging are foundational tenets for CITs with disabilities to fully engage in the academic process. The number of learners with disabilities in postsecondary higher education is on the rise. During the 2019–2020 academic year, approximately 21% of undergraduate and 11% of graduate learners reported having a disability diagnosis (Postsecondary National Policy Institute, 2023). Additionally, 28% of undergraduates and 20% of graduate learners reported that they were veterans (Postsecondary National Policy Institute, 2023). During the same academic year, the following undergraduate racial groups reported having a disability: Native Americans (24%), Pacific Islanders (23%), White (21%), Hispanic (22%), Black (18%), and Asian (14%) (Postsecondary National Policy Institute, 2023). Although learners with disabilities may have received accommodation during high school, transitioning from high school to higher education is a new landscape. Both undergraduate and graduate learners with disabilities oftentimes find themselves having to gain a deeper understanding of their disability and seek support to secure accommodations. Colleges and Universities house a division, Office of Disability and Veterans Support, which educates learners with disabilities about their rights and ensures that classroom accommodations are provided in both undergraduate and graduate programs. Likewise, faculty with disabilities must consider the nature of their disability when working in higher education. Mathews et al. (2020) reported on findings from the Collaborative on Academic Careers in Higher Education (COACHE) survey which focused on faculty with disabilities. Approximately 5% of faculty served were diagnosed with a disability. The most common disability reported was mobility impairment followed by a mental health disorder. Disability-related considerations often occur during the hiring and onboarding process. Faculty with disabilities are often unsure about when to disclose a disability diagnosis and are understandably concerned about the impact of such disclosure. The current chapter provides a practical guide on working with CITs with disabilities and navigating higher education as a counselor educator with a disability.

13.6 Disability in Higher Education

Two landmark federal laws protect learners with disabilities from discrimination in higher education. Section 504 of the Rehabilitation Act of 1973 (EEOC, 1973) and the Americans with Disabilities Act of 1990 (ADA, 1990) guarantee civil rights for persons with disabilities (Americans with Disabilities Act of 1990, 42 U.S.C. § 12101 et seq, 1990). The Rehabilitation Act of 1973 stated the following:

> no otherwise qualified disabled individual in the United States, shall, solely because of their disability, be excluded from the participation in, be denied the benefits of, or be subjected to discrimination under any program or activity receiving Federal financial assistance. (EEOC Rehabilitation Act of 1973, Section 504, 29 U.S.C. §794, Nondiscrimination Under Federal Grants section)

The ADA prohibits discrimination against persons with disabilities in the areas of employment, State and local government, public accommodations, commercial facilities, transportation, and telecommunications. Title II of the Americans with Disabilities Act (ADA) prohibits state and local governments, including public institutions of higher education, from discriminating against persons with disabilities. Some private universities are not exempt from this law (Americans with

Disabilities Act of 1990, 42 U.S.C. § 12101 et seq., 1990). If a private university receives federal financial assistance, it must also comply with both laws (Office for Civil Rights, 2023). The ADA regards disability as a legal term that defines a person with a disability as

(1) a physical or mental impairment that substantially limits one or more major life activities of such individual;
(2) a record of such an impairment; or
(3) being regarded as having such an impairment (U.S. Department of Justice Civil Rights Division, 2020, para 2).

The Americans with Disabilities Amendments Act of 2008 Amendments (ADAA) (U.S. Department of Justice Civil Rights Division, 2008) focused on narrowing the definition of disability. It also promoted the full inclusion of learners with disabilities through online platforms and course materials used (Phillippe et al., 2021). In higher education, the ADAA Amendments addressed "building accessibility, universal design, electronic accessibility, and academic accommodations in the college classroom" (Phillippe et al., 2021, pp. 31–32.).

Learners with disabilities are very diverse. Common types of disabilities represented in higher education include attention-deficit/hyperactivity disorder (ADHD), learning disabilities, blind or low vision, autism, deaf and hard of hearing, mobility, and speech or language impairments (American College Health Association, 2022).

Stop and Reflect: *As you reflect on the information provided in Case Scenario 1, here are some questions to consider as you read further:*

1. *What are the first steps in addressing the needs of this CIT with a disability?*
2. *Is Jennifer's need for accommodations unrealistic? Why or why not?*
3. *How would you change your syllabus to make sure to include CITs with disabilities in your class?*
4. *What changes would you make to the stated assignment above to make it more accommodating for Jennifer and her signer?*

Next, consider the information provided in Case Scenario 2, here are some questions to consider as you read further:

1. *How do you accept the new committee assignment as your new role as a faculty member in the department?*
2. *How will the diagnosis of ADHD play a part in your new role?*
3. *What are three strategies you can use to help you be successful as an assistant professor and committee chairperson?*
4. *Should you tell the department chair and committee members about your disability? Why or why not?*

13.7 Ableism and Disability-Related Bias in Counselor Education

As counselors and counselor educators with an ethical mandate to continue to work on our own biases, it is important to recognize how pervasive ableism is in our society and within our profession. This is also why we acknowledged the potential for ableism and ableist views to manifest in our writing, and why we encourage you to also reflect on your own biases related to disability.

A recent study of disability professionals found that 82% implicitly preferred non-disabled people, while 77% expressed an explicit preference for nondisabled people (Friedman, 2023). Available research indicates that counseling programs may not be using texts or requiring experiences of CITs that support preparation with disability demographics and that a minority of faculty consider their program to be "very effective" at addressing disability topics (Feather & Carlson, 2019). Given the high level of stigma surrounding discussion of disability experiences on a societal level, it is extremely important to ensure counselors in training and counselor educators in training are exposed to disability topics, engage with available disability competencies, and examine their own bias and ableism before working with disabled clients and CITs. Additionally, disability culture should be considered as a factor that helps to explain the differences that may appear in differing environments and locations as it relates to bias and ableism viewpoints.

Stop and Reflect: *Having a general understanding of disability legislation including the ADA's definition of a disability and Section 504 of the Rehabilitation Act of 1973 will help with advocacy for CITs with disabilities. In case scenario #1, you see that the CIT has not met with the office that will assist persons with disabilities. Encouraging CITs to access services from the appropriate office on campus will help with their overall academic success. They will also become familiar with other accommodations they may need. Most higher education institutions should have a disability culture that creates an openness to understanding the needs of persons with disabilities because of legislative mandates. However, the culture may vary in the understanding of differences related to disability type, gender, ableism, and cultural needs of CIT and faculty with disabilities.*

13.8 Disability Culture

While the disability community is remarkably diverse and norms between subcommunities vary widely, there is shared language, art, and expression which culminates into the "disability culture". Disabled people have shared experiences of oppression and a collective history of advocacy for their civil rights and right to self-determination. People with disabilities have their own symbols, from the International Symbol of Access to those associated with various disorders and subcommunities (the disability pride flag, zebras as a mascot for rare conditions, and various awareness ribbons).

This cultural component of disability indicates a need for multicultural competency related to disability (Chapin et al., 2018). It also suggests a need for disability awareness, including understanding the impacts of ableism on disabled people, empowering language choice and affirming disability identity, and implementing disability-affirming models including anti-ableist approaches such as Disability Justice.

13.9 Language

Language is an important element within the disability community. While person first language (person with a disability or person with [condition]) was a reaction to outdated, offensive, and overtly ableist language once common about disability and it is preferred by some people with disabilities, it has also been heavily enforced as the only correct approach by academics, APA guidelines, and non-disabled people. Person first language may have unintended consequences, such as reinforcing internalized ableism or preventing disability identity formation (Andrews et al., 2022). Person first language has not been mandated in the discussion of other historically marginalized groups. It may be considered to be euphemistic language (such as special needs or differently abled) designed to avoid either naming or fully acknowledging the disability, which is typically seen as a more subtle form of ableist language by some disabled people (Friedman & Gordon, 2023). Identity first language or disability forward language describes using disabled as an adjective (disabled person or disabled people). There is also within group language and a lot of individual preferences regarding disability identity expression, language, and the terminology used by disabled people themselves and by others to describe them. As with many cultural groups, it is important to broach and ask respectful questions to better understand and then respect and follow individual preferences around language choice.

Stop and Reflect: *As you reflect on both case scenarios, they provide views of self-awareness and understanding of one's disability and the ability to self-advocate in situations where assistance is needed. As the counselor educator in scenario #1 works with a CIT with a disability, being intentional about disability and language sensitivity is important. Asking CITs about their preferences or how they relate to their disability is a method of centering the individual's voice. Also, informing CITs of their ability to advocate for themself empowers them with language choice and disability awareness. In case scenario #2, similar issues apply to the counselor educator, you will need to have a clearer understanding of your new diagnosis, the ability to advocate for yourself, and knowledge of disability rights to accommodations in the workplace. Even though the counselor educator has used strategies in the past to overcome the perceived negative symptoms of the disability, the current situation requires more advocacy and a better understanding of disability accommodations in the workplace.*

13.10 Affirming Models of Disability and Disability Justice

There are several models rehabilitation professionals use to conceptualize and explain attitudes (historical and current) toward disabilities and the interaction of disability-related factors with interpersonal and environmental factors. A few of these models are the Moral Model (Retief & Letsosa, 2018), the Medical Model (Zaks, 2023), the Social Model (Ballahan et al., 2011), Disability Culture Model (Retief & Letsosa, 2018), and the International Classification of Functioning (McDougall et al., 2010). For more information, see the accompanying resource guide. While these models are important, for this chapter and in alignment with the goal of this textbook, we will focus on affirming models of disability and disability justice.

Disability-affirming models come from the work of disabled researchers or the disability community. This is another reason why immersion in disability culture is important for supporting CITs and educators with disabilities in ways that are culturally competent. Two examples of this are the disability identity development model and the disability justice framework.

13.11 Disability Identity Development Model

The disability identity development model, developed by Forber-Pratt and Zape (2017) is based on qualitative research with college learners with varying disabilities. The focus of the study was on college learners of traditional age, representing the "ADA generation". This generation has lived with the ADA for most or all of their lives. The researchers identified four statuses: acceptance, relationship, adoption, and engagement. The acceptance status speaks to accepting the disability, which may occur in different developmental periods depending on whether the disability is congenital or acquired, caused by illness or injury, and the exact circumstances and attached meaning. Relationship status describes the network built with disabled people, particularly those with similar circumstances. The adoption status describes the process of adopting values of disability culture and is a mediating status between relationship and engagement where the individual determines the level of identity expression and engagement they wish to integrate. In the engagement status, people are immersed in disability culture and disability community, serving as mentors and advocates and otherwise engaged in giving back. This model is particularly important to be aware of because disabling events and changes in diagnostic status can occur at any time. The barriers presented by academic environments may also highlight disability differences, causing engagement or re-engagement with disability identity development for disabled learners and educators.

13.12 Disability Justice

Disability Justice is a framework documented by Patty Berne, co-founder of the organization Sins Invalid. The framework reflects the collaborative advocacy work occurring in the disability community and is an attempt to document disabled voices, particularly those who hold multiple marginalized identities (Sins Invalid, 2015). Disability Justice explores complex intersections of factors of identity including ability, race, gender, sexuality, and more, and takes a holistic view of advocacy work. This framework allows allies and advocates to determine if their efforts are aligned with the values of disabled people and requires the involvement of disabled people in the issues that impact them. Disability Justice is informed by ten principles which are listed below.

- *Intersectionality*: "We do not live single issues lives"—Audre Lorde. Ableism, coupled with white supremacy, supported by capitalism, underscored by heteropatriarchy, has rendered the vast majority of the world "invalid".
- *Leadership of the most impacted*: "We are led by those who most know these systems"—Aurora Levins Morales.
- *Anti-capitalist politics*: In an economy that sees land and humans as components of profit, we are anti-capitalist by the nature of having non-conforming bodies/minds.
- *Commitment to cross-movement organizing*: Shifting how social justice movements understand disability and contextualize ableism, disability justice lends itself to politics of alliance.
- *Recognizing wholeness*: People have inherent worth outside of commodity relations and capitalist notions of productivity. Each person is full of history and life experience.
- *Sustainability*: We pace ourselves, individually and collectively, to be sustained long-term. Our embodied experiences guide us toward ongoing justice and liberation.
- *Commitment to cross-disability solidarity*: We honor the insights and participation of all our community members, knowing that isolation undermines collective liberation.
- *Interdependence*: We meet each others' needs as we build toward liberation, knowing that state solutions inevitably extend into further control over our lives.
- *Collective access*: As brown, black, and queer-bodied disabled people we bring flexibility and creative nuance that go beyond able-bodied/minded normativity, to be in community with each other.
- *Collective liberation*: No body or mind can be left behind. Only by moving together can we accomplish the revolution we require (Sins Invalid, 2015, 10 Principles of Disability Justice Section).

The principles of disability justice framework provide a disability-inclusive platform to engage in social justice and advocacy. The principles serve as a springboard to meet the diverse needs of learners with disabilities.

Stop and Reflect: *Disability justice can be seen in both scenarios as you evaluate the needs of the counselor educator and CIT to become more aware of their disabilities and the accommodations they may need. When addressing disability justice, you should also note the individuality of each person and the factors that relate to their self-efficacy and self-awareness. It includes those factors that relate to your ability to assist in advocating for yourself and/or your CITs.*

13.13 Best Practices for Working with Counselors-in-Training with Disabilities

Beginning with admissions, and throughout the matriculation process, it is imperative to reflect on the nature of university and program policies, and the impact of them on counselor education learners. This process of reflection should begin with counselor education and clinical training. As you begin to consider how to impart a social justice framework with respect to CITs with disabilities, the same principles of accessibility, inclusion, and belonging are vital as you integrate awareness of the unique needs of CITs and CES' with disabilities, and then broaden this information to, clients with disabilities and the disability community as a whole. In this section, we offer recommendations for best practices with respect to teaching CITs about disability culture and how as a CES you can provide an inclusive learning environment.

13.13.1 Admissions Process

Counselor educators should ensure that an open and welcoming environment is provided for CITs with disabilities. The ADA prohibits a university (including counselor educators) from asking an applicant or a CIT if he or she has a disability. To ensure that all legal rights of a CIT are adhered to, faculty can only inquire about the need for accommodations on the application or when an interview is granted. It is also prudent to provide information on disability support services, and the university's accommodations policy, and explain the program's sensitivity to CIT's academic needs, including diverse adult learners.

13.13.2 Universal Design

Ensuring equal access to learning is vital when working with CITs with disabilities. The importance of Universal Design (UD) is well documented in counseling literature (Dallas & Sprong, 2015; Dallas et al., 2016; Oswald et al., 2018). The Center for Universal Design in Education (CUD) defines Universal Design as "the design of products and environments to be usable by all people, to the greatest extent possible, without the need for adaptation or specialized design"

(Burgstahler, 2009, p. 1). As a counselor educator, preparing an all-inclusive learning environment that is accessible to all persons with disabilities requires a shift in thinking. The concept of UD ensures that accessibility is considered in the design of the educational environment for all persons with disabilities. Incorporating UD strategies also benefits CITs with disabilities with intersectional identities as it allows for flexible and dynamic instructional methods that are based on the adult learner's needs (Hennessey & Koch, 2007).

When implemented correctly, UD benefits all individuals, including CIT, faculty, and staff without disabilities. CUD details seven principles of UD which are listed below.

- *Equitable use.* The design is useful and marketable to people with diverse abilities.
- *Flexibility in use.* The design accommodates a wide range of individual preferences and abilities.
- *Simple and intuitive.* Use of the design is easy to understand, regardless of the user's experience, knowledge, language skills, or current concentration level.
- *Perceptible information.* The design communicates necessary information effectively to the user, regardless of ambient conditions or the user's sensory abilities.
- *Tolerance for error.* The design minimizes hazards and the adverse consequences of accidental or unintended actions.
- *Low physical effort.* The design can be used efficiently and comfortably and with a minimum of fatigue.
- *Size and space for approach and use.* The design provides appropriate size and space for approach, reach, manipulation, and use, regardless of the user's body size, posture, or mobility. (Burgstahler, 2009, para 6).

An example of *equitable use* in counselor education is providing adaptable seating in the classrooms, counseling labs, and conference rooms. An additional example is ensuring that the program's website, learning management system (e.g., Canvas, Blackboard, Moodle, etc.), and cloud-based systems used to track practicum and internship hours are accessible for individuals with visual impairments. *Flexibility of use* can be implemented by adopting textbooks that offer e-book versions containing a read-aloud and other accessibility functions. Incorporating a *simple and intuitive design* can be achieved by creating syllabi, assignment instructions, rubrics, and PowerPoint presentations that are clear, concise, and easy to understand. Examples of *perceptible information* include ensuring that videos used in class have both closed captioning and subtitles. Subtitles are especially useful for CITs to watch a video in their chosen language. *Tolerance for error* could be implemented by creating a quiz in a learning management system that allows the CIT to use the undo button to return to a previous response. A great example of *low physical effort* is having power doors or levers on doors that require minimal effort to open. Individuals without disabilities benefit from the use of powered doors as they minimize the level of effort needed to open heavy doors. Ensuring that the hallway is unobstructed and that teaching devices used (e.g., laptops, LCD monitors, whiteboards, etc.) are within site for all CITs in the classroom are examples of using a *size and space approach*. In addition to the UD principles, counselor educators should create a safe learning environment that is void of attitudinal barriers. The ACA Code of Ethics (2014) requires counselors to promote social justice and respect diversity. As such, it is critical to ensure that CITs with disabilities are not subject to discrimination or stereotyping. This principle applies to counselor educators with disabilities as well.

13.13.3 Office of Disability Support Services

Most universities have a division that is charged with ensuring that an inclusive community is created for CITs with disabilities. Traditionally the common name for this division is the Office of Disability Support Services (ODS), although these offices may use many names including Access and Accommodations or Student Disability Resources. ODS ensures the provision of accommodations, coordinates the provision of accommodations with program faculty without disclosing the nature of the disability, educates the campus about disability support services, advocates for CITs with disabilities, and provides necessary resources to CITs with disabilities and their families to ensure success. The types of accommodations frequently provided by ODS include (a) test accommodations including extended time to submit assignments or time and a half on quizzes and tests; (b) private low-noise space for testing; (c) adaptive technology, (d) note-taking services, (e) dictation software, and (f) screen reading software (Blasey et al., 2023). Worthy of note is that the CACREP requires that course syllabi contain a disability accommodation policy and procedure statement, along with institutional contacts, for enrolled CITs (CACREP, 2024). It is also important to be aware from a social justice perspective that the process to receive accommodations may be long due to the high volume of these offices and requires CITs to submit medical documentation. This may present a barrier for CITs who are seeking a diagnosis or require additional testing, which may be costly and may involve waiting for a specialist. One way counselor educators can support better equity in light of these barriers is to implement Universal Design principles in their course construction.

13.13.4 Disability Cultural Centers

While ODS is charged with the implementation of legally mandated academic accommodations, the University environment often presents multifaceted barriers. These may be physical or attitudinal and reflect systemic inequities and ableism in higher education (Dolmage, 2017). To best support CITs from a holistic and affirming framework, disability cultural centers (DCCs) or CIT organizations focused on disability are highly desirable (Elmore et al., 2018). Unfortunately, most colleges

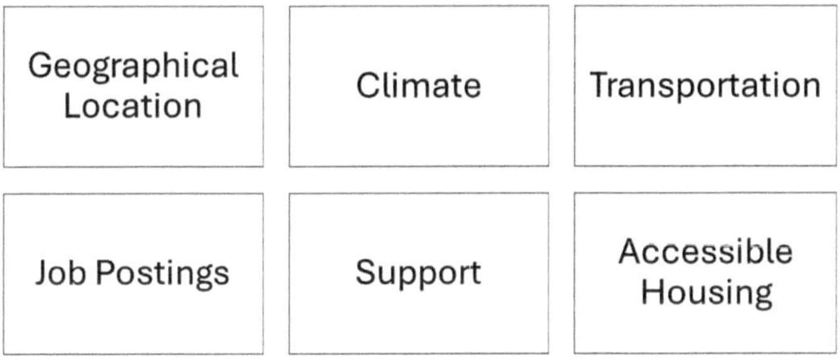

Fig. 13.1 Considerations When Finding Employment. *Note* This figure describes six employment considerations for both CES faculty and CES doctoral learners with disabilities

and universities have not yet adopted a DCC model and this is a current point of advocacy for disability equity and anti-ableism in higher education.

13.14 Best Practices for Counselor Educators with Disabilities

In this section, we will explore the unique needs of CES' with disabilities as they actively seek employment opportunities in counselor education. Though Chap. 10 is dedicated to finding and landing the job, there are unique considerations for CES' with disabilities, and this chapter delves into those nuances.

13.14.1 Finding Employment

CES doctoral learners are often inundated with conducting clinical supervision, serving as teaching or graduate assistants, conducting research, or working feverishly to finalize their dissertations. Those writing their dissertation often realize that they must update their Curriculum Vitae (CV) and apply for their first faculty position. When preparing to enter the job market, doctoral learners and seasoned faculty with disabilities have additional factors for consideration. Figure 13.1 offers a summary of the content in this section.

13.14.2 Geographical Location

It is important to consider the location of the job position when seeking employment in higher education. Counseling programs are housed at universities that are in large cities and rural areas. Some universities are near the beach while others are in the mountains. It is important to consider how the geographical location of the university may impact one's disability. For example, one of the authors worked at a university located in a rural area. One of her colleagues (pseudonym Heather) was diagnosed with Retinitis Pigmentosa (RP) which is a group of inherited eye diseases that cause progressive vision loss and may impact peripheral vision, night vision, and the ability to see color. Having RP impacted her ability to walk across campus and drive to department functions that were held at night, especially with limited lighting in the area.

13.14.3 Climate

Depending on the type of disability, some weather conditions may be more optimal than others. Extreme weather conditions trigger some disabilities. Individuals with a heart condition, chronic obstructive pulmonary disease (COPD), or a joint disorder may find working in extreme cold or heat challenging which may pose a health concern. As such, it is important to determine the impact of the external climate on the disabling condition. The goal is to secure an academic position in an environment that maximizes an individual's quality of life.

13.14.4 Transportation

Certain types of disabilities impact mobility which requires the need for transportation services. When applying for a position, it is important to determine the availability and scope of public transportation. Larger cities typically offer public transportation by bus, rail system, taxi, or ride-sharing services which provides more options for persons with physical disabilities. Smaller cities or rural communities may offer limited transportation services. We noted a faculty member named Heather in a previous section. There was one taxi service in the community that charged clients a significant amount because of the lack of competition. Heather had to pay for a taxi to transport her to work, to the market, and to other functions which became a financial burden as the community had limited resources for those with low vision. Heather eventually relocated to a larger city that was more accessible for individuals with visual impairments. As a result, her quality of life significantly improved.

13.14.5 Job Postings

The language used in job postings is quite telling. Perry (2016) argued that many job postings contain discriminatory language by including a laundry list of physical exertion requirements that are not necessarily required to perform the job task. For example, a faculty job posting for a position in an online program may indicate medium work which involves lifting no more than 50 pounds at a time with frequent lifting or carrying of objects weighing up to 25 pounds. One may question whether or not it is necessary to be able to lift 50 pounds to perform an online academic position. Although unintentional, some job postings dissuade persons with disabilities from applying due to the structure of the announcement. It is important to note that the ADA requires employers (including academic institutions) to outline a position's essential functions, which are the basic requirements to perform the job. It is encouraging to know that most academic positions maintain sedentary physical exertion requirements which should accommodate the majority of persons with disabilities.

13.14.6 Support

When seeking employment in higher education as a person with a disability, it is important to know the type and level of emotional, social, and medical support needed. These are key factors that are especially important for BIPOC community members with disabilities. If one's emotional support comes from being spiritually grounded, finding a church or group offering spiritual and emotional support may be an important factor in the search process. Medical support (both through medical insurance/benefits and through the location of doctors and specialists familiar with one's condition) can be a deciding factor. Additionally, it may be helpful to search the internet for existing support networks for persons with disabilities in the community. Doing so may allow you to "check the pulse" of the community to see their responsiveness to persons with disabilities.

13.14.7 Accessible Housing

Securing accessible housing is an important factor when seeking employment in higher education. Accessible housing allows persons with disabilities to have maximum independence and mobility in their home environment (Housing & Services Resource Center, 2023). The availability of accessible housing becomes critical when an academic institution is located in a rural community that may have older homes that are not accessible. In larger cities, a concern may be the availability of accessible housing apartments or condominiums. It is important to remember that the Fair Housing Act prohibits discrimination against persons with disabilities in most rental housing and also ensures the provision of reasonable accommodations and modifications (Jeter, 2016). It may be helpful to research the availability of accessible housing in the community in which the academic institution is housed as the findings may impact your decision to accept a position at the academic institution.

13.15 Hiring Considerations for Counselor Educators with Disabilities

The United States Equal Employment Opportunity Commission enforces laws that protect persons with disabilities in the hiring process and the workplace (n.d.-a). The United States Equal Employment Opportunity Commission (n.d.-a) offers persons with disabilities several fundamental rights. Two rights are critical to the interview process. One right is protection from adverse differential treatment by an employer due to having a disability, being associated with someone with a disability, or having had a disability. The second right is based upon the ADA which prohibits employers from asking any questions about an individual's disability or questions that may disclose an existing disability during the pre-offer period (United States Equal Employment Opportunity Commission, n.d.-b). Given these legal protections, the next logical question is when should an applicant disclose their disability status? According to the Job Accommodation Network (2023), applicants have the option to disclose their disability status at three key stages of the hiring process (a) pre-employment, (b) post-offer, and (c) post-employment.

13.15.1 Pre-employment

The timing of disability disclosure has been widely debated. Depending on the type of disability, hidden or visible, an individual may choose to not disclose his or her disability. Jans et al. (2011) conducted a qualitative study consisting of 41 individuals with disabilities who shared their decision to disclose or not disclose their disability status. Participants' decision to disclose was based on the type of disability, the need for accommodations, and the organization's openness to disability. Most counseling programs require applicants to deliver a teaching sample and present their research as part of the interview process. Depending on the type of disability, disclosure at this stage will allow an applicant to receive accommodations to fully participate in the interview process. In addition to the research and teaching sample, search committees often take the applicant on a walking tour of the university. Applicants with certain types of physical disabilities may require accommodations to engage in this type of activity. Jans et al. (2011) indicated that some applicants chose to wait until the interview to disclose their disability while others opted to not share at all. Their decision to disclose depended on their comfort level with the interviewers.

13.15.2 Post-offer

Counselor educators with disabilities (CED) may choose not to disclose their disability until an official job offer is made. Such disclosure is made when there is a need for workplace accommodations or restructuring of the work environment. For example, a faculty member who uses a wheelchair may need office and classroom space that is accessible. If the counseling program is housed in an older building, the faculty member may need to teach on the first floor of the building to allow for ease of access. It is important to note that a university cannot rescind a job offer due to disability disclosure unless it prevents the individual from performing the essential functions of the position (EEOC, n.d.-b).

13.15.3 Post-employment

Counselor educators with disabilities may choose to disclose disability-related information post-employment for various reasons. A CED who acquired a disability during employment may choose to disclose the disability, especially if the condition impacts their job performance. The Job Accommodations Network (JAN) (2023) suggests that when an employee chooses to disclose disability-related information, they should do so with an individual who can do something about it. In academia, this may be the department chair, Dean, and/or a Human Resources representative. CEDs should also document their request in writing if the history of the request is disputed (JAN, 2023). It is helpful to know that JAN advances equity and access for persons with disabilities by providing a comprehensive database of workplace accommodations for different types of disabilities. This invaluable resource is beneficial for both CED and employers to understand the diverse ways to provide workplace accommodations.

13.16 Anti-ableist Considerations for Counseling Programs

An anti-ableist approach to recruiting in counselor education would require consideration of barriers that may be present in your location and clear messaging around accessibility and requests for support. This might include offering options such as allowing an applicant to choose whether to be picked up from the airport or to secure their own ground transportation to and from the airport, which otherwise may require disclosure of a disability aid early in the process to ensure a suitable vehicle, or offering choices of restaurants in advance with allows the applicant to choose somewhere with food suitable to dietary needs without having to explain themselves. It is also worth noting that the long interview days common in higher education, often with short breaks and many changes of rooms and locations, may present challenges for applicants. When a disability has been disclosed early in the process, it may be supportive for the department chair or search chair to call and have a conversation with the applicant, describing as much as possible what to expect from the process, physical environment, and schedule and engaging in a collaborative process to determine where proactive changes can be made.

Stop and Reflect: *When reflecting on the second scenario, you should identify how the counselor educator has handled the situation related to their own disability in the workplace. Several factors as noted above should be considered as you search for employment in higher education. Factors to consider are disclosing your disability, requesting accommodations, and the job duties required. These are all areas that you should feel comfortable with and know your views before accepting a post-offer. Empowering yourself and the CITs you may work with broadens the disability culture at your university and provides a greater feeling of advocacy. When reflecting on the first scenario, you should understand the need to assist CITs with disabilities and teach the importance of self-advocacy.*

13.17 Conclusion

As CITs with disabilities enter the postsecondary experience, CITs experience many successes as well as challenges. To ensure that CITs with disabilities obtain an ideal experience from admission to graduation, counselor educators must create a welcoming environment that promotes equal access and safety. These foundational principles also apply to counselor educators with disabilities as they participate in the hiring process. Employing a universal design approach allows counselor educators and their colleagues with varying disabilities to fully engage in the academy thereby creating an experience grounded in diversity, equity, inclusion, belonging, accessibility and social justice.

References

American Counseling Association. (2014). *2014 ACA code of ethics*. https://www.counseling.org/docs/default-source/default-document-library/ethics/2014-aca-code-of-ethics.pdf

American College Health Association. (2022). *American college health association-national college health assessment III: Undergraduate student reference group data report spring 2022*. American College Health Association. https://www.acha.org/documents/ncha/NCHAIII_SPRING_2022_UNDERGRAD_REFERENCE_GROUP_DATA_REPORT.pdf

Americans With Disabilities Act of 1990, 42 U.S.C. § 12101 *et seq*. (1990). https://www.eeoc.gov/americans-disabilities-act-1990-original-text

Andrews, E. E., Powell, R. M., & Ayers, K. (2022). The evolution of disability language: Choosing terms to describe disability. *Disability and Health Journal, 15*(3), 1–5. https://doi.org/10.1016/j.dhjo.2022.101328

Ballahan, M. S., Romanelli, M., & Harper, J. N. (2011). The social model: A lens for counseling transgender individuals with disabilities. *Journal of Gay & Lesbian Mental Health, 15*(3), 260–280. https://doi.org/10.1080/19359705.2011.582073

Blasey, J., Wang, C., & Blasey, R. (2023). Accommodation use and academic outcomes for college students with disabilities. *Psychological Reports, 126*(4), 1891–1909. https://doi.org/10.1177/00332941221078011

Burgstahler, S. (2009). *Designing universal design of instruction (UDI): Definition, principles, guidelines, and examples.* DO-IT, University of Washington. https://www.washington.edu/doit/

Chapin, M., McCarthy, H., Shaw, L., Bradham-Cousar, M., Chapman, R., Nosek, M., Peterson, S., Yilmaz, Z., & Ysasi, N. (2018). *Disability-related counseling competencies.* American Rehabilitation Counseling Association.

Council for Accreditation of Counseling and Related Educational Programs. (2024). *2024 CACREP standards.* https://www.cacrep.org/wp-content/uploads/2024/04/2024-Standards-Combined-Version-4.11.2024.pdf

Dallas, B. K., & Sprong, M. E. (2015). Assessing faculty attitudes toward universal instructional techniques. *Journal of Applied Rehabilitation Counseling, 46*(4), 18–27.

Dallas, B. K., Sprong, M. E., & Kluesner, B. K. (2016). Multiuniversity comparison of faculty attitudes and use of universal design instructional techniques. *Rehabilitation Research, Policy, and Education., 30*(2), 148–160. https://doi.org/10.1891/2168-6653.30.2.148

Dolmage, J. (2017). *Academic ableism.* University of Michigan Press.

Elmore, K., Saia, T., & Thomson, E. A. (2018). *Special feature: An introduction to disability cultural centers in U.S. higher education, part I.* Association on Higher Education and Disability (AHEAD). https://www.ahead.org/professional-resources/publications/hub/hub-nov-2018/hub-nov-2018-special-feature-disability-cultural-centers

Feather, K. A., & Carlson, R. G. (2019). An initial investigation of individual instructors' self-perceived competence and incorporation of disability content into CACREP-accredited programs: Rethinking training in counselor education. *Journal of Multicultural Counseling and Development, 47*, 19–36.

Forber-Pratt, A. J., & Zape, M. P. (2017). Disability identity development model: Voices from the ADA generation. *Disability and Health Journal, 10*(2), 350–355. https://doi.org/10.1016/j.dhjo.2016.12.013

Friedman, C. (2023). Explicit and implicit: Ableism of disability professionals. *Disability and Health Journal, 16*(4), 101482. https://doi.org/10.1016/j.dhjo.2023.101482

Friedman, C., & Gordon, Z. (2023). *Ableist language & disability professionals: Differences in language based on professionals' demographics.* CQL The Council on Quality and Leadership. https://www.c-q-l.org/resources/articles/ableist-language-disability-professionals-differences-in-language-based-on-professionals-demographics/

Hennessey, M. L., & Koch, L. (2007). Universal design for instruction in rehabilitation counselor education. *Rehabilitation Education, 21*(3), 187–194.

Housing and Services Resource Center. (2023). *Accessible, affordable housing.* https://acl.gov/HousingAndServices/Accessible-Housing

Jans, L. H., Kaye, H. S., & Jones, E. C. (2011). Getting hired: Successfully employed people with disabilities offer advice on disclosure, interviewing, and job search. *Journal of Occupational Rehabilitation, 22*(2), 155–165. https://doi.org/10.1007/s10926-011-9336-y

Jeter, M. J. (2016). No handicapped people allowed. The need for objective accessibility standards under the Fair Housing Act. *Washington Law Review, 91*(1), 325–359.

Job Accommodation Network. (2023). *Disability disclosure and the Americans with disabilities act (ADA).* U.S. Dept. of Labor, Office of Disability Employment Policy.

Mathews, K., Benson, R.T., Trower, C., Azubuike, N.O., & Kumar, A. (2020). The collaborative on academic careers in higher education: Faculty job satisfaction survey. 2019–2020 (Research version). Harvard University.

McDougall, J., Wright, V., & Rosenbaum, P. (2010). The ICF model of functioning and disability: Incorporating quality of life and human development. *Developmental Neurorehabilitation., 13*(3), 204–211. https://doi.org/10.3109/17518421003620525

Oswald, G. R., Adams, R. D. N., & Hiles, J. A. (2018). Universal design for learning in rehabilitation education: Meeting the needs for equal access to electronic course resources and online learning. *Journal of Applied Rehabilitation Counseling, 49*(1), 19–22.

Perry, D. (2016). *Disabled people not apply.* Aljazeera America. http://america.aljazeera.com/opinions/2016/2/disabled-people-need-not-apply.html

Phillippe, L. K., Noble, N., Hendricks, B., Brendle, J., & Lock, R. H. (2021). The Americans with Disabilities Act implications for family counselors: Counseling students in higher education. *The Family Journal, 29*(1), 29–36. https://doi.org/10.1177/1066480720948869

Postsecondary National Policy Institute. (2023). *Students with disabilities in higher education.* https://pnpi.org/wp-content/uploads/2023/11/StudentswithDisabilities-Nov-2023.pdf

Retief, M., & Letsosa, R. (2018). Models of disability: A brief overview. *HTS Teologiese Studies/theological Studies, 74*(1), 1–8. https://doi.org/10.4102/hts.v74i1.4738

Sins Invalid. (2015). *10 principles of disability justice.* https://www.sinsinvalid.org/blog/10-principles-of-disability-justice

United States Department of Education. Office for Civil Rights. (2023). *Disability discrimination.* https://www2.ed.gov/about/offices/list/ocr/frontpage/faq/disability.html

United States Equal Employment Opportunity Commission. (1973). *Rehabilitation Act of 1973.* https://www.eeoc.gov/rehabilitation-act-1973-original-text

United States Equal Employment Opportunity Commission. (n.d.-a). *Disability discrimination.* https://www.eeoc.gov/youth/disability-discrimination-0

United States Equal Employment Opportunity Commission. (n.d.-b). *Disability discrimination and employment decisions.* https://www.eeoc.gov/disability-discrimination-and-employment-decisions#:~:text=After%20A%20Job%20Offer&text=An%20employer%20may%20only%20revoke,%2C%20if%20entitled%20to%20it. https://www.eeoc.gov/laws/guidance/job-applicants-and-ada

U.S. Department of Justice Civil Rights Division. (2008). *Americans with Disabilities Act (ADA) of 1990, ADA Amendments Act of 2008.* http://www.ada.gov

U.S. Department of Justice Civil Rights Division. (2020). *Information and technical assistance on the Americans with Disabilities Act: Introduction to the ADA.* https://www.ada.gov/ada_intro.htm

Zaks, Z. (2023). Changing the medical model of disability to the normalization model of disability: Clarifying the past to create a new future direction. *Disability & Society*, 1–28. https://doi.org/10.1080/09687599.2023.2255926

Tyra Turner Whittaker, RhD, LCMHC, CRC (she/her/hers) is a Professor in the Department of Counselor Education and Fami-ly Studies at Liberty University, with over 26 years of teaching experience prepar-ing counselors, counsselor educators, advanced researchers, and clinical supervi-sors to work effectively with diverse populations. As a grant writer, she has pro-cured over $8 million in grant funds to meet the needs of racial and ethnic minori-ties with disabilities and addictive behaviors. Her extensive leadership includes roles with the Arkansas Board of Examiners in Counseling, CRCC, NCRE, and CACREP.

Bridget Hollis Staten, Ph.D., LPC, NCC (she/her/hers) currently is a Professor in the Department of Human Services at South Carolina State University, with over 20 years of teaching experience in Re-habilitation Counseling. Her experience includes practicum and internship clinical supervision, student mentoring, and grant writing. Dr. Hollis Staten currently man-ages a 2.25 million dollar federal grant that focuses on educating counselors in the area of career development and transition for persons with disabilities. Dr. Hollis Staten's primary areas of research includes learning disabilities, intellectual disa-bilities and accommodations, minority issues in counseling and employment out-comes of persons with disabilities.

K. Lynn Pierce, Ph.D., CRC, LPC (she/her/hers) is a Certified Rehabilitation Counselor (CRC) and a Licensed Pro-fessional Counselor (GA). She is an Assistant Professor and Program Coordinator for the Ph.D. in Counselor Education and Supervision at Mercer University in At-lanta, Georgia. Her scholarship focuses on improving access to care for marginal-ized groups including people with disabilities, disability equity, and accessibility advocacy within counselor education and higher education.

The Promotion and Tenure Process

14

Janice Byrd, Christa J. Porter, and Amoaba Gooden

The secret of our success is that we never, never give up.

Wilma Mankiller

Abstract

This chapter describes the tenure process and uniquely attends to contingent appointments, historically marginalized faculty, and teaching. Authors contextualize the tenure process by providing a case scenario and conclude the chapter with four strategies to consider during the tenure process: (a) provide course release for hidden labor, (b) provide formal and informal opportunities for mentorship, (c) support affinity spaces, and (d) develop racial and gender capacity-building opportunities.

Learning Objectives After reading this chapter, you will be able to:

1. Articulate the specific steps in the tenure process for college- and university-level faculty in the United States.
2. Describe unique challenges and potential barriers in the tenure process, particularly for faculty of color.
3. Identify strategies to consider during the tenure process for faculty.

J. Byrd (✉)
The Pennsylvania State University, University Park, PA, USA
e-mail: byrdjanice91@gmail.com

C. J. Porter · A. Gooden
Kent State University, Kent, OH, USA
e-mail: cporte24@kent.edu

A. Gooden
e-mail: agooden@kent.edu

D. M. Stalnaker-Shofner and T. N. Sapp (eds.), *A Comprehensive Guide for Counselor Education*, Springer Texts in Education, https://doi.org/10.1007/978-3-031-68358-9_14

14.1 Statement of Reflexivity

We write this chapter as Black women faculty, having experienced both contingent and tenure-track appointments at several research institutions. Dr. Byrd is in her second tenure-track appointment; Dr. Porter served in a full-time contingent role at a different institution prior to her tenure-track appointment and is now a university-level administrator with tenure; Dr. Gooden serves as vice president who (at the same institution) received promotion to full professor and is a former department chairperson. Collectively, we as Black women carry a historical legacy of gendered racism in society as domestic workers and caregivers.

14.2 Case Scenario

Mary is a Black woman and CES faculty member in her sixth year in the academy. She graduated from a large research-focused university. Her current position is also her first academic appointment. She was appointed to a tenure-track position as an Assistant Professor at a predominantly White institution (PWI) with a Research Two Carnegie Classification®. In her current capacity, she has a workload ratio of 30% research, 60% teaching, and 10% service (see Chap. 13 referencing faculty workloads and institution classification).

Regarding the tenure process, she was reviewed in her third year and subsequently deemed eligible for tenure and promotion review in her sixth year. During her third-year review, she received favorable reviews in all major evaluation areas (research, teaching, and service), with no specific indications that she was not on a successful path to tenure and promotion. She has been admired, particularly for her university, community, and national service. She is active in professional associations and considered a 'good' citizen at her institution, having served on multiple university and departmental committees, as well as having served as a reviewer for two flagship CES journals. Her scholarship and publication record is solid, and exceeds her workload expectations. Notably, she was awarded a large foundation grant as the principal investigator and published two articles in a CES flagship journal. Mary's teaching was also reviewed favorably. Comments reflected on her content knowledge, clarity of expectations, professionalism, and effectiveness as an instructor.

Mary is the only faculty of color in her department. She has two mentors, who are not faculty members at her university as there was no formal mentoring structure for pre-tenured faculty. Mary has been working closely with one of her mentors to develop effective strategies to mitigate ongoing microaggressions from White learners in her classes, particularly in her social justice and multicultural counseling course. Learners often openly question her knowledge, ask other White faculty members if her content is relevant, and comment on her evaluations with statements such as "she does not speak to our experiences as real Americans," "she's unprofessional and doesn't smile enough," and "she focuses too much on race."

In developing and updating her course, she reflected on current national events such as the increased awareness of equity and anti-racism on college campuses, and made the decision to alter some of the content in her courses such as centering historically marginalized voices in assigned readings and openly encouraging learners to actively challenge and think more critically about the therapeutic approaches deemed foundational to the profession.

The microaggressions from learners continued, in the form of frequent pushback. Her most recent faculty evaluations had significantly more negative comments and lower satisfaction scores. Despite these challenges, she was deemed to have a strong dossier by her department chair, and external review letters were overwhelmingly positive. She submitted her tenure dossier for consideration; however, the negative comments on her course evaluations influenced her colleagues' perceptions of her ability to meet tenure guidelines. As a result, her colleagues in the department rendered a 2–3 vote to oppose her tenure and promotion to Associate Professor.

14.3 Introduction

In this chapter, we describe the tenure process and highlight unique experiences of faculty with historically marginalized identities and the implications for these individuals seeking tenure at their institutions. Additionally, we present Mary's case of tenure denial to guide readers to reflect on how university tenure-related processes and procedures affect historically marginalized faculty.

14.4 The Tenure Process

The tenure and promotion process is a career milestone for faculty and is often described as a multifaceted and politicized process (Youn & Price, 2009). Tenure is a concept resulting from a series of discussions among various educational associations, faculty members, administrators, and the American Association of University Professors (AAUP) that led to the *1940 Statement of Principles on Academic Freedom and Tenure* (AAUP, 2021). The AAUP defines tenure as an uninterrupted, rarely terminated appointment that provides academic faculty: (1) freedom in their teaching, research, and service and (2) relative economic security. These protections afforded to tenured faculty are what makes this designation so coveted in academia. Though these protections exist, there are specific causes for termination including but not limited to: financial stress, program discontinuation, or as a result of what the institution defines as due process (AAUP, 2021; Dutt-Ballerstadt, 2021). Furthermore, the protection of academic freedom is not a guarantee that was initially considered for non-White or non-male faculty when discussed in 1940, and this is apparent when considering the national statistics of those tenured.

According to the National Center for Education Statistics (NCES), Digest of Education Statistics in 2022, 65% of all full-time faculty in the United States were White (non-Hispanic), 6% were African American/Black, 6% identified as Latinx/e, 11% were Asian American, 0.4% were American Indian/Native American/

Pacific Islander, and 0.14% identified as Pacific Islander (NCES, 2023). White people continue to disproportionately have access to the protection of tenure despite representing approximately 62% of the U.S. population. Therefore, even though the United States continues to become more diverse, faculty of Color face significant barriers when attempting to secure tenure and enter into the *upper echelon* of academia (Bonner et al., 2015; Pérez, 2019).

Tenure can often be a process that is politicized, and this was recently brought to public attention with the case of Nikole Hannah-Jones, who was initially denied a tenure vote at the University of North Carolina Chapel Hill. The reasons for Hannah-Jones's denial were vaguely defined despite her significant academic and professional achievements, including the Pulitzer Prize for the development of *The New York Times Magazine's* 1619 Project, a historical body of work commemorating the 400th anniversary of the arrival of enslaved Africans (Hannah-Jones, 2019; June & O'Leary, 2021). Paul Harris at the University of Virginia (Hudson, 2021) and Lorgia García Peña at Harvard College (Mochkofsky, 2021) are other examples of highly publicized national cases of tenure denial.

Many people seeking tenure, regardless of identity, would describe the process as uniquely arduous, emotionally strenuous, and sometimes obscure and lacking clarity. This process can look different depending on the institution (i.e., research one (R1)/doctoral or baccalaureate/associate's colleges; Indiana University Center for Postsecondary Research, n.d.). However, the process generally involves the pre-tenured faculty member holding a probationary appointment for approximately three to five years before their completed dossier is reviewed at various levels (i.e., college and university) by university- and national-level tenured faculty. Dossier files include, but are not limited to, evidence of research (i.e., published manuscripts), teaching (i.e., faculty evaluations, peer evaluations, curricular innovation), and service (i.e., department administration, college, university, and national). At teaching institutions, the tenure and promotion process for faculty emphasizes excellence in teaching, service to learners, and contributions to the institution. Additionally, at some institutions individuals may be promoted (i.e., rank moves from Assistant to Associate) but tenure is not granted. Across the probationary period, tenure-track faculty are reviewed at various junctures depending on the institution; this can be annually, at the third-year mark, at two specific intervals during the probationary period, or at other specified intervals (Fig. 14.1).

14.4.1 Contingent Appointments

Faculty members serving in full-time tenured positions do not comprise the majority of academia. Many faculty appointments include those in part- and full-time contingent roles, as well as non-tenure track roles (AAUP, 2017). Unlike tenure-track or tenured appointments, contingent roles are often offered (and renewed or reappointed) on an annual basis. Some examples of contingent faculty include, but are not limited to, adjunct, teaching, clinical and visiting faculty. Contingent faculty are responsible for much of the teaching and administrative appointments in

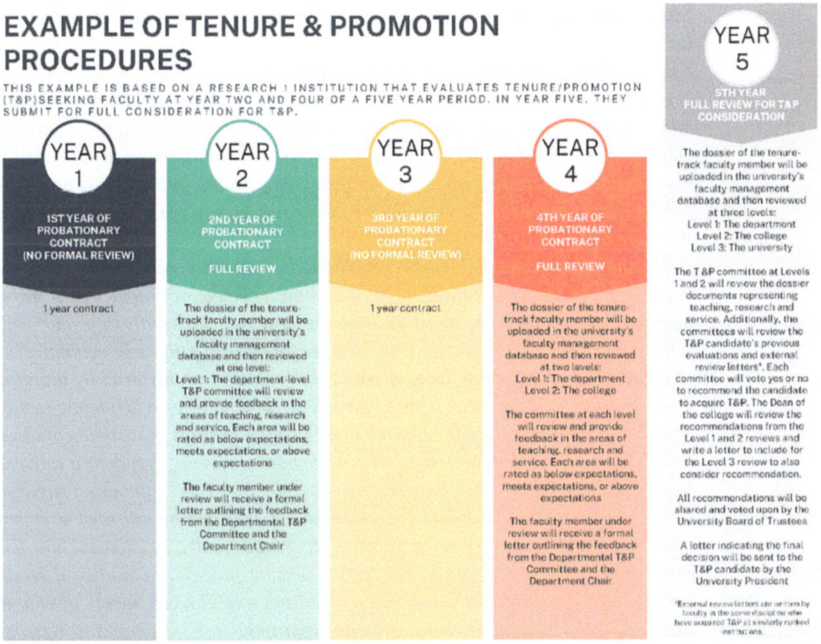

Fig. 14.1 The tenure and promotion process

the academy (Bradley, 2004; Kezar & Sam, 2010). They often face challenges such as job insecurity, lack of benefits, and lower pay compared to their tenure-track counterparts (Gappa et al., 2007). Teaching and clinical faculty often experience a different promotion process than tenure-track faculty. The nature of these processes varies from institution to institution and by contingent status. For example, teaching and clinical faculty may be reviewed to be promoted to associate or full teaching professor. However, if their promotion is not paired with tenure, they are still vulnerable due to the contingency of their appointment. While adjunct and lecturers are rehired on a year-by-year case and oftentimes do not qualify for university benefits. The NCES provided numerical data on full-time faculty in degree-granting postsecondary institutions across race/ethnicity, sex, and academic rank (NCES, 2023). Broadly, while these numerical data provide some clarity as to *who* makes up particular titles within the academy, qualitative data on *how* institutional structures name and title academic appointments are missing. In other words, these numerical data alone fail to capture the actual demography of the academic profession in terms of academic rank and tenure. Researchers and scholars must qualitatively examine and center individual and collective narratives to understand experiences, challenges, and opportunities concerning tenure and promotion (T&P) more fully in the academy.

Stop and Reflect: *Though the NCES provides data regarding faculty demographics and tenure appointments, with respect to the experiences of Black women contingent faculty,* Porter et al. (2020) *explained,*

These numbers, while valuable, do not confirm whether the positions of lecturer and/or instructor (or assistant professor for that matter) represent tenure-track or contingent status. Because of this lack of consistency in positional titles and the ways academic departments structure their budget lines, one's ability to account for the exact number of Black women in these full-time appointments becomes all the more difficult. (p. 675)

In the case scenario, learner evaluations of faculty performance weighed heavily in the tenure decision process. A more effective approach could involve institutional leaders specifically examining how and to what extent curricular innovations, teaching effectiveness, and learner satisfaction are evaluated and weighed differently among faculty, particularly those with historically marginalized identities. Additionally, tenured faculty are able to rely on academic freedom and take more risks in their research and teaching in ways that some contingent faculty cannot. Do committee members consider academic freedom a universal benefit for all tenure-track faculty? For example, does the committee engage in critical discourse about how academic freedom may not be afforded to historically marginalized faculty in the same way as White faculty. To examine how these disparities may play a role in the tenure-seeking process, institutional leaders are encouraged to conduct both macro- and microlevel assessments of who has attained tenure and from what academic programs.

14.5 Historically Marginalized Faculty

Faculty members across rank and status experience marginalization at the intersections of their historically marginalized identities, specifically, women, BIPOC individuals, those who identify as LGBTQQIP2SA, and others with historically marginalized identities (Boss et al., 2019; Davis et al., 2020; Niemann et al., 2020; Zambrana et al., 2015). These CES faculty are often engaging in teaching, research, service, and administrative responsibilities associated with tenure and promotion while combating *isms* (e.g., heterosexism, sexism, and racism), disrupting stereotypes, increasing sociopolitical awareness in their programs and/or campuses, and serving as allies to and for other historically marginalized groups at their institutions (Byrd & Porter, 2023; Mullings et al., 2020; Rockquemore & Laszloffy, 2008). When considering the tenure and promotion process for women, these types of service contributions (in addition to expected service commitments to learners, their respective department, and institution) are not accounted for in current evaluative processes (Gonzales, 2018; O'Meara et al., 2017). Academic discipline (e.g., STEM vs. social sciences) also plays a role in how historically marginalized faculty members are treated and experience tenure and promotion at the intersections of their gender, racial, and sexual identities (Griffin et al., 2015; Lisnic et al., 2020).

Additionally, faculty of Color experience high levels of mistreatment due to their racial and ethnic identities, with respect to their academic appointment (Harris & Tanksley, 2021; Haynes et al., 2020). Assigned teaching loads, research and service responsibilities, and/or academic administrative positions are compounded by the fact that faculty of Color "often engage in extensive emotional and psychological labor that is uncompensated, sometimes unrecognized, and almost always undervalued" (Davis et al., 2020, p. 24). Joseph and Hirschfield (2011) broadly coined this labor as the cultural taxation of faculty of Color. Turner (2002) described the multiple marginalities of women of Color as hidden labor. Offering a more poignant description, Carter Andrews (2015) proffered the exhaustion from this labor (and corresponding oppression) as gendered racial battle fatigue as Black women.

14.6 Teaching

Tenure-track faculty are expected to demonstrate effective andragogical praxis during their probationary period. Teaching is often evaluated by way of faculty personal reflection as described in their annual performance narrative as well as by utilizing peer evaluation, and faculty course evaluations. Faculty evaluations in particular, can be one of the more heavily weighted considerations in the tenure review process. The significance placed on teaching effectiveness in a tenure evaluation can vary among colleges and universities. For example, institutions with a Research One *Carnegie Classification*® designation may place more emphasis on evaluating faculty research, and teaching-focused institutions may focus more heavily on teaching performance.

Stop and Reflect: *Historically marginalized faculty often face marginalization and discrimination (i.e., racism, sexism) in almost all professional academic spaces. Often this marginalization can manifest in subtle ways, from varying persons within higher education. As noted in the case scenario, this marginalization can be evidenced by administrators as they assign service tasks, as well as by learners who may dismiss or diminish a Black women's foundation of knowledge. Marginalization can also be observed in faculty-to-faculty interactions, such as in the peer-review process of evaluating performance. In the case scenario, the faculty member was asked to take on additional service and was subjected to greater scrutiny because of the racially charged and gendered faculty evaluations. Leaders are encouraged to have a formal mentorship plan for pre-tenured faculty, (re)examine how service is counted and whether faculty members can name and measure their service differently and in innovative ways. In our case scenario, it is advised that the teaching evaluations should be contextualized and understood through a lens that acknowledges (1) the multiple and intersecting identities of the faculty; (2) the predominantly White composition of the class; (3) the focus of course content on exploring differences, privilege, and oppression; and (4) the influence of current social-political factors.*

14.7 Best Practices and Strategies for Tenure

Achieving success in academia can be influenced by different mitigating factors such as individual performance, evaluation criteria, and the university's *Carnegie Classification*®. Success for tenure-track faculty is often seen through a prism heavily influenced by patriarchal standards and a colonized view of how success should look and be determined. Examples of this perspective include positive peer reviews, and ultimately the granting of tenure by college-level administrators and/or the university's Board of Trustees. In this section, we will broadly describe four strategies to consider in the areas of teaching, research, and service from our perspective. Please be reminded of our positionalities as previously described in our opening reflexivity statement, as they can influence how we experience and respond to challenges in academic spaces. We offer the following four strategies to enhance the tenure process for faculty: (a) provide course release for hidden labor, (b) provide formal and informal opportunities for mentorship, (c) support affinity spaces, and (d) develop racial and gender capacity building opportunities.

14.7.1 Provide Course Release for Hidden Labor

We encourage university administration to consider providing an additional release for the hidden labor and often disproportionate service demands that can be a part of the lived experience of faculty with one or more historically marginalized identities in academia. Black faculty, particularly women, can face an extreme disadvantage in the tenure process because their service is typically undervalued (Garrett et al., 2023). When compared to their white-identifying counterparts, faculty of Color disproportionately spend time on service work that supports institutional missions and values such as mentoring learners with historically marginalized identities, and such work is typically undervalued. Institutions should also recognize that faculty of color, and in particular Black-identifying faculty also spend time managing their own racialized encounters in and out of the classroom, and this can impact their creative and intellectual energy and thus their productivity (Allen et al., 2000; Perlow et al., 2018). Individuals negotiating contracts for tenure-track positions are encouraged to ask about course releases to support potential invisible labor as equally meritorious as the time one spends developing their research and teaching.

14.7.2 Formal and Informal Opportunities for Mentorship

Mentorship within academic units is important to help faculty of Color navigate the nuances of institutional expectations, as well as formal and informal policies, practices, and procedures; this is especially true for Black women (Kelly & Fries-Britt, 2022). Often, a lack of local mentorship forces Black women to seek support and academic partnerships outside their departments and institutions (Porter et al.,

2023). Since the teaching requirement of the academic appointment for Black women is often uniquely race- and gender-based, opportunities for collaboration within units may be limited (Gregory, 2001). Mentoring can be an important step for them to receive needed support. A lack of community creates isolation, particularly in spaces where Blackness is unwelcomed and/or essentialized. Individuals negotiating tenure-track positions are encouraged to inquire if an infrastructure is in place for formal mentorship within the academic unit, college, and institution.

14.7.3 The Use and Need for Affinity Spaces

Consider offering brave spaces and communal opportunities for historically marginalized faculty to celebrate themselves, convene as a collective, and engage in open dialogue about their experiences (Boss et al., 2021; Byrd & Porter, 2023). More pointedly, researchers have asserted that Black women faculty are often alienated in their academic units. Examples include being excluded from collaborative research projects, as well as having their intellect, experiences, and qualifications called into question or openly devalued by White-identifying learners (Mullings et al., 2020; Williams et al., 2021). Affinity spaces can uplift and support historically marginalized faculty and counter the discrimination they endure. Such spaces can offer care and support, which has the potential to positively impact the success and thus retention of faculty with underrepresented identities, and in particular Black women faculty. Individuals seeking tenure-track positions are encouraged to contact leaders who coordinate faculty programming at the institution for resources and opportunities.

14.7.4 Racial and Gender Capacity-Building Opportunities

Historically Marginalized faculty can face gendered and racialized scrutiny and other forms of discrimination and are evaluated at a different and typically higher standard than their White counterparts (Mullings et al., 2020). Institutional leaders should consider creating an ongoing program of professional development and training related to gender and race equity and antiracism for *all* administrators and faculty to enhance awareness of the importance of social justice and to move academic units from a race-neutral position to an anti-racism position (Davis et al., 2020). We endorse that such professional development opportunities can provide administrators and faculty with a profound sense of the impact of *isms* on the professional lives of faculty with historically marginalized identities, especially for Black women faculty. Furthermore, such knowledge may have the potential to offset negative faculty evaluations and potentially improve the departmental climate for historically marginalized faculty.

Lastly, institutional leaders can consider providing multiple opportunities for faculty of Color and those with other historically marginalized identities to engage in professional development opportunities that are responsive to their unique experiences as they navigate higher education. For example, a session for faculty of Color may focus on how to manage the racialized and gendered issues that arise on their campuses, within and outside of the classroom. Such opportunities have the potential to demonstrate a commitment to supporting and retaining all faculty with diverse and intersecting identities.

14.8 Conclusion

The tenure and promotion process is multifaceted and arduous for many persons across institutions. We have offered a snapshot of the tenure process and also highlighted how the path looks different among individuals (i.e., historically marginalized faculty). Establishing a community wherein one can receive mentoring and support is vital for those seeking tenure. Institutional leaders and those reviewing dossiers must (re)examine the structural and procedural processes, such as rewarding hidden labor and service, faculty ability to utilize academic freedom, and ultimately what counts as valuable in the tenure and promotion process. This can advance a more equitable and just experience for all faculty.

References

Allen, W. R., Epps., E. G., Guillory, E. A., Suh, S. A., & Bonous-Hammarth, M. (2000). The Black academic: Faculty status among African Americans in U.S. higher education. *Journal of Negro Education, 69*(1–2), 112–127. https://www.jstor.org/stable/2696268

American Association of University Professors (AAUP). (2017). *Trends in the academic labor force 1975–2015.* https://www.aaup.org/sites/default/files/Academic_Labor_Force_Trends_1975-2015.pdf

American Association of University Professors (AAUP). (2021). *1940 statement of principles of academic freedom and tenure with 1970 interpretative comments.* https://www.aaup.org/report/1940-statement-principles-academic-freedom-and-tenure

Bonner, II., F., Marbley, A. F., Tuitt, F., Robinson, P. A., Banda, R. M., & Hughes, R. L. (2015). *Black faculty in academia: Narratives for negotiating identity and achieving career success.* Routledge.

Boss, G. J., Davis, T. J., Porter, C. J., & Moore, C. M. (2019). Second to none: Contingent women of color faculty in the classroom. In R. Jeffries (Ed.), *Diversity, equity, and inclusivity in contemporary higher education* (pp. 211–225). IGI Global.

Boss, G. J., Porter, C. J., & Davis, T. J. (2021). Co-conspirators and community care: Toward theorizing a post-COVID-19 academy. *Journal of the Professoriate, 12*(1). 30–54. https://caarpweb.org/wp-content/uploads/2021/04/Wellbeing_psychological_capital_Prasath-121.pdf

Bradley, G. (2004). Contingent faculty and the new academic labor system. *Academe, 90*(1), 28–31. https://doi.org/10.2307/40252585

Byrd, J. A., & Porter, C. J. (2023). Storying our mourning and resistance through teaching: Black women surviving (and thriving in) White spaces. *Journal of African American Women and Girls in Education, 3*(1), 93–113. https://jaawge-ojs-tamu.tdl.org/JAAWGE/article/view/146

Carter Andrews, D. J. (2015). Navigating raced-gender microaggressions: The experiences of tenure-track Black female scholars. In F. A. Bonner II, A. F. marbley, F. Tuitt, P. A. Robinson,

R. M. Banda, & R. L. Hughes (Eds.), *Black faculty in the academy: Narratives for negotiating identity and achieving career success.* Routledge.
Davis, T. J., Greer, T. W., Sisco, S., & Collins, J. C. (2020). "Reclaiming my time" amid organizational change: A dialectical approach to support the thriving and career development for faculty at the margins. *Advances in Developing Human Resources, 22*(1), 23–40. https://doi.org/10.1177/1523422319885115
Dutt-Ballerstadt, R. (2021). What did we provoke? BIPOC/WOC Calling out White supremacy in the academy. In *Civility, free speech, and academic freedom in higher education* (pp. 89–108). Routledge.
Gappa, J. M., Austin, A. E., & Trice, A. G. (2007). *Rethinking faculty work: Higher education's strategic imperative.* Jossey-Bass.
Garrett, S. D., Williams, M. S., & Carr, A. M. (2023). Finding their way: Exploring the experiences of tenured Black women faculty. *Journal of Diversity in Higher Education, 16*(5), 527–538. https://doi.org/10.1037/dhe0000213
Gonzales, L. D. (2018). Subverting and minding boundaries: The intellectual work of women. *The Journal of Higher Education, 89*(5), 677–701. https://doi.org/10.1080/00221546.2018.1434278
Gregory, S. T. (2001). Black faculty women in the academy: History, status, and future. *Journal of Negro Education, 70*(3), 124–138. https://doi.org/10.2307/3211205
Griffin, K., Gibbs, K. D., Bennett, J., Staples, C., & Robinson, T. (2015). 'Respect me for my science': A Bordieuian analysis of women scientists' interactions with faculty and socialization into science. *Journal of Women and Minorities in Science and Engineering, 21*(2), 159–179. https://doi.org/10.1615/JWomenMinorScienEng.2015011143
Hannah-Jones, N. (2019). Our democracy's founding ideals were false when they were written. Black Americans have fought to make them true. *New York Times Magazine.* https://www.nytimes.com/interactive/2019/08/14/magazine/black-history-american-democracy.html
Harris, J. C., & Tanksley, T. (2021). Multiracial faculty members' experiences with biculturalism. *The Journal of Higher Education, 92*(2), 279–302. https://doi.org/10.1080/00221546.2020.1803028
Haynes, C., Taylor, L., Mobley, S. D., Jr., & Haywood, J. (2020). Existing and resisting: The pedagogical realities of Black, critical men and women faculty. *The Journal of Higher Education, 91*(5), 698–721. https://doi.org/10.1080/00221546.2020.1731263
Hudson, W. (2021, May 11). After fighting to gain tenure, Dr. Paul Harris leaves UVA on his own terms. *Diverse Issues in Higher Education.* https://www.diverseeducation.com/tenure/article/15109207/after-fighting-to-gain-tenure-dr-paul-harris-leaves-uva-on-his-own-term
Indiana University Center for Postsecondary Research. (n.d.). *The Carnegie classification of institutions of higher education* (2021 ed.).
Joseph, T. D., & Hirschfield, L. E. (2011). "Why don't you get somebody new to do it?" Race and cultural taxation in the academy. *Ethnic and Racial Studies, 34*(1), 121–141. https://doi.org/10.1080/01419870.2010.496489
June, A. W., & O'Leary, B. (2021, May 27). How many Black women have tenure on your campus? Search here. *The Chronicle of Higher Education.* https://www.chronicle.com/article/how-many-black-women-have-tenure-on-your-campus-search-here?cid=gen_sign_in
Kelly, B. T., & Fries-Britt, S. (2022). *Building mentorship networks to support Black women: A guide to succeeding in the academy.* Routledge.
Kezar, A., & Sam, C. (2010). Understanding the new majority of non-tenure-track faculty in higher education: Demographics, experiences, and plans of action. *ASHE Higher Education Report, 36*(4), 1–133. https://doi.org/10.1002/aehe.3604
Lisnic, R., Zajicek, A., & Kerr, B. (2020). Women faculty in STEM disciplines: Experiences with the tenure process and departmental practices. *Humanity and Society, 46*(1), 52–77. https://doi.org/10.1177/0160597620978773
Mochkofsky, G. (2021, July 27). Why Lorgia García Peña was denied tenure at Harvard: A decision not to retain a beloved Latinx-studies professor raised questions about the university's commitment to students of color. *The New Yorker.* https://www.newyorker.com/news/annals-of-education/why-lorgia-garcia-pena-was-denied-tenure-at-harvest

Mullings, D., Gooden, A., & Brown Spencer, E. (2020). Catch me when I fall! Resiliency, freedom and Black sisterhood in the academy. *Cultural and Pedagogical Inquiry, 12*(1), 91–104. https://doi.org/10.18733/cpi29535

National Center for Education Statistics (2023). *Table 315.20. Full-time faculty in degree-granting postsecondary institutions, by race/ethnicity, sex, and academic rank: Fall 2020, fall 2021, and fall 2022.* https://nces.ed.gov/programs/digest/d23/tables/dt23_315.20.asp

Niemann, Y. F., Gutiérrez y Muhs, G., & González, C. G. (2020). *Presumed incompetent II: Race, class, power, and resistance of women in academia.* Utah State University Press.

O'Meara, K., Kuvaeva, A., & Nyunt, G. (2017). Constrained choices: A view of campus service inequality from annual faculty reports. *The Journal of Higher Education, 88*(5), 672–700. https://doi.org/10.1080/00221546.2016.1257312

Pérez, P. A. (2019). *The tenure-track process for Chicana and Latina faculty: Experiences of resisting and persisting in the academy.* Routledge.

Perlow, O. N., Wheeler, D. I., Bethea, S. L., & Scott, B. M. (2018). *Black women's liberatory pedagogies: Resistance, transformation, and healing within and beyond the academy.* Palgrave MacMillan.

Porter, C. J., Moore, C. M., Boss, G. J., Davis, T. J., & Louis, D. A. (2020). To be Black women and contingent faculty: Four scholarly personal narratives. *The Journal of Higher Education, 91*(5), 674–697. https://doi.org/10.1080/00221546.2019.1700478

Porter, C. J., Sulé, V. T., & Croom, N. N. (2023). *Applying Black feminist epistemology, research, and praxis: Narratives in and through the academy.* Routledge.

Rockquemore, K. A., & Laszloffy, T. (2008). *The Black academic's guide to winning tenure—Without losing your soul.* Lynne Rienner.

Turner, C. S. V. (2002). Women of Color in academe: Living with multiple marginality. *The Journal of Higher Education, 73*(1), 74–93. https://www.jstor.org/stable/1558448

Williams, J. M., Byrd, J. A., & Washington, A. R. (2021). Challenges in implementing antiracist pedagogy into counselor education programs: A collective self-study. *Counselor Education and Supervision, 60*(4), 254–273. https://doi.org/10.1002/ceas.12215

Youn, T. I., & Price, T. M. (2009). Learning from the experience of others: The evolution of faculty tenure and promotion rules in comprehensive institutions. *The Journal of Higher Education, 80*(2), 204–237. https://doi.org/10.1080/00221546.2009.11772139

Zambrana, R. E., Ray, R., Espino, M. M., Castro, C., Cohen, B. D., & Eliason, J. (2015). "Don't leave us behind": The importance of mentoring for underrepresented minority faculty. *American Educational Research Journal, 15*(1), 40–72. https://doi.org/10.3102/0002831214563063

Janice Byrd, Ph.D. (she/her), is an Associate Professor at The Pennsylvania State University. Dr. Byrd has previous experience as a school counselor, career counselor, teaching in secondary settings and serving as a university-wide DEI affiliate. She has been nationally recognized for her scholarship, teaching, and service, and her work appears in various peer-reviewed journals. Dr. Byrd's areas of research include: (1) policies and practices that influence the development and social determinants of health of Black girls/women in educational settings; (2) college and career readiness; and (3) culturally-responsive and trauma-informed research and teaching in counselor education and supervision.

Christa J. Porter, Ph.D. (she/her/hers) is interim dean of the Graduate College and Associate Professor in Higher Education Administration and Student Affairs at Kent State University. Guided by an equity-minded and engaged critical praxis, her teaching, clinical experience, and research examines trajectories of development, socialization, and praxis in higher education and student affairs, with particular interest and expertise in Black women's experiences into and through higher education. Her academic scholarship includes four edited texts, dozens of articles, and book chapters; and she has been nationally recognized for her scholarship, teaching, mentoring, and service in the academy.

Amoaba Gooden, Ph.D. (she/her/hers) serves as the Vice President for the Division of People, Culture, and Belonging at Kent State University where she is also a Professor of Africana Studies. Gooden's research focuses on racism, black feminism, gender and sexuality, and Black Canadian organizing. Her publications include an edited book, *Gender and Sexuality in Ghanaian Societies.* Other publications can also be found in a variety of peer-reviewed outlets including *African Canadian Leadership: Perspectives on Continuity, Transition, and Transformation*, S'Tenistolw-*Moving forward in Indigenous Higher Education*, the *Journal of Black Studies, and Wagadu: Journal of Transnational Women's and Gender Studies.*

Part IV

Counseling Specializations

Understanding the CACREP Standards and Self-Study Process

15

Mariaimeé Gonzalez, Katherine Fort, Jazmone Wilkerson, Letitia Johnson, and Stacy Henning

Pedagogy, regardless of its name, is useless without teachers dedicated to challenging systemic oppression with intersectional social justice.

Bettina Love

Abstract

This chapter facilitates knowledge and awareness of the CACREP Standards, integrating key performance indicators into course creation and development, and writing a CACREP self-study. Understanding the CACREP standards and developing a self-study is an important role as a counselor educator. This chapter focuses on understanding the importance of CACREP accreditation, the rationale for implementing the CACREP standards, developing a self-study within a counseling program, tips for addressing the CACREP standards, advocating for yourself or your program, and becoming involved with CACREP.

M. Gonzalez (✉) · K. Fort · J. Wilkerson · L. Johnson
Antioch University, Yellow Springs, OH, USA
e-mail: mymae78@hotmail.com

K. Fort
e-mail: kfort@antioch.edu

J. Wilkerson
e-mail: jwilkerson@antioch.edu

L. Johnson
e-mail: ljohnson21@antioch.edu

S. Henning
Webster University, Webster Groves, MO, USA
e-mail: stacyhenning67@webster.edu

D. M. Stalnaker-Shofner and T. N. Sapp (eds.), *A Comprehensive Guide for Counselor Education*, Springer Texts in Education, https://doi.org/10.1007/978-3-031-68358-9_15

Learning Objectives After reading this chapter, you will be able to:

1. Explain the relevance of CACREP accreditation and the rationale for future efforts towards unified accreditation processes.
2. Outline the ways in which CACREP supports CIT learning outcomes through the standardization of educational criteria thereby enhancing overall program quality framed by diversity and inclusion.
3. Incorporate the standards in curriculum through a social justice and advocacy lens.
4. Identify ways to become actively involved with CACREP as an organization.

15.1 Statement of Reflexivity

We approach this chapter as authors who have unique and shared experiences who regularly navigate various systems within mainstream society, the post-secondary education institution, and the counseling profession. Collectively, we have held multiple roles: individuals with disabilities (IWDs) in the counseling field, including student, professional counselor, and counselor educator; various leadership roles in counselor education including national, state, local, and in some cases, international counseling committees.

Dr. Mariaimeé' Gonzalez identifies as being a first-generation Latiné college graduate, cisgender, disabled, heterosexual woman. In recognizing that these positionalities hold both marginalization and privilege, she has actively utilized their intersections with her access in higher education to promote social justice, advocacy, and activism at multiple levels of leadership and administration within existing university hierarchies. Dr. Katherine Fort identifies as a White, Scandinavian-American cisgender woman, partner and mother. She is a doctoral counselor educator, program chair, counselor and advocate for social justice. She seeks to combine these roles and experiences in a meaningful way that has a positive impact on our society through creating a greater understanding and utilization of counseling by furthering access to quality, multiculturally representative counselor education programs, opening our frame and ideas regarding what experiences and attributes best support learning communities in our field. Dr. Jazmone Wilkerson identifies as a Black, cisgender woman, counselor educator, advocate for the dis/ability community as well as racial equity, and champion of social justice. Dr. Letitia Johnson identifies as a White, Italian American cisgender woman and mother. She is a counselor educator, a clinical supervisor, and a clinician. Dr. Stacy Henning identifies as White, cisgender woman, counselor educator, practitioner and mother. She has spent decades as a program and clinical administrator leading committees in the field of counselor education, teaching, supervising, and practicing, and is now focused on aiding her students in developing their professional identities, developing lessons in neuroscience and counseling, and working with women and couples in her part time practice.

Our participation in developing this chapter has been a celebration of women working with women and in sharing our knowledge regarding CACREP with you. It is truly a work of passion and includes our content knowledge and experience based on the above roles.

15.2 Case Scenario

A CES faculty member, who identifies as BIPOC and female, was recently informed that she will oversee writing the CACREP self-study for her counseling department. This is her first time writing a self-study and being in a leadership role overseeing this project. Most of her colleagues are new and they are unfamiliar with the self-study process. She is also teaching a full teaching load (4 courses per semester), writing several manuscripts for publication, conducting department and university service, and fulfilling her leadership and advocacy obligations.

The CES faculty member reaches out to her mentor to discuss best practices for writing a CACREP self-study and developing a plan to complete this project. They work together and determine that the CES faculty member needs to compile a list of the resources she needs for her journey, such as attending a CACREP workshop on how to write a self-study. The CES faculty member also creates a workload plan that she believes would be fair. After creating the resources list and action plan, her mentor advises her to seek out other persons who have completed a CACREP self-study in the past for more specific guidance. The CES faculty member looked at the CACREP list of site liaisons for potential persons who can offer her additional guidance. She contacted CACREP and asked to be connected with her program's assigned site reviewer to schedule a meeting and discuss the next steps.

15.3 Introduction

The Council for the Accreditation of Counseling Related Educational Programs, or CACREP, is a Council for Higher Education Accreditation (CHEA) accreditor for both master's and doctoral-level counseling-related degree programs in the United States. CACREP is essential to our profession as it sets forth requisite educational components for counseling-based degree programs with the expressed intent to enhance curricular standardization of education and training that CITs and doctoral learners receive as a part of their degree programs. As such, it is important for us to explore in this chapter the following: the history of the organization, how CACREP became integral to the counseling profession, and the development of the CACREP standards as seminal to curriculum development. Additionally, we want to explore how to appropriately implement the CACREP standards in a bifold manner—first, to support counseling educational curriculum and clinical training requirements, and second, to impart the requisite counseling knowledge and skills within a framework of social justice, inclusive practices, and multicultural awareness. We will also provide you with content and guidance that will support you should you choose to be involved in the CACREP-accreditation process to support the counseling programs and areas of specialized practice offered by your institution by elucidating recommendations and guidelines for developing a CACREP self-study. We will conclude with ways that you can actively become involved with CACREP as an element of institutional and professional service, which is an integral component to faculty workload as introduced in Chaps. 11 and 14.

As we discuss CACREP in this chapter, keep in mind that we are inextricably linked to the CACREP organization and counselor educators. In our roles as CES faculty, we are called to serve in varying capacities and at multiple touch points such as: (1) fulfilling the role of CACREP liaison within your program; (2) as a member of the program team responsible for developing and submitting the self-study report and supporting documents; (3) participating as a member of the CACREP site team integral to program accreditation; (4) engaging as a CACREP-Board representative with the opportunity to be involved in various committees that support the mission of CACREP. Essentially, CACREP is woven into the fabric of our professional identity as counselors and counselor educators. The more we understand CACREP as the accreditation body of counseling education, the more we can use our individual and collective voices in the representation, advocacy, and advancement of the counseling profession.

15.4 The History of CACREP and Its Mission and Vision for Counseling

CACREP is the primary accrediting organization of the counseling profession and has accredited over 600 graduate counseling programs at over 270 institutions in the United States and throughout the world (CACREP, 2013). With the increase in counseling education programs, the need for the development of professional and educational standards became clearer. The momentum towards standardization organically evolved for counseling, as other helping professions such as psychology and social work were beginning to develop their own professional standards. In 1981, CACREP was established when the ACES approached the APGA about the importance of developing professional standards (CACREP, 2015). In 1987, CACREP was admitted into The Council of Postsecondary Accreditation (COPA), which placed CACREP in a position of accreditation power parallel to other professional accreditation bodies such as the APA. As a result, the founding of CACREP and the educational standards that were created, would later come to define the counseling profession.

CACREP's vision is to "provide leadership and to promote excellence in professional preparation through the accreditation of counseling and related educational programs" (CACREP, 2023, Vision para 1). The purpose of CACREP is to set minimum standards for counseling and related educational programs. The CACREP standards are meant to promote a unified profession (CACREP, 2024). Additionally, CACREP focuses on encouraging and promoting the continuing development and improvement of preparation programs and preparing counseling and related professionals to provide services consistent with the idea of optimal human development (CACREP, 2024).

15.5 How CACREP Supports CIT Learning Outcomes and Program Quality

The influence and reach of CACREP as an organization has had a significant impact on the CITs learning and professional development as counselors. This is interlaced in the fabric of counselor preparation in a number of ways, but for our purpose we will explore CACREP as an organization that emphasizes social justice through diversity, inclusion, and multiculturalism, as integral to the education, training, and clinical practice of counselors.

The evolution of CACREP occurred in tandem with that of the counseling profession. As counseling has been impacted by societal shifts and changing awareness with respect to social issues, CACREP has responded accordingly with revisions or total re-imaginings of the curricular and training standards for program accreditation. As we reflect on current social movements, we delineate how CACREP has responded, and how these efforts directly influence CIT outcomes and program quality.

CACREP endorses and advocates for diversity and inclusive practices as integral to the counseling profession. This emphasis can most notably be seen in educational components for counseling programs such as curriculum development, clinical training requirements, and teaching praxis. It also underpins the standards related to broader educational systems such as the recruitment and retention of diverse faculty and learners. These efforts to increase the visibility and representation of individuals with multiple intersectional identities can be seen at a micro, meso, and macro level. Evident on the micro level is CACREP's requirement that counseling programs implement policies and practices supporting the intentional inclusion of persons who have been historically marginalized, oppressed, and educational disenfranchisement. At a meso level, CACREP as an organization has made efforts through internal changes that facilitate diversity and inclusion, with the goal of this representation permeating the internal structures that undergird standard creation and program accreditation. At a macro level, these systemic efforts impact CIT learning, development, and practice, and this influences the counseling services clients receive.

Social justice advocacy, multicultural competence, holistic mental health conceptualization, trauma-informed practice and strengths-based counseling approaches are modalities that evolved in response to the need to and call for counselors and counselor educators to address systemic factors fostering oppression. Such paradigms and philosophies rooted in liberation have begun to be factored into counselor education and training, and this can be traced to the influence of CACREP. Though not specifically named in singular accreditation standards, the recommendations, and delineated actions for how programs can meet specific CACREP standards often indicate their influence. For example, the importance of learner and faculty diversity is noted in Section 1 of the 2024 CACREP Standards, where a clear and documentable effort to recruit and retain diverse learners and faculty must be shown (CACREP, 2024). The standards can be viewed as aspirational, and though they do not specify a minimum threshold for programs, it is a requirement that programs make ongoing efforts to facilitate increased diversity. Further, CACREP (2015) states:

> Placing significant value on diversity, CACREP requires counseling programs to create and support an inclusive learning community. The CACREP Standards not only call for programs to recruit, employ, and retain a diverse faculty but also require programs to make systematic efforts to attract, enroll, and retain a diverse student body. Part of examining diversity within the counseling profession involves taking a close look at the individuals who are becoming professional counselors. (p. 5)

Within professional circles, counselor educators individually and collectively have shared their best practices, as well as their challenges, with respect to the recruitment and retention of diverse faculty, staff, and learners. In these conversations, these challenges have been attributed to a lack of representation in both the counseling and counselor education, as well as lags in administrative funding to properly support marketing and outreach specifically reaching out to diverse learner populations, noncompetitive diverse faculty salaries, and low rates of professional development funds for diverse learners and faculty (for conference attendance, educational materials, transportation, etc.). Supporting this assertion, Ju et al. (2020) stated that "faculty should be attentive to both common and unique personal and social challenges, experiences of marginalization and isolation, and acculturative challenges that learners from underrepresented minority (URM) backgrounds may face" to meet these CACREP benchmarks on recruitment and retention.

While it may be frustrating that CACREP does not hold programs to a more specific standard in regard to faculty and learner diversity, it is also important to see the value in this flexibility. CACREP gives programs latitude regarding their ability to set their own program objectives, mission, vision, and curriculum, done so within the boundaries of the CACREP standards. This allows programs to be unique, thereby distinguishing themselves from one another and fostering program diversity. This is a reflection of the social justice ideology held by CACREP. This distinction in CACREP-accredited counseling programs is reflected in the wide variety of theoretical orientations, learning environments, values systems, religious affiliation, geographic location, and enrollment size of the programs. What CACREP deems most important is that programs *actively work* toward creating program standards that address and meet the broader accreditation standards.

The importance of the afore-referenced constructs of diversity, social justice advocacy, and multicultural competence, as well as strength-centered, holistic, and systems-based approaches to conceptualizing mental health services have been explored. To further emphasize their significance, we want to provide an example of how programs can integrate the values and principles that are at the foundation of these constructs, thereby aligning their curriculum with the CACREP

Standards using a social justice framework. We will explore this in more detail in a subsequent section. Focusing on multicultural knowledge and skills training, programs seeking to truly "walk the talk," and demonstrate congruence between the integration of social justice tenets as a way to support learners' multicultural knowledge and skills development, crafting a concrete and actionable social justice curricular plan is the first step. How will CITs come to understand the meaning, function, and integration of cultural humility within their counseling practice? In which courses will CITs specifically learn about multiculturalism in the counseling field? How can that learning be scaffolded to align with the CITs current developmental stage? How can what they are learning be demonstrated? How can we as counselor educators assess the CIT's understanding that they "get it"? What teaching models and approaches will best support these objectives? Should there be uniformity in how the material is taught, or will it differ by professor? Which curricular aspects are important to replicate from CIT to CIT, and when is it important to provide more freedom or flexibility? Finally, is the material being taught consistent across programs, thus ensuring a baseline level of counselor multicultural competence? These questions are all better navigated through the support and standardization that accreditation provides. This accountability process further legitimizes the profession.

Ultimately, programs that not only align themselves to CACREP standards but also, more importantly, those that seek such continuous growth and improvement are much more likely to continue to advance the profession. In regard to program quality, this is arguably the paramount objective—to continue to advance the field of counseling through promotion, research, training, publication and broadening the scope of the foundational values that set our profession apart from other related fields.

15.6 CACREP Accreditation

In considering the importance and function of CACREP accreditation, we offer the following summarization of the accreditation process. First, accreditation:

> implies the setting of minimal standards which training programs must meet. In order to become accredited, a counselor education program must fulfill certain requirements or standards with regard to institutional settings, program mission and objectives, program content, practicum experiences, student selection and advising, faculty qualifications and workload, program governance, instructional support, and self-evaluation. (CACREP, 2023, Understanding para 1)

Accreditation serves multiple functions for the counseling profession. In this section, we will consider a broad view examining accreditation's utility and implications. Reflecting on the recency of the origins of counseling as a formalized profession, accreditation can ensconce our profession in validity and credibility. This is of particular importance as the terms *counseling* and *counselor* have been generally applied to and used in the description and nomenclature of other ancillary vocations (i.e. peer support counselor). It has also been invoked in unrelated professions such as financial counselor or camp counselor. For this reason, it is vital to the sustainability of our profession that we *own* our identity. CACREP supports this position as one of its primary guiding principles. This position is so strongly held that it is affirmed in its infusion throughout the 2024 CACREP Standards. Further, CACREP calls for a *unified* professional counselor identity as foundational, and the Standards ensure that CITs will graduate from their degree programs possessing a strong *professional counselor* identity (CACREP, 2024). Thus, the requirement for counselor educators to identify with the counseling profession (CACREP, 2024). We invite you to refer back to Chap. 11 where this was explored in greater detail.

Accreditation creates an agreed-upon set of parameters and boundaries that solidify the scope of professional practice, and supports this with standardized education, training, and professional expectations. Accreditation serves the purpose of minimizing as much as possible the potential for unqualified persons to essentially "hang a shingle" under the guise of providing counseling services. This has the ultimate goal of protecting individual clients and the greater community.

The educational standardization for accredited counseling-related programs determines and defines the requisite knowledge areas and content domains of counseling and its areas of specialized practice. These standards offer guidelines that touch on all aspects of counseling programs from the learning environment to the educational and credentialing requirements for core faculty teaching in counseling programs, and ultimately the curricular offerings of counseling programs as captured in The Foundational Counseling Curriculum section of the 2024 CACREP standards. This section supports the unification of our professional counseling identity through prescribed educational requirements or core content areas. These eight domains include:

1. Professional counseling orientation and ethical practice;
2. Social and cultural identities and experiences;
3. Lifespan development;
4. Career development;
5. Counseling practice and relationships;
6. Group counseling and group work;
7. Assessment and diagnostic processes; and
8. Research and program evaluation (CACREP, 2023).

Also addressed by the CACREP Standards are Entry-Level Specialized Practice Areas, which provide standards relevant to the knowledge and skills requisite for specialty practice areas. There are eight specialized practice areas that are accredited by CACREP:

1. Addiction counseling;

2. Career counseling;
3. Clinical mental health counseling;
4. Clinical rehabilitation counseling;
5. College counseling and student affairs;
6. Marriage, couple, and family counseling;
7. Rehabilitation counseling; and
8. School counseling (CACREP, 2023).

Now that we have articulated the importance of accreditation as a undergirding of professional counselor identity, as well as establishing a scope of education, clinical training and professional practice that ultimately serve to protect individual clients and the community at-large, we will begin an exploration of the processes of CACREP accreditation. The following section will offer an overview of the accreditation and review process, beginning with the CACREP self-study.

15.6.1 CACREP Self-study Process

Before delving into the self-study process, it is helpful to frame this section by extending the content from the prior section as a prelude and overview of the CACREP accreditation review process. From submission of the self-study, through review and the rendering of the final accreditation decision, the accreditation process can take approximately one to two years. In order to be considered for accreditation, programs must provide documentation demonstrating their eligibility. As a part of the overall CACREP review, counselor education programs being considered for accreditation must offer a self-study (the requisite components will be explored in the later content of this section). Once submitted, the CACREP representative assigned to work with the program's designated CACREP Liaison will advance the self-study for assigning to a review team. A site visit will be scheduled and a designated site visit team, composed of a group of CES professionals, will complete the required physical review process of the program. The purpose of the site visit is to provide a thorough evaluation that assesses the program's evidence of how they have addressed the CACREP Standards as documented in their self-study. Additionally, the site visit team will evaluate the program's ability to meet the CACREP Standards using collateral evidence. This includes meeting with and interviewing various constituents (i.e. CITs, faculty, staff, university administration) as well as a physical review of program data and records (i.e. vital statistics, website, learner files). The team may make recommendations to a program regarding additional actions that will help the program to meet a standard more accurately or adequately. Site team visits are approximately three days and can be virtual or in person. At the conclusion of the site visit, the review team provides the program CACREP liaison and other program constituents with verbal and written feedback, which is intended to enhance the quality of the program as well as the establishment of long-term planning and goals for the program. Once all data has been collected, the CACREP Board will offer a final review and subsequent accreditation decision. Program accreditation can be awarded for an eight-year period or a two-year period. Prior to the expiration of the current accreditation, the program must submit an application for re-accreditation (Foster, 2012).

When CACREP reviews programs being considered for accreditation, the primary focus is the *program* offering the graduate degree in counseling, rather than the larger university or institutional structure (CACREP, 2023, Understanding para 1). As programs submit for a review process, they undergo a significant and comprehensive self-evaluation process known as the CACREP Self-Study. In this process, programs review, delineate, and critique their strengths, weaknesses, and available resources. Additionally, the self-study includes documented evidence of the program's educational mission, goals, and objectives, as well as how these elements and the program curriculum align with the CACREP Standards, specifically Sections One through Five, with an additional focus on the Standards specific to the program's area of specialized practice (i.e. Section 5A for Addiction Counseling programs, which is more closely examined in Chap. 16). How the program addresses the requisite CACREP educational standards is delineated as key performance indicators (KPIs). KPIs are "student learning outcomes that are connected to the required curriculum and that program faculty have chosen to represent student knowledge and skills related to program objectives" (CACREP, 2024). While the scope of this chapter is to outline the general process of accreditation, further information regarding the specialized practice areas can be found in the subsequent chapters (Chaps. 16–22) housed in this part of the textbook.

Additionally, the program is required to document and report annual program data such as learner demographics, yearly program assessment and evaluation, and overall performance data; this must also be made available to the public. In doing so, the program "demonstrates its desire to be held accountable for its educational activities and assists prospective students in selecting an appropriate counselor education program" (CACREP, 2023, Why para 2). A program that is CACREP-accredited is accountable to meet the current CACREP standards, and this level of accountability can be helpful as the program seeks institutional support and resources from university administration to continually enhance the program's educational efficacy and quality.

15.6.1.1 Before You Begin

As you consider what is needed to craft the self-study, we want to offer you some guidance and resources as you embark on this journey. First, it is vital to have working knowledge and general understanding of the CACREP Standards. Additionally, it may also help you to become familiar with the CACREP Policy Document. The current standards and policy documents can be found on the CACREP website under the Programs link listed on the CACREP Home Page, or by searching https://www.cacrep.org/for-programs/.

The Programs link on the CACREP website can provide you with practical and logistical information and resources such as the CACREP Application for Accreditation fee schedule, and guides for best practices in writing a self-study. You will also find the CACREP Application for Accreditation, and other helpful documents and links useful for program development. Here are additional downloads and links offered by CACREP as supplemental self-study resources:

- Submitting Self-Studies via the Report Submission Page
- Consultation Considerations
- Application Due Dates and Extensions of Accredited Status
- A Reasoned Approach to FTE Faculty
- Program Evaluation Related Reports in the 2016 Standards.

It is important to review all of the resource documents CACREP provides before starting program and self-study development. An additional resource that may benefit you is the Webinar link, which can be found on the CACREP Program page. This link offers pre-recorded content sessions that provide supplemental information on a range of topics that include but are not limited to: (1) current CACREP standards; (2) how to write a self-study; and (3) navigating program requirements. There are a host of other relevant links to resources and support offered on the CACREP Programs page. We invite you to review these links as you begin your work.

Other offerings that can support you as you collect evidence to develop the self-study include "how-to" workshops, often sponsored by CACREP. These can be held independently or as a supplemental educational offering at counseling and counselor education conferences. You may also be able to secure funding to attend a workshop through your university by requesting financial assistance in the form of a stipend to cover related expenses.

The development of a self-study will take months. *It is best developed when most or many members of a department participate* so that range and diversity of thought is included and so the work is shared. We are better at care taking and protecting our program and colleagues when the work of accreditation self-studies is shared.

15.6.1.2 Self-advocacy and Self-care

Creating a self-study can feel isolating at times as you balance the requisite tasks and steps to accomplish this goal. It will be important to set boundaries, advocate for yourself, build community, and help others understand exactly what you need to meet your goals. You should also reflect on what kind of support or village you need along this journey. Self-advocacy is important to protect your time and energy. This is essential for faculty who identify as women and also hold the intersecting identity of being BIPOC. It is vital to communicate your needs to yourself and others. Be wary of the myth of "the strong Black woman," or the implicit or explicit expectation that you *should* be able to handle this alone. Delegation is also helpful as you consider balance.

Completing a self-study can be an opportunity for the program faculty to come together to examine areas of growth and celebrate areas of community and program effectiveness. Your leadership with this endeavor will impact your current and future stakeholders and can be part of the evolution of your program. Your stewardship will be rooted in the power of a community for the community. Celebrate your stewardship and honor your journey.

Stop and Reflect: *As she organizes her resources to begin her work creating the self-study of her institution's counseling graduate program, she learns that the Dean's Office is awarding grants to supplement the work of university faculty. She submits a request, secures a $2000 grant, which allows her to be able to attend a CACREP self-study workshop. Here, she received foundational knowledge about the history of CACREP and the importance of accreditation. Most importantly, she is educated about best practices in writing a self-study, as well as useful resources to help her in this endeavor. This helps her to begin to conceptualize the self-study, and to formulate a concrete plan denoting action steps to write the self-study. An added bonus of attending the workshop was the opportunity to develop relationships with other counselor educators serving as CACREP liaisons for their respective counseling programs. She determined that it would be helpful to surround herself with these colleagues also tasked with writing self-studies. She connects with another counselor educator at the workshop, and they plan to stay in communication to provide each other with support. She also decides to "create her village," specifically finding other women who are BIPOC who have been involved with the CACREP self-study process, who may be able to mentor her in this process. After connecting with other BIPOC faculty who are also female, Atia and her colleagues form a cohort of faculty writing a self-study. They each write a list of the support and resources they need for this journey. She decides to download at least five examples of self-study reports available online to gather ideas for resources and obtain a better understanding of the finished product. She will use the information to come up with more ideas for support and resources.*

Additionally, She extends the concept of advocacy for herself. She is going to write down a workload that she believes would be fair and then negotiate this list with her chair/program director. She is going to ask for course release and a stipend for the work related to writing the self-study, as well as for this work to be counted in her workload as program service and leadership. Additionally, she is going to honor the need for self-care. Writing a self-study and preparing for a site visit can be very stressful, and self-care is needed for this process. She will create a short- and long-term self-care plan, paying attention to how the project will impact her family time and share her concerns with her loved ones. Working with her chair/program director, they will explore ways in which she can continue to find/or maintain balance in her personal and professional life. She will continue to honor her feelings, emotions, expectations, and values during this journey. She will seek support when times become overwhelmed and lean into her village when in need.

15.7 Becoming Involved with CACREP

It has been said that we must be the change we want to see in the world. With this as a guiding principle, we want to provide you with ways that you can increase your service to the profession through involvement with CACREP.

15.7.1 As a Site Visitor

CACREP is a multifaceted organization with many avenues for service. The first way that you can become involved is as a site visitor. As previously mentioned, the accreditation process requires the support, time, and talents of dedicated professionals from the counselor education and supervision and clinical counseling practice fields to facilitate its mission and function. The CACREP Site Visit Team is integral to this process. The team is typically composed of counselor educators, who serve in varying roles. The site team includes a chair, who serves as the team coordinator and point of contact for the program CACREP Liaison. The additional members of the team (usually two other professionals) can be full-time core faculty in counselor education programs across the country, or adjunct faculty who are clinicians who also assist with the teaching and supervision of a counseling program.

Serving as a site visitor is a voluntary role. To become a site visitor, interested persons must complete an online application via the CACREP website. The application includes: (1) evidence of being a full-time faculty or clinician within the counseling field; (2) meeting the requisite experience of a minimum of three years as a counselor educator faculty or as a practicing clinician; (3) securing a letter of recommendation from a supervisor or colleague; (4) being an active member of a professional counseling organization; and (5) evidence regarding your service and advocacy in the field of counseling. Additionally, experience in writing or assistance in the development of an accreditation self-study is beneficial.

It seems evident that CACREP seeks to develop culturally diverse site teams. Accreditation standards include terms such as multicultural, diversity, pluralistic and equity. The application includes cultural-related items such as roles within the department or program; type of program including size and location in a region; teaching modality and organization classification such as for profit or non-profit. The application also includes the recognition of historically black colleges and universities (HBCUs), Hispanic-serving institutes (HSIs), and tribal program applicants and requests the ethnicity, gender and disability needs of the applicant. Accrediting bodies typically seek to place like-team members with like-programs such as school counseling faculty on a school counseling program accreditation and faith-based program faculty at a faith-based program. Combining the cultural and professional identities of a team member with the cultural and organizational structure identities of a program can help to create a match between the team and program. It also helps to create a culturally diverse team that provides a broader perspective when determining evidence of standards.

15.7.2 Advocacy with CACREP

There are advocacy opportunities linked to the advancement of CACREP's mission and purpose. As standards are re-evaluated and new standards are considered for inclusion in the next iteration, CACREP continually seeks feedback from counselor education faculty and learner stakeholders. For example, during the most recent CACREP Standards revision process, CACREP held several meetings where they elicited feedback from the public. There are opportunities to review upcoming CACREP standards for counselor educators, counseling professionals, and counseling program graduate learners. Such service is an invitation for you to engage in advocacy for and activism in the counseling profession. This is necessary because as the world around us changes, our programs and standards too must change.

Stop and Reflect: *In thinking about the case study, the CES faculty should consider what changes, if any, she might recommend to CACREP based on her on-the-ground experience in her program and as a CACREP liaison for her counseling program. CACREP depends on everyone to determine during their periodical review of their standards what revisions should be made. In the inverse, she should also consider, based on her self-study, what changes need to be made in her program to better address CACREP standards.*

15.8 CACREP Standards and How to Meet Them Using a Social Justice Framework

CACREP takes an active stance regarding DEIBASJ and elevating the representation of persons with historically marginalized identities. As such, the CACREP Standards have become vital in promoting diversity among faculty and CITs in counseling programs. In this way, the standards themselves actively help programs to become more anti-racist and inclusive.

CACREP allows programs to uniquely adhere to the curricular standards for counselor education needed to prepare CITs for the "real-world" of counseling. As such, there are many ways to meet these standards in a creative yet meaningful way. One topical area not directly addressed in the current iteration of the standards is *how* to infuse social justice in curriculum development and training. As counselors and counselor educators, we must view our counseling and teaching practice as well as the lived experiences of clients and CITs through a multicultural lens. This allows us to see the pervasiveness of social injustices from structural and systemic racism and how that oppression impacts both our clients and CITs. As clinicians, we are charged with advocacy by the 2014 ACA *Code of Ethics*, "to advocate at the individual, group, institutional, and societal level to address potential barriers and obstacles that inhibit client growth and development" (ACA, 2014, p. 5, Standard A.7.a.). As such, as counselors and counselor educators with a gatekeeping mandate, we have a professional obligation to actively work to dismantle and advocate against any oppressive forces in order to remove barriers to growth and development for clients and CITs. Further, in our roles as educators, we also must infuse advocacy in our education practices and teach through a social justice lens.

With this in mind, we invite you to consider these two questions: (1) how do I meet certain standards within the intricacies of my specific program, and (2) how do I infuse social justice into my programming while meeting the CACREP standards? As you reflect, we want to provide additional context for you as well as our recommendations. Please be advised that these are only suggestions based on our experiences, and you must consider the specific needs of your program. Using 2024 CACREP Standards, we offer specific examples of how to address the standard with social justice as a foundation in Table 15.1.

We want to emphasize that the recommendations offered in this section are not meant to be prescriptive. Rather, they are proffered to spark creative thinking. As you consider what is written here, we recognize that there may be challenges to implementation. As you work to incorporate the CACREP standards with social justice in mind, we encourage you to think broadly about the counseling field, and what is needed for new counseling professionals to address client and community needs while advancing the profession towards the 20/20 Vision for the Future of Counseling referenced at the opening of this chapter. As we close the circle, remember that we owe it to ourselves, CITs, and clients to consider the great impact of the inequities and disparities resulting from systemic oppression. This awareness will shape our teaching praxis as we prepare the next generation of counselors to advocate across the continuum effectively.

Stop and Reflect: *With a full-circle frame of reference, in tying back the information presented in this section to the case study, we ask you to reflect on requisite resources to address the current functioning and programmatic needs to support changes that incorporate CACREP accreditation standards through a social justice lens. What would you need in order to realize this goal of creating a socially-just counseling program that serves to advance equity for all?*

Table 15.1 Addressing the 2024 CACREP Standards through a social justice lens

Standard	Best practices though a social justice lens
Standard 1.M requires that CIT handbooks include specific things about programs such as (1) the mission, (2) information about professional counseling organizations and how to get involved, (3) matriculation requirements, (4) expectations needed of CITs, (5) academic appeals policies, (6) policies around the process for recommending CITs for employment and credentialing, and policies around CIT retention, dismissal, and remediation (CACREP, 2024)	As programs craft their handbooks, this is a unique opportunity to espouse your commitment to social justice and directly incorporate this commitment into these requisite materials. Remembering our advocacy charge, programs can use their handbooks as an invitation to CITs to avow their own commitment to social justice and advocacy. This is the beginning of holding ourselves and our respective programs accountable for being intentional about how we address and infuse this social justice into counselor education
Standard 1.O states that we should also have within our policies for retention, remediation, and dismissal, language specific to CIT disposition, and the need for CITs to exemplify a social justice approach to counseling that would require CITs to be able to effectively advocate for clients at an individual, group, institutional, and societal level (CACREP, 2024)	Infusing social justice principles into retention and remediation could begin with initial recruitment of applicants. Working in concert with admissions, counselor education programs could identify pathways of inclusion and diversity by widening efforts to liaise with undergraduate institutions such as Hispanic-serving Institutions (HSIs) as well as Historically Black Colleges and Universities (HBCUs). A relational approach is an ideal method to establish connections with faculty in departments that can serve as a pipeline to counseling graduate programs. Please refer back to Chap. 6 where this was explored. Incorporating social justice into CIT remediation would employ a strengths-based philosophy and should include identifying and incorporating supports and resources that will bolster CIT success efforts that will hopefully mitigate barriers that may have contributed to the need for remediation. Please refer back to Chap. 8 for specific strategies for implementation

(continued)

Table 15.1 (continued)

Standard	Best practices though a social justice lens
CACREP Standard 2.B. requires that program objectives reflect current knowledge and projected needs in a "diverse, multicultural, and global society" (CACREP, 2024, p. 8)	Infusing social justice to support this standard can involve specific curricular requirements that align with and extend the program's mission, values, and CIT learning objectives. An example of a CIT learning objective that meets this standard can be: *Learners will identify and implement effective advocacy strategies needed to address structural, institutional, and individual barriers that impede access to equity, fairness, and success for all clients.* Further, clearly delineating not only that the material taught will present underrepresented perspectives and approaches to promote diversity and inclusion in counseling-related curriculum is just the start. Teaching multicultural counseling skills and practices can employ a developmental approach that scaffolds learning. For example, curriculum developmentally matched to entering CITs can focus on enhancing multicultural *awareness*. In Year two, the next developmental level could address multicultural *knowledge*. Lastly, Year Three (which usually coincides with experiential courses such as Practicum and Internship) can focus on facilitating CIT's ability to appropriately *apply* multicultural skills in counseling practice through supervision. Utilizing formative and summative assessment measures that are implemented at specific junctures in the degree program can help determine if learning is occurring as outlined by program objectives. Collecting this data then allows for programs to measure and evaluate themselves as well as CITs learning to ensure that the infused social justice tenets support the CACREP standard and the program's commitment to address the needs of a multicultural society

15.9 Conclusion

As we shared at the beginning, CACREP is us, all of us. The more you learn about CACREP, the more you can use your voice using a social justice lens to create systemic change for our profession. Your leadership will provide community and promote excellence in professional preparation through the accreditation of counseling and related educational programs. Your stewardship can impact learner outcomes and program quality, site visits, advocacy with CACREP and for yourself.

Programs that are CACREP accredited make a commitment towards community care through the quality of education, effectiveness of the program, commitment to excellence, licensure preparedness, professional preparedness, and are to represent the community itself within the educational journey. Learning about CACREP can provide a shared understanding within the profession to maintain professional standards of practice and develop strong professional identities. The 2024 CACREP standards work to illuminate the power of one's professional identity and create intentionality regarding program evaluation and CIT assessment. The most recent CACREP standards were drafted during a historical time of a global pandemic and a movement of racial justice around the world due to systemic racism. As stated in the CACREP 2024 introduction,

The development of the 2024 CACREP Standards came at a time when the United States and many parts of the world were addressing issues in DEIBASJ; increased reliance and application of digital delivery in both higher education and counselor education; and a global pandemic that shifted the landscape of the profession, higher education, and broader global and societal opportunities and challenges. The 2024 CACREP Standards address the tenor of the time that they are published and seek to apply them to future societal, academic, and professional contexts (CACREP, 2024, p. 1).

Within the standards themselves, are opportunities for cultural stories to evolve and provide space for new knowledge, understanding and advocacy. The self-study process is part of our collective story as a profession, and your contribution is essential to the evolution of our professional identity, profession, educational journey, community care and connectedness.

References

American Counseling Association. (2014). *2014 ACA code of ethics*. https://www.counseling.org/docs/default-source/default-document-library/ethics/2014-aca-code-of-ethics.pdf?sfvrsn=55ab73d0_1

Council for Accreditation of Counseling and Related Educational Programs. (2013). *CACREP why CACREP.* https://www.cacrep.org/accreditation/why-should-my-program-seek-accreditation/

Council for Accreditation of Counseling and Related Educational Programs. (2015). *CACREP vital statistics 2014: Results from a national survey of accredited programs*. http://www.cacrep.org/wp-content/uploads/2019/05/2014-CACREP-Vital-Statistics-Report.pdf

Council for Accreditation of Counseling and Related Educational Programs. (2023). *About CACREP*. https://www.cacrep.org/about-cacrep/#understanding-accreditation

Council for Accreditation of Counseling and Related Educational Programs. (2024). 2024 CACREP Standards. https://www.cacrep.org/wp-content/uploads/2024/04/2024-Standards-Combined-Version-4.11.2024.pdf

Foster, L. H. (2012). Professional counselor credentialing and program accreditation in the United States: A historical review. *Journal for International Counselor Education, 4*(1), 42–56.

Ju, J., Merell-James, R., Coker, J. K., Ghoston, M., Péres, J. F., & Field, T. (2020). Recruiting, retaining, and supporting students from underrepresented racial minority backgrounds in doctoral counselor education. *Professional Counselor, 10*(4), 581–602.

Mariaimeé "Maria" Gonzalez, Ph.D., LPC (she/her/ella) is currently the co-founder of the Latinx Social Justice Mental Health Institute and serves as the Executive Director, Clinical Operations and Community Outreach at Antioch University Seattle. She has been a counselor educator, professionally licensed counselor and supervisor for over 16 years. Her extensive leadership background includes Chair of the Masters in Counseling at Antioch University Seattle (2019–2023), Presidencies of the American Counseling Association of Washington, and the Western Association for Counselor Education and Supervision (2023–2024), as well as serving in various leadership roles for American Counseling Assocation (ACA). She was a United Nations Delegate, served on a number of ACA committees, and served on the Association for Counselor Education and Supervision (ACES) governing council (2023–2024). Currently she advocates for global mental health rooted in liberation, human rights for marginalized communities, and social justice, advocacy, and positive change in the counseling profession.

Katherine Nordell Fort, Ph.D., LMHC (she/her/hers) is a Core Faculty at Antioch University, in the School of Counseling, Psychology, and Therapy. She has been a counselor educator and professionally licensed counselor and supervisor for 15 years. Her clinical experience includes providing individual and group counseling to college students, international students and clients in private practice who present with issues such as depression, anxiety, trauma, relationship challenges, grief and career exploration. Her primary research interests include resilience, cross-cultural counseling, student success, and social justice issues related to higher-education and the counseling profession.

Jazmone Wilkerson, Ph.D., LCPC, NCC (she/her/hers) currently serves as a Senior Lecturer, Adjunct Faculty Member at Antioch University, and a Program Manager with the U.S. Department of Justice, Office of Justice Programs, Office of Juvenile Justice & Delinquency Prevention. As a researcher, Dr Wilkerson has a special interest in racial and social justice for historically marginalized populations with a particular focus on Black and Latinx students with disabilities. More specifically, she is interested in bridging the gap between the legal and mental health system for students in K-12 to create a more equitable and just system for all.

Letitia D. Johnson, Ph.D., LicSW, LMHCA, CHT, CMHS (she/her/hers) is a Clinical Manager of School Based Mental Health Clinics at Neighborcare. She has served as adjunct faculty at Antioch University and has been a licensed mental health provider for over a decade. Letitia is also a certified transpersonal life coach, hypnotherapist and child mental health specialist. She has years of experience providing community, counseling and rehabilitation services to clients and their families dealing with mental health issues. She is currently providing therapeutic services to children, adolescents, adults and couples in a private practice in Seattle.

Stacy Henning, Ph.D., LPC, CCTHP, MHVDA-IRC (she/her/hers) is an Associate Professor at Webster University, Professional Counseling Department. She has been a counselor educator for over 17 years, counseling women and couples. Stacy has been active in American Counseling Assocation (ACA) Committees including the ACA Ethics Committee, Public Policy and Legislative Committee and the ACA Awards Committee. She is a Chair and Site Team member for the Council for Accreditation of Counseling and Related Educational Programs. Stacy has been active with university committees and dept committees. Current research includes the intersection of neuroscience and clinical counseling, and pedagogical efficacy in counselor education.

Addiction Counseling 16

Kathleen M. Ruscitto and Macie A. Hoover

Teaching is the greatest act of optimism.

Colleen Wilcox

Abstract

There is a pressing need for counselors to assist in providing quality substance and addictive behavior treatment and related services in response to the growing national mental health crisis. Counselor education programs can provide a CACREP addiction track of study using a social justice framework to help meet this need. This chapter will serve as an easy-to-follow guide for how to initiate a CACREP-aligned addiction track. We will use current literature, CACREP standards, and practical examples to demonstrate how counseling programs can offer an addiction counseling track for CITs.

Learning Objectives After reading this chapter, you will be able to:

1. Explore the professional identity of Addiction Counselors.
2. Explain the rationale and purpose of utilizing a CACREP-aligned addiction track and program of study.
3. Integrate best practices for creating an Addiction counseling program or track rooted in social justice and advocacy.

K. M. Ruscitto (✉) · M. A. Hoover
Buena Vista University, Storm Lake, IA, USA
e-mail: Ruscitto@bvu.edu

M. A. Hoover
e-mail: SteadMacie@cityu.edu

M. A. Hoover
City University of Seattle, Seatle, WA, USA

D. M. Stalnaker-Shofner and T. N. Sapp (eds.), *A Comprehensive Guide for Counselor Education*, Springer Texts in Education, https://doi.org/10.1007/978-3-031-68358-9_16

16.1 Statement of Reflexivity

Dr. Kathleen M. Ruscitto identifies as a cisgender, heterosexual, non-disabled white female of Northwestern European descent. She is anassistant professor and program director of a counselor education program in Iowa. She has over a decade of experience working as a licensed mental health counselor (LMHC) and addictions (IAADC) counselor before becoming a counselor educator. Dr. Ruscitto's clinical experience includes a range of treatment settings (e.g., inpatient, outpatient, residential), community demographics, and populations, as she has lived and worked in four different states. Dr. Ruscitto's personal and professional experiences have shaped her lens as a counselor educator, as she values fostering an inclusive learning environment that contributes to a more inclusive and equitable future for the counseling profession and the communities it serves.

Dr. Macie A. Hoover is a cisgender, heterosexual, non-disabled, white female of European descent. She is a licensed mental health counselor (LMHC) in Washington. She is a nationally certified counselor (NCC), clinical supervisor, substance use disorder professional trainee, and a child mental health specialist. She is the Digital Delivery Program Coordinator and a core faculty member in a clinical mental health counseling program. Her educational background impacts her theoretical orientation, which centers on mental health from a holistic perspective on wellness. Dr. Hoover provides outpatient counseling for people with obsessive–compulsive disorders, and she treats co-occurring substance use. As an outsider to addiction treatment herself, she acknowledges limitations in her ability to fully understand the lived experience of addiction. However, like many, she has been impacted by addiction as a family member and friend. Dr. Hoover promotes the use of counseling skills to work with people in addiction treatment. She finds clinical skills like the use of appropriate disclosures useful in developing trust, modeling vulnerability and the use of humor helpful in developing empathy and genuine connections with those in treatment.

16.2 Introduction

The prevalence and impact of addictive disorders are well documented and provide the rationale for addiction counseling programs. According to the National Institute of Mental Health (NIH), "Substance use disorder is a treatable mental condition that impacts an individual's brain and behavior, leading to their inability to control their use of substances like legal or illegal drugs, alcohol, or medications" (NIH, 2024, para 1). Additionally, the Substance Abuse and Mental Health Services Administration (SAMHSA) reports that approximately 46.3 million people, 12 years of age or older (or 16.5%) have a substance use disorder (SAMHSA, 2022).

The urgent need for qualified professionals is evident, with only 68,579 substance abuse counselors currently employed in the US (Zippia, 2024). Addiction affects people throughout their lifespan and can begin in the early stages of human development, most notably in adolescence. Adolescents often transition from initial experimentation and casual usage of a drug or substance to habitual use within the first three years (SAMHSA, 2022). It is not uncommon for a mental health diagnosis to exist alongside a substance use disorder. According to SAMHSA (2022), 22% of people with severe mental health symptoms will also develop a substance use disorder. Of those individuals, only 7.4% will receive treatment for both disorders, while 55% of people will not receive treatment at all. It is most effective to tailor treatment approaches to address both addiction and mental health symptoms concurrently (NIH, 2024). Substance use disorders and addictive disorders are among the most stigmatized health conditions (Adeyemy et al., 2021; Golubovic et al., 2021; Holman et al., 2019). Stigma can impact the allocation of funding, education, and resources that would help inform communities of treatment options for addiction disorders. Reducing stigma starts with counselor education (Adeyemy et al., 2021; Golubovic et al., 2021; Holman et al., 2019).

Counselor advocacy to reduce stigma, increase access to care, and develop social justice competencies begins within counselor education programs. The ACA Council outlined a conceptual framework for implementing social justice competencies such as power, privilege, and oppression into Counselor Education (Elliott & Downey, 2023; Ratts et al., 2016). Teaching is a form of political activism (Elliott & Downey, 2023). To develop effective intersectionality, counselor educators must address multiplicities of social identities while using collaborative and reflective approaches that challenge self-concept. In practice, counselors promote individualized and strengths-based care, and it is for these reasons that counselor educators and counseling education programs include social justice teaching praxess. Counselors are uniquely poised to address this need by offering evidenced-based approaches in a non-judgmental and confidential space that supports wellness. A Council for Accreditation of Counseling and Related Educational Programs (CACREP) addiction track affords CITs the knowledge that their program meets professional standards set in mental health and addiction studies (CACREP, 2024).

16.3 History of Addiction Counseling

The history of substance abuse treatment, including addiction counseling in the United States (US), has long been influenced by the public's perception of people with addiction and by social and political movements (Talchekar, 2023; Williams & Mee-Lee, 2019). During colonial times, it was a standard treatment practice to lock a person with alcohol use disorder (AUD) in wooden stocks to be publicly humiliated (Talchekar, 2023). Even today, similar treatment continues in jurisdictions through published records of instances of public intoxication (Talchekar, 2023). At the beginning of the twentieth century, it was common practice to treat AUDs in state mental hospitals. People with AUD were commonly outcasted and viewed as incurable by the medical community (Kurtz, 1979).

Addiction treatment and counseling have evolved in the last century. In the 1930s, a rehabilitation "recovery" system, commonly known as Alcoholics Anonymous (AA), was established by those recovering from AUD (Talchekar, 2023; Williams & Mee-Lee, 2019). Participants of AA were offered support and guidance from others who were all recovering from an AUD. AA emerged due to neglect by the medical community and operated independently of conventional health services (Hagedorn et al., 2012; Talchekar, 2023; Williams & Mee-Lee, 2019).

Treatment programs for SUDs began in the 1940s and 1950s. Established in 1949, the Hazelden Foundation was the first treatment program to offer a holistic approach to AUD treatment (Hagedorn et al., 2012; Hazelden Betty Ford Foundation, 2024; Williams & Mee-Lee, 2019). By the 1950s, paraprofessional helpers were immersed in addiction treatment, commonly applying the Minnesota model (Hagedorn et al., 2012; Williams & Mee-Lee, 2019). The return of soldiers addicted to heroin during the Vietnam War sparked the attention and concern of the US government and military (Hagedorn et al., 2012; Williams & Mee-Lee, 2019). The return of Vietnam soldiers also sparked a renewed interest from the medical and research communities. SUD treatment evolved from a focus on alcohol addiction to recognizing drug addiction, and in 1967, the American Medical Association (AMA) adopted the disease concept model of addiction.

The 1970s also saw the creation of the National Institute for Alcoholism and Alcohol Abuse (NIAAA) and the National Institute for Drug Abuse (NIDA). These professional groups were the start of formal education and training of professional helpers (Hagedorn et al., 2012). The continued development of AUD treatment models, the recognition and treatment of co-occurring disorders (addiction and mental health), the inclusion of behavioral addictions, and the advance in psychopharmacology have all led to the need for much higher levels of education and training for helping professionals to ensure that clients with SUDs receive the most efficacious treatment (Hagedorn et al., 2012; Williams & Mee-Lee, 2019). Thus, the development of standardized education and training, formal credentialing, and licensure.

16.4 CACREP Accreditation

The implementation of CACREP's standards (see Table 16.1), established over two decades, has legitimized the counseling profession. Colleges and universities benefit from CACREP approval, as it provides an accreditation that evaluates a program's quality and rigor to meet professional standards (CACREP, 2024). Accredited programs have been through an extensive approval process to ensure that they are continuously meeting standards in the field, such as coursework, evaluation methods, instructor qualifications, and classroom ratios.

All programs include the eight foundational curriculum areas required for *all* entry-level counselor education programs (professional counseling orientation and ethical practice, social and cultural diversity, human growth and development,

Table 16.1 Addiction counseling 2024 CACREP standards (Section 5.A)

Standards
5.A.1. Neurological, behavioral, psychological, physical, and social effects of psychoactive substances and addictive disorders on the user and significant others
5.A.2. Risk and protective factors for substance use disorders
5.A.3. Assessment for symptoms of psychoactive substance toxicity, intoxication, and withdrawal
5.A.4. Strategies for enhancing client motivation to change, managing cravings, and preventing relapse
5.A.5. Abstinence and harm reduction models of addiction recovery
5.A.6. Evaluating and identifying individualized strategies and treatment modalities relative to substance use disorder severity, stages of change, or recovery
5.A.7. Pharmacological interventions used to address substance use withdrawal, craving, and relapse prevention
5.A.8. Substance use recovery service delivery modalities and networks within the continuum of care, such as primary care, outpatient, partial treatment, inpatient, integrated behavioral healthcare, and aftercare
5.A.9. Recovery support tools and systems, including vocation, family, social networks, and community systems in the addiction treatment and recovery process
5.A.10. Culturally and developmentally relevant education programs that raise awareness and support addiction and substance use prevention and the recovery process
5.A.11. Regulatory processes, continuum of care, and service delivery in addiction counseling
5.A.12. Strategies for interfacing with the legal system and working with court-referred clients
5.A.13. Third-party reimbursement and other practice and management issues in addictions counseling
5.A.1. Neurological, behavioral, psychological, physical, and social effects of psychoactive substances and addictive disorders on the user and significant others

career development, counseling and helping relationships, group counseling and group work, assessment and testing, research, and program evaluation). These areas are addressed further in Chap. 15. In addition to the eight core areas, CITs enrolled in an addiction track or program will complete courses that are substance use and addiction-specific. Additionally, practicum and internship require CITsto obtain addiction and recovery-specific experience.

16.5 Developing an Addiction Counseling Training Program and Track

CACREP outlines three options to include addiction studies in counseling programs and curricula. The first option is to follow CACREP's policy and procedures to develop a new CACREP-accredited addiction counseling program. The second option is to add a new addiction focus within an existing area of specialized practice. The third option is to add an addiction track to an existing CACREP-accredited counseling program. All three are described in further detail with examples provided in the section on the Resources webpage of the textbook found online.

Substance use disorders and behavioral addictions significantly affect individuals across the United States. Professional counselors (excluding addiction counselors) have the highest proportion of clients with a diagnosis of an addictive disorder compared with closely related helping professionals such as social workers, psychologists, and psychiatrists (Lee, 2014). Furthermore, because of the prevalence of addictive disorders, faculty and CITs from accredited counseling programs have proposed that addiction education is necessary for all CITs enrolled in counseling programs, regardless of their concentration area (Golubovic et al., 2021; Lee, 2014).

When developing an addiction training program or track, faculty must consider their state addiction certification or licensing requirements in addition to the 2024 CACREP Standards. Some states require a higher degree in addiction counseling, while others require a high school diploma and continuing education credits. Counselor educators must be mindful of these requirements as well as the goals of the program when developing their addictions curriculum (see Table 16.2).

16.6 Addiction Counseling Specific Training Requirements

While CACREP clearly outlines program standards, it does not dictate how programs meet standards within course assignments, faculty specialty areas, or how programs integrate standards within existing curricula (CACREP, 2024). To meet the 2024 CACREP standards specific to addiction counseling, counselor educators might consider adding courses that balance theory with skill application. Additionally, with the rise in telehealth counseling services and digital delivery programs, it is critical to provide technologies that can enhance the practice of clinical skills related to counseling specialties.

The application of didactic and experiential praxess is at the center of the research recommendations and discussions (Golubovic et al., 2021; Holman et al., 2019). Experiential activities increase CITs advocacy competencies, awareness, and self-efficacy, and lessen anxiety. Furthermore, experiential methods successfully increase CITs cultural self-awareness as they encourage them to explore their own cultural experiences, biases, attitudes, and values (Elliott & Downey, 2023). Research on the topics of addiction counseling and training outlines considerations for curriculum development and programming. These recommendations also align with CACREP standards and may improve CITs learning outcomes. We offer an example of a course description, learning outcomes, and activities to illustrate the research and connection to the 2024 CACREP standards.

Table 16.2 Example addiction counseling program (60 credit hours) program plan of study

Name of course	Credits
Ethics and Professional Orientation[a]	3
Human Growth and Lifespan Development[a]	3
Counseling Theories[a]	3
Counseling Methods and Techniques[a]	3
Counseling and Advocacy with Diverse Populations[a]	3
Research Methodology and Program Evaluation[a]	3
Diagnosis and Treatment Planning in Counseling[a]	3
Career Counseling[a]	3
Group Counseling[a]	3
Assessment, Tests, and Measures in Counseling[a]	3
Psychopathology and Diagnosis in Counseling	3
Introduction to Trauma Informed Counseling	3
Orientation and Overview of Addictive Disorders[a]	3
Advanced Addiction Counseling	3
Practicum I	3
Practicum II	3
Internship I	3
Internship II	3
Internship III	3
Internship IV	3

[a] Indicates courses that address the 2024 CACREP Foundational Counseling Curriculum content area (CACREP, 2024, Section 3)

While every state has addiction education and training requirements, counselor educators should become familiar with certifications common among addiction professionals (see Table 16.3). Links to the agencies in each state that regulate the credentialing of addiction counseling are on the Addiction Treatment Technology Transfer Center (ATTC) website (https://attcnetwork.org/).

16.6.1 Orientation and Overview of Addictive Disorders

This course offers an overview of substance use and addictive disorders. CITs will learn about the historical, ethical, and legal implications of addiction counseling. CITs will gain knowledge of the correlation of neurological, behavioral, psychological, physical, and social effects of psychoactive substances and addictive disorders. CITs will foster culturally informed clinical practices that use a social justice framework for individual, group, and family counseling.

Table 16.3 Addiction counseling certification

Name of certifier	Website	Certification
The International Certification and Reciprocity Consortium (IC&RC)[a]	https://internationalcredentialing.org/	Internationally Certified Alcohol & Drug Counselor (ICADC) Internationally Certified Advanced Alcohol & Drug Counselor (ICAADC)
Association for Addiction Professionals (NAADAC)[b]	https://www.naadac.org/	National Certified Addiction Counselor, Level I National Certified Addiction Counselor, Level II Master Addiction Counselor (MAC)
The National Board of Certified Counselors (NBCC)	https://www.nbcc.org/	Master Addiction Counselor (MAC)
U.S. Department of Transportation (USDOT)	https://www.transportation.gov/odapc/SAP_Certification_Organizations	Substance Abuse Professional (SAP)

Note [a] The IC&RC offers a total of six certifications
[b] The NAADAC also offers additional certifications through its National Certification Commission for Addictions (NCC AP) program

16.6.2 Learning Outcomes

Objective 1 Learners will gain knowledge and skills in recognizing cultural, ethical, and legal issues related to substance abuse and addiction counseling (5.A. 10, 11, 12,13).

Objective 2 Learners will gain culturally competent knowledge and skills for screening and assessment instruments for substance use and addictive disorders (5.A.1, 2, 3).

Objective 3 Learners will gain culturally competent knowledge and skills for diagnosis and treatment of substance abuse and addictive disorders (5.A, 4, 5, 6).

Objective 4 Learners will gain knowledge and skills about the role of counselors, recovery supports, and stakeholders for integrated care and referral (5.A, 7, 8, 9, 10).

16.6.3 Activity Suggestions

Intersectionality and Pop Culture. The purpose of this assignment is to engage CITs in personal reflection and introspection about their intersectionality as it relates to the intersectionality of those with substance use and addictive disorders. CITswill reflect on their bias, privilege, or marginalized status through this assignment. Biases develop from the messages we receive from our environment and the larger systems we interact. Some people continue to question whether substance use or addictive behaviors such as eating, sex, and internet gaming can be addictive. In preparation for this assignment, CITs are strongly encouraged to thoughtfully reflect on what implicit biases are present and the experience with privilege and oppression. CITs will identify a movie that incorporates substance use or addictive behaviors. Then, CITs will complete the following phases:

1. First, identify three emotional, educational, or professional goals that demonstrate thoughtful consideration of personal biases the CITs wants to develop deeper insight and cultural humility towards as a result of participating in the assignment.
2. Next, the CIT will watch the movie they identified and will reflect on the portrayal of information presented about substance use disorders and addiction. What is accurate or credible? What is factual or biased?
3. The CIT will then write a paper:
   a. Identify and describe the intersections/ facets of the main character (s) identity. How do these intersections/facets impact the characters (s)
      i. substance use or addiction(s)
      ii. developmental considerations and relational impact
      iii. access to community support groups and resources, and
      iv. impact the stigma they experience,
   b. How do personal experiences compare to the main character(s)?
   c. How do these experiences impact CITs personal and professional relation ships?
   d. How do these experiences influence their worldview?
   e. How could these experiences affect work as an addiction counselor?
   f. Identify and discuss how to challenge bias.
   g. Reflect and revise the CITs original goals identified in Step 1.

Recovery Culture. This activity is designed to be experiential and expose CITs to the adjunctive support for individuals in recovery.

1. Attend a recovery meeting or alternative recovery program (ex, Alcoholics Anonymous, Narcotics Anonymous, SMART Recovery, Women for Sobriety, Lifering Secular Recovery).
2. Document the time, meeting date, and location.
3. What are the requirements of membership?
4. What is the purpose or mission of the program?
5. Provide a 1-page reflection on the experience:
   a. What are the initial reactions and biases when completing this assignment?
   b. What was it like to attend the meeting or program as an outsider of the recovery culture or the group subculture?
   c. How can CITs experience inform their roles as counselors and social justice advocates?

ASAM Case Evaluation. CITs will be assigned a case study of an individual presenting to the session with substance use and addiction issues (substance use or process addiction(s) and one or more mental health symptoms). CITs will complete an American Society of Addiction Medicine (ASAM) assessment with the following criteria.

1. Assessment—Identify two possible screening and assessment instruments for substance use disorders and process addictions.
2. ASAM Assessment includes
   a. Dimension I: A provisional diagnosis using the most recent edition of the Diagnostic and Statistical Manual of Mental Disorders (DSM-5-TR);
   b. Dimension II: Biomedical Conditions.
   c. Dimension III: Any co-occurring issues/diagnoses.
   d. Dimension IV: An assessment of the client's stage of change (Transtheoretical Model).
   e. Dimension V: Relapse, Continued Use, Continued Problem Potential, including any past attempts for recovery.
   f. Dimension VI: The client's support systems, particularly regarding couple/marriage and family-of-origin.
   g. Overall assessed level of need on the continuum of care.
3. Case Conceptualization. Provide a concise summary of the pertinent elements in the case and the underlying causes of mental disorders and addictions from a family systems perspective and the above-identified theory perspective. This summary should include information about the applicability of the disease concept of addictions.

Mock Sessions. CITs will watch segments of mock sessions that highlight ethical issues related to substance use treatment (one per week). CITs will respond to a video and demonstrate one skill they learned during the week. They can upload the video response directly to the platform online for review and feedback from their peers and instructor.

- Faculty may use a program such as Skillsetter for this activity.
- Actors in the mock sessions will represent diverse cultural groups.
- CITs will practice skills related to cultural humility, broaching, non-judgmental stance, empathy, and reflective processing.

Community Resource Interview and Analysis. CITs will be paired and will research two agencies within their community that provide treatment for substance use or behavioral addictions; each pair will receive a different form of addiction for the assignment. CITs will provide a descriptive report for the class. They will prepare an educational handout to share with peers and the instructor, which includes the 14 items below. All class peers must read each of the community reports and provide any clarification or related comments to which the presenting pair will respond. CITs prepare to receive questions from other CITs and the instructor about the agency. Each distributed report should cover the following:

1. Agency/program and contact information;
2. Focused population for agency services;
3. Type of treatment (e.g., in-patient, day-treatment, or out-patient);
4. Recommended length of treatment;
5. Therapeutic approach and models of treatment;
6. Continuum of treatment in program and referrals;
7. Program cost includes the type of funding (e.g., state, private, insurance);
8. What treatment approaches does the agency use?;
9. Credentials of staff;
10. Demographics of clients;
11. Information on the drugs of choice for this clientele;
12. The internal and external referral process for the agency;
13. Contact information for the agency (web page, phone number, email address);
14. Note any barriers to treatment.
15. CITs reactions to the program/agency.

16.7 Addiction Counseling Specific Field Placement

Two primary considerations for counselor education addiction tracks for field placement are the clinical supervision required and the services offered. Section 4 of the 2024 CACREP standards outlines the requirements for professional practice, specifically, clinical experience related to practicum and internship. Clinical experience is a time for CITs application and development of counseling skills under supervision. Practicum and internship sites offer diverse experiences and opportunities that counseling CITs need during their educational programming. Therefore, supervisors need to possess licensure or certification in substance abuse and addictive disorders, while sites need to offer these services to their clientele.

The faculty's role in field placements reflects their integration of substance use and addiction education into their program. Field placement will look different for CITs enrolled in an addiction counseling program vs. a mental health counseling program with an addiction counseling course(s). An addiction counseling program would require CITs to complete their practicum and internship with a supervisor with state licensure or certification. The site would also have to offer substance abuse and addiction-specific counseling services. The education and clinical requirements obtained in a mental health counseling program with an addiction track, or electives will often meet the requirements in states that recognize an addiction certification. Again, faculty must know state certification requirements when building their program to ensure their inclusion. If a CITs practicum and internship experience meet the 2024 CACREP Standards and a state's addiction certification requirements, a CIT could simultaneously complete their professional practice requirements toward their master's degree and gain experience for their addiction certification. A supervisor and site, in this case, would have to specialize and offer services specific to mental health counseling and substance use and addictive disorders. Commonly referred to as co-occurring disorders (mental health disorders and substance abuse and addictive disorders), it is not uncommon to see the co-occurrence in mental health or addiction-focused sites. See Chap. 5 to learn more about supervision.

16.8 Conclusion

The addiction epidemic in our society requires the knowledge and skills of qualified addiction counselors. CACREP provides a clear outline of standards with guidance for implementing addiction programs and addiction tracks in colleges and universities with programs in counselor education. Counselor educators can design effective course materials and assignments with a social justice framework that promotes cultural competencies in addiction studies. A social justice praxis supports transformative learning where a CIT's worldviews are challenged, and they must reflect on power, privilege, and oppression to elicit positive social change. By doing so, counseling programs can empower CITs to make a meaningful difference in people's lives and help communities overcome this crisis. To ensure that graduates are prepared to work as addiction counselors, counseling programs must focus on meeting state and national standards. Meeting these standards will prepare CITs with the skills, knowledge, and expertise necessary to provide effective care and support for individuals struggling with addiction. Investment in a CACREP specialty for addiction studies is vital to addressing the diverse needs of those impacted by substance use and addictive disorders.

References

Adeyemy, S., Yakasai, B., Solomon, J., & Abiola, T. (2021). Stigma from psychoactive substance use: Sociodemographic correlation of the perceiver. *Science World Journal, 16*(1), 45–47.

American Society of Addiction Medicine. (2023). *Definition of addiction.* https://www.asam.org/quality-care/definition-of-addiction

Council for Accreditation of Counseling and Related Educational Programs. (2024). *2024 CACREP standards.* https://www.cacrep.org/wp-content/uploads/2024/04/2024-Standards-Combined-Version-4.11.2024.pdf

Elliott, J. A., & Downey, L. E. (2023). Broaching intersectionality and social justice: Incorporating fruitvale station into multicultural counselor education. *Journal of Creativity in Mental Health, 18*(4), 604–615. https://doi.org/10.1080/15401383.2022.2035294

Golubovic, N., Dew, B., Rumsey, A., Murphy, T., Dispenza, F., Tabet, S., & Lebensohn, C. F. (2021). Pedagogical practices for teaching addiction counseling courses in CACREP-accredited programs. *Journal of Addictions & Offender Counseling, 42*(1), 3–18. https://doi.org/10.1002/jaoc.12086

Hagedorn, W. B., Culbreth, J. R., & Cashwell, C. S. (2012). Addiction counseling accreditation: CACREP's role in solidifying the counseling profession. *Professional Counselor, 2*(2), 124–133. https://doi.org/10.15241/wbh.2.2.124

Hazelden Betty Ford Foundation. (2024, May 26). *History of Hazelden Betty Ford Foundation.* https://www.hazeldenbettyford.org/about/history

Holman, L. F., Carlisle, K. L., Rapp, M., Moro, R., & Baker, C. (2019). A guide to integrating behavioral/process addictions into counselor education programs. *Journal of Counselor Preparation & Supervision, 12*(1), 1–28.

Kurtz, E. (1979). *Not-god. A short history of Alcoholics Anonymous.* Hazelden.

Lee, T. K. (2014). Addiction education and training for counselors: A qualitative study of five experts. *Journal of Addictions & Offender Counseling, 35*(2), 67–80. https://doi.org/10.1002/j.2161-1874.2014.00027.x

National Institute of Mental Health. (2024). *Substance use and co-occurring mental disorders.* https://www.nimh.nih.gov/health/topics/substance-use-and-mental-health#:~:text=Substance%20use%20disorder%20(SUD)%20is,most%20severe%20form%20of%20SUD

Ratts, M. J., Singh, A. A., Nassar-McMillan, S., Butler, S. K., & Rafferty McCullough, J. (2016). Multicultural and social justice counseling competencies: Guidelines for the counseling profession. *Journal of Multicultural Counseling and Development, 44*(1), 28–48. https://doi.org/10.1002/jmcd.12035

Substance Abuse and Mental Health Services Administration. (2022). *Key substance use and mental health indicators in the United States: Results from the 2021 National Survey on Drug Use and Health.* https://www.samhsa.gov/data/report/2021-nsduh-annual-national-report

Talchekar, A. (2023, October 19). *Timeline: History of addiction treatment.* American Addiction Centers. https://recovery.org/drug-treatment/history/

Williams, I. L., & Mee-Lee, D. (2019). Inside the black box of traditional treatment programs: Clearing the air on the original literary teachings of Alcoholics Anonymous (AA). *Addiction Research & Theory, 27*(5), 412–419. https://doi.org/10.1080/16066359.2018.1540692

Zippia. (2024, May 26). *Number of substance abuse counselors in the US.* https://www.zippia.com/substance-abuse-counselor-jobs/demographics/

Kathleen M. Ruscitto, Ph.D., LMHC, NCC ACS, IAADC (she/her/hers) is an Assistant Professor and Program Director of the Counseling Program at Buena Vista University. Dr. Ruscitto received her doctorate in Counselor Education and Supervision from Walden University. Dr. Ruscitto is a Past President of the American Counseling Association of Iowa, and she is passionate about mentoring future counselors and counselor leadership. Her research and interests include wellness, counselor development, cultural competencies, advocacy in counseling.

Macie A. Hoover, Ph.D., MS, LMHC, CMHS, NCC (she/her/hers) is the Digital Delivery Program Coordinator and Core Faculty at City University of Seattle. Dr. Hoover received her doctorate in Counselor Education and Supervision and a Master's in Mental Health Counseling from Walden University. Dr. Hoover specializes in Exposure and Response Prevention for Obsessive–Compulsive and Related Disorders. She is the owner of Skybridge Counseling and Psychiatry in Spokane, WA. Dr. Hoover has presented at conferences on supervision, diagnosis and assessment, ethics, social justice and advocacy, and positive psychology in counselor education.

Career Counseling 17

Devona M. Stalnaker-Shofner, Tanisha N. Sapp, and Tracey E. Robert

For me, education is absolutely a civil right because that is the key to being able to fully realize the American dream, access a livable wage, and participate in civil society.

Khadijah Williams

Abstract

Career counseling formed the foundation of the counseling profession in the early twentieth century and is currently a core course for all CACREP, as well as a specialized practice track. This chapter will guide you through the development of a career counseling program track and a training model for counselor educators. It will also incorporate best teaching practices for CES faculty, highlighting equity and diversity issues in career counseling. This chapter will discuss an approach to teaching career counseling in four key content areas: (1) career theories and application to practice, (2) career assessment, (3) career counseling process, and (4) career information and resources.

D. M. Stalnaker-Shofner (✉)
Antioch University, Yellow Springs, OH, USA
e-mail: dstalnakershofner@antioch.edu; cestextbookemail@gmail.com

T. N. Sapp
Liberty University, Lynchburg, VA, USA
e-mail: tsapp6@liberty.edu

T. E. Robert
Fairfield University, Fairfield, CT, USA
e-mail: trobert@fairfield.edu

D. M. Stalnaker-Shofner and T. N. Sapp (eds.), *A Comprehensive Guide for Counselor Education*, Springer Texts in Education, https://doi.org/10.1007/978-3-031-68358-9_17

Learning Objectives After reading this chapter, you will be able to:

1. Explain the professional identity and role of career counselors.
2. Integrate the current 2024 CACREP Standards as a foundation for curriculum development as well as educational and clinical training requirements for career counselors.
3. Utilize best practices for creating a career counseling program grounded in a social justice and advocacy framework.

17.1 Statement of Reflexivity

As we author this chapter, it is important for us to note our positionality and how it has contributed to the content you are going to read. As the first author identifies as an *unapologetically Black woman*, and as a licensed counselor who has worked in the carceral system, these intersections are evident in the writing of this chapter. Her identities and experiences are pronounced in writing recommendations about the necessity of re-entry programs.

The second author identifies as a Black, cisgender, woman, who is the first person in her family to have earned a doctoral degree. Her experiences in career counseling range from working with persons possessing historically marginalized identities helping them with employment resources, housing, and community-based resources. These experiences inform her work as a counselor and counselor educator. Her positionality frames her social justice lens and advocacy work for systemic change.

The third author identifies as a White, middle class, cisgender, heterosexual, Catholic, able-bodied female, whose ethnic background is a Western European, working class, second-generation college student and the first Ph.D. in her family. Her interest in career counseling began with her desire to help people who have migrated with work and employment issues. This manifests in her work with international students in a summer work program and her counseling of women re-entering the workforce. Additionally, she has advocated for the importance of career counseling training for professional counselors throughout her career. In this capacity, she emphasizes the cultural and societal contexts of career counseling by addressing social justice issues related to work and human rights, current global issues, such as the worldwide pandemic, and unemployment.

These experiences shared by the contributors are integral to the framing of this chapter.

17.2 Introduction

Career counseling formed the foundation of the counseling profession with its beginnings in the early twentieth century and remains an integral component with significant socioeconomic and cultural changes into the twenty-first century (Herr, 2001; Pope, 2000). Having counselor educators knowledgeable in the area of career development across the lifespan and across cultures has been essential to the profession's wellness orientation and effective practice.

Career counseling has been a core course since CACREP established counselor education accreditation in 1986. However, the career counseling course often has been met with disinterest from faculty and CITs and has been cited as the least favored counselor education course to teach or to take. In a qualitative study of graduate career counseling training, Lara et al. (2011) pointed to several issues about negative faculty and learner perceptions. For example, counseling programs tend to pay more attention to mental health counseling courses and issues than to career counseling. Also, faculty often do not want to teach career counseling courses because CITs do not want to take them. Lastly, faculty often focus on theory, while CITs want to explore applied concepts and the experiential aspects of career counseling.

Further, the lack of interest in teaching career counseling may result from a lack of training for faculty who teach the needed master's-level course in career counseling and doctoral-level training for future counselor educators. The training of CES faculty focuses primarily on scholarship, with a requisite course on teaching coupled with the practical experience gained during the doctoral internship. The NCDA attempted to address the lack of career counseling praxis in 2000 when it founded the ACES/NCDA Commission for Career Counselor Preparation. Recommendations for improved training for the needed career course outlined how counselor educators can enhance the skills, knowledge, and attitudes of CITs in career development.

In 2015, the NCDA created a Counselor Educator Academy (CEA) that addressed the need among faculty and doctoral learners for training in best practices in teaching a master's-level career counseling course. In a recent survey of CEA alumni conducted by Gibbons and Ford (2020), 91% of respondents found significant value in participating in the program. They noted improvement in their own career counseling course with additional and practical resources, the opportunity to collaborate with others in teaching, increased activity and engagement, and a feeling of greater empowerment and self-efficacy.

In a national survey, Osborn and Dames (2013) identified a gap in the counselor education literature on teaching praxis, educational content, and learner evaluation for a career development course. Barrio Minton et al. (2014) reviewed 315 articles about counselor education praxes published between 2001 and 2014 and found only four articles that covered learning and teaching practices for career counseling courses. To address this gap, this chapter will guide you through the development of a career counseling track, highlighting the specific professional identity of career counselors with a social justice perspective.

17.3 CACREP Accreditation

Whether clients work to live or live to work, career development is an essential part of their lives. Accordingly, the 2024 CACREP standards emphasize education for counselors in workplace issues as the client and the CIT need for help in the career and employment domain has increased. Professional counselors are the only mental health practitioners who have training in career and mental health issues. Many clients seek counseling because they have work issues. Furthermore, when considering the work experiences of persons of color (Flores et al., 2019), it is recommended that a continuing effort is needed in counselor training to address the many career and employment challenges and barriers faced by disadvantaged groups. Additionally, human rights issues in the workplace as well as workplace harassment issues have increased globally, and counseling programs need to address these concerns throughout the curriculum.

In order to respond to the needs of the individual client as well as in response to community need, professional counselors need to be trained in conceptualizing career issues, integrating mental health and personal issues in the career counseling process, and providing resources for clients to continue their personal growth and development in the work domain. Thus, in order for a program to meet the 2024 CACREP standards for accreditation at the master's level, the career counseling courses need to include four key content areas: (1) career theory, (2) career assessment, (3) the career counseling process (including interventions and job search strategies), and (4) career information and resources (including technology; CACREP, 2024). This content must include application to practice in individual and group counseling, P-12, university career centers, and adult programs. Table 17.1 outlines the 2024 CACREP Standards specific to Career Counseling.

Table 17.1 Career counseling 2024 CACREP standards (Section 5.B)

Standards
5.B.1. Factors that affect clients' attitudes toward work and their career decision-making processes
5.B.2. The unique needs and characteristics of diverse clients with regard to career exploration, employment expectations, and socioeconomic issues
5.B.3. Implications of gender roles and responsibilities for employment, education, family, and leisure
5.B.4. Impact of globalization on careers and the workplace
5.B.5. Education, training, employment trends, and labor market information and resources that provide information about job tasks, functions, salaries, requirements, and future outlooks related to broad occupational fields and individual occupations
5.B.6. Approaches and resources relevant to diverse clients acquiring a set of career planning, employability, job search, job creation, and life-work role transition skills
5.B.7. Strategies to assist clients in the appropriate use of technology for career information and planning
5.B.8. Strategies to market and promote career counseling resources and services

As mentioned in Chap. 16, all entry-level counselor preparation programs are required to incorporate the foundational curriculum content. The foundational curriculum content is addressed further in Chap. 15. With respect to implementing the track and teaching the developed courses, mentoring and support from career specialists can enhance the delivery of the material and expand faculty comfort with and mastery of career theory and assessment. This will facilitate imparting requisite knowledge to CITs, specifically career theories, assessments, processes, and available community resources to enhance overall client progress and ultimately improve their lives.

17.4 Developing a Career Counseling Training Program or Track

An interest in and an expressed need for trained career counselors by the community is one reason many programs are looking at the development and inclusion of a specialty focus of career counseling. This section offers a sample clinical mental health counseling program with a career counseling specialty focus that meets the 2024 CACREP standards. The need for clinical mental health and school counselors to be competent in career development is represented in the CACREP standards for each counseling track. Counselors are the only mental health providers who are specifically and directly trained in career counseling, their careers and thus they can fulfill the need to provide services to clients who are presenting for services as the result of career issues; examples include re-entry, career changes and transitions, underemployment, loss of employment, and discrimination. Established career tracks and clinical mental health tracks that have a career counseling specialized practice focus can provide needed training in career development, employment counseling, and career counseling and assessment, and they provide support for current research in the field.

The CACREP requirements for a single-track career counseling degree program would consist of 60 credit hours, including the CACREP core courses in counseling: ethics, cross-cultural issues, group counseling, foundations of career theory and development, techniques and theories, lifespan development, diagnosis and treatment planning, research methods, and assessment (CACREP, 2024). In addition, six courses that are specific to career counseling are required: career assessment; facilitating individual and group career counseling; creating career development programs and career information resources for clients across the lifespan; managing career centers in K-12, college campuses, and community outreach. Additionally, field experience is needed and should include one practicum and two semesters of internships at career counseling sites. Table 17.2 provides an example Career Counseling Program Plan of Study.

Another option available for counselor educators is to add a career counseling focus to an already existing program, such as clinical mental health counseling. This would enhance a CIT's marketability in that it provides the opportunity for licensure as well as having expertise in career counseling. Any courses added for

Table 17.2 Example career counseling program (60 credit hours) program plan of study

Name of course	Credits
Ethics and Professional Orientation[a]	3
Human Growth and Lifespan Development[a]	3
Counseling Theories[a]	3
Counseling Methods and Techniques[a]	3
Counseling and Advocacy with Diverse Populations[a]	3
Research Methodology and Program Evaluation[a]	3
Diagnosis and Treatment Planning in Counseling[a]	3
Career Counseling[a]	3
Group Counseling[a]	3
Assessment, Tests, and Measures in Counseling[a]	3
Career Testing and Assessment	3
Designing Career Development Programs Across the Lifespan	3
Vocational Theory and Career Development	3
Pre-Practicum in Career Counseling Skills and Consultation	3
Advanced Career Counseling	3
Introduction to Clinical Mental Health Counseling	3
Counseling Children and Adolescents	3
Practicum Career Counseling	3
Internship 1: Career Counseling	3
Internship 2: Career Counseling	3

[a] Indicates courses that address the 2024 CACREP Foundational Counseling Curriculum content area (CACREP, 2024, Section 3)

a career counseling focus would need to meet the same standards as the current CACREP accredited program. Therefore, the needed six courses for the career counseling focus would take the place of electives available in the current clinical mental health counseling program or be offered as an option to current requirements. The CACREP core would stay the same. To add a career counseling track, the institution would need to submit a *Substantive Change Report* with evidence that a few added electives or alternative courses meet the same requirements as the original accredited program.

17.4.1 Content Areas

In this section, experiential and engaging teaching strategies for the four key areas are outlined in alignment with the 2024 CACREP Standards for the master's-level career development and career counseling specialty courses. Further explored is a reflection of career issues for historically marginalized and disenfranchised populations and the use of a cross–cultural, socially-just approach to address their presenting concerns.

17.4.1.1 Career Development Theories

Career development theories provide a roadmap for the conceptualization of the client's presenting career issue and serve as a foundation for the treatment plan. Swanson and Fouad (2014) state that the counselor's theoretical orientation "interacts with one's view of career development" (p. 13), which facilitates the integration of personal and career counseling. Although the importance of this integration is known, it is often not addressed in an entry-level career theory course. Therefore, it is important that you incorporate this content into the development of your program curriculum.

Additionally, while most career counseling textbooks cover major career theories, one missing component is the integration of case studies. Doing so provides CITs with illustrative examples that facilitates their ability to integrate both counseling and career in practice. Moreover, case studies have the advantage of adaptivity and applicability in support of socially just clinical practice. For example, using an applied case study that presents varying career issues across diverse client groups aids students in their ability to retain theoretical knowledge and intentionally apply the appropriately related skills. As such, the case study approach presents career issues across the lifespan introducing CITs to each major theory (Swanson & Fouad, 2014). One suggestion we offer for a Key Performance Indicator (KPI) activity is to have CITs choose a specific theory to present and apply the selected theory to an identified case study. This will allow CITs to begin making the connection between theory and skills.

17.4.1.2 Career Assessment

Assessment is an integral part of career counseling training that helps students to learn about the importance of facilitating self-awareness and brainstorming career options with clients. It is essential for CITs to learn how to select, evaluate, and administer developmentally and culturally appropriate assessment materials. Another example of a KPI activity can involve CITs engaging in career assessment activities, which helps CITs to develop effective strategies to address the following CACREP career counseling track standards: career exploration; career decision making; career change; and work issues, including job loss, unemployment, career re-entry, career beliefs, and searching for meaning and purpose in life. Using assessment tools such as the Career Thoughts Inventory (CTI), Strong Interest Inventory (SII), Career Mastery Inventory (CMI), Self-Directed Search (SDS), and Career Decision-Making System-Revised (CDM-R) can enable CITs to facilitate their clients' understanding of their career values, interests, skills, personality traits, and decision-making abilities. Additionally, incorporating assessments such as the Multicultural Career Counseling Inventory (MCCI) can teach CITs the importance of assessing for the influence of environmental, socioeconomic, and multicultural factors. Doing so is integral to their learning of socially just counseling practices. One final recommendation is to teach CITs to integrate the use of multiple career assessments as a holistic approach, and more importantly a best practice.

17.4.1.3 Career Counseling Process

The career counseling process provides structure for clients to explore work/life concerns, career direction or change, job search strategies, and workplace issues. The integration of personal and career counseling strategies is essential to teach, as is the interrelationships between work, mental health, and wellness. CITs can adapt their personal model of counseling to include career development issues using a holistic and integrative approach as personal and career concerns are often interconnected. As noted in the 2024 CACREP standards, the career counseling process follows the same basic process as personal counseling, including an integration of a career intake, an identified career concern (assessment/diagnosis), and a career action plan utilizing client-specific career goals with appropriately matched career-based interventions.

Additionally, you can address the CACREP standards by creating three types of KPI assignments: reflection papers, discussion posts, and the career intake/interview project. Furthermore, to meet CACREP standards regarding developing and delivering career counseling services, we suggest a research-based group presentation as an example KPI assignment.

17.4.1.4 Career Information and Resources

When considering career information and resources, it is important for you to understand that both CITs and their respective clients may be equally overwhelmed and flooded by the vast amount of information accessible online. Thus, from a socially just perspective, you must help CITs to understand challenges to accessibility that impact their client's ability to make informed career decisions. As a future career counselor, CITs will assist their clients in evaluating resources and identifying appropriate career services. To assess the CIT's ability to demonstrate this CACREP standard, a suggested KPI assignment is to have CITs explore and critically evaluate career-based resources such as the US Department of Labor's O*NET Online website and write a reflection paper illustrating their learning. Ultimately, this facilitates the CIT's development of knowledge and applicable skills that support social justice through multicultural awareness.

17.5 Multicultural Implications and Social Justice Considerations

As has been explored throughout this textbook, social justice, advocacy, and activism are integral components of being a counselor providing mental health services, as well as being a counselor educator training the next generation of counseling practitioners. Career counseling as a specialized practice area has a unique opportunity to address the systemic challenges and oppressive structures related to the employment and vocational needs of persons who possess historically marginalized identities as they are experienced across multiple socio-ecological levels and often result in disenfranchisement.

As you reflect on the incorporation of these considerations within the development of career counseling programs or tracks, we want to provide you with recommendations to use in your role as counselor educators at multiple touchpoints. As career counselors work to address the needs of historically marginalized individuals experiencing varying levels of dispossession, counselor educators must train CITs to serve as practitioners as well as advocates. Examples of providing career-related services to marginalized populations can include job readiness and re-entry support for those impacted by the carceral system, adjunctive career planning and guidance for individuals with disabilities, as well as providing other points of access for individuals who have been relegated to the periphery in the upholding of the fallacies of patriarchy, capitalism, and other systems undergirded by white supremacy. As counselor educators, it is incumbent upon us to integrate the lived experiences of the oppressed as we train counselors to address their overall needs. Accordingly, our efforts related to curriculum design, clinical training, and supervision of future career counselors must be steeped in socially-just counseling practices that support the development of multicultural awareness in CITs, as well as facilitate their utilization of this knowledge and related skills as they serve their communities.

17.6 Conclusion

The counseling profession's need for counselor educators who are knowledgeable in career development across the lifespan has increased in recent years. This aligns with the increasing need for help expressed by clients and CITs with respect to the career and employment domain. The NCDA has offered recommendations for how counselor educators can enhance CITs' learning, and CACREP standards have placed a greater emphasis on education for counselors in workplace issues.

As we conclude our exploration of the requirements for career counseling programs and tracks, take a moment to reflect on the guidance offered that ideally will facilitate your development of a new career counseling track, or the creation of a single-track degree program. Accordingly, you want to ensure the incorporation of current best practices for career practitioners, as well as academic content that integrates personal and career counseling framed within a multicultural context. In adopting a practitioner approach to teaching career counseling, you can integrate the content offered in this textbook related to sample assignments that address KPIs.

The content offered here related to career development theories, career assessment, career counseling process, and career information and resources, can help you educate future career counselors in the provision of appropriate counseling services that are rooted in best practices. Using an active approach to teaching career counseling based on Amundson's (2009) model, and bringing experiential components into training, can greatly increase classroom engagement. The inclusion of experiential activities for learners can add significantly to the quantity and quality of their learning. With this experiential approach to teaching career development across the lifespan, the classroom content comes to life, enriching the learning and engaging the learner.

References

Amundson, N. E. (2009). *Active engagement: The being and doing of career counseling*. Ergon Communications.

Barrio Minton, C. A., Wachter Morris, C. A., & Yaites, L. D. (2014). Pedagogy in counselor education: A 10-year content analysis of journals. *Counselor Education and Supervision, 53*, 162–177. https://doi.org/10.1002/j.1556-6978.2014.00055.x

Council for Accreditation of Counseling and Related Educational Programs. (2024). *2024 CACREP standards.* https://www.cacrep.org/wp-content/uploads/2024/04/2024-Standards-Combined-Version-4.11.2024.pdf

Flores, L. Y., Martinez, L. D., McGillen, G. G., & Milord, J. (2019). Something old and something new: Future directions in vocational research with people of color in the United States. *Journal of Career Assessment, 27*(2), 187–208. https://doi.org/10.1177/1069072718822461

Gibbons, M., & Ford, D. (2020). Counselor education alumni survey results. https://ncda.org/aws/NCDA/pt/sp/counselor_academy

Herr, E. L. (2001). Career development and its practice: A historical perspective. *The Career Development Quarterly, 49*(3), 196–211. https://doi.org/10.1002/j.2161-0045.2001.tb00562.x

Lara, T. M., Kline, W. B., & Paulson, D. (2011). Attitudes regarding career counseling: Perceptions and experiences of counselors-in-training. *Career Development Quarterly, 59*(5), 428–440.

Osborn, D. S., & Dames, L. S. (2013). Teaching graduate course career classes: A national survey of career instructors. *Counselor Education and Supervision, 52*, 297–310.

Pope, M. (2000). A brief history of career counseling in the United States. *Career Development Quarterly, 48*(3), 194–211. https://doi.org/10.1002/j.2161-0045.2000.tb00286x

Swanson, J. L., & Fouad, N. A. (2014). *Career theory and practice: Learning through case studies.* Sage.

Devona M. Stalnaker-Shofner, Ed.D., LPC, NCC, MHP, SAP (she/her/hers) is an Associate Professor at Antioch University, School of Counseling, Psychology, and Therapy. She has been a counselor educator for more than 10 years, and in professional practice as a licensed counselor for more than 20 years. Her clinical experience includes providing individual, group, and couples and family counseling to clients presenting with treatment concerns such as depression, anxiety, trauma, as well as substance use, addiction, and recovery. She also provides clinical supervision to counselors-in-training and new counseling professionals. Dr. Stalnaker-Shofner has served in various leadership roles within the counseling and counselor education professions. Her research and scholarship includes numerous presentations at state, regional, national, and international conferences, as well as related publications. As a trainer, she has provided workshops on racial trauma and BIPOC mental health and wellness, and the decolonization of curriculum, teaching praxis, and educational policies to disrupt oppression and promote diversity, equity, inclusion, and access. Additionally, she serves as an educational and organizational consultant advising on implementing antiracist and social justice practices for leaders and organizational policies and culture.

Tanisha N. Sapp, Ed.D., LPC, CST, NCC, ACS, CPCS (she/her/Dr.) is an Assistant Professor of Counseling at Liberty University in the Department of Counseling and Family Studies. Dr. Sapp is a counselor educator, professional counselor, trainer, and clinical supervisor focused on training the next generation of helping professionals. She is the owner of Tanisha Sapp, LLC where she provides professional development training, clinical supervision services, and individual and couples sex therapy. With over 20 years of experience in the helping profession, Dr. Sapp brings a wealth of experience, insight, and a unique perspective into counselor education. Dr. Sapp is currently a member of the ACA ethics committee and serves on review panels for CACREP and NBCC where she offers her expertise to the profession in an effort to be the change she desires to see. Dr. Sapp has also served on a number of professional committees and provided leadership service to the profession and her community. Her areas of research, professional identity, and interests include: professional counselor identity, Anti-Racism in counseling and counselor education, DEIBASJ in counseling and counselor education, BIPOC sexual health and wellness, and professional advocacy in leadership.

Tracey E. Robert, Ph.D., LPC, NCC, NCCC (she/her/hers) is a Professor Emeritus of Counselor Education at Fairfield University. She has been a counselor educator for 20 years and in professional practice in career counseling and wellness for 30 years. Her clinical experience includes providing individual and group counseling for career change and career re-entry clients and clinical supervision, and integrating spirituality and religion into counseling.

Clinical Mental Health Counseling

18

Mary Kate Reese, Charmaine L. Conner, and Deanna Burgess

Education as the practice of freedom affirms healthy self-esteem in students as it promotes their capacity to be aware and live consciously.

bell hooks

Abstract

There is an ongoing need for mental health professionals who can work in a variety of settings with diverse individuals, groups, and families. This chapter will provide the information on the requirements for an entry-level Clinical Mental Health Counseling program that meets the requirements for accreditation by the CACREP, based on best practices from existing literature and the 2024 CACREP Standards. The chapter will include a history of CMHC, a description of the 2024 CACREP Standards specific to the CMHC specialized practice, an example of a CMHC program of study, and a discussion of important considerations when developing a CMHC program, with a particular focus on social justice and advocacy. The chapter will end with current and future trends in the CMHC field that should be considered in CMHC programs.

M. K. Reese (Deceased) (✉)
Walden University, Minneapolis, MN, USA
e-mail: tsapp6@liberty.edu

C. L. Conner
Roosevelt University, Chicago, IL, USA
e-mail: cconner@roosevelt.edu

D. Burgess
DePaul University, Chicago, IL, USA
e-mail: dburges4@depaul.edu

D. M. Stalnaker-Shofner and T. N. Sapp (eds.), *A Comprehensive Guide for Counselor Education*, Springer Texts in Education, https://doi.org/10.1007/978-3-031-68358-9_18

Learning Objectives After reading this chapter, you will be able to:

1. Distinguish the professional identity and role of clinical mental health counselors.
2. Explore the emergence of clinical mental health counseling as a distinct specialty that contributes to the unification of the counseling profession.
3. Implement best practices for creating a clinical mental health counseling program and preparing new professionals in the field using a social justice and advocacy framework.

18.1 Statement of Reflexivity

As the first author, Dr. Reese approached the writing of this chapter with the understanding that she knows a good bit about the subject matter, but certainly does not know everything about it. She is a doctoral-level licensed professional counselor. Additionally, she has been a full-time faculty member for 20+ years in two different counseling departments with CACREP-accredited programs (CMHC and CES). She has written CACREP self-studies for counseling programs first seeking accreditation and self-studies to apply for re-accreditation of existing programs. Further, she has served as a CACREP Site Team Member and Site Team Chair and conducted site visits to multiple universities with counseling programs which had applied for CACREP accreditation. Dr. Reese graduated from a campus-based program and has taught at both campus-based and hybrid (on campus and online) programs. She currently teaches in a fully online counselor education program. Curriculum development and program development for graduate-level counseling programs has been one of her favorite activities as a counselor educator. Lastly, she is also a counselor with a private practice and a counselor supervisor.

Dr. Reese recognizes the implications of her personal experiences, and the blind spots that she may have relative to her inherent privilege as a White, cisgender female counselor educator and supervisor. Her race and academic degree afford her certain ascribed privileges that are different from others. She has a passion for social justice and advocacy practices, particularly in topics related to sexuality and LGBTQ+ communities.

As the second and third authors, respectively, Drs. Conner and Burgess approached the writing of this content based on their collective experiences working within counselor education in the Midwest region of the United States. Both are educators and counseling practitioners with individual private practices. Their extensive clinical experience as independently licensed counselors includes providing mental health services in a variety of settings: residential, private practice, and nonprofit agencies. They approach their clinical work, advocacy, and teaching praxis with a focus on developing a strong therapeutic relationship with clients and learners through the utilization of the foundational counseling tenets of genuineness, unconditional positive regard, and empathy.

18.2 Introduction

Leaders in the counseling profession have been working diligently over recent years toward a more unified profession, and CMHC programs are one way this goal is being achieved. The specific CACREP requirements for a CMHC specialty have been used as a "gold standard" in discussions surrounding state licensure requirements, licensure portability across states, and approval for third-party insurance payment by federal payers such as the U.S. Veteran's Administration (VA) and the TRICARE system within the Department of Defense (Bobby, 2013). CACREP (2024b) defines CMHC programs as follows:

> Clinical Mental Health Counseling programs prepare graduates to work with clients across a spectrum of mental and emotional disorders, as well as to promote mental health and wellness. Clients may be seen individually, in couples, families, or group settings. Clinical Mental Health Counselors are knowledgeable in the principles and practices of diagnosis, treatment, referral and prevention and often work in interdisciplinary teams with other health professionals (e.g., psychiatrists, social workers, MDs). Employment opportunities may include private practice, community-based mental health centers, hospitals and other treatment centers. (para 3)

18.3 History of Clinical Mental Health Counseling

The question of whether counseling is a single profession, or a group of different professions has been a question within the counseling field for many years. An initiative known as *20/20: A Vision for the Future of Counseling*, cosponsored by ACA and the American Association of State Counseling Boards (AASCB), included 31 organizations representing the counseling profession working together from 2005 to 2013 to struggle with the issue of whether counseling could present itself as a single and unified profession (Bobby, 2013; Kaplan et al., 2014). In March 2010, delegates met and agreed upon a consensus definition of counseling, which is "Counseling is a professional relationship that empowers diverse individuals, families, and groups to accomplish mental health, wellness, education, and career goals" (Kaplan et al., 2014, p. 368). This was an important step for several reasons. First, if counseling could be defined and viewed as a unified profession, the understanding of what it is that counselors do and the visibility of counselors would be strengthened. In addition, a clear professional identity lends itself much more to the eventual process of licensure portability between states, which had been accomplished by older professions such as clinical social work. Along those same lines, a clear and unified definition of counseling as a profession provides some foundation for the development of academic and professional training programs (and the standards that govern these) to train competent, ethical counselors.

CACREP is a specialty accrediting body established in 1981. In 1984 CACREP standards had been developed and approved for three specialty areas: Student

Personnel in Education, Mental Health Counseling: Community and Agency Settings, and School Counseling (Bobby, 2013). Eventually, in the 1988 CACREP Standards, a decision was made to continue to have a Mental Health Counseling specialty that required a minimum 60 semester-hour program, and a Community Counseling specialty that required a minimum 48 semester-hour program, due to pressure and differing opinions from various stakeholders (Bobby, 2013). However, this split did not help further the mission toward a unified counseling profession and led to many questions about what distinguished a Mental Health Counseling program from a Community Counseling program. By the 2009 CACREP Standards, the decision was made to put these two areas together, to increase the credit hour requirement to 60 semester-hours, and to title the specialty area Clinical Mental Health Counseling (Bobby, 2013). See Chap. 15 for more information about the evolution of CACREP within the counseling profession.

Having a clearly defined specialty area in CMHC with specific requirements created opportunities for states to now work toward a national professional identity for counselors, and these efforts were rewarded when the U.S. Veteran's Administration (VA) began to recognize licensed counselors who had graduated from a CACREP accredited program and passed the National Clinical Mental Health Counselors Exam (NCMHCE) to work in the VA. Also in 2010, licensed counselors who met these criteria were approved to be providers within the TRICARE system of the Department of Defense (Bobby, 2013).

One other important evolution in the counseling profession and the development of CMHC programs has to do with the history of the very humanistic and wellness-based view of individuals long espoused by the counseling field as it intersects with the medical model of mental illness, with its focus on diagnosis and psychopathology (Cannon & Cooper, 2010). In the modern world, it is essential for mental health providers of all types to be able to speak the language of diagnosis in order to work within managed care and receive third-party reimbursement (Levers & Hyatt-Burkhart, 2019). Therefore, an important component of a program in CMHC is training in diagnosis and treatment planning. The important knowledge/skills for clinical mental health counselors continues to evolve over time. In the next section, we will discuss the development of a CMHC program that meets all of the CACREP requirements.

18.4 CACREP Accreditation

There are eight foundational curriculum areas required for all entry-level (master's) counselor education programs detailed in Section 3 of the 2024 CACREP Standards. These foundational curriculum areas include: Professional Counseling Orientation and Ethical Practice, Social and Cultural Identities and Experiences, Lifespan Development, Career Development, Counseling Practice and Relationships, Group Counseling and Group Work, Assessment and Diagnostic Processes, and Research and Program Evaluation (CACREP, 2024a). In addition to the eight foundational areas, there are nine additional standards specific to the CMHC specialized practice outlined in Section 5.C (see Table 18.1).

Table 18.1 Clinical mental health counseling 2024 CACREP standards (Section 5.C.)

Standards
5.C.1. Etiology, nomenclature, diagnosis, treatment, referral, and prevention of mental, behavioral, and neurodevelopmental disorders
5.C.2. Mental health service delivery modalities and networks within the continuum of care, such as primary care, outpatient, partial treatment, inpatient, integrated behavioral healthcare, and aftercare
5.C.3. Legislation, government policy, and regulatory processes relevant to clinical mental health counseling
5.C.4. Intake interview, mental status evaluation, biopsychosocial history, mental health history, and psychological assessment for treatment planning and caseload management
5.C.5. Techniques and interventions for prevention and treatment of a broad range of mental health issues
5.C.6. Strategies for interfacing with the legal system regarding court-referred clients
5.C.7. Strategies for interfacing with integrated behavioral healthcare professionals
5.C.8. Strategies to advocate for people with mental, behavioral, and neurodevelopmental conditions
5.C.9. Third-party reimbursement and other practice and management issues in clinical mental health counseling

18.5 Developing a Clinical Mental Health Counseling Training Program

According to CACREP (2023):

> All entry-level students are enrolled in at least one specialized practice area. Students are expected to develop and demonstrate the knowledge and skills necessary to address a wide range of issues in their specialized practice area in consideration of culturally sustaining practices across service delivery modalities. Counselor education programs must document where and in what manner each of the numbered standards listed for that specialized practice area is covered in the curriculum. The standards may be addressed in the foundational curriculum or in experiences specifically designed for each specialized practice area. (p. 190)

Thus, the specialty standards may be addressed by including specific knowledge and skills within existing courses that address the eight foundational curriculum areas or by creating courses specifically designed to meet the specialty standards. This decision is up to the program/university.

It is important, at minimum, to ensure that your CMHC program meets state licensing requirements for counselor licensure in the state in which your university is based. Some schools offer additional electives for individuals who may be living in or planning to move to another state so that they can meet any additional curriculum requirements for licensure in those states. With the increase in fully online counselor education programs, it is important to maintain awareness of the licensure requirements in all states in order to assist CITs in making sure that they are completing coursework and field experiences that meet their state's requirements for licensure after graduation. Olson et al. (2018) analyzed the differences between counselor licensure requirements in all states and found that while there was a fair amount of consistency in requirements for the eight foundational CACREP curriculum areas to be covered in licensure rules, there were sometimes very specific courses that are only required by certain states (e.g., Psychopharmacology or Human Sexuality). This is one reason that license portability is such a pressing issue for the counseling field; this is also why counselor education programs need to ensure that they include course offerings that will meet licensure requirements in multiple states, if possible, since license portability has not yet been endorsed by all states. With this in mind, below is one example of a CMHC program of study that meets CACREP requirements for the CMHC specialty area as well as some flexibility for varying state licensure requirements. Table 18.2 provides an example of a CMHC program plan of study.

18.5.1 Additional Curriculum Considerations

An important note on the curriculum within CMHC programs is about *how* it is being taught. Specifically, social justice and advocacy should be infused throughout the curriculum in relevant ways, and how we teach about these topics should be examined carefully. Goodman et al. (2015) describe ways in which counselor education still includes colonizing practices, defined as "educational practices that reproduce the existing conditions of oppression by failing to challenge the hegemonic views that marginalize groups of people, perpetuate deficit-based ideologies, and continue to disenfranchise the diverse clients and communities with whom our students will work" (p. 148). These authors describe and give specific examples of five areas that are essential to decolonizing practices within counseling and psychology training:

1. education for critical consciousness "... involves genuine questioning, having healthy dialogues and discourse, opportunities for independent and divergent thinking, and the freedom to arrive at one's own decisions regardless of the status quo" (Goodman et al., 2015, p. 149),
2. infusing multiculturalism and social justice throughout the curriculum,
3. voice (instead of perpetuating a voyeuristic curiosity about oppressed populations, finding ways to increase meaningful engagement and self-reflection),
4. community as integral (increasing opportunities for CITs to engage in meaningful ways with other communities, such as through service-learning projects versus standalone assignments), and
5. political engagement (because a position of "neutrality" is not in fact neutral and supports existing structures of power and privilege) (Goodman et al., 2015).

Table 18.2 Example clinical mental health counseling program (60 credit hours) program plan of study

Name of course	Credits
Foundations of Clinical Mental Health Counseling[a]	3
Counseling Theory[a]	3
Human Growth and Development[a]	3
Professional and Ethical Issues[a]	3
Social and Cultural Diversity[a]	3
Diagnosis and Treatment Planning[a]	3
Counseling Skills 1[a]	3
Counseling Skills 2[a]	3
Group Counseling[a]	3
Lifestyle and Career Development[a]	3
Appraisal and Assessment in Counseling[a]	3
Research and Program Evaluation[a]	3
Crisis, Trauma, and Grief Counseling[a]	3
Addictions Counseling[a]	3
Human Sexuality[a]	3
Counseling Practicum	3
Students select TWO elective courses from the options below (please consult with advisor and verify your state's coursework requirements for licensure before selection of these):	3
Internship 1: Clinical Mental Health Counseling	3
Internship 2: Clinical Mental Health Counseling	3
Psychopharmacology and Biological Bases of Behavior	3
Couples and Family Counseling	3
Advanced Skills in Couples and Family Counseling	3
Child and Adolescent Counseling	3

[a] Indicates courses that address the 2024 CACREP Foundational Counseling Curriculum content area (CACREP 2024a, Section 3)

Within the context of developing courses and programs that are sensitive to social justice and advocacy, there are several specific focus areas that have been recommended for inclusion in CMHC programs. These include child and adolescent counseling (with a specific focus on trauma), sexuality, neuroscience, and religion/spirituality.

18.5.1.1 Child and Adolescent Counseling: Attachment and Trauma

Counselors-in-training are expected to learn about traditional and emerging counseling theories (CACREP, 2023) and are expected to have identified a guiding counseling theory that is often taught from the perspective of counseling adults. Counselors-in-training who seek to work with children will need training on how to apply traditional and emerging counseling theories to children with regard to child development. For instance, modifications have been made to traditional counseling theories (person-centered, Adlerian, CBT, etc.) to better serve youth. Play therapy has been identified as a method of choice for counseling work with children, which also means that there is an increased need for universities to teach counselors-in-training about this practice (Anderson, 2022).

While attachment is often introduced as a component of the lifespan development course, it is also commonly linked to childhood and adolescent trauma. Distant or neglectful relational patterns and exposure to trauma in early life can significantly influence many facets of one's development. For this reason, it is important that counselors-in-training develop a firm understanding of interactive behaviors and early life experiences that influence long-term psychosocial and cognitive outcomes for youth. Gaining knowledge of attachment and trauma processes among children and adolescents can also facilitate case conceptualization and exploration of themes, identification of suitable treatment approaches, and development of appropriate goals for the treatment process. Furthermore, understanding early attachment and trauma allows one to explore underlying factors that influence maladaptive behaviors. Without this insight, novice counselors may have difficulty moving beyond surface-level conceptualizations to understand the developmental root cause of a client's presenting concerns.

According to the Substance Abuse and Mental Health Services Administration SAMHSA (2020), approximately two-thirds of children have reported trauma before the age of 16. Children often face adverse childhood experiences (ACEs), including but not limited to abuse, neglect, parental mental illness, domestic violence, loss of a parent, etc. (Felitti et al., 1998). The effects of ACEs on children may result in altered brain chemistry (Perry, 2006; Siegel, 2012), insecure attachment (van der Kolk, 2014), and substance abuse and mental health disorders (Wu et al., 2010). The impact of trauma on an individual goes beyond a single event; systems also contribute to re-victimizing the child. Therefore, it is important for counselors-in-training to engage in trauma-informed care as they prepare to work with children.

Trauma can pose a particular threat to adolescents who are more prone to high-risk internalizing and externalizing behaviors or observable and concealed behaviors (respectively) that signify psychological distress (Siegel, 2012). Therefore, it is imperative that counselor trainees understand how trauma uniquely impacts development within adolescence, discern internalizing and externalizing behaviors that potentially signify trauma, and learn best practices for trauma-informed care.

Finally, mandated reporting is an important and specific legal and ethical matter that child and adolescent counselors must grasp. Some states require counselors to report suspected child abuse and/or neglect as well as the potential for a child client to harm themselves or someone else. This process may cause emotional distress for trainees, as they may fear damaging the therapeutic relationship (Smith-Addock & Tucker, 2017).

18.5.1.2 Human Sexuality

Another important content area to include in the curriculum (as a standalone course or within a relevant course) is human sexuality. Counselors in many states are currently afforded many opportunities to focus on social justice and advocacy, as state legislatures have made decisions that oppress or limit rights for individuals within the LGBTQQIP2SA+ population. Rodenkirch (2023) conducted a study with counselors-in-training and found that sexuality training is correlated with greater sexual awareness, and greater sexual awareness is correlated with comfort with sexual discourse. This indicates that counselor education programs should recognize the importance of sexuality training and awareness development for CITs, so that they will be able to effectively manage conversations about sexual topics with clients. Blount et al. (2017) discussed the limited curriculum on sexual behavior and sexual counseling in CMHC programs and how lack of training/awareness in this area can result in counselor bias and lack of self-efficacy on sexual topics in counseling practice. The message is clear that clinical mental health counselors need to be able to effectively navigate sensitive topics such as sexuality with clients and that adding this topic into required coursework will help with this goal.

18.5.1.3 Spirituality/Religion in Counseling

Another topic that is sometimes sensitive and that is also important for counselors to be able to navigate with clients is religion/spirituality. Jangha (2023) discusses the fact that client spirituality and/or religion have been clearly identified as important considerations in counseling, yet there is still no consistent way in which it is incorporated into coursework in counselor education. Much like the topic of sexuality, CITs benefit from training that includes knowledge and self-awareness around religion/spirituality in order to work effectively with clients from various backgrounds. In counselor education, the topic of spirituality/religion is often assumed to be addressed in courses and conversations related to multicultural competence. However, most multicultural discourse tends to focus more on race and ethnicity than on other aspects of culture (Junfei et al., 2020). The Association for Spiritual, Ethical, and Religious Values in Counseling (ASERVIC, 2009) developed a list of competencies to help counselors appropriately address spiritual and religious issues in counseling, yet research has indicated that many counselors in training are not knowledgeable of these competencies. Clearly there is a need for better training in this topic area.

18.5.1.4 Neuroscience in Counseling

Field et al. (2022) noted that while the American Mental Health Counseling Association's (AMHCA) standards of practice include the only current comprehensive standards for neuroscience-informed counseling (titled the *Biological Basis of Behavior Standards*), not much has been done to incorporate this important topic area into counselor education programs. A taskforce developed to establish a pilot neuroscience program created a training model and suggestions for implementation of the model by counselor education programs so that CITs could be exposed to this important topic. Neuroscientific studies have indicated that neurophysiological changes occur as a result of trauma as well as provided evidence that psychotherapy can create neurophysiological changes.

In recent years, AMHCA developed a set of core practice standards that all clinical mental health counselors should have in addition to the common foundational standards from CACREP; these are updated regularly (AMHCA, 2023). The AMHCA Professional Standards Committee (now the Advancement of Clinical Practice Committee) initially identified four core areas where they believed further training is needed in clinical mental health counseling: the biological basis of behavior (neuroscience), psychological trauma, substance use, and specialized clinical assessment. In 2020 and 2021 they added to this list to include "technology-supported counseling, integrated behavioral healthcare, child and adolescent counseling, aging and older adults, forensic evaluation, and gender identity counseling" (Field et al., 2022, p. 267).

18.6 Clinical Mental Health Counseling Specific Field Placement

The 2024 CACREP Standards state, in Standard 4.A, that "the counselor education program provides on-going support to help students find fieldwork sites that are sufficient to provide the quality, quantity, and variety of expected experiences to prepare students for their roles and responsibilities as professional counselors within their CACREP specialized practice areas." Given the broad range of clients (individuals, couples, families, groups) and the potential settings for clinical mental health counselors (private practice, community-based mental health centers, hospitals, treatment centers, etc.) as described by CACREP (2024a), there should be numerous fieldwork site possibilities.

Clinical supervision throughout the practicum and internship experiences is an essential part of training clinical mental health counselors. In the 2024 CACREP Standards, it is clearly stated that throughout the practicum and the internship, CITs are required to receive regular individual and/or triadic supervision that averages one hour a week. This supervision may be provided by: "(1) a counselor education program core or affiliate faculty member, or (2) a doctoral student supervisor who is under the supervision of a qualified core or affiliate counselor education program faculty member, or (3) a fieldwork site supervisor who is working in consultation on a regular schedule with a counselor education program faculty member in accordance with the supervision agreement" (CACREP, 2024a, Standards 4.S. and 4.W.). In addition, throughout the practicum and the internship, CITs are required to receive regular group supervision that averages 1.5 h per week. This supervision may be provided by: "(1) a counselor education program faculty member or (2) a doctoral student supervisor who is under the supervision of a qualified core or affiliate counselor education program faculty member" (CACREP, 2024a, Standards 4.T. and 4.X.). Finally, counselor education faculty and site supervisors providing supervision to CITs are required to have: "(1) relevant certifications and/or licenses, (2) relevant training for in-person and/or distance counseling supervision, and (3) relevant training in the technology utilized for supervision" (CACREP, 2024a, Standards 4.N. and 4.P.). Based on the specific geographic area, field training site, and other factors, programs are allowed to develop their own specific criteria to define "relevant certifications and/or licenses" as well as "relevant training" in supervision and in technology. What is important is that these criteria are clearly laid out in program guides and supervision contracts developed by the program so that they are clearly articulated. More information about supervision can be found in Chap. 4 of this book.

18.7 Conclusion

As noted at the beginning of this chapter, there is a critical need for well-trained clinical mental health counselors who can work with various populations in various settings, in a socially and culturally sensitive way. Creating a CMHC program that provides the foundational knowledge and skills required by the 2024 CACREP Standards and CMHC specialty standards, as well as an underlying social justice and advocacy framework, will help to prepare future clinical mental health counselors to be effective in their work. Understanding the ways that counselor licensure is evolving and changing within state licensure rules as well as the move toward license portability is particularly important in this program area. Staying on top of current and emerging topics in the counseling field and making sure that these are included in your CMHC curriculum is a final best practice in counselor education.

References

American Mental Health Counselors Association (AMHCA). (2023). *AMHCA standards for the practice of clinical mental health counseling.* https://www.amhca.org/events/publications/standards

Anderson, C. (2022). Professional development in play therapy among counselors. *International Journal of Play Therapy, 31*(3), 153–164. https://doi.org/10.1037/pla0000181

Association for Spiritual, Ethical, and Religious Values in Counseling (ASERVIC). (2009). *Competencies for addressing spiritual and religious issues in counseling.* https://www.counseling.org/docs/default-source/competencies/competencies-for-addressing-spiritual-and-religious-issues-in-counseling.pdf

Blount, K. C., Booth, C., Webb, T., & Liles, R. G. (2017). Integration of sex and sexuality into counseling programs. In *Ideas and research you can use: VISTAS 2017.* https://www.counseling.org/docs/default-source/vistas/integration_of_sex_and_sexuality.pdf?sfvrsn=eb354c2c_4

Bobby, C. L. (2013). The evolution of specialties in the CACREP standards: CACREP's role in unifying the profession. *Journal of Counseling & Development, 91*(1), 35–43. https://doi.org/10.1002/j.1556-6676.2013.00068.x

Cannon, E., & Cooper, J. (2010). Clinical mental health counseling: A national survey of counselor educators. *Journal of Mental Health Counseling, 32*(3), 236–246. https://doi.org/10.17744/mehc.32.3.pl5r418241012481

Council for Accreditation of Counseling and Related Educational Programs. (2023, October 12). *CACREP 2024 standards guidance document, working draft version, October 12, 2023*. https://www.cacrep.org/wp-content/uploads/2023/10/2024-CACREP-Standards-Guidance-Document-DRAFT-10.12.2023.pdf

Council for Accreditation of Counseling and Related Educational Programs. (2024a). *2024 CACREP standards*. https://www.cacrep.org/wp-content/uploads/2024/04/2024-Standards-Combined-Version-4.11.2024.pdf

Council for Accreditation of Counseling and Related Educational Programs. (2024b). *Counseling specialties*. https://www.cacrep.org/counseling-specialities/

Felitti, V. J., Anda, R. F., Nordenberg, D., Williamson, D. F., Spitz, A. M., Edwards, V., Koss, M. P., & Marks, J. S. (1998). Relationship of childhood abuse and household dysfunction to many of the leading causes of death in adults: The adverse childhood experiences (ACE) study. *American Journal of Preventive Medicine, 14*(4), 245–258. https://doi.org/10.1016/S0749-3797(98)00017-8

Field, T. A., Moh, Y. S., Luke, C., Gracefire, P., Beeson, E. T., & Russo, G. M. (2022). A training model for the development of neuroscience-informed counseling competencies. *Journal of Mental Health Counseling, 44*(3), 266–281. https://doi.org/10.17744/mehc.44.3.05

Goodman, R. D., Williams, J. M., Chung, R. C., Talleyrand, R. M., Douglass, A. M., McMahon, H. G., & Bemak, F. (2015). Decolonizing traditional pedagogies and practices in counseling and psychology education: A move towards social justice and action. In R. D. Goodman & P. C. Gorski (Eds.), *Decolonizing "multicultural" counseling through social justice, international and cultural psychology* (pp. 147–164). https://doi.org/10.1007/978-1-4939-1283-4_11

Jangha, A. G. (2023). Teaching the integration of spirituality in counseling: A specialized course. *Counseling & Values, 68*(2), 138–168. https://doi.org/10.1163/2161007x-bja10004

Junfei, L., Li, C., Potts, C. A., & Joy, U. (2020). An exploration of variables that contribute to counseling students' spiritual competence development: Implications for counselor education. *International Journal for the Advancement of Counselling, 42*(2), 200–216. https://doi.org/10.1007/s10447-019-09391-9

Kaplan, D. M., Tarvydas, V. M., & Gladding, S. T. (2014). 20/20: A vision for the future of counseling: The new consensus definition of counseling. *Journal of Counseling & Development, 92*(3), 366–372. https://doi.org/10.1002/j.1556-6676.2014.00164.x

Levers, L. L., & Hyatt-Burkhart, D. (2019). Introduction to clinical mental health counseling and the underlying dynamics of practice. In L. L. Levers & D. Hyatt-Burkhart (Eds.), *Clinical mental health counseling: Practicing in integrated systems of care* (pp. 3–14). Springer. https://doi.org/10.1891/9780826131089.0001

Olson, S., Brown-Rice, K., & Gerodias, A. (2018). Professional counselor licensure portability: An examination of state license applications. *The Professional Counselor, 8*(1), 88–103. https://doi.org/10.15241/so.8.1.88

Perry, B. D. (2006). Applying principles of neurodevelopment to clinical work with maltreated and traumatized children: The neurosequential model of therapeutics. In N. B. Webb (Ed.), *Working with traumatized youth in child welfare* (pp. 27–52). The Guilford Press.

Rodenkirch, K. A. (2023). *Interaction of sexuality training, sexual awareness, and comfort with sexual discourse in counselors-in-training* (Order No. 30316004) [Doctoral dissertation], Northern Illinois University. ProQuest Dissertations & Theses Global (2827410899). https://www.proquest.com/dissertations-theses/interaction-sexuality-training-sexual-awareness/docview/2827410899/se-2

Siegel, D. J. (2012). *The developing mind: How relationships and the brain interact to shape who we are* (2nd ed.). The Guilford Press.

Smith-Addock, S., & Tucker, C. (2017). *Counseling children and adolescents* (1st ed.). Sage.

Substance Abuse and Mental Health Services Administration. (2020). *Understanding child trauma*. https://www.samhsa.gov/child-trauma/understanding-child-trauma

van der Kolk, B. A. (2014). *The body keeps the score: Brain, mind, and body in the healing of trauma*. Viking.

Wu, N. S., Schairer, L. C., Dellor, E., & Grella, C. (2010). Childhood trauma and health outcomes in adults with comorbid substance abuse and mental health disorders. *Addictive Behaviors, 35*(1), 68–71. https://doi.org/10.1016/j.addbeh.2009.09.003

Mary Kate Reese (Deceased), Ph.D., LPC, CPCS (she/her/hers) is a Core Faculty Member in the School of Counseling at Walden University. She has been a licensed counselor for over 30 years and a counselor educator and supervisor for over 25 years. Her clinical experience includes work with children, adolescents, adults, couples, and groups. Currently her focus areas are presenting concerns such as anxiety, depression, and sexual issues and providing supervision and training to counselors.

Charmaine Conner, Ph.D., LPC, NCC, CCPT-S, CPRT S (she/her/hers) is the Department Chair and Assistant Professor at Roosevelt University in the Counseling and Human Services Program. She has been a counselor educator for 5 years, and in professional practice as a licensed counselor for more than 10 years. Her clinical experience includes providing individual and group counseling to children and adolescents who have presented with treatment concerns such as depression, anxiety, trauma, and academic issues.

Deanna Burgess, Ph.D., LCPC (she/her/hers) is an Assistant Professor in the Counseling and Special Education Department of the College of Education at DePaul University. Her research interests include exploring social justice integration considerations within school settings, and investigating developmental trajectories for youth and practitioners engaged in social justice education and advocacy. Dr. Burgess supports social justice programming and training efforts in collaboration with school districts in Pennsylvania, and her expertise includes providing equity training grounded in critical race pedagogy.

Clinical Rehabilitation and Rehabilitation Counseling

19

K. Lynn Pierce

The only thing worse than being blind is having sight but no vision.

Helen Keller

Abstract

Rehabilitation counselors work with individuals who possess any number or combination of visible and/or invisible disabilities to achieve their individual treatment goals, and with the overall goal of increasing their autonomy and capacity for independent living. Rehabilitation Counseling is an underrecognized specialty within counseling as a profession and Counselor Education and Supervision as a discipline. Rehabilitation counselors have their own professional history, professional identity, and specific needs in their training. This chapter briefly explores key disability-related knowledge, rehabilitation counseling as a profession and as a specialty counseling area, and the unique skills and knowledge essential for rehabilitation counselors (rehabilitation counselors) to be successful.

Learning Objectives After reading this chapter, you will be able to:

1. Outline the major historical and legislative events that have shaped rehabilitation counseling, including within the counseling profession.
2. Distinguish the unique elements of the rehabilitation counselor's professional identity.
3. Implement best practices for developing a rehabilitation counseling program or track using a social justice and advocacy framework.

K. Lynn Pierce (✉)
Mercer University, Atlanta, GA, USA
e-mail: pierce_k03@mercer.edu

D. M. Stalnaker-Shofner and T. N. Sapp (eds.), *A Comprehensive Guide for Counselor Education*, Springer Texts in Education, https://doi.org/10.1007/978-3-031-68358-9_19

19.1 Statement of Reflexivity

I completed a master's degree in clinical mental health counseling and then took a specialty area of rehabilitation counseling for my doctoral program emphasis. I have taught rehabilitation classes and am a Certified Rehabilitation Counselor (CRC) in good standing in addition to being a Licensed Professional Counselor (LPC). I have successfully led the early stages of program development for the creation of a clinical rehabilitation track aligned with CACREP standards, CRCC eligibility requirements, and state licensing board requirements.

19.1.1 Language Statement

Person-first language is used for the purposes of this chapter due to established academic and APA conventions; however, it is worth noting that many in the disability community disagree with person-first language and prefer identity first language for themselves and their communities.

19.2 History of Rehabilitation Counseling

Rehabilitation counseling has its roots in state-federal vocational rehabilitation programs. It is unique in its legislated roots—the passage of the Smith-Fess Act established the federal-state vocational rehabilitation program in 1920. Rehabilitation counselors now work across a variety of settings to meet the needs of people with disabilities. Regardless of setting, rehabilitation counselors are unique among helping professionals due to their specialized knowledge of disability models, medical aspects of disability, disability-related laws, and disability programs and services at federal, state, and local levels. Many rehabilitation counselors work in vocational rehabilitation programs, while others work in settings across the public, private, and not-for-profit rehabilitation sectors. Rehabilitation counselors can be found in independent living centers, hospitals, private practices, colleges and universities, public schools, and many other settings.

While rehabilitation counseling has a long history and unique professional identity, there has been a longstanding debate regarding whether it is an independent profession or a specialty area of counseling. With the merger of accrediting bodies detailed more below, this argument has in many ways been settled. Subsequently, the rehabilitation counseling profession has had to reexamine their contributions as the field is redefined through these significant changes. This has led to an increasing tension within rehabilitation counseling culture between those who felt rehabilitation was naturally a specialty within counseling and those who believed rehabilitation counselors were best trained under a rehabilitation practice model that was distinct from counseling. In rehabilitation settings, this has sometimes been referred to as the "big hat" versus "two hat" theory or approach to rehabilitation counseling. One benefit of rehabilitation counseling developing in a largely separate way from the broader counseling field is a resulting strong professional identity as well as clear ties to the policy and advocacy movements of people with disabilities. One detriment has been a certain degree of siloing, where neither the rehabilitation field nor the broader counseling field has been easily able to collaborate and share ideas and knowledge.

In this time of bridging the gap between rehabilitation counseling and professional counseling, and navigating changes that are at times challenging, it is of note that Myers (2012) observed that as a counseling specialty, rehabilitation counseling "stands at the forefront in creating sustained positive change in the holistic well-being of persons with disabilities … to be effective advocates and change agents for themselves, their families, their communities, and society" (p. xvi).

19.2.1 Council on Rehabilitation Education

The Council on Rehabilitation Education (CORE) was the primary accreditation body for rehabilitation counselor education programs from 1972 until 2017. In 2015, CORE and CACREP signed a merger agreement. One significant impact of this is the replacement of the CORE Standards for programs, which in some cases were more clearly aligned with rehabilitation counseling identity and with CRCC (Commission on Rehabilitation Counselor Certification) knowledge domains with the CACREP clinical rehabilitation counseling and rehabilitation counseling standards.

19.2.2 CACREP/CORE Merger

The CACREP/CORE merger has settled the question of whether rehabilitation is a counseling specialty or distinct profession with rehabilitation added to counseling specialties under CACREP but has led to fear that there may be a loss of rehabilitation knowledge and rehabilitation counseling identity. As further addressed in the section below, the merger also invites a situation where rehabilitation counselors may not be trained by rehabilitation professionals or where core classes taught in programs that did not previously have rehabilitation CITs may miss key content areas for rehabilitation CITs to prepare them both for the CRCC exam and for their future work sites.

Due to the complexity of the merger, rehabilitation is currently in a unique position of having two entries: rehabilitation counseling and clinical rehabilitation counseling. There have been a number of criticisms of this divide, including a lack of clarity on the difference between rehabilitation and clinical rehabilitation, a lack of reflection of the history or practical reality of the profession, and concern regarding the absence of important elements including vocational placement and case management in clinical rehabilitation specialty standards (Bishop, 2020).

One clear opportunity of the CORE and CACREP merger is better implementation of disability competencies across CACREP areas in future standards.

Depending on how this is implemented, it could help facilitate discussions of disability that may not have been happening in counselor training programs. In the 2024 CACREP Standards, "disability status" is included in CACREP's definitions of *cultural identity*, *diversity*, and *marginalized populations* (CACREP, 2024). However, disability is often not addressed across core content areas or included in conversations about multicultural competency. In a survey of faculty from 141 CACREP programs, 36% of faculty indicated that their program was ineffective at addressing disability topics (Feather & Carlson, 2019). Programs may also not use texts with disability topics and sections (Smart & Smart, 2006), as many commonly used texts do not address disability demographics, and counselors in training not specifically working in rehabilitation sites often do not have internship experiences that support preparation to work with people with disabilities. Due to the prevalence and complexity of disability, it is essential that counselors in training receive information on disability and work through their own ableism and disability-related bias, whether they are in a rehabilitation specialty or not.

19.3 CACREP Accreditation

Clinical rehabilitation and rehabilitation counseling programs can be accredited by CACREP which may also allow for the program to meet state licensure requirements. Additionally, programs ensure that their rehabilitation CITs are eligible for and prepared for the National Certified Rehabilitation Counselor (CRC) examination.

All programs include the eight core areas for entry level programs (this is addressed further in Chap. 15), in addition to the standards for that specific specialized practice area in Section 5. Due to the two categories for rehabilitation counseling under the 2024 standards, programs must determine whether they wish to implement 5.D: Clinical Rehabilitation Counseling or 5.G: Rehabilitation Counseling standards for their program (CACREP, 2024) (see Table 19.1).

19.4 Developing a Clinical Rehabilitation or Rehabilitation Counseling Training Program and Track

A primary focus of clinical rehabilitation and rehabilitation programs is to ensure CITs in the rehabilitation specialty are eligible for the CRC examination. The Commission on Rehabilitation Counselor Certification (CRCC) is the primary certifying body for rehabilitation counselors and sets the scope of practice for rehabilitation counseling. While CRCC is not an additional accreditation, the knowledge assessed in the CRC examination is empirically derived based on the knowledge domains and roles and functions of rehabilitation counselors (Leahy et al., 2013). More information on the knowledge domains and CRC examination can be found in *Certified Rehabilitation Counselor Examination Preparation* (Chan

Table 19.1 Clinical rehabilitation counseling and rehabilitation counseling 2024 CACREP standards (Sections 5.D and 5.G.)

Clinical rehabilitation counseling standards	Rehabilitation counseling standards
5.D.1. Effects of the onset, progression, and expected duration of disability on clients' holistic functioning	5.G.1. Individual response to disability, including the role of families, communities, and other social networks
5.D.2. Environmental, attitudinal, and individual barriers for people with disabilities	5.G.2. Strategies to enhance adjustment and adaptation to disability
5.D.3. Impact of disability on sexuality	5.G.3. Effects of socioeconomic trends, public policies, stigma, access, and attitudinal barriers as they relate to disability
5.D.4. Rehabilitation service delivery systems, including housing, independent living, case management, public benefits programs, educational programs, and public/proprietary vocational rehabilitation programs	5.G.4. Principles of independent living, self-determination, and informed choice
5.D.5. Clinical rehabilitation counseling services within the continuum of care, such as inpatient, outpatient, partial hospitalization and aftercare, integrated behavioral healthcare, and the rehabilitation counseling services networks	5.G.5. Rehabilitation counseling services and organizational settings, including independent living, community rehabilitation, and public/proprietary vocational rehabilitation programs
5.D.6. Transferable skills, functional assessments, and work-related supports for achieving and maintaining meaningful employment for people with disabilities	5.G.6. Benefit systems used by individuals with disabilities, including but not limited to social security, governmental monetary assistance, workers' compensation insurance, long-term disability insurance, and veterans' benefits
5.D.7. Role of family, social networks, and community in the provision of services for and treatment of people with disabilities	5.G.7. Classification, terminology, etiology, functional capacity, and prognosis of disabilities
5.D.8. Assistive technology to reduce or eliminate barriers and functional limitations	5.G.8. Career- and work-related assessments, including job analysis, worksite modification, transferable skills analysis, job readiness, and work hardening
5.D.9. Intake interview, mental status evaluation, biopsychosocial history, mental health history, and psychological assessment for treatment planning and caseload management for people with disabilities	5.G.9. Evaluation and application of assistive technology with an emphasis on individualized assessment and planning
5.D.10. Strategies to advocate for people with disabilities related to accessibility, accommodations, and disability law adherence	5.G.10. Career development and employment models and strategies for achieving and maintaining meaningful employment for people with disabilities

(continued)

Table 19.1 (continued)

Clinical rehabilitation counseling standards	Rehabilitation counseling standards
5.D.11. Third-party reimbursement and other practice and management issues in clinical rehabilitation counseling	5.G.11. Strategies to analyze work activity and labor market data and trends to facilitate the match between an individual with a disability and targeted jobs
	5.G.12. Case management strategies that facilitate rehabilitation and independent living planning
	5.G.13. Consultation and collaboration with employers regarding the legal rights and benefits of hiring individuals with disabilities, including Americans with Disabilities Act adherence, accommodations, universal design, and workplace disability prevention
	5.G.14. Strategies to promote self-advocacy skills of individuals with disabilities
	5.G.15. Facilitating client knowledge of and access to community and technology services and resources
	5.G.16. Strategies to advocate on behalf of people with disabilities as related to disability and disability legislation

et al., 2021). The knowledge domains that define the rehabilitation counselor scope of practice are as follows:

- Assessment and appraisal
- Diagnosis and treatment planning
- Career (vocational) counseling
- Individual and group counseling treatment interventions focused on facilitating adjustments to the medical and psychosocial impact of disability
- Case management, referral, and service coordination
- Program evaluation and research
- Interventions to remove environmental, employment, and attitudinal barriers
- Consultation services among multiple parties and regulatory systems
- Job analysis, job development, and placement services, including assistance with employment and job accommodations
- Provision of consultation about and access to rehabilitation technology (CRCC, 2020).

19.4.1 CRCC Eligibility

An important element of planning the development of a clinical rehabilitation counseling or rehabilitation counseling program is to ensure CITs' eligibility for the CRC Exam. CRCC has three categories of eligibility:

- **Category 1**: Student in or graduate of a masters level CACREP-Accredited Program in clinical rehabilitation counseling or clinical rehabilitation counseling.

  Highlighted Additional Requirements: 75% of coursework completed by testing date and a practicum/internship of 100/600 clock hours with 40/240 direct clock hours supervised by CRC (as the on-site supervisor or faculty supervisor) providing direct services to individuals with disabilities.
- **Category 2**: Student in or graduate of a master's level non-CACREP-Accredited Program in clinical rehabilitation counseling or clinical rehabilitation counseling.

  Highlighted Additional Requirements: 75% of coursework completed by testing date and a practicum/internship of 100/600 clock hours with 40/240 direct clock hours supervised by CRC (as the on-site supervisor or faculty supervisor) providing direct services to individuals with disabilities.
- **Category 3**: Graduate of a master's or doctoral program in a related field of study.

Additional requirements include specific coursework and either internship or employment experience (CRCC, 2021).

Because new programs will have a delay in CACREP approval, it is important to ensure that programs meet the requirements under Category 2. This category has more specific coursework requirements, outlined below from the Category 2 verification form:

- Professional orientation and ethics in rehabilitation counseling
- Medical and psychosocial aspects of disabilities
- Assessment
- Career development theories and job development and placement techniques
- Case management and community partnerships
- Theories and techniques of counseling
- Research, methodology, and performance management (CRCC, 2023).

19.4.2 State Licensure

Historically, it was not always common or possible for rehabilitation counselors to be licensed. Since the transition to CACREP accreditation, it is typical that rehabilitation programs meet licensure requirements in their state.

19.5 Rehabilitation Counseling Specific Training Requirements

Each program will have slightly different needs, based on license requirements, the schedule of eligibility under CRCC, and other factors. However, the following are common considerations in specialty area course requirements for each rehabilitation specialty. Clinical rehabilitation programs may offer the following classes as required specialty area courses:

- Principles of Rehabilitation or Introduction to Rehabilitation
- Medical and Psychosocial Aspects of Disability (sometimes combined, sometimes separately)
- Vocational Planning or Vocational Evaluation
- Case Management (sometimes grouped with other topics such as placement).

Rehabilitation counseling programs are similarly structured but are more likely to require additional courses such as forensic rehabilitation or psychiatric rehabilitation, as well as a more robust choice of electives such as those specifically designed to support blind and vision services (BVS) or deaf and hard-of-hearing-related career trajectories. An example plan of study is offered in Table 19.2.

19.6 Rehabilitation Counseling Specific Field Placement

For professional identity development, it is generally considered important for rehabilitation counselors in training to be supervised by faculty who are rehabilitation counselors who understand the unique roles and scope of practice their CITs may encounter. Ideally, in order to ensure CRC examination eligibility, faculty supervisors for rehabilitation CITs will be CRCs and rehabilitation CRCs will work at sites that specifically serve individuals with disabilities.

Many programs also have Rehabilitation Services Administration (RSA) grants and learners receiving these grants are required to work at a Vocational Rehabilitation (VR) agency or VR-contracted agency for two years for each year of support received during the program. It is therefore beneficial for rehabilitation programs to have field placement relationships with state VR agencies in addition to other disability-serving sites and agencies.

Table 19.2 Example clinical rehabilitation counseling program (60 credit hours) program plan of study

Name of course	Credits
Professional Orientation and Ethics[a]	3
Social and Cultural Foundations[a]	3
Counseling Skills[a]	3
Assessment and Appraisal[a]	3
Diagnosis in Counseling[a]	3
Research Methods in Counseling[a]	3
Career Development[a]	3
Group Counseling[a]	3
Theories and Techniques[a]	3
Human Growth and Development[a]	3
Introduction to Addictions[a]	3
Crisis and Trauma Counseling[a]	3
Elective of Choice	3
Rehabilitation Foundations and Ethics	3
Medical Aspects of Disability	3
Psychosocial Aspects of Disability	3
Vocational Planning and Case Management	3
Practicum in Clinical Rehabilitation Counseling	3
Internship in Clinical Rehabilitation Counseling I	3
Internship in Clinical Rehabilitation Counseling II	3

[a] Indicates courses that address the 2024 CACREP Foundational Counseling Curriculum content area (CACREP, 2024, Section 3)

19.7 Conclusion

In conclusion, rehabilitation counseling is at an important time of development. As the field of rehabilitation counseling solidifies its place as a counseling specialty within CACREP accreditation, attention must be paid to maintaining the specialty knowledge of disability related laws, systems and services, and biopsychosocial impacts rehabilitation counselors which uniquely equips rehabilitation counselors to advocate for and with people with disabilities. Those developing rehabilitation counselor training programs must carefully navigate meeting accreditation, certification, and licensure requirements.

References

Bishop, M. (2020). Editorial on the rehabilitation counseling curricular standards revision. *Rehabilitation Research, Policy, and Education, 34*(3), 140–144. https://doi.org/10.1891/RE-20-17

Chan, F., Bishop, M., Chronister, J., Lee, E., & Chiu, C. (2021). *Certified rehabilitation counselor examination preparation.* Springer Publishing Company.

Commission on Rehabilitation Counselor Certification. (2020). *CRC exam knowledge domains.*

Commission on Rehabilitation Counselor Certification. (2021). *CRC certification guide certified rehabilitation counselor*.

Commission on Rehabilitation Counselor Certification. (2023, April 6). *Category 2—Student enrolled in a non-CACREP accredited program verification form.* Commission on Rehabilitation Counselor Certification. https://crccertification.com/wp-content/uploads/2020/10/Category-2-Student-Enrolled-in-a-Non-CACREP-Accredited-Program-Verification-Form.pdf

Council for Accreditation of Counseling and Related Educational Programs. (2024). *2024 CACREP standards.* https://www.cacrep.org/wp-content/uploads/2024/04/2024-Standards-Combined-Version-4.11.2024.pdf

Feather, K. A., & Carlson, R. G. (2019). An initial investigation of individual instructors' self-perceived competence and incorporation of disability content into CACREP-accredited programs: Rethinking training in counselor education. *Journal of Multicultural Counseling and Development, 47*, 19–36. https://doi.org/10.1002/JMCD.12118

Leahy, M. J., Chan, F., Sung, C., & Kim, M. (2013). Empirically derived test specifications for the certified rehabilitation counselor examination. *Rehabilitation Counseling Bulletin, 56*(4), 199–214. https://doi.org/10.1177/0034355212469839

Myers, J. E. (2012). Forward. In D. R. Maki & V. M. Tarvydas (Eds.), *The professional practice of rehabilitation counseling* (pp. xv–xvii). Springer Publishing Company.

Smart, J. F., & Smart, D. W. (2006). Models of disability: Implications for the counseling profession. *Journal of Counseling & Development, 84*, 29–40. https://doi.org/10.1002/j.1556-6678.2006.tb00377.x

K. Lynn Pierce, Ph.D., CRC, LPC, (she/her/hers) is a Certified Rehabilitation Counselor (CRC) and a Licensed Professional Counselor (GA). She is an Assistant Professor and Program Coordinator for the Ph.D. in Counselor Education and Supervision at Mercer University in Atlanta, Georgia. Her scholarship focuses on improving access to care for marginalized groups including people with disabilities, disability equity, and accessibility advocacy within counselor education and higher education.

College Counseling and Student Affairs 20

Jocelyn Novella and Krista Dobson

Education is the passport to the future, for tomorrow belongs to those who prepare for it today.

Malcolm X

Abstract

College counseling and student affairs work has changed dramatically over the past twenty years. The college counseling center began as a free resource to support learners trying to balance academics with other life stressors. It has evolved into the establishment of campus mental health clinics. While this is challenging enough, many counselor education master's programs with a college counseling and student affairs track continue to present the environment as one of privilege, wealth, and safety. This chapter will set the stage by offering a realistic understanding of the college environment. Next, we will delineate steps for program development of a college counseling track based on the 2024 CACREP Standards. Lastly, we will provide useful strategies for integrating social justice and advocacy into curriculum development and outline best practices regarding pedagogical implementation.

Learning Objectives After reading this chapter, you will be able to:

1. Identify the CACREP 2024 standards for a college counseling and student affairs track.
2. Develop curriculum for a college counseling track utilizing a social justice framework grounded in a critical consciousness orientation.

J. Novella (✉)
Fairfield University, Fairfield, CT, USA
e-mail: jnovella@fairfield.edu

K. Dobson
Yale University, New Haven, CT, USA
e-mail: krista.dobson@yale.edu

D. M. Stalnaker-Shofner and T. N. Sapp (eds.), *A Comprehensive Guide for Counselor Education*, Springer Texts in Education, https://doi.org/10.1007/978-3-031-68358-9_20

3. Integrate identified best practices related to curriculum design, course development, and teaching praxis of college counseling and student affairs track that incorporates extant research and current social and global influences.

20.1 Statement of Reflexivity

We approach this chapter as college counselors with different identities and diverse experiences. However, we both recognize the shortcomings of college campuses in addressing issues of systemic racism and inequity. This chapter is born from our varied experiences and the desire to prepare future college counselors to meet learner's needs from a social justice perspective. The first author is a cisgender, heterosexual, able-bodied White female who is an assistant professor in a CACREP-accredited counselor education program. She identifies strongly with her Armenian heritage, is an LPC, and is a Board-Certified Telemental Health Provider. She worked in a college counseling center for over 20 years before taking a faculty position. The second author is a cisgender, heterosexual, able-bodied Black female who is a licensed professional counselor working at a university in the northeast. She is of African American descent whose family has roots in rural Virginia and North Carolina.

20.2 Introduction

The dynamic and fluid environment of college counseling/student affairs creates challenges for educators teaching the specialty. If faculty are not working in this environment daily, it is difficult to remain on top of the ever-changing world of college counseling. This applies to the development of the requisite skills and knowledge for the role, and, more importantly for new CES faculty, how to best train CITs to meet these requirements. The 2024 CACREP Standards lay the foundation for the essential elements of the program curriculum for a college counseling track. Key to these standards is the understanding of student development theory, as well as the various roles that college counselors play in the college or university system, whether the "campus" is online or on-ground.

This chapter will offer guidelines for developing a college counseling track in a counselor education program. This will include understanding the key issues that counselor educators need to discuss with CITs interested in this specialty, such as campus environment, specific support services, and the unique needs of college learners. Our focus is to look at curriculum development from a social justice/critical consciousness framework, for CITs to recognize and understand the needs of the college learner in today's environment.

We begin the chapter with a brief history of college counseling over the last century to provide a background. Next, we outline both the 2024 CACREP Standards for this track as well as a possible program plan of study. Some of the college-specific courses outlined in the plan of study will be discussed in more detail with a rationale for their importance in preparing CITs to enter the profession. Finally, we discuss the placement process in college counseling and what is best practice in terms of training and preparation for college counseling and student affairs work.

20.3 History of College Counseling and Student Affairs

In the days when colleges and universities were seen as operating "in loco parentis," institutions had a great deal of power in how they addressed learner behavioral and mental health issues (Lee, 2011). Since colleges were educational institutions, the belief was that "educators" could address these issues. Also, since many of those coming to college were part of a privileged population, the parents saw college as a rite of passage and were supportive of the authority that colleges wielded (Hodges, 2017).

Much changed with the influence of World War II and veterans attending higher education through the G.I. Bill (Sharkin, 2012). During this time, college learners represented those with more experiences and more needs in terms of mental health support and career counseling. This continued into the 1960s and 1970s where young adults were advocating for their rights to make independent choices around their futures, including their education (Sharkin, 2012). In 1961, "in loco parentis" was no longer deemed legal, and the U.S. Family Educational Rights and Privacy Act (FERPA) was passed in 1974 (Sharkin, 2012).

The college counseling center began to change based on the needs of the learners at the institution, whether it be a community college or 4-year institution. The perception that there was an increase in the pathology of presenting learners and the severity of their issues may have been based on incorrect perception (Sharkin, 1997); however, these counseling centers began to establish crisis services to deal with what was seen as an increase in risk level for learners.

When the Americans with Disability Act (ADA) was passed in 1990, colleges needed to be accessible for learners with disabilities, including chronic mental illnesses (Keenan et al., 2019). Universities had to increase funding to counseling centers to ensure these needs were addressed, and services were increased. It is possible that the focus on diagnostic criteria in order to qualify under ADA created a "medical model" for the typical counseling center, rather than the support and resource focus it had been in the past.

The 2000s saw a continuing increase in the need and use of counseling services on campuses (Gorman et al., 2020). The increased awareness around mental health diagnoses and the challenges of emerging adulthood continue to overwhelm the resources available to learners. In addition, parental involvement has increased as tuition costs have skyrocketed (Gorman et al., 2020). This has led to many student affairs administrators, including college counselors, being stuck between triaging services to those who most need them and trying to keep parents satisfied (given they were often footing the bill) (Long, 2018). Finally, the prevalence of school-based shootings, including on college campuses, has created a focus on early assessment and intervention in potentially dangerous situations.

Finally, when the trauma of the COVID-19 pandemic occurred and most campuses were shut down, colleges lost their identity as a social community; they became a place simply to get an online education. Traditional age learners were isolated, confused, and depressed; there was more need for counseling than ever before, but there were limitations on providing that counseling across state lines, depending on the location of the school to the learners' home (Bradford, 2021).

Most importantly, college counseling centers have been challenged to engage in social justice and advocacy work. The traditional model of predominantly white counselors offering individual counseling appointments in a medically-based office on campus does not address the needs of the marginalized communities within the college environment. We see this as the greatest challenge for CITs graduating from this track in Counselor Education programs and hope to address some of those issues in the upcoming sections.

20.4 CACREP Accreditation

While CACREP is currently the only accrediting body for college counseling and student affairs tracks in a CES program, college counseling centers are governed by the AUCCCD. For the purpose of this chapter, we will focus on CACREP accreditation. As previously mentioned in the preceding chapters of this text, all programs must include the eight foundational curriculum areas required for entry-level counselor education programs (see Chap. 15 for more information). In addition, programs specializing in college counseling and student affairs must meet additional CACREP standards located in Section 5.E. (CACREP, 2024). We have outlined these standards for you in Table 20.1 is the CACREP 2024 Standards for inclusion in this track.

20.5 Developing a College Counseling and Student Affairs Training Program and Track

Having a foundational understanding of the college environment is crucial for today's work on campuses. New counselor educators and student affairs professionals are beginning their career in a time like no other. Pressing financial constraints, lack of full-time appointments, and expanding learner populations call for creative and unorthodox ways of engaging with the college learner (Gorman et al., 2020). Therefore, CITs should have a foundational awareness and understanding of the factors that may impact the campus environment and ultimately, the college learner. As you consider the developmental needs of your program, we have provided you with an example college counseling and student affairs program plan of study in Table 20.2. This example program provides CITs with the ability

Table 20.1 College counseling and student affairs 2024 CACREP standards (Section 5.E.)

Standards
5.E.1. Principles of student development and the effect on life, education, and career choices
5.E.2. Organizational, management, and leadership theories relevant in higher education settings
5.E.3. Organizational culture, budgeting and finance, and personnel practices in higher education
5.E.4. Current trends in higher education
5.E.5. Diversity of higher education environments
5.E.6. The influence of institutional, systemic, interpersonal, and intrapersonal barriers on learning and career opportunities in higher education
5.E.7. Policies, programs, and services that are equitable, preventative, and responsive to the unique needs of students in higher education settings
5.E.8. Higher education resources to improve student learning, personal growth, professional identity development, and mental health
5.E.9. Models of threat assessment and violence prevention in higher education settings
5.E.10. Roles of college counselors and student affairs professionals in collaborating with personnel from other educational settings to facilitate college and postsecondary transitions

to be eligible for professional counselor licensure as well. While this is an example, your program will need to verify your specific state and local requirements for licensure.

20.5.1 Curriculum Suggestions and Practices Using a Social Justice Lens

Within your program, it will be important that you are intentional with diffusing social justice and diversity throughout the curriculum. As such, we thought it may be helpful to provide you with some best practices and ideas for how to do this within your programs. Additionally, in this section, we provide you with a few best practices for course implementation to help you as you begin to design or redesign your college counseling and student affairs courses, program, or track.

20.5.1.1 Social Justice and Diversity in College Course

This college-specific course is essential for preparing CITs for the field. College campuses are recognizing the influence of racial and social unrest on learners, and the need to appropriately and meaningfully address deficits in DEIBASJ in administrative practice, policy, and teaching praxis. Teaching praxis and related curriculum must highlight the unique position of college counselors and student affairs professionals to be agents of change in this environment (Paladino & Davis, 2006).

Table 20.2 Example college counseling and student affairs program (60 credit hours) program plan of study

Name of course	Credits
Counseling Skills and Helping Relationships[a]	3
Lifespan Development[a]	3
Theories of Psychotherapy[a]	3
Career Counseling[a]	3
Diagnosis and Treatment Planning[a]	3
Assessment Methods in Counseling[a]	3
Research Methodology[a]	3
Introduction to Family Systems[a]	3
Social Justice and Diversity in Colleges[a]	3
Introduction to College Counseling and Student Development[a]	3
Ethics and Legal Considerations in College Counseling[a]	3
Group Counseling in the College Environment[a]	3
Substances and the College Student	3
Organizational Behavior and Leadership in Higher Education	3
Integrated Care and Prevention on College Campuses	3
Electives [2]	6
Practicum in a College Counseling Center	3
Internship 1 in a College Counseling Center	3
Internship 2 in a College Counseling Center	3

[a] Indicates courses that address the 2024 CACREP Foundational Counseling Curriculum content area (CACREP, 2024, Section 3)

College counselors who fully understand their identity and how it may be perceived are key to being able to establish good therapeutic relationships going forward. Having an acute sense of one's own limitations and biases provides a model for college learners who are going through an identity exploration phase of their development. Failure to examine privilege and oppression in gender, race, sex, sexual orientation, color, socioeconomics, age, ability, hair texture, education, etc. impacts the day-to-day life of a learner is not working from a social justice perspective. This lack of examination results in distrust, which may manifest as skipped appointments, 'resistance,' medication management issues, and disconnection. Counselor educators would do well to help their CITs go beyond cultural competence and intentionally interrogate how power, privilege, and oppression impact a college learner's mental health and academic functioning (Kumagai & Lypson, 2009).

One core way of increasing intentionality in engaging in social justice work within the college environment is to practice critical consciousness. Rooted in the work of Paulo Freire, critical consciousness asks us to engage in reflective awareness of how oppression and privilege are embedded in social relationships (Freire,

1968; Kumagai & Lypson, 2009). This includes an understanding of one's own biases and assumptions to become aware of how our own privileges are constructed and leveraged (Kumagai & Lypson, 2009). This is critical in how we interact with our CITs. Lack of self-awareness increases the likelihood of perpetrating harm, i.e., implicit bias and microaggressions. Practicing critical consciousness is extremely important for counselors and student affairs administrators who hold multiple levels of privilege. By naming how we as practitioners engage in the politics of difference, identity, and culture, we shine a light on systemic inequity. For the CIT, it conveys that we have taken the time to invest in our own development, which gives them license and agency to do so as well. Including critical consciousness practices into CES curriculum on a college counseling track is key for preparing counselors to engage in social justice work at this level.

Furthermore, traditional counseling models, (e.g. evidence-based practices) purport to be value-neutral and reinforce these methodologies as irrefutable. This is all predicated on the concept that mental illness is due to a deficiency of the "ill" and that it is the individual's responsibility to address (Smith et al., 2003). Counseling skills are rooted in these constructs which include discouragement from advice-giving or offering suggestions, little to no self-disclosure, no bargaining or accepting of gifts. However, for some cultures this enhances trust and credibility (Sue, 2015).

While the counseling profession strives for multicultural humility, in many ways it falls short of its goal, including in college counseling centers. Our many social systems are based on mono-cultural values and do not always consider social and cultural conditioning stemming from systemic inequity. This often results in well-intentioned counselors not creating space for, or outright, ignoring discussions of oppression from clients who experience its effects (Sue, 2015). A counselor's inability to engage in how systemic oppression affects clients creates harm. Therefore, CITs operating from a social justice perspective interrogate cultural norms, explore and actively engage in their own biases and privilege, and advocate for equity for diverse individuals (CACREP, 2024, standards 5.E.5., 5.E.6., and 5.E.7.). This is not to say that there is no value in traditional therapy models for some. It is not an either/or proposition; however, we seek to look at therapeutic interventions through a social justice lens in which to better meet the needs of college learners.

College counseling and student affairs professionals seek to best enhance the learners functioning and development. Often overlooked are the various communities both, within and outside of the campus, in which a college learner operates. The tendency to focus on the learner as an autonomous being misses the very subjective nature of a learner's lived experience. Not incorporating space for intergenerational impacts, expressions of cultural heritage, relations to nature, religious and spiritual affiliation and practices, perpetuate oppressive structures that value individualism and little else (Atkinson et al., 2019). Teaching future college counselors how to engage with their future clients in a culturally humble way will go far in preparing them for the campuses of the future.

20.5.1.2 Integrated Healthcare and Prevention on College Campuses Course

A course focusing on prevention is key to the work that needs to be done in future college counseling centers. The standard approach to mental health care in these settings has been a "reactive" one, allowing the college learner to engage with services once a problem exists. By 2015, the number of counseling center appointments increased by 30–40% from 6 years prior, and the allocation of college counselor time for crisis or immediate access services increased by 28% (Center for Collegiate Mental Health (CCMH), 2019). As discussed above, current mental health needs far outweigh the ability of staff to provide adequate, individual services (LeViness et al., 2017), and waiting for distress to occur does not make sense as a behavioral healthcare strategy. As our colleagues in public health understand, addressing issues from a preventative community perspective can create an environment of wellness and support (Cramer et al., 2020).

The accrediting body for university and college counseling centers, the International Association of Counseling Services (IACS) (2021) understands this need and states the counseling service outreach must

> offer preventive programming focused on the developmental needs of students, to maximize the potential to benefit from their academic experience. These prevention programs should help college students acquire new knowledge, skills and behaviors; encourage positive and realistic self-appraisal; foster personal, academic and career choices; enhance the ability to relate mutually and meaningfully with others; and increase the capacity to engage in a personally satisfying and effective style of living. Counseling centers may use social media and/or passive programming in their outreach efforts. These programs should be responsive to sexual/relational orientation, gender identity, racial, cultural, disability and ethnic diversity among students, and reach students who are less likely to make use of traditional counseling services. Counseling centers should effectively market their services to the university community – communicating the range of services available to students in order to maximize awareness and utilization. (p. 4)

Most prevention work is structured using Substance Abuse and Mental Health Administration's (SAMHSA) Strategic Prevention Framework (2019), which describes the process from assessment through evaluation, with an underlying emphasis on sustainability and cultural competence.

In addition to this approach, the three-tiered system for implementation that has been used for decades, not only in colleges but also at the K-12 level, provides guidance for ensuring that all levels of prevention are addressed. Primary prevention focuses on increasing awareness and educating the entire campus community to reduce the incidence of emotional difficulties or challenges. An example would be discussing some of the emotional challenges in transitioning to college and wellness resources at first-year orientation. Secondary prevention is to address issues that have started to arise or to direct outreach to high-risk behaviors of specific community members. An example of this may be eating disorder screenings with college athletes. Tertiary prevention helps those individuals who have already experienced negative outcomes of emotional difficulties return to their previous wellness state. An example of this may be a recovery house on campus or programming for BIPOC learners to discuss and process a campus racial incident. These approaches to prevention can ensure a comprehensive, evidence-informed strategy for reducing mental health concerns on a college campus and should be emphasized in our learning outcomes for our college counseling courses.

Research demonstrates that peer education programs are an effective way to engage learners in the overall mental and physical wellness of the community (Dubovi & Sawyer, 2018). The theory of peer education is based on Bandura's social cognitive theory (1994, 2004), which discusses the process of making behavior changes based on knowledge of the desired behavior and a sense of self-efficacy to reach that desired behavior. College peers who are trained in health promotion and in various prevention strategies can be considered credible sources of health strategies by their peers (White et al., 2009). They also can reduce barriers in the college environment that cause stress and increase mental health issues (CACREP, 2024, Standard 5.E.6.).

In addition to the impact these peer educators can have on their classmates, one of the largest effects may be on these educators themselves. From the perspective of career construction theory (Savickas, 2019), individuals begin to make meaning of their career goals as part of a larger life purpose. Learners who apply to become peer educators will have an interest in helping others as well as an interest in promoting healthy behaviors. The training in strategies for changing behaviors gives them a foundation upon which to start building their sense of self-efficacy in this area. They can begin to construct a sense of what addressing public health concerns in a community truly looks like. Additionally, their presence in their own social circles, teams, and classrooms allows for a perspective of health promotion to begin to permeate the campus in ways that would not be possible otherwise. Therefore, this course should address the structure of peer education programs, training for peer educators, and how these prevention programs can be integrated into counseling or wellness centers on college campuses.

20.6 College Counseling and Student Affairs Specific Field Placement

The best way for CITs to be prepared to enter this field is to do both field placements on a college campus. Our suggestion is that at least one or two of those semesters be in a college counseling center in order to understand the distinctive short-term model of this treatment approach. However, there are other key offices in colleges that would add to the CIT's growth in this track. Table 20.3 denotes college departments that can potentially serve as short-term internship sites and the key learning objectives for each.

Another issue with field placements is that CITs often are placed at one institution. It can be helpful to explore more than one type of campus for fieldwork in this track. If there are options for a community college setting, this provides

Table 20.3 Alternative field placement options for college counseling and student affairs programs

Department	Learning objective
Office of Accessibility	Understanding of the needs of students with documented disabilities and the accommodations that are possible
Residential Life Office	Interacting with Residential Assistants (RAs) and others in this department gives a "first responder" perspective to some of the issues that students are experiencing
Career Counseling Office	Career is an essential part of counselor education and working with first- and second-year students on choosing a major/exploring possible interests is helpful
Substance Use Prevention Office	This provides a key perspective into one of the most prevalent issues on campuses, while also educating on best practices in prevention
Peer Education or Health Education Office	Can be eye-opening for counselors to appreciate the work of mental health prevention in a college community

the distinction between a 2-year campus, the needs of those particular learners and best practices in integrating traditional therapy with case management.

20.7 Conclusion

College counseling and student affairs is a changing discipline that requires counselor educators to remain in touch with the transitions in higher education. We have discussed the following key changes in the discipline throughout this chapter, from addressing the needs of learners with marginalized identities to a comprehensive, integrated, prevention strategy for mental health issues. The stressors in this population are great, and we need to be more creative in order to engage them in their quest for mental wellness. These will be the necessary areas of focus for the future of this track in counselor education, and the hope is that we can produce counselors who know how to navigate the complexity of the college setting.

References

Atkinson, S., Bagnall, A. M., Corcoran, R., South, J., & Curtis, S. (2019). Being well together: Individual subject and community well-being. *Journal of Happiness Studies, 21*, 1903–1921.

Bandura, A. (1994). Self-efficacy. In R. J. Corsini (Ed.), *Encyclopedia of psychology* (2nd ed., pp. 368–369). Wiley.

Bandura, A. (2004). Self-efficacy. In E. W. Craighead & C. B. Nemeroff (Eds.), *The concise Corsini encyclopedia of psychology and behavioral sciences* (pp. 859–862). Wiley.

Bradford, N. (2021). Understanding COVID-19's impact on college students. *Teaching & Learning in Nursing, 16*(3), 1–11. https://doi.org/10.1016/j.teln.2020.10.002

Center for Collegiate Mental Health. (2019, January). *2018 annual report (Publication No. STA 19-180).* https://ccmh.psu.edu/files/2019/09/2018-Annuual-Report-9.27.19-FINAL.pdf

Council for Accreditation of Counseling and Related Educational Programs. (2024). *2024 CACREP standards.* https://www.cacrep.org/wp-content/uploads/2024/04/2024-Standards-Combined-Version-4.11.2024.pdf

Cramer, R. J., Judah, M. R., Badger, N. L., Holley, A. M., Judd, S., Peterson, M., Hager, N., Vandecar-Burdin, T., & Foss, J. J. (2020). Suicide on college campuses: A public health framework and case illustration. *Journal of American College Health, 70*(1), 1–8. https://doi.org/10.1080/07448481.2020.1739053

Dubovi, A. S., & Sawyer, J. S. (2018). Evidence-based peer health education. In M. D. Cimini & E. M. Rivero (Eds.), *Promoting behavioral health & reducing risk among students: A comprehensive approach.* Routledge.

Freire, P. (1968). *Pedagogy of the oppressed.* Bloomsbury.

Gorman, K. S., Bruns, C., Chin, C., Fitzpatrick, N. Y., Koenig, L., LeViness, P., & Sokolowski, K. (2020). *Association for university and college counseling center directors annual survey: 2020.* https://www.aucccd.org/assets/documents/Survey/2019-2020%20Annual%20Report%20FINAL%204-2021.pdf

Hodges, S. J. (2017). College counseling: Past, present & future. In S. J. Hodges, K. Shelton, & M. M. King Lyn (Eds.), *The college & university counseling manual* (pp. 1–12). Springer.

International Accreditation of Counseling Services. (2021). *IACS standards for university and college counseling services.* https://iacsinc.org/wp-content/uploads/2023/11/IACS-2023-STANDARDS.pdf

Keenan, W. R., Madaus, J. W., Lombardi, A. R., & Dukes, L. L. (2019). Impact of the Americans with disabilities act amendments act on documentation for students with disabilities in transition to college: Implications for practitioners. *Career Development and Transition for Exceptional Individuals, 42*(1), 56–63. https://doi.org/10.1177/2165143418809691

Kumagai, A. K., & Lypson, M. L. (2009). Beyond cultural competence: Critical consciousness, social justice, and multicultural education. *Academic Medicine, 84*(7), 782–787.

Lee, P. (2011). The curious life of in loco parentis in American universities. *Higher Ed in Review, 8*, 68–90.

LeViness, P., Bershad, C., & Gorman, K. (2017). *Association for university and college counseling center directors annual survey: 2017.* https://www.aucccd.org/assets/documents/Governance/2017%20aucccd%20survey-public-apr26.pdf

Long, C. (2018, October 12). *Educators weigh in on lawnmower parents.* https://www.nea.org/nea-today/all-news-articles/educators-weigh-lawnmower-parents

Paladino, D. A., & Davis, H. (2006). Counseling and outreach strategies for assisting multiracial college students. *Journal of College Student Psychotherapy, 20*, 19–31.

Savickas, M. (2019). *Career construction theory: Life portraits of attachment, adaptability and identity.* Mark Savickas.

Sharkin, B. S. (1997). Increased severity of presenting problems at college counseling centers: A closer look. *Journal of Counseling & Development, 75*, 275–281. https://doi.org/10.1002/j.1556-6676.1997.tb02342.x

Sharkin, B. S. (2012). *Being a college counselor on today's campus: Roles, contributions & special challenges.* Routledge.

Smith, L., Baluch, S., Bernabei, S., Robohm, J., & Sheehy, J. (2003). Applying a social justice framework to college counseling center practice. *Journal of College Counseling, 6*(1), 3–13. https://doi.org/10.1002/j.2161-1882.2003.tb00222.x

Substance Abuse and Mental Health Administration (SAMHSA). (2019). *SAMHSA strategic prevention framework guide.* https://www.samhsa.gov/sites/default/files/20190620-samhsa-strategic-prevention-framework-guide.pdf

Sue, D. W. (2015). Therapeutic harm and cultural oppression. *Counseling Psychologist, 43*(3), 359–369. https://doi.org/10.1177/0011000014565713

White, S., Park, Y. S., Israel, T., & Cordero, E. D. (2009). Longitudinal evaluation of peer health education on a college campus: Impact on health behaviors. *Journal of American College Health, 57*, 497–505. https://doi.org/10.3200/JACH.57.5.497-506

Jocelyn Novella, Ph.D., LPC, (she/her/hers) is an assistant professor of Counselor Education at Fairfield University and a Licensed Professional Counselor in the state of CT. She received her Ph.D. at Oregon State University and worked at a college counseling center in the northeast for 24 years, most recently as Director of Counseling. She worked within a Wellness Center and led efforts in establishing a Body Image Task Force on campus. Her research interests include efficacy of telemental health, interprofessional education in behavioral health, and specialized issues with emerging adults.

Krista Dobson, M.A., LPC, (she/her/hers) is a LPC whose passion is empowering students to reach their highest potential. She earned her Master's degree in Clinical Mental Health Counseling at Fairfield University. Krista's experiences have included clinical counseling in universities, colleges and community outpatient mental health agencies. Her approach is intentional, collaborative and compassionate informed by interpersonal, psychodynamic and intersectional perspectives. Professional interests include identity exploration and development and how power, privilege and oppressive systems influence mental health. Krista is currently a counselor at Yale University supporting graduate and technical interns in the Schools of Art, Architecture, and Drama.

Marriage, Couple, and Family Counseling

21

Dontè R. Corey, Katrina Y. Billingsley, Charmaine L. Conner, Deanna Burgess, and Lynn Bohecker

We cultivate love when we allow our most vulnerable and powerful selves to be deeply seen and known.

Brene Brown

Abstract

This chapter provides counselor educators with the guidance needed to create a marriage, couple, and family counseling (MCF) specialized practice within their counselor training program. Included in this chapter is an overview of the CACREP MCF counseling specialized practice standards, recommendations for developing a specialized practice area using a social justice and advocacy framework within the program.

D. R. Corey
True Living Counseling Services PLLC, Burlington, NC, USA
e-mail: drcorey08@gmail.com

K. Y. Billingsley
Albany State University, Albany, GA, USA

C. L. Conner
Roosevelt University, Chicago, IL, USA
e-mail: cconner@roosevelt.edu

D. Burgess
DePaul University, Chicago, IL, USA
e-mail: dburges4@depaul.edu

L. Bohecker (✉)
Liberty University, Lynchburg, VA, USA
e-mail: lrbohecker@liberty.edu

D. M. Stalnaker-Shofner and T. N. Sapp (eds.), *A Comprehensive Guide for Counselor Education*, Springer Texts in Education, https://doi.org/10.1007/978-3-031-68358-9_21

Learning Objectives After reading this chapter, you will be able to:

1. Outline the history of MCF counseling in relation to its inclusion as a counseling specialized practice area.
2. Apply the 2024 CACREP Standards specific to MCF counseling curriculum and program development, as well as relevant MCF training requirements.
3. Conceptualize curriculum and program development emphasizing diversity, inclusion and other multicultural considerations using a social justice and advocacy framework.
4. Identify the common presenting issues counselors may encounter in client seeking MCF counseling services.

21.1 Statement of Reflexivity

The first and second authors of this chapter are counselor educators and licensed professional counselors who enjoy working with CITs. Drs. Corey and Billingsley believe that counseling is important at all developmental stages. They believe that individuals interact and live in communities with others who can influence their values, beliefs, and behaviors. The influences of family, community, and societal systems on an individual can drastically impact their lives in both positive and negative ways. People from historically marginalized communities also experience the additional impact of intergenerational trauma. The intensifying effect of the multiple and intersecting identities that comprise each individual is a compounding network of interacting forces.

Drs. Corey and Billingsley both believe that their goal as counseling professionals is to understand *every* client as they are *uniquely* made. They strive to explore and identify systemic factors and highlight these factors for the client. Their teaching praxis involves facilitating CITs' exploration of their lived experiences and the impact of experienced or inherited trauma through assignments and supportive feedback. This is done to ensure that CITs understand themselves before working with couples, children, and family systems. As CITs may be reluctant to engage in CFT counseling due to the complexity of their counselor identity development, Drs. Corey and Billingsley believe that as counselor educators, it is important to provide a safe zone for CITs to begin this requisite personal exploration to become competent professional counselors. The researching of content and the writing of this chapter is shaped by all that they understand about culture, theory, relationships, learner engagement and best practices.

The third and fourth authors have extensive experience working with children and adolescents. The authors hold doctoral degrees in counselor education and practice in the Midwest region of the United States. Both work as counselor educators and engage in private practice work, with one author owning their practice. Both authors are independently licensed, and one is a national certified counselor. Their combined experience includes providing mental health services to clients with diverse backgrounds presenting in a variety of treatment settings (e.g. residential, private practice, nonprofit agencies). Both seek to develop a strong therapeutic relationship by providing genuineness, unconditional positive regard, and empathy.

Drs. Conner and Burgess both operate from an anti-racist/anti-oppressive lens and are LGBTQIA+ affirming. Their substantial clinical experience includes providing trauma-informed care as they provide services to clients with varying treatment issues such as relational and attachment challenges, self-esteem, grief, depression, anxiety, anger management, and substance use disorders. They believe that relationships can be a catalyst for healing. In addition to our professional experiences and thoughts on relationships, they include this context for how cultural, social, and historical structures and influences shape the needs of clients and communities.

The fifth author holds a doctoral degree in counselor education and supervision and teaches in both master's and doctoral level CACREP accredited programs. Dr. Bohecker is a licensed marriage and family therapist and is also the CEO of a professional counseling agency. She is the senior editor of a peer-reviewed journal and enjoys teaching, research, and scholarship.

21.2 Introduction

In a CACREP accredited counseling program, all CITs are to choose at least one of the specialized practice areas in which to focus and complete the program. The specialized practice area options are addiction counseling, clinical mental health counseling, clinical rehabilitation counseling, college counseling and student affairs, rehabilitation counseling, school counseling, or MCF counseling. Program and curricular developers need to evaluate which specialized practice areas to offer CITs. Each specialized practice area is individually reviewed to determine if CACREP accreditation standards are met.

A counseling program that includes the MCF specialized practice area provides a unique perspective to the foundational counselor professional identity, specifically, the focus on systems and relationships. This perspective situates the MCF specialized practice area as ideal to integrate social justice and advocacy as integral to the contextual factors in which every individual lives. The knowledge and skills requirements identified by CACREP cover a wide range of issues found in relationships and families. Social justice perspectives and advocacy can be integrated seamlessly into an already systemic view of individuals, couples, and families.

21.3 History of Marriage, Couple, and Family Counseling

The movement from working with individuals in psychotherapy or counseling to a more systemic view began in the early twentieth century. This change created new terms and language in clinical work which formed the foundation of the marriage and family therapy movement (Bitter & Carlson, 2017). It is important to note that during this time, family therapy was established for White Anglo-Saxon heterosexual couples. Divorce was not an option because the dominant religion at that time was Christianity, and divorce was not allowed. BIPOC and lesbian, gay, bisexual or transgender (LGBTQQIP2SA) individuals were not recognized in the early formation of family therapy. Biracial marriages were legalized in 1967 and only in 2015 did gay marriages become legal in the U.S. (Head, 2021; Liptak, 2015).

Additional changes to marriage and family therapy evolved during the 1970s, then a third evolutionary period was in the late 1980s influenced by postmodern and social constructivism. The position of the clinician transitioned from the all-knowing expert to viewing the client as the expert in their own lives.

Knowing the purpose of MCF while understanding the impact on the family system is the model used to create a curriculum where all persons and varied relationship types are acknowledged, protected and honored. Social justice and cultural competence are at the epicenter of what is needed to ensure that counseling training programs adequately prepare CITs for working with a variety of clients. Counselors must be prepared to understand, confront and guide clients who present differently or the same in a professional and ethical manner. It is important that biases are acknowledged prior to working with any client and, more specifically, with diverse clients.

MCF counseling should be expansive in the definition of who is being served. All types of romantic and affectional relationships, families, and marriages should be considered and interwoven into the counseling training program. When speaking to diversity in working with families and couples, this includes but is not limited to those who are ethnically and culturally diverse, divorced families, step or blended families, same-sex couples and families, transgender couples, single parent families, childfree families, dual career families, together but living separately families, aging families, multigenerational families, military families, new couples, the single-unattached, young adult, new couples, families with young children, families with school-age children or adolescents, empty nesters, families in retirement and later in life and interracial families.

As with most specialized practice areas within the field of counseling, MCF has a division of the broader counseling organization that is dedicated to educating and celebrating the specialization. Counselor educators must encourage CITs to become familiar with their state, national and international professional organizations (International Association for Marriage and Family Counselors [IAMFC], 2024). CITs need to also know how they can benefit from becoming members of these organizations. CITs should also become very familiar with their state licensure boards as well as NBCC. The NBCC provides professional learning, research and social advocacy opportunities for its members. It also offers a listing of approved supervisors, professional liability insurance and networking opportunities. The purpose of this organization is to represent marriage and family therapists as they serve their communities by offering effective and evidenced-based practices to marriages, couples and families.

21.4 CACREP Accreditation

When designing a MCF specialized practice area that aligns with the 2024 CACREP Standards, it will be important to keep in mind the areas specific to couples and marriage, children and adolescents, and the family system overall while maintaining a keen focus on the influence of cultural factors and legal and ethical requirements (ACA, 2014; CACREP, 2024). Counselor educators developing the MCF specialized practice area coursework are reminded that CITs in the MCF specialized practice are expected to demonstrate the knowledge and skills necessary to address a wide range of issues in this specialized practice area. Throughout the development of a MCF specialized practice area, course designers must document where and in what manner each of the MCF specific CACREP standards is covered in the curriculum. Table 21.1 contains the 2024 CACREP Standards for the MCF specialized practice area. While the specialized practice area standards are identified separately, they may be addressed in either the foundational core coursework or courses designed for the MCF specialized practice area.

In addition to the CACREP program accreditation standards, counselor educators can integrate social justice and advocacy components as a golden thread woven throughout each course. Culturally sustaining practices can be integrated

Table 21.1 Marriage, couple, and family counseling 2024 CACREP standards (Section 5.F.)

Standards	
5.F.1.	Sociology of the family, family phenomenology, and family of origin theories
5.F.2.	Aging and intergenerational influences and related family concerns
5.F.3.	Impact of interpersonal violence on marriages, couples, and families
5.F4.	Interactions of career, life, and gender roles in marriages, couples, and families
5.F.5.	Impact of unemployment, under-employment, and changes in socioeconomic standing on marriages, couples, and families
5.F.6.	The impact of migration on family functioning
5.F.7.	Theories and models of marriage, couple, and family counseling
5.F.8.	Principles and models of assessment and case conceptualization from a systems perspective
5.F.9.	Family assessments, including genograms and family mapping
5.F.10.	Techniques and interventions of marriage, couple, and family counseling
5.F.11.	Conceptualizing and implementing treatment, planning, and intervention strategies in marriage, couple, and family counseling
5.F.12.	Service delivery modalities and networks within the continuum of care, such as primary care, outpatient, partial treatment, inpatient, integrated behavioral healthcare, and aftercare
5.F.13.	Strategies for interfacing with the legal system relevant to marriage, couple, and family counseling
5.F.14.	Third-party reimbursement and other practice and management issues in marriage, couple, and family counseling

across service delivery modalities. One example is using the MSJCC model (Ratts et al., 2016) and integrating social and cultural movements of the current societal milieu.

21.5 Marriage, Couple, and Family Diversity Considerations

In 2020, COVID-19 created an unprecedented public health crisis (Kumar, 2020). Working adults stayed at home limited to electronic communications. Children stayed home from school and participated in remote learning. In addition to impacting the world, moving work and school from outside to inside the home impacted entire family systems. Some families (e.g. low SES and racially marginalized) faced a digital divide and did not have adequate resources to properly engage in work or school and many other activities. Along with COVID-19, another global pandemic, racism, was accentuated in June 2020 (Elias et al., 2021). The Black Lives Matter protests spread throughout the U.S. and across the world after the murders of Breonna Taylor, Ahmaud Arbery, and George Floyd. As a result, many Black people experienced the emotional trauma associated with overcoming racism, discrimination, and marginalization. These two pandemics as well as discrimination against youth with disabilities, various gender identities, religious backgrounds, ethnicities, immigration status, etc., are often minimized and are not highlighted as factors contributing to the mental health of families (Haight et al., 2016). Counselor educators developing an MCF specialized practice area are advised to integrate advanced multicultural and social justice training for counseling couples, children, and families.

Advanced diversity training involves understanding the difference between culture, development, and pathology. Clients who identify with traditional marginalized populations are diagnosed with mental health disorders and arrested at higher rates than those who are not (Haight et al., 2016; U.S. Department of Education, 2018). These actions lead to disparities in mental health treatment for those who are subjected to abuse of privilege, power, and oppression. Counselor educators can support CITs as they develop the skill to be critically conscious regarding their conceptualization of mental health concerns, especially within a cultural lens.

Counselor educators need to incorporate into the MCF training program how to work with historically marginalized populations. Some MCF programs only provide diversity and multicultural training in one counseling course (Ratts et al., 2016). However, multicultural, and social justice training and advocacy can also be infused into every course. Counselor educators can begin by incorporating textbooks and published works from BIPOC individuals. Intentionally reviewing all the curricular materials with an eye on centering authors and scholars whose voices are underrepresented will establish the expectations as norms within your MCF program. Diversity needs to be addressed in diagnosis and treatment planning, assessments, and research counseling courses.

21.5.1 Legal and Ethical Considerations Specific to Children and Couples

Legal and ethical matters impact counseling practices across all specialty areas but are particularly important to consider when providing services for children and couples. There are a number of legal and ethical considerations that are unique to child and adolescent counseling and also when working with couples. Counselor educators must be mindful of how to integrate these topics into coursework in the MCF specialized practice area.

Counselor educators rely on several ethical and legal principles when preparing CITs to serve children and couples. CITs must first understand legal guidelines concerning children and adolescents, which include state and federal laws that govern counseling practice. The Freedom of Information Act and privileged communication are two laws that inform counseling practice across all settings and regulate the privacy of client information shared in counseling settings. Education and health care laws and regulations that direct child welfare include The Family Education Rights and Privacy Act of 1974 (FERPA), The Health Insurance Portability and Accountability Act (HIPAA), the Americans with Disabilities Act (ADA), Individuals with Disabilities Education Act (IDEA) and Section 504 of the Rehabilitation Act. Although some of these laws do not directly apply to counselors, it is important for counselors providing clinical services to children and adolescents to understand the legal standards and parameters in relation to counseling activities.

Counseling children and adolescents presents nuanced challenges given that they are not yet at an age where they are granted complete power over their choices and are identified as a protected class of citizens. The ACA (2014) Code of Ethics requires professional counselors to be responsible to establish collaborative relationships with parents and guardians inform parents and guardians of the confidential nature of counseling children and simultaneously maintaining a sensitivity to the diverse cultural values and beliefs of families (ACA, 2014, B.5.b.). Each state has differing laws related to counseling children and MCF coursework can integrate activities for CITs to look into their respective state to understand the laws they will be working under when counseling children and families.

Couples counseling is another area that presents unique challenges in counseling. The counseling ethical codes require the counselor to determine who is the "client". This can be an individual who brings in a partner or the couple. Each of these options brings different expectations and limitations of confidentiality. It is important to identify that without this delineation, the couple or family is considered to be the client (ACA, 2014, B.4.b.). This singular aspect can become problematic when one person shares a secret with the counselor. Counselor educators are advised to integrate this specific teaching in the MCF program.

CITs are often provided with content related to these legal and ethical concerns, yet more opportunities to share their understanding of the implications and consequences are needed. Counselor educators might begin incorporating additional activities into their teaching methods. Professors could contact their state licensing board and coordinate an opportunity for the board to speak with their CITs about recent ethical violations with minors. Introducing case studies that illuminate ethical dilemmas is an additional approach in expanding CITs' understanding of legal and ethical matters. CITs can be directed to utilize ethics codes in counseling as a resource guide, such as the ACA's code of ethics, and apply decision-making steps to resolve legal and ethical scenarios. Another example might include attending an ethical board review as a class or tuning in virtually, if possible. In addition, a mock ethical board review may be held in class with CITs facilitating the process. Legal and ethical issues can also be reinforced in clinical courses such as practicum and internship and may even benefit from holding a mock review board when ethical violations occur. Each of the listed exercises allows CITs to familiarize themselves with governing codes as well as process complexities and ambiguities that commonly emerge when counseling couples, children, and adolescents.

Counselors must also develop skills to understand and apply ethical standards that direct decision-making. Counseling professionals and CITs are guided by ethical standards outlined by counseling organizations, including but not limited to the ACA, American School Counseling Association (ASCA), and AMHCA. Common ethical dilemmas that may present when working with adolescent populations involve informed consent, boundaries, and autonomy. Given age regulations for consent and assent of services, counselor educators must work to establish awareness of the ability for consent, exceptions to consent, and reporting issues. Other important topics involve sharing information to parents and caregivers and navigating subpoenas of clinical documentation. Furthermore, counselors must be mindful to establish appropriate boundaries and avoid dual relationships with youth, as well as work to prioritize practices that allow autonomy, particularly for adolescent populations. In addition to increasing awareness of legal and ethical principles, CITs would benefit from learning decision-making models, which outline steps for ethical and legal decision-making processes (Corey et al., 2024; Remley & Herlihy, 2024; Sileo & Kopala, 1993; Stone, 2013).

Mandated reporting is a final legal and ethical matter that child and adolescent counselors must grasp. Some states require counselors to report suspected child abuse and/or neglect and the potential for a child client to harm themselves or someone else. This process may cause emotional distress for CITs, as they may fear damaging the therapeutic relationship (Smith-Addock & Tucker, 2017).

Failure to follow legal and ethical guidelines may result in grave consequences for the CIT, supervisor, and even the university program. Despite the daunting feelings that are typically associated with discussing laws and ethics, CITs benefit from being equipped with tools to navigate these situations. Integrating legal and ethical aspects related to children and adolescents is a key component in developing an MCF program.

21.6 Developing a Marriage, Couple, and Family Training Program and Track

When developing a program, keep in mind that CITs in the MCF specialized practice area will spend the first 36 credit hours learning the foundational and basic knowledge and skills needed for counseling (CACREP, 2024). The next 15 credit hours will move into the MCF specific topical areas such as advanced systemic theories, working with couples and children, assessment techniques specific to MCF, and connecting theory to practice within a range of delivery applications (CACREP, 2024). The remaining nine (9) credit hours will be focused on skill building through field study in practicum and internship courses. In addition to earning a master's degree, graduates of a CACREP accredited program are positioned to meet state educational licensure requirements to practice as a professional counselor. With a CACREP accredited MCF counseling program, graduates may additionally qualify to obtain a marriage and family therapy (MFT) license in some states, this may not be the case in other states. The program and CIT will need to determine eligibility based on your specific state licensure requirements.

In Table 21.2, we provide you with an example MCF program plan of study. Within this example, we identify courses that are commonly found in MCF programs across the nation. Foundational courses will include, but are not limited to diversity, family theories, ethical and legal issues, and family development across the lifespan. Additionally, some programs may have courses targeted toward special populations including working with children, adolescents and their families, career interventions, substance abuse, sexuality and sex therapy and gender issues in counseling. There are assessments and research courses as well as psychopharmacology and treatment and diagnosis.

While this is one example of an MCF program, counselor educators developing MCF programs are encouraged to develop their own unique conceptualization and curricular overview (CACREP, 2024). In addition to social and diversity courses, social justice and advocacy competencies can be systematically integrated into the syllabus created for each course throughout the program curriculum. As you are developing your program, there are specific aspects of MCF counselor training and development that we recommend that you include within your courses such as: learning about developing a therapeutic alliance with couples, children, and adolescents, common presenting concerns, and developmentally appropriate interventions and assessments. We explain these in greater detail throughout the chapter.

21.6.1 Common Presenting Issues

This chapter highlights developmental, attachment and trauma considerations that most commonly affect working with couples, children, and families. In addition to learning core tenets of each topic, it is critical that CITs recognize how each of these factors underlie common presenting concerns. The ability to accurately

Table 21.2 Example marriage, couple, and family counseling program (60 credit hours) program plan of study

Name of course	Credits
Introduction to Marriage and Family Counseling[a]	3
Ethical and Legal Issues in Counseling[a]	3
Human Growth and Development[a]	3
Social and Cultural Diversity in Counseling[a]	3
Counseling Techniques and the Helping Relationship[a]	3
Theories of Counseling[a]	3
Group Methods and Processes[a]	3
Research and Program Evaluation[a]	3
Assessment Techniques in Counseling[a]	3
Career Development and Counseling[a]	3
Psychopathology[a]	3
Theories of Family Systems[a]	3
Advanced Systemic Theories in MFC	3
Assessment, Diagnosis, and Treatment Planning in MFC	3
Advanced Couple and Marital Counseling	3
Counseling Children, Adolescents, and Their Families	3
Practice Delivery and Applications in MFC	3
Counseling Practicum	3
Counseling Internship I	3
Counseling Internship II	3

[a] Indicates courses that address the 2024 CACREP Foundational Counseling Curriculum content area (CACREP, 2024, Section 3)

identify the client's primary and secondary concerns within the early stages of counseling allows the CIT to quickly concentrate on appropriate interventions to alleviate distress. CITs who familiarize themselves with common presenting concerns are better equipped to develop goals, objectives, and interventions that address the client's core issues.

CITs must also develop skills to accurately identify and address mental health concerns that are present among specific populations. Young children, whose parents seek therapy, may be experiencing attachment issues within the child–parent relationship (Lin & Bratton, 2015). Middle-aged and older children may begin to show internalizing and externalizing behaviors (Ray, 2016). Furthermore, common concerns that prompt adolescents to engage in counseling include identity issues, interpersonal relationships, academic issues and developmental concerns (Smith-Addock & Tucker, 2017). Clients of all ages may work through traumatic events, including abuse and neglect (Haight et al., 2016), bullying, racism and discrimination (Jernigan & Daniel, 2011), as well as mental health diagnoses, including ADHD, ODD, anxiety and depression (Cokley et al., 2015).

Counselor educators can prepare CITs to address these issues by creating assignments that evaluate their comprehensive understanding from previous counseling courses. CITs could be assigned a research paper in which they investigate a common presenting therapeutic problem and are asked to develop a diagnosis and treatment plan for a potential client. Another activity is for counselor educators to present case scenarios and prompt CITs to develop case conceptualizations based on the information provided. CITs can explore affective, behavioral, and cognitive features associated with a client's presenting problem. Directing CITs to develop probing questions based on case scenarios can facilitate and promote awareness of common presenting concerns while also fostering core counseling skills. Furthermore, counselor educators might encourage CITs to attend professional development workshops geared toward topics common to couples and children reporting their findings to their peers.

21.6.1.1 Developing a Therapeutic Alliance with Couples, Children, and Adolescents

Therapeutic alliance is one of the greatest determinants of positive counseling outcomes in working with families (Rogers, 1957). People who feel seen, heard, and understood may be more willing to engage in the therapeutic process. However, counseling couples, children, and adolescents presents unique challenges to establishing a strong therapeutic alliance. For instance, when counseling couples, it is important to learn how to balance each partner equally. When counseling children the therapeutic relationship is with the client and also with their parents. Similarly, adolescents are generally more likely to express a lack of trust in perceived authority figures and confide in peers than adults when confronted with personal challenges (Smith-Addock & Tucker, 2017).

Furthermore, children and adolescents engaged in counseling services are more likely to be mandated participants in counseling or enlisted by parents or caregivers when compared to adult populations. Mandated participation presents additional obstacles to establishing a positive therapeutic alliance (Rogers, 1957). CITs in a MCF program are required to learn about both traditional and emerging counseling theories (ACA, 2014; CACREP, 2024) and are expected to have identified a guiding counseling theory that is often taught from the perspective of counseling individual adults. CITs who seek to work with couples and children will need additional training on theories specific to couples and children. For example, modifications have been made to traditional counseling theories (person-centered, Adlerian, CBT) to better serve couples and youth. MCF programs can incorporate theories to assist MCF CITs to develop therapeutic alliance with couples, children, and adolescents that differs from working with only individuals. Overall, it is critical that MCF CITs learn to effectively cultivate strong therapeutic relationships, particularly among couples, children, and adolescent populations.

21.6.1.2 Child and Adolescent Counseling

Children develop at a rapid pace, and given the uniqueness of each child, it can be difficult to discern when presenting characteristics outside of the parameters of healthy development. Developmental and maturation models have been generated as criteria to help educators, parents, health professionals, and counselors better characterize emotional, social, and behavioral attributes among children and adolescents. Understanding the theorized developmental stages and maturation processes of children and adolescents allows CITs to (1) discern the behaviors, cognitions, and emotions of children within the context of what is considered normal for their stage, (2) identify behavior that falls outside of what is considered developmentally normal or typical, and (3) explore best-practice treatment approaches according to one's cognitive, social and emotional abilities and realities.

CITs specializing in child and adolescent counseling could also benefit from understanding the basic principles of development (Ray, 2016) and the various types of developmental models (maturational, psychosocial, ego, cognitive, moral and emotional) and receiving training on how to communicate with parents about their client's developmental areas (Smith-Addock & Tucker, 2017). Explaining the connection between development and mental health can be a challenge for CITs; counselor educators can support CITs by fostering a learning environment conducive for practical application. There are five key takeaways when introducing developmental and maturation processes that occur across childhood and adolescence. It is important that CITs commit to memory general cognitions, social and emotional behaviors, and moral reasoning that align with developmental ages. It is also important that CITs understand how milestones for each of the listed models fit together to inform the full person based on a client's development age. MCF CITs should also be able to recognize when cognitions, moral reasoning, and social and emotional behaviors do not align with expectations for a given age. It is also imperative that CITs are able to describe various environmental and biological factors that influence child and adolescent development. In preparation for clinical practice, CITs should be able to conceptualize presenting concerns within the context of one's developmental level. Finally, counseling CITs should be able to identify appropriate goals, objectives and treatment approaches based on developmental stages.

The ultimate objective of introducing developmental and maturation content is for CITs to understand how developmental milestones can influence and inform mental health considerations. Counselor educators can teach child development to CITs in various ways. One method of teaching child development might include a lecture format, which may involve teaching the content across the academic semester or a two-to-three-week time span. Child development could also be taught from an experiential perspective. For example, one of the authors provided CITs with readings on child development prior to the class meeting. During the scheduled class, CITs guessed the ages of the child based on descriptors provided by the professor. The professor utilized handouts from Ray and Jayne (2016) to create descriptions of children of different ages and placed them on a PowerPoint slide for the class activity. Their understanding of child development was also strengthened through a child interview in which they conceptualized their interviewee's developmental stage. As a result, CITs reported deepening their understanding of child development and what to expect when working with children. A combination of course readings, interactive class activities, and practical application assignments may be helpful in expanding CITs' understanding of child development. A range of practical application exercises, including role-play, fishbowl, case study, and self-exploration activities.

Conceptualizing a client through a theoretical lens is an advanced counseling skill that can be strengthened through course assignments. CITs may be asked to record a mock session with a child and write a case presentation conceptualizing the child's presenting concerns. In an effort to help CITs become more comfortable working with parents, CITs can be asked to demonstrate a parent consultation. This is a process in which the CIT seeks to understand how the parent views the child and may even provide the parent with tools to use at home. Through this assignment, CITs will be able to demonstrate competence in their skills and ability to conceptualize through theory, additionally gaining confidence when interacting with parents. In the event that a child client is not available, counselor educators may ask CITs to conceptualize a client from a children's movie. Strengthening this skill will be imperative for working with child clients.

21.6.1.3 Attachment and Trauma

While attachment is often introduced as a component of the lifespan development course, it is also commonly linked to childhood and adolescent trauma. Distant or neglectful relational patterns and exposure to trauma in early life can significantly influence many facets of development. It is important that MCF CITs develop a firm understanding of interactive behaviors and early life experiences that influence long-term psychosocial and cognitive outcomes for working with families. Gaining knowledge of attachment and trauma processes can also facilitate case conceptualization and exploration of themes, identification of suitable treatment approaches, and development of appropriate goals for the treatment process. Furthermore, understanding early attachment and trauma allows MCF CIT to explore underlying factors that influence maladaptive behaviors that manifest in couples and families. Without this insight, novice counselors may have difficulty moving beyond surface-level conceptualizations to understand the developmental root cause of a client's presenting concerns.

According to SAMHSA (2020), approximately two-thirds of those surveyed have reported trauma before the age of 16. Children often face adverse childhood experiences (ACEs), including but not limited to abuse, neglect, parental mental illness, domestic violence, loss of a parent, etc. (Felitti et al., 1998). The effects of ACEs during childhood may result in altered brain chemistry (Perry, 2006; Shonkoff et al., 2012), insecure attachment (Herman & van der Kolk, 2020), and mental health disorders (Haight et al., 2016). The lasting impacts of ACEs experiences influence relationships, many of which manifest in couple and family functioning. The impact of trauma on an individual goes beyond a single event; systemic social and environmental factors also can contribute to re-victimizing the individual. Therefore, it is important for MCF CITs to engage in trauma-informed care as they prepare to work with children, couples, and families.

Attachment is commonly introduced using Bowlby's theory of attachment (Bowlby, 1969). Bowlby asserted that children are born with an innate need for attachment and that early attachment behaviors are determinants of lifelong social interactive styles. The research of Ainsworth (1973) built upon Bowlby's original work by proposing three major attachment styles that are developed based on one's early interactions with caregivers: secure attachment, ambivalent-insecure attachment, and avoidant-insecure attachment, with disorganized-insecure later being added as a fourth attachment style. In addition to recognizing the patterns and lasting effects of early attachment, it is crucial to increase CITs awareness of variables that promote attachment. Factors that influence attachment patterns are summarized as quality of caregiving and opportunities for attachment (Bowlby, 1958).

Counselor educators, at the programmatic level, can review curriculum development and infuse trauma content across counseling courses. CITs may be introduced to both relational and cognitive-behavioral trauma approaches in their counseling theories course. Efforts to infuse trauma in the curriculum can also be maintained by using the MSJCCs (Ratts et al., 2016) to discuss how privilege, power, and oppression influence clients' overall mental health with regard to trauma in a multicultural counseling course as well as a practicum and internship course. CITs could also demonstrate their understanding of trauma and the impact of traumatic events on their clients' lives through case presentations and assignments such as interviewing a trauma-informed therapist.

Trauma often manifests itself in a wide range of presentations. Furthermore, trauma can pose a particular threat to adolescents who are more prone to high-risk internalizing and externalizing behaviors or observable and concealed behaviors that signify psychological distress (Brown et al., 2020; Haller & Chassin, 2012). Therefore, it is imperative that CITs understand how trauma uniquely impacts development within adolescence, discern internalizing and externalizing behaviors that potentially signify trauma, and learn best practices for trauma-informed care. Trauma-informed care has often been a phrase used to describe how mental professionals work with clients who have experienced trauma. Trauma-informed care involves both organizational and clinical practices (Menschner & Maul, 2016) and involves the four Rs of working with clients whose lives have been impacted by trauma: realization about trauma and how it can affect people and groups, recognizing the signs of trauma, having a system that can respond to trauma, and resisting re-traumatization (SAMHSA, 2020).

The demands of teaching and preparing course curriculum are common barriers when preparing trauma-informed counselors. However, CITs can benefit from utilizing relational trauma-focused approaches as well as culturally responsive counseling practices. We are aware of the barriers counselor educators may face (course prep and curriculum development) when preparing to engage CITs in trauma-informed practices. Therefore, we provide recommendations in the next section. Given the complexity of trauma and treatment approaches to trauma, it is also important to stress that this topic should be an ongoing area of development for counselors throughout their training and professional careers. There are a number of entities that offer continuing education opportunities within the area of trauma among specialized groups, including children and adolescents, including ASCA, PESI, and Darkness To Light.

Counselor educators may use a range of methods to increase CIT knowledge of trauma and attachment styles. One method is to introduce fundamental principles of attachment through didactic instruction. It can also be beneficial to supplement class lectures with videos that demonstrate internalizing and externalizing patterns of behavior among children and adolescents. Other materials can focus on how attachment styles show up in couples. Visual representations of behavioral patterns can allow CITs to better discern trauma responses and attachment styles that may present within the clinical setting. Attachment can also be taught using self-reflective life analyses. Mayo (2001) introduced *life analysis* as a teaching exercise for exploring patterns of lifespan development and attachment. CITs who engaged in this activity were able to better understand theoretical content by describing tangible examples of interactive patterns within their own lives. Life analyses are completed by directing CITs to critically examine early-life relationships and interactive styles that were instrumental in shaping their relational development. CITs can begin by completing personal journals as well as interviews with parents, former teachers, friends, and other significant individuals in their lives and ultimately synthesize their findings into an anecdotal representation of their behavioral and attachment styles.

21.6.2 Developmentally Appropriate Interventions and Assessments

Knowing common presenting mental health concerns is important for counseling CITs. Identifying presenting concerns only provides a small aspect of the whole client. To generate systemic client conceptualizations and provide effective, lasting counseling intervention, CITs must also identify a holistic picture that includes biological, psychological, developmental, spiritual, and environmental factors that interact with the presenting concern. Developmentally appropriate assessments are critical for illuminating latent factors that might otherwise go undetected. Furthermore, incorporating appropriate counseling interventions significantly increases outcome effectiveness by allowing CITs to address underlying causes of presenting distress and provide clients with strategies for ongoing self-intervention (Gordon & Russo, 2009).

CITs must learn how to (1) identify the presenting problem, (2) determine the client's readiness for change, (3) conceptualize the case based on their theoretical orientation, (4) collaboratively develop client goals, and (5) determine interventions that align with identified goals. Furthermore, counselors must utilize assessments that allow them to adequately inform case conceptualizations and track client progress over time. Assessments must align with developmental levels as well as with the presenting concerns and identified goals. When used appropriately, assessments help CITs generate suitable interventions aimed at promoting positive therapeutic change.

Generating appropriate counseling interventions for children, adolescents, and families is a complex skill and one that takes practice for CITs to gain proficiency. The following interventions are developmentally appropriate for counseling children and adolescents: play therapy (Ray, 2011), activity therapy (Smith-Addock & Tucker, 2017), and interventions targeted to improve child–parent relationships (Lin & Bratton, 2015). Play therapy is an evidence-based intervention for all ages, particularly children between the ages of 3–10. Play therapy helps children learn self-control, problem-solving skills, emotional regulation, and limits for their behaviors (Landreth, 2012). Activity therapy, expressive arts and sand trays, appropriate for children 10 and up, help children express their emotions through experimental experiences. Child–parent relationship therapy (CPRT) and parent–child interaction therapy (PCIT) is used to strengthen the child–parent relationship for children as young as three. Exposure to such therapeutic modalities may nudge CITs to seek additional certifications beyond graduate school, and they will be prepared to work effectively with children and families.

One approach that can allow CITs to effectively identify and integrate interventions and assessments is by directing CITs to construct mock treatment plans based on case scenarios. The range of psychotherapy treatment planners can be a useful resource in guiding CITs through the treatment planning and intervention process. Therefore, counselor educators can develop case vignettes that highlight common presenting issues for couples, children, and adolescent clients. Counselor educators can direct CITs to develop a treatment plan, which summarizes overarching counseling goals, objectives for meeting each goal, and at least two potential counseling interventions for each of the identified objectives. It is critical that CITs also utilize developmentally and topic-relevant instruments when incorporating assessments into the counseling process. Therefore, CITs can be asked to examine several counseling instruments and provide critiques of appropriateness based on their holistic understanding of their clients.

21.7 Marriage, Couple, and Family Specific Field Placement

Practicum and fieldwork courses round out master-level courses in counseling, giving CITs real work experience and a chance to apply what they have learned to helping clients. The experiences that will increase competence in MCF CITs is working specifically with children, adolescents, couples, and families. Counselor educators who are developing fieldwork courses can help the CITs understand the roles and responsibilities related to faculty class supervision, site supervision, and clinical supervision. Site supervisors may or may not be clinical and it will be important to identify who will be providing administrative supervision, such as hiring, timekeeping, and paperwork requirements and who will be providing clinical supervision, such as evaluating skills, providing feedback, and reporting to the academic institution. The faculty supervisor will be responsible for the classroom experience, evaluating counseling skills, and facilitating group processing with CITs.

Even when working with individuals, MCF CITs can conceptualize the client from a systems theorctical perspective. MCF CITs may need to seek out diverse clients from themselves to increase their experiences in working with diverse populations. Faculty supervisors can assist CITs in this advocacy and conceptualizing their clients from a systems lens. MCF CITs will benefit from seeking clinical supervision from a licensed professional counselor supervisor who has training in MCF or from a licensed marriage and family therapist supervisor. Supervision is covered more thoroughly in Chap. 4 of the text, however, MCF CITs may need to advocate for themselves at their internship sites for seeing couples, children or adolescents with their parents in session, or engaging in family sessions.

21.8 Conclusion

In conclusion, when creating a MCF specialized practice area, it is important to utilize the most current CACREP accreditation standards as a guide. It is also important to integrate social justice and advocacy components and provide CITs with resources that will help inform how they work with diverse couples and families. Providing CITs with mentorship within the program of study will aid in how they approach the profession and will garner an appreciation for the profession and the clients they serve.

References

Ainsworth, M. D. S. (1973). The development of infant-mother attachment. In B. Cardwell & H. Ricciuti (Eds.), *Review of child development research* (pp. 1–94) University of Chicago Press. https://doi.org/10.1037/0003-066X.34.10.932

American Counseling Association. (2014). *2014 ACA code of ethics*. https://www.counseling.org/docs/default-source/default-document-library/ethics/2014-aca-code-of-ethics.pdf?sfvrsn=55ab73d0_1

Bitter, J. R., & Carlson, J. (2017). The history of marriage, family, and couples therapy. In J. Carlson & S. B. Dermer (Eds.), *The SAGE encyclopedia of marriage, family, and couples counseling* (pp. 1767–1787). Sage.

Bowlby, J. (1958). The nature of the child's tie to his mother. *International Journal of Psychoanalysis, 39*, 350–371. https://doi.org/10.4324/9780429475931-15/nature-child-tie-mother-1-john-bowlby

Bowlby, J. (1969). *Attachment. Attachment and loss: Vol. I11. Loss—Sadness and depression*. Basic Books.

Brown, J. A., Hattouni, E., & Russell, S. (2020). School-based mind–body interventions in the treatment of childhood trauma. In C. Maykel & M. A. Bray (Eds.), *Promoting mind–body health in schools: Interventions for mental health professionals* (pp. 373–386). American Psychological Association. https://doi.org/10.1037/0000157-025

Cokley, K., Cody, B., Smith, L., Beasley, S., Miller, I. S. K., Hurst, A., Awosogba, O., Stone, S., & Jackson, S. (2015, January). Bridge over troubled waters: Meeting the mental health needs of Black CITs. *Kappan Magazine, 96*(4), 40–45. https://doi.org/10.1177/0031721714561445

Corey, G., Corey, M. S., & Corey, C. (2024). *Issues and ethics in the helping professions* (11th ed.). Cengage.

Council for Accreditation of Counseling and Related Educational Programs. (2024). *2024 CACREP standards.* https://www.cacrep.org/wp-content/uploads/2024/04/2024-Standards-Combined-Version-4.11.2024.pdf

Elias, A., Ben, J., Mansouri, F., & Paradies, Y. (2021). Racism and nationalism during and beyond the COVID-19 pandemic. In *Race and ethnicity in pandemic times* (pp. 65–75). Routledge.

Felitti, V. J., Anda, R. F., Nordenberg, D., Williamson, D. F., Spitz, A. M., Edwards, V., Koss, M. P., & Marks, J. S. (1998). Relationship of childhood abuse and household dysfunction to many of the leading causes of death in adults. The Adverse Childhood Experiences (ACE) Study. *American Journal of Preventive Medicine, 14*(4), 245–258. https://doi.org/10.1016/s0749-3797(98)00017-8

Gordon, M., & Russo, K. (2009). Children's views matter too! A pilot project assessing children's and adolescents' experiences of clinical psychology services. *Child Care in Practice, 15*(1), 39–48. https://doi.org/10.1080/13575270802504396

Haight, W., Kayama, M., & Gibson, P. A. (2016). Out-of-school suspensions of Black youths: Culture, ability, disability, gender, and perspective. *Social Work, 61*(3), 235–243. https://doi.org/10.1093/sw/sww021

Haller, M., & Chassin, L. (2012). A test of adolescent internalizing and externalizing symptoms as prospective predictors of type of trauma exposure and posttraumatic stress disorder. *Journal of Traumatic Stress, 25*(6), 691–699. https://doi.org/10.1002/jts.21751

Head, T. (2021, August 31). *Interracial marriage laws history and timeline.* https://www.thoughtco.com/interracial-marriage-laws-721611

Herman, J. L., & van der Kolk, B. A. (2020). *Treating complex traumatic stress disorders in adults: Scientific foundations and therapeutic models.* Guilford Publications.

International Association for Marriage and Family Counselors. (2024). https://www.IAMFConline.org

Jernigan, M. M., & Daniel, J. H. (2011). Racial trauma in the lives of Black children and adolescents: Challenges and clinical implications. *Journal of Child & Adolescent Trauma, 4*(2), 123–141. https://doi.org/10.1080/19361521.2011.574678

Kumar, A. (2020). COVID-19 and domestic violence: A possible public health crisis. *Journal of Health Management, 22*(2), 192–196. https://doi.org/10.1177/0972063420932765

Landreth, G. (2012). *Play therapy: The art of the relationship.* Routledge.

Lin, Y., & Bratton, S. C. (2015). A meta-analytic review of child-centered play therapy approaches. *Journal of Counseling & Development, 93*, 45–58. https://doi.org/10.1002/j.1556-6676.2015.00180.x

Liptak, A. (2015, June 27). *Supreme court ruling makes same-sex marriage a right nationwide.* https://www.nytimes.com/2015/06/27/us/supreme-court-same-sex-marriage.html

Mayo, J. A. (2001). Life analysis: Using life-story narratives in teaching life-span developmental psychology. *Journal of Constructivist Psychology, 14*(1), 25–41. https://doi.org/10.1080/10720530125850

Menschner, C., & Maul, A. (2016). *Key ingredients for successful trauma-informed care implementation.* Center for Health Care Strategies, Incorporated.

Perry, B. D. (2006). Applying principles of neurodevelopment to clinical work with maltreated and traumatized children: The neurosequential model of therapeutics. In N. B. Webb (Ed.), *Working with traumatized youth in child welfare* (pp. 27–52). The Guilford Press.

Ratts, M. J., Singh, A. A., Nassar-McMillan, S., Butler, S. K., & McCullough, J. R. (2016). Multicultural and social justice counseling competencies: Guidelines for the counseling profession. *Journal of Multicultural Counseling and Development, 44*(1), 28–48. https://doi.org/10.1002/jmcd.12035

Ray, D. (2011). *Advanced play therapy: Essential conditions, knowledge, and skills for child practice*. Routledge.
Ray, D. (2016). *A therapist's guide to child development: The extraordinarily normal years*. Routledge.
Ray, D. C., & Jayne, K. M. (2016). Humanistic psychotherapy with children. In D. J. Cain, K. Keenan, & S. Rubin (Eds.), *Humanistic psychotherapies: Handbook of research and practice* (2nd ed., pp. 387–417). American Psychological Association. https://doi.org/10.1037/14775-013
Remley, T., & Herlihy, B. (2024). *Ethical, legal, and professional issues in counseling* (7th ed.). Pearson.
Rogers, C. R. (1957). The necessary and sufficient conditions of therapeutic personality change. *Journal of Consulting Psychology, 21*, 95–103. https://doi.org/10.1037/h0045357
Shonkoff, J. P., Garner, A. S., Committee on Psychosocial Aspects of Child and Family Health, Committee on Early Childhood, Adoption, and Dependent Care, and Section on Developmental and Behavioral Pediatrics, Siegel, B. S., Dobbins, M. I., Earls, M. F., Garner, A. S., McGuinn, L., Pascoe, J., & Wood, D. L. (2012). The lifelong effects of early childhood adversity and toxic stress. *Pediatrics, 129*(1), e232–e246. https://doi.org/10.1542/peds.2011-2663
Sileo, F., & Kopala, M. (1993). An A-B-C-D-E worksheet for promoting beneficence when considering ethical issues. *Counseling & Values, 37*(2), 89–95. https://doi.org/10.1002/j.2161-007X.1993.tb00800.x
Smith-Addock, S., & Tucker, C. (2017). *Counseling children and adolescents* (1st ed.). Sage.
Stone, C. (2013). *School counseling principles: Ethics and law* (3rd ed.). American School Counselor Association.
Substance Abuse and Mental Health Services Administration. (2020). *Understanding child trauma*. https://www.samhsa.gov/child-trauma/understanding-child-trauma
U.S. Department of Education. (2018). *2015–2016 civil rights data collection (CRDC). Public use data file user's manual*. https://www.aclu.org/report/cops-and-no-counselors

Dontè R. Corey, Ph.D., LCMHCS, NCC (she/her/hers) is a practitioner in the fields of mental health and education. Since 2015 she has taught a variety of courses within clinical mental health counseling programs in the United States and Canada. She currently manages a private mental health practice that she opened in 2010. In her practice, she provides counseling to adults, children and families. She also provides licensure supervision. Dr. Corey has diverse research interests including trauma and racial issues.

Katrina Y. Billingsley, Ph.D., LPC, NCC, (she/her/hers) is a National Certified Counselor (NCC), a licensed professional counselor and counselor educator. She currently serves as a high school counselor in a public school in rural Georgia where she has worked for three years. Prior to taking on this role, Dr. Billingsley's professional career was primarily in higher education focusing on program management and student development work. Her research focus is on anti-racist, anti-oppressive research centered around Black and Brown people.

Charmaine L. Conner, Ph.D., LPC, NCC, CCPT-S, CPRT-S (she/her/hers) is the Department Chair and Assistant Professor at Roosevelt University in the Counseling and Human Services Program. She has been a counselor educator for 5 years, and in professional practice as a licensed counselor for more than 10 years. Her clinical experience includes providing individual and group counseling to children and adolescents who have presented with treatment concerns such as depression, anxiety, trauma, and academic issues.

Deanna Burgess, Ph.D., LCPC (she/her/hers) is an Assistant Professor in the Counseling and Special Education Department of the College of Education at DePaul University. Her research interests include exploring social justice integration considerations within school settings, and investigating developmental trajectories for youth and practitioners engaged in social justice education and advocacy. Dr. Burgess supports social justice programming and training efforts in collaboration with school districts in Pennsylvania, and her expertise includes providing equity training grounded in critical race pedagogy.

Lynn Bohecker, Ph.D., LMFT (she/her/hers) is a licensed marriage and family therapist, an AAMFT Approved Supervisor, and has taught counselor education in academic institutions for the past 20 years. She is a full professor in the Department of Counselor Education and Family Studies at Liberty University and the Senior Editor of the Journal of Faith Integration in Counseling. Dr. Bohecker is also the Chief Executive Officer of The Counseling Center at Tree City and has provided professional presentations at state, regional, national, and international events. She has over 50 publications in peer-reviewed journals, book chapters, and textbooks.

School Counseling

22

Syntia Santos Dietz, Katrina Y. Billingsley, and Taqueena S. Quintana

Every child deserves a champion—an adult who will never give up on them, who understands the power of connection and insists that they become the best that they can possibly be.

Rita Pierson

Abstract

Supporting the mental health and wellbeing of all our children and adolescents is a priority in our profession. Prevention, education, support, early intervention, and advocacy are fundamental in these critical years, and school counselors are positioned to walk alongside them in their journey. This chapter will focus on understanding the relevance of the field of school counseling, the challenges school counselors face, and identifying some useful resources and strategies to navigate a career in the field. School counseling training will also be addressed, especially in relation to creating specialty programs that are centered on social justice and advocacy practices and are also aligned with the current standards issued by the CACREP.

S. S. Dietz (✉) · T. S. Quintana
Antioch University, Yellow Springs, OH, USA
e-mail: sdietz@antioch.edu

T. S. Quintana
e-mail: tquintana@antioch.edu

K. Y. Billingsley
Albany State University, Fitzgerald, GA, USA

D. M. Stalnaker-Shofner and T. N. Sapp (eds.), *A Comprehensive Guide for Counselor Education*, Springer Texts in Education, https://doi.org/10.1007/978-3-031-68358-9_22

Learning Objectives After reading this chapter, you will be able to:

1. Distinguish the professional identity and role of school counselors as a distinct specialized practice area of counseling.
2. Influence the preparation of new school counselors through the development of relevant curriculum rooted in the 2024 CACREP Standards as well as extant literature regarding best practices in their education and training.
3. Develop rigorous education curriculum and training protocols that are grounded in a social justice and advocacy framework.
4. Identify the potential pitfalls and challenges school counselors may face with respect to systemic and administrative demands and constraints.

22.1 Statement of Reflexivity

We bring ourselves to this chapter as doctoral-level licensed school counselors, National Certified Counselors, and counselor educators, with various experiences in the field as counselors, educators, and administrators, both nationally and internationally. More importantly, we share a passion and commitment for social justice, anti-racism, and advocacy practices that we trust is evident throughout this chapter. We were all trained at the graduate level in the United States, and we are all members of historically marginalized communities. These cultural lenses impact our worldview and inform our work. They can also be the reason for potential bias and particular perspective, especially as referring to social justice and advocacy.

22.2 Introduction

The ACA, through its 20/20: A Vision for the Future of Counseling task force, stated that counseling "involves professional relationships designed to assist individuals, families, and groups toward mental health, wellness, educational, and career goals" (Kaplan et al., 2014, p. 368). Kaplan et al. (2014) further expounds upon this definition, stating that school counseling is

> a professional relationship that empowers diverse individuals, families, and groups to accomplish mental health, wellness, education, and career goals. Using counseling theories and techniques to accomplish these goals by fostering educational and social equity, access, and success. The professional school counselor serves as a leader and as an assertive advocate for students, consultant to families and educators, and team member to teachers, administrators and other school personnel to help each student succeed. (p. 368)

School Counseling is considered a specialized practice area within the counseling profession that focuses on supporting children and adolescents through their PK-12 education. CACREP includes in its 2024 standards a section dedicated specifically to school counseling as a specialty area (CACREP, 2024) denoting the relevance of school counselors in promoting the academic, career, and personal/social development of all CITs and the need for quality training programs in the area. They also highlight the requirement of utilizing evidence-based and culturally sustaining interventions in school counseling programs. This chapter will inform new counselor educators on what is needed to create a comprehensive school counseling program that will benefit CITs. It is important to formulate a program that is inclusive and meets the needs of all CITs. It is also important to create a comprehensive program that prepares CITs to execute what is needed in schools. To that end, it is imperative to examine the American School Counseling Association (ASCA) national standards for school counseling programs and suggested mindsets and behaviors for CIT success created around the three primary domains of the profession: academic, career, and social/emotional development (Erford, 2019).

22.3 History of School Counseling

The history of school counseling dates back to the 1900s when vocational guidance began and counselors helped instruct students in secondary education programs on how to find jobs (Gysbers, 2010). Gysbers (2010) listed the progression of the history of school counseling noting the following events: In the 1920s, there was a shift from vocational guidance to counseling for personal adjustment; the 1940s and 1950s saw an increase in school counseling training and an increase in the number of school counseling positions legislated by the federal government; in 1952, the ASCA was formed; in the 1960s, school counseling was launched in elementary schools; the formation of school counseling programs came into fruition during the 1960s and 1970s; in the 1980s and 1990s, states began adopting models for school counseling programs; in 2001, by federal legislation, there was a switch from guidance counseling to school counseling; and ASCA released its National School Counseling Program model for the first time in 2003, where it became the standard nationwide. There has been an adoption of the ASCA model by many states since then and there have been four editions with the last update in 2019 of the model. The evolution of school counseling has grown from a position to a service and to a program. School counseling programs are now found at every level to include elementary, middle and high school. Guidance counselors versus school counselors continue to perplex many today. Guidance counselors were deemed reactive, worked in isolation and served a limited number of students. School counselors, on the other hand, work with all students and are considered school leaders who develop, manage, and evaluate comprehensive school counseling programs (Gysbers, 2010). School personnel and even school counselors still refer to themselves and others as guidance counselors. As stated above, the transition from guidance to school has been an ongoing battle for quite some time. The focus on guidance is slowly falling away. The term change was to embody the expansion of the duties and responsibilities that are needed by school counselors.

The education system in the United States offers students services that include school counseling programs. Unfortunately, school counselors are not always included as a part of the leadership team and therefore their voices and expertise are often overlooked in the decision-making process. Regardless of the legislation that has been passed and the models created, school counselors and programs vary from district to district and school to school. Actions toward advocacy for the profession and professional identity are of high priority to combat role ambiguity and confusion, and clearly defined roles and responsibilities in the profession (Havlik et al., 2018). According to the U.S. Bureau of Labor Statistics (2024), employment for school counselors is projected to grow 5% between 2022 and 2032, with approximately 26,600 job openings each year, faster than the average growth rate for any other occupation. Thus, the need and demand of school counselor training programs is undeniable.

Counselor educators have the great responsibility to train, supervise, and walk alongside the future generations of counselors that will be entering the field and, in this case, be entrusted with the wellbeing and development of children and adolescents. As we choose to create or evaluate school counseling training programs, it is indispensable to reflect on the rationale behind it, the impact that it may have on those who we served, and the requirements that should be fulfilled in the training. As we contemplate the idea of creating a new program or adding to existing specialized practice area offerings, planning and reflection should accompany the process, especially as we consider offering programs that respond to the current demands of the field and society.

22.4 School Counseling Program Accreditation

School counseling training programs have varied throughout the United States in response to the need, rules, and regulations in each state, accreditation status of the program, and the requirements for state credentials needed to practice. For example, some states, such as Texas, require applicants to have a degree in education prior to pursuing a career in school counseling, which also speaks of the divided identity that school counselors must navigate between being counselors and educators. It is relevant to mention that some institutions have decided not to pursue accreditation and therefore have different requirements that align more with their state mandates for licensure.

School counseling as a profession has been influenced by societal changes, professional organizations, and professional leaders (Betters-Bubon et al., 2021). School counseling has responded to societal and educational priorities through a variety of efforts that most recently and notably include a focus on social justice, advocacy, and antiracist school counseling practice (Betters-Bubon et al., 2021; Song et al., 2020). Professional organizations such as the International School Counselor Association (ISCA), the American School Counseling Association (ASCA), the ACA, and ACES have guided the practice of the profession and influence policy at the national and international levels (Betters-Bubon et al., 2021). Accreditation bodies greatly influence the policy and preparation of future school counselors as well. CACREP is the main accrediting body for counseling master's and doctoral programs across specialty areas, including school counseling, in the United States. The Council for the Accreditation of Educator Preparation (CAEP) adds to the accreditation standards from the perspective of teacher education (Betters-Bubon et al., 2021). Each accreditation body has its unique emphasis delineated by their standards. We outline this further in Table 22.1.

22.4.1 CACREP Accreditation

CACREP standards address school counseling program coursework, faculty requirements, credit hours, fieldwork experiences, CIT and faculty evaluations, and other program-related specifications. CACREP standards are founded on quality assurance principles and the vision of a unified counselor identity in the profession (CACREP, 2024). All accredited programs include and must adhere to the 8 core areas for entry level programs that are discussed in Chap. 15 in this book. The 2024 CACREP standards specific to school counseling, also include an emphasis on advocacy towards enacting change. Standards for the school counseling specialty area required training programs to focus on theoretical foundations, skills, and strategies, including evidence-based and culturally sustaining interventions (CACREP, 2024, Section 5.H.). Additionally, CACREP emphasizes the importance of leadership skills, social-emotional and trauma-informed counseling, and collaboration and consultation as essential to the work in place.

22.4.2 CAEP Accreditation

CAEP, on the other hand, provides content-specific standards and recognition for specialized professional associations (SPAs), including areas such as school administration, school psychology, and special education (CAEP, 2022). The CAEP SPA standards solely address the CIT's knowledge, recognizing the differences among programs and focusing on the competencies that school counselors need to meet (CAEP, 2022). In 2019, the ASCA offered SPA recognition to school counseling training programs. National recognition is based on ASCA SPA standards, emphasizing school counselors' roles as educators while valuing mental health services for students (ASCA, 2021a). Thus, CACREP and CAEP SPA professional standards must be considered when developing a new school counseling training program or track. Table 22.1 provides an overview of both the CACREP and CAEP standards for school counselor training programs.

Table 22.1 School counseling 2024 CACREP standards (Section 5.H.) and 2022 CAEP standards

2024 CACREP standards	2022 CAEP standards
5.H.1. Models of school counseling programs 5.H.2. Models of PK-12 comprehensive career development 5.H.3. Models of school-based collaboration and consultation 5.H.4. Development of school counseling program mission statements and objectives	Standard 1. Content and pedagogical knowledge The provider ensures that candidates develop, through curriculum and experiences, a deep understanding of the critical concepts and principles of their discipline that integrate equity and diversity throughout candidates' courses and their developmental clinical experiences with diverse P-12 students. Upon completion, candidates can use discipline-specific practices and understand student culture and differing needs to advance learning by all students
5.H.5. Design and evaluation of school counseling curriculum, lesson plan development, diverse classroom management strategies, and differentiated instructional strategies 5.H.6. School counselor roles as leaders, advocates, and systems change agents in PK-12 schools	Standard 2. Clinical partnerships and practice The provider ensures effective partnerships and high-quality clinical practice are central to candidate preparation. These experiences should be designed to develop candidate's knowledge, skills, and professional dispositions to demonstrate positive impact on diverse students' learning and development. High quality clinical practice offers candidates experiences in different settings and modalities, as well as with diverse P-12 students, schools, families, and communities. Partners share responsibility to identify and address real problems of practice candidates experience in their engagement with P-12 students
5.H.7. Qualities and styles of effective leadership in schools 5.H.8. Advocacy for comprehensive school counseling programs and associated school counselor roles	Standard 3. Candidate recruitment, progression, and support The provider demonstrates that the quality of candidates is a continuous and purposeful focus from recruitment through completion. The provider demonstrates that development of candidate quality is the goal of educator preparation and that the EPP provides support services (such as advising, remediation, and mentoring) in all phases of the program so candidates will be successful
5.H.9. School counselor roles and responsibilities in relation to the school crisis and management plans	Standard 4. Program impact The provider demonstrates the effectiveness of its completers' instruction on P-12 student learning and development, and completer and employer satisfaction with the relevance and effectiveness of preparation

(continued)

Table 22.1 (continued)

2024 CACREP standards	2022 CAEP standards
5.H.10. School counselor consultation with families, PK-12 and postsecondary school personnel, community agencies, and other referral sources	Standard 5. Quality assurance system and continuous improvement The provider maintains a quality assurance system that consists of valid data from multiple measures and supports continuous improvement that is sustained and evidence-based. The system is developed and maintained with input from internal and external stakeholders. The provider uses the results of inquiry and data collection to establish priorities, enhance program elements, establish goals for improving, and highlight innovations
5.H.11. Skills to critically examine the connections of social, cultural, familial, emotional, and behavioral factors to academic achievement	
5.H.12. Skills to screen PK-12 students for characteristics, risk factors, and warning signs of mental health and behavioral disorders	Standard 6. Fiscal and administrative capacity The EPP has the fiscal and administrative capacity, faculty, infrastructure (facilities, equipment, and supplies) and other resources as appropriate to the scale of its operations and as necessary for the preparation of candidates to meet professional, state, and institutional standards. For EPPs whose institution is accredited by an accreditor recognized by the U.S. Secretary of Education (e.g., SACSCOC, HLC), such accreditation will be considered sufficient evidence of compliance with Standard 6. If an EPP's institution is not accredited by an accreditor recognized by the U.S. Secretary of Education, the EPP must address each component of Standard 6 in narrative supported by evidence
5.H.13. Strategies for implementing and coordinating school-based interventions	
5.H.14. Techniques of social-emotional and trauma-informed counseling in school settings	
5.H.15. Evidence-based and culturally sustaining interventions to promote academic development	
5.H.16. Approaches to increase promotion and graduation rates	Standard 7. Record of compliance with Title IV of the Higher Education Act Freestanding EPPs relying on CAEP accreditation to access Title IV of the Higher Education Act must demonstrate 100% compliance with their responsibilities under Title IV of the Act, including but not limited to on the basis of student loan default rate data provided by the Secretary, financial and compliance audits, and program reviews conducted by the U.S. Department of Education. Freestanding EPPs will need to provide narrative and evidence for all components of Standard 7
5.H.17. Interventions to promote postsecondary and career readiness	
5.H.18. Strategies to facilitate school and postsecondary transitions	
5.H.19. Strategies to promote equity in student achievement and access to postsecondary education opportunities	

Note Summary table presenting the school counseling 2024 CACREP standards, Section 5.H. (CACREP, 2024) and the 2022 CAEP Standards (CAEP, 2022)

22.5 Developing a School Counseling Training Program and Track

Upon describing the foundations of the school counseling profession, the high demand for professionals in the field, especially those from historically marginalized populations, and the standards needed from training programs, we can explore the process of creating a new program or specialized practice area in school counseling. The process, based on the authors' experience, is composed of a series of stages conducive to reflection, planning, action, and evaluation, is captured on Fig. 22.1. The proposed model includes considerations based on the authors' experience; however, it is important to acknowledge that there are particularities of each institution and therefore of each program that need to be carefully considered. Adjustments will be needed to address specific needs and challenges, and to meet the goals of your program and institution. In addition, it is important to note that the stages are flexible, and they mean to be in revision, adjustment, and continue evaluation. The authors expect that their experience will aid others in the process of building or evaluating a school counseling training program, and moreover, it is their hope to open the door to more conversations and knowledge sharing on the myriad of experiences and historical accounts of school counseling as a profession and counselor education in the field.

22.5.1 Stage 1: Initial Assessment

Assessment should be conducted throughout the process, starting with a needs and interest assessment gathering information from all stakeholders. There are different assessment models that can be used, it is important to choose one that best fits your needs and objectives. The information gathered should inform decision making moving forward. In each stage potential challenges or threats should also be examined. One area that is of critical importance for the authors and should also be intentionally included throughout the process is a social justice lens founded on anti-racist practices, advocacy and action toward dismantling systems of inequity and oppression. Questions needed to be asked in this stage to frame the work include: Is the program needed in your area? How competitive is recruitment? Do you have qualified professionals to lead the program? What type of resources are available? Is there interest from potential learners and if so, do they have specific needs to be met? What are potential challenges or threats to be considered? What social justice considerations should you address in this stage?

22.5.2 Stage 2: Professional Credentials

Reviewing the most current professional standards in the field should be one of the first steps in the process, along with early discussions on whether or not potential accreditation will be sought out. Even if the leaders decide not to seek accreditation

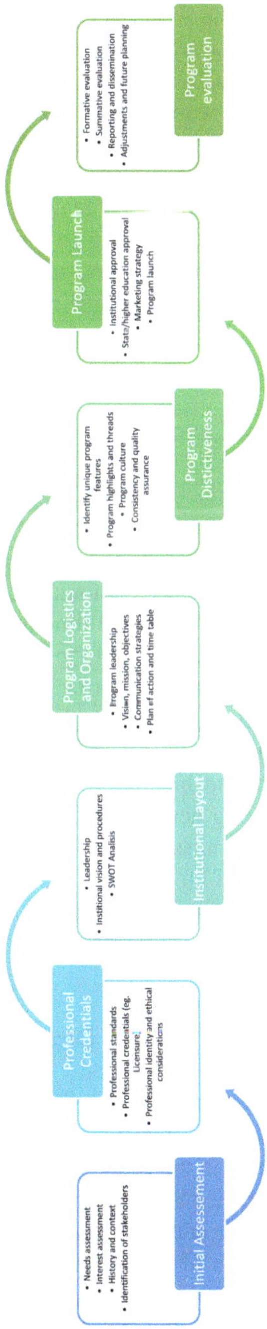

Fig. 22.1 Program development model

at that time, it is still important to consider the standards being used in the profession for quality assurance. The same is true for professional credentials required in the state(s) for graduates to enter the workplace. Questions for guidance in this stage: Are you considering CACREP accreditation or ASCA CAEP recognition or both? What are the implications for each? What are the available resources to support the accreditation process? What would the requirements be for the program under design to meet the accreditations standards? What type of credentials are required for professionals in the field in the state and nearby states? What is the process that graduates would need to follow to obtain the corresponding credentials and what would the requirements be related to their training program (e.g. credit hours, specific coursework, internship hours, etc.). What are potential challenges or threats to be considered? What social justice considerations should you address in this stage?

22.5.3 Stage 3: Institutional Layout

Conversations and reflections around the vision for the program and its connection to the institutional vision and mission are fundamental. The leaders in the process should maintain constant communication and be aware of their own goals and expectations. Professionals leading the process should also be or become familiar with the institutional procedures, regulations, and timeline to propose and support a new program. It is also important to be aware of the potential resources that may be available and those who will be needed in order to effectively launch a new program. A SWOT analysis or similar strategy may be of great value at this stage. Who is leading the program development? What are their credentials, experience, goals and expectations? What are the institutional procedures, regulations, and timeline for proposing and supporting new programs? How would your program align with the institutional vision and mission? How would it respond to the needs and challenges of the community and the field? What are potential challenges or threats to be considered? What social justice considerations should you address in this stage?

22.5.4 Stage 4: Program Logistics and Organization

Upon gathering all the information regarding requirements, working sessions are in order to get organized and address all the logistics. It is important to gather information and get stakeholders involved in the process once again. Participation may contribute to the feelings of belonging and commitment to see it through. Details in this stage will differ by institution and will be influenced by the institutional culture. Leaders should lay out a plan of action and timetable with stakeholder's input. How is the leadership team organized? What resources do they have access to (e.g. class release, stipend, teaching assistants, etc.)? How would you build an action plan? What should it include? What would be a realistic and attainable timetable? What are potential challenges or threats to be considered? What social justice considerations should you address in this stage?

22.5.5 Stage 5: Program Distinctiveness

Apart from recognizing professional standards that should lead the path toward quality assurance, it is also important to decide the aspects of the program that will make it distinct from others. Once decided, make sure to reflect on how these aspects or distinct characteristics will take place in the program and how to ensure consistency. For the authors for example, the social justice lens is critical and so it has been having their voices as BIPOC professionals as part of the leadership team. Framing questions: How would you envision your program? What would be unique about it? What do you want to be known for? What would your contributions be to the school counseling field? What are potential challenges or threats to be considered? What social justice considerations should you address in this stage?

22.5.6 Stage 6: Program Launch

Obtaining the corresponding approval and needed support are indispensable for the success of the program. After obtaining the approval needed, marketing will be an important step to take to ensure program enrollment. Identifying effective means of communication is also important and can aid the process. Questions to consider: What are the steps that you need to take to obtain approval? What are the requirements and deadlines? What are the marketing resources available? What would you need? What are potential challenges or threats to be considered? What social justice considerations should you address in this stage?

22.5.7 Stage 7: Program Evaluation

Setting a process of evaluation is important to document the work, collect evidence, reflect on strengths and challenges, make the necessary changes, and work toward accountability and sustainability. Formative evaluation should be included throughout and should support the flexibility of the process. It should help determine when to continue or when you would need more time to address the challenges faced. A summative evaluation is also important as you will need to record and very likely present your outcomes. Ultimately the launch of the program is the goal supported by mechanisms of evaluation and sustainability. Final questions for reflection: How would you like the evaluation to take place? What information do you need to gather in the process? What would your process be to make decisions? How can you incorporate summative and formative evaluations strategies throughout the process and who would be monitoring it? What are potential challenges or threats to be considered? What social justice considerations should you address in this stage?

22.6 School Counseling Specific Training Requirements

Aligned with the 2024 CACREP Standards (CACREP, 2024), school counseling training programs are required to have 60 semester hours or 90 quarter hours of credits with a course sequence that meets the standards. We provide an example School Counseling program plan of study in Table 22.2. The example program of study includes the foundational courses along with the school counseling specialized practice courses. Your program's course of study may deviate slightly to allow for elective courses. Apart from aligning with CACREP, programs should also consider their state licensure or certification requirements. For example, Maine requires school counselors to take a course on teaching exceptional students, whereas Arkansas requires an examination on the principles of learning and teaching. A complete list of certification/licensure requirements by state is available on the ASCA's website https://www.schoolcounselor.org/. It is also worth mentioning that in some states the credential to practice as a school counselor is referred to as license while in others is known as certification.

22.7 School Counseling Specific Field Placement

The journey of becoming a school counselor formally starts with the training program. The curriculum sequence of the program lays down a developmental path to discuss, reflect, and learn the theoretical foundations and skills necessary to practice effectively in the field. Prior to entering the workforce, CITs are required to successfully complete a supervised field placement in school settings. This experience offers opportunities to CITs to dive into the roles and responsibilities of school counselors at either level, elementary, middle, or high school. Throughout the experience and following CACREP regulations, CITs are supervised by a counselor educator program faculty member or a doctoral learner under supervision themselves, and by a qualified site supervisor with the education and training to serve as such (ASCA, 2022; CACREP, 2024).

22.7.1 School Counseling Supervision

School counselor educators play an integral role in supporting the development of emerging school counselors. The ASCA Ethical Standards for School Counselor Educator Faculty (2018) state that school counselor educators "provide assistance to graduate students in gaining supervised practice experience in a school setting" (p. 1). As faculty supervisors, school counselor educators are leaders and

Table 22.2 Example school counseling program (60 credit hours) program plan of study

Name of course	Credits
Human Growth and Development[a]	3
Counseling Theories[a]	3
Professional Orientation and Ethical Practice[a]	3
Counseling Skills and Helping Relationships[a]	3
Group Counseling[a]	3
Social and Cultural Diversity[a]	3
Career Development[a]	3
Assessment and Testing[a]	3
Research and Evaluation[a]	3
Addictions Counseling[a]	3
Diagnosis and Treatment[a]	3
Crisis Counseling[a]	3
Counseling Couples and Families[a]	3
Introduction to School Counseling[b]	3
Program Development[b]	3
Collaboration and Consultation[b]	3
Counseling Children and Adolescents[b]	3
Practicum	3
Internship 1	3
Internship 2	3

[a] Indicates courses that address the 2024 CACREP Foundational Counseling Curriculum content area (CACREP, 2024, Section 3)
[b] Indicates school counseling specialty courses

mentors in preparing the next generation of school counselors through collaboration with school districts. It is critical that school counselor educators ensure adequate and appropriate field experiences to support CITs in effectively addressing the academic, social/emotional and career development needs of K-12 students. Supervision is explored in greater detail in Chap. 4.

22.7.2 Supervisory Roles

School counselor educators, site supervisors and district coordinators work together to train and support emerging school counselors (ASCA, 2019). Supervision can be facilitated through individual, dyadic, triadic and/or group sessions (Dollarhide & Miller, 2006). School counseling supervisors on various levels have a direct impact on trainees during field experience and throughout their careers, as they serve as gatekeepers of the profession (Wood & Rayle, 2006). Understanding the role of the supervisor is imperative in that it helps to ensure clear expectations and minimizes role confusion.

22.7.2.1 School Counseling Faculty Supervisors

School counseling faculty supervisors possess the education, formal training, and experience in supervision, as coursework within this area is typically offered during doctoral-level training. Faculty supervisors train supervisees during their training program to ensure the quality and effectiveness of school counseling programs in the K-12 setting (ASCA, 2017). Along with facilitating supervision through practicum and internship courses, faculty supervisors may also be expected to manage a variety of tasks, such as maintaining administrative documents (e.g., developing/updated training guides, site contracts/agreements, MOUs/affiliate agreements, CIT liability insurance) conducting site visits, tracking field experience hours, supporting CITs in navigating case conceptualizations, and providing orientation, professional development and consultation to site supervisors and district coordinators (CACREP, 2024; Lazovsky & Shimoni, 2007; Quintana & Gooden-Alexis, 2020). The faculty supervisor's role is multifaceted and essential to the supervisee's overall development when transitioning from trainee to school counselor.

22.7.2.2 School Counseling Site Supervisors

School counselors play a critical role in facilitating successful supervision in school settings as site supervisors (Dollarhide & Miller, 2006). The primary responsibility of the site supervisor is to provide relevant on-site guidance and training experiences to school counseling supervisees to prepare them to enter the field (Roberts et al., 2001). Specifically, site supervisors train supervisees in developing a professional identity, implementing a comprehensive school counseling program, understanding student issues, and navigating school settings (Studer & Diambra, 2010). When school counselors serve as site supervisors, they directly contribute to the training of emerging school counselors who, in the near future, will be responsible for developing, implementing and assessing their comprehensive school counseling program to support all students (Quintana & Gooden-Alexis, 2020). To serve as a site supervisor, ASCA (2022) states that school counselors must have the education and training to provide counseling supervision. Without formal supervision training or supervision coursework, which is rarely offered within master's level school counseling programs (Borders et al., 1991; Nelson & Johnson, 1999), site supervisors may feel unfamiliar with, overwhelmed by or unequipped to navigate the challenges that come with supporting a supervisee (Quintana & Gooden-Alexis, 2020). As models who are responsible for training future school counselors, it is critical for site supervisors to be competent and prepared within the area of supervision (Dollarhide & Miller, 2006; Herlihy et al., 2002; Roberts et al., 2001).

Because supervision is a key component in the training of emerging school counselors, the relationship between universities and school districts serves to benefit all school counseling professionals. In training supervisees, it is imperative that universities and school districts—school counseling education faculty supervisors, coordinators and site supervisors—establish and maintain collaborative partnerships. Given the high demands and complex issues within school settings, collaborative partnerships between school counseling supervisors comprehensively address the various needs of school counseling supervisees and are critical to the professional development of both emerging and practicing school counselors (Quintana & Gooden-Alexis, 2020).

22.7.2.3 Collaborative Partnerships

The partnership between universities and school districts is key to the development of emerging school counselors. At the district level, school counseling supervisors are responsible for supporting the development, implementation and assessment of school counseling programs and related activities including professional development for school counselors (ASCA, 2019). School counseling supervisors at the university, district and school levels ensure effective professional relationships and high-quality training that is essential to school counselor preparation. The ASCA Ethical Standards for School Counselor Education Faculty Section E (2018) highlights collaboration and specific responsibilities of faculty supervisors when working with schools and school districts. These collaborative partnerships are necessary to ensure that supervisees develop the knowledge, skills and professional dispositions needed to demonstrate a positive impact on K-12 student development and achievement (ASCA, 2019). Collaborative partnerships may include:

1. Individual/group supervision for site supervisors facilitated by faculty supervisors (Quintana & Gooden-Alexis, 2020).
2. The development of a university advisory committee made up of site supervisors and school counselors to inform and support university-level programming (Quintana & Gooden-Alexis, 2020).
3. Collaboration between district-level school counseling supervisors and school counseling graduate program directors to provide counseling workshops for supervisees and supervision training for site supervisors (ASCA, 2019).
4. Consultation among school counseling graduate programs and district-level school counseling supervisors to locate and secure field placements for supervisees (ASCA, 2018).
5. Partnerships with district-level school counseling supervisors, site supervisors and faculty supervisors to address concerns that arise on-site with school counseling trainees (ASCA, 2018).
6. Advocacy efforts on the state level related to issues affecting K-12 education policy and school counseling programs (Quintana & Gooden-Alexis, 2020).

Because supervision is a key component in the training of emerging school counselors, the relationship between universities and school districts serves to benefit all school counseling professionals. In training supervisees, it is imperative that universities and school districts—school counseling education faculty supervisors, coordinators and site supervisors—establish and maintain collaborative partnerships. Given the high demands and complex issues within school settings, collaborative partnerships between school counseling supervisors comprehensively address the various needs of school counseling supervisees and are critical to the professional development of both emerging and practicing school counselors (Quintana & Gooden-Alexis, 2020).

22.7.3 Anti-racist School Counseling Supervision Practices

Racism is deeply woven into the fabric of American society and its structures, including educational institutions (ASCA, 2021b). As racism, bias and oppression continue to impact K-12 institutions, university programs, in collaboration with school districts, have the unique opportunity to train supervisees through anti-racist school counseling supervision. University programs, specifically faculty supervisors, are ethically responsible for ensuring they possess "the knowledge and skills to support social justice and advocacy efforts and to teach graduate students to become culturally competent school counselors and leaders" and emphasize "social justice, advocacy, multiculturalism and preparation to work with a diverse population" (ASCA, 2018, pp. 1–2). Through an anti-racist lens, school counseling education programs can prepare CITs to interrogate systems of power that shape racist policies and practices, address disparities that affect BIPOC students, and promote equity and access for historically underserved, underrepresented and marginalized student populations.

Quintana and Gooden-Alexis (2020) highlight specific strategies to increase cultural competence in counselor education programs and school districts that can be helpful when engaging in anti-racist school counseling supervision. These strategies include:

1. Providing supervision in a manner that is uplifting of nondominant cultures. An example of this could be to highlight strengths in culture and observe ways to incorporate for supervisee success.
2. Monitoring personal levels of power and privilege. Supervisors have a level of power and influence that cannot be ignored. Having an understanding of intersecting identities and how the history of oppression impacts this is critical when supervising BIPOC supervisees.
3. Reflecting regularly on cultural worldviews (values, beliefs, assumptions, biases) to understand how these views influence supervision practices.
4. Initiating and/or instigating "courageous conversations" that challenge discomfort on topics of injustice, racism, privilege, oppression and related issues.
5. Offering training experiences that engage both site supervisors and supervisees in recognizing and responding to incidents of racism and bias at their sites.
6. Providing a diversified site list and site supervisors for CITs to obtain increased exposure to different challenges that exist among various racial communities.
7. Providing support for BIPOC supervisees who may demonstrate issues surrounding racial trauma and stress as a result of racist policies and practices.

As school counselors are called upon to serve as social justice advocates and change agents, it is imperative that their training programs equip them with the tools necessary to critically examine and dismantle systems of racism, bias and oppression. As university programs and school districts collaborate in supporting supervisees within their field experiences, it is the ethical and professional responsibility of these partners to ensure that emerging school counselors "engage in anti-racist actions by advocating to change racist policies, procedures, practices, guidelines and laws contributing to inequities in students' academic, career and social/emotional development" (ASCA, 2021b, p. 1).

It is the recommendation of the authors to create a school counseling program that intentionally and consciously prepares emerging counselors to support diverse student populations as they navigate an ever-changing world. Additionally, collaborating and consulting with university and community stakeholders, including program leaders, accrediting bodies, university marketing teams, admissions personnel, and school districts, is critical to the foundation when developing a graduate-level school counseling program. Last, ensuring that graduate-level programs are rooted in social justice and advocacy is crucial, as programs are responsible for preparing emerging school counselors to serve as change agents who critically examine and dismantle systems of inequity and oppression to increase access, opportunity and advancement for historically marginalized K-12 student populations.

22.8 Conclusion

The school counseling field provides the first line of defense toward prevention and early intervention in the school setting toward the wellbeing of our new generations. Because the field is of great importance, the training of those entering the field is also of high relevance. Creating a new program or specialized practice in this area or evaluating an existing program provides a great opportunity to respond to the current needs, challenges, and demands in the field. It is necessary to create a program that will effectively equip counselors in training with the knowledge, skills, strategies, and experience needed to enter the workforce to support new generations of children and adolescents in schools. In this chapter we detailed the field of school counseling and present the major components of a school counseling training program. We summarized the history of school counseling as a specialized practice area, the role and responsibilities of school counselors, the rationale for quality school counseling training programs and respective accreditation standards and described the process of creating a school counseling program and all that it implies including supervision practices. The authors shared their expertise in hopes of providing a layout and foundation key points to those planning on developing a new school counseling program or evaluating an existing program.

References

American School Counselor Association. (2017). *The essential role of school counselor educators/practicum and internship supervisors.* https://www.schoolcounselor.org/asca/media/asca/Careers-Roles/WhySCE.pdf

American School Counselor Association. (2018). *ASCA ethical standards for school counselor education faculty.* https://www.schoolcounselor.org/asca/media/asca/Ethics/SCEEthicalStandards.pdf

American School Counselor Association. (2019). *The essential role of school counseling directors/coordinators.* https://www.schoolcounselor.org/getmedia/48ae6ab8-7140-4d12-8ad8-a8ce8ddc03fa/Why-Director-Coord.pdf

American School Counselor Association. (2021a). *ASCA school counselor education/preparation program frequently asked questions.* https://www.schoolcounselor.org/Recognition/ASCA-Recognized-School-Counselor-Preparation-Progr/School-Counselor-Preparation-Program-Standards-FAQ

American School Counselor Association. (2021b). *Standards in practice—Eliminating racism and bias in schools: The school counselor's role.* https://www.schoolcounselor.org/getmedia/542b085a-7eda-48ba-906e-24cd3f08a03f/SIP-Racism-Bias.pdf

American School Counselor Association. (2022). *ASCA ethical standards for school counselors.* https://schoolcounselor.org/About-School-Counseling/Ethical-Responsibilities/ASCA-Ethical-Standards-for-School-Counselors-(1)

Betters-Bubon, J., Goodman-Scott, E., & Bamgbose, O. (2021). School counselor educators' reactions to changes in the profession: Implications for policy, evaluation, and preparation. *Journal of School-Based Counseling Policy and Evaluation, 3*(2), 40–50. https://doi.org/10.25774/gkr1-j228

Borders, L. D., Bernard, J. M., Dye, H. A., Fong, M. L., Henderson, P., & Nance, D. W. (1991). Curriculum guide for training counseling supervisors: Rationale, development, and implementation. *Counselor Education and Supervision, 31*, 58–80. https://doi.org/10.1002/j.1556-6978.1991.tb00371.x

Bureau of Labor Statistics. (2024). *U.S. Department of Labor, occupational outlook handbook, school and career counselors and advisors.* https://www.bls.gov/ooh/community-and-social-service/school-and-career-counselors.htm

Council for Accreditation of Counseling and Related Educational Programs. (2024). *2024 CACREP standards.* https://www.cacrep.org/wp-content/uploads/2024/04/2024-Standards-Combined-Version-4.11.2024.pdf

Council for the Accreditation of Educator Preparation. (2022). *2022 CAEP standards.* https://caepnet.org/standards/2022-itp/introduction

Dollarhide, C. T., & Miller, G. M. (2006). Supervision for preparation and practice of school counselors: Pathways to excellence. *Counselor Education & Supervision, 45*, 242–252. https://doi.org/10.1002/j.1556-6978.2006.tb00001.x

Erford, B. T. (Ed.). (2019). *Transforming the school counseling profession* (5th ed.). Pearson.

Gysbers, N. C. (2010). *Remembering the past, shaping the future: A history of school counseling.* American School Counselor Association.

Havlik, S., Ciarletta, M., & Crawford, E. (2018). "If we don't define our roles, someone else will": Professional advocacy in school counseling. *Professional School Counseling, 22*(1), 1–11.

Herlihy, B., Gray, N., & McCollum, V. (2002). Legal and ethical issues in school counselor supervision. *Professional School Counseling, 6*(1), 55–60.

Kaplan, D. M., Tarvydas, V. M., & Gladding, S. T. (2014). 20/20: A vision for the future of counseling: The new consensus definition of counseling. *Journal of Counseling and Development, 92*(3), 366–372.

Lazovsky, R., & Shimoni, A. (2007). The working contract between the on-site mentor and school counseling students during internship—Contents and processes. *Mentoring & Tutoring: Partnership in Learning, 13*, 367–382. https://doi.org/10.1080/13611260500105857

Nelson, M. D., & Johnson, P. (1999). School counselors as supervisors: An integrated approach for supervising school counseling interns. *Counselor Education and Supervision, 39*, 89–101. https://doi.org/10.1002/j.1556-6978.1999.tb01220.x

Quintana, T. S., & Gooden-Alexis, S. E. (2020). *Making supervision work: An ASCA national model publication.* American School Counselor Association.

Roberts, W. B., Morotti, A. A., Herrick, C., & Tilbury, R. (2001). Site supervisors of professional school counseling interns: Suggested guidelines. *Professional School Counseling, 4*, 208–215.

Song, S. Y., Eddy, J. M., Thompson, H. M., Adams, B., & Beskow, J. (2020). Restorative consultation in schools: A systematic review and call for restorative justice science to promote anti-racism and social justice. *Journal of Educational and Psychological Consultation, 30*(4), 462–476. https://doi.org/10.1080/10474412.2020.1819298

Studer, J. R., & Diambra, J. F. (2010). *A guide to practicum and internship for school counselors-in-training.* New Routledge Press.

Wood, C., & Rayle, A. D. (2006). A model of school counseling supervision: The goals, functions, roles, and systems model. *Counselor Education & Supervision, 45*, 253–266. https://doi.org/10.1002/j.1556-6978.2006.tb00002.x

Syntia Santos Dietz, Ph.D., NCC (she/her/ella) is a Licensed School Counselor and is an Associate Professor at Antioch University. She has held varying leadership roles such as program coordinator in the school counseling program at the Universidad Pedagógica Nacional Francisco Morazán (UPNFM) in her native country of Honduras, creating a School Counseling Program at her institution, as well as co-founder/director of the Latinx Mental Health and Social Justice Institute. Her research includes cultural competence, school counseling, and international counseling and counselor education addressing mental health counseling for historically marginalized populations and how future counselors can support them.

Katrina Y. Billingsley, Ph.D., LPC, NCC (she/her/hers) is a National Certified Counselor (NCC), a licensed professional counselor and counselor educator. She currently serves as a high school counselor in a public school in rural Georgia where she has worked for three years. Prior to taking on this role, Dr. Billingsley's professional career was primarily in higher education focusing on program management and student development work. Her research focus is on anti-racist, anti-oppressive research centered around Black and Brown people.

Taqueena S. Quintana, Ph.D., LPC, NCC, ACS (she/her/hers) is a National Certified Counselor (NCC), Licensed Professional Counselor (LPC-DC and GA) Certified School Counselor and Approved Clinical Supervisor. She currently serves as a counselor educator and therapist. Prior to this, Dr. Quintana was the School Counseling Practicum and Internship Coordinator at a public institution in Arkansas. Her research interests include school counseling supervision, supporting military-connected students and families and counseling students with disabilities.

Part V

Personal and Professional Development

Leadership and Administrative Roles in Counselor Education

23

Erika Cameron, Jung H. Hyun, and Mariaimeé Gonzalez

There is always a light, if only we're brave enough to see it. If only we're brave enough to be it.

Amanda Gorman

Abstract

Doctoral degree programs in Counselor Education and Supervision are intended to prepare graduates to be leaders and advocates in the profession. As such, Leadership and Advocacy is designated as one of the five core areas outlining the roles and responsibilities of being a counselor educator. Understanding the CACREP leadership standards and how this may intersect with your developing leadership framework is important as a counselor educator in training, and as a new CES professional who may one day become an administrator. This chapter focuses on understanding leadership from a liberation paradigm, learning the CACREP leadership standards, wellness and self-care for leaders, and leader development models.

E. Cameron (✉)
Palo Alto University, Palo Alto, CA, USA
e-mail: erikacameron@paloaltou.edu

J. H. Hyun
Agnes Scott College, Decatur, GA, USA
e-mail: jhyun@agnesscott.edu

M. Gonzalez
Antioch University, Yellow Springs, OH, USA
e-mail: mymae78@hotmail.com

D. M. Stalnaker-Shofner and T. N. Sapp (eds.), *A Comprehensive Guide for Counselor Education*, Springer Texts in Education, https://doi.org/10.1007/978-3-031-68358-9_23

Learning Objectives After reading this chapter, you will be able to:

1. Identify potential leadership and administrative opportunities available to counselor educators.
2. Explain the importance and relevance of the CACREP Standards related to leadership and our advocacy role as counselor educators.
3. Evaluate different models of and approaches to leadership with respect to advantages, challenges, and efficacy.
4. Understand how leadership can effectively utilize social justice, advocacy, and activism to promote and facilitate liberation in the counseling profession as well as within counselor education.
5. Incorporate wellness strategies and an active self-care plan as an integral component to one's leadership journey.

23.1 Statement of Reflexivity

As the authors of this chapter, we each have unique backgrounds and leadership paths. We share our reflexive narratives, offering insightful perspectives on our diverse experiences. Dr. Erika Cameron identifies as a multiethnic, cisgender, heterosexual, able-bodied individual, and is a devoted wife and mother of two. She currently serves as the provost at a university and has 15 years of experience as a counselor educator. She has held various leadership positions within the profession throughout her tenure. Her leadership journey is deeply rooted in her upbringing and motivated by a desire to contribute to the greater good.

Dr. Jung (June) H. Hyun identifies as a Korean American, cisgender, heterosexual, able-bodied female. She is an Associate Professor in a Community Mental Health Counseling Program. She has 13 years of counselor education experience and a wealth of leadership experience in various roles. Dr. Hyun's perception of leadership revolves around recognizing and leveraging each member's strengths and weaknesses to achieve shared goals. Her leadership journey traces back to her early years, where she demonstrated innate leadership traits, taking initiatives and setting goals.

Dr. Mariaimeé "Maria" Gonzalez identifies as a first-generation Latiné college graduate, cisgender, disabled, heterosexual woman. To the writing of this chapter, she brings 16 years of experience as a counselor educator and a wealth of leadership experience in the profession. Her leadership journey began in her childhood, influenced by her mother and father's advocacy for Puerto Rican and Latiné human rights, and guided by the collective values of her Latiné community. Mariaimeé emphasizes the value of collaborative leadership in academia, rooted in liberation and mental well-being, as she continues to contribute to global community building through teaching, supervision, research, consultation, counseling, and advocacy.

Together, Drs. Cameron, Hyun, and Gonzalez contribute richly to the collective narrative of women, BIPOC, and leaders, shedding light on their reflexive journeys and perspectives within the often-underrepresented realm of higher education leadership and administration.

23.2 Case Scenario

Picture yourself as a newly appointed faculty member in a CES program, where your fresh perspective and enthusiasm position you as a potential leader. The challenge you face is to propose a transformative initiative within your department, aimed at enhancing inclusivity, cultural responsiveness, and advocating for social justiceprinciples you deeply believe in.

As you navigate this scenario, you encounter resistance from colleagues who are deeply rooted in traditional practices. Some express concerns about disrupting established structures and question the need for a shift towards a more inclusive curriculum. Here, your experience becomes critical in addressing these barriers. Drawing from your cultural capital—the deep understanding of diverse perspectives gained through your experiences and education—you leverage your unique insights to make a compelling case for change.

You recognize that effective leadership in counselor education requires the ability to lean into your cultural capital, effectively communicate the benefits of the proposed initiative, and bridge the gap between tradition and innovation. Your experience enables you to navigate the complexities of leading in new ways, emphasizing the importance of a liberation paradigm that aligns with contemporary counseling education principles. Simultaneously, you acknowledge the barriers and potential resistance, but your cultural capital empowers you to build bridges, fostering collaboration and understanding.

In this case scenario, your journey as a faculty member becomes a testament to the transformative power of leadership rooted in cultural capital. By embracing a liberation leadership paradigm, navigating barriers, and leaning into your rich cultural insights, you not only champion positive change within your department but also exemplify a leadership model that inspires others to embrace inclusivity and advocacy in counselor education.

23.3 Introduction

We want you to close your eyes and think about what leadership is to you. What do you see as the typical images of leadership? What do those leaders look like? What are those leaders doing? Did you envision images of an individual standing out in front of a group? Did you envision that individual to be a man? Was he white? If you did, that's what we would have expected you to visualize, because in the media and throughout literature on leadership, leaders are often described and depicted as "individuals who impact meaning as a way of providing direction to their followers" (Bass & Bass, 2008). In addition, the racial ethnic makeup of higher education and corporate leadership is predominantly White males. A 2020 study conducted by the College and University Professional Association for Human Resources (CUPA-HR) reported that racial minorities make up 20% of higher education administrators and that BIPOC individuals make up only 13% of the top higher education executive officers (President, Provost, Chancellor,

Vice President). While the percentage of learners from BIPOC communities has been rapidly growing in US higher education institutions, the growth of diversity among higher education leaders has not kept pace. While administrative positions in higher education are dominated by White people, diversity in academic leadership is crucial for institutions to be able to relate to and educate the collective learner community.

It is documented in the counseling literature that successful leaders have the ability to cultivate and maintain relationships that encourage individuals to invest in a common goal (Hogan & Kaiser, 2005; Jacob et al., 2013; Kaslow et al., 2012). West et al. (2006) emphasized three dimensions in counseling leadership: context, vision, and action. Leaders in counselor education should have a clear vision for their organization, which includes a deep understanding of the organization's needs, a sense of the steps that are necessary to implement certain plans, and methods for celebrating success and applying feedback. While there are many different leadership styles that align with a counselor's more general goals of being relational, inspiring, and helpful, the following section will provide you with a high-level overview of five leadership styles across a social justice paradigm.

23.4 Models of Leadership Through a Social Justice Lens

Leadership styles play a crucial role in shaping organizational culture, values, and practices. In the context of social justice, leadership styles can either perpetuate or challenge systemic inequalities. This section explores various leadership styles, ranging from authoritative to servant, and discusses how they align with a social justice paradigm. By examining these leadership styles through the lens of colonialism and liberation, we can better understand their implications for promoting equity and inclusion.

23.4.1 Authoritative Leadership

Authoritative leadership, positioned at the initial end of the leadership spectrum, is characterized by a rigidly hierarchical structure in which decisions are unilaterally made by a single leader or a small group of leaders at the top of the organizational hierarchy. This leadership style tends to stifle collaboration, creativity, and shared decision-making, as the decision-making power is concentrated in the hands of a few individuals (Ahmed Iqbal et al., 2021). This concentration of power can result in a lack of empowerment for followers, as their input and perspectives may be overlooked or disregarded in the decision-making process. Ultimately, authoritative leadership is a restrictive leadership paradigm from a social justice lens because it tends to perpetuate power imbalances and limit the participation and empowerment of historically marginalized or underrepresented groups within the organization.

23.4.2 Democratic Leadership

Democratic leadership represents a shift from the authoritative paradigm towards a more inclusive and participatory approach to decision-making. Unlike authoritative leadership, where decisions are made solely by a single leader or a small group at the top, democratic leadership encourages shared decision-making among team members. This collaborative approach allows for a broader range of perspectives and experiences to be considered, potentially leading to more equitable and inclusive outcomes. However, democratic leadership still carries the risk of perpetuating existing power dynamics within the organization. This leadership style can also bring an absence of leadership and direction which could have two potential impacts: (1) decision-making processes may still be dominated by certain individuals or groups, while others may feel excluded or historically marginalized and (2) low morale and interest in the work (Bhatti et al., 2012). This can limit the effectiveness of democratic leadership in promoting social justice.

23.4.3 Adaptive Leadership

Adaptive leadership marks a shift towards flexibility and inclusivity, allowing leaders to navigate and initiate change in response to evolving challenges. Adaptive leadership embodies a more dynamic and responsive approach to leadership. Unlike democratic leadership, which focuses on shared decision-making, adaptive leadership embraces change and uncertainty, recognizing that challenges and opportunities are constantly evolving. This style of leadership encourages leaders to be flexible and adaptable, adjusting their strategies and approaches as needed to address new and emerging issues. This approach, however, is focused on navigating change, adapting to the shifting needs, and finding solutions (Nelson & Squires, 2017). When there are times of uncertainty or challenges adaptive leaders who are not decisive could potentially fall back on tried-and-true ways of operating that could be rooted in continuing systemic oppression. To combat this tendency, adaptive leaders must engage in introspection and honest assessment of their biases, have emotional intelligence, strong character, and believe in organizational justice.

23.4.4 Transformational Leadership

Transformational leaders inspire and motivate followers by articulating a compelling vision and setting high standards of performance (Bass & Bass, 2008). They use their influence to empower their team members to achieve their goals. In a social justice paradigm, this style is more liberated, as it emphasizes vision, empowerment, and the importance of addressing systemic injustices. Transformational leaders are characterized as inspirational and intellectually stimulating. They tend to consider individuals as assets, and they are influential (Piccolo & Colquitt,

2006) in motivating and inspiring followers to achieve their potential while also recognizing their followers' values and ideals (Bass, 1997). Because it is well suited for organizations that are hoping to go beyond simply meeting its collective needs, transformational leadership has been favored in the counseling field and studied often (Lopez-Perry, 2020). At the same time, considering institutions of higher education and the people who tend to be part of them, more flexible leadership styles, including transactional-transformational leadership, have also been introduced. This model embraces a liberative approach, focusing on individual and collective potential.

23.4.5 Servant Leadership

At the pinnacle of our spectrum stands servant leadership, embodying inclusivity and liberation. Servant leadership, when it is defined as "one wants to serve, to serve first" (Greenleaf, 1977), is another leadership style that has been welcomed in helping professions in medical fields and faith organizations. Prioritizing altruism, humility, and empowering others, servant leadership stands as the least restrictive and most socially just model of leadership. Servant leaders, who are characterized by altruism, humility, and an ability to inspire others to press on toward goals in situations (Monaghan, 2018), put their followers first and literally serve as a guide, mentor, and coach. Although they provide a vision for the organization—similar to the way other leadership styles do—the ultimate responsibility of the servant leader is the enduring investment of the leader's life in the lives of those who follow (Allen et al., 2016). Servant leaders focus on empathy, listening, and empowering others (Greenleaf, 1977). In a social justice paradigm, this style aligns with a more liberated perspective, as it emphasizes equality, empowerment, and the importance of serving marginalized communities.

Leadership plays a crucial role in shaping organizational culture and practices. In the context of social justice, leadership styles can either perpetuate or challenge systemic inequalities. By examining various leadership styles through the lens of colonialism and liberation, we can better understand their implications for promoting equity and inclusion. Figure 23.1 illustrates the spectrum of leadership styles aligned with a social justice paradigm. The diagram visually represents how different leadership styles, ranging from authoritative to servant leadership, align with social justice principles.

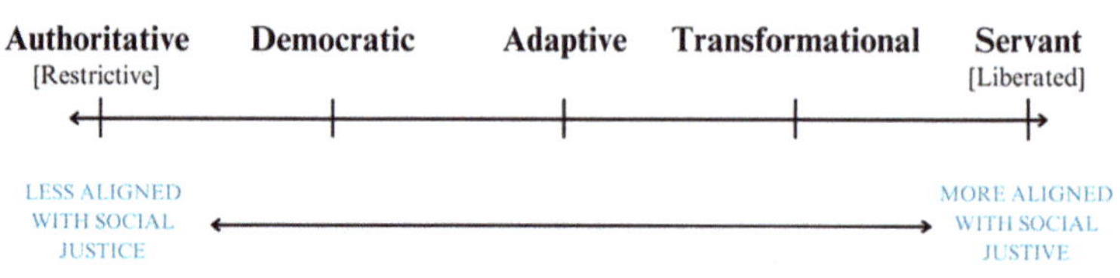

Fig. 23.1 Spectrum of leadership styles aligned with a social justice paradigm

The spectrum places authoritative leadership at one end, representing a restrictive approach that is less aligned with social justice principles. On the other end of the spectrum, servant leadership is positioned as the most liberated and closely aligned with social justice. Between these two extremes, democratic, adaptive, and transformational leadership styles are situated, reflecting their increasing alignment with social justice as they move towards the liberated end of the spectrum.

This visual representation helps to contextualize the discussion of leadership styles and their relationship to social justice, providing a clear and concise overview of the concepts explored in the chapter. By understanding where various leadership styles fall on this spectrum, counselor educators and CITs can better assess their own leadership approaches and work towards adopting more socially just and liberating practices.

Servant, transformational, and adaptive leadership styles align more closely with a social justice paradigm, emphasizing equality, empowerment, and the importance of building strong relationships. On the other hand, authoritative and democratic leadership styles may perpetuate inequalities and reinforce power imbalances.

Stop and Reflect: *As you reflect on the spectrum of leadership styles presented, which of these models do you find most resonant with your personal beliefs and values about leadership? Do you see any potential challenges or opportunities in applying these models within your own leadership context, particularly in a setting where there is a need for greater diversity and inclusion?*

23.5 Liberated Lens of Counselor Education Leadership

As administrators and counselor educators dedicated to molding the next generation of mental health change agents, engaging in social justice leadership and fostering mental liberation transcends mere choice—it becomes a calling. As liberators, the imperative is to leverage cultural gifts, forge inclusive communities, and lead with a commitment to critical transformation. This form of leadership involves actively supporting others in navigating the intricate, interconnected systems of oppression that hinder the realization of a liberated world. Leadership for liberation envisions a transformative process challenging the systems, structures, and cultural norms perpetuating harmful and inequitable realities. It encompasses both individual liberation for the oppressed and the oppressor, as well as collective liberation for all of humanity. This approach often demands resistance against traditional power structures and prevailing methods of instigating change.

According to hooks (1994), individual liberation marks a historical moment when one critically reflects on self and identity in relation to political circumstances. She emphasizes the interlocking, interdependent nature of systems of domination and stresses that understanding and dismantling these systems are vital for both personal freedom and collective liberation struggles (hooks, 2006). Collective liberation asserts that all forms of oppression are interconnected, necessitating a communal responsibility for the work of liberation. As Freire (1996) notes, both the oppressed and the oppressor are victims in the cycle of oppression, binding us all in each other's struggles for liberation. Leadership, in this context, becomes a form of liberation, inviting intentional exploration of ways to dismantle oppressive systems and internal narratives, fostering a new culture grounded in equity, passion, compassion, and love (Harro, 2010).

Approaching leadership through a lens of liberation involves decolonizing the dominant narratives that surround it. The etymology of the word "leadership" itself, originating from the Old English word "lædere," meaning "one who leads," suggests a shift from an individualistic paradigm to a collective approach. Liberation leadership aligns with counseling competencies, emphasizing listening, reflective practice, cultural humility, vulnerability, risk-taking, paraphrasing, critical thinking, and openness to new knowledge. It requires leaders to sit in multiplicity, holding space for others and contributing to the creation of a new culture grounded in personal agency and collaborative efforts for collective freedom.

Khalifa et al. (2019) developed a framework for indigenous decolonizing school leadership that could be adapted in higher education and specifically Counselor Education to provide an alternate approach to leadership in schools that are colonized, westernized, and oppressed. Leaders should focus on: "(1) the prioritization of self-knowledge and self-reflection, (2) the empowerment of community through self-determination, (3) the centering of community voices and values, (4) service based in altruism and spirituality, and (5) approaching collectivism through inclusive communication practices" (Khalifa et al., 2019). These themes closely resemble the framework of the ACA's MSJCCs (Ratts et al., 2016).

ACA's Multicultural and Social Justice Counseling Competencies provide a comprehensive framework for infusing social justice principles into leadership practices. These competencies include cultural awareness, knowledge, and skills, emphasizing the significance of cultural humility, empathy, and advocacy (ACA, 2015). Leaders committed to social justice integrate these competencies into their approach, acknowledging the diverse ways of knowing and fostering connectedness. Furthermore, ACA's advocacy (ACA, 2020) for the equitable treatment of all individuals aligns seamlessly with the ideals of liberated leadership, promoting a collective approach to dismantling inequality.

Sentipensante (Sensing/Thinking) Pedagogy, conceived by Laura Rendon (1992), addresses the intricate challenges faced by BIPOC scholars in academic settings. Rendon's exploration of *academic shock* demonstrated the struggle scholars undergo in affirming themselves through past experiences and navigating the complexities of living in two distinct worlds without complete acceptance. Sentipensante Pedagogy critiques dominant Western ways of knowing that separate epistemology from ontology and advocates for a *participatory epistemology*, highlighting the unity of the knower and the known. Rendon's renowned *validation theory* challenges conventional views of academic success and integration theory, taking an assets-based approach that seeks to reshape the educational environment to recognize the richness of the individual's knowledge and cultural perspectives.

Sentipensante Pedagogy presents a case for a new approach to leadership. The liberative leadership practices outlined in Table 23.1 resonate with Rendon's vision, challenging the privileged agreements that perpetuate inequality and perpetuate a belief system hindering social change and inclusion. Towards a liberated agreement where leadership cultivates individual voices to be heard and valued. The liberated leadership agreements align with the commitment to justice, equity, and collective well-being, as outlined in the ACA's Multicultural and Social Justice Counseling Competencies (2015).

The incorporation of liberated practices in counselor education and supervision is pivotal for cultivating leaders and advocates who are attuned to the complexities of diverse and dynamic professional landscapes. Doctoral degree programs are designed to equip graduates with the theoretical foundations and practical skills necessary for leadership roles and advocacy within the counseling field. CACREP sets forth comprehensive standards to guide doctoral learners in their journey toward leadership and advocacy. These standards encompass various dimensions, including leadership theories and skills, organizational leadership, crisis response strategies, multicultural and social justice issues, and ethical advocacy practices (CACREP, 2024). Notably, these standards acknowledge the importance of addressing current topical and political issues in counseling, highlighting the interconnectedness of leadership, advocacy, and cultural competence.

As counselor educators and supervisors embark on the development of their professional identity as leaders, they navigate a transformative journey influenced by cultural nuances. The 2024 CACREP standards foster active reflection on one's leadership beliefs, recognizing the impact of culture on leadership styles. In this context, the term "misogynoir" becomes relevant, denoting the intersectionality of race and gender, particularly the unique challenges faced by Black women. Misogynoir sheds light on the oppressive situations linked to race and gender stereotypes that female leaders of color may encounter during their leadership experiences. Research by Black and Magnuson (2005) reinforces the dynamic nature of leadership styles, emphasizing a shift toward collective action over individual needs

Table 23.1 Privileged versus liberated leadership agreements

Privileged leadership agreements	Liberated leadership agreements
Privilege intellectual/rational knowing	Work with diverse ways of knowing
Privilege separation	Embrace connectedness, collaboration, transdisciplinarity
Privilege competition	Engage diverse leadership strategies
Privilege perfection	Be open about being grounded in knowing/not knowing of multiculturalism and respect for diverse cultures
Privilege monoculturalism	Balance our personal and professional lives with work, rest, and replenishment
Privilege the avoidance of self-examination	Take time for self-reflexivity

among female leaders. The researchers interviewed female leaders, and the experiences shared emphasize the necessity of understanding the influence of race and gender stereotypes. Specifically, the study participants indicated that these stereotypes contributed to the isolation they experienced. Participants in the study defined leadership as a shared, intergenerational, and dynamic activity driven by a collective commitment to fulfilling a mission, vision, or calling (Black & Magnuson, 2005).

In essence, incorporating liberative practices involves not only meeting accreditation standards but also fostering an environment that recognizes the unique challenges faced by leaders of diverse backgrounds. Doctoral programs play a crucial role in shaping future leaders and advocates who are equipped to navigate and challenge oppressive systems. By embracing cultural competence, acknowledging intersectionality, and promoting collective, dynamic leadership, these programs contribute to the development of counselors and counselor educators who are not only leaders in their field but also advocates for social justice and inclusivity.

Stop and Reflect: *As you reflect on the concept of liberated leadership within counselor education and supervision, how do you see the incorporation of these principles aligning with your personal experiences and beliefs about leadership? How might this framework challenge or expand your understanding of leadership, particularly in terms of advocating for social justice and inclusivity within a counseling context?*

23.6 Preparing for Leadership

Race and gender have continued to be under researched areas in leadership (Ospina & Foldy, 2009). While race is often an integral part of how individuals define themselves, it also plays an important role in how an individual defines leadership. Shore et al. (2011) define leadership as "the action of leading people or an organization" (Shore et al., 2011). However, cultural variables such as race, ethnicity, gender, sexuality, which would provide context to leadership are missing from this definition, however. We have found that it is important to provide this crucial cultural context, which allows us to build a more complete picture of leadership, leader development, and the various methods of addressing barriers as a leader of color. By understanding how race fits into organizational leadership, individuals can better prepare for roles in leadership and administration. As seen from the collection of experiences included in the authors' leadership journeys, none of us began our academic careers intending to be leaders and administrators. Along the way, we have encountered systemic barriers and personal insecurities. In addition, although our professional journeys began out of a passion to do more to connect and serve as advocates, our leadership styles have evolved as our professional identities have developed. As new leadership opportunities have presented themselves, we have gained knowledge, and we have realized and capitalized on our potential.

23.6.1 Development

Oftentimes, the terms leadership development and leader development are confused or used interchangeably. However, according to Day (2001), the difference between the two is significant. *Leadership* development occurs when multiple methods are employed in a systematic way to develop leaders. On the other hand, leader development is individualized and mirrors the development of individuals into adulthood (Day & Sin, 2009; Day et al., 2014). *Leader* development is focused on developing an individual's skills and capacities by assessing their strengths and areas of growth, encouraging self-reflection, and mentoring or coaching (Day, 2001). It is important to note that an individual's cultural background (e.g., race, ethnicity, gender, sexual orientation) can influence the leader's development experience.

The cyclical diagram in Fig. 23.2 illustrates how key leadership development methods are interconnected and influenced by cultural capital, self-care, and wellness.

At the center of the diagram is cultural capital, highlighting its significance in influencing all aspects of leadership development. Multirater feedback, a comprehensive assessment method that collects input from various sources, feeds into executive coaching. Executive coaching, a personalized approach to leadership development, then leads to leadership training, which equips individuals with essential leadership competencies.

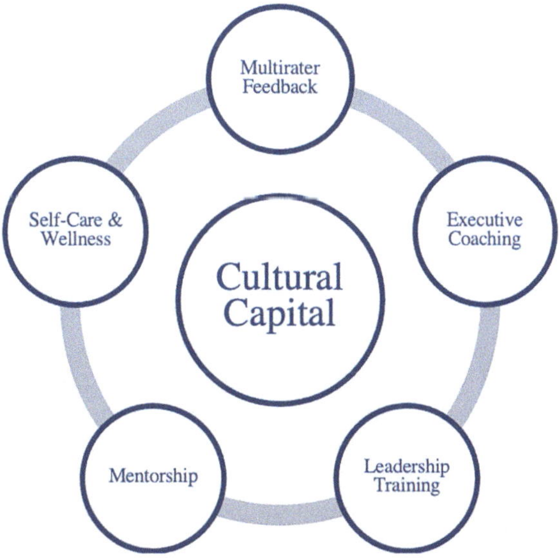

Fig. 23.2 The cyclical nature of leader development

Mentorship, another crucial component of leadership development, connects back to cultural capital, emphasizing the importance of learning from experienced leaders who can provide guidance and support. Self-care and wellness complete the cycle, reflecting their vital role in sustainable leadership and the prevention of burnout.

The cyclical nature of the diagram emphasizes the continuous growth process and the interconnectedness of these leadership development methods. By placing cultural capital at the center and incorporating self-care and wellness, this model underscores the importance of a holistic approach to leadership development that considers the unique challenges and strengths of diverse leaders.

BIPOC individuals in leader development will have individualized experiences and unique ways of viewing and understanding the world (Vinnicombe & Singh, 2002). Consequently, the experiences of BIPOC individuals in leadership and administration, which are often shaped by their experiences in a society marked by racism, systemic oppression, and bias, will likely be different from those of their White peers. The microaggressions a leader of color may experience, as well as their feelings of being an impostor, could impact the leader's development process as well.

In addition to the influence of cultural background on leadership development, counselor educators, doctoral learners, and CITs may face various barriers that hinder the cultivation of their leadership skills. These barriers can include limited resources, such as funding for professional development opportunities, or institutional constraints that prioritize other areas of growth. Time constraints and competing responsibilities, such as teaching, research, and service, can also make it challenging for counselor educators to prioritize their leadership development. Recognizing these barriers is crucial for finding creative solutions and advocating for the necessary resources and support to foster leadership growth within counselor education programs.

23.6.2 Cultural Capital

In 1970, the French sociologist Pierre Bourdieu coined the term cultural capital as a way to explain how power is transferred and social class is maintained. Believing that capital involves more than just economic power, Bourdieu (1984) argued that cultural capital is the bedrock of one's social life and ultimately determines one's position within society. Cultural capital consists of those social assets that allow an individual to have social mobility within society. Bourdieu developed three distinct types: embodied (e.g., language, mannerisms, and preferences); objectified (e.g., cultural goods, books, and works of art); and institutional (e.g., qualifications, educational credentials, and professional credentials). There are other indicators of social standing that can add or detract from one's cultural capital, including race, class, gender, sexuality, ethnicity, nationality, religion, and age. One's cultural capital also varies based on the environment one is operating in. In its simplest form, however, within the right environment, the more cultural capital an individual has, the more social power they have.

Too often, faculty and CITs of color do not realize they possess cultural capital that makes them viable candidates for leadership positions. Leaders of color, who could serve as visible role models for aspiring leaders, are not the norm in higher education leadership. Additionally, the leadership structure is typically hierarchical and not collectivist, the politics of leadership and administration often operate using a Eurocentric framework, and the pressure of being an effective leader of color can jeopardize the social capital a faculty member may already possess. However, faculty of color who have exposure to mentors, who participate in leadership training, who self-evaluate their own leadership skills, and who realize their leadership potential are often able to utilize their cultural capital to open doors of opportunity in leadership and administration for others. Cultural capital allows us to question why something is the way it is. It can also be used to develop new opportunities to build cultural capital within an institution, and it can be imparted to others by increasing their accessibility to opportunities. For both aspiring and seasoned leaders, understanding cultural capital's role at an institution and for leadership positions can help create more effective leaders and administrators. It can also push institutions in directions that are more equitable, inclusive, and just.

Leadership development is a multifaceted process that encompasses various methods to enhance an individual's leadership skills. These methods are essential for cultivating effective leaders who can navigate the complexities of their roles. Here, we highlight key leadership development methods, including multirater feedback, executive coaching, mentorship, and leadership training, backed by research findings and industry best practices.

23.6.3 Multirater Feedback

Multirater feedback, also known as 360-degree feedback, is a comprehensive assessment method that collects input from various sources, including peers, subordinates, and supervisors. This method provides leaders with a holistic view of their performance and behaviors, offering insights into their strengths and areas for improvement. Research indicates that multirater feedback enhances self-awareness and promotes targeted development, contributing to leadership effectiveness (Atwater & Yammarino, 1997).

23.6.4 Executive Coaching

Executive coaching is a dynamic and personalized approach to leadership development. It involves a collaborative partnership between an individual and a coach, fostering a reflective process to maximize personal and professional potential. The coaching process integrates counseling, mentoring, consulting, and training to leverage the leader's strengths and address growth areas. Studies suggest that executive coaching positively impacts leadership skills, self-efficacy, and overall job performance (de Haan et al., 2018; Jones et al., 2016).

23.6.5 Mentorship

Mentorship serves as a valuable component in leadership development, pairing individuals with experienced mentors to facilitate knowledge transfer and skill enhancement. This relationship focuses on providing guidance regarding the mentee's current skills, overall professional development, and career trajectory. Research highlights the importance of mentorship in leadership development, emphasizing the role mentors play in modeling effective leadership practices and expanding mentees' networks (Allen et al., 2016; Ragins & Cotton, 1999).

23.6.6 Leadership Training

Leadership training programs are structured initiatives designed to equip individuals with essential leadership competencies. One example is the Emerging Leaders programs, offered by the regions in the Association for Counselor Education and Supervision, which provides training in leadership, advocacy, and social justice for counselor educators. These programs often incorporate workshops, seminars, and experiential learning to enhance leadership skills. Research supports the effectiveness of leadership training in developing specific competencies, such as communication, decision-making, and conflict resolution (Day et al., 2014). However, it is important to note that counselor education programs often lack formal leadership training, experiential learning opportunities, and research training focused on leadership. While programs like the Emerging Leaders initiative by the Association for Counselor Education and Supervision provide valuable training, it is crucial for counselor education programs to integrate leadership development and research on leadership into their core curriculum. By offering practicum and internship experiences focused on leadership, as well as incorporating leadership theory, research methodology, and practice specific to leadership into coursework, counselor education programs can better prepare learners for future leadership roles and equip them with the necessary skills to conduct and evaluate research on leadership in the field. This integration can include case studies, role-playing exercises, research projects on leadership theories and practices, and reflective assignments that encourage doctoral learners and CITs to explore their leadership styles, develop essential competencies, and engage in research activities relevant to leadership in counselor education. By emphasizing both leadership skills and research on leadership, counselor education programs can foster a new generation of leaders who are well-prepared to advance the field through evidence-based practices and innovative research on leadership development and effectiveness. Tailoring training to address the unique challenges faced by diverse leaders contributes to more inclusive leadership development (Ely & Thomas, 2001).

Incorporating these diverse methods into a comprehensive leadership development plan ensures a well-rounded approach to fostering effective and adaptable leaders. As the leadership landscape evolves, staying attuned to emerging strategies and incorporating evidence-based practices remains integral to continuous improvement.

23.7 Self-care and Wellness in Leadership

Navigating the leadership landscape as a BIPOC individual is fraught with the challenges posed by systemic barriers as well as a pervasive lack of representation. In this intricate web of difficulties, cultivating self-care and wellness practices is not just a means of personal sustenance but a strategic approach to recognize, understand, and prepare for the multifaceted challenges unique to individuals of color in leadership positions. The importance of self-care becomes increasingly apparent when we delve into the intricacies of these challenges, seeking to unravel the reasons behind the often-overlooked potential of faculty and CITs of color for leadership roles.

One prevailing issue is the scarcity of visible role models within higher education leadership who mirror the diverse faces of faculty members and CITs. This absence perpetuates the notion that leadership is an arena exclusive to certain demographics, inadvertently discouraging individuals of color from envisioning themselves in such positions. Furthermore, the prevailing hierarchical structure of leadership often clashes with collectivist values, presenting an additional barrier for those who identify with more communal approaches to governance.

The politics of leadership and administration add another layer of complexity, often perpetuating Eurocentric perspectives that may not align with the cultural backgrounds of faculty and CITs of color. Negotiating the pressure to conform to predetermined notions of effective leadership can be daunting, as it may compromise the social capital that faculty members currently possess within their academic circles.

The very definition of *leadership* itself can carry different connotations, especially when viewed through the lens of cultural diversity. It is imperative to reframe leadership into a liberated concept that accommodates diverse perspectives, allowing individuals of color to bring their unique cultural assets and strengths to the forefront. Decolonizing leadership messages and expectations becomes crucial in challenging preconceived notions and fostering an environment that values inclusivity. The demand for individuals to change to fit into existing leadership paradigms is yet another obstacle, often requiring a compromise between authentic identity and assumed leadership norms. This dynamic reinforces the need for a shift in the narrative surrounding leadership—one that embraces the rich cultural capital possessed by faculty and CITs of color.

Lastly, the lack of community and expertise to aid mentors exacerbates the challenges faced by BIPOC individuals in leadership roles. Establishing networks and mentorship programs specifically tailored to address the unique struggles and strengths of faculty and CITs of color becomes an integral part of dismantling barriers. Self-care and wellness, in this context, are not merely personal choices but strategic tools for resilience, providing the necessary fortitude to confront and overcome these challenges. By acknowledging, understanding, and preparing for the barriers to leadership, individuals of color can unlock their inherent cultural capital, transforming themselves into formidable and empowered candidates for leadership positions.

Throughout our leadership journeys, each of us encountered reservations and barriers that tested our resilience. Purposeful attempts to silence and sabotage collective goals were draining experiences faced by many in our positions. Recognizing that not everyone will respect the values or honor the person in our line of work, we navigated challenges posed by oppressive working styles. Dealing with gaslighting and the dangers of being underrepresented in academia were common struggles. However, leaning into community support, seeking education, and learning from the stories of those who paved the way became crucial steps in dismantling oppression through liberation.

Taking risks in leadership positions revealed the need to sit with multiplicity when communicating, honoring the lived realities of those targeted by oppression. The ongoing work of liberation, while challenging and slow, requires intentional unpacking of harms and complexities with community support and compassion. Embracing self-care and wellness became integral in the journey of leadership. The primary lesson learned and valued collectively is to be kind and compassionate to oneself during this transformative journey. In a collective pursuit of excellence for our communities, recognizing and mitigating internalized oppression stands as a mindful barrier to overcome.

Imposter syndrome emerged as a shared challenge, raising questions about competence and the persistent struggle to break free from preconceived notions of leadership. The difficulty of finding relatable examples in administration, especially for underrepresented individuals, made gauging abilities a complex task. The balance between professional and personal life, particularly for those who prioritize familial roles, presented a unique barrier. Despite these challenges, stubbornness emerged as an asset, enabling a march to the beat of one's own drum. Hearing barriers, preparing for challenges, and thriving by trusting abilities, approach, and work ethic became pivotal in the leadership journey.

Leadership, initially viewed as daunting by some, brought forth negative experiences. The assumption that leadership requires charisma and extensive responsibilities conflicted with comfort zones. Yet, many found themselves elected to leadership positions unexpectedly, discovering their ability to navigate diverse roles. Negative experiences, such as feeling responsible for the dissolution of a group, taught the importance of acknowledging others' struggles. Despite these challenges, each story underscores the multifaceted nature of leadership, revealing valuable lessons learned through experience. We conclude this chapter by offering self-care tips for leaders, recognizing that collective stories and shared wisdom contribute to the ongoing journey of effective and inclusive leadership.

23.7.1 Wellness Plans for Self-care

While Chap. 24 will thoroughly explore the nuances of wellness, it remains paramount to underscore its indispensability for individuals in leadership positions. Research consistently underscores the value of leaders prioritizing self-care, revealing that such prioritization reduces the risk of burnout and enhances overall effectiveness and sustained performance (Maslach et al., 2001). This prioritization of wellness is particularly vital, given that leaders often invest themselves deeply in guiding others.

Amidst the prevailing misconception that self-care is a selfish endeavor, it stands as a crucial component of effective leadership. Advocating for personal needs is not only a demonstration of leadership's importance but also a fundamental aspect of fostering sustained performance. This becomes even more pronounced for women of color and BIPOC individuals, who statistically encounter higher rates of health concerns due to environmental factors (Williams & Mohammed, 2009). Crafting wellness plans tailored to address these unique needs is, therefore, imperative.

In the context of social justice and liberative leadership practices, Lorde's (1988) quote becomes profoundly relevant: "Caring for myself is not self-indulgence, it is self-preservation, and that is an act of political warfare." This quote underscores the profound link between self-care, wellness, and the broader pursuit of social justice. Leaders, especially those from marginalized communities, engage in an act of resistance against oppressive systems when they prioritize their well-being. Leadership literature echoes the importance of cultural competence in effective leadership. Recognizing the significance of cultural gifts and understanding diverse perspectives contribute significantly to achieving better outcomes in leadership (Greenleaf, 1977). This highlights the essential interplay between cultural awareness and effective leadership practices within the broader context of wellness.

A holistic wellness plan should address physical, social, emotional, and cultural dimensions, enabling leaders to tailor their focus according to culturally specific interpretations and involvements with well-being. Resilience, a concept emphasized in leadership literature (Luthar et al., 2000), plays a crucial role in effective leadership. Leaders who incorporate resilience strategies into their wellness routines are better prepared to confront challenges and navigate the inherent stressors of leadership roles. Empowering women and BIPOC faculty, this integration of cultural gifts and resilience strategies into self-care practices proves particularly valuable in helping them navigate the stresses within oppressive higher education systems.

Leadership involves acknowledging both strengths and growth areas while celebrating the collective journey. Viewing mistakes not as failures but as learning opportunities propels leaders toward future successes. Overcoming negative experiences requires self-reflection and embracing both strengths and weaknesses. Leaders benefit from understanding and appreciating their unique qualities to continue thriving in their roles.

A key component of an effective wellness strategy is the establishment of a personal support network, a factor acknowledged by Myers and Sweeney (2005) as a substantial predictor of wellness. In the pursuit of challenging oppressive systems, leaders must replenish their energy. It is commonplace to encounter challenges, face attempts to derail efforts, and experience discrediting of work, underscoring the necessity for a robust support network. Colleagues, family, friends, mentors, or those who share the vision can play a pivotal role in navigating barriers and fostering essential resiliency. The importance of a personal support network, highlighted by Myers and Sweeney (2005), is substantiated by research, with studies indicating that social support significantly predicts well-being and is crucial for leaders navigating adversity (Cohen & Wills, 1985). In essence, wellness and self-care are integral components of effective leadership, ensuring leaders can sustain themselves while driving meaningful change.

Stop and Reflect: *As you consider the importance of self-care and wellness in the context of leadership, how might you incorporate these practices into your own leadership journey? How can a focus on wellness not only benefit you personally but also contribute to your effectiveness and sustainability as a leader, particularly within the context of social justice and inclusivity?*

23.8 Conclusion

At the outset of this chapter, we prompted you to visualize a leader standing out at the forefront of the pack. In reflecting on our collective experiences in higher education and counseling, the paramount theme that emerged is the profound significance of embracing authenticity and cultural assets in leadership. Recalling the challenges we faced approximately two decades ago, we grappled with integrating our cultural assets into an academic landscape that often-pressured conformity to westernized theories and leadership styles. However, over time, the realization of the vital importance of congruence surfaced, empowering us to intricately weave cultural narratives into both our personal and professional spheres, thereby honoring our individual and collective identities.

As women of color navigating dual roles in client engagement and higher education, we encountered the intricate challenges of balancing cultural identity with academic expectations. Recognizing the intrinsic value, we bring to the profession became a cornerstone. Essential to our journey was the embrace of our cultural identity, coupled with a steadfast resistance to being relegated to mere token colleagues. In the early stages of our academic careers, the expectation to be experts in multicultural counseling and diversity work proved burdensome. It was in acknowledging that none of us holds all the answers that space for imperfection and genuine growth was cultivated. Leadership, we discovered, is an ongoing journey, and genuine success is found in fostering a community where learning is reciprocal, transcending cultural boundaries.

Amidst assimilation pressures, the pivotal realization emerged that celebrating our cultural gifts is not only viable but essential. A seasoned colleague once suggested adopting a "think like a white man" approach for success in academia. Rejecting this notion, we chose instead to celebrate our cultural strengths, redefining leadership not as conformity but as the creation of inclusive spaces where diverse narratives contribute to collective growth. As women of color, this transformative approach involves dispelling stereotypes, embracing our passions, and rejecting the notion of having to think or lead like others. Our vision extends towards a career dedicated to cultural celebration, fostering spaces where collaboration and liberation thrive.

As the counseling profession continues to evolve and face new challenges, it is imperative for counselor education programs to prioritize the development of leadership skills among CITs and faculty. By integrating leadership training into the curriculum, providing experiential learning opportunities, conducting research on leadership theory/skills, and addressing the barriers to leadership development, counselor education programs can cultivate a pipeline of effective and diverse leaders. This investment in leadership development will not only benefit individual counselor educators but also strengthen the profession's ability to advocate for social justice, promote wellness, and meet the evolving needs of the communities they serve.

Central to our individual journeys was the crafting of comprehensive wellness plans to navigate leadership experiences effectively. Adapting these plans to reflect growth, prioritizing balance, self-care, and setting boundaries emerged as essential elements. Key steps included attending workshops, seeking mentorship from BIPOC leaders, and actively participating in the co-creation of supportive communities. In this shared space, we contribute wisdom, support one another, and collectively engage in a journey of leadership development, fostering a powerful community where learning is reciprocal, and leadership becomes a collective voyage towards liberation.

References

Ahmed Iqbal, Z., Abid, G., Arshad, M., Ashfaq, F., Athar, M. A., & Hassan, Q. (2021). Impact of authoritative and laissez-faire leadership on thriving at work: The moderating role of conscientiousness. *European Journal of Investigation in Health, Psychology and Education, 11*(3), 667–685.

Allen, G. P., Moore, W. M., Moser, L. R., Neill, K. K., Sambamoorthi, U., & Bell, H. S. (2016). The role of servant leadership and transformational leadership in academic pharmacy. *American Journal of Pharmaceutical Education, 80*(7), 1–7. https://doi.org/10.5688/ajpe807113

American Counseling Association. (2015). *Multicultural and social justice counseling competencies.*

American Counseling Association. (2020). *ACA advocacy competencies.*

Atwater, L. E., & Yammarino, F. J. (1997). Self–other ratings agreement: A review and model. *Journal of Management, 23*(5), 711–738.

Bass, B. M. (1997). Does the transactional–transformational leadership paradigm transcend organizational and national boundaries? *American Psychologist, 52*(2), 130–139. https://doi.org/10.1037/0003-066X.52.2.130

Bass, B. M., & Bass, R. (2008). *Handbook of leadership: Theory, research, and application* (4th ed.). Free Press.

Bhatti, N., Maitlo, G. M., Shaikh, N., Hashmi, M. A., & Shaikh, F. M. (2012). The impact of autocratic and democratic leadership style on job satisfaction. *International Business Research, 5*(2), 192–201. https://doi.org/10.5539/ibr.v5n2p192

Black, L., & Magnuson, S. (2005). Women of spirit: Leaders in the counseling profession. *Journal of Counseling & Development, 83*(3), 337–342. https://doi.org/10.1002/j.1556-6678.2005.tb00352.x

Bourdieu, P. (1984). *Distinction: A social critique of the judgment of taste.* Harvard University Press.

Cohen, S., & Wills, T. A. (1985). Stress, social support, and the buffering hypothesis. *Psychological Bulletin, 98*(2), 310–357.

Council for Accreditation of Counseling and Related Educational Programs. (2024). *2024 CACREP standards.* https://www.cacrep.org/wp-content/uploads/2024/04/2024-Standards-Combined-Version-4.11.2024.pdf

Day, D. V. (2001). Leadership development: A review in context. *The Leadership Quarterly, 11*, 581–613. https://doi.org/10.1016/S1048-9843(00)00061-8

Day, D. V., Harrison, M. M., & Halpin, S. M. (2014). *An integrative approach to leader development: Connecting adult development, identity, and expertise.* Psychology Press.

Day, D. V., & Sin, H. (2009). Leader development, identity, and goal orientation: A study of personal change trajectories. *Academy of Management Proceedings, 2009*, 1–6. https://doi.org/10.5465/ambpp.2009.44243040

de Haan, E., Duckworth, A., Birch, D., Jones, C., & Middlehurst, R. (2018). Evidence-based coaching: Flourishing or floundering? *International Coaching Psychology Review, 13*(1), 6–28.

Ely, R. J., & Thomas, D. A. (2001). Cultural diversity at work: The effects of diversity perspectives on work group processes and outcomes. *Administrative Science Quarterly, 46*(2), 229–273.

Freire, P. (1996). *Pedagogy of the oppressed* (revised ed.). Continuum.

Greenleaf, R. K. (1977). *Servant leadership—A journey into the nature of legitimate power and greatness.* Paulist Press.

Harro, B. (2010). The cycle of liberation. In M. Adams, W. J. Blumenfeld, C. Castaneda, H. W. Hackman, M. Peters, & X. Zuniga (Eds.), *Readings in diversity and social justice* (2nd ed., pp. 618–625). Routledge.

Hogan, R., & Kaiser, R. B. (2005). What we know about leadership. *Review of General Psychology, 9*(2), 169–180.

hooks, b. (1994). *Teaching to transgress: Education as the practice of freedom.* Routledge.

hooks, b. (2006). *Outlaw culture: Resisting representations.* Routledge.

Jacob, C. J., McMaster, M., Nestel, L., Metzger, N., & Olesky, D. (2013). Collaborating with seemingly unrelated disciplines: Connecting transformational leadership and counseling research. *Journal of Creativity in Mental Health, 8*(3), 293–304. https://doi.org/10.1080/15401383.2013.821931

Jones, R. J., Woods, S. A., & Guillaume, Y. R. F. (2016). The effectiveness of workplace coaching: A meta-analysis of learning and performance outcomes from coaching. *Journal of Occupational and Organizational Psychology, 89*(2), 249–277.

Kaslow, N. J., Falender, C. A., & Grus, C. L. (2012). Valuing and practicing competency-based supervision: A transformational leadership perspective. *Training and Education in Professional Psychology, 6*(1), 47–54. https://doi.org/10.1037/a0026704

Khalifa, M. A., Khalil, D., Marsh, T. E. J., & Halloran, C. (2019). Toward an indigenous, decolonizing school leadership: A literature review. *Educational Administration Quarterly, 55*(4), 571–614. https://doi.org/10.1177/0013161X18809348

Lopez-Perry, C. (2020). Transformational leadership and the big five personality traits of counselor educators. *Journal of Counselor Leadership & Advocacy, 7*(2), 132–146. https://doi.org/10.1080/2326716X.2020.1820406

Lorde, A. (1988). *A burst of light: And other essays.* Ibis Press.

Luthar, S. S., Cicchetti, D., & Becker, B. (2000). The construct of resilience: A critical evaluation and guidelines for future work. *Child Development, 71*(3), 543–562.

Maslach, C., Schaufeli, W. B., & Leiter, M. P. (2001). Job burnout. *Annual Review of Psychology, 52*(1), 397–422.

Monaghan, P. (2018, May 20). When power plays fail, you can lead by example. *Chronicle of Higher Education.* https://www.chronicle.com/article/when-power-plays-fail-you-can-lead-by-example/

Myers, J. E., & Sweeney, T. J. (2005). The indivisible self: An evidence-based model of wellness. *The Journal of Individual Psychology, 61*(3), 269–279.

Nelson, T., & Squires, V. (2017). Addressing complex challenges through adaptive leadership: A promising approach to collaborative problem solving. *Journal of Leadership Education, 16*(4), 111–123. https://doi.org/10.12806/V16/I4/T2

Ospina, S., & Foldy, E. (2009). A critical review of race and ethnicity in the leadership literature: Surfacing context, power and the collective dimensions of leadership. *The Leadership Quarterly, 20*(6), 876–896. https://doi.org/10.1016/j.leaqua.2009.09.005

Piccolo, R. F., & Colquitt, J. A. (2006). Transformational leadership and job behaviors: The mediating role of core job characteristics. *Academy of Management Journal, 49*, 327–340. https://doi.org/10.5465/AMJ.2006.20786079

Ragins, B. R., & Cotton, J. L. (1999). Mentor functions and outcomes: A comparison of men and women in formal and informal mentoring relationships. *Journal of Applied Psychology, 84*(4), 529–550.

Ratts, M., Singh, A., Nassar-McMillan, S., Butler, S., & McCullough, J. (2016). *Multicultural and social justice counseling competencies.* https://doi.org/10.13140/RG.2.1.1989.8002

Shore, L., Randel, A., Chung, B., Dean, M., & Ehrhart, K. (2011). Inclusion and diversity in work groups: A review and model for future research. *Journal of Management, 37*(4), 1262–1289. https://doi.org/10.1177/0149206310385943

Vinnicombe, S., & Singh, V. (2002). Sex role stereotyping and requisites of successful top managers. *Women in Management Review, 17*(3/4), 120–130. https://doi.org/10.1108/09649420210425264

West, J. D., Bubenzer, D. L., Osborn, C. J., Paez, S. B., & Desmond, K. J. (2006). Leadership and the profession of counseling: Beliefs and practices. *Counselor Education & Supervision, 46*(1), 2–16. https://doi.org/10.1002/j.1556-6978.2006.tb00008.x

Williams, D. R., & Mohammed, S. A. (2009). Discrimination and racial disparities in health: Evidence and needed research. *Journal of Behavioral Medicine, 32*(1), 20–47.

Erika Cameron, Ph.D., NCC, ACS (she/her/hers) is the Provost and Vice President of Academic and Student Affairs at Palo Alto University. She has worked as a teacher, counselor, and clinical supervisor in a variety of settings including a primary, middle, and secondary school, university, residential treatment facility, and community agencies. She is an active counselor educator who enjoys teaching in creative and innovative ways. She has assumed leadership roles and delivered presentations at the conferences hosted by the American Counseling Association (ACA), Association for Counselor Education and Supervision (ACES), and International Counselling Association (IAC).

Jung (June) H. Hyun, Ph.D., LMHC, NCC (she/her/hers) is an Associate Professor in the CMHC program at Agnes Scott College. Her scholarly pursuits center around presenting and publishing in the areas of multicultural counseling as well as social justice issues and fostering the resiliency of Asian American Native Hawaiian and Pacific Islanders. She is actively engaged in leadership roles in the counseling profession on a national level. She is a licensed mental health counselor in the State of Washington providing play therapy for children and adolescents and parenting workshops for Asian American populations.

Mariaimeé "Maria" Gonzalez, Ph.D., LPC, (she/her/ella) is currently the co-founder of the Latinx Social Justice Mental Health Institute and serves as the Executive Director, Clinical Operations and Community Outreach at Antioch University Seattle. She has over 16 years of experience as a counselor educator. Her extensive leadership background includes Presidencies of the American Counseling Association of Washington, and the Western Association for Counselor Education and Supervision, as well as serving in various leadership roles for ACA. She was a United Nations Delegate, advocating for global mental health support, social justice, advocacy, and positive change in the counseling profession.

Maintaining and Promoting Wellness for Faculty and Counselors-in-Training

24

Brianne Scott, Cathy Lounsbury, and Jocelyn Novella

Caring for myself is not self-indulgence, it is self-preservation, and that is an act of political warfare.

-Audre Lorde

Abstract

This chapter highlights the importance of wellness for counselor educators and CITs. Specifically, this chapter focuses on exploring the systemic influences that hinder wellness, current wellness practices and models, and best practices for achieving total wellness for individuals within counselor training and counselor education.

Learning Objectives After reading this chapter, you will be able to:

1. Identify varying definitions and models of wellness that can be used within counselor education programs.
2. Explore the influence of systemic challenges on personal and professional wellness that are endemic in institutions of higher education, and how these challenges may serve to foster and further oppression.
3. Explore the signs, symptoms, and prevention strategies for burnout and compassion fatigue.

B. Scott (✉)
Walden University, Minneapolis, MN, USA
e-mail: briannescott@isu.edu

C. Lounsbury
Antioch University, Yellow Springs, OH, USA
e-mail: clounsbury@antioch.edu

J. Novella
Fairfield University, Fairfield, CT, USA
e-mail: jnovella@fairfield.edu

D. M. Stalnaker-Shofner and T. N. Sapp (eds.), *A Comprehensive Guide for Counselor Education*, Springer Texts in Education, https://doi.org/10.1007/978-3-031-68358-9_24

4. Implement holistic wellness practices within counselor education programs via the infusion of best practices into curriculum development and training for CITs, and also as a component of professional development for counselor educators.

24.1 Statement of Reflexivity

The authors are counselor educators at predominantly white institutions who, through their own experiences within institutions of higher education and within the counseling field, recognize the importance of wellness practices. Brianne E. Scott is a contributing faculty member at a predominantly White institution (PWI). She is also a licensed professional counselor working within a community mental health agency. She is a cisgender, able-bodied, queer woman, and a second-generation college student. Her ethnic background is primarily of European descent.

Cathy Lounsbury is a full professor in counselor education at a PWI and has been a counselor and counselor educator for 30+ years in the Northeast. She is a cisgender, heterosexual, able-bodied, white-identifying mother of three. She is a first-generation college student. Her ethnic background is primarily Italian, and the Italian culture continues to be an important aspect of her identity. Jocelyn K. Novella is in her fifth year as an assistant professor in counselor education at a PWI. She is a cisgender, heterosexual, able-bodied female of Armenian and Dutch/English heritage. Her connection to an Armenian heritage influences how she works within the counseling profession and her interpretation of wellness.

The authors' perspective is influenced not only by their own experiences with wellness but also by those who have shared their journeys, triumphs, and challenges providing the "stories" and cases for the chapter, as well as those who have contributed to the research on wellness practices in counselor education.

24.2 Case Scenario

You are a new counselor educator that was recently hired as an Assistant Professor in a CACREP accredited master's level counseling program at a PWI. Your new position is tenure-track which requires a higher level of time dedicated to research. In this scenario, consider that you are the only BIPOC and openly LGBTQQIP2SA faculty member. You are excited to bring your antiracist advocacy and praxis to the program. You are encouraged to continue her work from your dissertation research and felt inspired by some of your mentors of color from your doctoral program. Outside of counselor education, you also own a small private practice in your community where you work with young adults who have experienced varying levels of interpersonal trauma.

As you begin her position, you notice how much work needs to be done within the program to address issues regarding diversity and equity. While your colleagues and department chair state that they will protect your time so that you can focus on her teaching and research, you find it hard to do so given the demands of her program. To address these needs, you joined the newly formed DEIBASJ (Diversity, Equity, Inclusion, Belonging, Advocacy, & Social Justice) committee for the graduate school and stepped in as interim chair while the current chair was on sabbatical. Additionally, several LGBTQQIP2SA CITs approach you about their goal of forming an organization focused on supporting graduate CITs with diverse gender and sexual identities. You are inspired by these CITs as they remind you of the clients you serve in your practice. You agree to be their advisor.

During your first term and courses, some of the CITs present as defensive towards your antiracist teachings. While you were prepared for differences of opinion and you enjoyed the discussions with the CITs, some CITs expressed anger and talked about you trying to "brainwash" them to share your "political" viewpoints. You discussed these statements and experiences with other faculty in the department. While they were able to sympathize with you, they had difficulty relating to your situation. They often told her not to "take it personally" or "I'm sure they didn't mean it like that." One of your colleagues even told you to "have thicker skin". She begins to seek support from your mentors from your doctoral program. You notice how you are struggling with preparing course material, wanting to present the information well, however you feel very worried about the CIT interactions.

In your clinical work, you find yourself thinking about your clients between sessions. You also begin experiencing some difficulty sleeping and hypervigilance when leaving campus after classes at night. After your first term, you realize that you are exhausted, you have not completed any research or writing, and you are feeling resentful toward the program.

24.3 Introduction

Counselors have embraced wellness practices for their clients since the origin of the profession. Additionally, the importance of having effective strategies to maintain counselor wellness has been increasingly accepted (Gibson et al., 2021). However, CES' are facing challenges with utilizing these practices in their own lives. As CES, we must not only prepare CITs for incorporating wellness practices when they enter the profession but also find ways to integrate wellness throughout the curriculum. This chapter begins with an overview of wellness models and the importance of self-care. We explore approaches to wellness used within counselor education. Additionally, we will discuss systemic influences that encourage or inhibit best practices in self-care, especially for faculty and CIT with historically marginalized identities. Finally, we will provide practical applications for incorporating wellness practices within counselor education programs.

24.4 What Is Wellness?

As mentioned throughout this text, CES faculty encompass many roles and functions including teacher, mentor, supervisor, and/or researcher to name a few. Additionally, CES faculty often have other responsibilities outside of counselor education (i.e. family, caretaking, clinical practice) making the process of maintaining our own wellness quite challenging (Lackritz, 2004). When considering wellness, Harrichand et al. (2021) considers the focus of wellness practices to be both a pedagogical priority and critical imperative to promote CIT development. Wellness is defined as "a way of life oriented toward optimal health and well-being, in which body, mind, and spirit are integrated by the individual to live life more fully within the human and natural community" (Myers et al., 2000, p. 250). More broadly speaking, wellness is defined as a balance between the mind, body and spirit (CACREP, 2023a).

Stop and Reflect: *In the case scenario above, it is becoming more apparent that you are struggling with wellness physically and emotionally. You have realized that you have not been able to take daily walks for physical and mental wellness and you have sometimes forgotten to eat regularly. These symptoms are related to the time you have dedicated to the many responsibilities you have acquired in your faculty role. Additionally, your clinical work seems to be having more of an impact than usual, with the increased sleep disruption and hypervigilance. Since you have not had time to make progress in your research or writing (a requirement for your position and rank promotion), you find yourself feeling overwhelmed and ineffective in your work. Additionally, due to the increased stress and lack of self-care, you have noticed that you have been feeling more agitated and you have not been able to practice your daily self-care practices (i.e. mindfulness, meditation, journaling for emotional wellness). Because the experience of stress diminishes your executive functioning, without intervention, this trajectory could lead to further emotional and/or physical symptoms and lead to experiences of compassion fatigue and burnout.*

24.4.1 Wellness Frameworks

One of the most researched paradigms of holistic wellness used in counselor education is based upon the Wellness Wheel created by Sweeney and Witmer in 1991. The purpose of the Wellness Wheel was to have a framework to identify and promote personal wellness plans (Myers et al., 2000). Evolving from this holistic perspective, Myers and Sweeney (2014) developed the Five Factor Wellness Inventory (FFWEL) to assess wellness through the five dimensions of self: creative, coping, social, essential, and physical. The creative self-dimension addresses how thinking, emotions, control, positive humor, and work impact a client's wellness. The coping self-dimension includes the leisure, stress management, self-worth, and realistic beliefs subscales. The subscales of social self-dimension are friendship and love. The essential self-dimension subscales include spirituality, gender identity, cultural identity, and self-care. Lastly, the physical self-dimension includes the exercise and nutrition subscales. At any point in time, we can give more or less attention to each of these dimensions. This inventory is helpful in giving us a holistic picture of the status of our wellness. From this framework, wellness is viewed as a lifestyle, with a focused balance among spirit, mind, and body.

A promising framework for a counselor education wellness paradigm is the development of counselor wellness competences (Gibson et al., 2021) that will ideally generate a shared understanding and value of wellness within the field of counseling. These competencies, additionally, will provide counselor educators with guideposts for integration into counselor training programs. Initiated by the Chi Sigma Iota Executive Council, the framework includes nine wellness competencies relevant to the counseling profession: self-care, personal relationships, boundaries, stress and burnout, professional supports, wellness promotion, wellness research, wellness assessment, and wellness-based goals.

As applied to counselor educators, the first competency, self-care, refers to the ability of counselor educators to interpersonally monitor personal wellness, identify needs, and implement strategies that maintain wellness. Personal relationships refer to the counselor educator's ability to identify and maintain close relationships that promote optimal well-being. Boundaries encompass counselor educators' ability to recognize needs and limitations and to set and communicate boundaries to support wellness. The fourth component is stress, burnout, and impairment, which refers to counselor educators' ability to self-reflect and recognize signs of burnout and compassion fatigue and maintain professional effectiveness whilst addressing these concerns. Professional support practices encapsulate counselor educators' ability to seek out professional support when needed including personal counseling, consultation, and supervision. Wellness promotion enlists the ability to promote the use of wellness practices to maintain holistic wellness. Wellness research and assessment refers to counselor educators' ability to incorporate wellness assessment and use of empirically based wellness models as tools within their own counseling, supervision, and interpersonal roles. The final component of Wellness-based goal setting refers to counselor educators' ability to utilize wellness models and individualize them to the person with specific goals based to optimize wellness (Gibson et al., 2021).

Within this framework, counselors and counselor educators are provided with a realistic breakdown of wellness practices that can be tailored to CIT needs. This model could serve as a potential framework for counselor educators when discussing wellness and self-care in their courses. We believe wellness must be discussed throughout a counseling program, as stressors may shift depending on the semester. Unlike other wellness models, the counselor wellness competencies (Gibson et al., 2021) highlight the importance of self-care while also highlighting boundaries, professional support, and personal relationships as a way to mitigate stress and burnout. The role of relationships and support remains a powerful mitigator of perceived stress. Other researchers have identified how relationships play a positive role in mitigating stress and burnout. All of the aforementioned wellness models could be considered an important framework to help begin conversations related to wellness between CITs and faculty.

It is important to consider how hierarchical systems may impact the ability to adequately incorporate wellness models into curriculum. Mekhail (2019) reported how wellness initiatives need to be supported by university and program administration through cross-cultural partnerships within the university and surrounding community, representation of differing ideas, and the need for DEIBASJ to be a consideration for all faculty.

Therefore, wellness is not seen as static but rather as an evolving process requiring consistent attention and growth, as well as an ethical imperative. As such, the ACA *Code of Ethics* (ACA, 2014) mandates that "counselors engage in self-care activities to maintain and promote their own emotional, physical, mental, and spiritual wellbeing to best meet their professional responsibilities" (p. 8, Ethical Standard C.2.g). Additionally, CACREP (2023a) requires that counselor educators provide their CITs with instruction on self-care strategies appropriate to the counselor role. This professional imperative to monitor oneself and one's colleagues against professional impairment is compounded for counselor educators as the ethical standards create accountability to provide our CITs with the skills and strategies to maintain wellness in addition to incorporating our own self-care practices. Accordingly, ethical Standards F.6.a. and F.6.b. address the responsibility of counselor educators to implement evaluation and remediation practices to support supervisee growth and promote self-care practices (ACA, 2014). So as we move forward in this chapter, we ask the question: How do we find this balance? Without the proactive presence of wellness, counseling CITs and CES' can be wholly impacted by the daily stressors associated with the profession.

24.5 Systemic Influences on Wellness

To truly understand and implement strategies for wellness practices within your counselor education program, it is necessary to gain awareness of the systemic influences and barriers to wellness at the macro and micro levels. We will begin with the macro level, which encompasses cultural and societal aspects that impact a person's development (Bronfenbrenner & Morris, 2006). Using the ecological systems theory of human development as a framework (Bronfenbrenner & Morris, 2006), it is clear that to create a CIT who prioritizes wellness, the entire educational system within which that CIT develops must be evaluated (Harrichand et al., 2021; Myers et al., 2016). To promote a more holistic consideration, we will first examine the role of societal influences along with the counselor education system and work our way inward, while identifying the disparities that exist for counselor educators, CITs, and clients.

24.5.1 Societal Influences with Wellness

Outside of the institutional barriers of higher academia, there remain further wellness considerations for faculty and CITs of historically marginalized identities. It is necessary for higher administration and faculty to consider the current political and social climate that CITs and faculty are living within and how this may affect overall wellness and feelings of safety. In considering individual safety and wellness, considerations can be made to the current protections toward and lack of legislative protections for African Americans, Asian Americans, women of all races and ethnicities, LGBTQQIP2SA individuals and people with intersecting historically marginalized identities. Following the televised murder of George Floyd, there was a reported significant increase in depression and anxiety among African Americans (Fowers & Wan, 2020). Accordingly, linked with an increase in anti-Asian hate crimes, Asian Americans have reported an increase in anxiety and depression (Abrams, 2021). The experiences are compounded in consideration of the mercurial LGBTQQIP2SA protections that are available or have been recently retracted for LGBTQQIP2SA faculty and CITs (American Civil Liberties Union, 2021) as well as the changes in legislation that affect women's reproductive health (Berg & Woods, 2023).

As we know, the concept of personal and professional identities has been broadened to encompass intersectionality, the interaction of various identities in one individual. In the academic context, McDowell and Hernández (2010) describe:

> In the context of participatory and democratic ideals attending to multiple voices from the ground (e.g., faculty and students) and creating a culture of inclusion involves having spaces where input, visions, cultural norms, and values can be assessed and weighted to negotiate how differences will be handled, promotions will be granted, programming decisions will be made, curriculum will be developed, and so on. (p. 102)

This intersectionality of historically marginalized identities compounds the stress on faculty, CITs, and clients and needs to be a priority in considering wellness concerns (Moe et al., 2023). A "culture of inclusion" represents the potential for a well academic environment and requires faculty who represent aspects of the dominant culture to engage in open conversation about how their privilege presents in the dynamics of the department, the policies and procedures, and in pedagogical decisions in the classroom (McDowell & Hernández, 2010).

The historical events listed above are by no means a comprehensive list of societal considerations because they do not encompass all persons and all identities. However, we included this section to highlight the importance of how societal climate and change can be linked to counselor educator faculty and counseling CITs' perceptions of overall wellness. Moving forward, we will highlight the role of counseling governing bodies and how they may influence wellness.

24.5.2 Organizational Influences on Wellness

CACREP is one crucial element of the macrosystem in the ecological model. It establishes the norms of the profession and accredits programs for their ability to achieve these normative goals. Counseling organizations have worked hard over the years to establish credibility within a chaotic mental health marketplace, and the standards set in place by CACREP go a long way toward doing that. Counseling programs can communicate with each other through shared language and standards that allow for much-needed collaboration. These requirements for accreditation also provide information for CITs as they navigate the programs available to them (CACREP, 2023b). Harrichand et al. (2021) highlighted the importance of the incorporation and facilitation of self-care / wellness strategies within CACREP standards.

However, as with any standards for any profession, these requirements can create pressure and stress for faculty members, administrators, and even CITs. When we look at the impact of these standards from the point of view of eustress versus distress, the kind of stress experienced by all of the previously listed constituents depends on a variety of factors; however, we believe that one stands out above the rest. That is, what is the level of support from administrators for this accreditation process, and how many resources are they willing to contribute to make it happen? This may be an important question for new counselor educators to ask as part of the job application process, especially if their role will involve participation in this process.

Stop and Reflect: *In considering the case scenario, you are excited to be a new faculty member at a CACREP program; however, you have vetted the program to determine the level of support offered regarding the accreditation process, which faculty members handle that process and what administrative support exists for this work? This could alter your sense of what programs are a good fit for you.*

The ACA *Code of Ethics* is another example of a macrosystem impact on wellness. Most counselors believe in and resonate with the standards established here and understand the importance of upholding the highest ethical values in providing care to clients. However, there is a message in those standards that we should prioritize our clients' wellness needs, but we also have to reflect on ourselves, our own needs, and take a step back if we feel compromised emotionally (Hollingsworth, 2015; Yager & Tovar-Blank, 2007). How often do we, as a profession, talk about this conflict within ourselves or discuss with our CITs the challenges inherent in walking this fine line? Having continuous conversations will be key to understanding and integrating these standards into a healthier profession.

Both areas of the macrosystem also reflect the chronosystem (Bronfenbrenner, 1992) impact on wellness for counselor educators. As we all know, standards are constantly changing, being updated, and becoming more stringent. This makes sense for a relatively new profession on the mental health stage. However, each change can feel like an edict from the external world to faculty members who are trying to ensure a quality program. This lack of control over what is happening in the larger system can be a factor in feeling overwhelmed, unappreciated, or just exhausted. Again, the support of the graduate school environment can make all the difference here. Finally, any standards established for an entire profession can be subject to the dominant perspectives of that profession. Considerations of all voices in the profession is crucial for the organizational wellness of our field.

Stop and Reflect: *As identified in the scenario, you could ask questions of other junior faculty in the program or the graduate school at large to gauge the place of the Dean's Office in understanding and collaborating with departments on accreditation issues.*

24.5.3 Institutional Influences on Wellness

The graduate school and overall university environment have an enormous impact on the wellness of a counseling program, from the faculty to the individual CIT. This exosystem (Bronfenbrenner, 1992) provides a framework for the program and the processes that either aid or hinder its functioning. As a new faculty member or when applying for a job, it is essential to evaluate specific, intentional initiatives offered by the school to support this level of wellness. In the case scenario at the beginning of the chapter, it appears that you have become a "go-to" faculty for CITs who wanted to work on antiracist initiatives, largely because no system was in place in the graduate school for this kind of work. The lack of institutional support experienced through the vignette is indicative of how higher academia can be unresponsive to the needs of historically marginalized groups and individuals.

Within higher academia, there still remains a disproportionately high number of White faculty, particularly White cisgender male faculty within higher academia (U.S. Department of Education, 2020), despite the overall increase of faculty of color, female faculty, etc. Over time, there has been an increase in the number of Asian American, Black, Latinx, and Native American scholars in higher academia (Finkelstein et al., 2016); however, cisgender White male faculty remain the majority. Accordingly, though female faculty outnumber male faculty at 2-year institutions they are less likely to receive tenure or be employed in a tenure-track position (Finkelstein et al., 2016).

Given the historical dominance of White male faculty in academia, institutional procedures and policies have been created and maintained in accordance with the needs of this subgroup. These policies are created in accordance with White and male faculty needs and could prove to be disadvantageous for those of differing identities and their differing needs. Some common examples include lack of consideration for family and home life. Particularly within counselor education, the presence of a "competition culture" (Johnson, 2002) can lead faculty to feel disconnected and overworked.

Within in an institution and program, faculty need to review their DEIBASJ statements and collaborate on how they are actively practicing these statements within the classroom, within CIT clinical placement, within their research, and within their interactions with others (Mekhail, 2019) The faculty represents part of the microsystem (Bronfenbrenner, 1992) in this context. At this level, individual faculty members have an enormous impact on the wellness of CITs for a variety of reasons. One of the most obvious is the expectations in the classroom and the instructor's own relationship with wellness/self-care. Within academia, the emphasis on high drive work culture can lead to burnout for many academics (Linder et al., 2015).

Finally, CITs represent the core of the microsystem of the counselor education world. They may enter the program with their own individual understandings of the meaning of wellness, self-care, and self-priority. They then begin hearing about the importance of wellness from the individual program (hopefully). They may understand what these terms mean, or they may assume they understand. Added to that is the experience of historically marginalized CITs in counselor education programs, where discussions of self-care can take on a privileged voice.

Common challenges for CITs include time related demands and increased workload (Hill, 2009). CITs are typically juggling personal and professional development throughout their program, alongside overall workload, high need clients, and lack of support (Lawson & Myers, 2011). All of these factors contribute to potential mental health struggles; however, BIPOC counselors in training face unique stressors that are not encountered by their White counterparts. On top of the time demands and increased workload, BIPOC CITs also experience racial discrimination, microaggressions, and prejudice, both within their school program and their clinical site (El-Ghoroury et al., 2012). The experiencing of discrimination has been linked with higher rates of anxiety and depression, low self-esteem, and post-traumatic stress disorder (Carter et al., 2017; El-Ghoroury et al., 2012; Museus et al., 2017).

BIPOC CITs have reported higher rates of social isolation, burnout, reduced quality of life, increased anxiety and depressive symptoms (Jang et al., 2008). Discrimination has also been linked to low rates of wellness and higher rates of exhaustion by CITs (Museus et al., 2017). Experiences of prolonged discrimination can ultimately lead to minority stress status (Banks, 2010; McClain et al., 2016) and racial battle fatigue (Delgado et al., 2000; Parker & Lynn, 2002). To review, minority stress status is described as the increased cognitive load and stressors experienced by historically marginalized people and is linked to lower academic success and increased mental health concerns (Museus et al., 2017). Accordingly, racial battle fatigue is

> physical, mental, and/or emotional/behavioral response to racial microaggressions, which are subtle, conscious or unconscious, intentional or unintentional, layered, cumulative, verbal and nonverbal, behavioral, and environmental insults directed at People of Color based on race… [that] cause unnecessary stress while benefiting White people. (Furr, 2018, p. 3)

Furr (2018) noted that BIPOC individuals experience both psychological and physiological symptoms of Racial Battle Fatigue (RBF). These symptoms range from high blood pressure, fatigue, and insomnia (Gee & Ford, 2011) to increased social isolation and poor job/school performance (Smith, 2004).

As noted with the vignette, you have been confronted with overt/covert racism and microaggressions from your university and CITs, while also balancing your teaching responsibilities and your dedication to promoting equity within your university. Towards the end of your first semester, you have experienced similar symptoms (feeling exhausted and resentful) which align with Racial Battle Fatigue. Because you have received minimal overt support from your colleagues, you are at continued risk for social isolation and health concerns.

As we continue to highlight the case scenario above, we find it important to note that as White persons, we will never truly understand the daily racism and discrimination experienced by BIPOC communities. However, that does not excuse us from knowing about the long term effects, speaking out for equity, and learning what our role is as humans, counselors, and counselor educators in promoting wellness within higher academia.

Often when considering wellness with the counseling profession, there remains the tendency to emphasize the individual and an internal locus of control in enacting change. This internalized focus leaves disempowered CITs to experience isolation while struggling within the program, often leading to compassion fatigue and burnout for new counselors.

24.6 Compassion Fatigue and Burnout

Researchers have indicated that counselors experience negative cognitive, emotional, physical, and behavioral responses due to their secondary exposure to the trauma material of their clients (Furr, 2018; Lackritz, 2004; Woo et al., 2019). While the term Compassion Fatigue first appeared in the literature to describe the experience of nurses exposed to trauma in their work (Joinson, 1992), the potentially deleterious effects on counselors themselves gained recognition through literature on Compassion Fatigue (CF) (Figley, 1995), Secondary Traumatic Stress (STS) (Stamm, 1997) and Vicarious Traumatization (VT) (Saakvitne & Pearlman, 1996). Figley (1995) described the symptoms of secondary traumatic stress (which he used interchangeably with STS) as nearly identical to Post-Traumatic Stress Disorder (PTSD), including re-experiencing, avoidance/numbing, and persistent arousal. Vicarious Traumatization is defined as the "transformation of the therapist's or helper's inner experience as a result of empathic engagement with survivor clients and their trauma material" (Saakvitne & Pearlman, 1996, p. 25). These reactions can occur as a short-term response to working with one or more particular clients or as a long-term transformation (McCann & Pearlman, 1990).Burnout, on the other hand, is most often characterized as a result of stressors in the work environment, such as long hours and large caseload, as opposed to STS, which is directly related to the material presented by the client. Burnout is viewed as a gradual wearing down of workers who feel overwhelmed and ineffective in their work. There is evidence (e.g., Lackritz, 2004; Woo et al., 2019) that approximately 20%

of university faculty (regardless of discipline) may experience burnout and, thus, the stressors related to academic life may contribute to the burnout experienced by counselor educators. The compounding stressors for those within counselor education who are also engaging in clinical work require a more intentional holistic approach to wellness than one might have previously incorporated.

Accordingly, when the issue of self-care and wellness trickles down to CITs, it speaks to the pervasive concern about how wellness is modeled and whether faculty have the necessary systemic supports to adequately model wellness practices. The following section will address the practical application of wellness practices alongside the consideration of institutional program influences to promote CIT and faculty wellness.

24.7 Addressing the Gap for Wellness

Although there is an apparent wealth of research that speaks towards the importance of self-care practices and wellness within counselor education (Furr, 2018; Gibson et al., 2021; Woo et al., 2019), there remains minimal, accessible information about the practical application of wellness strategies within counselor education. However, there are some practical ways to incorporate wellness practices while considering systemic influences and CIT development (See Fig. 24.1).

Within the institutional/program level, there is research to support the implementation of wellness /stress management courses within CES curriculum. These potential courses could be required as part of the overall curriculum and could be taken concurrently with other classes. Past researchers have reported that the

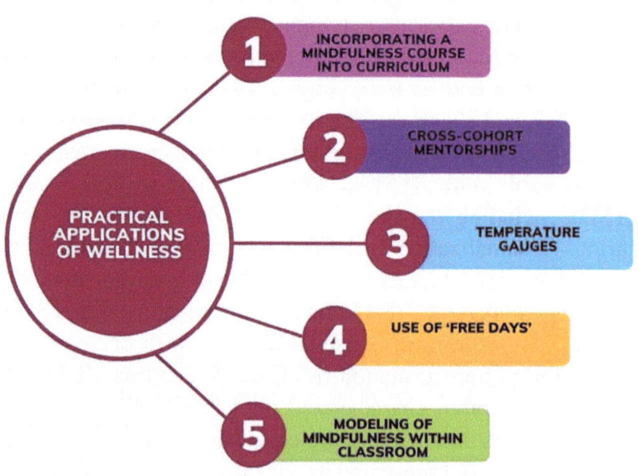

Fig. 24.1 Practical applications of wellness

inclusion of a course focused on learner wellness has shown to positively impact CIT self awareness to stressors, practical self-care, and assessing wellness needs (Abel et al., 2012; Wolf et al., 2014). Concurrently, Fung (2019) reported that even shortened exposure to wellness practices promoted CIT self awareness towards overall wellness needs. Accordingly, ongoing experiences of increased isolation have been reported as a major stressor for historically marginalized CITs and faculty (Jang et al, 2008). Thus, a cross-cohort approach and faculty mentorship can provide active support and connection for CITs and faculty (Linder et al., 2015; Mitchell & Binkley, 2021; Salazar, 2009).

The incorporation of mindfulness practices within counselor training has shown to have a positive impact on both faculty and CIT wellness and decrease the intensity of emotions after a negative event (Arch & Craske, 2006; Newsome et al., 2012). Mindfulness can be incorporated from the beginning of the program and be used for CITs to "check-in" with themselves during difficult classes and counseling sessions. Mitchell and Binkley (2021) recommend *temperature gauges*, which includes CITs using mindfulness strategies to gauge their emotional temperature to the presented subject and utilize reflective exercises and mindful breathing practices (Dye et al., 2020) to promote emotional regulation. The use of mindfulness practices within CIT programs can lead to higher ambiguity tolerance, increased self-reflection skills, and increased reported empathy towards clients (Bohecker et al., 2016; Leppma & Young, 2016). Faculty can accordingly model these practices in the classroom to encourage CIT engagement. Accordingly, with the use of mindfulness practices, it is suggested that faculty consider a *free day* within their curriculum. The purpose of this free day is meant to encourage CIT practice of mindfulness, stepping away from academic stressors, and intentional connection with others (Mitchells & Binkley, 2021). Within the consistent practice of mindfulness, CITs can recognize the signs of burnout and more quickly acknowledge when they need to take a break (Grise-Owens et al., 2018).

24.8 Conclusion

Wellness remains to be an ethical imperative and pedagogical priority within counselor education. Counselor educators, counselors, and counseling CITs face unique stressors that can easily affect overall wellness. Without the proactive focus on wellness by administration, counselor educators and counselors, individuals can easily begin to experience symptoms of burnout and compassion fatigue. There are many systemic influences that overtly and covertly affect our ability to focus on wellness. Historically marginalized CITs and faculty experience many similar stressors to the majority, but these are compounded with daily experiences of microaggressions and campus climate. There are several accessible wellness frameworks, including the CSI counselor competencies model, which provides a more inclusive framework for wellness practices. There are also several practical wellness/self-care strategies that could be incorporated into counseling programs. Overall, this chapter hopes to further the call to action for counselor education departments in their ability to foster a sense of community and belonging for all CITs and faculty.

References

Abel, H., Abel, A., & Smith, R. L. (2012). The effects of a stress management course on counselors-in-training. *Counselor Education and Supervision, 51*(1), 64–78. https://doi.org/10.1002/j.1556-6978.2012.00005.x

Abrams, Z. (2021). The mental health impact of anti-Asian racism. *American Psychological Association, 52*(5), 22. https://www.apa.org/monitor/2021/07/impact-anti-asian-racism

American Civil Liberties Union (ACLU). (2021). *Legislation affecting LGBT rights across the country.* American Civil Liberties Union. https://www.aclu.org/legislation-affecting-lgbt-rights-across-country

American Counseling Association. (2014). *2014 ACA code of ethics.* https://www.counseling.org/docs/default-source/default-document-library/ethics/2014-aca-code-of-ethics.pdf?sfvrsn=55ab73d0_1

Arch, J. J., & Craske, M. G. (2006). Mechanisms of mindfulness: Emotion regulation following a focused breathing induction. *Behaviour Research and Therapy, 44*(12), 1849–1858. https://doi.org/10.1016/j.brat.2005.12.007

Banks, K. H. (2010). African American college students' experiences of racial discrimination and the role of the college hassles. *Journal of College Student Development, 51*(1), 23–34. https://doi.org/10.1353/csd.0.0115

Berg, J. A., & Woods, N. F. (2023). Overturning Roe v. Wade: Consequences for midlife women's health and well-being. *Women's Midlife Health, 9*, Article 2. https://doi.org/10.1186/s40695-022-00085-8

Bohecker, L., Vereen, L. G., Wells, P., & Wathen, C. (2016). A mindfulness experiential small group to help students tolerate ambiguity. *Counselor Education and Supervision, 55*(1), 16–30.

Bronfenbrenner, U. (1992). Ecological systems theory. In U. Bronfenbrenner (Ed.), *Making human beings human: Bioecological perspectives on human development* (pp. 106–173). Sage.

Bronfenbrenner, U., & Morris, P. A. (2006). The bioecological model of human development. In R. M. Lerner & W. Damon (Eds.), *Handbook of child psychology: Theoretical models of human development* (pp. 793–828). Wiley.

Carter, R. T., Lau, M., Johnson, V., & Kirkinis, K. (2017). Racial discrimination and health outcomes among racial/ethnic minorities: A meta-analytic review. *Journal of Multicultural Counseling and Development, 45*(4), 232–259. https://doi.org/10.1002/jmcd.12076

Council for Accreditation of Counseling and Related Educational Programs. (2023a). *2024 CACREP standards.* https://www.cacrep.org/wp-content/uploads/2023/12/2024-CACREP-Standards.pdf

Council for Accreditation of Counseling and Related Educational Programs. (2023b). *About CACREP.* https://www.cacrep.org/about-cacrep/#understanding-accreditation

Delgado, R., & Stefancic, J. (Eds.). (2000). *Introduction. Critical race theory: The cutting edge* (2nd ed., pp. xv–xix). Temple University Press.

Dye, L., Burke, M. G., & Wolf, C. (2020). Teaching mindfulness for the self-care and well-being of counselors-in-training. *Journal of Creativity in Mental Health, 15*(2), 140–153. https://doi.org/10.1080/15401383.2019.1642171

El-Ghoroury, N. H., Galper, D. I., Sawaqdeh, A., & Bufka, L. F. (2012). Stress, coping, and barriers to wellness among psychology graduate students. *Training and Education in Professional Psychology, 6*(2), 122–134. https://doi.org/10.1037/a0028768

Figley, C. (1995). *Compassion fatigue: Toward a new understanding of the costs of caring.* In B. H. Stamm (Ed.), Secondary traumatic stress: Self-care issues for clinicians, researchers, and educators (pp. 3–28). Lutherville, ME: Sidran Press.

Finkelstein, M. J., Conley, V. M., & Schuster, J. H. (2016). *Taking the measure of faculty diversity*. TIAA Institute.

Fowers, A., & Wan, W. (2020). Depression and anxiety spiked among black Americans after George Floyd's death. *The Washington Post: Health*. https://www.washingtonpost.com/health/2020/06/12/mental-health-george-floyd-census/

Fung, S. C. (2019). Effects of an experiential training group on psychological wellness and professional efficacy for counsellors-in-training. *Global Journal of Health Science, 11*(9), 1–22.

Furr, S. (2018). Wellness interventions for social justice fatigue among student affairs professionals. *Dissertations*. 2803. https://ecommons.luc.edu/luc_diss/2803

Gee, G., & Ford, C. (2011). Structural racism and health inequities: Old issues, new directions. *Du Bois Review: Social Science Research on Race, 8*(1), 115–132. https://doi.org/10.1017/S1742058X11000130

Gibson, D. M., Pence, C., Kennedy, S. D., Gerlach, J., Degges-White, S., & Watson, J. (2021). Development of the counselor wellness competencies. *Journal of Counselor Leadership and Advocacy, 8*(2), 130–145. https://doi.org/10.1080/2326716X.2021.1925997

Grise-Owens, E., Miller, J., Escobar-Ratliff, L., & George, N. (2018). Teaching note; Teaching self-care and wellness as a professional practice skill: A curricular case example. *Journal of Social Work Education, 54*(1), 180–186. https://doi.org/10.1080/10437797.2017.1308778

Harrichand, J., Litam, S. D., & Ausloos, C. D. (2021). Infusing self-care and wellness into CACREP curricula: Pedagogical recommendations for counselor educators and counselors during COVID-19. *International Journal of Advanced Counseling*. Advance online publication. https://doi.org/10.1007/s10447-021-09423-3.

Hill, N. R. (2009). An empirical exploration of the occupational satisfaction of counselor educators: The influence of gender, tenure status, and minority status. *Journal of Counseling and Development, 87*(1), 55–61. https://doi.org/10.1002/j.1556.2009.tb00549.x

Hollingsworth, M. A. (2015). Wellness: Paradigm for training & practice. *VISTAS Online*, Article 39. ACA Knowledge Center.

Jang, Y., Chiriboga, D. A., & Small, B. J. (2008). Perceived discrimination and psychological well-being: The mediating and moderating role of sense of control. *The International Journal of Aging & Human Development, 66*(3), 213–227. https://doi.org/10.2190/AG.66.3.c

Johnson, W. B. (2002). The intentional mentor: Strategies and guidelines for the practice of mentoring. *Professional Psychology: Research and Practice, 33*, 88–96. https://doi.org/10.1037/0735-7028.33.1.88

Joinson, C. (1992). Coping with compassion fatigue. *Nursing, 22*(4), 116, 118–119, 120.

Lackritz, J. R. (2004). Exploring burnout among university faculty: Incidence, performance, and demographic issues. *Teaching and Teacher Education, 20*(7), 713–729. https://doi.org/10.1016/j.tate.2004.07.002

Lawson, G., & Myers, J. E. (2011). Wellness, professional quality of life, and career-sustaining behaviors: What keeps us well? *Journal of Counseling and Development, 89*(2), 163–171. https://doi.org/10.1002/j.1556-6678.2011.tb00074.x

Leppma, M., & Young, M. E. (2016). Loving-kindness meditation and empathy: A wellness group intervention for counseling students. *Journal of Counseling & Development, 94*(3), 297–305.

Linder, C., Harris, J. C., Allen, E. L., & Hubain, B. (2015). Building inclusive pedagogy: Recommendations from a national study of students of color in higher education and student affairs graduate programs. *Equity & Excellence in Education, 48*(2), 178–194. https://doi.org/10.1080/10665684.2014.959270

McClain, S., Beasley, S. T., Jones, B., Awosogba, O., Jackson, S., & Cokley, K. (2016). An examination of the impact of racial and ethnic identity, imposter feelings, and minority status on the mental health of Black college students. *Journal of Multicultural Counseling and Development, 44*(2), 101–117. https://doi.org/10.1002/jmcd.12040

McDowell, T., & Hernández, P. (2010). Decolonizing academia: Intersectionality, participation, and accountability in family therapy and counseling. *Journal of Feminist Family Therapy, 22*(2), 93–111. https://doi.org/10.1080/08952831003787834

Mekhail, M. (2019). Culture in mind: Fostering a sense of belonging for students of color in wellness-affiliated Spaces. *M.A. in Higher Education Leadership: Action Research Projects, 20,* 1–63.
Mitchell, M., & Binkley, E. (2021). Self-Care: An Ethical Imperative for Anti-Racist Counselor Training. *Teaching and Supervision in Counseling, 3*(2), 5. https://doi.org/10.7290/tsc030205
Moe, J., Perera, D. M., & Rodgers, D. (2023). Promoting wellness at the intersections of gender, race and ethnicity, and sexual-affectional orientation identities. *Journal of Mental Health Counseling, 45*(3), 231–246. https://doi.org/10.17744/mehc.45.3.04
Museus, S. D., Yi, V., & Saelua, N. (2017). How culturally engaging campus environments influence sense of belonging in college: An examination of differences between white students and students of color. *Journal of Diversity in Higher Education, 10*(3), 1–17. https://doi.org/10.1037/dhe0000069
Myers, J. E., & Sweeney, T. J. (2014). *Five factor wellness inventory (FFWEL): Adult, teenage, and elementary school versions* (2nd ed. manual). Mind Garden.
Myers, J. E., Sweeney, T. J., & Witmer, J. M. (2000). The wheel of wellness counseling for wellness: A holistic model for treatment planning. *Journal of Counseling & Development, 78,* 251–266. https://doi.org/10.1002/j.1556-6676.2000.tb01906.x
Myers, J. E., Trepal, H., Ivers, N., & Wester, K. L. (2016). Wellness of counselor educators: Do we practice what we preach? *Journal of Counselor Leadership and Advocacy, 3*(1), 22–30. https://doi.org/10.1080/2326716X.2016.1139479
Newsome, S., Waldo, M., & Gruszka, C. (2012). Mindfulness group work: Preventing stress and increasing self-compassion among helping professionals in training. *The Journal for Specialists in Group Work.*. https://doi.org/10.1080/01933922.2012.690832
Parker, L., & Lynn, M. (2002). What's race got to do with it? CRT's conflicts with and connections to qualitative research methodology and epistemology. *Qualitative Inquiry, 8,* 7–22.
Saakvitne, K. W., & Pearlman, L. A. (1996). *Transforming the pain: A workbook on vicarious traumatization.* WW Norton & Co.
Salazar, C. F. (2009). Strategies to survive and thrive in academia: The collective voices of counseling faculty of color. *International Journal for the Advancement of Counselling, 31*(3), 181–198. https://doi.org/10.1007/s10447-009-9077-1
Smith, W. A. (2004). Black faculty coping with racial battle fatigue: The campus racial climate in a post-civil rights era. In D. Cleveland (Ed.), *A long way to go: Conversations about race Franklin et al. 321 by African American faculty and graduate students at predominantly White institutions* (pp. 171–190). Peter Lang.
Sweeney, T. J., & Witmer, J. M. (1991). Beyond social interest: Striving toward optimum health and wellness. *Individual Psychology: The Journal of Adlerian Theory, Research & Practice, 47*(4), 527–540.
U.S. Department of Education, National Center for Education Statistics. (2020). *Digest of education statistics, 2020.* Indicator 47. http://nces.ed.gov
Wolf, C. P., Thompson, I. A., Thompson, E. S., & Smith-Adcock, S. (2014). Refresh your mind, rejuvenate your body, renew your spirit: A pilot wellness program for counselor education. *The Journal of Individual Psychology, 70*(1), 57–75.
Woo, H., Kim, H., & Park, S. (2019). Burnout and turnover intentions among junior counseling faculty: Moderating role of mentoring. *Journal of Employment Counseling, 56*(2), 85–94. https://doi.org/10.1002/joec.12114
Yager, G. G., & Tovar-Blank, Z. G. (2007). Wellness and counselor education. *The Journal of Humanistic Counseling, 46,* 142–153. https://doi.org/10.1002/j.2161-1939.2007.tb00032.x

Brianne Scott, Ph.D., LCPC, (she/her/hers) is a contributing faculty member at Walden University. Her research areas include intersectionality, addictions curriculum integration, and LGBTQ+ topics. She is a Licensed Clinical Professional Counselor (LCPC) and works full time at a community mental health agency; her specialities include neurodivergence, queer identities, and trauma counseling. She has held several community leadership roles and is currently on the board of two local queer nonprofits in Idaho, focused on providing support within her community.

Cathy Lounsbury, EdD, LCPC, (she/her/hers) is an Associate Professor as well as serving as the current Chair of the Counselor Education Department, at Antioch University. She has been a LCPC for 30 years working with children and adults who have experienced trauma. In addition to serving on national and global trauma response teams, Dr. Lounsbury has provided consultation, training, and supervision to organizations on trauma-informed care, fostering resilience, and mitigating secondary traumatic stress. She has held varying national and community leadership roles and is the Director of the Institute for Counselor Wellness at Antioch University New England.

Jocelyn Novella, Ph.D., LPC, (she/her/hers) is an assistant professor of Counselor Education at Fairfield University and a Licensed Professional Counselor in the state of CT. She received her Ph.D. at Oregon State University and worked at a college counseling center in the northeast for 24 years, most recently as Director of Counseling. She worked within a Wellness Center and led efforts in establishing a Body Image Task Force on campus. Her research interests include efficacy of telemental health, interprofessional education in behavioral health, and specialized issues with emerging adults.

Imposter Phenomenon–Recognizing, Managing, and Preventing

25

Samantha Airhart-Larraga

> *If we really want to change the world, we must dig deep into our own healing from oppression and injustice. Only then can we begin to interrogate systems and structures that maintain these inequities.*
>
> *Anneliese Singh*

Abstract

The imposter phenomenon (IP) is the belief that you are a fraud or not good enough, a sense of non-belonging, and the fear of being discovered as a fraud resulting in one being removed or fired. IP is more common for BIPOC learners, for first-generation college learners, in the early stages of professional identity creation, and for academics early in their careers. In this chapter, using the case of Maria as an illustration, we will explore the features and potential predictors of IP as well as IP in counselor education faculty. Additionally, we will discuss ways to manage IP at the intrapersonal, interpersonal, and institutional levels with recommendations for implementing formal mentorship programs.

Learning Objectives After reading this chapter, you will be able to:

1 Explain the definition of imposter phenomena, noting its key characteristics.
2 Recognize internal and external signs of the imposter phenomenon and the ways it can manifest and the adverse impact it can have.
3 Identify one intrapersonal, one interpersonal, and one institutional strategy for managing imposter phenomena.

S. Airhart-Larraga (✉)
Texas A&M University–Central Texas, Killeen, TX, USA
e-mail: s.airhart-larraga@tamuct.edu

D. M. Stalnaker-Shofner and T. N. Sapp (eds.), *A Comprehensive Guide for Counselor Education*, Springer Texts in Education, https://doi.org/10.1007/978-3-031-68358-9_25

25.1 Statement of Reflexivity

I am a first-generation Mexican American and I identify as a Hispanic, BIPOC, cisgender female. I am an Assistant Professor of counseling at a small university, and I have been a professional counselor for over 20 years. I am also a counselor supervisor. since 2003 and a counselor supervisor since 2007. I am the first female in my family to get a Ph.D. I returned to school in my 40 s and pursued my Ph.D. as a second career. I have experienced the imposter phenomenon; it is part of my narrative as a counselor educator and something I actively manage.

I conceptualize the imposter phenomenon as a worry that I am going to be found lacking and unable to do my job as an assistant professor. Essentially, it manifests as the idea that I will be found to be a fraud and fired. IP is not new to me; I believe it is an extension of existing anxiety and negative cognitions. My IP does intensify in a new setting, or in this case, a new career. It is exhausting to think this way and to work through daily thoughts questioning being good enough. Over the last few years, I have learned ways to manage IP and have carved out my own space at my institution to gain a sense of belonging. Thus, this chapter is written from these perspectives.

25.2 Case Scenario

Maria is currently pursuing a doctoral degree in counselor education from a well-known counselor education program. She is a cisgender heterosexual female. in her mid-30 s, unpartnered, and has one male child that is 5 years old. She identifies as Hispanic and is a first-generation college learner. Her parents are immigrants from northern Mexico and own a Mexican food restaurant in her hometown.

Maria is a Licensed Professional Counselor Associate working part-time for a small private practice to satisfy the 3000-h direct experience requirement for full licensure. She is a graduate research assistant at her university, and she receives tuition and a monthly stipend for her research. She has limited financial support from family and currently lives with her parents and son.

Maria graduated with a bachelor's degree in psychology ten years ago and immediately went to work for the local office of the state department of child welfare as an investigator. While working in this capacity, she realized she enjoyed working with children and their families and decided to enroll in graduate school to pursue a master's degree in counseling; she completed her degree one year ago. Maria also continued to work full-time as an investigator while obtaining her master's degree and completed her studies with a 4.0 GPA. She was encouraged to pursue a Ph.D. by colleagues and a former professor. Maria applied for and was accepted to the doctoral program in her hometown.

Maria began the doctoral program in counselor education six months ago. Though she was always good at learning, she has come to believe that her writing is not at the same level as the rest of her cohort. Unlike other members, she has not connected with a current faculty mentor to provide guidance and support related to writing and research. She is quiet in class because she often feels she does not have anything significant to contribute. She feels like an outsider within the program and her cohort, as well as with faculty. As a single mother it is difficult for her to dedicate the same time commitment to school as her peers, which contributes to her belief that she does not have much in common with them as her peers do not have the same responsibilities she has. She has begun to question whether academia is the right setting for her and is contemplating leaving the program.

25.3 Introduction

The imposter phenomenon (IP), also known as imposter syndrome, was first identified by Pauline Clance and Suzanne Imes in 1978 and linked primarily to women. We now understand that IP is experienced regardless of gender identity and may be more common among racial and ethnic minorities (Peteet et al., 2015; Trotman, 2009). The imposter phenomenon is an experience of feelings of inadequacy and fearing discovery as not belonging, as well as the persistent belief that you are not good enough despite high academic and professional achievements (Clance & Imes, 1978). In their seminal research on IP, Clance and Imes (1978) further the previous statement by stating the following: "women who experience the impostor phenomenon maintain a strong belief that they are not intelligent; in fact, they are convinced that they have fooled anyone who thinks otherwise" (p. 241). The imposter phenomenon could lead to emotional distress, job dissatisfaction, and eventually professional burnout (Chandra et al., 2019).

Reviewing the literature, empirical evidence suggests that the imposter phenomenon is more common in the academic setting for CITs of racial and ethnic minorities (Haskins et al., 2019; Lige et al., 2016; Peteet et al., 2015; Smedley et al., 1993). Similarly, IP occurs more often for first-generation college learners (McCarthy et al., 2023), learners and professionals in the early stages of their professional identity development (Hutchins & Rainbolt, 2017), and academics early in their careers in higher education (Haskins et al., 2019; Parkman, 2016). When we consider this research, it seems to support the general vulnerability of faculty with racially marginalized identities. This vulnerability to imposter phenomenon could potentially stunt their academic growth as the experiencing of IP could cause them "to disengage from academic endeavors, avoid evaluative situations, have constant feelings of inadequacy, and exhibit an unhealthy pressure to succeed" (Peteet et al., 2015, p. 176). Additional related research on IP focuses on specifying the nuances of IP and their impact. Below, the specific features of IP as proffered by Clance and O'Toole (1987) are delineated.

The first noted feature is referred to as the *imposter cycle.* This often manifests as anxiety related to the completion of an assigned task. In an effort to manage the anxiety, an individual may either overprepare or procrastinate. In spite of the anxiety and the coping attempts, the task is completed successfully. However, the successful completion of the task creates a pattern, and this pattern of thinking and coping is unfortunately reinforced. The second characteristic of IP is that it is more common in people who are introverted. Third, people who experience IP have apprehension about being assessed; this can be formally as in the form of an annual performance evaluation, or informally as in the perceived judgment of others. This contributes to the fourth feature of IP, which is dreading failure. The fifth trait of IP is an underlying sense of shame about achieving success, the sixth is difficulty accepting positive feedback, and the seventh is a pervasive feeling of anxiety. The eighth characteristic is a tendency to overestimate others while undervaluing self, and the ninth is the idea that aptitude is to be perfect which is unachievable. Finally, the tenth characteristic is negative messages from family about their ability to achieve success or need to achieve success. As we further explore the nature and impact of IP, we will move into a discussion of the predictors of IP.

Stop and Reflect: *Referring back to our case scenario, Maria is experiencing imposter phenomenon. She is questioning if she belongs in the doctoral program and is wondering if she is good enough despite having evidence (i.e., a 4.0 in her master's degree) to the contrary. She has a fear of evaluation and failure, has anxiety, tends to overestimate others while underestimating herself, and possibly has a skewed definition of intelligence and success. Perhaps if we were to talk to her about her feelings of imposture, she would demonstrate that she goes through the imposter cycle frequently and has throughout her entire higher education experience.*

25.4 Predictors of Imposter Phenomenon

Bernard et al. (2002) found that depression, anxiety, and a tendency to experience negative feelings may be predictors of IP in college learners. Similarly, Lane (2015) conducted a qualitative study of 29 individuals transitioning from learners to professional life and found that 80% of the participants described feelings of imposter phenomenon. Lane developed a grounded theory of imposter phenomenon that included both internal and external factors contributing to the development of feelings of imposture. Internal factors include a high drive for success, a tendency toward perfectionism, and a need for external validation. External factors include comparing professional performance to colleagues, exaggerated perceived abilities of others, and a general fear of being evaluated and found lacking. Furthermore, Vergauwe et al. (2015) found that imposter feelings are related to higher neuroticism and lower conscientiousness. Neuroticism is associated with perfectionism tendencies, a tendency to experience negative feelings, and less ability to adapt realistic expectations. Conscientiousness includes the tendency to self-evaluate in a negative manner across multiple situations. Relatedly, Peteet et al. (2015) looked at 161 Black and Hispanic first-generation college learners and found that lower levels of emotional health and ethnic belonging were predictors of IP. A furtherance of Lane's research, Fraenza (2016) compared online learners to traditional college learners and found a positive relationship between perfectionism and imposter phenomenon. Perfectionism was found to be the most significant predictor of imposter feelings, with social influence or peer pressure driving the feelings of fraudulence. In 2017, Chapman discussed that learners with diverse identities, for example, learners who are parents, first generation, or from underrepresented groups, can experience feelings of disengagement. These negative feelings could contribute to the development of imposter phenomena or make existing IP worse. Finally, in a study examining how early attachment styles relate to imposter phenomenon in university learners, Jensen and Deemer (2020) found that avoidant attachment to early caregivers may lead to feelings of fraudulence, and this may be due to having less close relationships and the subsequent overreliance on self. In other words, experiences with avoidant early attachment may lead to a sense of imposture.

Stop and Reflect: *For Maria, if we consider that she had a less than ideal early attachment, and as a consequence, she may have had fewer close relationships on which she could rely for support. This could contribute to feelings of alienation, followed by a sense of being overwhelmed. Additionally, as a single mother, she may not have the same amount of time to spend on her doctoral studies and research opportunities, which may contribute to her thoughts of inadequacy with respect to her ability to engage and contribute in a manner on par with her peers. She also has a high drive for success, as evidenced by her pursuit of higher education, however, she is comparing her own academic performance with that of her peers. This may promote an exaggeration of her peers' abilities, and this could trigger feelings of inadequacy supported by thoughts that she is not good enough. Finally, as her doctoral program lacks ethnic representation in both learners and faculty, Maria may feel more isolated without a clear sense of her identity. All of these factors contribute to the experiencing of imposter phenomenon.*

25.5 Imposter Phenomenon and Higher Education Faculty

There are several factors and events that can contribute to faculty experiencing imposter phenomenon. These factors include foundational events of professional development, the influence of the culture of academia, being subjected to frequent microaggressions, and their pursuit of acceptance. Additionally, particularly for women and BIPOC faculty, there exists a fear of presenting as their authentic selves and being subjected to "damaging gender-based stereotypes" (O'Connell et al., 2020, p. 76). These factors can create barriers for women and BIPOC faculty as they endeavor to achieve successful careers. It can also adversely impact the choices they may make both professionally and personally. Lastly, these factors perpetuate the inequalities that are prevalent and insidious within academic institutions (Arnold et al., 2016; Reddick et al., 2021; Settles et al., 2020). Below, we explore these factors in detail.

25.6 Foundational Events

Hutchins and Rainbolt (2017) examined the founding events that trigger feelings of fraudulence in faculty. The researchers incorporated Erik Erikson's work on professional identity development to suggest that faculty may experience increased feelings of fraudulence in response to critical professional events that increase psychological distress (e.g., a rejection letter from a journal editor or grant application) (Hutchins & Rainbolt, 2017). The more distressful the events that occur during the early stages of professional development are, the more faculty begin to examine their own professional legitimacy, leading to perceived shortcomings in their performance and abilities. The feelings of imposture potentially lead these faculty to avoid submitting their work to journals for fear of rejection, which in turn reinforces the feelings of fraudulence. Beneath this is a fear that they will be exposed as a fraud and fired from the job they worked so hard to get. This is particularly noteworthy for faculty who are early in their careers and at institutions where the culture is "publish or perish."

25.7 Culture

Culture may also play a role in feelings of imposture for BIPOC faculty in the academy, as they may experience a disconnection between their own racial/ethnic culture and that of academia (Settles et al., 2020). There are countermeasures for this. For example, Hispanic/Latinos may thrive in work environments that offer more support and are less competitive (De Luca & Escoto, 2012). Similarly, Winkle-Wagner et al. (2019) suggest that African American faculty thrive in an environment where they feel "emotionally, physically, and socially supported" (p. 661). Additionally, Black faculty report that they find it challenging to find a community that is supportive and often feel "siloed" and isolated by their experiences in academia (Reddick et al., 2021). Furthermore, at institutions where the culture is "publish or perish," the expectation to meet this standard can contribute to the onset of IP, or exacerbate existing feelings of IP.

25.8 Microaggressions

Being subjected to microaggressions factors into the development of imposter phenomenon. For faculty outside of the dominant group (i.e., white, middle-class males), microaggressions are a common occurrence. Microaggressions are committed by those with power, then are perpetuated and protected by the traditional hierarchies of academia (Avent Harris et al., 2019). Examples include systemic impediments such as pay inequity, and delaying the tenure and promotion process, to self-imposed barriers like the feelings of inadequacy and not belonging, which may also inadvertently support the existing systemic barriers. Also, there **is** the inherent implicit bias of devaluing meaningful contributions of BIPOC faculty, placing more value on certain types of research or service (Arnold et al., 2016; Domingo et al., 2020). This unwritten policy is explored in the research of Settles et al. (2020), noting that faculty of color at a research-intensive institution experienced "epistemic exclusion." This "experience in which faculty of color are deemed illegitimate members of the academy and their scholarship is devalued" (p. 1) is a systemic microaggression and impedes BIPOC faculty's professional experiences. Examples include the devaluing research efforts of BIPOC faculty, the lack of acknowledgment of any significant contributions they have made by the institution and their peers, and unclear expectations or ambiguous standards for BIPOC faculty. Another more furtive effect is the internalization by BIPOC faculty of these misattributions leading them to devalue their research, which is a manifestation of IP. Ultimately, microaggressions experienced by BIPOC faculty exacerbate existing feelings of imposture, intensify feelings of isolation, and lead to difficulties with belonging (Smedley et al., 1993). Though the focus of this content addresses the impact of microaggressions on BIPOC faculty, it is important to note that individuals possessing historically marginalized identities may experience microaggressions based on various intersecting identities including but not limited to gender, sexuality, and disability.

25.9 Social Acceptance

Regarding the concept of social acceptance. faculty with historically marginalized identities, particularly BIPOC faculty, experience a lower rate of social acceptance by their colleagues. As they are often underrepresented in academia, they may experience further isolation as the result. Furthermore, having first-generation status intersecting with their BIPOC identity may also contribute to their experience of reduced social acceptance. This occurs not only with their colleagues, but also within their own families due to lack of family members' understanding of or experience with higher education (De Luca & Escoto, 2012). The subsequent isolation BIPOC faculty experience can be especially difficult for them as the family unit can have cultural significance. Specific to being Black-identifying faculty, the struggle to find social connections is experienced within the institutions where they work and the communities where they live (Reddick et al., 2021). The lack of acceptance across multiple dimensions can sow the seeds of imposter phenomenon.

25.10 The Exceptions

Obviously, not everyone experiences imposter phenomenon. Although the transition from learner to faculty is a time when IP is most likely to occur, not everyone develops feelings of fraudulence. In Sanford et al.'s (2017) investigation into factors mitigating IP, female participants who self-identified as successful noted that they did not experience IP, and this was attributed to several factors. First, these participants reported a high sense of self-confidence, nurturing from strong and supportive relationships with professional mentors as well as having supportive personal relationships (e.g. friends and intimate partners). Lastly, they also report receiving the support of other women in leadership positions. The interlocking network of the combined support of relationship partners, personal friends, and professional mentors facilitated the development and maintenance of the confidence needed to prevent or move through initial feelings of imposture. The factors identified in Sanford et al. (2017), lay the foundation for the exploration of ways to manage IP, with specific focus on both prevention and remediation.

Stop and Reflect: *As we consider the case of Maria, Maria's feelings of fraudulence are impacting her ability to actively engage in her learning, specifically manifesting as a lack of participation in class as well as her avoidance of opportunities to professionally network. One criterion for promoting learning and growth in a doctoral program is the importance of constructive feedback. For Maria, already feeling out of place and questioning her abilities, this constructive feedback from professors has the result of exponentially magnifying her sense of inadequacy as further evidence that she does not belong and will be exposed as a fraud. Additionally, Maria has been the target of microaggressions from both her peers and the faculty in her program. An example of this is the faculty's failure to engage Maria with opportunities to collaborate on writing and research projects. This form of implicit bias is often resultant from institutional culture that devalues the scholarship efforts of BIPOC individuals.*

25.11 Managing Imposter Phenomenon

The prevention and remediation of imposter phenomenon begins with recognition. Thus far, we have examined a working definition of IP, explored features and predictors of IP, and reflected on its manifestation in faculty. Additionally, we considered the implications of culture and gender on IP through the delineation of how faculty, particularly women and BIPOC, have higher vulnerability to IP. In this section, we will explore strategies to prevent and remediate IP at different levels: intrapersonal, interpersonal, and institutional. As we explore IP from a systems perspective, we will then revisit the case of Maria and discuss how implementing strategies at these different levels could help address IP.

25.12 Intrapersonal Strategies

There are several intrapersonal strategies that we can implement as countermeasures to prevent or remediate imposter phenomenon. We begin with an inside-out approach, with an initial focus on the intrapersonal. An intrapersonal perspective of IP involves the work that happens from within. As applied to IP, one intrapersonal approach is to diminish the need for external validation and approval from others. One way to do this is to remind yourself of your successes, and to also find ways to intrinsically validate your achievements. Engaging in this internal discourse can help you to self-regulate the negative thoughts of fraudulence associated with IP and to temper behaviors connected with those thoughts. The work of Puchalska-Wasyl and Zarzycka (2020) supports the efficacy of this intervention. The research proffered that internal dialogue from a spiritual foundation (i.e. prayer) had a positive impact on well-being. Additionally, positive self-talk can help create a more realistic perception of your ability (Jensen & Deemer, 2020) and promote self-confidence. Self-dialogue may also mitigate the negative comparison of self to others (Lane, 2015), and help you to root out the source of that insecurity (Tiefenthaler, 2018). Finally, it is important to celebrate your achievements coupled with putting setbacks into proper perspective (Hutchins & Rainbolt, 2017). Shifting the source of validation from an external to internal may be the first course of action to prevent or remedy IP.

Several other intrapersonal approaches may prove helpful in managing IP. Seeking out and engaging in new experiences may enhance your courage and self-confidence, which then can mitigate the effects of IP (Sanford et al., 2017). Additionally, securing mentorship, and also changing mentors as your professional needs and goals evolve is an effective strategy for managing IP. You also want to incorporate adaptability to counter rigidity, and actively engage in reflection to facilitate self-awareness. Both can mitigate IP. and help a new academic effectively evolve from learner to professional (Purgason et al., 2018). Finally, focusing on resilience-building, or our ability to bounce back, also has efficacy in preventing and mitigating IP; let's explore this more in depth.

Factors that contribute to resilience include a work-life balance, facilitating physical and emotional wellbeing, engaging in meaningful self-care, sustaining personal and professional relationships, participating in professional development and growth opportunities, externalization of problems, open-mindedness, and use of humor and fun (Clark et al., 2022; Lawson & Myers, 2011). Additionally, there are various strategies to build and maintain personal and professional resilience. These include being intentional about self-care practices, prioritizing time with family or other significant support networks, and establishing a spiritual foundation all are important countermeasures to IP (Airhart-Larraga et al., 2021). A specific suggestion for CES doctoral learners and new faculty who possess nondominant and intersectional identities (i.e., racial/ethnic minorities, female-identifying, LGBTQQIP2SA, persons with disabilities) is to connect with and integrate at least two of these practices, given the potential predisposition to IP.

25.13 Interpersonal Strategies

In extending the afore-mentioned intrapersonal strategies, we will explore interpersonal strategies in which we can engage to counter IP. Interpersonal relates to our association with and connection to others within established relationships. Social support from our interpersonal relationships (i.e. friendships, romantic pairings) has been strongly associated with self-reported higher levels of overall wellness

(Myers & Sweeney, 2005). Thus, we can suggest that your connection to a personal network can serve to moderate IP, or to prevent its development.

As we explore specific interventions, one approach is to ask for feedback from non-evaluating colleagues as a way to offer a reality-check, thus examining the accuracy of our self-perceptions (Zanchetta et al., 2020). Another measure is thoughtfully utilizing our established relationships for help and at times when support is needed (Griffin et al., 2014). Examples of interpersonal relationships that can meet this need include strategic mentorship (formal or informal) from senior faculty with whom we share similar backgrounds and experiences. These intentional relationships can be vital for managing IP (Griffin et al., 2014). Through this mentorship relationship, the mentor can help validate and normalize your experiences of working in higher education, while also providing tips for navigating the separate roles and responsibilities of faculty. Further, a mentoring relationship with the added dimension of connecting with a person in leadership may have the two-fold benefit of enhancing your self-confidence and helping establish meaningful connections within higher education (Sanford et al., 2017). Another approach is to find and engage with a peer group who also share similar identities (i.e. affinity groups). These groups can ameliorate feelings of disconnection that can provide fertile ground for IP's onset (Chapman, 2017). If such a peer group is not available at your university, there are options for connection available via social media. Examples of these on Facebook include pages and groups for those in academia, those new to academia, academic mothers, tenure-track mothers, as well as BIPOC individuals completing doctoral degrees. Finally, engaging your cultural supports (i.e., spending time with people with similar backgrounds), giving back, and giving back to and supporting future generations may foster resilience building and temper the effects of IP (Airhart-Larraga et al., 2021).

As CES professionals, it is important that we not forget the importance of personal counseling to maintain wellness and prevent IP. As new faculty, working with a counselor can help you to focus on processing feelings of IP, identity development, improving your self-confidence, and reducing the tendency to compare your achievements with others (Peteet et al., 2015). A counselor can help you externalize problems, identify validating connections, and work on empowerment (Haskins et al., 2019). Ideally, engaging in personal counseling should be a best practice and included as a part of our self-care as a way to achieve and maintain our wellness. Thus, increased wellness could be an effective countermand or arrest the effects of imposter phenomenon.

25.14 Institutional Interventions and Strategies

Above we discussed strategies that we can engage in at an individual level to help manage imposter phenomenon. It would be remiss to not include a reflection on institutional responsibility in the prevention and mitigation of IP in their faculty. One approach is for colleges and universities to offer IP-specific resources such as training, coaching, formal mentoring, and workplace support. For new professionals, facilitated socialization as they transition from learner to faculty can help manage the experience of IP. This can be achieved through using direct observation of established peers and tenured faculty as an intervention to manage IP (Lamar et al., 2019). A second consideration to mitigate IP at the institutional level is the strategic orientation of new faculty to help them to learn the values of importance at the program and department levels, as well as the priorities of the institution. Essentially, the act of promoting this understanding of faculty expectations may also effectively reduce feelings of IP (Parkman, 2016). Institutions can also provide regular formal and informal feedback during nonevaluative times (Vergauwe et al., 2015). Additionally, they can offer related training to educate and normalize IP in faculty (Armstrong & Shulman, 2019). Armstrong and Shulman (2019) further suggest that institutions can create space at the program and department levels for conversation about IP, and to incorporate routine check-ins with new faculty members. Another practical strategy that colleges and universities can support is a cultural shift of promoting faculty's ability to and the necessity of being able to establish appropriate professional boundaries and offer resources to faculty members that facilitate healthy work-life balance (Parkman, 2016). Finally, a specific suggestion for BIPOC faculty is offered. As they experience underrepresentation in academia both as learners and faculty (Arnold et al., 2016; De Luca & Escoto, 2012; Reddick et al., 2021) further minoritizing them, institutions can work to create affinity communities and push to increase minority representation (Haskins et al., 2019; Peteet et al., 2015).

For doctoral learners, CES programs can implement formal mentoring practices. Protivnak and Foss (2009) explored the influential experiences of CES doctoral learners, and noted that the departmental culture, the presence of available support systems, as well as understanding how these when combined with learners' personal issues all influenced their doctoral experience. It was suggested that mentoring was the "most helpful experience in their doctoral studies" (Protivnak & Foss, 2009, p. 246). Similarly, Miller and Stone (2011) offered that BIPOC learners described mentorship as "a positive factor in promoting self-confidence" (p. 106). Finally, Kent et al. (2020) explored how mentorship can mitigate attrition and noted that mentoring "served as a protective factor in helping navigate barriers, providing academic and emotional encouragement, reducing isolation, and creating realistic timelines" (p. 532).

Anekstein and Vereen (2018) put forth recommendations for how CES programs can implement formal mentoring. First, they suggest implementing a peer-mentoring program with more advanced doctoral learners paired with newer doctoral learners. This could be a good way for programs to help newer CES doctoral learners who identify as BIPOC, older, parents, or possess any other non-traditional learner identities to encourage connection and outreach to peers with similar backgrounds. Second, they recommend that new doctoral learners be paired with a faculty mentor in the first semester of their program. Pairing with a faculty mentor can help mitigate these feelings. A formal mentoring program embedded in CES programs would endorse the university's commitment to reduce IP in learners and faculty through the increase of self-esteem, and the support of nontraditional learners to find connections within their CES programs. Finally, Bano and O'Shea (2023) recommend that higher education institutions should help doctoral learners with social and emotional support by way of peer support groups and accessibility of mental health resources on campus. Figure 25.1 provides an illustrative graphic summarizing the major points of this chapter.

Stop and Reflect: *Turning our attention back to Maria, we will focus on ways she can begin to address her IP. One suggestion is for Maria to complete the Clance Impostor Phenomenon Scale (CIPS), which can be found online. This inventory can help illuminate the specific impacts of Maria's IP as the results of this self-assessment may offer her insight into how IP can be undergirding her doubts about being a doctoral learner. Another intervention for Maria to manage IP is to help her implement intrapersonal and interpersonal strategies as discussed in the chapter.*

Specifically, from an intrapersonal approach, Maria can manage her internal dialogue by realistically reframing her negative self-perceptions and her inflated perceptions of others. Further, she can begin writing in a journal, where she can document her wins and achievements. While it is important for the institution to facilitate a supportive environment for learners, particularly those with historically marginalized identities, Maria can begin to develop and nurture meaningful connections via *social media by joining online affinity groups that will connect her with other doctoral learners with similar identities. While ideally her doctoral program would have created a mentorship program for learners as outlined by the 2024 CACREP Standards, in the absence of this, Maria can reach out to a faculty to provide her with mentorship. It would be ideal for her to reach out to a BIPOC faculty member to create an affinity connection, either within her program, department, or university, or if necessary, outside of her institution, and to faculty at other universities. The mentorship can also create opportunities for Maria to engage in research and advance her academic writing. As Maria reframes her negative cognitions, she can then focus on resilience-building, by engaging in some of the practices outlined in the chapter to mitigate her IP. Finally, Maria can seek personal counseling. Some universities may have counseling centers that offer free or low-cost mental health services to their current learners. In her therapy, her counselor can work with her to begin to uproot and challenge her negative cognitions, as well as working with her to enhance her self-confidence.*

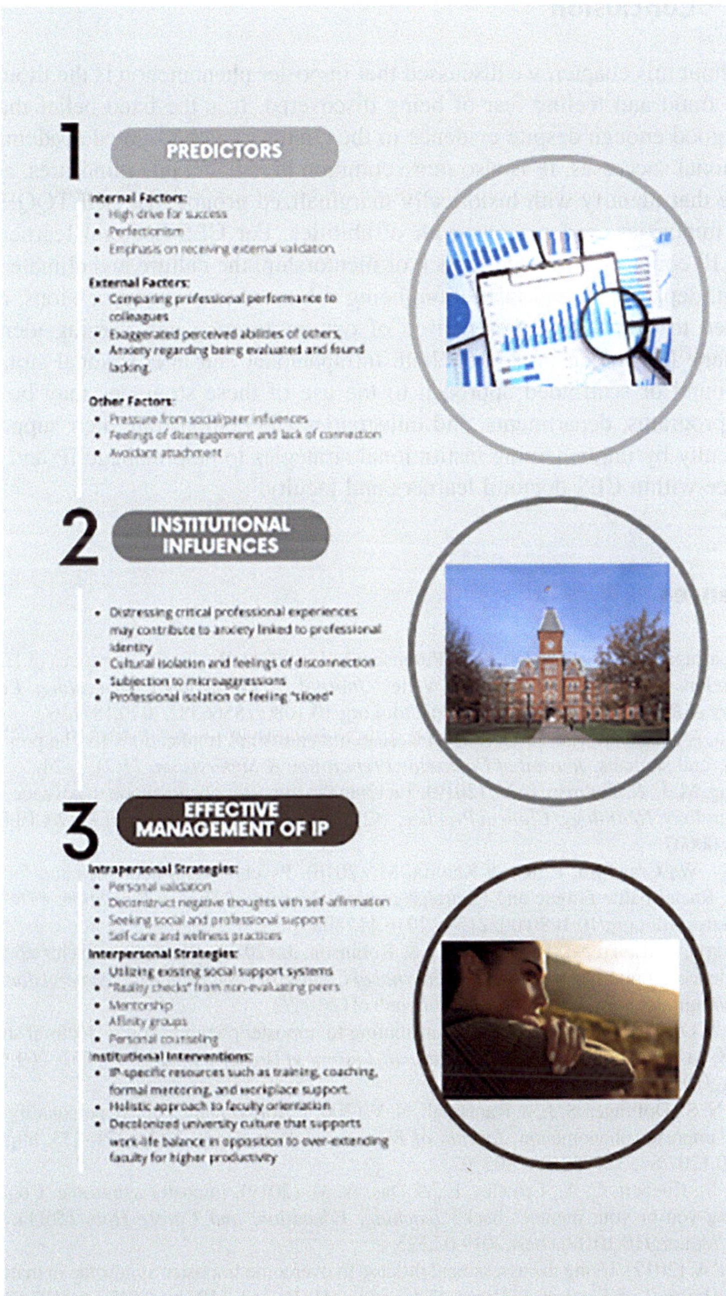

Fig. 25.1 Understanding Impostor Phenomenon

25.15 Conclusion

Throughout this chapter, we discussed that imposter phenomenon is the thought of being a fraud and feeling fear of being discovered. It is the fixed belief that you are not good enough despite evidence to the contrary, such as noted academic and professional successes. IP is also more common in racial/ethnic minorities, as well as those that identify with historically marginalized groups like LGBTQQIP2SA, gender minorities, and persons with disabilities. For CES doctoral learners and faculty, IP could be attributed to lack of mentorship, the culture and climate of the program, department, and institution, being subjected to microaggressions, and as correlated to a lack of representation of our intersecting and varying identities. To manage IP, we can implement both intrapersonal and interpersonal strategies; a compound or scaffolded approach to the use of these strategies may be ideal. Lastly, programs, departments, and universities can demonstrate their support for their faculty by implementing institutional strategies to help manage IP and foster resilience within CES doctoral learners and faculty.

References

Airhart-Larraga, S., Lloyd-Hazlett, J., & Purgason, L. L. (2021). Resilience narratives of Hispanic counselors in the Texas Rio Grande Valley. *Journal of Professional Counseling: Practice, Theory & Research, 48*(1), 15–30. https://doi.org/10.1080/15566382.2020.1871260

Anekstein, A. M., & Vereen, L. G. (2018). Research mentorship: Implications for the preparation of doctoral students. *Journal of Counselor Preparation & Supervision, 11*(2), 1–24.

Armstrong, M. J., & Shulman, L. M. (2019). Tackling the imposter phenomenon to advance women in neurology. *Neurology: Clinical Practice, 9*(2), 155–159. https://doi.org/10.1212/CPJ.0000000000000607

Arnold, N. W., Crawford, E. R., & Khalifa, M. (2016). Psychological heuristics and faculty of color: Racial battle fatigue and tenure/promotion. *Journal of Higher Education, 87*(6), 890–919. https://doi.org/10.1080/00221546.2016.11780891

Avent Harris, J. R., Trepal, H., Prado, A., & Robinson, J. (2019). Women counselor educators' experiences of microaggressions. *The Journal of Counselor Preparation and Supervision, 12*(2). https://digitalcommons.sacredheart.edu/jcps/vol12/iss2/2

Bano, S., & O'Shea, C. (2023). Factors contributing to imposter phenomenon in doctoral students: A U.S. based qualitative study. *International Journal of Doctoral Studies, 18*, 251–269. https://doi.org/10.28945/5195

Bernard, N. S., Dollinger, S. J., & Ramaniah, N. V. (2002). Applying the big five personality factors to the impostor phenomenon. *Journal of Personality Assessment, 78*(2), 321–333. https://doi.org/10.1207/S15327752JPA7802_07

Chandra, S., Huebert, C. A., Crowley, E., & Das, A. M. (2019). Impostor syndrome: Could it be holding you or your mentees back? *Teaching, Education, and Career Hub, 156*(1), 26–32. https://doi.org/10.1016/j.chest.2019.02.325

Chapman, A. (2017). Using the assessment process to overcome Imposter Syndrome in mature students. *Journal of Further & Higher Education, 41*(2), 112–119. https://doi.org/10.1080/0309877X.2015.1062851

Clance, P. R., & Imes, S. A. (1978). The imposter phenomenon in high achieving women: Dynamics and therapeutic intervention. *Psychotherapy: Theory, Research & Practice, 15*(3), 241–247. https://doi.org/10.1037/h0086006

Clance, P. R., & O'Toole, M. A. (1987). The imposter phenomenon: An internal barrier to empowerment and achievement. *Women & Therapy, 6*(3), 51–64. https://doi.org/10.1300/J015V06N03_05

Clark, P., Holder, C., Russell, M., & Downs, H. (2022). The impostor phenomenon in mental health professionals: Relationships among compassion fatigue, burnout, and compassion satisfaction. *Contemporary Family Therapy, 44*(22), 185–197. https://doi.org/10.1007/s10591-021-09580-y

De Luca, S. M., & Escoto, E. R. (2012). The recruitment and support of Latino faculty for tenure and promotion. *Journal of Hispanic Higher Education, 11*(1), 29–40. https://doi.org/10.1177/1538192711435552

Domingo, C. R., Gerber, N. C., Harris, D., Mamo, L., Pasion, S. G., Rebanal, R. D., & Rosser, S. V. (2020). More service or more advancement: Institutional barriers to academic success for women and women of color faculty at a large public comprehensive minority-serving state university. *Journal of Diversity in Higher Education, 15*(3), 365–379. https://doi.org/10.1037/dhe0000292

Fraenza, C. (2016). The role of social influence in anxiety and the imposter phenomenon. *Online Learning, 20*(2), 230–243. https://doi.org/10.24059/olj.v20i2.618

Griffin, R. A., Ward, L., & Phillips, A. R. (2014). Still flies in buttermilk: Black male faculty, critical race theory, and composite counterstorytelling. *International Journal of Qualitative Studies in Education, 27*(10), 1354–1375. https://doi.org/10.1080/09518398.2013.840403

Haskins, N. H., Hughes, K. L., Crumb, L., Smith, A. R., Brown, S. S., & Pignato, L. (2019). Postmodern womanism: Dismantling the imposter phenomenon for Black American college students. *Negro Educational Review, 70*(1–4), 5–25.

Hutchins, H. M., & Rainbolt, H. (2017). What triggers imposter phenomenon among academic faculty? A critical incident study exploring antecedents, coping, and development opportunities. *Human Resource Development International, 20*(3), 194–214. https://doi.org/10.1080/13678868.2016.1248205

Jensen, L. E., & Deemer, E. D. (2020). Attachment style and self-handicapping: The mediating role of the imposter phenomenon. *Social Psychology of Education, 23*(5), 1259–1276. https://doi.org/10.1007/s11218-020-09580-0

Kent, V., Runyan, H., Savinsky, D., & Knight, J. (2020). Mentoring doctoral student mothers in counselor education: A phenomenological study. *Professional Counselor, 10*(4), 532–547. https://doi.org/10.15241/vk.10.4.532

Lamar, M. R., Clemens, E., & Dunbar, A. S. (2019). Promoting doctoral student researcher development through positive research training environments using self-concept theory. *The Professional Counselor, 9*(4), 298–309. https://doi.org/10.15241/mrl.9.4.298

Lane, J. A. (2015). The imposter phenomenon among emerging adults transitioning into professional life: Developing a grounded theory. *Adultspan Journal, 14*(2), 114–128. https://doi.org/10.1002/adsp.12009

Lawson, G., & Myers, J. E. (2011). Wellness, professional quality of life, and career sustaining behaviors: What keeps us well? *Journal of Counseling & Development, 89*, 163–171. https://doi.org/10.1002/j.1556-6678.2011.tb00074.x

Lige, Q. M., Peteet, B. J., & Brown, C. M. (2016). Racial identity, self-esteem, and the impostor phenomenon among African American college students. *Journal of Black Psychology, 43*(4), 345–357. https://doi.org/10.1177/0095798416648787

McCarthy, K., Chavez, K., Gastelum, K., Gomez, J., Salas, J., Severson, Y., & Zabat, J. (2023). Imposter phenomenon: The occupational experience of first-generation college students. *The Open Journal of Occupational Therapy, 11*(2), 1–18. https://doi.org/10.15453/2168-6408.2011

Miller, J. K., & Stone, D. J. (2011). Voices of family therapy doctoral students of color: Aspirations and factors influencing careers in academia. *Journal of Multicultural Counseling & Development, 39*(2), 101–113.

Myers, J. E., & Sweeney, T. J. (2005). The indivisible self: An evidence-based model of wellness. *The Journal of Individual Psychology, 61*(3), 269–279.

O'Connell, C., Eranki, P., & Landis, A. (2020). Empowering women's voices in STEM and banishing the inner impostor. *The International Journal of Diversity in Education, 21*(1), 75–87. https://doi.org/10.18848/2327-0020/CGP/v21i01/75-87

Parkman, A. (2016). The imposter phenomenon in higher education: Incidence and impact. *Journal of Higher Education Theory and Practice, 16*(1), 51–60.

Peteet, B. J., Montgomery, L., & Weekes, J. C. (2015). Predictors of imposter phenomenon among talented ethnic minority undergraduate students. *The Journal of Negro Education, 84*(2), 175–186. https://doi.org/10.7709/jnegroeducation.84.2.0175

Protivnak, J. J., & Foss, L. L. (2009). An exploration of themes that influence the counselor education doctoral student experience. *Counselor Education & Supervision, 48*(4), 239–256.

Puchalska-Wasyl, M. M., & Zarzycka, B. (2020). Prayer and internal dialogical activity: How do they predict well-being? *Psychology of Religion and Spirituality, 12*(4), 417–427. https://doi.org/10.1037/rel0000255

Purgason, L. L., Lloyd-Hazlett, J., & Avent Harris, J. R. (2018). Mentoring counselor education students: A delphi study with leaders in the field. *Journal of Counselor Leadership and Advocacy, 5*(2), 122–136. https://doi.org/10.1080/2326716X.2018.1452080

Reddick, R. J., Taylor, B. J., Nagbe, M., & Taylor, Z. W. (2021). Professor beware: Liberating faculty voices of color working in predominantly White institutions and geographic settings. *Education & Urban Society, 53*(5), 536–560. https://doi.org/10.1177/0013124520933349

Sanford, A. A., Ross, E. M., Blake, S. J., & Cambiano, R. L. (2017). Finding courage and confirmation: Resisting impostor feelings through relationships with mentors, romantic partners, and other women in leadership. *Advancing Women in Leadership, 35*, 31–41. https://doi.org/10.21423/awlj-v35.a140

Settles, I. H., Jones, M. K., Buchanan, N. T., & Dotson, K. (2020). Epistemic exclusion: Scholar(ly) devaluation that marginalizes faculty of color. *Journal of Diversity in Higher Education, 14*(4), 493–507. https://doi.org/10.1037/dhe0000174

Smedley, B. D., Myers, H. F., & Harrell, S. P. (1993). Minority-status stresses and the college adjustment of ethnic minority freshmen. *The Journal of Higher Education, 64*(4), 434–452. https://doi.org/10.2307/2960051

Tiefenthaler, I. (2018). Conquering imposter syndrome. *University of Montana Journal of Early Childhood Scholarship and Innovative Practice, 2*(1), Article 4, 1–3. https://scholarworks.umt.edu/ecsip/vol2/iss1/4

Trotman, F. K. (2009). The imposter phenomenon among African American women in U.S. institutions of higher education: Implication for counseling. In G. R. Walz, J. C. Bluer, & R. K. Yep (Eds.), *Compelling counseling interventions: VISTAS 2009* (pp. 77–87). American Counseling Association.

Vergauwe, J., Wille, B., Feys, M., De Fruyt, F., & Anseel, F. (2015). Fear of being exposed: The trait-relatedness of the impostor phenomenon and its relevance in the work context. *Journal of Business and Psychology, 30*(3), 565–581. https://doi.org/10.1007/s10869-014-9382-5

Winkle-Wagner, R., Forbes, J. M., Rogers, S., & Reavis, T. B. (2019). A culture of success: Black alumnae discussions of the assets-based approach at Spelman College. *Journal of Higher Education, 91*(5), 653–673. https://doi.org/10.1080/00221546.2019.1654965

Zanchetta, M., Junker, S., Wolf, A.-M., & Traut-Mattausch, E. (2020). "Overcoming the fear that haunts your success"—The effectiveness of interventions for reducing the impostor phenomenon. *Frontiers in Psychology, 11*, Article 405. https://doi.org/10.3389/fpsyg.2020.00405

Samantha Airhart-Larraga, Ph.D., LPC, LCDC, NCC is an Assistant Professor in the Counseling and Psychology Department of Texas A&M University–Central Texas, and is the Program Coordinator for the CMHC Program. She has over 20 years of experience as a counselor, focusing on providing culturally relevant counseling services to underserved and underrepresented clients, as well as culturally relevant supervision. She believes in advocacy, and is currently the

Chair of the Addictions Counseling Advisory Council for the National Board for Certified Counselors Foundation Minority Fellowship Program and on the Board of Directors for the Center for Credentialing and Education.

Conclusion—Our Letter to You

Tap someone in.

S. Kent Butler

Dear Reader,

As co-editors, we had a vision for this textbook. First, to pull together a resource that will serve you as a doctoral learner and throughout your career as a new faculty, your tenured/promotion process, and into other areas of academia such as leadership. We sought to do this through a socially-just paradigm that thoughtfully, eloquently, and most importantly, intentionally elevates the voices of those who have historically been silenced in academia, and whose experiences can provide a rich and diverse contextual perspective about life as an academic. As we highlighted in the Preface of this book, each of the chapter contributors identify as female, about 65% identify as BIPOC, and most also possess additional intersecting identities with respect to sexuality, gender expression, size, spirituality, neurodivergence, and various forms of physical, cognitive, and psychological disability, both overt and invisible.

Again, these are voices, experiences, and perspectives that are often deliberately oppressed through the hegemony of hierarchy, power, privilege, and patriarchy that uphold white supremacist ideology. These very systems were never designed for inclusion and were developed with the expressed purpose of elevating, expanding, and supporting principles that were only conducive to those who looked like those in power and whose lived experiences represented a narrow concept of learning and illustrative of outdated pedagogical practices. Such a collaborative approach is liberative and aligns with the established principles of social justice—equity, diversity, belonging, accessibility, and mutuality. It also serves to dismantle systems of oppression that were designed to quash and exclude persons who possess traditionally marginalized and historically disenfranchised intersectional identities.

D. M. Stalnaker-Shofner and T. N. Sapp (eds.), *A Comprehensive Guide for Counselor Education*, Springer Texts in Education, https://doi.org/10.1007/978-3-031-68358-9

The Hard Truth About Life in the Ivory Tower

We want to take a minute to acknowledge a hard truth—for those with marginalized identities and those with a greater level of ascribed privilege. We preface this portion of our letter to you with the caveat that what we share herein is through the lens of our experiences, and we acknowledge that this may not be true for every person with a historically marginalized identity. First, we want to speak to the reader who will be and are counselor educators with historically marginalized identities. We want to be as transparent and as authentic with you about what you are likely to experience upon the completion of your doctoral studies, and at multiple touchpoints in your career as an educator. The harsh reality is that you may find yourself teaching within environments that may not be welcoming or appreciative of you and the identities you possess, and that is the malevolence of the academy, its oppressive systems, and those who uphold them. You will likely encounter microaggressions and microinvalidations, overt acts of discrimination, and the experiences of *isms.* The progenitor of all -isms is white supremacist ideology, which can manifest in other forms of weaponized discrimination such as tokenization, differential racialization (the pitting of those with intersecting identities against each other), as well as other acts of marginalization and oppression. These experiences may leave you with a pervasive sense un-belonging, insecurity, and a lingering malaise that fosters isolation and disengagement, as it has for us at many different times in our respective careers. It left us with the realization that while our professors and mentors collectively taught us "how to teach," they failed to teach us about these experiences that often come with teaching in higher education. As such, we thought of how we could best capture these experiences without compromising the integrity and professionalism of this textbook. So we thought that it was important to share this with you here. What better place than in the conclusion and our closing letter to you.

As people who both identify as Black women, our experiences in the academy have bound us in a sisterhood and in community with others who have had similar experiences of marginalization. We each have experienced microaggressions in the learning environment and in other environments and communities. We have witnessed CIT's and doctoral learners being microaggressed by their peers, and we also have been the target of microaggressions by CITs and doctoral learners whom we are charged with facilitating their cultural sensitivity, awareness, and competency, as well as by colleagues who present as allies, which often is perfunctory in commitment and performative in nature. These are injurious on multiple interpersonal levels and have contributed to actual and perceived threats to our sense of self as well as our mental and emotional wellness. Further, these encounters have left us at times struggling against imposter syndrome. The anguish of these experiences that we have endured left us feeling deflated and defeated, and changed our perception of what it means to be a counselor educator. Quite honestly, the resulting trauma and racial battle fatigue almost corrupted our purpose and diminished our abilities, talents, and gifts as educators. These experiences when culminated ultimately have the goal to extinguish our light and the light of others who look like who. However, by having affinity spaces and communities that build you up, you can stand against the forces that were designed to tear you down. Finding your community will be an integral countermeasure for self-preservation as you enter this profession and navigate these spaces.

Next, we want to speak to the experiences of our White accomplices, persons who may not identify as having historically marginalized or disenfranchised identities, and persons with ascribed privilege based on their dominant identities. We acknowledge that your lived experiences may not be parallel to those with historically marginalized identities; however, there are moments of intersection. As a culturally aware counselor educator, you may witness the injustices of those who endure racism, discrimination, and oppression. As such, it becomes *your* imperative as an accomplice to take the risk of losing it all on the battlefield of social justice alongside those with whom and for whom you fight. For longevity and sustainability in this fight, it is important that you align yourself in community with like-minded accomplices that will unapologetically fight *with* you to dismantle such systems.

Our Experiences in the Creation of This Book

The road to Hell is paved with good intentions. When we began this journey, our intention was to provide a platform for those whose voices have not been heard. We also encouraged contributors to share their personal and professional experiences in the Academy. While this was rooted in the desire to elevate historically marginalized voices and perspectives, we as the pilots of this project were subjected to marginalization, racism, white fragility, privilege, and white supremacy. These experiences attempted to cloud our better judgment and distract us from the original idea, passion for this work, and steal the joy from this monumental experience.

As we deliberated about how to share these experiences with you. We felt an urgency to balance what we experienced with the expressed purpose of this book and the charge we took on as co-editors. We also felt the need to consider the importance of this project tempered with the antiquated and at times racist idea of professionalism notwithstanding the emotional labor and cultural taxation that comes with developing a project of this magnitude. Yet, we are still here, and this project is complete.

Our Parting Words of Wisdom for You

While we are unified in voice as co-editors of this project, we recognize that we are individuals with unique experiences as we have shared within the preface of the textbook. We understand that we are members of a system that is bigger than one individual and this work is only one part of the whole. We also recognize that change can be slow and does not happen overnight, while keeping in mind that the system is working the way that it was designed to work. Thus, it is important to also contend with the reality of the illusion of inclusion in which those in power and privilege attempt to maintain the status quo by *allowing* persons with historically marginalized identities to have a *seat at the table*, while giving the overt and covert message that *we* are not all welcomed at *their* table. Moreover, when there are no seats left, this book was intended to establish our own table and burn down the tables that uphold these oppressive systems and beliefs. As you step into your role as a counselor educator, we invite you to do the same with the understanding that advocacy and activism are integral to your work in this profession.

It remains evident that there is much to do. Therefore, we hope that this book empowers you to continue this work. As an agitator and disruptor, we invite you to continue chipping away at this system. It is our aspiration that you, the next generation of Counselor Educators and Supervisors, will take up this mantle and carry this work forward. Each one, teach one.

In Solidarity,

Drs. Devona and Tanisha

Index

A

B

C

D

D. M. Stalnaker-Shofner and T. N. Sapp (eds.), *A Comprehensive Guide for Counselor Education*, Springer Texts in Education, https://doi.org/10.1007/978-3-031-68358-9

MIX
Papier aus verantwortungsvollen Quellen
Paper from responsible sources
FSC® C105338

If you have any concerns about our products,
you can contact us on
ProductSafety@springernature.com

In case Publisher is established outside the EU,
the EU authorized representative is:
Springer Nature Customer Service Center GmbH
Europaplatz 3, 69115 Heidelberg, Germany

Printed by Libri Plureos GmbH
in Hamburg, Germany